Lecture Notes in Artificial Intel

Subseries of Lecture Notes in Computer Sci

Edited by J. G. Carbonell and J. Siekmann

Lecture Notes in Computer Science

Edited by G. Goos, J. Hartmanis and J. van Leeuwen

Springer
Berlin
Heidelberg
New York
Barcelona
Hong Kong
London
Milan
Paris
Singapore
Tokyo

Evelina Lamma   Paola Mello (Eds.)

AI*IA 99:
Advances in
Artificial Intelligence

6th Congress of Italian Association
for Artificial Intelligence
Bologna, Italy, September 14-17, 1999
Selected Papers

 Springer

Series Editors

Jaime G. Carbonell,Carnegie Mellon University, Pittsburgh, PA, USA
Jörg Siekmann, University of Saarland, Saarbrücken, Germany

Volume Editors

Evelina Lamma
Paola Mello
University of Bologna
DEIS
Viale Risorgimento, 2, 40136 Bologna, Italy
E-mail:{elamma/pmello}@deis.unibo.it

Cataloging-in-Publication Data applied for

Die Deutsche Bibliothek - CIP-Einheitsaufnahme

Advances in artificial intelligence : Bologna, Italy, September 14 -
17, 1999 ; selected papers / Evelina Lamma ; Paola Mello (ed.). -
Berlin ; Heidelberg ; New York ; Barcelona ; Hong Kong ; London ;
Milan ; Paris ; Singapore ; Tokyo : Springer, 2000
(... congress of the Italian Association for Artificial
Intelligence, AIIA ... ; 6)
    (Lecture notes in computer science ; Vol. 1792 : Lecture notes in
    artificial intelligence)
    ISBN 3-540-67350-4

CR Subject Classification (1991): I.2

ISBN 3-540-67350-4 Springer-Verlag Berlin Heidelberg New York

Springer-Verlag is a company in the BertelsmannSpringer publishing group.
© Springer-Verlag Berlin Heidelberg 2000
Printed in Germany

Typesetting: Camera-ready by author
Printed on acid-free paper   SPIN 10720068   06/3142   5 4 3 2 1 0

Preface

This book contains the extended versions of 33 papers selected among those originally presented at the Sixth Congress of the Italian Association for Artificial Intelligence (AI*IA). The congress of the AI*IA is the most relevant Italian event in the field of Artificial Intelligence, and has been receiving much attention from many researchers and practitioners of different countries. The sixth congress was held in Bologna, 14-17 September 1999, and was organized in twelve scientific sessions and one demo session.

The papers here collected report on significant work carried out in different areas of artificial intelligence, in Italy and other countries. Areas such as automated reasoning, knowledge representation, planning, and machine learning continue to be thoroughly investigated. The collection also shows a growing interest in the field of multi-agent systems, perception and robotics, and temporal reasoning.

Many people contributed in different ways to the success of the congress and to this volume. First of all, the members of the program committee who efficiently handled the reviewing of the 64 papers submitted to the congress, and later on the reviewing of the 41 papers submitted for publication in this volume. They provided three reviews for each manuscript, by relying on the support of valuable additional reviewers. The members of the organizing committee, namely Rosangela Barruffi, Paolo Bellavista, Anna Ciampolini, Marco Cremonini, Enrico Denti, Marco Gavanelli, Mauro Gaspari, Michela Milano, Rebecca Montanari, Andrea Omicini, Fabrizio Riguzzi, Cesare Stefanelli, and Paolo Torroni, worked hardy supporting at solving problems during and after the congress.

We wish to thank Giovanni Soda who, as director of AI*IA Bulletin, helped us in promoting the congress, and Maurelio Boari for encouraging us in organizing the event.

The financial support of the Fondazione CARISBO, Bologna, Italy, for partially covering the publication cost of this book, is acknowledged.

Finally, a special thank to our families and husbands, Claudio and Paolo, who have made our life and work easier.

January 2000

Evelina Lamma and Paola Mello

Program Chairs

Evelina Lamma, Paola Mello (Università di Bologna)

Program Committee

Giovanni Adorni (Università di Parma)
Andrea Bonarini (Politecnico di Milano)
Ernesto Burattini (CNR - Napoli)
Luigia Carlucci Aiello (Università di Roma "La Sapienza")
Riccardo Cassinis (Università di Brescia)
Amedeo Cesta (CNR - Roma)
Mauro Di Manzo (Università di Genova)
Floriana Esposito (Università di Bari)
Salvatore Gaglio (Università di Palermo)
Fausto Giunchiglia (Università di Trento)
Liliana Ironi (CNR - Pavia)
Leonardo Lesmo (Università di Torino)
Patrizia Marti (Università di Siena)
Gianni Morra (Centro Ricerche FIAT, Orbassano)
Lorenza Saitta (Università di Torino)
Giorgio Satta (Università di Padova)
Marco Schaerf (Università di Roma "La Sapienza")
Roberto Serra (Montecatini S.p.A., Ravenna)
Carlo Tasso (Università di Udine)
Franco Turini (Università di Pisa)

Referees

Adorni Giovanni
Amigoni Francesco
Andretta Massimo
Armando Alessandro

Battiti Roberto
Bellazzi Riccardo
Benedetti Marco
Bergamaschi Sonia
Bergenti Federico
Bianchi Dario
Blanzieri Enrico
Bonarini Andrea
Bracciali Andrea
Brogi Antonio

Cagnoni Stefano
Cappelli Amedeo
Carlo Ferrari
Castelfranchi Cristiano
Castellini Claudio
Cattoni Roldano
Chella Antonio
Contiero Simone
Cossentino Massimo

D'Aloisi Daniela
Damiano Rossana
Danieli Morena
De Carolis
De Falco Ivanoe
De Rosis
Di Gregorio Salvatore

Fabio Massacci
Falcone Rino
Fanelli Anna Maria
Ferilli Stefano
Focacci Filippo

Giordano Laura

Giunchiglia Enrico

Liberatore Paolo

Maccione Maria Grazia
Malerba Donato
Manco Giuseppe
Melucci Massimo
Milani Alfredo
Milano Michela

Nardi Daniele

Oddi Angelo
Omicini Andrea

Pianesi Fabio
Pilato Giovanni
Poggi Agostino

Quenda Valter

Raffaetà Alessandra
Ramoni Marco
Riguzzi Fabrizio
Roli Andrea

Secco Suardo Gian Maria
Semeraro Giovanni
Simi Maria
Suggi Liverani Furio

Tacchella Armando
Terenziani Paolo

Vitabile Salvatore
Vivo Giulio

Zaccaria Renato
Zanardo Alberto
Zanichelli Francesco

Table of Contents

Generalized default logic: minimal knowledge, autoepistemic and default reasoning reconciled

Daniele Nardi and Riccardo Rosati

Dipartimento di Informatica e Sistemistica
Università di Roma "La Sapienza"
Via Salaria 113, 00198 Roma, Italy
{nardi,rosati}@dis.uniroma1.it

Abstract. Logical approaches to nonmonotonic reasoning have been developed within different technical settings, thus making it difficult to establish correspondences among them and to identify common underlying principles. In this paper we argue that the most well-known nonmonotonic reasoning formalisms are actually characterized by two closure assumptions: a minimal knowledge assumption and an autoepistemic assumption. We justify this thesis by introducing generalized default logic (*GDL*), obtained through a simple and natural generalization of Reiter's default logic, which fully captures both closure assumptions. We then analyze the relationship between *GDL* and nonmonotonic modal logics, in particular Moore's autoepistemic logic and Lifschitz's logic of minimal knowledge and negation as failure, showing the existence of a full correspondence between these modal formalisms and *GDL*. Such a correspondence gives us a unified reading of nonmonotonic reasoning formalisms in terms of the above two assumptions; in particular, it clarifies the relationship between default and autoepistemic logic.

1 Introduction

Research in the formalization of commonsense reasoning through nonmonotonic logics aims at finding suitable ways to complete the knowledge of a reasoning agent (see e.g. [Levesque, 1990]). The main ingredient of a nonmonotonic reasoning formalism is therefore the kind of closure assumption which is chosen in order to enrich the set of conclusions beyond those derivable from a first-order theory.

However, it is difficult to give a precise characterization of the various closure assumptions, because they are hidden in the formal setting that is adopted: defaults are expressed as special inference rules, epistemic closure assumptions are phrased in the setting of modal nonmonotonic logic, predicate circumscription characterizes minimal first-order preferred models, while minimization of knowledge is expressed as a preference criterion on possible-world structures.

As a consequence of this variety, attempts have been made to find common roots for apparently different proposals. This has lead not only to discover many relationships among the formalizations of commonsense reasoning, but also to develop several refinements of the basic approaches.

E. Lamma and P. Mello (Eds.): AI*IA 99, LNAI 1792, pp. 1–12, 2000.
© Springer-Verlag Berlin Heidelberg 2000

In particular, the correspondence between Reiter's default logic (DL) [Reiter, 1980] and Moore's autoepistemic logic (AEL) [Moore, 1985] has been analyzed e.g. in [Konolige, 1988, Gottlob, 1995, Chen, 1994, Schwarz, 1996, Janhunen, 1996]. Such studies have shown both similarities and differences between the two formalisms. In particular, it has been argued that defaults and autoepistemic logic make similar assumptions for completing the knowledge of the agent. Following this intuition, one can find cases where default rules can naturally be represented as modal sentences in autoepistemic logic and viceversa. Moreover, both approaches, although developed within different formal settings, are based on a fixed-point definition to characterize the knowledge of the agent.

Indeed, in order to find a precise correspondence between the two formalisms, several difficulties arise. On the one hand, it has been shown that the translation of defaults into modal sentences leads to modal nonmonotonic formalisms different from AEL [Marek and Truszczyński, 1993]. On the other hand, it has been shown that it is impossible to find an "easy" (i.e. modular) translation of DL in AEL [Gottlob, 1995], while a (not easy) translation exists in the restricted case of finite default theories [Gottlob, 1995, Schwarz, 1996]. By analyzing these results one might conclude that, despite intuitive similarities, DL and AEL embed different notions of closure of the agent's knowledge.

Another family of *modal* formalisms for nonmonotonic reasoning is obtained by modifying the semantics of a classical modal logic through the definition of a preference criterion among the models of the agent's initial knowledge (i.e. a *preference semantics* [Shoham, 1987]). All the proposed criteria reflect the general idea of selecting those models in which knowledge is "minimal". The relationship between preference-based and fixed-point modal nonmonotonic formalisms has been thoroughly investigated [Schwarz, 1992, Donini *et al.*, 1997]. It turns out that both fixed-point definitions can be given a semantic counterpart through a preference relation on possible-world structures, and that the notion of minimal knowledge [Halpern and Moses, 1985] can be captured through a fixed-point definition. This suggests that, in a modal nonmonotonic setting, one can capture in a unified framework several principles underlying nonmonotonic reasoning formalisms. In fact, the relationship between nonmonotonic modal logics and other formalisms for nonmonotonic reasoning has been highlighted by resorting to modal systems such as nonmonotonic S4F [Schwarz and Truszczyński, 1994] or the bimodal logic of minimal knowledge and negation as failure $MKNF$ [Lifschitz, 1991]. In particular, $MKNF$ has been shown to capture, by carefully using both modalities, other formalizations of nonmonotonic reasoning.

However, the relationship between $MKNF$ and AEL, analyzed e.g. in [Lin and Shoham, 1992, Schwarz and Lifschitz, 1993], has only recently been fully described [Rosati, 1997a]. This result completes the overall picture, by establishing a new important connection between DL and AEL, which enables for a characterization of the main nonmonotonic formalisms according to two principles: minimal knowledge and autoepistemic assumptions.

The goal of this paper is to show that the above two principles are sufficient to characterize nonmonotonic reasoning. The claim is justified by showing that such principles can not only be formulated in a modal setting, but are actually also captured in the framework of default logic. To this end, we present generalized default logic (*GDL*), which is obtained through a simple and natural extension of Reiter's default logic. First, we study the relationship between *GDL* and nonmonotonic modal logics, in particular Moore's autoepistemic logic and Lifschitz's logic of minimal knowledge and negation as failure *MKNF*. Then, we show the existence of a strong correspondence between these modal formalisms and *GDL*. In particular, we show that the expressive power of *GDL* and *MKNF* is the same. Based on such a correspondence, we suggest a new interpretation of both (generalized) defaults and autoepistemic logic, which provides a new reading of the embedding of default logic into autoepistemic logic.

The paper is structured as follows. In Section 2 we define generalized default logic *GDL*, and in Section 3 we study the relationship between *GDL* and *MKNF*. In Section 4 we focus on the problem of embedding *DL* into *AEL*, and we conclude in Section 5. Due to space limitations, detailed proofs of theorems are not reported in this version of the paper.

2   Generalized default logic

We start by briefly recalling Reiter's default logic [Reiter, 1980]. Let $\mathcal{L}$ be the propositional language built in the usual way from an alphabet $\mathcal{A}$ of propositional symbols (atoms) and the propositional connectives $\vee, \wedge, \neg, \supset$. A *default rule* is a rule of the form

$$\frac{\alpha : M\beta_1, \ldots, M\beta_n}{\gamma} \tag{1}$$

where $n \geq 0$ and $\alpha, \beta_1, \ldots, \beta_n, \gamma \in \mathcal{L}$. A *default theory* is a pair (D, W) where $W \subseteq \mathcal{L}$ and D is a set of default rules.

The characterization of default theories is given through the notion of extension, i.e. a deductively closed set of propositional formulas.

Definition 1. *Let $E_1, E_2 \subseteq \mathcal{L}$. We say that a default rule $d = \frac{\alpha : M\beta_1, \ldots, M\beta_n}{\gamma}$ is applicable wrt E_1, E_2 if:*

1. $\alpha \in E_1$;
2. $\gamma \notin E_1$;
3. $\neg\beta_i \notin E_2$ for each $i \in \{1, \ldots, n\}$.

Definition 2. *Let (D, W) be a default theory. A consistent set of formulas $E \subset \mathcal{L}$ is an extension for (D, W) iff the following conditions hold:*

1. $E_0 = Th(W)$;
2. $E_{i+1} = Th(E_i \cup \{\gamma | d = \frac{\alpha : M\beta_1, \ldots, M\beta_n}{\gamma} \in D$ and d is applicable wrt $E_i, E\})$;
3. $E = \bigcup_{i=0}^{\infty} E_i$.

where $Th(E)$ denotes the deductive closure of the set E, i.e. the set of propositional formulas logically implied by E.

We recall that an extension can be constructed starting from the set of facts W, and increasing such a set by applying the special inference rules in D, until no rule can be applied. In order to apply an inference rule of the form (1), the prerequisite α must be implied by the theory built so far (*local* check), while the justifications must be *globally* consistent, i.e. each formula $\neg\beta_i$ must not be implied by the theory obtained at the end of the construction.

In [Gelfond *et al.*, 1991] default logic has been extended to the case of disjunctive conclusions, in the following way. A *disjunctive default rule* is a rule of the form

$$\frac{\alpha : M\beta_1, \ldots, M\beta_n}{\gamma_1|\ldots|\gamma_m}$$

where $n, m \geq 0$ and $\alpha, \beta_1, \ldots, \beta_n, \gamma_1, \ldots, \gamma_m \in \mathcal{L}$. A disjunctive default theory is a pair (D, W) where $W \subseteq \mathcal{L}$ and D is a set of disjunctive default rules. The characterization of disjunctive default theories is given by changing (in a conservative way) the above notion of extension as follows.

Definition 3. *A disjunctive default rule* $d = \frac{\alpha : M\beta_1, \ldots, M\beta_n}{\gamma_1|\ldots|\gamma_m}$ *is applicable wrt* $E_1, E_2 \subseteq \mathcal{L}$ *if:*

1. $\alpha \in E_1$;
2. $\gamma_i \notin E_1$ *for each* $i \in \{1, \ldots, m\}$;
3. $\neg\beta_i \notin E_2$ *for each* $i \in \{1, \ldots, n\}$.

Definition 4. *Given two sets* $E, E' \subseteq \mathcal{L}$, *and a disjunctive default theory* (D, W), *we say that* E' *is* comparable *with* E *wrt* (D, W) *if* E' *is such that:*

1. $E'_0 = Th(W)$;
2. $E'_{i+1} = Th(E'_i \cup \{\gamma_i | d = \frac{\alpha : M\beta_1, \ldots, M\beta_n}{\gamma_1|\ldots|\gamma_m} \in D$ *and* d *is applicable wrt* $E'_i, E\})$;
3. $E' = \bigcup_{i=0}^{\infty} E'_i$.

The definition of comparable sets of formulas allows for the formulation of the minimality condition on the extensions. Intuitively, two extensions are comparable if they are built using the same justifications.

Definition 5. *Let* (D, W) *be a disjunctive default theory. A consistent set of formulas* $E \subset \mathcal{L}$ *is an* extension *for* (D, W) *if:*

1. $E_0 = Th(W)$;
2. $E_{i+1} = Th(E_i \cup \{\gamma_i | d = \frac{\alpha : M\beta_1, \ldots, M\beta_n}{\gamma_1|\ldots|\gamma_m} \in D$ *and* d *is applicable wrt* $E_i, E\})$;
3. $E = \bigcup_{i=0}^{\infty} E_i$;
4. *for each* $E' \subset E$, E' *is not comparable with* E *wrt* (D, W).

From the above definition it follows that, in the disjunctive case, one cannot build an extension independently of the others, since it is necessary to check minimality of the conclusions chosen in the construction of the extension.

We now extend (disjunctive) default logic by simply adding the possibility of expressing not only the notion of *global consistency* assumption, but also the dual notion of *global validity* assumption. In fact, notice that the justifications

$M\beta_1, \ldots, M\beta_n$ in (1) are satisfied iff none among the formulas $\neg\beta_1, \ldots, \neg\beta_n$ belongs to E; hence, $M\beta_1, \ldots, M\beta_n$ can be considered as *negative* global assumptions. Now, it appears natural and plausible to consider also the symmetric notion of *positive* global assumption in the justification part of the default, i.e. assuming that a propositional formula β belongs to the extension E. Notice that this is different from *locally* checking the validity of a formula, which is done with the prerequisite part of the default.

Formally, we call *generalized default rule* a rule of the form

$$\frac{\alpha : M\beta_1, \ldots, M\beta_n, \overline{M}\beta}{\gamma_1 | \ldots | \gamma_m} \tag{2}$$

where $n, m \geq 0$ and $\alpha, \beta_1, \ldots, \beta_n, \beta, \gamma_1, \ldots, \gamma_m \in \mathcal{L}$. A generalized default theory is a pair (D, W) where $W \subseteq \mathcal{L}$ and D is a set of generalized default rules.

We thus extend the definition of applicable default rule to the case of positive justifications in the following way.

Definition 6. *A generalized default rule* $d = \frac{\alpha : M\beta_1, \ldots, M\beta_n, \overline{M}\beta}{\gamma_1 | \ldots | \gamma_m}$ *is applicable wrt* $E_1, E_2 \subseteq \mathcal{L}$ *if:*

1. $\alpha \in E_1$;
2. $\gamma_i \notin E_1$ for each $i \in \{1, \ldots, m\}$;
3. $\beta \in E_2$;
4. $\neg\beta_i \notin E_2$ for each $i \in \{1, \ldots, n\}$.

By using this new notion of applicable default in Definition 4 we again realize the idea that comparable extensions are built using the same justifications, which in this case include also positive global assumptions.

Definition 7. *Let* (D, W) *be a generalized default theory. A consistent set of formulas* $E \subset \mathcal{L}$ *is an extension for* (D, W) *iff:*

1. $E_0 = Th(W)$;
2. $E_{i+1} = Th(E_i \cup$
   $\{\gamma_i | d = \frac{\alpha : M\beta_1, \ldots, M\beta_n, \overline{M}\beta}{\gamma_1 | \ldots | \gamma_m} \in D$ *and* d *is applicable wrt* $E_i, E\})$;
3. $E = \bigcup_{i=0}^{\infty} E_i$;
4. *for each* $E' \subset E$, E' *is not comparable with* E *wrt* (D, W).

We now present some very simple examples of generalized default theories.

Example 1. Let

$$(D, W) = (\{\frac{: \overline{M}p}{p}\}, \emptyset)$$

It is easy to see that the theory (D, W) has the two extensions $E_1 = Th(\emptyset)$, $E_2 = Th(\{p\})$. In fact, if we do not make any global validity assumption, then the generalized default is not applicable, and we get the extension E_1; on the other hand, if we assume that p holds (i.e., p belongs to the extension), then the default is applicable and we conclude p, thus obtaining the extension E_2. $\square$

Example 2. Let

$$(D, W) = (\{\frac{: \overline{Mp}}{p}\}, \{\neg p\})$$

has the only extension $E = Th(\{\neg p\})$. In fact, if we do not make any global validity assumption, then the generalized default is not applicable, and we get the extension E. On the other hand, if we assume that p holds (i.e., p belongs to the extension), then the default is applicable and we conclude p: however, since $\neg p \in W$, we obtain an inconsistent set of formulas. Therefore, E is the only extension for (D, W). $\qquad\square$

We remark that, despite the different nature of the characterization, the framework of generalized default logic has a tight relationship with the framework of generalized disjunctive logic programming defined in [Inoue and Sakama, 1994] (analogous to the relationship between disjunctive default logic and extended logic programs [Gelfond and Lifschitz, 1991, Gelfond *et al.*, 1991]), and can be considered as an extension of that framework to the case of the full propositional language.

3   Relationship between *GDL* and *MKNF*

In this section we show that there exists a strict correspondence between *GDL* and the logic of minimal knowledge and negation as failure *MKNF*. We start by briefly introducing *MKNF* [Lifschitz, 1991].

We assume that the reader is familiar with the basics of modal logic [Hughes and Cresswell, 1968]. We denote with $\mathcal{L}_M$ the modal extension of $\mathcal{L}$ with the modalities K and A.[1] Moreover, we denote with $\mathcal{L}_K$ the set of formulas from $\mathcal{L}_M$ in which the modality A does not occur, and call *flat* any formula from $\mathcal{L}_M$ in which each propositional symbol appears in the scope of exactly one modality.

We now recall the notion of *MKNF* model. An *interpretation* is a set of propositional symbols. Satisfiability of a formula in a structure (I, M_k, M_a), where I is an interpretation and M_k, M_a are sets of interpretations (worlds), is defined inductively as follows:

1. if φ is an atom, φ is true in (I, M_k, M_a) iff $\varphi \in I$;
2. $\neg\varphi$ is true in (I, M_k, M_a) iff φ is not true in (I, M_k, M_a);
3. $\varphi_1 \wedge \varphi_2$ is true in (I, M_k, M_a) iff φ_1 is true in (I, M_k, M_a) and φ_2 is true in (I, M_k, M_a);
4. $\varphi_1 \vee \varphi_2$ is true in (I, M_k, M_a) iff φ_1 is true in (I, M_k, M_a) or φ_2 is true in (I, M_k, M_a);
5. $\varphi_1 \supset \varphi_2$ is true in (I, M_k, M_a) iff φ_1 is not true in (I, M_k, M_a) or φ_2 is true in (I, M_k, M_a);
6. $K\varphi$ is true in (I, M_k, M_a) iff, for every $J \in M_k$, φ is true in (J, M_k, M_a);

---

[1] We adopt the modality A as in [Lin and Shoham, 1992]; in Lifschitz's original proposal [Lifschitz, 1991] the modality *not* was used, which corresponds to $\neg A$ in our notation.

7. $A\varphi$ is true in (I, M_k, M_a) iff, for every $J \in M_a$, φ is true in (J, M_k, M_a).

Given a pair (M_k, M_a) of sets of interpretations, and a formula $\varphi \in \mathcal{L}_M$, we write $(M_k, M_a) \models \varphi$ iff for each $I \in M_k$, φ is true in (I, M_k, M_a).

Definition 8. *A set of interpretations M, where $M \neq \emptyset$, is an MKNF model of a theory $\Sigma \subseteq \mathcal{L}_M$ iff each formula φ from Σ is such that $(M, M) \models \varphi$ and, for each set of interpretations M', if $M' \supset M$ then at least one formula from Σ is such that $(M', M) \not\models \varphi$.*

We say that a formula φ is entailed by Σ in *MKNF* (and write $\Sigma \models_{MKNF} \varphi$) iff φ is true in every *MKNF* model of Σ.

Example 3. Let
$$\Sigma = \{Kp\}$$
The only *MKNF* model for Σ is $M = \{J : J \models p\}$. Hence, $\Sigma \models_{MKNF} Kp$, and $\Sigma \models_{MKNF} \neg K\varphi$ for each $\varphi \in \mathcal{L}$ such that $\not\models p \supset \varphi$. Therefore, the agent modeled by Σ has minimal knowledge, in the sense that she only knows p and the objective facts logically implied by p. □

Example 4. Let
$$\Sigma = \{\neg Ap \supset q\}$$
It is easy to see that the only *MKNF* model for Σ is $M = \{J : J \models q\}$, since $\neg p$ can be "assumed by default" by the agent modeled by Σ, which is then able to conclude q. □

We now show that there exists a full correspondence between generalized default logic and *MKNF*. In particular, we prove that there exists a faithful (i.e. model-preserving) and modular translation [Gottlob, 1995] of *GDL* into *MKNF* and viceversa.

Let d be a generalized default rule of the form 2. Then, $\tau(d) \in \mathcal{L}_M$ is the following formula:

$$\neg K\alpha \vee A\neg\beta_1 \vee \ldots \vee A\neg\beta_n \vee \neg A\beta \vee K\gamma_1 \vee \ldots \vee K\gamma_m$$

Definition 9. *Let (D, W) be a generalized default theory. Then, we denote with $\tau(D, W) \subset \mathcal{L}_M$ the modal theory*

$$\tau(D, W) = W \cup \{\tau(d)|d \in W\}$$

Let $E \subseteq \mathcal{L}$ be an extension. We denote with $\mathcal{M}(E)$ the set of interpretations satisfying each formula in E.

The following property easily follows by extending previous results on the relationship between *MKNF* and (disjunctive) default logic.

Theorem 1. *Let (D, W) be a GDL theory. Then, E is an extension for (D, W) iff $\mathcal{M}(E)$ is an MKNF model for $\tau(D, W)$.*

The above theorem allows for establishing a computational characterization of reasoning in GDL (we refer to [Johnson, 1990] for the definition of the complexity classes mentioned in the following).

Theorem 2. *Let* (D, W) *be a generalized default theory, and let* $\varphi \in \mathcal{L}$. *Then, the problem of establishing whether* φ *belongs to all extensions of* (D, W) *is* Π_2^p-*complete.*

Proof sketch. Membership in Π_2^p follows from Theorem 1 and from known computational properties of the flat fragment of propositional $MKNF$ (see [Rosati, 1997b, Theorem 12]). Hardness immediately follows from the fact that GDL is a conservative extension of Reiter's default logic.   □

The above theorem shows that the proposed generalization of default logic does not change the computational properties of reasoning with propositional default theories.

Let us now turn our attention to the problem of translating $MKNF$ theories into GDL. We denote with $\mathcal{L}_{DNF}$ the subset of $\mathcal{L}_M$ composed of formulas of the form

$$\neg K\alpha \vee A\neg\beta_1 \vee \ldots \vee A\neg\beta_n \vee \neg A\beta \vee K\gamma_1 \vee \ldots \vee K\gamma_m \tag{3}$$

with $n, m \geq 0$, $\alpha, \beta_1, \ldots, \beta_n, \beta, \gamma_1, \ldots, \gamma_m \in \mathcal{L}$.

Let $\varphi \in \mathcal{L}_{DNF}$ be a formula of the form (3). We denote with $\tau^-(\varphi)$ the generalized default rule (2).

It is possible to show that the translation τ^- realizes the embedding of $MKNF$ theories in disjunctive normal form into GDL. Moreover, it is easy to prove that, for each $\Sigma \subseteq \mathcal{L}_M$ there exists an equivalent theory $\tau_{DNF}(\Sigma) \in \mathcal{L}_{DNF}$, which can be constructed by computing the flat disjunctive normal form of each formula in Σ (see [Lin and Shoham, 1992]).

Let M be a set of interpretations. We denote with $\mathcal{E}(M)$ the set of propositional formulas which are satisfied by all the interpretations in M.

Theorem 3. *Let* $\Sigma \subseteq \mathcal{L}_M$. *Then,* M *is an* $MKNF$ *model for* Σ *iff* $\mathcal{E}(M)$ *is a* GDL *extension for* $\tau^-(\tau_{DNF}(\Sigma))$.

Hence, it is possible to faithfully translate any (either finite or infinite) GDL theory into $MKNF$ and viceversa, which implies that the expressive power (that is, the ability of expressing sets of models [Gottlob, 1995]) of GDL is the same as $MKNF$.

We remark that such equivalence in terms of expressive power is not reflected from a computational viewpoint. In fact, it turns out that reasoning in $MKNF$ is harder than reasoning in GDL, specifically the entailment problem in $MKNF$ lies at the third level of the polynomial hierarchy [Rosati, 1997b]. In fact, the above translation of $MKNF$ into GDL is not polynomial, since putting the theory Σ in flat disjunctive normal form requires, in general, space exponential in the size of Σ.

4   On embedding default logic into autoepistemic logic

We finally briefly recall Moore's autoepistemic logic (AEL) [Moore, 1985]. In order to keep notation to a minimum, we change the language of AEL, using the modality K instead of L. Thus, in the following a formula of AEL is a formula from $\mathcal{L}_K$.

A consistent set of formulas T from $\mathcal{L}_K$ is a *stable expansion* for a set of initial knowledge $\Sigma \subseteq \mathcal{L}_K$ if T satisfies the following equation:

$$T = Cn_{\mathsf{KD45}}(\Sigma \cup \{\neg K\varphi \mid \varphi \notin T\})$$

where Cn_{KD45} is the logical consequence operator of modal logic KD45.

Given a theory $\Sigma \subseteq \mathcal{L}_K$ and a formula $\varphi \in \mathcal{L}_K$, $\Sigma \models_{AEL} \varphi$ iff φ belongs to all the stable expansions of Σ.

Notably, each stable expansion T is a *stable set* [Stalnaker, 1993], i.e.:

1. T is closed under propositional consequence;
2. if $\varphi \in T$ then $K\varphi \in T$;
3. if $\varphi \notin T$ then $\neg K\varphi \in T$.

We recall that each stable set S corresponds to a *maximal* universal S5 model $\mathcal{M}_S$ such that S is the set of formulas satisfied by $\mathcal{M}_S$ (see e.g. [Marek and Truszczyński, 1993]).

With the term AEL *model* for Σ we will refer to an S5 model whose set of theorems corresponds to a stable expansion for Σ in AEL: without loss of generality, we will identify such a model with the set of interpretations it contains.

Finally, notice that, as in e.g. [Marek and Truszczyński, 1993], we have adopted the notion of *consistent* autoepistemic logic, i.e. we do not allow the inconsistent theory containing all modal formulas to be a (possible) stable expansion. The results we present can be easily extended to this case (corresponding to Moore's original proposal).

It turns out that there exists a close relationship between AEL and $MKNF$: in fact, AEL theories can be embedded into $MKNF$ theories. In particular, it has been proven [Lin and Shoham, 1992, Schwarz and Truszczyński, 1994] that AEL theories with no nested occurrences of K (called *flat* theories) can be embedded into $MKNF$. And since in AEL any theory can be transformed into an equivalent flat theory (which has in general size exponential in the size of the initial theory), it follows that any AEL theory can be embedded into $MKNF$.

Moreover, a stronger result has been recently proven [Rosati, 1997a]: negation as failure in $MKNF$ *exactly* corresponds to negative introspection in AEL, i.e. AEL's modality $\neg K$ and $MKNF$'s modality *not* are semantically equivalent. Hence, such a correspondence is not restricted to modal theories without nested modalities, and induces a polynomial-time embedding of *any* AEL theory into $MKNF$.

Definition 10. *Let $\varphi \in \mathcal{L}_K$. Then, $tr_M(\varphi)$ is the MKNF formula obtained from φ by substituting each occurrence of K with A. Moreover, if $\Sigma \subseteq \mathcal{L}_K$, then $tr_M(\Sigma)$ denotes the MKNF theory $\{tr_M(\varphi)|\varphi \in \Sigma\}$.*

It can be shown [Rosati, 1997a] that the translation $tr_M(\cdot)$ embeds AEL into $MKNF$.

Proposition 1. *Let $\Sigma \subseteq \mathcal{L}_K$. Then, M is an AEL model for Σ iff M is an MKNF model of $tr_M(\Sigma)$.*

This result allows for interpreting the modality A in $MKNF$ *exactly* as Moore's autoepistemic operator, thus strengthening the generality of the logic $MKNF$ and its underlying principles. In particular, since the fragment of $MKNF$ built upon the modality K corresponds to Halpern and Moses' logic of minimal knowledge [Halpern and Moses, 1985], it becomes clear that $MKNF$ can be completely characterized by the two notions of minimal knowledge and autoepistemic assumption.

Now, due to the full correspondence between $MKNF$ and GDL, it also follows that generalized default logic is based on the same two principles. This allows us to view many modal nonmonotonic formalisms in terms of special (default) inference rules, which has strong connections with previous studies [Bochman, 1996] relating nonmonotonic modal logics with biconsequence relations. However, our aim here is to ground these results to the basic intuitive notions underlying nonmonotonic reasoning.

The correspondence between $MKNF$ and GDL provides a new reading of the embedding of default logic into autoepistemic logic, since it clarifies that both Reiter's default logic and Moore's autoepistemic logic are actually special cases of a more general framework. In fact, Reiter's default logic can be obtained by omitting positive justifications in generalized defaults, while autoepistemic logic is obtained by eliminating the minimal knowledge operator from $MKNF$. This explains the difficulties and problems encountered in establishing the correspondences between the two formalisms.

Moreover, this result allows for the characterization of autoepistemic logic in terms of default logic. This problem has been studied e.g. in [Janhunen, 1996], which provides a *non-faithful* translation of *finite* autoepistemic theories in terms of standard defaults. From the above proposition and the results shown in the previous section, it follows that, if we simply allow for the presence of positive justifications in default rules,[2] then we are able to overcome both limitations in the translation. That is, it is possible to faithfully translate both finite and infinite AEL theories in terms of GDL theories. Hence, the following property holds.

Theorem 4. *There exists a faithful and modular translation of AEL into GDL.*

Notice that (as shown in [Gottlob, 1995]) a faithful translation of autoepistemic theories in terms of Reiter's default logic is impossible. Hence, extending default rules with positive justifications actually increases the expressive power of defaults.

---

[2] Notice that the presence of disjunctive conclusions in default rules is not necessary in order to prove Theorem 4.

5   Conclusions

In this paper we have proposed a revisitation of the work on nonmonotonic reasoning, showing that there are two basic closure assumptions which are made by the most well-known nonmonotonic reasoning formalisms. Specifically, we have shown that, by extending Reiter's default logic with the ability of expressing positive global assumptions, one gets the ability to express the kind of self-supported conclusions that are typical of autoepistemic reasoning.

On the other hand, the ability to express the prerequisites of defaults in AEL can only be gained if one introduces a way of minimizing knowledge, that in $MKNF$ is captured by the minimal knowledge epistemic operator.

In this way, default logic, autoepistemic logic, and minimal knowledge with negation as failure can all be viewed as special cases of a unique framework, whose underlying closure principles are autoepistemic assumptions and minimal knowledge.

Acknowledgments

This research has been partially supported by MURST 60%, "Rappresentazione di azioni e ragionamento non monotono".

References

[Bochman, 1996] A. Bochman. Biconsequence relations for nonmonotonic reasoning. In *Proc. of the 5th Int. Conf. on the Principles of Knowledge Representation and Reasoning (KR'96)*, 1996.

[Chen, 1994] J. Chen. The logic of only knowing as a unified framework for nonmonotonic reasoning. *Fundamenta Informaticae*, 21:205–220, 1994.

[Donini et al., 1997] Francesco M. Donini, Daniele Nardi, and Riccardo Rosati. Ground nonmonotonic modal logics. *J. of Logic and Computation*, 7(4):523–548, August 1997.

[Gelfond and Lifschitz, 1991] M. Gelfond and V. Lifschitz. Classical negation in logic programs and disjunctive databases. *New Generation Computing*, 9:365–385, 1991.

[Gelfond et al., 1991] M. Gelfond, V. Lifschitz, H.Przymusinska, and M. Truszczynski. Disjunctive defaults. In *Proc. of the 2nd Int. Conf. on the Principles of Knowledge Representation and Reasoning (KR'91)*, pages 230–237. Morgan Kaufmann, Los Altos, 1991.

[Ginsberg, 1987] Matthew L. Ginsberg, editor. *Readings in Nonmonotonic Reasoning*. Morgan Kaufmann, Los Altos, 1987.

[Gottlob, 1995] G. Gottlob. Translating default logic into standard autoepistemic logic. *J. of the ACM*, 42:711–740, 1995.

[Halpern and Moses, 1985] Joseph Y. Halpern and Yoram Moses. Towards a theory of knowledge and ignorance: Preliminary report. Technical Report CD-TR 92/34, IBM, 1985.

[Hughes and Cresswell, 1968] G. E. Hughes and M. J. Cresswell. *An Introduction to Modal Logic*. Methuen University Press, London, 1968.

[Inoue and Sakama, 1994] K. Inoue and C. Sakama. On positive occurrences of negation as failure. In *Proc. of the 4th Int. Conf. on the Principles of Knowledge Representation and Reasoning (KR'94)*, pages 293–304. Morgan Kaufmann, Los Altos,
1994.

[Janhunen, 1996] Tomi Janhunen. Representing autoepistemic introspection in terms
of default rules. In *Proc. of the 12th European Conf. on Artificial Intelligence
(ECAI'96)*, 1996.

[Johnson, 1990] D. S. Johnson. A catalog of complexity classes. In J. van Leuven,
editor, *Handbook of Theoretical Computer Science*, volume A, chapter 2. Elsevier
Science Publishers (North-Holland), Amsterdam, 1990.

[Konolige, 1988] K. Konolige. On the relationship between default and autoepistemic
logic. *Artificial Intelligence*, 35:343–382, 1988.

[Levesque, 1990] Hector J. Levesque. All I know: a study in autoepistemic logic. *Artificial Intelligence*, 42:263–310, 1990.

[Lifschitz, 1991] Vladimir Lifschitz. Nonmonotonic databases and epistemic queries.
In *Proc. of the 12th Int. Joint Conf. on Artificial Intelligence (IJCAI'91)*, pages
381–386, 1991.

[Lin and Shoham, 1992] F. Lin and Y. Shoham. Epistemic semantics for fixed-point
non-monotonic logics. *Artificial Intelligence*, 57:271–289, 1992.

[Marek and Truszczyński, 1993] W. Marek and M. Truszczyński. *Nonmonotonic Logics – Context-Dependent Reasoning*. Springer-Verlag, 1993.

[Moore, 1985] R. C. Moore. Semantical considerations on nonmonotonic logic. *Artificial Intelligence*, 25:75–94, 1985.

[Reiter, 1980] Raymond Reiter. A logic for default reasoning. *Artificial Intelligence*,
13:81–132, 1980. Republished in [Ginsberg, 1987].

[Rosati, 1997a] Riccardo Rosati. Embedding minimal knowledge into autoepistemic
logic. In *Proc. of the 5th Conf. of the Italian Association for Artificial Intelligence
(AI*IA'97)*, number 1321 in Lecture Notes In Artificial Intelligence, pages 231–241.
Springer-Verlag, 1997.

[Rosati, 1997b] Riccardo Rosati. Reasoning with minimal belief and negation as failure: Algorithms and complexity. In *Proc. of the 14th Nat. Conf. on Artificial Intelligence (AAAI'97)*, pages 430–435. AAAI Press/The MIT Press, 1997.

[Schwarz and Lifschitz, 1993] G. Schwarz and V. Lifschitz. Extended logic programs
as autoepistemic theories. In *Proc. of the 2nd Int. Workshop on Logic Programming
and Non-monotonic Reasoning (LPNMR'93)*, pages 101–114. The MIT Press, 1993.

[Schwarz and Truszczyński, 1994] G. Schwarz and M. Truszczyński. Minimal knowledge problem: a new approach. *Artificial Intelligence*, 67:113–141, 1994.

[Schwarz, 1992] G. Schwarz. Minimal model semantics for nonmonotonic modal logics.
In *Proc. of the 7th IEEE Sym. on Logic in Computer Science (LICS'92)*, pages 34–43.
IEEE Computer Society Press, 1992.

[Schwarz, 1996] G. Schwarz. On embedding default logic into Moore's autoepistemic
logic. *Artificial Intelligence*, 80:388–392, 1996.

[Shoham, 1987] Y. Shoham. Nonmonotonic logics: Meaning and utility. In *Proc. of
the 10th Int. Joint Conf. on Artificial Intelligence (IJCAI'87)*, pages 388–392, 1987.

[Stalnaker, 1993] Robert Stalnaker. A note on non-monotonic modal logic. *Artificial
Intelligence*, 64(2):183–196, 1993.

A Description Logic for Image Retrieval

Eugenio Di Sciascio, Francesco M. Donini, Marina Mongiello

Dipartimento di Elettrotecnica ed Elettronica
Politecnico di Bari
Via Re David, 200 - 70125 Bari
{disciascio,donini,mongiello}@poliba.it

Abstract. We present a simple description logic for semantic indexing in image retrieval. The language allows to describe complex shapes as composition of more simple ones, using geometric transformations to describe the relative positions of shape components. An extensional semantics is provided, which allows us to formally define reasoning services – such as recognition, subsumption, and satisfiability – and to study the computational properties of the formalism. The logic is devised for exact recognition of complex shapes, but it can be extended to include similarity degrees.

1 Motivations

Recent years have seen an extreme increase of the size of digital image collections. In order to use these images, tools and techniques are needed to efficiently index and retrieve them. Traditional approaches to image databases have been based on the association to images of a textual description and then use text-based Database management systems to perform image retrieval ([3,4]). There are two major drawbacks in this approach. First, the amount of human effort needed to annotate images when collections are large. Second, the difficulties in representing by textual descriptions the rich content of images, and the difference in human perception of the same image.

Lately there has been a growing interest towards content-based image retrieval. Techniques and systems have been proposed to index and retrieve images by their own visual properties, e.g. color, shape, texture, etc. ([8,11]). All these techniques require image analysis and processing prior to indexing. While color and texture based retrieval have been widely experimented with good results, retrieval by shape is still a challenging problem. As a matter of fact, retrieval by shape requires image segmentation. Good results have been obtained also in this field, but a blind automatic segmentation provides a partition of images in regions, which is quite different from actual objects. Most systems overcome this difficulty either indexing regions [12] or reducing the domain of interest to limited classes of objects ([5,14]) or also reverting to human assistance [7]. Reasons for these difficulty are clear: there is a gap to bridge between the low-level features obtainable by a vision algorithm and the complex structures of objects. Here

E. Lamma and P. Mello (Eds.): AI*IA 99, LNAI 1792, pp. 13–24, 2000.

we propose to bridge the gap with a structured approach based on Description Logics.

The use of structural descriptions of objects for the recognition of their images can be dated back to Minsky's frames. The idea is to associate parts of an object (and generally of a scene) to the regions an image can be segmented into. Description logics can help by giving an established framework for the structural descriptions of objects and scenes. Structured descriptions of three-dimensional images are already present in languages for virtual reality like VRML [10]. However, the semantics of such languages is operational, and no effort is made to automatically classify objects with respect to the structure of their appearance.

We believe that the use of a language for describing parts of images can provide several benefits. First of all, it semantically clarifies the process of image retrieval (which we consider to be a recognition) as model checking. Secondly, it allows to express complex queries to an image database, such as "retrieve all images with a portal between two smaller portals". Third, it allows a compilation of recognition (i.e., images are classified along the hierarchy of shape descriptions as soon as they are entered in the database) which can considerably speed up query answering. Finally, if the parts of an object are given a name — as in our proposal — this name can be used as part of the explanation of the recognition: i.e., the system can reasonably argue that an image contains a car, pointing to the chassis, the wheels, and the front screen.

We present here a logic, developed along the same lines of Description Logics, which deals only with *exact* recognition of two-dimensional objects in images, i.e., recognition of objects by matching exactly their contour, modulo transformations. Obviously, image recognition should allow for a certain degree of vagueness in matching shapes and identifying colors. However, we believe that before giving a logic of approximate recognition, the logic of exact recognition must be clearly stated as such, and (at least some of) its complexity studied. We claim that the logic we present can be adapted along the same lines of [17, 16] to accommodate for rough recognition, preserving the original framework.

The paper is organized as follows: in Section 2, we present the syntax of a language for composing shapes into shape descriptions, and some examples. In Section 3, we give an extensional (i.e., set-based), compositional semantics to complex shape descriptions. In Section 4, we list the reasoning services that can be set up in our formalism, and in Section 5 we deal with the computational aspects of such services. In the last section we compare our proposal with existing ones we know about, and illustrate how this proposal is driving our current research.

2   Syntax

We assume that each image is divided into *regions*, where a region (denoted by letter r) is a connected part of an image with homogeneous color inside. Uniform color will be replaced by "almost uniform" (fuzzy) in the next version of the logic which we are currently working on. An image I is identified by the set of all its regions. Each region in an image comes with a color $c(r)$ and a contour (or, edge set) $e(r)$.

Our framework does not require a particular method to represent edges and contours, and also the representation of the color c is free.

Given a transformation τ (a rotation, a uniform scaling, and a translation) we denote as $\tau(e(r))$ the (pointwise) transformation of $e(r)$. We recall that such transformations are a mathematical group. *Throughout the paper, transformations are always compositions of rotations, uniform scaling, and translations.*

Any shape which is likely to come with a uniform color in an image — such as rectangles, circles, squares, but also the chassis of a car — is a *basic shape*. Basic shapes are given a concept name B, and are defined by a *prototypical* contour $e(B)$. Intuitively, a region r is recognized as a shape B iff there exists a transformation τ mapping $e(B)$ in $e(r)$, i.e., such that $\tau(e(B)) = e(r)$. In this way, we can abstract from the method used to recognize basic shapes, as long as the method is robust wrt rotations, scaling, and translations. The equality $\tau(e(B)) = e(r)$ will be relaxed to approximate equality (distance within a given range) in the next (fuzzy) version of the logic.

Definition 1. *A basic shape is a pair $(B, e(B))$ where B is a concept name, and $e(B)$ (the prototypical contour of B) is the contour of an image region corresponding to the shape.*

Following hierarchical representations, the contour $e(B)$ can be assumed to be given with respect to the centroid of the region — i.e., coordinates for $e(B)$ are given considering the centroid of the region as the origin.

As an example, one can define the two basic shapes `rectangle` and `arch` by giving their contours $e(\mathtt{rectangle})$ and $e(\mathtt{arch})$ (see Fig. 1, left).

Definition 2. *A basic role is a triple (R, τ, c), where R is a role name, τ is a transformation, and c is a color.*

Definition 3. *A basic component is denoted as $\exists(R, \tau, c).B$, where B is a basic shape.*

Intuitively, a basic component describes a region whose contour is $\tau(e(B))$, which is filled with color c. For example, the right pier (of a white complex shape) could be denoted as $\exists(\mathtt{rightPier}, \tau_2, white).\mathtt{rectangle}$. Anticipating semantics, we point out that the role name R here is just a label: it gives only the name of the component as part of a complex shape, defined as follows:

Definition 4. *A complex shape is a conjunction of components, denoted as $C_1 \sqcap \cdots \sqcap C_n$, where C_i is either a basic component, or a complex component (see Definition 6). A complex shape description is denoted as $D \doteq C$, where D is a shape name and C is a complex shape.*

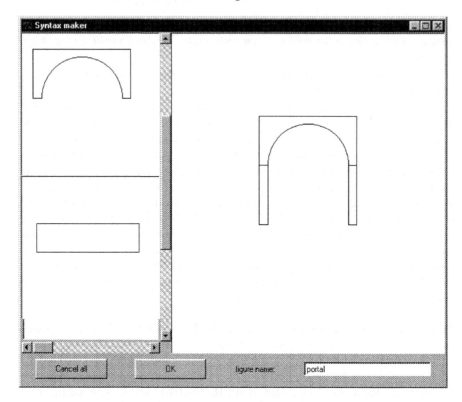

Fig. 1. The construction of a complex shape with a graphical user interface.

For example, the shape of a white portal can be defined as an arch (depicted as a white **arch**) over two piers (depicted as white **rectangles**), with suitable positioning of the three parts with the three transformations τ_1, τ_2, τ_3:

$$\text{portal} \doteq \exists(\text{vault}, \tau_1, white).\text{arch}$$
$$\sqcap \exists(\text{rightPier}, \tau_2, white).\text{rectangle}$$
$$\sqcap \exists(\text{leftPier}, \tau_3, white).\text{rectangle}$$

The contour of the whole portal $e(\text{portal})$ is the familiar arch contour, composed of the edges of the three basic shapes joined together (Fig. 1, right).

Definition 5. *A general role is a pair* (R, τ), *where* R *is a role name, and* τ *is a transformation.*

A general role has the same properties of basic roles, but for the color. The color of a complex shape results from the colors of the basic components, which cannot be overridden. General roles apply to complex shapes, to build nested structures.

Definition 6. *A complex component is denoted as* $\exists(R, \tau).C$, *where* C *is a complex shape.*

For complex components, the transformation τ is rigidly applied to all subcomponents. E.g., the complex component $\exists(R_1, \tau_1).(\exists(R_2, \tau_2, c_2).B2 \sqcap \exists(R_3, \tau_3, c_3).B3)$ describes all shapes obtained by applying the transformation $(\tau_1 \circ \tau_2)$ to $e(B2)$, and filling the region $\tau_1(\tau_2(e(B2)))$ with color c_2, and applying $\tau_1 \circ \tau_3$ to $e(B3)$, and filling $\tau_1(\tau_3(e(B3)))$ with c_3. Observe that $(\tau_1 \circ \tau_2)$ and $(\tau_1 \circ \tau_3)$ are still transformations.

Continuing the example, a (kind of) ancient roman city gate, which we may name `threePortalsGate`, could be defined as two small portals on the two sides of a bigger one, using transformations τ_4, τ_5, τ_6:

$$\text{threePortalsGate} \doteq \exists(\text{leftPortal}, \tau_4).\text{portal}$$
$$\sqcap \ \exists(\text{rightPortal}, \tau_5).\text{portal}$$
$$\sqcap \ \exists(\text{mainPortal}, \tau_6).\text{portal}$$

Intuitively, such description is satisfied by all images containing a shape which can be matched with the above one, modulo a transformation — i.e., any image containing a scaled-rotated-translated gate satisfies the above description. Observe that other kinds of gates can be defined. They would all be classified as shapes containing special kinds of portals.

A usual description logic can be added on top of the constructs above, allowing to state, e.g., that both **portals** and **doors** (with different shapes and parts) are subclasses of **entrances**.

3 Semantics

We give a Tarski-style extensional semantics to our language for shape compositions. Such a semantics is not present in other proposals using Description Logics for image processing (see Section 6 for a comparison).

Each image I corresponds to an interpretation $\mathcal{I}$. The domain Δ of $\mathcal{I}$ is the set of regions which I can be segmented into.

An interpretation maps a shape to a set of regions. An interpretation comes in two ways: either a transformation is specified (written $\mathcal{I}(\tau)$), or not (we write simply $\mathcal{I}$). In the second case, we assume that *there exists* a transformation with particular properties.

An interpretation $\mathcal{I}(\tau)$ maps every basic shape B with prototypical contour $e(B)$ to the set of all regions in Δ whose contour is transformed by τ into $e(B)$. In formulae, $B^{\mathcal{I}(\tau)} = \{r \in \Delta | e(r) = \tau(e(B))\}$ The region is said to be "recognized as a B, with transformation τ". Then, dropping the transformation, the interpretation of a basic shape is:

$$B^{\mathcal{I}} = \{r \in \Delta | \exists \tau : r \in B^{\mathcal{I}(\tau)}\} = \{r \in \Delta | \exists \tau : e(r) = \tau(e(B))\}$$

E.g., **rectangle**$^{\mathcal{I}}$ is interpreted as all rectangular regions in Δ.

A similar interpretation is assumed for basic components, taking color into account: $(\exists(R, \tau_1, c).B)^{\mathcal{I}(\tau)} = \{r \in \Delta | e(r) = \tau(\tau_1(e(B))) \wedge c(r) = c\}$

Again, dropping the transformation one obtains the interpretation of the basic component as regions that can be matched with the basic shape by some transformation:

$$(\exists(R, \tau_1, c).B)^{\mathcal{I}} = \{r \in \Delta | \exists \tau : r \in (\exists(R, \tau_1, c).B)^{\mathcal{I}(\tau)}\}$$
$$= \{r \in \Delta | \exists \tau : e(r) = \tau(\tau_1(e(B))) \wedge c(r) = c\}$$

Thus, a region in the interpretation of a component is said "the R-part" of a complex shape. E.g., the region previously recognized as an isolated **rectangle** can be further recognized as "the **rightPier** of a portal", if also the other parts of the portal are recognized, in the proper positions. Complex components are interpreted in the same way, excluding the color.

Complex shapes are interpreted as sets of regions in one image, such that there exists one transformation, mapping rigidly all parts of the complex shape definition to (sets of) regions in the image. When the complex shape is composed by basic shapes only, it is sufficient to find as many different regions as the components of the complex shape — each region mapped into a component. However, when the complex shape is composed by nested complex shapes, the interpretation requires to have different *sets of* regions $s_1 \ldots, s_n$, where each set can be mapped into a complex component.

$$(C_1 \sqcap \cdots \sqcap C_n)^{\mathcal{I}(\tau)} = \{ \{r_1, \ldots, r_m\} \in \Delta |$$
$$\exists s_1 \cdots \exists s_n \subseteq \{r_1, \ldots, r_m\} :$$
$$(i \neq j \Rightarrow s_i \neq s_j)$$
$$\wedge \;\; \forall i \in 1..n : s_i \in (C_i)^{\mathcal{I}(\tau)}\}$$

Dropping τ, one obtains the interpretation of a complex shape.

$$(C_1 \sqcap \cdots \sqcap C_n)^{\mathcal{I}} = \{ \{r_1, \ldots, r_m\} \in \Delta |$$
$$\exists \tau \exists s_1 \cdots \exists s_n \subseteq \{r_1, \ldots, r_m\} :$$
$$(i \neq j \Rightarrow s_i \neq s_j) \tag{1}$$
$$\wedge \;\; \forall i \in 1..n : s_i \in (C_i)^{\mathcal{I}(\tau)}\}$$

Note that τ is *not* dropped in the last condition of (1) — i.e., the same interpretation $\mathcal{I}(\tau)$ maps all complex components $C_1, \ldots, C_n$ (otherwise the overall shape would not be preserved). In this way, the recognition of a complex shape in an image is restricted to rigid motions of all components.

This semantics deals with the (simple) case in which regions of basic components are always properly segmented. This is not true whenever two touching regions of basic components in a complex shape have the same color; in that case, a single region formed by the union of regions with the same color would be segmented. To deal with this case, the contour of the complex shape should be taken into account — e.g., $\mathtt{portal}^{\mathcal{I}}$ should contain also a single region with the shape of a (completely white) $\mathtt{portal}$. However, we observe that dealing with this problem would entail also a correct treatment of mimesis, which is outside the scope of this work. Hence, we keep here the simpler semantics of differently colored touching regions.

Definition 7. *An interpretation $\mathcal{I}$ related with image I satisfies a shape description D if there exists a subset of Δ which belongs to $D^{\mathcal{I}}$. A shape description is satisfiable if there exists an interpretation (image) satisfying it.*

Observe that descriptions could be unsatisfiable: if two components have overlapping regions, no image can be segmented in a way that satisfies both components. This constraint would be dropped if we moved to describing images of three-dimensional scenes.

Definition 8. *A description D_1 subsumes a description D_2 if every interpretation satisfying D_2 satisfies also D_1.*

For example, the description $\mathtt{portal}$ subsumes $\mathtt{threePortalsGate}$, because to satisfy $\mathtt{threePortalsGate}$ an image I should contain the regions corresponding to the three portals, hence I must satisfy also $\mathtt{portal}$.

We note that although we did not introduce *backgrounds*, they could be added to our framework as special basic components $\exists(\mathtt{background}, c).\top$ with the property that a region b satisfies the background simply if colors match. Also, more than one background could be added; in that case background regions should not overlap, and the matching of background regions should be considered after the regions of all the basic shapes recognized are subtracted to the background regions.

4   Reasoning services

An image *is* an interpretation. Technically, one might think about an image as an ABox; however, observe that usually a *Domain Closure Assumption* (DCA) is made for images — that is, there are no regions but the ones which can be seen in the images themselves. This transforms the problem of instance checking to simpler model checking. Obviously, DCA should be dropped for a description logic dealing with three-dimensional shapes (and scenes). The possible reasoning services in a description logic for image retrieval are:

1. image recognition: given a new image and a collection of descriptions, the new image is classified by finding the most specific descriptions it satisfies;
2. description satisfiability: verify if a given description may contain at least one image — e.g., there are no overlapping regions in the description;
3. image retrieval: given a set of images and the description of a scene, retrieve all images that satisfy the description;

4. description subsumption (and classification): given a (new) description D and a set of descriptions $D_1, \ldots, D_n$, decide if D subsumes/is subsumed by each D_i, $i \in 1..n$.

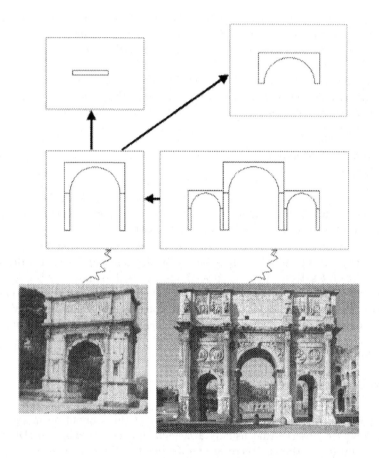

Fig. 2. The subsumption hierarchy for the examples. Thick arrows denote subsumption; the thin arrows link an image to a description it satisfies.

Observe that the expensive process of image retrieval can be simplified by image recognition, in the usual way a classification wrt a TBox (semantic indexing) can help query answering. In fact, given a query description D, if there exists a collection of descriptions $D_1, \ldots, D_n$ and all images in the database are already classified wrt $D_1, \ldots, D_n$, then it may suffice to classify D wrt $D_1, \ldots, D_n$ to find (most of) the images satisfying D. E.g., to answer the query asking for images containing a `portal`, a system may classify `portal` and find that it subsumes `threePortalsGate`; then the system can include in the answer all images recognized as containing ancient roman gates, without recomputing whether these images contain a portal or not — see Figure 2. The whole process will be convenient if classifying the query description on-line is computationally less demanding than computing the answer from scratch. The problem of computing subsumption between descriptions is dealt with in the next section.

5   Computing satisfiability, recognition, and subsumption

Deductive services in this simple description logic rely on the prototypical contours of basic shapes. Intuitively, the existential symbols in the shape descriptions are skolemized with their prototypical contours.

Definition 9. *The* prototypical image $I(D)$ *of a shape description D is an image containing a set of regions defined recursively as follows:*

1. *if D is a basic shape B, then $I(B) = \{r\}$ where r is the region with contour $e(B)$;*
2. *if D is a basic component $\exists(R, \tau, c).B$, then $I(D) = \{r\}$, where r is the region with contour $\tau(e(B))$, filled with color c;*
3. *if D is a complex shape $C_1 \sqcap \ldots \sqcap C_n$ then $I(D) = I(C_1) \cup \cdots \cup I(C_n)$, where $I(C_i)$ is the prototypical image of the i-th component C_i;*
4. *if D is a complex component $\exists(R, \tau).C$, then $I(D) = \tau(I(C))$, where $\tau(I(C))$ is $\tau(\{r_1, \ldots, r_n\})$ and denotes the set of regions obtained from $\{r_1, \ldots, r_n\}$ by transforming each contour $e(r_i)$ to $\tau(e(r_i))$.*

In practice, from a shape description one builds its prototypical image just applying the stated transformations and color fillings to its components. We envisage this prototypical image to be built directly by the user, with the help of a drawing tool, with basic shapes and colors as palette items — see Figure 1. The system will just keep track of the transformations corresponding to the user's actions, and use them in building the (internal) shape descriptions stored with the previous syntax.

Satisfiability of a shape description D can now be easily decided by trying to build $I(D)$, and see if there are not overlapping regions.

Proposition 1. *A shape description D is satisfiable iff its prototypical image $I(D)$ contains no overlapping regions.*

Ideally, every complex description built with the help of a graphical tool — as envisaged in Figure 1 — is satisfiable. Hence we do not deal with this problem any more.

Subsumption can be decided exploiting the following general property relating subsumption to recognition of prototypical images:

Proposition 2. *A shape description D_1 subsumes a shape description D_2 if and only if the prototypical image $I(D_2)$ satisfies D_1.*

The above property allows us to concentrate on complex shape recognition.

Observe that, since there is always the inverse of a transformation τ, if D_1 and D_2 are basic shapes, either they are equivalent (each one subsumes the other) or neither of the two subsumes the other. If we adopt for the segmented regions an invariant representation, (e.g. Fourier transforms of the contour) deciding equivalence between basic shapes, or recognizing whether a basic shape appears in an image, is just a call to an algorithm computing the similarity between shapes. This is what usual image recognizers do — allowing for some tolerance in the matching of the shapes.

For recognizing a complex shape D in an image $\mathcal{I}$, we concentrate on complex shapes made of basic components only — we call such descriptions to be in *normal form*. It is easy to prove that every complex shape description can be turned into a normal form one, just composing the transformations. E.g., the shape $\exists(R_1, \tau_1).(\exists(R_2, \tau_2, c_2).B2 \sqcap \exists(R_3, \tau_3, c_3).B3)$ is equivalent to $\exists((R_1 R_2), (\tau_1 \circ \tau_2), c_2).B2 \sqcap \exists((R_1 R_3), (\tau_1 \circ \tau_3), c_3).B3)$. Therefore, we assume that D is always formed by basic components.

Theorem 1. *Let $D = \sqcap_{i=1}^{k}(\exists(R_i, \tau_i, c_i).B_i)$ be a complex shape in normal form, and let I be an image, segmented into regions $\{r_1, \ldots, r_n\}$. I satisfies D iff there exists a transformation τ such that for each $i \in 1..k$ there exists a $j \in 1..n$ such that $\tau(\tau_i(e(B_i))) = r_j$.*

The fact that we look only for *rigid* transformations of the complex shape D in a given image $\mathcal{I}$ reduces the number of possible matches between the regions of D and those of $\mathcal{I}$, as stated in the following theorem.

Theorem 2. *Given a complex shape with k basic components and an image segmented in n regions, there are at most n^2 possible matches between the k basic shapes and the n regions.*

The above theorem leads to the algorithm Recognize, in which we exploit the fact that each region has a centroid, and to match regions, their centroids should be matched first. This simplifies the computation of possible matches.

Algorithm Recognize (D, I);
input a complex shape description $D = \sqcap_{i=1}^{k}(\exists(R_i, \tau_i, c_i).B_i)$, and
   an image I, segmented into regions $r_1, \ldots, r_n$
output True if D appears in I, False otherwise
begin
   compute the centroids $\mathbf{v}_1, \ldots, \mathbf{v}_n$ of $r_1, \ldots, r_n$;
   extract the centroids $\mathbf{p}_1, \ldots, \mathbf{p}_k$ of the regions of $I(D)$ from $\tau_1, \ldots, \tau_k$;
   for $i, j \in \{1, \ldots, n\}$ with $i \neq j$ **do**
      compute the transformation τ such that $\tau(\mathbf{p}_1) = \mathbf{v}_i$ and $\tau(\mathbf{p}_2) = \mathbf{v}_j$;
      if (**for** $h \in \{3, \ldots, k\}$ it is $\tau(p_h) \in \{\mathbf{v}_1, \ldots, \mathbf{v}_n\}$) **and**

(for $h \in \{1, \ldots, k\}$ **it is**
$\tau(\tau_h(e(B_h))) = e(r)$ **and** $c_h = c(r)$ for some r in I)
   then return True
endfor
return False
end

Theorem 3. *Let D_1 be a complex shape with k basic components, and let $\mathcal{I}$ be an image of $N_h \times N_v$ pixels, segmented into n regions. D can be recognized in $\mathcal{I}$ with $O(n^2 k N_h N_v)$. The same upper bound holds for checking subsumption between D_1 and a complex shape D_2 with n basic components.*

6   Related work and perspectives

In [13] a formalism integrating Description Logics and image retrieval is proposed, while in [9] Description Logics are integrated with spatial reasoning. Both proposals build on the clean integration of Description Logics and *concrete domains* of [1]. However, neither of the formalisms can be used to build complex shapes by nesting more simple shapes. Moreover, the proposal in [9] is based on the logic of spatial relations named RCC8, which is enough for specifying meaningful relations in a map, but it is too qualitative to specify the relative sizes and positions of regions in a complex shape. More similar to our approach is the proposal in [6], where parts of a complex shape are described with a Description Logic. However, the composition of shapes does not consider their positions, hence reasoning cannot take positions into account. Relative position of parts of a complex shape can be expressed in a constraint relational calculus in [2]. However, reasoning about queries (containment and emptiness) is not considered in this approach. Compositions of parts of an image are considered in [15] for character recognition. Note that in our framework, the shape "F" composed by three lines, is subsumed by the shape Γ—something unacceptable in recognizing characters. Apart from the different task, the approach in [15] does not make use of an extensional semantics for composite shapes, hence no reasoning is possible.

This work is still in progress. We are currently extending the formalism to *approximate* matching of shapes and colors. In particular, observe that the similarity degree that is presently computed by all image retrieval systems should be extended to a similarity degree of complex shapes, taking into account both the (usual) similarity degree between simple shapes, and a (new) similarity degree between the *relative positions* of shape components in an image and in a shape description. To this aim, we envisage the application of frameworks for "fuzzy" description logics such as [17, 16]. We believe that the extensional Tarski-style semantics given to our formalism, if suitably extended with a fuzzy recognition, contributes to a smooth integration of Description Logics and existing image retrieval systems, which interpret a user query as a set of images matching the image query — up to a given threshold. We are designing an implementation of the algorithm, to experiment the recognition of complex shapes.

Acknowledgments

We thank Marco Schaerf for useful discussions about VRML, and anonymous referees for useful suggestions and pointers to relevant literature. This research has been supported by project CNR-DeMAnD, and by project MURST 60% "Sistemi informativi di immagini". Francesco Donini acknowledges the Dipartimento di Informatica e Sistemistica, Università di Roma "La Sapienza", for supporting this research through project CNR-LAICO.

References

1. Franz Baader and Philipp Hanschke. A schema for integrating concrete domains into concept languages. In *Proc. of IJCAI'91*, pages 452–457, Sydney, 1991.
2. E. Bertino and B. Catania. A constraint-based approach to shape management in multimedia databases. *Multimedia Systems*, 6:2–16, 1998.
3. N.S. Chang and K.S. Fu. Query by pictorial example. *IEEE Trans. Software Engineering*, 6(6), 1980.
4. S.K. Chang and et al. Intelligent image database system. *IEEE Trans. Software Engineering*, 14(5), 1988.
5. E. Di Sciascio and M. Mongiello. Query by sketch and relevance feedback for content-based image retrieval over the web. *Journal of Visual Languages and Computing*, 10(6), 1999.
6. E. Ardizzone et al. Hybrid computation and reasoning for artificial vision. In V. Cantoni, S. Levialdi, and V. Roberto, editors, *Artificial Vision*, pages 193–221. Academic Press, 1997.
7. M. Flickner and et al. The QBIC system. *IEEE Computer*, 28(9), 1995.
8. V.N. Gudivada and J.V.Raghavan. Special issue on content-based image retrieval. *IEEE Computer*, 28(9), 1995.
9. V. Haarslev, C. Lutz, and R. Moeller. Foundations of spatioterminological reasoning with descrition logics. In *Proc. of KR'98*, pages 112–123, 1998.
10. Jed Hartman and Josie Wernecke. *The VRML 2.0 Handbook*. Addison-Wesley, 1996.
11. R. Jain. Special issue on visual information systems. *Communications of the ACM*, 40(12), Dec. 1997.
12. W.Y. Ma and B.S. Manjunath. NETRA: A toolbox for navigating large image database. In *Proc. of IEEE ICIP*, 1997.
13. C. Meghini, F. Sebastiani, and U. Straccia. The terminological image retrieval model. In *Proc. of ICIAP-97*, number 1311 in LNCS, pages 156–163. Springer-Verlag, 1997.
14. Y. Rui, A.C. She, and T.S. Huang. Automated shape segmentation using attraction-based grouping in spatial-color-texture space. In *Proc. of IEEE ICIP*, 1996.
15. A. Sanfeliu and K. Fu. A distance measure between attributed relational graphs for pattern recognition. *IEEE Trans. on Systems, Man, and Cybernetics*, 13(3):353–362, 1983.
16. U. Straccia. A fuzzy description logic. In *Proc. of AAAI'98*, pages 594–599, 1998.
17. John Yen. Generalizing term subsumption languages to fuzzy logic. In *Proc. of IJCAI'91*, pages 472–477, 1991.

Certainty-factor-like Structures in Bayesian Networks

Peter Lucas

Department of Computing Science, University of Aberdeen
Aberdeen AB24 3UE, Scotland, UK
E-mail: plucas@csd.abdn.ac.uk

Abstract. The certainty-factor model was one of the most popular models for the representation and manipulation of uncertain knowledge in the early rule-based expert systems of the 1980s. After the model was criticised by researchers in artificial intelligence and statistics as being ad-hoc in nature, researchers and developers have stopped using the model. Nowadays, it is often stated that the model is merely interesting from a historical point of view. Its place has been taken by more expressive formalisms for the representation and manipulation of uncertain knowledge, in particular by the formalism of Bayesian networks. In this paper, it is shown that this view underestimates the importance of the principles underlying the certainty-factor model. In particular, it is shown that certainty-factor-like structures occur frequently in practical Bayesian network models as causal independence assumptions. In fact, the noisy-OR and noisy-AND models, two probabilistic models frequently employed, appear to be reinventions of combination functions previously introduced as part of the certainty-factor model. This insight may lead to a reappraisal of the certainty-factor model.

1 Introduction

In the early rule-based expert systems as developed in the 1980s, the representation and manipulation of uncertain knowledge was accomplished by various ad-hoc schemes. Typical examples of such schemes are the certainty-factor calculus of Shortliffe and Buchanan [2, 13] and the subjective Bayesian method as designed by Duda, Hart and Nilsson [4]. At the time the certainty-factor model enjoyed much popularity, possibly due to its mathematical and computational simplicity.

However, after the introduction of more expressive, and mathematically sound, probabilistic methods for the representation and manipulation of uncertainty the early methods have been criticised, sometimes severely, by researchers. Examples of such criticism are easily found in the literature; a selection is shown below (explanations added for the purpose of this paper are written in parentheses). For example, Heckerman states ([5], page 309):

> "... it is recommended that those who intend to build a system incorporating the certainty factor model consider these more general techniques (i.e. Bayesian networks)."

E. Lamma and P. Mello (Eds.): AI*IA 99, LNAI 1792, pp. 25–36, 2000.
© Springer-Verlag Berlin Heidelberg 2000

whereas Neapolitan states ([11], pages 70–71):

> "The calculus for combining certainty factors . . . is of interest primarily for its historical significance."

Jensen's opinion is even stronger ([8], page 3):

> ". . . it is not possible to capture reasoning with uncertainty with inference rules for production rules."

In contrast, the criticism of Pearl is more moderate ([12], page 6):

> "The price attached to extensional systems (e.g. rule-based systems) is that they often yield updating that is incoherent, i.e. subject to surprise and counterintuitive conclusions."

Nowadays, most AI researchers probably agree with the opinions summarised above. The general consensus now is that the framework of Bayesian networks offers a coherent, expressive, and flexible formalism for the representation and manipulation of uncertain knowledge, and there seems to be little reason to revert to the use of the early models of uncertainty. The author of this paper shares this opinion. Yet, the situation is not as clear-cut as it appears.

In this paper it is shown that the certainty-factor model has in fact been reintroduced by Bayesian network theoreticians, and is used as an essential ingredient of many practical network models. The results of this study are significant, because it indicates that particular practically important probabilistic models have been introduced by various research traditions independently, indicating their general significance. Furthermore, this study sheds some light on current Bayesian-network modelling practice. As we have not been able to find similar results in the literature, we believe these results to be new.

In the next section, the certainty-factor model is introduced. Next, we study various probabilistic models that seem good candidates for their mapping to fragments of the certainty-factor model, and also their significance in building real-world Bayesian networks. The paper is rounded off by a discussion of the practical consequences of the results achieved.

2   The Certainty-factor Model

In this section, the basic principles of the certainty-factor model, so far as needed for the reading of this paper, are briefly reviewed.

2.1   Certainty Factors

The certainty-factor model was introduced by Shortliffe and Buchanan as a method for the representation and manipulation of uncertain knowledge in the rule-based expert system MYCIN [13, 2], and later incorporated, in slightly modified form, in the prototypical rule-based expert-system shell EMYCIN [2]. The basic idea underlying the method is that when representing knowledge as production rules of the form **if** e **then** h_x **fi**, a measure of uncertainty x is associated with the hypothesis h, expressing the degree to which the observation of evidence e influences the confidence in h. In developing the certainty-factor model Shortliffe and Buchanan have chosen two basic measures of uncertainty: the *measure of belief* $\mathrm{MB}(h,e)$ expressing the degree to which an observed piece of evidence e increases the belief in a hypothesis h, and the *measure of disbelief* $\mathrm{MD}(h,e)$, expressing the degree to which an observed piece of evidence e decreases the belief in a hypothesis h. Each of these measures lie in the closed interval $[0,1]$.

The measure of belief $\mathrm{MB}(h,e)$ and the measure of disbelief $\mathrm{MD}(h,e)$ are defined in terms of probability theory as relative changes with respect to the prior probability $\Pr(h)$, based on available evidence e. Although intuitively attractive at first sight, Heckerman [5] and Van der Gaag [15] showed that this choice renders the certainty-factor model inconsistent with the basic axioms of probability theory. Heckerman, however, has been able to find alternative definitions for these measures in terms of likelihood ratios, yielding mathematically sound probabilistic interpretations of the model [5].

A *certainty factor* $\mathrm{CF}(h,e)$ is just a numerical measure between -1 and $+1$, defined in terms of measures of belief and disbelief. The actual definition is not relevant for this paper (cf. [9]). A negative certainty factor indicates that the hypothesis h is disconfirmed by the evidence e; a positive certainty factor indicates that the hypothesis h is confirmed by the evidence e. A certainty factor equal to zero indicates that the evidence e does not influence the belief in the hypothesis h. In most implementations of the certainty factor model, the measures of belief $\mathrm{MB}(h,e)$ and disbelief $\mathrm{MD}(h,e)$ are no longer used; only the certainty factor is employed. Consequently, with each production rule **if** e **then** h **fi** is now associated a certainty factor $\mathrm{CF}(h,e)$.

2.2   Combination Functions

For the manipulation of certainty factors, Shortliffe and Buchanan have defined a number of *combination functions*, expressed in terms of certainty factors. For an extensive motivation underlying their design, the reader is referred to [2].

The combination function for the propagation of uncertain evidence from the antecedent of a production rule to its consequence is the following:

$$\mathrm{CF}(h,e') = \mathrm{CF}(h,e) \cdot \max\{0, \mathrm{CF}(e,e')\} \tag{1}$$

Here, $\mathrm{CF}(h,e)$ is the certainty factor associated with the hypothesis h by the production rule **if** e **then** h **fi** if the evidence e has been observed with absolute certainty; $\mathrm{CF}(e,e')$ represents the actual confidence in e based on some prior evidence e' and acts as a weighting factor to $\mathrm{CF}(h,e)$. If the rule's antecedent is false, the resulting weighting factor will be 0, as indicated in formula (1).

The function for combining two certainty factors $\mathrm{CF}(e_1,e')$ and $\mathrm{CF}(e_2,e')$ of two constituting pieces of evidence e_1 and e_2 to obtain a certainty factor for the conjunction e_1 **and** e_2 of these pieces of evidence is as follows:

$$\mathrm{CF}(e_1 \text{ and } e_2, e') = \min\{\mathrm{CF}(e_1,e'), \mathrm{CF}(e_2,e')\} \tag{2}$$

For the disjunction of two pieces of evidence, we have the following formula:

$$\mathrm{CF}(e_1 \textbf{ or } e_2, e') = \max\{\mathrm{CF}(e_1, e'), \mathrm{CF}(e_2, e')\} \tag{3}$$

The combination functions (2) and (3) are commutative and associative in their first argument; so the order in which conjunctions and disjunctions are evaluated has no effect on the resulting certainty factor.

Finally, the combination function for combining two certainty factors $\mathrm{CF}(h, e_1')$ and $\mathrm{CF}(h, e_2')$ which have been derived from two co-concluding production rules **if** e_i **then** h **fi**, $i = 1, 2$, is as follows:

$$\mathrm{CF}(h, e_1' \textbf{ co } e_2') = \begin{cases} x + y(1 - x) & \text{if } x, y > 0 \\ \frac{x+y}{1 - \min\{|x|, |y|\}} & \text{if } -1 < xy \leq 0 \\ x + y(1 + x) & \text{if } x, y < 0 \end{cases} \tag{4}$$

where $\mathrm{CF}(h, e_1') = x$ and $\mathrm{CF}(h, e_2') = y$. Combination function (4) is commutative and associative in its second argument; so, the order in which production rules are applied has no effect on the final result.

As an example, consider the following medical rule base $\mathcal{R}$:

$$\mathcal{R} = \{R_1 : \textbf{ if } \textit{flu} \textbf{ then } \textit{fever}_{\mathrm{CF}(\textit{fever},\textit{flu})=0.8} \textbf{ fi},$$
$$R_2 : \textbf{ if } \textit{common-cold} \textbf{ then } \textit{fever}_{\mathrm{CF}(\textit{fever},\textit{common-cold})=0.3} \textbf{ fi}\}$$

Furthermore, assume that we have the following facts concerning a patient: $\mathrm{CF}(\textit{flu}, e') = 0.6$ and $\mathrm{CF}(\textit{common-cold}, e') = 1$, where e' denotes background knowledge; in words: we are uncertain to some extent whether the patient has the flu, but we are completely certain that the patient has a common cold. The certainty of whether or not the patient has a fever is then calculated as follows, using the combination functions discussed above. First, the uncertainty with respect to the presence of the flu is propagated to the conclusion of rule R_1:

$$\mathrm{CF}(\textit{fever}, e_1') = \mathrm{CF}(\textit{fever}, \textit{flu}) \cdot \max\{0, \mathrm{CF}(\textit{flu}, e')\}$$
$$= 0.8 \cdot 0.6 = 0.48$$

The same is done for rule R_2, with $\mathrm{CF}(\textit{fever}, e_2') = 0.3$ as a result. Next, the results of the two co-concluding rules are combined:

$$\mathrm{CF}(\textit{fever}, e_1' \textbf{ co } e_2') = \mathrm{CF}(\textit{fever}, e_1') + \mathrm{CF}(\textit{fever}, e_2')(1 - \mathrm{CF}(\textit{fever}, e_1'))$$
$$= 0.48 + 0.3(1 - 0.48) = 0.636$$

This result is higher than the individual certainty factors, but still lower than the maximum of the certainty factors attached to the rules, 0.8. This seems intuitively right, because we are not particularly certain about the presence of the flu, whereas knowing that a patient has a common cold is only weak evidence for the presence of fever.

As mentioned above, Heckerman has proposed a number of suitable transformations of the certainty-factor model to probability theory [5]; it is therefore known that the model, with slightly altered definitions, permits a probabilistic interpretation. Although important as a result, this work is still in line with the basic ideas of Shortliffe and Buchanan, in the sense that the original model was the central focus of the study; the meaning of certainty factors as changes to belief states was left unchanged. Our goals are different, because we employ the certainty-factor model without modification as a tool in the analysis of Bayesian-network models. Thus, we are actually interested in the inverse problem. Taking solving the inverse problem as our aim, it seems unnecessary complicated to maintain the idea of certainty factors as modelling belief changes, and we shall therefore abandon this idea. In facts, although certainty factors were originally defined in terms of probability theory, they have never been used in this way, not even in the MYCIN system for which the model was originally developed.

3   Certainty-factor Interpretation of Bayesian Networks

Above, we have summarised the principles of the certainty-factor model. In this section, we trace probabilistic models that correspond to fragments of the certainty-factor model.

3.1   Employed Notation

Stochastic variables will be denoted by upper-case letter, e.g. X; values of variables will be denoted by lower-case letters, e.g. x. In the case of binary variables, the value $X = true$ will be denoted by $X = x$, or simply x; the value $X = false$ is denoted by $X = \neg x$, or simply $\neg x$. All variables are assumed to be discrete. By an expression like

$$\sum_{f(X_1,\ldots,X_n)=c} \psi(X_1,\ldots,X_n)$$

is indicated a summation of function values of a function ψ, ranging over all possible values of the variables $X_1,\ldots,X_n$ satisfying the functional constraint $f(X_1,\ldots,X_n) = c$. A probability distribution will be denoted by Pr.

3.2   Causal Independence

In building Bayesian networks for practical purposes it has been argued that considering the assumption of *causal independence* may be very fruitful [6]. The global structure of a causal-independence model is shown in Fig. 1; it expresses the idea that causes $C_1,\ldots,C_n$ influence a given common effect E through intermediate variables $I_1,\ldots,I_n$ and a deterministic function f. The influence of each cause C_k on the common effect E is independent of each cause C_j, $j \neq k$. The function f represents in which way the intermediate effects I_k, and indirectly also the causes C_k, interact to yield a final effect E. Hence, this function f is defined in such way that when a relationship between $I_k = i_k$, $k = 1,\ldots,n$, and $E = e$ is satisfied, then $e = f(i_1,\ldots,i_n)$.

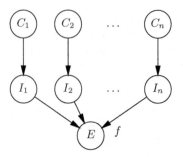

Fig. 1. Causal independence model.

In terms of probability theory, the notion of causal independence can be formalised for a *distinguished value* e of E as follows:

$$\Pr(e|C_1,\ldots,C_n) = \sum_{f(I_1,\ldots,I_n)=e} \Pr(e|I_1,\ldots,I_n)\Pr(I_1,\ldots,I_n|C_1,\ldots,C_n)$$

meaning that the causes $C_1,\ldots,C_n$ influence the common effect E through the intermediate effects $I_1,\ldots,I_n$ only when $e = f(I_1,\ldots,I_n)$ for certain values $I_k = i_k$, $k = 1,\ldots,n$. Under this condition, it is assumed that $\Pr(e|i_1,\ldots,i_n) = 1$; otherwise, when $f(i_1,\ldots,i_n) = e' \neq e$, it holds that $\Pr(e|i_1,\ldots,i_n) = 0$. Note that the effect variable E is conditionally independent of $C_1,\ldots,C_n$ given the intermediate variables $I_1,\ldots,I_n$, and that each variable I_k is only dependent on its associated variable C_k; hence, it holds that

$$\Pr(e|I_1,\ldots,I_n,C_1,\ldots,C_n) = \Pr(e|I_1,\ldots,I_n)$$

and

$$\Pr(I_1,\ldots,I_n|C_1,\ldots,C_n) = \prod_{k=1}^{n} \Pr(I_k|C_k)$$

The formula above can now be simplified to:

$$\Pr(e|C_1,\ldots,C_n) = \sum_{f(I_1,\ldots,I_n)=e} \prod_{k=1}^{n} \Pr(I_k|C_k) \tag{5}$$

Based on the assumptions above, and using marginalisation and conditioning, it also holds that

$$\Pr(e|C_1,\ldots,C_n) = \sum_{I_1,\ldots,I_n} \Pr(e|I_1,\ldots,I_n) \prod_{k=1}^{n} \Pr(I_k|C_k) \tag{6}$$

Formula (5) above is practically spoken still not very useful, because the size of the specification of the function f is exponential in the number of its arguments. The resulting probability distribution is therefore in general computationally intractable, both in terms of space and time requirements. An important subclass

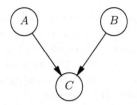

Fig. 2. Three-node model.

of causal independence models, however, is formed by models in which the deterministic function f can be defined in terms of separate binary functions g_k, also denoted by $g_k(I_k, I_{k+1})$. Such causal independence models have been called *decomposable* causal independence models [6]; these models are of significant practical importance. Usually, all functions $g_k(I_k, I_{k+1})$ are identical for each k; a function $g_k(I_k, I_{k+1})$ may therefore be simply denoted by $g(I, I')$. Typical examples of decomposable causal independence models are the noisy-OR and noisy-AND models [6, 7, 12, 14]. These two models will be studied below.

3.3 Noisy-OR Model

As shown above, it is the precise definition of the function f of a causal independence model that distinguishes one model from the other. Hence, for simplicity's sake, it is allowed to discard intermediate variables. Also, since only the use of decomposable causal independence models is practically feasible, it seems justified to merely consider three-node models as shown in Fig. 2, without loss of generality.

Now, suppose that the three variables A, B and C are binary variables, and assume that node C represents a logical OR, i.e.:

$$\Pr(c|A, B) = \begin{cases} 0 \text{ if } A = \neg a \text{ and } B = \neg b \\ 1 \text{ otherwise} \end{cases}$$

The binary functions g_k as defined above correspond to a logical OR. The marginal probability $\Pr(C)$ is now obtained as follows, using formula (6):

$$\Pr(c) = \sum_{A,B} \Pr(c|A, B) \Pr(A, B)$$
$$= \Pr(a) \Pr(b) + \Pr(\neg a) \Pr(b) + \Pr(a) \Pr(\neg b)$$

since the variables A and B are independent. We can rewrite this result in two different ways:

1. $\Pr(a) \Pr(b) + \Pr(\neg a) \Pr(b) + \Pr(a) P(\neg b) = \Pr(a) + \Pr(b)(1 - \Pr(a))$, which corresponds to the combination function for co-concluding production rules (4) in the certainty-factor model for positive certainty factors;
2. $\Pr(a) \Pr(b) + \Pr(\neg a) \Pr(b) + \Pr(a) \Pr(\neg b) = 1 - \Pr(\neg a, \neg b) = 1 - \Pr(\neg a) \Pr(\neg b)$ (because, $\Pr(\neg a, \neg b)$ was discarded in the sum above), which is a well-known formula used to define the noisy-OR model [12].

Note that $\Pr(\neg c) = 1 - \Pr(c) = \Pr(\neg a)\Pr(\neg b)$ is unspecified in the certainty-factor model, because certainty factors only concern positive literals. This limitation is not too important, because we can just stick to the standard probabilistic interpretation of $\Pr(\neg c)$. Alternatively, this limitation might be dealt with by the method discussed in the next section, compensating for not dealing with negative literals in the certainty-factor model.

Hence, it appears that the noisy-OR model has exactly the same mathematical structure as combination function (4) for co-concluding production rules of the certainty-factor model for binary variables.

3.4   Noisy-AND Model

The noisy-OR appears to be one of the most popular probabilistic models used in building practical Bayesian networks. However, this model is not suitable when one is primarily interested in modelling the conjunctive effect of particular causes. This idea naturally leads to the concept of the noisy-AND model. Using again the topology of the graph depicted in Fig. 2, the noisy-AND model can be defined in terms of a probabilistic representation of the logical AND:

$$\Pr(c|A, B) = \begin{cases} 1 \text{ if } A = a \text{ and } B = b \\ 0 \text{ otherwise} \end{cases}$$

where A, B and C are binary stochastic variables. The binary functions g_k now correspond to the logical AND. Using again formula (6), it follows that:

$$\Pr(c) = \sum_{A,B} \Pr(c|A, B)\Pr(A, B) = \Pr(a)\Pr(b)$$

because A and B are independent. This result does not correspond to the combination function for co-concluding production rules (4). However, it is possible to represent the noisy-AND model in terms of the combination function for the propagation of evidence (1), using two production rules as follows:

> **if** a **then** $b_{\Pr(b)}$ **fi**
> **if** b **then** $c_{1.0}$ **fi**

given the probability distributions $\Pr(A)$ and $\Pr(B)$, and assuming that the subscript 1.0 attached to c represents a certainty factor. Using combination function (1) twice yields the required result for C.

3.5   Generalised Noisy Interactions

When we drop the restriction that variables are binary, generalisations of the noisy-OR and noisy-AND model, known as the *noisy-MAX* and *noisy-MIN model*, respectively, are obtained [6]. In both models, the values of the variables are assumed to be linearly ordered. The maximum (noisy-MAX) or minimum (noisy-MIN) according to this order of two given values of variables are determined. For the value highest (noisy-MAX) or lowest (noisy-MIN) in the order,

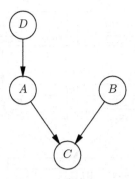

Fig. 3. Propagation of evidence.

the results are the same as for the noisy-OR and noisy-AND models. For the other values, however, the results are different from the certainty-factor model, simply because in the certainty-factor model, the uncertainties with respect to values are always produced using the same combination functions. In both the noisy-MAX and noisy-MIN model, however, the actual combination function varies with the position of values in the linear order. Still, there is much similarity in mathematical structure between the noisy-MAX and noisy-MIN models on the one hand, and the combination functions on the other hand.

3.6 Propagation of Evidence

Consider the probabilistic network shown in Fig. 3; it is identical to the network model in Fig. 2, except that a node D is added. Let us assume that the corresponding variable D only influences the uncertainty with respect to A for the distinguished value d (D is present); if D is absent, i.e. $\neg d$, it holds that A cannot occur, formally: $\Pr(a|\neg d) = 0$. We only consider the noisy-OR probabilistic model of causal independence in this section.

Now, when assuming that evidence with respect to D has been observed with certainty, it holds that:

$$\Pr(C|D) = \sum_{A,B} \Pr(C, A, B|D)$$
$$= \sum_{A,B} \Pr(C|A, B) \Pr(A|B, D) \Pr(B|D)$$
$$= \sum_{A,B} \Pr(C|A, B) \Pr(A|D) \Pr(B)$$

by the (conditional) independence information represented in the network. Let node C again model a logical OR, as defined in Section 3.3. Under this condition, it holds that when $D = d$: $\Pr(c|d) = \Pr(a|d) \Pr(b) + \Pr(a|d) \Pr(\neg b) + \Pr(\neg a|d) \Pr(b)$, which is equal to $\Pr(a|d) + \Pr(b)(1 - \Pr(a|d))$. This equation combines the effects of combination function (1), the propagation of evidence

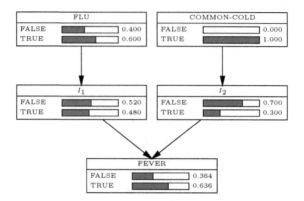

Fig. 4. Bayesian-network example.

from D to A, and combination function (4) for co-concluding production rules. Note that $\Pr(c|\neg d) = \Pr(\neg a|\neg d)\Pr(b) = \Pr(b)$, which result corresponds to the situation when the rule **if** d **then** a **fi** fails; only B contributes to C. This result is again in accordance with the certainty-factor model.

Next, assume that D in Fig. 3 is not known with certainty. We then get:

$$\Pr(C) = \sum_{A,B,D} \Pr(C, A, B, D) = \sum_{A,B,D} \Pr(C, A, B|D)\Pr(D)$$

Substituting results from the derivation of $\Pr(C|D)$ above in this equality, we obtain:

$$\Pr(C) = \sum_{A,B,D} \Pr(C|A, B)\Pr(A|D)\Pr(B)\Pr(D)$$

Again, using the causal independence assumption of the logical OR, the following result is obtained:

$$\begin{aligned}
\Pr(c) &= \Pr(c|d)\Pr(d) + \Pr(c|\neg d)\Pr(\neg d) \\
&= (\Pr(a|d) + \Pr(b)(1 - \Pr(a|d)))\Pr(d) + \Pr(b)\Pr(\neg d) \\
&= \Pr(a|d)\Pr(d) + \Pr(b)(1 - \Pr(a|d)\Pr(d))
\end{aligned}$$

This result corresponds again to the successive application of combination functions (1) and (4) in the certainty-factor model.

As an example, consider the Bayesian network shown in Figure 4. This Bayesian network expresses that both flu and common cold may cause fever, but with different probability. The effects of flu and common cold on the presence of fever are modelled through intermediate variables I_1 and I_2: $\Pr(i_1|flu) = 0.8$, and $\Pr(i_2|common\text{-}cold) = 0.3$. Furthermore, it is assumed that $\Pr(i_k|w) = 0$, $k = 1, 2$, if $w \in \{\neg flu, \neg common\text{-}cold\}$. The interaction between the variables FLU and COMMON-COLD has been modelled as a noisy-OR:

$$\Pr(fever|I_1, I_2) = \begin{cases} 0 \text{ if } I_1 = false \text{ and } I_2 = false \\ 1 \text{ otherwise} \end{cases}$$

Now, suppose that we know for certain that the patient has a common cold, whereas the probability that the patient has the flu is only 0.6. Using the method above, the marginal probability distribution for each variable in the network has been computed, as shown in the figure. The probability that the patient has a fever is 0.636. It now appears that this example corresponds to the certainty-factor formulation of the same problem as discussed in Section 2.2.

4   Practical Significance

Above we have seen that important Bayesian network models can be mapped to fragments of the certainty-factor model. However, the results of this paper would have little significance when in almost all practical network models the assumptions underlying decomposable, causal independence would not be satisfied. But the opposite appears to be the case: in many practical Bayesian network models, a lot of causal independence assumptions are made. This is to be expected, because the technology of Bayesian networks is only practically useful when a large amount of information concerning independence, with causal independence as a special case, is available in a domain. A number of actual network models, as described in the literature, is briefly discussed to illustrate this point.

Heckerman and colleagues have described a probabilistic network for printer trouble shooting [6]. Assumptions of causal independence are rather essential ingredients of the network, and the arguments developed in this paper seem to fully apply to this network. Díez and colleagues [3] have developed a Bayesian network for the diagnosis of heart disease, in which the noisy-OR and noisy-MAX models are used to represent interactions among causes. Another well-known example is the probabilistic reformulation of Internist-1/QMR [10]. In this network model, assumptions of causal independence are used intensively.

In applications of prediction and planning it is in principle possible to use the certainty-factor calculus as a method for probabilistic inference if the structure of the network follows the principles discussed in this paper. An example of such a Bayesian network, meant to assist medical specialists in the treatment of infectious diseases, is described in [1]. This observation is interesting from the perspective of the design of efficient algorithms for probabilistic inference [16].

5   Discussion

We have studied the mapping of probabilistic structures to fragments of the certainty-factor model. As was to be expected, only very specific probabilistic models can be dealt with in this way. Nevertheless, these structures appear to be of major practical importance to developers of Bayesian networks for specific problem domains. The conclusion that the certainty-factor model is more important than most researcher nowadays think, seems inescapable. There can be learnt something from the early models of uncertainty in terms of probabilistic structures that have general significance. We believe that the results of this paper ought to be common knowledge to artificial-intelligence researchers.

We finally would like to plea for a more balanced view of the certainty-factor model; too often researchers have expressed opinions about the model that are not supported by scientific facts.

References

1. S. Andreassen, C. Riekehr, B. Kristensen, H.C. Schønheyder and L. Leibovici. Using probabilistic and decision-theoretic methods in treatment and prognosis modeling, *Artificial Intelligence in Medicine* 15, 1999, 121–134.
2. B.G. Buchanan and E.H. Shortliffe (Eds.). *Rule-Based Expert Systems: The MYCIN Experiments of the Stanford Heuristic Programming Project* (Addison-Wesley Publishing Company, Reading, Massachusetts, 1984).
3. F.J. Díez, J. Mira, E. Iturralde and S. Zubillage. DIAVAL: a Bayesian expert system for echocardiography, *Artificial Intelligence in Medicine* 10, 1997, 59–73.
4. R.O. Duda, P.E. Hart and N.J. Nilsson. Subjective Bayesian methods for rule-based inference systems. In: *AFIPS Conference Proceedings of the 1976 National Computer Conference* 45, 1075–82.
5. D. Heckerman. Probabilistic interpretations for MYCIN's certainty factors. In: L.N. Kanal and J.F. Lemmer (Eds.), *Uncertainty in Artificial Intelligence* (North-Holland, Amsterdam, 1986) 298–312.
6. D. Heckerman and J.S. Breese. Causal independence for probabilistic assessment and inference using Bayesian networks, *IEEE Transactions on Systems, Man and Cybernetics* 26(6), 1996, 826–831.
7. M. Henrion. Some practical issues in constructing belief networks. In: J.F. Lemmer and L.N. Kanal (Eds.), *Uncertainty in Artificial Intelligence* 3 (Elsevier, Amsterdam, 1989) 161–173.
8. F.V. Jensen. An Introduction to Bayesian Networks (UCL Press, London, 1996).
9. P.J.F. Lucas and L.C. van der Gaag. *Principles of Expert Systems* (Addison-Wesley, Wokingham, 1991).
10. B. Middleton, M.A. Shwe, D.E. Heckerman, M. Henrion, E.J. Horvitz, H.P. Lehmann and G.F. Cooper. Probabilistic diagnosis using a reformulation of the INTERNIST-1/QMR knowledge base, II – Evaluation of diagnostic performance, *Methods of Information in Medicine* 30, 1991, 256–267.
11. R.E. Neapolitan. *Probabilistic Reasoning in Expert Systems — Theory and Algorithms* (John Wiley & Sons, New York, 1990).
12. J. Pearl. *Probabilistic Reasoning in Intelligent Systems: Networks of Plausible Inference* (Morgan Kaufmann Publishers, San Mateo, California, 1988).
13. E.H. Shortliffe. *Computer-Based Medical Consultations: MYCIN* (Elsevier, New York, 1976).
14. S. Srinivas. A generalization of the noisy-OR model. In: *Proceedings of the 9th Conference on Uncertainty in Artificial Intelligence*, 1993, 208–215.
15. L.C. van der Gaag. *Probability-based Models for Plausible Reasoning*, PhD Thesis, University of Amsterdam, 1990.
16. N.L. Zhang and D. Poole. Exploiting causal independence in Bayesian network inference, *Journal of Artificial Intelligence Research* 5, 1996, 301–328.

Sensitivity Analysis for Threshold Decision Making with Bayesian Belief Networks*

Linda C. van der Gaag [1] and Veerle M.H. Coupé [2]

[1] Department of Computer Science, Utrecht University, P.O. Box 80.089, 3508 TB Utrecht, The Netherlands; linda@cs.uu.nl
[2] Center for Clinical Decision Sciences, Erasmus University Rotterdam, P.O. Box 1738, 3000 DR Rotterdam, The Netherlands; coupe@mgz.fgg.eur.nl

Abstract. The probability assessments of a Bayesian belief network generally include inaccuracies. These inaccuracies influence the reliability of the network's output. An integral part of investigating the output's reliability is to study its robustness. Robustness pertains to the extent to which varying the probability assessments of the network influences the output. It is studied by subjecting the network to a sensitivity analysis. In this paper, we address the issue of robustness of a belief network's output in view of the threshold model for decision making. We present a method for sensitivity analysis that provides for the computation of bounds between which a network's assessments can be varied without inducing a change in recommended decision.

1 Introduction

Bayesian belief networks are widely accepted in artificial intelligence as intuitively appealing representations of domain knowledge. A Bayesian belief network basically is a concise representation of a joint probability distribution. It encodes, in a qualitative, graphical part, the variables of importance in the domain that is being represented, along with their probabilistic interrelationships; the strengths of these relationships are quantified by conditional probabilities, that with each other constitute the network's quantitative part. The increasing number of knowledge-based systems that build upon the framework of Bayesian belief networks for knowledge representation and inference, clearly demonstrate its usefulness for addressing complex real-life problem domains in which uncertainty is predominant. Most notably, applications are being realised in the medical domain, for diagnosis, prognostic assessment, and treatment planning.

Bayesian belief networks are generally constructed with the help of experts from the domain of application. Experience shows that, although it may require considerable effort, building the qualitative part of a belief network is quite practicable. In fact, as it has parallels to designing a domain model for a more traditional knowledge-based system, well-known knowledge-engineering techniques

---

* The investigations were (partly) supported by the Netherlands Computer Science Research Foundation with financial support from the Netherlands Organization for Scientific Research (NWO).

E. Lamma and P. Mello (Eds.): AI*IA 99, LNAI 1792, pp. 37–48, 2000.
© Springer-Verlag Berlin Heidelberg 2000

can be employed. Constructing a belief network's quantitative part is generally considered a far harder task, not in the least because it tends to be much more time-consuming. It amounts to assessing various conditional probabilities for the variables represented in the network's qualitative part. Although, for most application domains, probabilistic information is available from literature or from statistical data, it often turns out that this information does not provide for estimating all probabilities required [DV95]. For most domains, therefore, many probabilities remain to be assessed by domain experts. Upon eliciting judgemental probabilities from experts, various problems of bias and poor calibration are typically encountered [KST82]. The probability assessments obtained for a belief network as a consequence tend to be inaccurate.

The inaccuracies in the probability assessments of a Bayesian belief network influence the reliability of its output. An integral part of investigating the reliability of a network's output is to study its robustness. Robustness pertains to the extent to which varying the probability assessments of the network influences its output. For gaining detailed insight in output robustness, a Bayesian belief network can be subjected to a sensitivity analysis [CV98]. Sensitivity analysis is a general technique for investigating the effects of the inaccuracies in the parameters of a mathematical model on the model's output [MH90]. The basic idea of performing a sensitivity analysis of a belief network is to systematically vary the assessments for the network's conditional probabilities and study the effects on the output. Upon such an analysis, some conditional probabilities will show a considerable impact, while others will hardly reveal any influence.

In this paper, we address the issue of output robustness of a Bayesian belief network in view of applications in which the output is used for decision making. To this end, we focus on the threshold model for decision making. Although generally applicable, this model is used most notably for patient management in medical applications [PK80]. With the threshold model, an attending physician decides whether or not to gather additional information from diagnostic tests and whether or not to give treatment based upon the probability of disease for a patient under consideration. The robustness of the output of a belief network now pertains not just to the probability of disease computed from the network, but also to the decision for patient management based upon it. For some conditional probabilities, varying their assessment may have a considerable effect on the probability of disease and yet not induce a change in patient management; for other probabilities, variation may have little effect on the probability of disease and nonetheless result in a different management decision. Studying the effects of varying the assessments for the network's conditional probabilities on the probability of disease therefore no longer suffices for establishing robustness: the effects on the recommended decision need also be taken into consideration.

To provide for studying output robustness of a Bayesian belief network in view of the threshold model for decision making, we enhance the basic method of sensitivity analysis with the computation of upper and lower bounds between which a belief network's assessments can be varied without inducing a change in recommended decision. Informally speaking, the more a belief network's probability assessments can be varied, the more robust the decision based upon the network is.

The paper is organised as follows. In Section 2, we briefly review the formalism of Bayesian belief networks. In Section 3, we outline the threshold model for decision making. In Section 4, we detail the basic method of sensitivity analysis and its enhancement for threshold decision making. The paper ends with some conclusions and directions for further research in Section 5.

2   Bayesian Belief Networks

A *Bayesian belief network* basically is a representation of a joint probability distribution on a set of statistical variables [Pea88]. It consists of a qualitative part and an associated quantitative part. The network's qualitative part takes the form of an acyclic directed graph, or digraph, for short. Each node in this digraph represents a statistical variable that takes its value from a finite set of discrete values. In this paper we will restrict the discussion to binary variables, taking one of the values *true* and *false*. If a variable V has the value *true*, we will write v; the notation $\neg v$ is used to indicate that $V = false$. The arcs in the digraph represent the influential relationships among the represented variables. The tail of an arc indicates the cause of the effect at the head of the arc. Absence of an arc between two variables means that these variables do not influence each other directly and, hence, are conditionally independent.

For our running example we consider the following fragment of (fictitious and incomplete) medical information, adapted from [Coo84]:

> Consider a primary tumour with an uncertain prognosis in an arbitrary patient. The cancer can metastasize to the brain and to other sites. We are interested in the course of the cancer within the next few years, especially with regard to the development of a brain tumour and its associated problems. Metastatic cancer (denoted MC) may be detected by an increased level of serum calcium (ISC). The presence of a brain tumour (B) may be established from a CT scan (CT). Severe headaches (SH) are indicative of the presence of a brain tumour. Both a brain tumour and an increased level of serum calcium are likely to cause a patient to fall into a coma (C) in due course.

In this fragment of information, six statistical variables are identified. The influential relationships among these variables are encoded in the digraph depicted in Figure 1. The digraph for example reflects, by means of the arc $B \rightarrow SH$, that the presence of a brain tumour is a possible cause of severe headaches.

The relationships among the variables that are represented in the qualitative part of a Bayesian belief network basically are probabilistic dependences. The strengths of these dependences are described by conditional probabilities: for each variable, the probabilities of its values are specified conditional on the various possible combinations of values for its parents in the digraph. For our

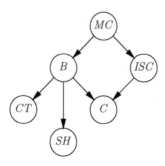

Fig. 1. The digraph of an example belief network; it expresses information concerning the presence of a brain tumour and its associated problems in an arbitrary patient.

running example, we assume the following probabilities:

$p(b \mid mc) =$	0.20	$p(mc) =$	0.20	$p(ct \mid b) =$	0.95
$p(b \mid \neg mc) =$	0.05			$p(ct \mid \neg b) =$	0.10

$$p(c \mid b, isc) = 0.80$$

$p(isc \mid mc) =$	0.80	$p(c \mid \neg b, isc) =$	0.80
$p(isc \mid \neg mc) =$	0.20	$p(c \mid b, \neg isc) =$	0.80

$p(sh \mid b) =$ 0.80
$p(sh \mid \neg b) = 0.60$

$$p(c \mid \neg b, \neg isc) = 0.05$$

The probabilities specified for the variable ISC, for example, express that knowing whether or not metastatic cancer is present has a considerable influence on the probability of an increased level of serum calcium in an arbitrary patient. The relationship between metastatic cancer and increased total serum calcium therefore is a strong dependence. On the other hand, severe headaches are expressed as quite common in both patients with and without a brain tumour. Severe headaches thus have a low predictive value for a brain tumour. The probabilities with each other constitute the network's quantitative part.

The qualitative and quantitative parts of a Bayesian belief network with each other uniquely define a joint probability distribution. A belief network therefore allows for the computation of any probability pertaining to its variables. For this purpose, various algorithms are available, that provide for computing probabilities of interest and for processing evidence, that is, for entering observations into the network and subsequently computing the revised probability distribution given these observations [Pea88,LS88]. The details of these algorithms are not relevant for the present paper.

3   Threshold Decision Making

In the medical domain, Bayesian belief networks are often used for diagnostic purposes. A diagnostic belief network typically comprises one or more variables modeling the presence or absence of disease, various variables modeling findings and results from diagnostic tests, and a number of intermediate variables modeling unobservable pathophysiological states. In our example network, for instance, the variable B models the disease of interest, being the presence or absence of a brain tumour; the variable MC models an unobservable state and the remaining variables capture findings and test results. A medical diagnostic belief network is used for computing a most likely diagnosis for a patient given his or her presentation findings and test results.

The most likely diagnosis for a patient, along with its uncertainty, is generally taken by an attending physician to decide upon management of the patient. The physician may decide, for example, to start treatment rightaway. For our running example, the physician may decide to perform neurosurgery if a brain tumour is indicated. Alternatively, the physician may defer the decision whether or not to treat the patient until additional diagnostic information has become available, for example from a CT scan. Or, the physician may decide to withhold treatment altogether. To support choosing among these decision alternatives, the threshold model for patient management can be used.

The *threshold model for patient management*, or for decision making more in general, builds upon various threshold probabilities of disease [PK80]. The *treatment threshold probability* of disease, written $P^*(d)$ for disease d, is the probability at which an attending physician is indifferent between giving treatment and withholding treatment. If, for a specific patient, the probability of disease $\Pr(d)$ exceeds the treatment threshold probability, that is, if $\Pr(d) > P^*(d)$, then the physician will decide to treat the patient as if the disease were known to be present with certainty. Alternatively, if $\Pr(d) \leq P^*(d)$, the physician will basically withhold treatment from the patient.

As a consequence of the uncertainty concerning the presence of disease in a patient, additional information from a diagnostic test may affect an attending physician's basic management decision. If the probability of disease exceeds the treatment threshold probability, then interpreting a negative test result may result in an updated probability of disease *below* the threshold probability. Alternatively, if the pretest probability of disease falls below the treatment threshold probability, a positive test result may raise the probability of disease to a value *above* the threshold probability. To reckon with such effects, the threshold model for patient management includes another two threshold probabilities. The *no treatment-test threshold probability* of disease, written $P^-(d)$, is the probability at which the attending physician is indifferent between the decision to withhold treatment and the decision to obtain additional diagnostic information. The *test-treatment threshold probability* of disease, written $P^+(d)$, is the probability at which the physician is indifferent between obtaining additional information and starting treatment rightaway.

Figure 2 summarises the basic idea of the threshold model for patient management. As long as the diagnostic test under consideration has not been performed, a physician has three decision alternatives at his or her disposal. If the probability of disease $\Pr(d)$ for a patient falls below the no treatment-test threshold probability, that is, if $\Pr(d) < P^-(d)$, then the physician will withhold treatment from the patient without gathering additional diagnostic information.

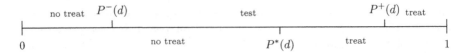

Fig. 2. The threshold model for patient management, indicating three threshold probabilities and the various decision alternatives at a physician's disposal.

If the probability of disease exceeds the test-treatment threshold probability, that is, if $\Pr(d) > P^+(d)$, then the physician will start treatment rightaway. Otherwise, that is, if $P^-(d) \leq \Pr(d) \leq P^+(d)$, the physician will perform the diagnostic test. After testing, there are only two decision alternatives left. If the updated probability of disease for the patient exceeds the treatment threshold probability, the physician will start treatment; otherwise, treatment will be withheld from the patient.

The treatment threshold probability of disease $P^*(d)$ used in the threshold model is typically established by a physician after carefully weighing the various utilities involved. These utilities pertain to the presence or absence of disease on the one hand and giving or withholding treatment on the other hand. From the expected utilities for giving and withholding treatment in view of the uncertainty concerning the presence of disease, the probability of disease at which the physician is indifferent between the two decision alternatives is readily determined; the basic idea is illustrated in Figure 3(a). For our running example, the physician will typically take into consideration the life expectancy for a patient, with and without a brain tumour, and the patient's attitude towards impaired health states; we assume that the physician sets the treatment threshold probability of a brain tumour at 0.15. The two threshold probabilities $P^-(d)$ and $P^+(d)$ for deciding whether or not to perform a diagnostic test are established from the test's characteristics. For our example, the physician will typically weigh the discomfort of a CT scan for a patient against the additional

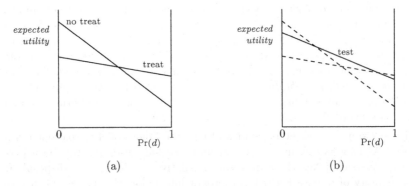

(a)   (b)

Fig. 3. The basic idea of establishing the treatment threshold probability of disease, (a), and the no treatment-test and test-treatment threshold probabilities, (b).

diagnostic information yielded by the scan; we assume that the physician sets the no treatment-test threshold probability of a brain tumour at 0.045 and the test-treatment threshold probability at 0.56. The basic idea of establishing these two threshold probabilities is illustrated in Figure 3(b).

Although we have discussed the threshold model for decision making in a medical context, we would like to note that the model's use is not restricted to the medical domain but in fact is broadly applicable.

4   Sensitivity Analysis for Threshold Decision Making

In our introduction, we have argued that the various probability assessments of a Bayesian belief network tend to be inaccurate. To gain insight into the effects of the inaccuracies involved, a belief network can be subjected to a sensitivity analysis. In Section 4.1, we outline sensitivity analysis of a Bayesian belief network with regard to a probability of interest. In Section 4.2, we address sensitivity analysis of a belief network in view of threshold decision making.

4.1   Sensitivity analysis of a Bayesian belief network

For a Bayesian belief network, sensitivity analysis amounts to systematically varying the assessments for the network's conditional probabilities and investigating the effects on a probability of interest [CV98]. In essence, for every conditional probability of the network, a number of deviations from the original assessment are investigated. For every investigated value, the probability of interest is computed from the network. The results thus obtained reflect the probability of interest as a function of the conditional probability under study.

We illustrate performing a sensitivity analysis of our example belief network, taking the prior probability of the presence of a brain tumour in an arbitrary patient for the probability of interest. The effects of varying the assessments for the probabilities $p(mc)$ and $p(b \mid \neg mc)$ on this probability of interest are shown in Figure 4. Figure 4(a) shows that systematically varying, from 0 to 1, the assessment for the probability $p(mc)$ of the presence of metastatic cancer has a rather small effect on the probability of interest: $\Pr(b)$ increases from 0.05 to 0.20. Figure 4(b) shows that varying the assessment for the conditional probability $p(b \mid \neg mc)$ of the presence of a brain tumour in the absence of metastatic cancer has a much stronger effect: $\Pr(b)$ now ranges from 0.04 to 0.84. As long as no further information is available about the degrees of inaccuracy in the assessments for the two probabilities under study, we conclude that the probability of interest is more robust with regard to the assessment for the probability $p(mc)$ than with regard to the assessment for $p(b \mid \neg mc)$.

A sensitivity analysis of a Bayesian belief network with regard to a prior probability of interest allows for assessing the robustness of the network in its reflecting a prior probability distribution for the domain of application. In the presence of case-specific observations, however, a belief network may very well

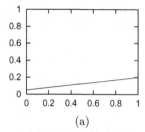
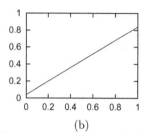

(a)   (b)

Fig. 4. A sensitivity analysis of the example belief network; the effects of varying the assessments for the probabilities $p(mc)$, (a), and $p(b \mid \neg mc)$, (b), on the prior probability of disease $\Pr(b)$ are shown.

show different sensitivities. To reveal these, a sensitivity analysis can be performed with regard to a *posterior* probability of interest. Such an analysis allows for investigating the robustness of the network's output for specific cases or for case profiles.

We once again perform a sensitivity analysis of our example belief network, this time taking for the probability of interest the *posterior* probability $\Pr(b \mid sh)$ of the presence of a brain tumour in a patient who is *known* to suffer from severe headaches. By doing so, we assess the robustness of the diagnosis of a brain tumour for an arbitrary patient with severe headaches. The effects of varying the assessments for the conditional probabilities $p(b \mid \neg mc)$ and $p(sh \mid \neg b)$ on the posterior probability of interest are shown in Figure 5. Figure 5(a), when compared with Figure 4(b), reveals that the observation that a patient suffers from severe headaches has little impact on the robustness of the probability of disease with regard to the assessment for $p(b \mid \neg mc)$. Figure 5(b) shows that varying the assessment for the conditional probability $p(sh \mid \neg b)$ can have a considerable effect on the posterior probability of disease; small deviations from the original assessment 0.60 have little effect, however.

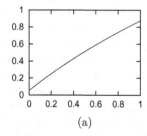
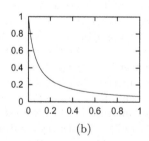

(a)   (b)

Fig. 5. A sensitivity analysis of the example belief network; the effects of varying the assessments for the conditional probabilities $p(b \mid \neg mc)$, (a), and $p(sh \mid \neg b)$, (b), on the posterior probability of disease $\Pr(b \mid sh)$ are shown.

In a sensitivity analysis of a Bayesian belief network, the relation between a probability of interest and a conditional probability under study is a simple mathematical function. In general, the probability of interest relates to a conditional probability under study as a quotient of two linear functions. For the posterior probability of interest $\Pr(d \mid o)$, given some observations o, and a conditional probability x, we have that

$$\Pr(d \mid o) = \frac{a \cdot x + b}{e \cdot x + f}$$

where a, b, e, and f are constants. For an example, we reconsider Figure 5(b) showing for our belief network the posterior probability of interest $\Pr(b \mid sh)$ as a function of the conditional probability $x = p(sh \mid \neg b)$; this function equals

$$\Pr(b \mid sh) = \frac{0.06957}{x + 0.06957}$$

If the conditional probability under study pertains to a variable without any observed descendants, that is an ancestor of the variable of interest in the network's qualitative part, the mathematical function reduces to a linear function. For the probability of interest and a conditional probability x as indicated, we then have that

$$\Pr(d \mid o) = a \cdot x + b$$

where a and b are constants. In particular, a prior probability of interest relates linearly to any conditional probability from the network. For an example, we reconsider Figure 4(b) showing for our belief network the prior probability of interest $\Pr(b)$ as a function of the conditional probability $x = p(b \mid \neg mc)$; the function equals

$$\Pr(b) = 0.8 \cdot x + 0.04$$

The constants in the mathematical functions involved in a sensitivity analysis of a Bayesian belief network are readily determined by computing the probability of interest from the network for a small number of values for the conditional probability under study and solving the resulting system of linear equations. For further technical details, we refer the reader to [CV98].

4.2   Sensitivity analysis in view of threshold decision making

Sensitivity analysis of a Bayesian belief network with regard to a probability of interest yields a functional relation between this probability of interest and every single conditional probability from the network. These relations indicate how the probability of interest will shift upon varying the assessments for the various conditional probabilities. For a probability of interest that is used in the threshold model for decision making, not every shift is significant. In fact, only a shift that results in a different decision recommendation is of interest. In sensitivity analysis in view of threshold decision making, therefore, we have to take the various threshold probabilities employed into consideration. To this end, we enhance sensitivity analysis of a Bayesian belief network with the computation of upper and lower bounds between which the network's assessments can be varied without inducing a change in decision.

The computation of bounds on variation of a belief network's probability assessments builds upon the mathematical functions that we have detailed before, relating a probability of interest to the network's conditional probabilities. Once again focusing on patient management, we begin by considering a probability of disease $\Pr(d \mid o)$ and a conditional probability x to which it is linearly related, that is, we have

$$\Pr(d \mid o) = a \cdot x + b$$

for some constants a and b. For ease of exposition, we assume that $\Pr(d \mid o)$ increases with increasing values for x; we will return to this assumption presently. If, in view of the threshold model, the probability of disease indicates withholding treatment, that is, if $\Pr(d \mid o) < P^-(d)$, then the decision will remain unaltered as long as the conditional probability x is smaller than the value x^- that is computed from

$$a \cdot x^- + b = P^-(d)$$

More precisely, the decision to withhold treatment remains unaltered for any value of the conditional probability x within the interval $(-\infty, x^-) \cap [0, 1]$. If the probability of disease on the other hand indicates starting treatment rightaway, that is, if $\Pr(d \mid o) > P^+(d)$, then the decision will remain unaltered as long as the conditional probability x is greater than the value x^+ that is computed from

$$a \cdot x^+ + b = P^+(d)$$

More precisely, the decision to start treatment rightaway remains unaltered for any value of the conditional probability x within the interval $(x^+, +\infty) \cap [0, 1]$. If the probability of disease indicates testing, that is, if $P^-(d) \leq \Pr(d \mid o) \leq P^+(d)$, then this decision will be the same for any value of the conditional probability x within the interval $[x^-, x^+] \cap [0, 1]$.

So far, we have addressed the computation of bounds on the variation of a conditional probability that is related linearly to the probability of disease. For a conditional probability that is related to the probability of disease by a quotient of two linear functions, bounds on variation are computed in a similar fashion. We have further assumed so far that the probability of disease increases with increasing values of the conditional probability x under study. With this assumption, we have implicitly assumed that $x^- \leq x^+$. For a conditional probability x of which increasing values serve to decrease the probability of disease, we have that $x^- \geq x^+$. Using this observation, the bounds derived above are readily adjusted.

We illustrate the computation of bounds on variation for our example belief network; we recall from Section 3 that the three threshold probabilities of disease have been set at $P^*(b) = 0.15$, $P^-(b) = 0.045$, and $P^+(b) = 0.56$. We begin by addressing the robustness of the decision for management of an arbitrary patient. From our belief network, the prior probability of disease is computed to be $\Pr(b) = 0.08$. For this probability, we have that $P^-(b) \leq \Pr(b) \leq P^+(b)$. Using the threshold model for patient management, therefore, the physician will decide to gather additional information from a CT scan. We investigate the robustness of this decision by computing an upper and lower bound on variation of the assessment for the conditional probability $x = p(b \mid \neg mc)$. The lower bound x^- on variation is computed from

$$\Pr(b) = 0.8 \cdot x^- + 0.04 = 0.045$$

yielding $x^- = 0.00625$; the upper bound x^+ on variation is computed from

$$\Pr(b) = 0.8 \cdot x^+ + 0.04 = 0.56$$

yielding $x^+ = 0.65$. For any value of the conditional probability $p(b \mid \neg mc)$ within the interval $[0.00625, 0.65]$, therefore, the decision to gather additional diagnostic information will remain unaltered. Since the conditional probability under study has been assessed at 0.05, we conclude that the decision is fairly robust with regard to this assessment; variation of the assessment to smaller values, however, may change the decision to the recommendation to withhold treatment without gathering additional diagnostic information.

To conclude, we address the robustness of the management decision for a patient with a primary tumour who is known to suffer from severe headaches. From our belief network, the posterior probability of disease is computed to be $\Pr(b \mid sh) = 0.1039$. For this probability, we observe that $P^-(b) \leq \Pr(b \mid sh) \leq P^+(b)$. The physician will therefore order a CT scan for the patient. We investigate the robustness of this decision by computing the upper and lower bound on variation of the assessment of the conditional probability $x = p(sh \mid \neg b)$. Note that the probability of disease decreases with increasing values for this conditional probability. The lower bound x^+ on variation is computed from

$$\Pr(b \mid sh) = \frac{0.06957}{x^+ + 0.06957} = 0.56$$

yielding $x^+ = 0.1938$. Upon computing the upper bound x^- on variation, we find a value greater than one. For any value of the conditional probability $p(sh \mid \neg b)$ within the interval $[0.1938, 1]$, therefore, the decision to gather additional diagnostic information for the patient will remain unaltered. Since the conditional probability under study has been assessed at 0.60, we conclude that the decision is quite robust with regard to this assessment.

5   Conclusions

The probability assessments of a Bayesian belief network tend to be inaccurate. The belief network as a consequence will yield inaccurate output. If the network's output is used for decision making, its inaccuracy influences the reliability of a decision that is based upon it. An integral part of investigating reliability is to study output robustness. To investigate the robustness of a belief network's output in view of threshold decision making, we have presented an enhanced method for sensitivity analysis that provides for the computation of upper and lower bounds between which a network's assessments can be varied without inducing a change in decision.

We have addressed the issue of robustness in view of a simplified threshold model for decision making, involving binary variables and a single diagnostic test. The more general threshold model addresses variables that have multiple discrete values and provides for selecting among multiple tests. Our method of sensitivity analysis will be further elaborated upon for use with this more general model. Although often used in practice, the threshold model is a simple model for decision making. With a Bayesian belief network, more complex models can be used. More specifically, a belief network can be extended to an influence diagram to provide for addressing more elaborate trade-offs in decision making. The results put forward in this paper hold unabatedly for influence diagrams. In the near future, we hope to extend our method of sensitivity analysis for decision making to apply to influence diagrams.

References

[Coo84] G.F. Cooper (1984). *NESTOR: a Computer-based Medical Diagnostic Aid that Integrates Causal and Probabilistic Knowledge*, Report HPP-84-48, Stanford University.

[CV98] V.M.H. Coupé, L.C. van der Gaag (1998). Practicable sensitivity analysis of Bayesian belief networks. In: M. Hušková, P. Lachout, J.A. Víšek (Editors). *Prague Stochastics '98*, Union of Czech Mathematicians and Physicists, Prague, pp. 81 – 86; also available as Report UU-CS-1998-10, Utrecht University.

[DV95] M.J. Druzdzel, L.C. van der Gaag (1995). Elicitation of probabilities for belief networks: combining qualitative and quantitative information. In: P. Besnard, S. Hanks (Editors). *Proceedings of the Eleventh Conference on Uncertainty in Artificial Intelligence*, Morgan Kaufmann, Palo Alto, pp. 141 – 148.

[LS88] S.L. Lauritzen, D.J. Spiegelhalter (1988). Local computations with probabilities on graphical structures and their application to expert systems. *Journal of the Royal Statistical Society, Series B*, vol. 50, pp. 157 – 224.

[MH90] M.G. Morgan, M. Henrion (1990). *Uncertainty, a Guide to Dealing with Uncertainty in Quantitative Risk and Policy Analysis*, Cambridge University Press, Cambridge.

[Pea88] J. Pearl (1988). *Probabilistic Reasoning in Intelligent Systems. Networks of Plausible Inference*, Morgan Kaufmann, Palo Alto.

[PK80] S.G. Pauker, J.P. Kassirer (1980). The threshold approach to clinical decision making. *New England Journal of Medicine*, vol. 302, pp. 1109 – 1117.

[KST82] D. Kahneman, P. Slovic, A. Tversky (1982). *Judgement under Uncertainty: Heuristics and Biases*, Cambridge University Press, Cambridge.

Abduction with Negation as Failure
for Active and Reactive Rules

Fariba Sadri and Francesca Toni

Department of Computing, Imperial College, London SW7 2AZ, UK
{fs,ft}@doc.ic.ac.uk

Abstract. Recent work has suggested abductive logic programming as a suitable formalism to represent active databases and intelligent agents. In particular, abducibles in abductive logic programs can be used to represent actions, and integrity constraints in abductive logic programs can be used to represent active rules of the kind encountered in active databases and reactive rules incorporating reactive behaviour in agents. One would expect that, in this approach, abductive proof procedures could provide the engine underlying active database management systems and the behaviour of agents. We analyse existing abductive proof procedures and argue that they are inadequate in handling these applications. The inadequacy is due to the inappropriate treatment of negative literals in integrity constraints. We propose a new abductive proof procedure and give examples of how this proof procedure can be used to achieve active behaviour in (deductive) databases and reactivity in agents. Finally, we prove some soundness and completeness results for the new proof procedure.

1 Introduction

Abductive logic programming is a powerful knowledge representation framework, that can be used to realise many diverse applications [9]. An **abductive logic program** $\langle P, \mathcal{A}, I \rangle$ consists of
- a logic program, P, seen as an "incomplete" theory,
- a set of **abducible predicates**, $\mathcal{A}$,
  whose (variable-free) **abducible atoms** are used to expand the theory,
- a set of first-order sentences, I, the integrity constraints,
  that must be "satisfied" by any sets of abducibles expanding the theory.
Earlier work [11, 16] shows promise in using abductive logic programming to understand and implement active databases (e.g. see [17]) and intelligent agents (e.g. see [7]). In particular, *beliefs* and *desires* of agents as conceptualised in the BDI architecture [15] can be understood as logic programs and integrity constraints, respectively.

In general, (many) *active rules* in active databases and rules determining the reactive behaviour of agents in multi-agent systems (*reactive rules*) can be understood as integrity constraints in abductive logic programming. For example, the active/reactive rule

E. Lamma and P. Mello (Eds.): AI*IA 99, LNAI 1792, pp. 49–60, 2000.

on *rise-temperature-to(T)*, if *T>90* then *raise-alarm*
can be understood declaratively as an integrity constraint

$\forall T$ [*rise-temperature-to(T)* $\wedge$ *T>90* $\rightarrow$ *raise-alarm*], or, more accurately

$\forall T, T'$ [*rise-temperature-to(T, T')* $\wedge$ *T>90* $\rightarrow$ *raise-alarm(T' + 1)*].

Reactive rules like the one above can be interpreted as production rules.

Given a goal (conjunction of literals) G, a set of abducible atoms $\mathcal{D}$, and a variable substitution θ for the variables in G, a pair $(\mathcal{D}, \theta)$ is an **abductive answer** for G, wrt an abductive logic program $\langle P, \mathcal{A}, I \rangle$, iff

1) $P \cup \mathcal{D}$ entails $G\theta$, and
2) $P \cup \mathcal{D}$ satisfies I.

Various notions of entailment and satisfaction can be adopted (see [9]). Fulfillment of other properties is sometimes required, e.g. minimality, wrt set inclusion, of the set of abducibles in the answer.

Under the abductive interpretation of multi-agent systems and active databases, abductive answers are understood as acceptable sets of actions to be performed as a consequence of given transactions, in the case of active databases, and of given observations and goals, in the case of agents. In the above example, given the observation *rise-temperature-to(95)* (or more accurately *rise-temperature-to(95,now)*), the only acceptable set of actions (abductive answer) is {*raise-alarm*} (or more accurately {*raise-alarm(now + 1)*}). In general the actions can be internal, for example changing the database, or external, affecting the environment, for example communication actions. Any selected abductive answer corresponds to an *intention* in the BDI architecture for agents [15].

A number of proof procedures for the computation of abductive answers (**abductive proof procedures**) have been proposed, e.g. [10, 2, 5, 3, 12, 14, 16].[1] Reactivity in active database management systems and agents can be obtained by interleaving the execution of the proof procedures, the selection of abducibles (actions) in partially computed abductive answers (plans) and the processing of outside observations, that might trigger active/reactive rules. This interleaving gives rise to an observe-think-act cycle [11, 16].

Our investigation indicates that none of the existing procedures produces the required active/reactive behaviour, due to the inadequate treatment of negative literals in integrity constraints. We propose an alternative abductive proof procedure, obtained by modifying the proof procedure of [5]. We prove soundness of the new proof procedure wrt the semantics of abductive answers in [5] and, in a special case, soundness and completeness wrt the stable model semantics [6].

The paper is organised as follows. In section 2 we describe some preliminary notions. In section 3, through a number of examples, we analyse the behaviour of some existing abductive proof procedures, in particular [5], [10] and [3]. On the basis of the examples, we demonstrate the inadequacy of these proof procedure to be applied in the context of active databases and multi-agent systems. In section 4 we revise the proof procedure of [5] to define the new abductive proof procedure, illustrating its application to examples. In section 5 we prove some

---

[1] Theorist, the procedure presented in [14], computes answers wrt more general logic programs where P, in addition to I, is a set of first-order sentences.

formal properties of the proof procedure, in particular its relationshoip to the proof procedure of [5] and its soundness. In section 6 we conclude.

2   Preliminaries

A **logic program** is a set of rules of the form
$$A \leftarrow L_1 \wedge \ldots \wedge L_n,$$
with A atom, $L_1, \ldots, L_n$ (positive or negative) literals, and $n \geq 0$. All variables in A, L_i are implicitly universally quantified, with scope the entire rule. If $A = p(t)$, for some vector of terms t, the rule is said to *define* p. In the sequel, t, s and t_i represent vectors of terms and X represents a vector of variables.

Our proof procedure relies upon the **completion** [1] of logic programs. The completion of a predicate p defined by the set of rules
$$\{p(t_1) \leftarrow D_1, \ldots, p(t_k) \leftarrow D_k\}$$
is the **iff-definition**
$$p(X) \leftrightarrow [X = t_1 \wedge D_1] \vee \ldots \vee [X = t_k \wedge D_k]$$
where X is a vector of variables, implicitly universally quantified with scope the entire definition, and every variable in t_j and D_j not in X is implicitly existentially quantified on the righthand side of the definition. The left and righthand side are called the *head* and the *body*, respectively. The completion of a predicate p not defined in a given logic program is $p(X) \leftrightarrow false$.

The **selective completion** $comp_S(P)$ of a logic program P wrt a set of predicates S in the language of P is the union of the completions of all the predicates in S.

In this paper, **integrity constraints** are implications of the form
$$L_1 \wedge \ldots \wedge L_n \rightarrow A$$
with $L_1, \ldots, L_n$ literals, possibly *true*, $n > 0$, and A atom, possibly *false*. All variables in A, L_i are implicitly universally quantified, with scope the entire implication. A is called the *head* and $L_1 \wedge \ldots \wedge L_n$ is called the *body*.

Without loss of generality [9] we can assume that the abducible predicates in an abductive logic program $\langle P, \mathcal{A}, I \rangle$ are not defined in P. In the sequel, $\overline{\mathcal{A}}$ will refer to the complement of the set $\mathcal{A}$ wrt the set of all predicates in the language of P, i.e. $\overline{\mathcal{A}}$ is the set of non-abducible predicates.

3   Motivating examples

A number of abductive proof procedures have been defined, e.g. [14, 10, 2, 5, 3]. In this section, we will examine the behaviour of the proof procedures of [10, 5, 3], here referred to as KM, FK and SLDNFA, respectively, for some simple abductive logic programs. Analogous considerations apply for the remaining proof procedures. Note that KM and SLDNFA employ only (*denial*) integrity constraints with the special atom *false* in the head, and assume that integrity constraints $L_1 \wedge \ldots \wedge L_n \rightarrow A$, with $A \neq false$, are rewritten as $L_1 \wedge \ldots \wedge L_n \wedge not\,A \rightarrow false$. Also, the literal *not false* is implicitly conjoined to every initial goal in SLDNFA. Finally, similarly to [2], FK uses $comp_{\overline{\mathcal{A}}}(P)$ rather than P.

In the absence of negation, KM, FK and SLDNFA all produce the required results, as illustrated by the following example.

Example 1. Let $\langle P, \mathcal{A}, I \rangle$ be the abductive logic program with
$$P = \{\ emp(mary), emp(joe), tax\text{-}form(mary, 32B98), tax\text{-}form(joe, nil)\}$$
$$\mathcal{A} = \{print, date\}$$
$$I = \{date(may) \wedge emp(E) \wedge tax\text{-}form(E, nil) \rightarrow print(\text{``E to fill tax form''})\}.$$
The program P represents a database for the personnel of a department, defined in terms of the relations $emp(Employee)$ and $tax\text{-}form(Employee, Code)$. The integrity constraint in I represents the active rule
    on $date(may)$, if $emp(E)$ and $tax\text{-}form(E, nil)$
                                                        then $print(\text{``E to fill tax form''})$
whose procedural interpretation is: when the event $date(may)$ takes place, the rule is triggered, the condition "$emp(E)$ and $tax\text{-}form(E, nil)$" is evaluated, and, for each instance of E satisfying the condition, the printing action is executed.

Given the input $date(may)$, KM, FK and SLDNFA compute the only intuitively correct answer $\{print(\text{``joe to fill tax form''})\}$.

However, in the presence of negation KM, FK and SLDNFA can produce unintuitive answers, as illustrated by the following examples.

Example 2. Let $\langle P, \mathcal{A}, I \rangle$ be the abductive logic program with $P = \emptyset$ and
$$\mathcal{A} = \{cleaning\text{-}day, temperature\text{-}rise, dust, sound\text{-}alarm, evacuate\}$$
$$I = \{\ cleaning\text{-}day \wedge not\ sound\text{-}alarm \rightarrow dust,$$
$$\qquad temperature\text{-}rise \rightarrow sound\text{-}alarm,$$
$$\qquad sound\text{-}alarm \rightarrow evacuate\}.$$
Intuitively, the integrity constraints represent the reactive rules
    on $cleaning\text{-}day$, if $not\ sound\text{-}alarm$, then $dust$
    on $temperature\text{-}rise$, then $sound\text{-}alarm$
    on $sound\text{-}alarm$, then $evacuate$
Given only the observation $cleaning\text{-}day$, KM, FK and SLDNFA compute the intuitively correct answer $\{cleaning\text{-}day, dust\}$ as well as the unintuitive answer $\{cleaning\text{-}day, sound\text{-}alarm, evacuate\}$. The second answer arbitrarily abduces $sound\text{-}alarm$, and is incorrect according to the active database and multi-agent system interpretations. (Note that both answers are minimal wrt set inclusion.)

Example 3. Let $\langle P, \mathcal{A}, I \rangle$ be the abductive logic program with
$$P = \{\ pregnant \leftarrow naturally\text{-}inseminated,$$
$$\qquad pregnant \leftarrow artificially\text{-}inseminated\}$$
$$\mathcal{A} = \{weight\text{-}gain, naturally\text{-}inseminated, diet, artificially\text{-}inseminated\}$$
$$I = \{weight\text{-}gain \wedge not\ pregnant \rightarrow diet\}.$$
Intuitively, the integrity constraint represents the reactive rule
    on $weight\text{-}gain$, if $not\ pregnant$, then $diet$
whose procedural interpretation is: when the event $weight\text{-}gain$ occurs and the condition $pregnant$ does not hold, the action $diet$ is executed. Given the observation $weight\text{-}gain$, KM, FK and SLDNFA compute three alternative (minimal) answers, $\{weight\text{-}gain, diet\}$, $\{weight\text{-}gain, naturally\text{-}inseminated\}$, and $\{weight\text{-}gain, artificially\text{-}inseminated\}$. Only the first is intuitively correct.

The unintuitive behaviour of KM, FK and SLDNFA is due to the inappropriate treatment of the negative literals, occurring in the body of integrity constraints, whose atoms are either abducibles or are defined via abducibles. Indeed, these proof procedures seem to treat negations, implicitly, classically rather than as negation as failure, and the implication → as material implication. In example 3, the classical interpretation of negation occurring in the body of integrity constraints leads to treating *weight-gain* ∧ *not pregnant* → *diet* as the material implication *weight-gain* → [*diet* ∨ *pregnant*] rather than as the reactive rule the integrity constraint aims at representing.

We will define a modification of FK computing only the intuitively correct answers to goals and observations in an active database/agent perspective.

4   The proof procedure

Like FK, our proposed proof procedure uses the selective completion $comp_{\overline{A}}(P)$ of P in the given abductive logic program $\langle P, A, I \rangle$. Moreover, like FK, it derives a sequence of goals, starting from an **initial goal**, which is a conjunction of literals, conjoined with the integrity constraints in I. All variables in the literals in the initial goal are free. All variables in the integrity constraints in the initial goal are universally quantified. Goals in the sequence are derived by applying a number of inference rules. To simplify the treatment of quantifiers, both iff-definitions in $comp_{\overline{A}}(P)$ and integrity constraints in I are assumed to be range-restricted, i.e. all variables in the head must appear in at least one (positive) atom in the body, and this atom must not be an equality between two variables.

In the simplest case, goals derived by the proof procedure are disjunctions of **simple goals**, which are conjunctions of the form
$$A_1 \wedge \ldots \wedge A_n \wedge I_1 \wedge \ldots \wedge I_m \wedge D_1 \wedge \ldots \wedge D_k$$
where $n, m, k \geq 0$, $n+m+k > 0$, the A_i are atoms, the I_i are **implications**, with the same syntax of integrity constraints, except that in addition to universally quantified variables, they can also contain existentially quantified or free variables, occurring elsewhere in the goal, and the D_i are disjunctions of conjunctions of literals and implications. Implications are obtained by repeatedly applying the inference rules of the proof procedure to either integrity constraints in the given $\langle P, A, I \rangle$ or to the result of rewriting negative literals *not A* as $A \to false$.

FK assumes that the inference rules below are applied in such a way that every goal in a sequence derived by the proof procedure is a *disjunction of simple goals*. (Note that every initial goal is a simple goal with the integrity constraints and the rewriting of negative literals as the only implications.) Our proof procedure will make the same assumption.

4.1   FK proof procedure

Given an abductive logic program $\langle P, A, I \rangle$ and an initial goal G, a **derivation** for G wrt $comp_{\overline{A}}(P), I$ is a sequence of goals, $G_1, \ldots, G_n$, such that $G_1 = G \wedge I$ and each G_{i+1} is obtained from the previous formula G_i by application of one of the following (basic) inference rules:

Unfolding: given an atom $p(t)$ and $p(X) \leftrightarrow D_1 \vee \ldots \vee D_n$ in $comp_{\overline{A}}(P)$

- if the atom is a conjunct of a simple goal in G_i, then G_{i+1} is G_i with the atom replaced by $(D_1 \vee \ldots \vee D_n)\theta$, where $\theta = \{X/t\}$;
- if the atom is a conjunct L_i in the body of an implication $L_1 \wedge \ldots \wedge L_m \rightarrow A$, $m \geq 1$ which is a conjunct of a simple goal of G_i, then G_{i+1} is G_i with the implication replaced by the conjunction $[L_1 \wedge \ldots \wedge D_1\theta \wedge \ldots \wedge L_m \rightarrow A] \wedge \ldots \wedge [L_1 \wedge \ldots \wedge D_n\theta \wedge \ldots \wedge L_m \rightarrow A]$, where $\theta = \{X/t\}$.

Propagation: given an atom $p(s)$ and an implication $L_1 \wedge \ldots \wedge L_m \rightarrow A$, $m \geq 1$, with $L_i = p(t)$, both conjuncts of the same simple goal in G_i, then, if the implication $L_1 \wedge \ldots L_{i-1} \wedge t = s \wedge L_{i+1} \wedge \ldots \wedge L_m \rightarrow A$ is not already a conjunct of the simple goal, then G_{i+1} is G_i with the new implication conjoined to the simple goal.

Negation elimination: given an implication $not\ A_1 \wedge \ldots \wedge not\ A_m \rightarrow A$ which is a conjunct of a simple goal in G_i, then G_{i+1} is G_i with the implication replaced by the disjunction $A \vee A_1 \vee \ldots \vee A_m$. [2]

Logical simplification replaces:
$[B \vee C] \wedge E$ by $[B \wedge E] \vee [C \wedge E]$ (**splitting**)
$B \wedge true$ by B; $B \wedge B$ by B; $B \wedge false$ by $false$;   etc.

Equality rewriting applies the equality rewrite rules, simulating the unification algorithm [13] and the application of substitution.

Case analysis: given an implication $B \wedge X = t \rightarrow A$, where X is a free or existentially quantified variable and t does not contain X and is not a universally quantified variable, if the implication is a conjunct in a simple goal in G_i, then G_{i+1} is G_i with the implication replaced by the disjunction $[X = t \wedge [B \rightarrow A]] \vee [X = t \rightarrow false]$. Any variables in t which are universally quantified in the implication correctly become existentially quantified in the first disjunct and universally quantified in the second disjunct.

Factoring: given a simple goal $a(t) \wedge a(s) \wedge C$ in G_i, with a abducible, G_{i+1} is G_i with the given simple goal replaced by the disjunction $[a(t) \wedge a(s) \wedge C \wedge [t = s \rightarrow false]] \vee [a(t) \wedge C \wedge t = s]$.

Note that for goals in a derivation to be guaranteed to be disjunctions of simple goals, it is sufficient that every step of unfolding, negation elimination and case analysis is followed by a step of splitting.

Given an initial goal G, an FK-derivation $(G_1 = G \wedge I), \ldots (G_n = N \vee Rest)$, for some conjunction N of literals and implications, is a **successful FK-derivation** for G iff no inference rule can be applied to N and $N \neq false$. Given such a successful FK-derivation, an **FK-answer extracted from** N is a pair $(\mathcal{D}, \sigma)$ such that

- σ' is a substitution replacing all free and existentially quantified variables in N by ground terms, and σ' satisfies all equalities and disequalities in N,
- σ is the restriction of σ' to the variables in G,
- $\mathcal{D}$ is the set of all abducible atoms in $N\sigma$.

---

[2] In [5], negation elimination is defined as follows: $not\ A_1 \wedge Rest \rightarrow A$ is replaced by $Rest \rightarrow A \vee A_1$. Operationally, our definition is equivalent to the one in [5].

Every FK-answer extracted from a disjunct in a successful FK-derivation for an initial goal G is called an **FK-computed answer** for G.

In example 3, a possible FK-derivation for *weight-gain* is

$G_1 = weight\text{-}gain \land [weight\text{-}gain \land not\,pregnant \rightarrow diet]$

$G_2 = G_1 \land [not\,pregnant \rightarrow diet]$	by propagation
$G_3 = G_1 \land [pregnant \lor diet]$	by negation elimination
$G_4 = [G_1 \land pregnant] \lor [G_1 \land diet]$	by splitting
$G_5 = [G_1 \land [naturally\text{-}inseminated \lor artificially\text{-}inseminated]] \lor [G_1 \land diet]$	
	by unfolding in the first disjunct

$G_6 = [G_1 \land naturally\text{-}inseminated] \lor$
$\qquad [G_1 \land artificially\text{-}inseminated] \lor \qquad\qquad\qquad$ by splitting
$\qquad [G_1 \land diet].$

Since no inference rule can be applied to any of the resulting disjuncts, the derivation $G_1, \ldots, G_6$ is a successful derivation. The FK-answers

$\{weight\text{-}gain, naturally\text{-}inseminated\},$
$\{weight\text{-}gain, artificially\text{-}inseminated\}$ and
$\{weight\text{-}gain, diet\}$

can be extracted from the first, second and third disjunct of G_6, respectively. Note that the derivation $G_1, \ldots, G_4$ is also a successful derivation, since no inference rule can be applied to the second disjunct in G_4. The answer $\{weight\text{-}gain, diet\}$ can be extracted from this disjunct.

4.2 Modified proof procedure

In the modified proof procedure, implications in goals are either **marked** (by means of the * symbol) or **non-marked**. In the initial goal, integrity constraints are marked whereas implications obtained by rewriting negative literals are non-marked. All inference rules of FK except negation elimination can be applied to marked implications. We define a new inference rule to handle negation in the conditions of marked implications.

Negation rewriting: a *marked* implication

$*[not\,A_1 \land \ldots \land not\,A_m \rightarrow A], m \geq 1,$

is replaced by the disjunction $[provable(A_1)] \lor \ldots \lor [provable(A_m)] \lor [*[A_1 \rightarrow false] \land \ldots \land *[A_m \rightarrow false] \land A].$

All inference rules of FK leave the marked/non-marked status unchanged, except that $*[true \rightarrow A]$ is automatically rewritten as A.

Example 4. In example 2, a possible derivation for *cleaning-day* is

$G_1 = cleaning\text{-}day \land *[cleaning\text{-}day \land not\,sound\text{-}alarm \rightarrow dust] \land$
$\qquad *[temperature\text{-}rise \rightarrow sound\text{-}alarm] \land *[sound\text{-}alarm \rightarrow evacuate]$

$G_2 = G_1 \land *[not\,sound\text{-}alarm \rightarrow dust]$	by propagation
$G_3 = G_1 \land [[[*[sound\text{-}alarm \rightarrow false] \land dust] \lor [provable(sound\text{-}alarm)]]$	
	by negation rewriting
$G_4 = [G_1 \land [*[sound\text{-}alarm \rightarrow false] \land dust] \lor [G_1 \land provable(sound\text{-}alarm)]$	
	by splitting

to which no inference rule can be applied.

Given an initial goal G, a derivation $(G_1 = G \wedge I), \ldots, (G_n = N \vee Rest)$, for some conjunction N of literals and implications, is a **successful derivation** for G iff no inference rule can be applied to N. Given such a successful derivation, an **answer extracted from** N is a pair $(\mathcal{D}, \sigma)$ such that

- if no conjunct in N is of the form $provable(A)$ then $(\mathcal{D}, \sigma)$ is an FK-answer extracted from N,
- otherwise, let
    1. σ' be a Skolemisation for free and existentially quantified variables in N,
    2. $\mathcal{D}'$ be the set of all abducible atoms in $N\sigma'$, and T be $comp_A(\mathcal{D}') \cup comp_{\overline{A}}(P)$,
    3. $provable(A)$ be a conjunct of $N\sigma'$,
    4. $G'_1 = A, \ldots, G'_k$ be a derivation wrt $T, \emptyset$ such that $G'_k = N' \vee Rest'$ for some conjunction $N' \neq false$ to which no inference rule can be applied,
    5. N'' be the deSkolemisation of N' wrt σ'.

If N'' satisfies all (in)equalities in N, $(\mathcal{D}, \sigma)$ is an *answer extracted from* the conjunction obtained by replacing $provable(A)$ in N by N''.

Every answer extracted from a disjunct in a successful derivation for an initial goal G is called a **computed answer** for G.

Given the derivation in example 4, $(\{dust\}, \emptyset)$ is the only (FK-)answer extracted from the first disjunct in G_4. No answer can be extracted from the second disjunct in G_4. Indeed, $provable(sound\text{-}alarm)$ belongs to it, and the only derivation from $sound\text{-}alarm$, wrt $T = comp_{\overline{A}}(\emptyset) \cup comp_A(\{cleaning\text{-}day\}) = \{dust \leftrightarrow false, sound\text{-}alarm \leftrightarrow false, temperature\text{-}rise \leftrightarrow false, cleaning\text{-}day \leftrightarrow true\}$ and wrt the empty set of integrity constraints, is the derivation

$sound\text{-}alarm, false$.

To illustrate the requirement that equalities and inequalities must be satisfied during the answer extraction process, let $\langle P, \mathcal{A}, I \rangle$ be

$P = \{p(a) \leftarrow r(a)\}$
$\mathcal{A} = \{r, s, t\}$
$I = \{t(X) \wedge not\, p(X) \rightarrow s(X)\}$.

A possible derivation for $G = r(Y) \wedge t(Y) \wedge [Y = a \rightarrow false]$ is

$G_1 = G \wedge *[t(X) \wedge not\, p(X) \rightarrow s(X)]$
$G_2 = G_1 \wedge *[not\, p(Y) \rightarrow s(Y)]$
$G_3 = [G_1 \wedge *[p(Y) \rightarrow false] \wedge s(Y)] \vee [G_1 \wedge provable(p(Y))]$.

G_1, G_2, G_3 is a successful derivation, as no inference rule can be applied to the second disjunct in G_3. To extract an answer from the second disjunct, let

1. σ' be the Skolemisation $\{Y/\alpha\}$,
2. T be $comp_{\overline{A}}(P) \cup comp_A(\{r(\alpha), t(\alpha)\}) = \{p(X) \leftrightarrow r(X) \wedge X = a, r(X) \leftrightarrow X = \alpha, t(X) \leftrightarrow X = \alpha, s(X) \leftrightarrow false\}$
3. $provable(p(\alpha))$ be the chosen conjunct of the Skolemised disjunct,
4. $G'_1 = p(\alpha)$, $G'_2 = [r(\alpha) \wedge \alpha = a]$, $G'_3 = [\alpha = \alpha \wedge \alpha = a]$, $G'_4 = [\alpha = a]$ be a derivation, wrt $T, \emptyset$,
5. $Y = a$ be the deSkolemisation of $\alpha = a$ wrt σ'.

Since $Y = a$ does not satisfy the denial $Y = a \rightarrow false$ in the second disjunct in G_3, correctly no answer for G can be extracted from that disjunct.

5   Formal results

Our proof procedure is a specialisation of FK in the sense that every answer computed by our modified proof procedure is also computed by FK.

Theorem 1. *If (D, σ) is a computed answer for an initial goal G then (D, σ) is an FK-computed answer for G.*

Proof (sketch): we construct a successful FK-derivation from the given successful derivation by mapping every step except negation rewriting and logical simplification onto itself, every negation rewriting step replacing an implication $*[not\, A_1 \wedge \ldots \wedge not\, A_m \to A]$ with $A \neq false$ by the disjunction

$$[provable(A_1)] \vee \ldots \vee [provable(A_m)] \vee [*[A_1 \to false] \wedge \ldots \wedge *[A_m \to false] \wedge A]$$

onto a negation elimination step replacing $not\, A_1 \wedge \ldots \wedge not\, A_m \to A$ by the disjunction $A_1 \vee \ldots \vee A_m \vee A$, and every negation rewriting + logical simplification steps replacing an implication $*[not\, A_1 \wedge \ldots \wedge not\, A_m \to false]$ first (negation rewriting) by the disjunction

$$[provable(A_1)] \vee \ldots \vee [provable(A_m)] \vee$$
$$[*[A_1 \to false] \wedge \ldots \wedge *[A_m \to false] \wedge false]$$

and then (logical simplification) by the disjunction $[provable(A_1)] \vee \ldots \vee [provable(A_m)] \vee false$, onto a single negation elimination step replacing $not\, A_1 \wedge \ldots \wedge not\, A_m \to false$ by the disjunction $A_1 \vee \ldots \vee A_m \vee false$.

It is easy to see that, if $A \wedge *[I'] \wedge provable(p_1) \wedge \ldots \wedge provable(p_m)$ is the disjunct (from which the answer has been extracted) of the final goal in the given successful derivation, with A a set of (abducible) atoms, $*[I']$ a set of (marked and non-marked) implications and each p_i an atom ($m \geq 0$), then $A \wedge I' \wedge p_1 \wedge \ldots \wedge p_m$ is a disjunct of the final goal in the constructed FK-derivation. This might not be a successful derivation yet, since some p_i might be non-abducible and additional steps might have to be performed on the p_is. However, the constructed FK-derivation can be extended to a successful FK-derivation from which $(\mathcal{D}, \sigma)$ can be extracted, by mapping all operations in the process of answer extraction onto FK operations. In particular, every step except unfolding is mapped onto itself, every step of unfolding of non-abducible atoms at step 4 is mapped onto a step of unfolding in the FK-derivation, and every step of unfolding of abducible atoms at step 4 is mapped onto a step of logical simplification ($p \wedge p$ is replaced by p) or factoring.   □

The converse of this theorem does not hold, e.g. for example 2.

FK is sound wrt the semantics of abductive answers in [5], i.e. every FK-computed answer $(\mathcal{D}, \sigma)$ for an initial goal G satisfies the following conditions:

1) $comp(P \cup \mathcal{D}) \cup CET \models G\sigma$, and
2) $comp(P \cup \mathcal{D}) \cup CET \models I$,

where $\models$ is either ordinary two-valued logical consequence or logical consequence in Kunen's three-valued logic. We will refer to abductive answers as defined above as **FK-abductive answers**. The following soundness result wrt the semantics of FK-abductive answers is a direct corollary of theorem 1:

Corollary 1 *If $(\mathcal{D}, \sigma)$ is a computed answer for an initial goal G then $(\mathcal{D}, \sigma)$ is an FK-abductive answer for G.*

FK is complete (in a weak sense) wrt the semantics of FK-abductive answers: for every FK-abductive answer $(\mathcal{D}, \sigma)$ for an initial goal G, there exists a subset $\mathcal{D}'$ of $\mathcal{D}$ such that $(\mathcal{D}', \sigma)$ is an FK- computed answer for G. Our procedure is not complete, even in the weak sense, wrt the semantics of FK- abductive answers. Indeed, it was specifically designed not to compute the unintuitive FK-computed answers. So, it is the semantics, rather than the proof procedure, that is at fault here. However, our procedure is complete wrt the semantics of FK- abductive answers in some cases, e.g when no negation occurs in integrity constraints and goals (in this case our procedure is equivalent to FK).

In the special case in which the given logic program is empty and all atoms occurring in the integrity constraints and the initial goal are abducibles, then our proof procedure computes the **stable model semantics** [6] of the integrity constraints and the goal, both seen as logic programs. In the agent setting, this special case corresponds to purely reactive agents. Every ground negative literal $not\,p$ in the goal is seen as a logic programming rule $false \leftarrow p$.

Theorem 2. *Let $\langle P, \mathcal{A}, I \rangle$ be an abductive logic program with $\mathcal{P} = \emptyset$ and G be an initial goal, and let all predicates occurring in I and G belong to $\mathcal{A}$. Then:*

- *if $(\mathcal{D}, \sigma)$ is a computed answer for G then $\mathcal{D}$ is a stable model of $I \cup G\sigma$;*
- *if M is a stable model of $I \cup G\sigma$, for some variable-free substitution σ for the variables of G, and $false \notin M$, then (M, σ) is a computed answer for G.*

Note that $false$ might be the head of some rule in $I \cup G\sigma$ and thus belong to some stable model of $I \cup G\sigma$.

This theorem is a corollary of theorem 3 below, relating our procedure, in the special case considered in theorem 2, and the procedure of [8], which is proved sound and complete wrt the stable model semantics. Given a logic program T, the proof procedure of [8] applies the model generation theorem prover (MGTP) to the disjunctive logic program $tr(T)$ obtained from T by replacing every rule of the form $A \leftarrow A_1 \wedge \ldots \wedge A_n \wedge not\,A_{n+1} \wedge \ldots \wedge not\,A_{n+m}$ with A, A_i atoms and $n \geq 0$, $m \geq 1$, by a (disjunctive) rule of the form
$$[A, \neg K A_{n+1} \wedge \ldots \wedge \neg K A_{n+m}] \vee [K A_{n+1}] \vee \ldots \vee [K A_{n+m}] \leftarrow A_1 \wedge \ldots \wedge A_n.$$
[8] computes the set $MGTP(tr(T), \{\emptyset\})$ of all (minimal) models of $tr(T)$ satisfying the denials $A \wedge \neg K A \rightarrow false$ and $K A \wedge \neg K A \rightarrow false$, for all atoms A, and ignoring the models containing KA but not containing A, for some atom A. [8] proves that for each model M in $MGTP(tr(T), \{\emptyset\})$, the set of all atoms in M is a stable model of T and, conversely, every stable model of T is the set of all atoms of some model in $MGTP(tr(T), \{\emptyset\})$.

Theorem 3. *Let $\langle P, \mathcal{A}, I \rangle$ and G be as in theorem 2.*

- *if $(\mathcal{D}, \sigma)$ is a computed answer for G then $\mathcal{D} \in MGTP(tr(I \wedge G\sigma), \{\emptyset\})$;*
- *if $M \in MGTP(tr(I \wedge G\sigma), \{\emptyset\})$, for some variable-free substitution σ for the variables of G, and $false \notin M$, then (M, σ) is a computed answer for G.*

Proof (sketch): $MGTP(tr(I \wedge G\sigma), \{\emptyset\})$ is constructed as follows, starting with $S_0 = \{\emptyset\}$:

1. if there exists a (disjunctive) rule $H_1 \vee \ldots \vee H_m \leftarrow B \in tr(I \wedge G\sigma)$ and a substitution θ such that, for some $M \in S_i$, $B\theta \subseteq M$ and no $H_i\theta \subseteq M$, then $S_{i+1} = S_i - \{M\} \cup \{M \cup \{H_1\theta\}\} \cup \ldots \cup \{M \cup \{H_m\theta\}\}$;
2. if there exists an atom A such that, for some $M \in S_i$, either
   (a) both A and $\neg KA$ belong to M, or
   (b) both KA and $\neg KA$ belong to M,
   then $S_{i+1} = S_i - \{M\}$.
   until $S_{i+1} = S_i$. Then
3. $MGTP(tr(I \wedge G\sigma), \{\emptyset\}) = S_i - \{M | KA \in M$ but $A \notin M\}$.

It is easy to see that the construction of every M not containing $false$ in $MGTP(tr(I \wedge G\sigma), \{\emptyset\})$ corresponds to a derivation from G to a disjunct $N \vee Rest$ such that $(\mathcal{D}, \sigma)$ can be extracted from N, where $\mathcal{D}$ is the set of all "non-K-atoms" in M. Indeed:

• Every step of type 1 for $H_1 \vee \ldots \vee H_m \leftarrow B$ with B non-empty and $m = 1$ corresponds to a series of propagation steps (one for each atom in B) with the integrity constraint (without negation) $B \rightarrow H_1$;

• Every step of type 1 for $H_1 \vee \ldots \vee H_m \leftarrow B$ with B empty and $m = 1$ corresponds to no step in our proof procedure (H_1 is an atom in every disjunct of any goal in any derivation from G));

• Every step of type 1 for $H_1 \vee \ldots \vee H_m \leftarrow B$ with B non-empty and $m > 1$ corresponds to a series of propagation steps (one for each atom in B) with the integrity constraint from which $H_1 \vee \ldots \vee H_m \leftarrow B$ has been obtained by tr, followed by a step of negation rewriting and a step of splitting (in this sequence); for every atom A, $\neg KA$ corresponds to $A \rightarrow false$ in the derivation and KA corresponds to $provable(A)$ in the derivation;

• Every step of type 2a corresponds to a step of propagation of $false$ from $A \rightarrow false$ and A;

• Every step of type 3 corresponds to eliminating disjuncts from successful derivations by answer extraction, which, in the special case considered, amounts to checking that if $provable(A)$ belongs to the disjunct then so does A.

The corresponding steps of type 2b in the proof procedure is that $provable(A)$ and $A \rightarrow false$ do not both belong to any computed answer. Such steps do not correspond to any explicit steps in the proof procedure. However, answer extraction guarantees that $provable(A)$ and $A \rightarrow false$ do not both belong to any computed answer. □

6   Conclusions and future work

We have defined a new abductive proof procedure and compared it to a number of existing similar proof procedures. We have argued that the new procedure is suitable as the engine underlying active database management systems as well as (rational and reactive) logic-based agents. Indeed, our proof procedure can be used as the underlying procedure in the agent architecture of [11].

Our integrity constraints seem closely related to the production rules with negation as failure proposed by [4]. The formal study of the relationships between the two is a subject for future work.

Our proof procedure needs to be extended to handle built-ins such as $<$, e.g. as in [12]. This extension is needed, in particular, to cater for temporal reasoning in agents.

Finally, future work includes refining existing prototype implementations of the proof procedure.

Acknowledgements

This reasearch was supported by the UK EPSRC project "Logic-based multi-agent systems". The authors are grateful to Bob Kowalski for challenging discussions and to the anonymous referees for their comments.

References

1. Clark, K.L.; 1978. Negation as failure. *Logic and Data Bases*, 293–322, Plenum, NY.
2. Console, L.; Theseider Dupré, D.; Torasso, P.; 1991. On the relationship between abduction and deduction. *Journal of Logic and Computation* 2(5): 661–690, OUP.
3. Denecker, M.; De Schreye, D.; 1997. SLDNFA: an abductive procedure for abductive logic programs. *Journal of Logic Programming* 34(2): 111–167, Elsevier.
4. Dung, P.M.; Mancarella, P.; 1996. Production systems need negation as failure. *Proc. 13th AAAI*, AAAI Press.
5. Fung, T.H.; Kowalski, R.A.; 1997. The iff procedure for abductive logic programming. *Journal of Logic Programming* 33(2):151–165, Elsevier.
6. Gelfond, M.; Lifschitz, V.; 1988. The stable model semantics for logic programming. *Proc. 5th ICLP* 1070–1080, MIT Press.
7. Huhns, M.N.; Singh M.P. (eds); 1997. *Readings in Agents*, Morgan Kaufman.
8. Inoue, K.; Koshimura, M.; Hasegawa, R.; 1992. Embedding negation as failure into a model generation theorem prover. *Proc. 11th CADE*, LNAI 607:400–415, Springer.
9. Kakas, A.C.; Kowalski, R.A.; Toni, F.; 1998. The role of abduction in logic programming. *Handbook of Logic in AI and Logic Programming* 5:235–324, OUP.
10. Kakas, A.C.; Mancarella, P.; 1990. Abductive Logic Programming. *Workshop on Non-Monotonic Reasoning and Logic Programming*.
11. Kowalski, R.A.; Sadri, F.; 1999. From Logic Programming to Multi-agent Systems. *Annals of Mathemathics and Artificial Intelligence* (Forthcoming).
12. Kowalski, R.A.; Toni, F.; Wetzel, G.; 1998. Executing suspended logic programs. *Fundamenta Informaticae* 34(3):203–224, ISO Press.
13. Martelli, A.; Montanari, U.; 1982. An efficient unification algorithm. *ACM Trans. on Prog. Lang. and Systems* 4(2):258–282.
14. Poole, D.; 1988. A logical framework for default reasoning. *Artificial Intelligence* 36:27–47, Elsevier.
15. Rao, A.S.; Georgeff, M.P.; 1992. An abstract architecture for rational agents. *Proc. 3rd Int. Conf. on Principles of Knowledge Representation and Reasoning*.
16. Shanahan, M.; 1997. Event calculus planning revisited. *Proc. 4th European Conference on Planning* 390–402, LNAI 1348, Springer.
17. Widom, J.; Ceri, S.; 1996. *Active Database Systems: Triggers and Rules for Advanced Database Processing*, Morgan Kaufmann.

An Implementation for Abductive Logic Agents

A. Ciampolini[1], E. Lamma[1], P. Mello[1], C. Stefanelli[2] and P. Torroni[1]

[1] DEIS, Università di Bologna, Viale Risorgimento 2, 40136 Bologna, Italy
{aciampolini,elamma,pmello,ptorroni}@deis.unibo.it
[2] Dip. di Ingegneria, Università di Ferrara, Via Saragat 2, 44100 Ferrara, Italy
cstefanelli@ing.unife.it

Abstract. This paper presents the distributed implementation of *ALIAS*, an architecture composed of several cooperating intelligent agents. This system is particularly suited to solve problems in cases where knowledge about the problem domain is incomplete and agents may need to form reasonable hypotheses. In *ALIAS* agents are equipped with hypothetical reasoning capabilities, performed by means of abduction: if the knowledge available to a logic agent is insufficient to solve a query, the agent could abduce new hypotheses. Each agent is characterized by a local knowledge base represented by an abductive logic program. Agents might differ in their knowledge bases, but must agree on assumed hypotheses. That *global knowledge base* is dynamically created and managed by means of a shared tuple space. The prototype, developed using Java and Prolog, can run on a TCP/IP network of computers. In the paper, we also discuss some experimental results to evaluate prototype efficiency.

1 Introduction

The agent concept has become of great significance in distributed artificial intelligence. An intelligent agent is a software or hardware system that is autonomous, interactive with and *reactive* to its environment and other agents. An agent can also be *pro-active* in taking the initiative in goal-directed behavior. Thus, the agent concept is systematically used to represent entities with the ability to solve problems, reflecting the results on the environment. Moreover, intelligent agents have goals to solve but have also to work in environments not completely under their control. In recent years, the interest for intelligent agents has considerably grown from both theoretical and practical point of view [12]. Intelligent agents need deductive and pattern-matching capabilities to perform goals and activity requests on them. In this respect, the knowledge of an agent can be specified by using the logic programming paradigm [15], and a logic language in particular.

In knowledge-intensive (distributed) applications, it is often the case that an intelligent agent requires some sort of *guess* about a computation (viz., a goal in a logic programming perspective) which cannot be performed (viz., solved) locally since the local knowledge is incomplete. In this respect, the Closed World Assumption [4] usually adopted in logic programming can be no longer assumed,

E. Lamma and P. Mello (Eds.): AI*IA 99, LNAI 1792, pp. 61–71, 2000.

and some form of *open* or *abductive* reasoning has to be considered. Abduction has been widely recognized as a powerful mechanism for hypothetical reasoning in presence of incomplete knowledge [5, 6, 9]. Abduction is generally understood as reasoning from effects to causes, and also captures other important issues such as reasoning with defaults and beliefs (see for instance [11, 13]). Incomplete knowledge is handled by labelling some pieces of information as abducibles, i.e., possible hypotheses which can be assumed, provided that they are consistent with the current knowledge base. In the context of intelligent agents, abduction can be regarded as a way of *dynamically* enlarging the agent's knowledge with abducible atoms. In a multi-agent environment, abductive reasoning requires a form of coordination among agents in order to guarantee that abduced hypotheses are assumed *consistently*. When one agent wants to abduce a hypothesis h, it has to check not only the consistency of its knowledge base with the new assumption h, but also that the knowledge bases of all the other agents are consistent with the new assumption. Furthermore, when h is assumed, one has to guarantee that any other subsequent assumption will be consistent with the new enlarged knowledge base. In this work, we present the distributed implementation of the Abductive LogIc Agents System (from now on, *ALIAS*), an architecture composed of several cooperating intelligent agents. In *ALIAS*, logic agents are equipped with hypothetical reasoning capabilities, obtained by means of abduction. In this framework, agents can perform standard deduction and also *abduce* new hypotheses, provided that they are consistent with the knowledge of other agents. To this purpose, a mechanism to coordinate agent reasoning is introduced. In particular, reasoning and coordination are integrated within the Distributed Abduction Algorithm (DAA, for short). Each agent is characterized by statically defined local knowledge represented by an abductive logic program [8]. Moreover, a global knowledge (represented by the assumed hypotheses posted into a shared tuple space) is dynamically built. While static knowledge is peculiar to each agent and might differ from agent to agent, all agents must agree on the global set of assumed abducibles. To this purpose, a set of integrity constraints is used - together with program clauses - to confirm or discard new hypotheses. In this respect, an agent is *pro-active* when it executes (its own) goals, while it is *reactive* to its environment, and cooperate with other agents when it checks the consistency of hypotheses raised by other agents. The properties of *ALIAS* make it very suitable for the solution of problems in a distributed environment where knowledge might be incomplete, multiple and even conflicting. We are experimenting, for instance, the employment of *ALIAS* agents for the solution of distributed diagnosis problems in the automotive industry. In the paper we describe the distributed implementation of *ALIAS*, based on Java and *Amzi!* Prolog. The first prototype executes on a TCP/IP network of computers. The analysis of experimental results lead us to focus on future improvements and optimizations.

2   The architecture of $ALIAS$

In $ALIAS$, the computation is carried out by several parallel agents that cooperate for solving goals. Each agent has its own (possibly incomplete) knowledge
base, and uses abduction as a way of hypothetical reasoning. Agents can be
grouped into *bunches*: each bunch of *arguing* agents is associated with a set of
abducible hypotheses (*i.e.*, the set of hypotheses that could be possibly raised).
Moreover, agents of the same bunch refer to the common set of hypotheses, Δ,
assumed so far (the dynamic knowledge of the bunch). When an agent A tries
to raise a new hypothesis h, agents belonging to the same bunch cooperate with
A (by means of the coordination protocol) in order to check that h is consistent with the knowledge of the other agents and with the assumptions made so
far: if all agents agree about the assumption of h, h is assumed; otherwise it
is discarded. The composition of a bunch can be statically specified or can be
dynamically determined. In this latter case, when an agent dynamically wants
to enter a bunch, it expresses its interest by raising a suitable event thus starting
a protocol aimed at checking the consistency of its local knowledge base with
the global knowledge of the bunch, Δ.

The inner structure of each $ALIAS$ agent is shown in Fig. 1: each agent is
composed of three functional blocks: a *reasoning* module, which contains the
abductive (and deductive) reasoning mechanisms, a *coordination* module which
interfaces the agent with other agents in the system, and a user interface module
for the interaction with external users. Each agent A can accept queries from
external users by means of the *user interface* module; each query q is passed to
the *reasoning* module which performs a local computation in order to calculate
an answer for q. If the local knowledge of A is insufficient to solve the query,
the solution of q could be possibly obtained by making additional assumptions.
Each time A tries to abduce a new hypothesis h, the coordination module starts
a message exchange session involving A and other agents in the bunch, in order
to check the consistency of h with the knowledge of the other agents and with
the assumptions made so far. At the end of this coordination activity, if all
agents agree in assuming h, the hypothesis is inserted in the common set of
assumptions associated to the bunch, and the computation can proceed. At the
end of the computation (if successful) the set of assumptions is stored in the
bunch tuple space, and the answer is returned to the external user (through the
user interface). Agents are autonomous and parallel: this means that within the
same bunch more than one computation could be started in parallel. For this
reason, accesses to the tuple space have to be suitably synchronized, in order to
preserve the consistency of the dynamic knowledge.

3   Agent Reasoning and Coordination

As described in Section 2, an $ALIAS$ multi-agent application is composed of
several agents, possibly grouped into bunches. Each bunch consists of $n + 1$
agents *arguing* out a common set of abducibles. Each bunch is also associated

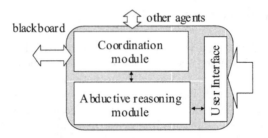

Fig. 1. *ALIAS* agent functional structure

with a dynamic knowledge, represented by the set Δ, containing the hypotheses so far assumed by all agents in the group. Each agent A_i, for $i = 0, \ldots, n$, encapsulates (in its reasoning module) an abductive logic program $\langle P_i, A_i, IC_i \rangle$

An *abductive logic program* is a triple $\langle P, A, IC \rangle$ where P is a logic program possibly with abducible atoms in clause bodies; A is a set of *abducible predicates*, i.e., *open* predicates which can be used to form explaining sentences; IC is a set of integrity constraints: each constraint is a denial containing at least one abducible[1]. Given an abductive program $\langle P, A, IC \rangle$ and a formula G, the goal of abduction is to find a (possibly minimal) set of atoms Δ which together with P entails G. It is also required that the program $P \cup \Delta$ is consistent with respect to IC. According to [6], negation as default, possibly occurring in clause bodies, can be recovered into abduction by replacing negated literals of the form *not a* with a new positive, abducible atom *not_a* and by adding the integrity constraint $\leftarrow a, not\_a$ to IC. The natural syntactic correspondence between a standard atom and its negation by default is given by the following notion of complement

$$\bar{l} = \begin{cases} \alpha & \text{if } l = not\_\alpha \\ not\_\alpha & \text{otherwise} \end{cases}$$

where α is an atom.

We suppose that each integrity constraint in IC_i of an agent A_i has at least one abducible in the body. We suppose that abducible predicates have no definition as in [10]. As concerns integrity constraints, the user-defined ones are partitioned among the various agents, while those for handling negation as default, like the constraint $\leftarrow p, not\ p$, are left implicit and replicated in each agent's knowledge base. The set Δ contains the hypotheses so far assumed by all agents. The set of program clauses and integrity constraints might differ from agent to agent, but we assume that the set of abducible predicates (default predicates included) is the same for all the agents in a bunch.

---

[1] In the following, for the sake of simplicity, we consider only ground programs, thus assuming that P and IC have already been instantiated.

3.1   The Distributed Abduction Algorithm

The DAA algorithm we adopt for abductive reasoning in a multi-agent system is based on a proof procedure, defined originally in [6] by Eshgi and Kowalski and further refined by Kakas and Mancarella [10], which is correct with respect to the abductive semantics defined in [3]. The proof procedure presented in [10] extends the basic resolution mechanism adopted in logic programming by introducing the notion of *abductive* and *consistency* derivation. Intuitively, an *abductive* derivation is the usual logic programming derivation suitably extended in order to consider abducibles. When an abducible atom h is encountered during this derivation, it is assumed, provided this is consistent. The consistency check of a hypothesis, then, starts the second kind of derivation. The *consistency* derivation verifies that, when the hypothesis h is assumed and added to the current set of hypotheses, any integrity constraint containing h fails (i.e., the bodies of all the integrity constraints containing h are false). During this latter procedure, when an abducible L is encountered, in order to prove its failure, an abductive derivation for its complement, $\overline{L}$, is attempted. The DAA algorithm extends the Kakas and Mancarella approach in the sense of distribution: now knowledge is distributed among various agents, and consistency derivations have to be coordinated within a pool of logic agents.

Abductive derivation
An abductive derivation from $(G_1 \, \Delta_1)$ to $(G_n \, \Delta_n)$ for an agent A_0 (with arguing agents $A_1, \ldots, A_m$) with knowledge base given by the abductive logic program $\langle P, Ab, IC \rangle$ via a selection rule R is a sequence $(G_1 \, \Delta_1), (G_2 \, \Delta_2), \ldots, (G_n \, \Delta_n)$ such that each G_i has the form $\leftarrow L_1, \ldots, L_k$, $R(G_i) = L_j$ and $(G_{i+1} \, \Delta_{i+1})$ is obtained according to one of the following rules:

(1) If L_j is not abducible, then $G_{i+1} = C$ and $\Delta_{i+1} = \Delta_i$ where C is the resolvent of some clause in P with G_i on the selected literal L_j;
(2) If L_j is abducible and $L_j \in \Delta_i$ then
$G_{i+1} = \leftarrow L_1, \ldots, L_{j-1}, L_{j+1}, \ldots, L_k$ and $\Delta_{i+1} = \Delta_i$;
(3) If L_j is abducible, $L_j \notin \Delta_i$ and $\overline{L_j} \notin \Delta_i$ and for each arguing agent A_k ($k = 1, \ldots, m$) there exists a *consistency derivation* from $(\{L_j\} \, \Delta_i \cup \{L_j\})$ to $(\{\} \, \Delta_k')$ and the union set $\cup_{k=1,\ldots,n} \Delta_k'$ is consistent (i.e., L and $\overline{L}$ do not belong to the union set for any literal L), then
$G_{i+1} = \leftarrow L_1, \ldots, L_{j-1}, L_{j+1}, \ldots, L_k$ and
$\Delta_{i+1} = \cup_{k=1,\ldots,n} \Delta_k'$.

Steps (1) and (2) are local SLD-resolution steps using only the rules of A_0 and abductive hypotheses, respectively. Step (3) requires the coordination of all agents in the bunch: the new hypothesis L_j could be possibly assumed if all arguing agents perform a successful consistency derivation for L_j, starting from $\Delta_i \cup \{L_j\}$. In general, the consistency of each hypothesis L_j is checked concurrently by all the arguing agents. Each consistency check, when successful, might require the assumption of other hypotheses. If all consistency derivation are successful, L_j, together with the additional hypotheses Δ_i returned by the arguing agents, is added to the current set of hypotheses, provided that the union set of these hypotheses is consistent; then, the computation proceeds within A_0 by assuming L_j and the set $\Delta_{out} = \bigcup_{i=1,\dots,n} \Delta_i$.

Consistency derivation

Given an agent A_0 (with arguing agents $A_1, \dots, A_m$) whose knowledge base is given by the abductive logic program $\langle P, Ab, IC \rangle$, a consistency derivation for an abducible literal α from $(\alpha\ \Delta_1)$ to $(F_n\ \Delta_n)$ is a sequence $(\alpha\ \Delta_1), (F_1\ \Delta_1), (F_2\ \Delta_2), \dots, (F_n\ \Delta_n)$ where :

(i) F_1 is the union of all goals of the form $\leftarrow L_1, \dots, L_n$ obtained by resolving the abducible α with the denials in IC with no such goal been empty, $\leftarrow$;

(ii) for each $i > 1$, F_i has the form $\{\leftarrow L_1, \dots, L_k\} \cup F_i'$ and for some $j = 1, \dots, k$ $(F_{i+1}\ \Delta_{i+1})$ is obtained according to one of the following rules:

(C1) If L_j is not abducible, then $F_{i+1} = C' \cup F_i'$ where C' is the set of all resolvents of clauses in P with $\leftarrow L_1, \dots, L_k$ on the literal L_j and $\leftarrow \notin C'$, and $\Delta_{i+1} = \Delta_i$;

(C2) If L_j is abducible, $L_j \in \Delta_i$ and $k > 1$, then
$$F_{i+1} = \{\leftarrow L_1, \dots, L_{j-1}, L_{j+1}, \dots, L_k\} \cup F_i' \text{ and } \Delta_{i+1} = \Delta_i;$$

(C3) If L_j is abducible, $\overline{L_j} \in \Delta_i$ then $F_{i+1} = F_i'$ and $\Delta_{i+1} = \Delta_i;$

(C4) If L_j is abducible, $L_j \notin \Delta_i$ and $\overline{L_j} \notin \Delta_i$, and there exists a (local) *abductive derivation* from $(\leftarrow \overline{L_j}\ \Delta_i)$ to $(\leftarrow\ \Delta')$ then $F_{i+1} = F_i'$ and $\Delta_{i+1} = \Delta'.$

It is worth to notice that the consistency derivation involves only local computation. In fact, abducible predicates have no definition (as in [6, 9]); if, during a consistency derivation, an abducible atom h is encountered, a local abductive derivation is performed. That corresponds to assume h and then, during this local abductive derivation, to ask each arguing agent for the *consistency* check of h.

3.2   An Example

Agents coordinate themselves on the basis of the set of assumed hypotheses Δ by using a global repository for knowledge. All agents have to access the global repository for getting the current set of assumed hypotheses to be considered in their further computations. The global repository can be realized by a tuple space accessed in a reading, reading and consuming, and writing mode through Linda-like primitives **read**, **in** and **out** [7].

It is worth noting that several agents may issue distinct hypotheses, in parallel and independently one of each other. This may lead to a situation where two agents may try to store into the tuple space two conflicting sets of hypotheses.

Example 1. Let us consider a system composed of four agents (A_0, A_1, A_2, A_3) whose knowledge base is structured as follows:

$A0)$ s : $-$p. $A1) : -$q, not b. $A2) : -$p, not c. $A3)$ r : $-$q.
                                                                        : $-$b, c.

where p, q, b, and c are abducible atoms. Let the current set of hypotheses Δ be empty. Suppose that agent A_0 raises the goal $\leftarrow$s and agent A_3 the goal $\leftarrow$r. Each single request is processed in parallel, producing two different and conflicting sets of hypotheses ($\{$p, c, not b, not q$\}$ for A_0 and $\{$q, b, not c, not p$\}$ for A_3).

A possible solution to the conflict is to guarantee the mutual exclusion of agents in accessing the set of hypotheses in the tuple space, so that the first agent succeeding in extracting the current Δ blocks further accesses until the consistency check terminates. Other computations are *de facto* serialized on the basis of the agent relative speeds in accessing the tuple space. However, two different computations starting with the same set of current hypotheses might result in two sets which are consistent with each other. In that case, agents may read in parallel the tuple space, while the blackboard checks the consistency of consequent updates.

4   The Implementation

The implementation has been obtained by using Java and *Amzi!* Prolog [2]. With reference to the terminology adopted in Fig. 1, Java is adopted to implement the *User Interface* and the *Coordination Module*, Prolog to implement the *Abductive Reasoning Module*. The implementation scheme of a single agent is shown in Fig. 2, where each block represents a software module. The user interacts with the system through the *User Interface* by invoking the methods provided by the class *agentFrame*. In particular, it is possible to start an abductive derivation process by specifying the goal to prove. Moreover, a blackboard is used to store the current list of abducibles. This way, we separate shared *dynamic* knowledge (the list of abducibles which is available from the blackboard and can be updated at run-time by the agents) from agent-specific local knowledge base, which is statically specified.

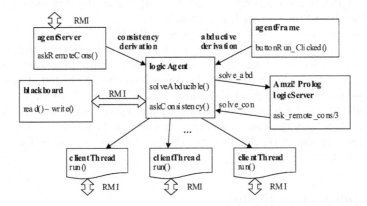

Fig. 2. The implementation scheme of a single agent.

Class *blackboard*, which implements the tuple space, handles the current list of abducibles and basically provides the access to the global knowledge. For a better comprehension of the relationships among the classes, let us consider the case of a user that asks a query to an agent through the *User interface*. Each agent of the bunch has an instance of class *agentServer* listening to an *IP address:port* waiting for remote requests. Then, the *User Interface* creates a *logicAgent* which is asked to demonstrate the goal (method *solveAbducible()*). First of all, *logicAgent* invokes the remote method *read()* of the blackboard in order to obtain the list of abducibles, Δ. As it receives an answer, it gives control to a Prolog engine, instantiating an object of class *logicServer*. During the *logicServer* initialization phase, it loads its knowledge base and its interface with Java. Then it starts the abductive derivation for the query. If no abducible is encountered during the abductive derivation phase, the *logicServer* returns control to the *logicAgent*, which displays the result. In that case, no coordination protocol among agents is required since the computation is performed locally. In some other cases, instead, the Prolog engine could attempt to abduce a hypothesis h. The consistency of the new abducible has to be checked by all the agents of the bunch. Therefore, Prolog returns the control to Java (*ask_remote_cons/3*), which creates one thread for each other agent in the bunch (*clientThread*) for communication purposes. Each thread sends the consistency request (by means of method *askRemoteCons()* of *agentServer*) to a specific remote agent. The remote *agentServer* receiving the request starts a *consistency derivation* for h, for which a new Prolog engine is dynamically created. It is worth to notice that the consistency derivation could start nested abductive and consistency derivations. After a remote consistency check returns the result (which will be positive iif all of the *clientThreads* returned *true*) the initial Prolog engine proceeds in its abductive derivation. This process of asking remote consistency might be invoked several times before a goal is demonstrated. As *logicServer* returns control to the *logicAgent*, it invokes method *write()* of object *blackboard* in order to store in the blackboard the current list of abducibles.

The source code, whose latest version is available at [1], has been written in Java 1.2 and imports class *logicSever* of *Amzi!* Prolog [2] in order to interface with the Prolog engine. *Amzi!* has been chosen among the other Prolog interpreters since it allows multiple instances of class *logicServer* to be created at the same time inside a single Java process. In fact, for the sake of deadlock avoidance, the *agentServer* which answers to remote requests must create a new instance of class *logicAgent* any time the consistency of a new abducible has to be proved. As our tests demonstrate, this sequence of operations is responsible for most of the overhead.

5   Experimental Results

We tested the prototype in order to trace the behavior of the protocol when specific parameters change. The Prolog knowledge bases we generated on purpose consist in general of a certain number of goals to prove, a set of rules organized in a hierarchy to form an AND/OR tree, a set of integrity constraints and a list of abducibles. We made experiments with bunches ranging from two to four agents and with different depths of the program (depth is intended to be the maximum number of nodes between a goal and the leaves, constituted by rules having abducibles in the body). Other parameters are the number of atoms, of abducibles, of integrity constraints, and the average length of the body of a clause.

From the experimental results emerged that there is evidence of a dependency between the number of consistency checks (c) requested by a computation, and the response time (t). In Fig. 3, we report t/c, calculated for different values

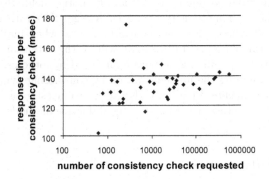

number of consistency check requested

Fig. 3. Average consistency check cost

of c. From these results we can see that t/c remains almost constant. We can say that in our architecture t depends linearly on c. A closer analysis of the single consistency request cost allows us to focus on two different sources of overhead. The *communication overhead* is the cost of pure message exchange. The *Prolog engine load time* is the time spent by the *agentServer* creating a thread and loading a Prolog engine. In order measure these sources of overhead we considered a bunch composed of two agents, the former running a standard program, the latter playing the role of an *agentServer* having no computation to do but a list of abducibles. Prolog engine load time resulted responsible for 82% of the whole response time, while communication overhead is of 17%.

The performance results show that the implementation can be improved and optimized. In particular, we are considering to provide the *agentServer* with a pool of threads ready to answer to remote queries, in order to reduce the overhead produced by both thread creation and Prolog engine management. We are also considering the opportunity of using other Prolog engines, for instance some lighter interpreter with a shorter load-time. Another way is to reduce the number of consistency check requests itself, for instance by indexing the broadcast and implementing a consistency derivation driven by the characteristics of each agent constraints (multicast in place of broadcast).

6 Conclusions and Future Work

We have presented the implementation of *ALIAS*, an architecture composed of several cooperating abductive logic agents. We defined a basic protocol to coordinate the reasoning of abductive (rational) agents, in order to introduce abduction in a (logic) multi-agent environment. *ALIAS* is currently available in its prototypical implementation obtained with Java and *Amzi!* Prolog. We evaluated the performance of *ALIAS* executing simple applications without any concrete meaning; current work is now devoted to test the system effectiveness with real applications. To this purpose we are working at the definition of an application for distributed diagnosis in the automotive field. However, we are aware that the strict monotonicity of the DAA algorithm with respect to the set of abduced hypotheses may represent an obstacle when implementing real applications: for this reason, a future topic will be the extension of the system with respect to the capability of retracting abduced hypotheses. Current work focuses also on extending the implementation by considering dynamic composition of agents into bunches. Finally we also intend to investigate the application of the coordination protocol to other existing abductive methods, in addition to the one here considered.

7 Acknowledgements

We would like to thank Stefano Tampieri for his contribution in the implementation of *ALIAS*. This work has been supported by M.U.R.S.T. Project on *Intelligent agents: interaction and knowledge acquisition*.

References

1. *Abductive LogIc Agent System*. http://www.lia.deis.unibo.it/Software/ALIAS/.
2. AMZI! *Amzi!* Prolog + Logic Server 4.1. http://www.amzi.com.
3. A. Brogi, E. Lamma, P. Mancarella, and P. Mello. A Unifying View for Logic Programming with Non-Monotonic Reasoning. In *Theoretical Computer Science*, Vol. 184, 1–49, North Holland, 1997.
4. K. L. Clark. Negation as Failure. In H. Gallaire and J. Minker, eds., *Logic and Databases*. Plenum Press, New York, 1978.
5. P. T. Cox and T. Pietrzykowski. Causes for events: Their computation and applications. In *Proc. CADE-86*, 608, 1986.
6. K. Eshgi and R. A. Kowalski. Abduction compared with negation by failure. In G. Levi and M. Martelli, editors, *Proc. 6th International Conference on Logic Programming*, 234. MIT Press, 1989.
7. D. Gelernter. *Generative Communication in Linda*. *ACM Toplas*, 7(1):80–112, 1985. V.7, N.1, 80–112, 1985.
8. A. C. Kakas, R. A. Kowalski, and F. Toni. Abductive Logic Programming. *Journal of Logic and Computation*, 2(6):719–770, 1993.
9. A. C. Kakas, and P. Mancarella. Generalized stable models: a semantics for abduction. In *Proc. 9th European Conference on Artificial Intelligence*. Pitman Pub., 1990.

10. A. C. Kakas, and P. Mancarella. On the relation between Truth Maintenance and Abduction. In *Proc. PRICAI90*, 1990.
11. R. A. Kowalski. Problems and promises of computational logic. In *Proc. Symposium on Computational Logic*, 1-36. Springer-Verlag, Nov. 1990.
12. N. R. Jennings, M. J. Wooldridge, eds., *Agent Technology*. Springer-Verlag, 1998.
13. D. L. Poole. A logical framework for default reasoning. *Artificial Intelligence*, 36:27. Elsevier, 1988.
14. K. Sicara, et al. Distributed Intelligent Agents. *IEEE Expert*, 36–46, Dec. 1996.
15. M. H. van Emden and R. A. Kowalski. The semantics of predicate logic as a programming language. *Journal of the ACM*, 23(4):733–742, 1976.

Solving the Satisfiability Problem
Through Boolean Networks

Michela Milano   Andrea Roli

DEIS Università di Bologna

V.le Risorgimento, 2 – 40136 Bologna ITALY

email: mmilano@deis.unibo.it, roli.a@mail.aitec.it

Abstract.   In this paper we present a new approach to solve the satisfiability problem (SAT), based on boolean networks (BN). We define a mapping between a SAT instance and a BN, and we solve SAT problem by simulating the BN dynamics. We prove that BN fixed points correspond to the SAT solutions. The mapping presented allows to develop a new class of algorithms to solve SAT. Moreover, this new approach suggests new ways to combine symbolic and connectionist computation and provides a general framework for local search algorithms.

1 Introduction

The satisfiability problem (SAT) [Garey and Johnson, 1979] has an important role in computer science and it has been widely investigated. The SAT problem is a NP-complete problem concerning the satisfiability of boolean formulas, i.e., find an assignment of boolean values to variables such that the formula is satisfied. SAT is very important in several Artificial Intelligence areas, like propositional calculus, constraints satisfaction and planning. For its theoretical and practical relevance, many specialized (complete and incomplete) algorithms have been developed.

We present a novel approach to solve SAT, based on Boolean Networks (BN). Up to this time, boolean networks have been used for modeling complex adaptive systems [Cowan *et al.*, 1994], and in the field of machine learning (see for instance [Dorigo, 1994]). In this approach, we map a SAT instance in a BN, and we simulate its dynamics; the stationary states of the net correspond to the solutions of SAT. Due to the BN structure and dynamics used, the resulting algorithms are incomplete.

We have developed and tested three algorithms, each of them is derived from a variant of boolean networks: synchronous, probabilistic and asynchronous boolean nets. The first algorithm has led to disappointing results, while the second and the third had performed better.

The new approach represents a bind between symbolic and connectionist computation, and it allows to develop new algorithms to solve SAT.

This work represents a first investigation on the subject and it mainly refers to the founding principles. The algorithms presented are based on elementary dynamics of boolean networks, without using any heuristic function to guide the search, nor optimization criteria.

E. Lamma and P. Mello (Eds.): AI*IA 99, LNAI 1792, pp. 72–83, 2000.

2 Preliminaries

In this section we recall the boolean network model (for more details see for instance [Kauffman, 1993]). Then, we briefly define the satisfiability problem and recall some algorithms.

2.1 Boolean Networks

Boolean networks (BN) have been introduced by Kauffman [Kauffman, 1993] as a model of genetic networks (models of genes activity and interactions) and as a framework to study complex adaptive systems (see [Kauffman, 1993; Cowan *et al.,* 1994]).

A BN is a directed graph of *n* nodes; each node *i* of the graph is associated with a boolean variable (v_i) and a boolean function (F_i). The inputs of the boolean function F_i are boolean variables associated with the neighboring nodes (i.e., nodes whose outgoing arcs lead to the node *i*). See, for instance, fig.1 (left part).

The network is initialized with a random or deterministically selected initial state; the dynamics of the net is given by the state transition of the nodes (see fig.1 right part), depending on the results of the corresponding boolean functions. In the main definition of boolean networks the dynamics is synchronous, i.e., nodes are updated in parallel. We will consider, also, asynchronous dynamics, i.e., nodes are sequentially updated, and probabilistic dynamics, i.e., each node has a set of boolean functions and it is updated choosing one of them.

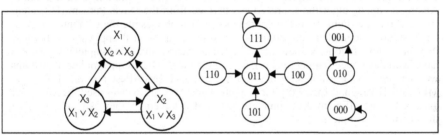

Fig.1 A synchronous boolean network and its trajectories

A BN is a discrete-time dynamic system with boolean variables; we can analyze it observing the *trajectory* in the state space, the length of the *transient phase*, the type of the *attractors* and the *stability*. The state of the system is given by the array $\mathbf{x}=(x_1,...,x_n)$, $x_i \in \{0,1\}$, $1 \le i \le n$.

Since the number of states is finite (2^n) and the transition rules are deterministic, eventually the system will reach a state already found, that is, after a transient, it will find a *cyclic attractor* and it will repeat the same sequence of states (*cycle of states*). The number of states constituting the cycle represents the *length* (*period*) of the attractor; the minimum period is 1 (i.e., the attractor is a *fixed point*) and the maximum period is the number of states of the system (2^n).

The dynamics of the network is given by the transition rules: $x_i(t+1)=F_i(x_{i_1}(t),...,x_{i_{k(i)}}(t))$, where x_{i_j} ($j = 1,2,...,k(i)$) are the inputs of the boolean function F_i, for $i = 1,2,...,n$.

We define *basin of attraction* of an attractor the collection of states such that, if selected as initial states, will converge to the attractor. See fig.1 for an example of a boolean network dynamics.

2.2 The Satisfiability Problem

The satisfiability problem (SAT) is a well-known NP-complete problem (see [Garey and Johnson, 1979]) and it has an important role in computer science; in fact, it is possible to transform every NP problem in SAT in polynomial time. Furthermore, many applications (e.g., planning, VLSI testing, Boolean CSP) can be expressed in terms of SAT.

We will refer to the following definition of SAT: given a boolean expression in conjunctive normal form (CNF), i.e., a conjunction of clauses, each of them constituted by disjunction of variables, negated or not, find an assignment of boolean variables which satisfies the expression. For example, consider the expression $\Phi = (x_1 \vee x_2 \vee \sim x_3) \wedge (\sim x_2 \vee x_3) \wedge (\sim x_1 \vee \sim x_2 \vee x_3) \wedge (\sim x_1 \vee x_2)$; Φ is constituted by four clauses, each of them contains the disjunction of some *literals* (i.e., positive or negative variables). Given a truth assignment T (that is, we assign the value 'True' (1) or 'False' (0) to each variable) we say that Φ is satisfied by T if and only if every clause contains at least one literal with the 'True' value. In this case, Φ is satisfied by the assignments $\{x_1 = 0, x_2 = 0, x_3 = 0\}$ and $\{x_1 = 0, x_2 = 1, x_3 = 1\}$.

Two kinds of algorithms for solving SAT have been proposed in the literature: complete and incomplete algorithms. Complete algorithms always find a solution, if it exists, in finite time; incomplete algorithms could not find a solution, even if it exists. Among complete algorithms, procedures derived from the Davis-Putnam (DP) algorithm [Davis and Putnam, 1960] are the most efficient. Despite the guarantee of finding a solution, complete algorithms are seldom used for real applications, because they are computationally inefficient. In recent years, some incomplete algorithms have been developed (*model finders*); among the most efficient incomplete algorithms we mention GSAT [Selman *et al.*, 1992], WalkSAT [McAllester *et al.*, 1997] and MSLSAT [Liang and Li, 1998]. Incomplete algorithms are widely used, because they are much more efficient then complete ones and, on average, they can solve most of the satisfiable instances.

3 Solving SAT Problems with BNs

In this section, we present a new approach to solve the satisfiability problem, which consists in the transformation of a SAT problem in a BN. For this purpose we define a *mapping* that generates, given a SAT instance, a BN whose dynamics is characterized by the presence of fixed points corresponding to the solutions of the SAT instance. Then we simulate the dynamics of the network until a steady state is reached. The steady state represents the solution of the problem. The algorithms derived are incomplete. We are currently investigating if, by changing the mapping and dynamics, we can obtain complete procedures.

3.1 The Mapping

The core of the application is the particular transformation that allows to switch from the symbolic space of the propositional satisfiability to the BN sub-symbolic space, preserving the correctness of the results.

The fundamental requirement of a mapping is to give a correspondence between the solutions of the SAT instance and the BN fixed points. More precisely, if we assume a one-to-one correspondence between the boolean variables of the propositional formula and the nodes of the network, the mapping should be such that a satisfying assignment for the formula corresponds to a fixed point of the network (*completeness* property); moreover, every fixed point of the boolean network corresponds to a solution of the SAT instance (*soundness* property).

We designed a simple mapping (called $\mu1$) which has the desired requirements; the BN has n nodes if n are SAT variables. For each variable, the corresponding boolean function is computed as follows:

Input: $\Phi = c_1 \wedge c_2 \wedge ... \wedge c_m$ (a boolean formula in CNF);
Output: Boolean functions F_i ;
For each variable x_i **define** $O_i = \{c_j,\ j = 1,..,m\ |\ x_i \in c_j\}$, $A_i = \{c_j,\ j = 1,..,m\ |\ \sim x_i \in c_j\}$
For i:=1 **to** n **define** $F_i = (x_i \wedge And[A_i]) \vee \sim And[O_i]$

where the function «*And*» is the logical operator '$\wedge$' applied to the elements of A_i, being '1' the result of its application to an empty set.

For example, consider the following SAT instance: $\Phi_1 = (x_1 \vee \sim x_2) \wedge (\sim x_1 \vee x_2) \wedge (x_2 \vee x_3)$ $= c_1 \wedge c_2 \wedge c_3$; we use a boolean network of three nodes with (x_1, F_1), (x_2, F_2), (x_3, F_3). The sets O_i and A_i are: $O_1 = \{c_1\}$, $A_1 = \{c_2\}$; $O_2 = \{c_2, c_3\}$, $A_2 = \{c_1\}$; $O_3 = \{c_3\}$, $A_3 = \varnothing$. The boolean functions are: $F_1 = (c_2 \wedge x_1) \vee \sim c_1$, $F_2 = (c_1 \wedge x_2) \vee \sim c_2 \vee \sim c_3$, $F_3 = x_3 \vee \sim c_3$. Note that Φ_1 is satisfied iff $(x_1, x_2, x_3) \in \{(0,0,1), (1,1,0), (1,1,1)\}$ representing the only fixed points of the network.

It is possible to prove that the mapping $\mu1$ is sound and complete.

Proposition 1: given an instance Φ of SAT (with n variables), the boolean network $\Re$ of n nodes induced by the mapping $\mu1$ is such that its fixed points are in one-to-one correspondence with the solutions of Φ (see Appendix A for the proof).

Note that the mapping $\mu1$ can be efficiently implemented. If the SAT has n variables, m clauses and l_{max} is the maximum number of literals per clause, the definition of A_i and O_i can be executed in time $O(m\ l_{max})$.

3.2 The Dynamics of the Network

The second phase of the algorithm is the simulation of the dynamics of the network. The boolean net associated (by means of $\mu1$) with the problem is now the dynamic system that performs the computation. The goal of the simulation is to find a fixed point. Note that the mapping obeys only the condition about fixed points, nothing has been imposed about cycles. If during the simulation of a synchronous and deterministic dynamics the network reaches a cycle, it has to be reinitialized and restarted with a new trajectory in the state space. In order to avoid deterministic cycles, we have investigated also probabilistic and asynchronous BNs, for which we proved that (deterministic) cycles do not exist.

We have tried three different kind of dynamics, i.e., synchronous, probabilistic and asynchronous, while maintaining the same mapping ($\mu1$). In the next subsections we will describe each of them.

3.2.1 Synchronous Boolean Networks

Given a SAT instance we apply $\mu1$ to obtain a boolean network; in a Synchronous Boolean Network (hereinafter referred to as SBN), variables are updated in parallel and transitions are deterministic.

Example: given the boolean formula $\Phi_2 = (x_1 \vee x_2) \wedge (x_1 \vee \sim x_3) \wedge (\sim x_1 \vee \sim x_3) \wedge (x_2 \vee x_3) \wedge (x_1 \vee x_3) = c_1 \wedge c_2 \wedge c_3 \wedge c_4 \wedge c_5$, $\mu1$ generates a boolean network with three nodes, defined by these functions: $F_1 = (c_3 \wedge x_1) \vee \sim c_1 \vee \sim c_2 \vee \sim c_5$, $F_2 = x_2 \vee \sim c_1 \vee \sim c_4$, $F_3 = (c_2 \wedge c_3 \wedge x_3) \vee \sim c_4 \vee \sim c_5$. The solution of Φ_2 is $(x_1, x_2, x_3) \in \{(1,1,0)\}$ and corresponds to the transition graph fix point depicted in fig.2.

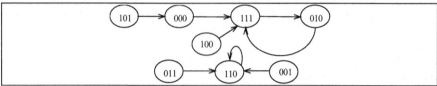

Fig. 2. Transition graph of the BN associated with Φ_2: the fixed point has a basin of attraction of 3 states. There is also a cycle which has period 2 and a basin of attraction of 5 states.

The algorithm for SBN, depicted in figure 3, simulates the network dynamics until a fixed point is found or the maximum number of iterations is reached. If the network is trapped in a cycle, the procedure restarts the network from a new random initial state. SAT-SBN1 detains disappointing performances: it gave not better performance than a *generate and test* procedure. Experimental results suggest that the lower is the number of satisfiable assignments, the lower the size of the fixed points basin of attraction.

Note that the inefficiency of the algorithm comes from the combination of the specific mapping with synchronous dynamics and it is not an intrinsic characteristic of the approach.

```
procedure SAT-SBN1;
begin
  iterations := 1;
  while (iterations ≤ MAX_ITER) do
  begin
    attractor := False; trajectory := [];
    select_random_initial_state;
    while (attractor==False && iterations≤ MAX_ITER) do
    begin
      compute_new_state;
      Append(trajectory, state);
      if end_of_transient(trajectory) then attractor := True
        else iterations++;
    end;
    if fixed_point(trajectory) then return solution;
    else iterations++;
  end;
end;
```

Fig. 3. SAT-SBN1 algorithm

3.2.2 Probabilistic BNs

One way to avoid cycles is to introduce a non-deterministic system transition function where a system state has more than one successor state, each one with a given probability.

The probabilistic version of a boolean network (PBN) is obtained by associating more than one boolean function with each node and specifying a *function probability*, which gives the probability of selecting a particular boolean function. Each state transition is obtained by selecting one boolean function per node and synchronously updating all nodes involved in the selected function. Since for each state several transitions are possible, the transition graph has nodes with more than one outcoming arc and each arc has a transition probability.

A fixed point for a PBN transition graph is a node with a self-arc whose transition probability is equal to 1. PBN can present *(probabilistic) cycles*, which are cycles composed by arcs with a probability less than 1. We call *deterministic cycles* those whose arcs have transition probability equal to 1.

In this paper, we consider PBNs obtained by generating a SBN with $\mu 1$ and adding to each node an identity boolean function ($F_i = x_i(t+1) = x_i(t)$); the transition probability of the first boolean function is p, and for the identity function is 1-p. Thus, each node changes its value according to the original boolean function with probability p, and maintains the same value with probability 1-p.

The algorithm that simulates the dynamics of the PBN is reported in figure 4. The algorithm must recognize true fixed points, distinguishing them from repetition of the same state, even if it is not a fixed point. This is done by verifying if the current assignment (i.e., the current state) satisfies the original formula (see the statement "if (satisfied_formula(state)) then return solution" in fig.4), or by executing a SBN1-like step. Even if this operation has a computational high cost if frequently executed, SAT-PBN1 strongly outperformed SAT-SBN1. We experimentally found that an *optimal probability p* exists for which the algorithm gets the best performance; for 3-SAT *p* is near 0.2.

```
procedure SAT-PBN1;
begin
   iterations := 1;
   select_random_initial_state;
   while (iterations ≤ MAX_ITER) do
   begin
      old_state := state;
      compute_new_state_with_transition_prob_p;
      if (old_state == state) then
         if (satisfied_formula(state) ) then return solution;
      iterations++;
   end;
end;
```

Fig. 4 SAT-PBN algorithm

PBN1 has the following property:
Proposition 2: If the network is generated by means of $\mu 1$ from a satisfiable boolean formula, for every initial state the probability that the network reaches a fixed point tends to 1; that is:

$$\lim_{time \to \infty} \text{Prob}\{"\text{ the net reaches a fixed point"}\} = 1$$

(see Appendix B for a proof). As a consequence of the previous proposition PBNs of this application are "deterministic cycle – free".

Proposition 2 allows to formally define the convergence of the algorithm SAT-PBN1 in terms of *Probabilistic Asymptotic Completeness* [Hoos, 1999] asserting that the algorithm SAT-PBN1 is Probabilistically Approximately Complete (PAC).

3.2.3 Asynchronous BNs

Asynchronous boolean networks (ABN) are characterized by the sequential update of the nodes. There are several ways to update the nodes, either fixed or random sequences or sequences obtained by other kinds of probabilistic distributions. In this work, we use random update sequences: at each iteration only one randomly selected node is updated. The algorithm for ABN (SAT-ABN1) is depicted in fig.5. Since the computational cost of the "true fixed point" test is high, we structured the update sequences in this way: the dynamics of the network is divided in *macro-transitions*, which are random sequential update of all the N nodes (each single update is called *micro-transitions*). Since, if a state is a fixed point, every micro-transition is such that the variable maintains the old value, after a macro-transition the fixed point is correctly recognized. Vice versa, a simple repetition of a state, which is not a fixed point, is possible only during the macro-transition (that is: between micro-transitions) and, after the macro-transition, the new state is surely different from the old one. The asynchronous dynamics allows a kind of *communication* between the nodes: since they are updated one at a time, two or more variables do not change their value to satisfying the same clause. The use of macro-transitions gains the performance of the SAT-ABN1 algorithm.

```
procedure SAT-ABN1;
begin
   iterations := 1;
   select_random_initial_state;
   while(iterations≤ MAX_ITERATIONS) do
   begin
      old_state := state;
      compute_new_state_with_random sequence;
      if (old_state == state) then return solution;
      else iterations++;
   end;
end;
```

Fig. 5. SAT-ABN1 algorithm

Proposition 2, presented in the previous subsection, is also valid in the ABNs case. Therefore, we can assert that ABNs of this application are "deterministic cycle-free" and the algorithm SAT-ABN1 is PAC.

3.3 Experimental Results

We compared the BN-based algorithms on 3-SAT random generated satisfiable (*forced*) formulas with n variables and m clauses. Since the synchronous version showed non competitive performances, even for 20 variables, we tested only SAT-PBN1 (with $p=0.2$) and SAT-ABN1. The run time was limited and a negative result was reported if a solution was not found. ABN and PBN were restarted after a number of transitions proportional to n^2. In Tables 1,2 are shown samples of the experimental results. The algorithms have been implemented in C and run on a PentiumII 233 Mhz.

SAT-PBN1 is competitive with SAT-ABN1 for $n>500$ and $m<3n$. When $m/n<3$, 3-SAT instances have many solutions and the parallel search is most efficient. For $m/n>3$ more conflicting constraints have to be satisfied and the sequential search works better.

n	m	SAT-ABN1			SAT-PBN1			GSAT		
		time (msec)	iter.	solved	time (msec)	iter.	solved	time (msec)	iter.	solved
50	100	10	3	100%	<1	22	100%	<1	11	100%
50	150	10	9	100%	10	156	100%	<1	26	100%
50	215	310	894	99%	3155	34073	88%	10	105	100%
80	160	20	4	100%	<1	29	100%	<1	22	100%
80	240	20	14	100%	30	257	100%	10	72	100%
80	344	9113	15958	55.5%	13550	97891	12.5%	30	428	100%
100	200	<1	4	100%	10	34	100%	<1	33	100%
100	300	20	19	100%	90	598	100%	10	97	100%
100	430	21681	28526	16.5%	-	-	0%	60	590	100%
200	400	20	5	100%	30	50	100%	20	94	100%
200	600	121	64	100%	1011	3664	100%	60	287	100%
200	860	-	-	0%	-	-	0%	471	2435	100%

Table 1
Median execution time and iterations over 200 satisfiable instances.

We also compared these procedures with GSAT, but we obtained disappointing results: GSAT is faster and more effective than the BN-procedures. This is due to the fact that GSAT is based on heuristic criteria, which guide the search, while the simple BN-procedures perform a "blind" search. Nevertheless, even without heuristic, BN-procedures perform better than GSAT when $m<3n$, as we can see from Table 2. The number of GSAT maxflips was fixed to $5n$ (according to [Selman et al., 1992]).

We also tested the procedures on random non-forced instances and we observed the same qualitative behavior (in this case, BN-procedures perform better than GSAT for $m<2.5n$).

n	m	SAT-ABN1			SAT-PBN1			GSAT		
		time (msec)	iter.	solved	time (msec)	iter.	solved	time (msec)	iter.	solved
300	600	41	6	100%	50	57	100%	61	174	100%
300	750	90	14	100%	120	180	100%	100	253	100%
500	1000	140	7	100%	130	70	100%	201	363	100%
500	1250	220	18	100%	231	225	100%	330	722	100%
700	1400	250	9	100%	190	76	100%	391	601	100%
700	1750	450	23	100%	390	282	100%	721	1186	100%
1000	2000	481	9	100%	341	84	100%	851	914	100%
1000	2500	871	27	100%	670	343	100%	1432	1688	100%

Table 2
Median execution time and iterations over 100 satisfiable instances.

3.4 Discussion

The asynchronous version of the algorithm (with μ1) is analogous to a local repair algorithm; in fact, variables that belong to unsatisfied clauses are forced to change their value. The WalkSAT algorithm, with random choice of the variable within an unsatisfied clause, is indeed very similar to ABN-based algorithms. Furthermore, SAT-ABN1 is a kind of WalkSAT with random choice and variable-length tabu list. Main differences are:

- ABN-based algorithms are intrinsically concurrent and, when sequentialized, they update even those variables which belongs to satisfied clauses; this implies many "void updates", which decrease the performance (notice that SAT-PBN1 can be viewed as a sort of parallelized version of WalkSAT).

- WalkSAT shows the best performance with heuristic function which guides the search; such heuristic is completely absent in SAT-ABN1. We are currently working on the introduction of heuristic knowledge in BN-algorithms.

Finally, it is worth noticing that the boolean functions defined by μ1 explicitly make the *pure literals* simplification (only in the first processing phase), since they fix the values 1 (0) to those updating variables which compare only non-negated (negated).

The combination of functional computation and dynamics can be generalized using a General Framework (see fig.6). Moving along the two dimensions (which represent the functional/dynamics complexity) it is possible to design new algorithms (like SAT-ABN1) and redesigning old ones. For example, with a particular choice of dynamics and mapping, local search algorithms, like GSAT, WalkSAT and their variants can be reinterpreted in the BN framework. The mapping in this case creates boolean functions imposing a simple flip of the updating variable, $F_i = x_i(t+1) = \sim x_i(t) \; \forall i$. The search mechanism is performed by the asynchronous (sequential) dynamics which selects the updating variable according to the heuristic criteria of the search procedures.

This framework allows compared analysis and generalization of local search and local repair procedures. A first result of this approach is that, as a consequence of Proposition 2, GSAT and WalkSAT with noise can find a solution with probability 1 (with unlimited time).

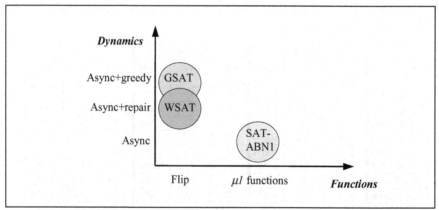

Fig. 6 The separation between functions and dynamics allows to consider old and new algorithms in a unique framework.

4 Conclusion and Future Work

In this paper we have introduced a new approach to the solution of SAT, based on boolean networks. The transformation from a SAT instance to a boolean network is allowed by a mapping, which is sound and complete. The dynamics of the SAT-generated networks corresponds to the computation phase and the stationary state of the system is the solution of the problem.

We designed a mapping (μl) and we developed three simple algorithms, derived by synchronous, probabilistic and asynchronous BN. The probabilistic and asynchronous algorithms have shown interesting behaviors.

The contribution of this work is twofold: first, we proved that it is possible to switch from the propositional space to the boolean network space, preserving the correctness of the results; second, BN-computation provides a general framework for local search procedures.

We are currently working on the introduction of heuristics into BNs algorithms; future works concern the design of more complex mappings and the extension of BNs model.

Appendix A

Proposition 1: the mapping μl between a SAT instance Φ (with n variables) and the corresponding BN $\mathfrak{R}$ of n nodes is sound and complete.
Proof:
1- completeness) Suppose that $(x_1, \dots, x_n)$ is a solution of Φ, then all the clauses are satisfied, that is $c_1 = c_2 = \dots = c_m = 1$. All the boolean function are: $F_i = (1 \wedge \dots \wedge 1 \wedge x_i) \vee 0 \vee \dots \vee 0 \Leftrightarrow F_i = x_i$, this is equivalent to a dynamics given by the evolution equations $x_i(t+1) = x_i(t)$ $\forall i$ $(1 \le i \le n)$ corresponding to a fixed point trajectory.
2- soundness) The current hypothesis is that $(x_1, \dots, x_n)$ is a fixed point for $\mathfrak{R}$; suppose, *ab absurdo*, that $(x_1, \dots, x_n)$ is not a satisfying assignment for Φ; therefore a non satisfied clause c_j exists, i.e., $c_j = 0$. Take a variable x_i such that x_i belongs to c_j; there are two cases:
a) $c_j = (\dots \vee x_i \vee \dots) = 0$, this implies that $x_i = x_i(t) = 0$ and then all the clauses containing literal $\sim x_i$ are satisfied; we have $F_i = x_i(t+1) = (1 \wedge x_i) \vee \dots \vee \sim c_j = 0 \vee \sim c_j = 1$, that is $x_i(t) \neq x_i(t+1)$ and this contradicts the hypothesis.
b) $c_j = (\dots \vee \sim x_i \vee \dots) = 0$, this implies that $x_i = x_i(t) = 1$ and then all the clauses which contain the literal x_i are satisfied; we have $F_i = x_i(t+1) = (\dots \wedge c_j \wedge x_i) \vee 0 \vee \dots \vee 0 = (0 \wedge 1) \vee 0 = 0$, that is $x_i(t) \neq x_i(t+1)$ and this contradicts the hypothesis.

Appendix B

Proposition 2: If the PBN (ABN) is generated by means of μl from a satisfiable boolean formula, for every initial state the probability that the network reaches a fixed point tends to 1.
Proof (sketched): to prove the proposition we need to use some results about Markov chains (MCs) ([Feller, 1968]). The main result we use is the following: given a MC, if C is the closed set given by all the persistent states of the MC, the chain will eventually reach C with probability 1.

Obs1: The state space trajectory described by a PBN (ABN) is a MC.

Lemma1: If x^* is a fixed point, then x^* is an *absorbing state* for the MC (that is x^* is an irreducible set of only one state).

Proof: it is easy to prove that the sum of the probabilities of all the transitions from any node is 1 (by using combinatorial analysis). Since x^* is a fixed point, for $i=1,...,n$ is $x_i(t+1) = F_i = x_i(t)$. Then, each variable has probability 1 to maintain the old value and the only transition is represented by a self-arc, which has probability 1. Each fixed point can communicate only with itself, then it is an absorbing state.

Lemma2: The states which are not fixed points are *transient states*, in the MC sense.

Proof: we will prove that a state x, which is not a solution, communicates with a solution s; then, since solutions communicate only with themselves, x is a transient state. We will prove that there exists a path (constituted by 1-Hamming transitions), with positive probability, between x and s. The trajectory is the result of two overlapped mechanisms: the dynamics mechanism and the functional mechanism. The first quantifies the probability of any transition, while the second specifies which transitions are allowed and which are not. Suppose that the network has only one fixed point $s = (s_1,...,s_n)$, $x = (x_1,...,x_n)$, $x \neq s$ and define $V=\{x_1,...,x_n\}$, $I = \{x_i \in V$ s.t. $x_i \neq s_i\}$. Since x is not a solution, there exists a subset Γ of unsatisfied clauses. There is, at least, one $x_i \in I$ such that $x_i \in c_j \in \Gamma$, then the transition $(x_1,..,x_i,..,x_n) \rightarrow (x_1,..,\sim x_i,..,x_n)$ is allowed (by the functional mechanism). If such transition does not exist, Γ would be constituted only by clauses involving variables belonging to $V \backslash I$; but those variables have a value that satisfies the formula, then also the subset Γ and this is a contradiction. The probability of the transition (given by the dynamics mechanism) is $p(1-p)^{n-1}$ for the PBN and $1/n$ for the ABN. By iterating this step it is possible to reach s with a succession of transitions, each one obtained by a single variable update. The probability of this path is the product of the transition probabilities and it is positive. Suppose, now, that the network has a set S of fixed points, with $|S|>1$. If we take $s \in S$ and $x \notin S$ we can repeat the previous proof. Thus every $x \notin S$ can reach every $s \in S$ with positive probability.

Conclusion: the states of the network can be represented by $E = T \cup \{s_1\} \cup...\cup \{s_h\}$, where T is the set of transient states, and $\{s_1\} \cup...\cup \{s_h\} = C$ is the closed set of the absorbing states. A theorem states that the MC reaches C with probability 1.

References

[Cowan et al., 1994] G.A. Cowan, D. Pines, D. Meltzer eds. *Complexity: metaphors, models, and reality.* Addison-Wesley Publishing Company, Redwood City, CA, 1994.

[Davis and Putnam, 1960] M. Davis, H. Putnam. A computing procedure for quantification theory. *JACM*,7:201-215, 1960.

[Dorigo, 1994] M. Dorigo. Learning by Probabilistic Boolean Networks. *Proceedings of World Congress on Computational Intelligence* - IEEE International Conference on Neural Networks,   887-891, 1994.

[Feller, 1968] W. Feller. *An Introduction to Probability Theory and its Applications.* Third Edition, John Wiley.

[Garey and Johnson, 1979] M. R. Garey, D. S. Johnson. *Computers and intractability.* Freeman, 1979.

[Hoos, 1999] H. H. Hoos. On the Run-time Behaviour of Stochastic Local Search Algortihms for SAT. *Proceedings of AAAI-99*, p.661-666, MIT Press, 1999.

[Kauffman, 1993] S. A. Kauffman. *The Origins of Order.* Oxford University Press, New York, 1993.

[Liang and Li, 1998] D. Liang, W. Li. Multi-strategy local search for SAT problem. *Proceeding ECAI98*, H. Prade ed. John Whiley & sons. 1998.

[McAllester *et al.*, 1997] D. McAllester, B. Selman, H. Kautz. Evidence for invariants in local search. *Proceedings of AAAI-97*,1997.

[Selman *et al.*, 1992] B. Selman, H. Levesque, D. Mitchell. A new method for solving hard satisfiability problems. *Proceedings of AAAI-92*, 440-446, San Jose, CA, 1992.

Applying the Davis-Putnam procedure to non-clausal formulas [*]

Enrico Giunchiglia[1] and Roberto Sebastiani[2]

[1] DIST, Università di Genova, Viale Causa, 13 – 16145 Genova, Italy
[2] DISA, Università di Trento, Via Inama, 5 – 38100 Trento, Italy

Abstract. Traditionally, the satisfiability problem for propositional logics deals with formulas in Conjunctive Normal Form (CNF). A typical
way to deal with non-CNF formulas requires (i) converting them into
CNF, and (ii) applying solvers usually based on the Davis-Putnam (DP)
procedure. A well known problem of this solution is that the CNF conversion may introduce many new variables, thus greatly widening the
space of assignments in which the DP procedure has to search in order
to find solutions.
In this paper we present two variants of the DP procedure which overcome the problem outlined above. The idea underlying these variants
is that splitting should occur only for the variables in the original formula. The CNF conversion methods employed ensure their correctness
and completeness. As a consequence, we get two decision procedures for
non-CNF formulas (i) which can exploit all the present and future sophisticated technology of current DP implementations, and (ii) whose
space of assignments they have to search in, is limited in size by the
number of variables in the original input formula.
In [11], it is showed that limiting the splitting step to a subset of the
set of variables (the truth values of the others being consequentially
determined) can lead to significant speeds up.

1 Introduction

In the last few years the satisfiability problem for CNF propositional formulas
(SAT) has been widely investigated both theoretically and empirically and very
efficient solvers have been developed (see e.g. [2]). Among the correct and complete solvers, the most popular are variants of the DP procedure [7, 6]. Highly
sophisticated DP implementations include smart splitting heuristics and efficient
data structures for manipulating CNF formulas (see, e.g., [9, 4, 22]).

---

[*] The ideas underlying this work have benefited from some discussions with Alessandro Armando, Alessandro Massarotto, David McAllester, Bart Selman, Armando
Tacchella and Toby Walsh. Fausto Giunchiglia provided very useful feedback. Pier-
giorgio Bertoli and Luciano Serafini provided valuable help with the proofs of the
theorems. All people mentioned above are thanked for their help.

E. Lamma and P. Mello (Eds.): AI*IA 99, LNAI 1792, pp. 84–94, 2000.
© Springer-Verlag Berlin Heidelberg 2000

On the other hand, many applications require decision procedures for *non-CNF* propositional formulas. For instance, the decision procedures for modal and terminological logics presented in [12, 13] —which proved to be empirically and theoretically superior to standard tableau systems [13, 10]— are built on top of non-CNF propositional procedures. In the field of digital hardware design, the correctness of a boolean circuit is showed by proving the equivalence between the propositional encodings of the circuit and its specification. In order to apply the DP procedure also in these applications, the standard solution is to pre-convert the formula to a CNF form using methods based on [15] (lately optimized in [8]).[1] The problem with this solution is that these conversions produce CNF formulas possibly containing many new variables. These new variables greatly widen the space of assignments in which the DP procedure has to search in order to find solutions.

In this paper we present two variants of the DP procedure which (when applied to CNF conversions of non-CNF formulas) overcome the problem outlined above. The idea underlying these variants —called DP* and DP**— is that splitting should occur only for the variables in the original formula. The CNF conversion methods employed ensure that the newly introduced variables get assigned either by unit propagation or by the pure literal rule. As a consequence, we get two correct and complete decision procedures for non-CNF formulas

1. which can exploit all the present and future sophisticated technology of current DP implementations, and
2. whose space of assignments they have to search in, is limited in size by the number of variables in the original input formula.

In [11], it is showed that limiting the splitting step to a subset of the set of variables (the truth values of the others being consequentially determined) can lead to significant speeds up (up to 4 orders of magnitude when using a time limit of 2700 seconds).

2   Preliminaries

We assume all the standard definitions and results of propositional logic. To simplify the presentation, we consider only formulas built from propositional literals – i.e., atoms and their negations – through finitely many applications of the connectives $\wedge, \vee, \equiv$. As customary in implementations, we allow conjunctions and disjunctions of an arbitrary number of formulas. Notationally, we use the capital letters $A_1, A_2, \ldots$ for propositional atoms; $l, l_1, \ldots$ for literals; $\Phi, \Phi_1, \ldots$ for CNF formulas; $\varphi, \varphi_1, \ldots$ for generic propositional formulas; and $\mu, \mu', \mu_1, \ldots$ for (partial) truth assignments. We use the symbols T and F as the logical constants for truth and falsity, and the same symbols denote also their respective truth values. If $l_i = \neg A_i$, $\neg l_i$ stands for A_i. We represent truth assignments as

---

[1] Actually, the methods in [15, 8] were proposed in the setting of first-order logic. We are simply considering their restriction to propositional logic.

	$\varphi = (\bigvee_{i=1}^{m} \varphi_i)$	$\varphi = (\bigwedge_{i=1}^{m} \varphi_i)$	$\varphi = (\varphi_1 \equiv \varphi_2)$
$ren_\equiv(\varphi)$	$(\neg B \vee \bigvee_{i=1}^{m} B_i) \wedge$ $(B \vee \neg B_1)$ $\dots$ $(B \vee \neg B_m)$	$(B \vee \bigvee_{i=1}^{m} \neg B_i) \wedge$ $(\neg B \vee B_1)$ $\wedge \dots$ $(\neg B \vee B_m)$	$(\neg B \vee B_1 \vee \neg B_2) \wedge$ $(\neg B \vee \neg B_1 \vee B_2) \wedge$ $(B \vee B_1 \vee B_2)$ $\wedge$ $(B \vee \neg B_1 \vee \neg B_2)$
$ren_\supset(\varphi)$	$(\neg B \vee \bigvee_{i=1}^{m} B_i)$	$(\neg B \vee B_1)$ $\dots$ $(\neg B \vee B_m)$	$(\neg B \vee B_1 \vee \neg B_2) \wedge$ $(\neg B \vee \neg B_1 \vee B_2)$

Table 1. Definition of $ren_\equiv(\varphi)$ and $ren_\supset(\varphi)$.

sets of literals like $\{A_1, \neg A_2, \dots\}$, with the intended meaning $\{A_1 := \mathsf{T}, A_2 := \mathsf{F}, \dots\}$.

By $assign(l, \varphi)$ we denote the formula obtained

1. substituting every occurrence of l $[\neg l]$ in φ with T $[\mathsf{F}]$, and
2. recursively evaluating the result according to the standard propositional simplification rules ($\varphi \vee \mathsf{T} \Rightarrow \mathsf{T}$, $\varphi \wedge \mathsf{T} \Rightarrow \varphi$, $\varphi \equiv \mathsf{T} \Rightarrow \varphi$, etc.).

If $\mu = \{l_1, \dots, l_k\}$, then $assign(\mu, \varphi)$ denotes the formula

$$assign(l_k, assign(\dots, assign(l_1, \varphi) \dots)). \tag{1}$$

It is easy to check that for any two literals l_1 and l_2 with $l_1 \neq l_2$, and for any formula φ,

$$assign(l_1, assign(l_2, \varphi)) = assign(l_2, assign(l_1, \varphi))$$

so that the specific ordering used in (1) does not matter.

For any assignment μ and formula φ, we say that

- μ *evaluates* φ *to* T $[\mathsf{F}]$ if $assign(\mu, \varphi)$ returns T $[\mathsf{F}]$, and
- μ *evaluates* φ if μ evaluates φ either to T or to F.

Finally, the *size* $|\varphi|$ of a formula φ is the number of atoms occurring in it.

2.1   CNF conversions

Consider a propositional formula φ. φ may be converted into CNF by the "classical" method: First, φ is converted into negative normal form. Second, the rule

$$(\bigwedge_i \bigvee_j \varphi_{ij}) \vee (\bigwedge_k \bigvee_m \varphi_{km}) \Longrightarrow \bigwedge_{i,k} (\bigvee_j \varphi_{ij} \vee \bigvee_m \varphi_{km}).$$

is recursively applied to distribute $\wedge$'s over $\vee$'s. Notationally, we will call *cnf* the function implementing such a conversion. As result of this conversion, we get a formula Φ which is logically equivalent to φ. However, this transformation may lead to a considerable increase in the size of the formula (in the worst case, $|\Phi|$ is $O(2^{|\varphi|})$), which makes the method of no practical utility in many cases.

A more convenient way to convert φ into CNF is based on the idea of renaming the subformulas of φ (see e.g. [20, 15]). In this method, a newly introduced atom B_{φ_i} is associated to each non-literal subformula φ_i of φ. Then, each B_{φ_i} substitutes every occurrence of φ_i inside φ, and the expression $(B_{\varphi_i} \equiv \varphi_i)$ is added to the result. In the rest of the paper, given a formula φ we will use B_φ to represent

- a new atom (the atom associated to φ), if φ is not a literal; and
- φ, otherwise.

For sake of readability we will abbreviate B_φ and B_{φ_i} with B and B_i respectively. One straightforward implementation of this method is given by the function ct^*, which is described by the recursive equation:

$$ct^*(\varphi) := \begin{cases} \mathsf{T} & \text{if } \varphi \text{ is a literal,} \\ (\bigwedge_{i=1}^m ct^*(\varphi_i) \ \wedge \ ren_\equiv(\varphi)) & \text{if } \varphi = (\bigvee_{i=1}^m \varphi_i) \text{ or } \varphi = (\bigwedge_{i=1}^m \varphi_i), \\ (\bigwedge_{i=1}^2 ct^*(\varphi_i) \ \wedge \ ren_\equiv(\varphi)) & \text{if } \varphi = (\varphi_1 \equiv \varphi_2), \end{cases}$$

where $ren_\equiv(\varphi)$ is defined in Table 1. It is easy to show that the formula $(B \wedge ct^*(\varphi))$ is a CNF formula which is satisfiable if and only if φ is satisfiable.

A variant of the latter method has been proposed in [15] and lately optimized in [8]. If a formula φ_i is not a literal, and is not a subformula of an equivalence in φ, then we can substitute B_i for φ_i in φ and add the expression $(\neg B_i \vee \varphi_i)$ to the result. A straightforward implementation of this method is given by the function ct^{**} described by the following recursive equation:

$$ct^{**}(\varphi) := \begin{cases} \mathsf{T} & \text{if } \varphi \text{ is a literal,} \\ (\bigwedge_{i=1}^m ct^{**}(\varphi_i) \ \wedge \ ren_\supset(\varphi)) & \text{if } \varphi = (\bigvee_{i=1}^m \varphi_i) \text{ or } \varphi = (\bigwedge_{i=1}^m \varphi_i), \\ (\bigwedge_{i=1}^2 ct^*(\varphi_i) \ \wedge \ ren_\supset(\varphi)) & \text{if } \varphi = (\varphi_1 \equiv \varphi_2), \end{cases}$$

where $ren_\supset(\varphi)$ is defined in Table 1. The above transformation is equivalent to that described in [15]. In that paper, the authors show that $(B \wedge ct^{**}(\varphi))$ is a CNF formula which is satisfiable if and only if φ is satisfiable.

Notice that both $|ct^*(\varphi))|$ and $|ct^{**}(\varphi))|$ are $O(|\varphi|)$. However, ct^* generally returns bigger formulas than ct^{**}. For instance, if $\varphi = (\bigvee_{i=1}^m \varphi_i)$, then $ren(B \equiv \varphi)$ contains one $m+1$-ary clause plus m binary clauses, while $ren(\neg B \vee \varphi)$ contains only one $m+1$-ary clause (see Table 1).

2.2 DP

There are many variants of the Davis-Putnam [7,6] procedure, each variant differing for the set of rules implemented. Figure 1 is an high-level description of the Davis-Putnam procedure in its minimal form. In one of its most popular variants, an extra step after the unit step and before the split step is added:[2]

---

[2] A literal l occurs *only positively* in a CNF formula Φ if l occurs in Φ while $\neg l$ does not.

function $DP(\Phi, \mu)$
    if $\Phi = \mathsf{T}$ **then return** μ;   /* base   */
    if $\Phi = \mathsf{F}$ **then return** *False*;   /* backtrack */
    if $\{$a unit clause (l) occurs in $\Phi\}$ /* unit   */
        then return $DP(assign(l, \Phi), \mu \cup \{l\})$;
    $l := choose\text{-}literal(\Phi, \mu)$;   /* split   */
    return $DP(assign(l, \Phi), \mu \cup \{l\})$ **or**
              $DP(assign(\neg l, \Phi), \mu \cup \{\neg l\})$;

Fig. 1. Schema of the DP procedure.

    if $\{l$ occurs only positively in $\Phi\}$ /* pure literal */
        then return $DP(assign(l, \Phi), \mu \cup \{l\})$;

Independently from whether the pure literal rule is implemented or not, the procedure has to be invoked by the call $DP(\Phi, \{\})$, where Φ is the CNF formula to be proved (un)satisfiable and $\{\}$ is the empty assignment. $DP(\Phi, \{\})$ returns an assignment μ (satisfying Φ) if Φ is satisfiable, and *False* otherwise. If N is the number of distinct atoms in Φ, DP searches in a space of 2^N assignments. Notice that the number of atoms N is thus much more critical than the size $|\Phi|$ of the formula. A more fine-grained analysis can be found, e.g., in [22].

3   Applying DP to non-CNF formulas

Suppose we want to check the satisfiability of a non-CNF formula φ in the variables $A_1, \ldots, A_N$. Before applying DP, we must pre-convert φ by either ct^* or ct^{**}, obtaining a CNF formula Φ in the original variables $A_1, \ldots, A_N$ and in a set of K newly added variables. Therefore standard DP will have to search in a space of 2^{N+K} assignments, for it may backtrack on the newly added variables.

In this section we propose an alternative approach. We present two ad-hoc variants of DP, called DP* and DP**, which perform no backtracking on the newly added variables, eliminating thus the 2^K factor. The underlying idea of these variants is that splitting should occur only for the variables in the original non-CNF formula.

3.1   DP*

Consider a formula φ over $A_1, \ldots, A_N$. The intuition underlying ct^* is that each new variable B_i labels a subformula φ_i of φ, so that it should be assigned the same truth value as φ_i is. As the truth value to which a subformula φ_i is evaluated is a deterministic consequence of the values assigned to $A_1, \ldots, A_N$, the value assigned to B_i should be deterministically derived from those assigned to $A_1, \ldots, A_N$ too. This is achieved by the occurrence of the conjunct $ren_\equiv(\varphi_i)$

in $ct^*(\varphi)$, which forces the truth value of B_i to be *deterministically derived* from that of φ_i, and thus, recursively, from the truth values of $A_1, \ldots, A_N$. This suggests that no backtracking should be performed on the newly added variables.

Following these considerations, we introduce here DP*, a variant of DP which exploits variable dependency to avoid extra search over dependent variables. In this section, given a CNF formula Φ, the *independent* variables of Φ are the variables in

- φ, if $\Phi = (B \wedge ct^*(\varphi))$ for some formula φ,
- Φ otherwise.

We will call *dependent* the variables in Φ which are not independent.

Definition 1. Let Φ be a CNF formula. DP*(Φ, μ) is the procedure in Figure 1 in which *choose-literal*(Φ, μ)

- returns an unassigned literal whose atom is among the *independent* variables of Φ, if there is some, and
- loops forever, otherwise.

This means that DP* cannot branch on the dependent variables in the input formula Φ, so that these can be assigned only by unit propagation. We show that DP*$(\Phi, \{\})$ returns an assignment if Φ is satisfiable, F otherwise. To prove this fact we need to show that DP*$(\Phi, \{\})$ terminates. In the following lemma, we say that DP*(Φ, μ) *returns* $\mu \cup \mu'$ *by unit propagation* meaning that DP*(Φ, μ) returns $\mu \cup \mu'$ after a sequence eventually empty of unit steps.

Lemma 2. Let φ be a formula in the variables $A_1, \ldots, A_N$. Let μ be a total assignment over $A_1, \ldots, A_N$ which evaluates φ to T [F]. DP*$(assign(\mu, ct^*(\varphi)), \mu)$ returns an assignment $\mu \cup \mu'$ by unit propagation, such that $\mu \cup \mu'$ evaluates B to T [F].

Proof. By induction on the structure of φ. In the base case, φ is a literal, $ct^*(\varphi)$ is T and the thesis trivially follows. All the step cases are similar. We elaborate the case in which $\varphi = (\bigvee_{i=1}^m \varphi_i)$. In this case

$$ct^*(\varphi) = \bigwedge_{i=1}^m ct^*(\varphi_i) \wedge (\neg B \vee \bigvee_{i=1}^m B_i) \wedge \bigwedge_{i=1}^m (B \vee \neg B_i).$$

By induction hypothesis, for each $i \in \{1, \ldots, m\}$, DP*$(assign(\mu, ct^*(\varphi_i)), \mu)$ returns an assignment $\mu \cup \mu_i$ by unit propagation which evaluates

- $ct^*(\varphi_i)$ to T ($1 \leq i \leq m$) by unit propagation,
- B_i to T [F],

(notice that B does not occur in $ct^*(\varphi_i)$, and thus B does not get evaluated by μ_i). Assume that μ evaluates φ to T [F], i.e. that for some [each] $i \in \{1, \ldots, m\}$,

μ evaluates φ_i to T [F]. Then, $DP^*(assign(\mu, ct^*(\varphi)), \mu)$ returns by unit propagation the assignment $\mu \cup_{i=1}^{m} \mu_i \cup \{B\}$ $[\mu \cup_{i=1}^{m} \mu_i \cup \{\neg B\}]$.[3]

Theorem 3. *Let φ be an arbitrary formula. Let Φ be $(B \wedge ct^*(\varphi))$. $DP^*(\Phi, \{\})$ terminates, returning an assignment if φ is satisfiable, False otherwise.*

Proof. $DP^*(\Phi, \{\})$, in each branch of its search tree,

- either terminates (i.e. returns an assignment or *False*) before generating a complete assignment over the independent variables of Φ,
- or generates such an assignment, after which it will terminate by Lemma 2.

Obviously, the result returned by $DP^*(\Phi, \{\})$ is correct.

3.2   DP**

We introduce here DP**, a further variant of DP* which is suitable for working with CNF formulas obtained using ct^{**}. Analogously to the previous section, given a CNF formula Φ, the *independent* variables of Φ are the variables in

- φ, if $\Phi = (B \wedge ct^{**}(\varphi))$ for some formula φ,
- Φ otherwise.

We will call *dependent* the variables in Φ which are not independent.

Definition 4. Let Φ be a CNF formula. $DP^{**}(\Phi, \mu)$ is the procedure in Figure 1 in which

- the pure literal rule is added,[4] and
- *choose-literal*(Φ, μ)
    - returns an unassigned literal whose atom is among the *independent* variables of Φ, if there is some, and
    - loops forever, otherwise.

Similarly to DP*, DP** exploits variable dependency to avoid extra search over dependent variables. Roughly speaking, the usage of pure literal in DP** compensates for the one-way implication of $ren_\supset$ in ct^{**}.

  Again, we need to show that $DP^{**}(\Phi, \{\})$ terminates. In the following lemma, we say that $DP^{**}(\Phi, \mu)$

- *assigns l by unit propagation* meaning that $DP^{**}(\Phi, \mu)$ assigns l to T after a sequence (eventually empty) of unit steps.

---

[3] This relies on the fact that for any disjunct φ_i of φ, any atom assigned by $DP^*(assign(\mu, ct^*(\varphi_i)), \mu)$ is assigned in the same way by $DP^*(assign(\mu, ct^*(\varphi)), \mu)$. Why this is indeed the case, is an easy consequence of the fact that, for any assignment μ' extending μ, the set of unit clauses in $assign(\mu', ct^*(\varphi_i))$ is a subset of the set of unit clauses in $assign(\mu', ct^*(\varphi))$.

[4] Actually, for proving the following Lemma, we may assume that the pure literal rule be applicable only to assign the newly introduced atoms to T.

– *returns* $\mu \cup \mu'$ *without splitting* meaning that $\mu \cup \mu'$ is a possible assignment returned by $DP^{**}(\Phi, \mu)$ after a sequence (eventually empty) of unit and/or pure literal steps.

Lemma 5. *Let* φ *be a formula in the variables* $A_1, \ldots, A_N$. *Let* μ *be a total assignment over* $A_1, \ldots, A_N$.

– *If* μ *evaluates* φ *to* F *then* $DP^{**}(assign(\mu, ct^{**}(\varphi)), \mu)$ *assigns* $\neg B$ *by unit propagation and returns an assignment* $\mu \cup \mu'$ *without splitting.*
– *If* μ *evaluates* φ *to* T *then* $DP^{**}(assign(\mu, ct^{**}(\varphi)), \mu)$ *returns an assignment* $\mu \cup \mu'$ *without splitting, such that* $\mu' \setminus \mu$ *does not evaluate* B.

Proof. By induction on the structure of φ. In the base case, φ is a literal, $ct^{**}(\varphi)$ is T and the thesis trivially follows. As in Lemma 2, we elaborate only the case in which $\varphi = (\bigvee_{i=1}^{m} \varphi_i)$. The case $\varphi = (\bigwedge_{i=1}^{m} \varphi_i)$ is similar, while the case $\varphi = (\varphi_1 \equiv \varphi_2)$ —given Lemma 2— is simple. In this case

$$ct^{**}(\varphi) = \bigwedge_{i=1}^{m} ct^{**}(\varphi_i) \wedge (\neg B \vee \bigvee_{i=1}^{m} B_i).$$

There are two possibilities:

1. μ evaluates φ to T, i.e., μ evaluates to T a nonempty subset S of $\{\varphi_1, \ldots, \varphi_m\}$. By induction hypothesis, for each disjunct φ_i of φ and not in S, the call $DP^{**}(assign(\mu, ct^{**}(\varphi_i)), \mu)$ returns without splitting an assignment $\mu \cup \mu_i$. Now consider a formula φ_i in S. $DP^{**}(assign(\mu, ct^{**}(\varphi_i)), \mu)$ by induction hypothesis returns without splitting an assignment $\mu \cup \mu_i$ such that $\mu_i \setminus \mu$ does not evaluate B_i. There are two cases:
   – either B_i gets evaluated by μ. This means that $B_i = \varphi_i$ and thus B_i is evaluated to T;
   – or B_i is not evaluated by μ. This means that $\mu \cup \mu_i$ does not evaluate B_i and evaluates $ren_\supset(\varphi_i)$ to T. As a consequence, if φ_i is a subformula of an equivalence in φ, (i.e. if $ren_\equiv(\varphi_i)$ is a subformula of $ct^{**}(\varphi)$) then B_i occurs as a unit clause in $assign(\mu \cup \mu_i, ct^{**}(\varphi))$; otherwise B_i occurs only positively in $assign(\mu \cup \mu_i, ct^{**}(\varphi))$. In any case, $DP^{**}(assign(\mu \cup \mu_i, ct^{**}(\varphi)), \mu \cup \mu_i)$ may assign B_i to T.
   In both cases, $DP^{**}(assign(\mu, ct^{**}(\varphi)), \mu)$ returns without splitting the assignment $\mu \cup_{i=1}^{m} \mu_i \cup_{\varphi_i \in S} \{B_i\}$. This assignment does not evaluate B.[5]

---

[5] This relies on the fact that for any disjunct φ_i of φ, any atom assigned by $DP^{**}(assign(\mu, ct^{**}(\varphi_i)), \mu)$ may be assigned in the same way by $DP^{**}(assign(\mu, ct^{**}(\varphi)), \mu)$. In fact, let μ' be an assignment extending μ, and let B_j be an atom occurring only positively in $assign(\mu', ct^{**}(\varphi_i))$.
– If $ren_\equiv(\varphi_j)$ is a subformula of $ct^{**}(\varphi)$ then B_j occurs as a unit clause in $assign(\mu', ct^{**}(\varphi))$,
– otherwise, B_j occurs only positively in $assign(\mu', ct^{**}(\varphi))$.
See also Footnote 3 in Lemma 2.

2. μ evaluates φ to F. Hence, μ evaluates to F also $\varphi_1, \ldots, \varphi_m$. By induction hypothesis, for each $i \in \{1, \ldots, m\}$, $\mathrm{DP}^{**}(assign(\mu, ct^{**}(\varphi_i)), \mu)$ assigns $\neg B_i$ by unit propagation and returns without splitting an assignment $\mu \cup \mu_i$. Then, $\mathrm{DP}^{**}(assign(\mu, ct^{**}(\varphi)), \mu)$
   - assigns $\neg B$ by unit propagation, and
   - returns without splitting the assignment $\mu \cup_{i=1}^{m} \mu_i \cup \{\neg B\}$.

Theorem 6. *Let φ be an arbitrary formula. Let Φ be $(B \wedge ct^{**}(\varphi))$. $\mathrm{DP}^{**}(\Phi, \{\})$ terminates, returning an assignment if φ is satisfiable, False otherwise.*

Proof. As in Theorem 3, the essential fact is to guarantee that $\mathrm{DP}^{**}(\Phi, \{\})$ terminates, which is an obvious consequence of Lemma 5.

4   Related work

Armando and Giunchiglia [1] introduced PTAUT, a variant of DP working directly with non-CNF formulas. The procedure is based on a method to detect "unit clauses" for non-CNF formulas φ (roughly speaking, l is a "unit clause" for φ if φ has the form $(l \wedge \varphi_1)$). *assign* is implemented by lazy evaluation. PTAUT has been used inside the first implementations of the procedure KSAT [12, 13, 10]. Nevertheless, PTAUT efficiency is far below the current implementations of CNF DP. For instance, so far we do not know of any non-CNF DP implementation exploiting fast unit-propagation and inexpensive backtracking techniques, like those used by TABLEAU [4] or SATO [22].

D'Agostino and Mondadori [5] introduced an evolution of the propositional tableau framework, called KE, and a decision procedure for non-CNF formulas based on KE. Unlike tableau, it branches on truth values rather than on disjunctions. Unlike DP, it assigns truth values to subformulas rather than to variables. We are not aware of any efficient implementation of this procedure available.

In the area of digital hardware design, the solvers traditionally used are based on Ordered Binary Decision Diagrams (OBDD) [3]. Though these solvers may require an exponential amount of space, they proved to very highly effective in this area. Interestingly, Uribe and Stickel [21] presented and discussed the results of an empirical comparison between an OBDD based solver and various DP implementations. While none of the two procedures was proved to be definitely superior to the other in general, OBDD outperformed in time DP over formulas encoding boolean circuits. These are the only formulas, in the test set, which are not in CNF, and thus which had to be pre-converted into CNF before applying DP procedures. According to [21], one of the causes of DP implementations poor performances is that in the CNF conversion, the difference between the original and the newly added variables is lost. They suggest that a good branching heuristic for DP implementations would probably have it distinguish them again. However, they do not push this idea any further.

Considering correct but incomplete SAT procedures, Sebastiani [16] suggested how to modify GSAT [17] to be applied to non-CNF formulas. The idea was to use a particular "score" function returning the number of clauses in $cnf(\varphi)$ which are false under a given truth assignment. This value is computed from φ in linear time, without constructing $cnf(\varphi)$. This method was not implemented. Kautz, McAllester and Selman [14] implemented an extension of WALKSAT [18] (called DAGSAT) in which search concentrates only on the independent variables. They present a comparative analysis between WALKSAT and DAGSAT, and show that on 7 out of the 8 problems they consider, DAGSAT performs better than WALKSAT.

Finally, we have already showed in [11] that limiting the splitting step in DP implementations to a subset of the set of variables (the truth values of the others being assigned by unit propagation, analogously to what happens in ct^*+DP^*) can lead to significant speeds up. In particular, we considered 114 SAT problems, and on each of them we run both the TABLEAU system and TABLEAU*, a version of TABLEAU modified in order to split only over the "independent" variables. The results show that:

- The search space effectively searched by TABLEAU* (i.e. the number of nodes in the search tree) is up to 4 orders of magnitude less than the search space analyzed by TABLEAU.
- The CPU time requested by TABLEAU* to solve a problem is up to 4 orders of magnitude less than the CPU time requested by TABLEAU on the same problem.

References

1. A. Armando and E. Giunchiglia. Embedding Complex Decision Procedures inside an Interactive Theorem Prover. *Annals of Mathematics and Artificial Intelligence*, 8(3–4):475–502, 1993.
2. *Artificial Intelligence*, 81(1,2), 1996. Special Volume on Frontiers in Probelm Solving: Phase Transitions and Complexity.
3. R. E. Bryant. Graph-Based Algorithms for Boolean Function Manipulation. *IEEE Transactions on Computers*, C-35(8):677–691, August 1986.
4. J. Crawford and L. Auton. Experimental results on the crossover point in 3SAT. *Artificial Intelligence*, 81, 1996.
5. M. D'Agostino and M. Mondadori. The Taming of the Cut. *Journal of Logic and Computation*, 4(3):285–319, 1994.
6. M. Davis, G. Longemann, and D. Loveland. A machine program for theorem proving. *Journal of the ACM*, 5(7), 1962.
7. M. Davis and H. Putnam. A computing procedure for quantification theory. *Journal of the ACM*, 7:201–215, 1960.
8. T. Boy de la Tour. Minimizing the Number of Clauses by Renaming. In *Proc. CADE-90*, pages 558–572. Springer-Verlag, 1990.
9. DIMACS. *The Second DIMACS International Algorithm Implementation Challenge*, Rutgers University, USA, 1993.
10. E. Giunchiglia, F. Giunchiglia, R. Sebastiani, and A. Tacchella. More evaluation of decision procedures for modal logics. In *Proc. KR'98*, 1998.
11. E. Giunchiglia, A. Massarotto, and R. Sebastiani. Act, and the rest will follow: Exploiting determinism in planning as satisfiability. In *Proc. AAAI-98*, 1998.

12. F. Giunchiglia and R. Sebastiani. Building decision procedures for modal logics from propositional decision procedures - the case study of modal K. In *Proc. CADE-96*, Lecture Notes in Artificial Intelligence. Springer Verlag.

13. F. Giunchiglia and R. Sebastiani. A SAT-based decision procedure for ALC. In *Proc. KR'96*, Cambridge, MA, USA, November 1996.

14. Henry Kautz, David McAllester, and Bart Selman. Exploiting variable dependency in local search. In *Abstracts of the Poster Sessions of IJCAI-97*, August 23-29 1997. Available at http://www.research.att.com/~kautz/papers-ftp/index.html.

15. D.A. Plaisted and S. Greenbaum. A Structure-preserving Clause Form Translation. *Journal of Symbolic Computation*, 2:293–304, 1986.

16. R. Sebastiani. Applying GSAT to Non-Clausal Formulas. *Journal of Artificial Intelligence Research*, 1:309–314, 1994.

17. B. Selman, H. Levesque., and D. Mitchell. A New Method for Solving Hard Satisfiability Problems. In *Proc. AAAI-92*, pages 440–446, 1992.

18. Bart Selman, Henry A. Kautz, and Bram Cohen. Noise strategies for improving local search. In *Proc. AAAI-94*, pages 337–343. AAAI Press.

19. Jörg Siekmann and Graham Wrightson, editors. *Automation of Reasoning: Classical Papers in Computational Logic 1967–1970*, volume 2. Springer-Verlag, 1983.

20. G. Tseitin. On the complexity of proofs in propositional logics. *Seminars in Mathematics*, 8, 1970. Reprinted in [19].

21. T. E. Uribe and M. E. Stickel. Ordered Binary Decision Diagrams and the Davis-Putnam Procedure. In *Proc. of the 1st International Conference on Constraints in Computational Logics*, 1994.

22. H. Zhang and M. Stickel. Implementing the Davis-Putnam algorithm by tries. Technical report, University of Iowa, August 1994.

The SAT-Based Approach for Classical Modal Logics*

Enrico Giunchiglia[1], Fausto Giunchiglia[2], and Armando Tacchella[1]

[1] DIST, Università di Genova, Viale Causa, 13 – 16145 Genova, Italy
[2] DISA, Università di Trento. IRST, 38050 Povo, Trento, Italy.

Abstract. We present a set of SAT-based decision procedures for various classical modal logics. The decision procedures are implemented in our system *SAT. For some of the logics we deal with, we are not aware of any other implementation. For the others, we define a testing methodology which generalizes the 3CNF$_K$ methodology by Giunchiglia and Sebastiani. The experimental evaluation shows that our decision procedures perform better than or as well as other state-of-the-art decision procedures.

1 Introduction

In recent years there has been a growing interest in efficient decision procedures for modal logics. Researchers tried to push performances either by building optimized version of tableau algorithms, or by finding reductions to logics for which state-of-the-art systems are already available. The SAT-based approach, first suggested by Giunchiglia and Sebastiani [1], features yet a different recipe: (*i*) take out off the shelf one of the fastest SAT procedures available, and (*ii*) use it as the basis for your modal decider.

In this paper we present a set of SAT-based decision procedures for various classical modal logics. We have implemented the procedures in our system *SAT which improves on previous works by Sebastiani and ourselves [2, 3, 1]. *SAT is built on top of the SAT decider SATO [4] one of the fastest and better engineered among the publicly available SAT solvers. *SAT is able to deal with eight modal logics and, for some of these logics, we do not know of any other implemented decision procedure, nor of any reduction to a formalism for which a decision procedure is available.

In [5], we experimentally tested *SAT performances on various benchmarks for K against other state-of-the-art deciders. Here, we define a testing methodology which generalizes the 3CNF$_K$ methodology by Giunchiglia and Sebastiani [2] and we test *SAT performances in the modal logic E. The experimental analysis shows that *SAT performs better than or as well as other state-of-the-art systems.

---

* We are grateful to Ullrich Hustadt, Peter F. Patel-Schneider, and Hantao Zhang for the assistance they provided on their systems. Thanks to Roberto Sebastiani for useful discussions related to the subject of this paper.

E. Lamma and P. Mello (Eds.): AI*IA 99, LNAI 1792, pp. 95–106, 2000.

2   Classical modal logics

Following [6], a *modal logic* is a set of formulas (called *theorems*) closed under tautological consequence. Most modal logics are closed under the rule

$$\frac{(\varphi_1 \wedge \ldots \wedge \varphi_n) \supset \psi}{(\Box\varphi_1 \wedge \ldots \wedge \Box\varphi_n) \supset \Box\psi} \, .$$

for certain values of n. If $n = 1$ then the logic is said to be *monotone*. If $n = 2$ then the logic is said to be *regular*. If $n \geq 0$ then the logic is said to be *normal*. The smallest monotone, regular and normal modal logics are called M, R and K respectively (see, e.g., [6]).

Classical modal logics [7, 8] are weaker than normal modal logics. In fact, the only requirement is that the set of theorems is closed under the rule

$$\frac{\varphi \equiv \psi}{\Box\varphi \equiv \Box\psi} \, .$$

As a consequence, the schemas[1]

N: $\Box\top$,   M: $\Box(\varphi \wedge \psi) \supset \Box\varphi$,   C: $(\Box\varphi \wedge \Box\psi) \supset \Box(\varphi \wedge \psi)$,

which are theorems in K do not necessarily hold in classical modal logics. The three principles N, M, and C enforce closure conditions on the set of provable formulas which are not always desirable, especially if the $\Box$ operator has an epistemic (such as knowledge or belief) reading. If we interpret $\Box\varphi$ as "a certain agent a believes φ", then N enforces that a believes all the logical truths, M that a's beliefs are closed under logical consequence, and C that a's beliefs are closed under conjunction. These three closure properties are different forms of omniscience, and —as such— they are not appropriate for modeling the beliefs of a real agent (see, e.g., [9] Chapter 9). We can easily imagine situations involving a's beliefs, where only an arbitrary subset of the above properties holds.

There are eight possible ways to add the three schemas M, C, and N to the smallest classical modal logic E. The resulting modal logics are called E, EM (equivalent to the logic M), EN, EMN, EC, EMC (equivalent to R), ECN, EMCN (equivalent to K), where EX denotes the logic obtained adding the schemas in X to E.

3   SAT-based procedures for classical modal logics

We say that a conjunction μ of propositional literals and formulas of the form $\Box\varphi$ or $\neg\Box\varphi$ is an *assignment* if, for any pair ψ, ψ' of conjuncts in μ, it is not the case that $\psi = \neg\psi'$. An assignment μ *satisfies* a formula φ if μ entails φ by propositional reasoning. A formula φ is *consistent* in a logic L (or *L-consistent*) if $\neg\varphi$ is not a theorem of L, i.e., if $\neg\varphi \notin$ L.

---

[1] The symbols $\top$ and $\bot$ are 0-ary connectives representing truth and falsity respectively.

Consider a formula φ. Let S be a set of assignments satisfying φ, and let L be a modal logic. As noticed by Sebastiani and Giunchiglia [10], the following two facts hold:

- If at least one assignment in S is L-consistent then φ is L-consistent.
- If no assignment in S is L-consistent then φ is not L-consistent as long as the set S is *complete for* φ, i.e., as long as the disjunction of the assignments in S is propositionally equivalent to φ.

From these facts, it follows that the problem of determining whether φ is L-consistent can be decomposed in two steps:

- *generate* an assignment μ satisfying φ, and
- *test* whether μ is L-consistent.

In all the logics we consider, testing the consistency of an assignment μ amounts to determining the consistency of other formulas whose depth (i.e., the maximum number of nested $\square$ operators) is strictly minor than the depth of μ. This implies that we can check the consistency of these other formulas by recursively applying the above methodology, at the same time ensuring the termination of the overall process. The above methodology can be implemented by two mutually recursive procedures:

- LSAT(φ) for the generation of assignments satisfying φ, and
- LCONSIST(μ) for testing the L-consistency of each generated assignment μ.

3.1   Lsat(φ)

Consider a formula φ. Let L be a modal logic. The generation of assignments satisfying φ is independent of the particular logic L being considered. Furthermore, it can be based on any procedure for SAT:

- if the SAT decider is complete, then we can generate a finite and complete set of assignments for φ as follows:
  - at step 0, ask for an assignment satisfying φ, and
  - at step $i + 1$, ask for an assignment satisfying φ and the negation of the assignments generated in the previous steps.
  By checking the L-consistency of each assignment, we obtain a correct and complete decider for L.
- if the SAT decider is correct but incomplete, then we cannot generate a complete set of assignments for φ, but we can still build a correct but incomplete decider for L by checking each generated assignment. Of course, whether an incomplete effective procedure for SAT can be turned into an effective incomplete procedure for a modal logic L, is still an open point.

The above method for generating a complete set of assignments for φ has the advantage that the SAT decider is used as a blackbox. The obvious disadvantage is that the size of the input formula checked by the SAT solver may become

function LSAT(φ)
  return LSAT$_{\text{DP}}$($cnf(\varphi)$, $\top$).

function LSAT$_{\text{DP}}$(φ, μ)
  if $\varphi = \top$ **then return** LCONSIST(μ);   /* base */
  if $\varphi = \bot$ **then return** *False*;   /* backtrack */
  if { a unit clause (l) occurs in φ }   /* unit */
     then return LSAT$_{\text{DP}}$($assign(l, \varphi)$,$\mu \wedge l$);
  $l := choose\text{-}literal(\varphi, \mu)$;
  return LSAT$_{\text{DP}}$($assign(l, \varphi)$,$\mu \wedge l$) **or**   /* split */
     LSAT$_{\text{DP}}$($assign(\bar{l}, \varphi)$,$\mu \wedge \bar{l}$).

Fig. 1. LSAT and LSAT$_{\text{DP}}$

exponentially bigger than the original one. A better solution is to invoke the test for L-consistency *inside* the SAT procedure whenever an assignment satisfying the input formula is found. In the case of the Davis-Putnam (DP) procedure [11], we get the procedure LSAT represented in Figure 1. In the figure,

- $cnf(\varphi)$ is a set of clauses —possibly with newly introduced propositional variables— such that, for any assignment μ in the extended language:[2]
    • if μ satisfies $cnf(\varphi)$ then the restriction of μ to the language of φ satisfies φ, and
    • if μ satisfies φ then there exists an assignment in the language of $cnf(\varphi)$ which (*i*) extends μ and (*ii*) satisfies $cnf(\varphi)$.
- $choose\text{-}literal(\varphi, \mu)$ returns a literal occurring in φ and chosen according to some heuristic criterion.
- if l is a literal, $\bar{l}$ stands for A if $l = \neg A$, and for $\neg A$ if $l = A$;
- for any literal l and formula φ, $assign(l, \varphi)$ is the formula obtained from φ by (*i*) deleting the clauses in which l occurs as a disjunct, and (*ii*) eliminating $\bar{l}$ from the others.

As can be observed, the procedure LSAT$_{\text{DP}}$ in Figure 1 is the DP-procedure modulo the call to LCONSIST(μ) when it finds an assignment μ satisfying the input formula.

3.2   Lconsist(μ)

Whether an assignment is consistent, depends on the particular logic L being considered. Furthermore, depending on the logic L considered, the consistency problem for L (i.e., determining whether a formula is consistent in L) belongs to different complexity classes. In particular, the consistency problem for E, EM, EN, EMN is NP-complete, while for EC, ECN, EMC, EMCN it is PSPACE-complete (see [12, 9]). Here, to save space, we divide these eight logics in two

---

[2] Let μ be an assignment in a language L. Let $L' \subseteq L$ be a language. The *restriction* of μ to L' is the assignment obtained from μ by deleting the conjuncts not in L'. Let μ' an assignment. μ' *extends* μ if each conjunct of μ is also a conjunct of μ'.

groups. We present the algorithms for checking the L-consistency of an assignment first in the case in which L is one of E, EM, EN, EMN, and then in the case in which L is one of the others.

Logics E, EM, EN, EMN The following conditions are an easy consequence of the results presented in [12]. Let $\mu = \bigwedge_i \Box\alpha_i \wedge \bigwedge_j \neg\Box\beta_j \wedge \gamma$ be an assignment in which γ is a propositional formula. Let L be one of the logics E, EM, EN, EMN. μ is consistent in L if for each conjunct $\neg\Box\beta_j$ in μ one of the following conditions is satisfied:

- $(\alpha_i \equiv \neg\beta_j)$ is L-consistent for each conjunct $\Box\alpha_i$ in μ, and L=E;
- $(\alpha_i \wedge \neg\beta_j)$ is L-consistent for each conjunct $\Box\alpha_i$ in μ, and L=EM;
- $\neg\beta_j$ and $(\alpha_i \equiv \neg\beta_j)$ are L-consistent for each conjunct $\Box\alpha_i$ in μ, and L=EN;
- $\neg\beta_j$ and $(\alpha_i \wedge \neg\beta_j)$ are L-consistent for each conjunct $\Box\alpha_i$ in μ, and L=EMN.

```
function LCONSIST(⋀_i □α_i ∧ ⋀_j ¬□β_j ∧ γ)
  foreach conjunct □β_j do
    foreach conjunct □α_i do
      if M[i,j] = Undef then M[i,j] := LSAT(α_i ∧ ¬β_j);
      if L ∈ {EN,EMN} and M[i,j] = True then M[j,j] := True;
      if L ∈ {E,EN} and M[i,j] = False then
        if M[j,i] = Undef then M[j,i] := LSAT(¬α_i ∧ β_j);
        if L = EN and M[j,i] = True then M[i,i] := True;
        if M[j,i] = False then return False
    end
    if L ∈ {EN,EMN} then
      if M[j,j] = Undef then M[j,j] := LSAT(¬β_j);
      if M[j,j] = False then return False
  end;
  return True.
```

Fig. 2. LCONSIST for E, EM, EN, EMN

When implementing the above conditions, care must be taken in order to avoid repetitions of consistency checks. In fact, while an exponential number of assignments satisfying the input formula can be generated by LSAT, at most n^2 checks are possible in L, where n is the number of "$\Box$" in the input formula. Given this upper bound, for each new consistency check, we can cache the result for a future possible re-utilization in a $n \times n$ matrix M. This ensures that at most n^2 consistency checks will be performed. In more detail, given an enumeration $\varphi_1, \varphi_2, \ldots, \varphi_n$ of the boxed subformulas of the input formula, M[i,j], with $i \neq j$, stores the result of the consistency check for $(\varphi_i \wedge \neg\varphi_j)$. M[i,i] stores the result of the consistency check for $\neg\varphi_i$. Initially, each element of the matrix M has value *Undef* (meaning that the corresponding test has not been done yet). The result is the procedure LCONSIST in Figure 2.

function $\text{LCONSIST}(\bigwedge_i \Box\alpha_i \wedge \bigwedge_j \neg\Box\beta_j \wedge \gamma)$
  $\Delta := \{\alpha_i \mid \Box\alpha_i \text{ is a conjunct of } \mu\};$
  foreach conjunct $\Box\beta_j$ **do**
    $\Delta' := \Delta;$
    if $L \in \{EC, ECN\}$ **then**
      foreach conjunct $\Box\alpha_i$ **do**
        if $M[j, i] = Undef$ **then** $M[j, i] := \text{LSAT}(\neg\alpha_i \wedge \beta_j);$
        if $M[j, i] = True$ **then** $\Delta' = \Delta' \setminus \{\alpha_i\}$
      end;
    if $L \in \{ECN, EMCN\}$ **or** $\Delta' \neq \emptyset$ **then**
      if not $\text{LSAT}(\bigwedge_{\alpha_i \in \Delta'} \alpha_i \wedge \neg\beta_j)$ **then return** *False*
  end;
  return *True*.

Fig. 3. LCONSIST for EC, ECN, EMC (R), EMCN (K)

Consider Figure 2 and assume that L=E or L=EN. Given a pair of conjuncts $\Box\alpha_i$ and $\neg\Box\beta_j$, we split the consistency test for $(\alpha_i \equiv \neg\beta_j)$ in two simpler sub-tests:

– first, we test whether $(\alpha_i \wedge \neg\beta_j)$ is consistent, and
– only if this test gives *False*, we test whether $(\neg\alpha_i \wedge \beta_j)$ is consistent.

Notice also that, in case L=EN or L=EMN, if we know that, e.g., $(\alpha_i \wedge \neg\beta_j)$ is consistent, then also $\neg\beta_j$ is consistent and we store this result in M[j,j].

Logics EC, ECN, EMC, EMCN The following conditions are an easy consequence of the results presented in [12]. Let $\mu = \bigwedge_i \Box\alpha_i \wedge \bigwedge_j \neg\Box\beta_j \wedge \gamma$ be an assignment in which γ is a propositional formula. Let Δ be the set of formulas α_i such that $\Box\alpha_i$ is a conjunct of μ. Let L be one of logics EC, ECN, EMC, EMCN. μ is consistent in L if for each conjunct $\neg\Box\beta_j$ in μ one of the following conditions is satisfied:

– $((\bigwedge_{\alpha_i \in \Delta'} \alpha_i) \equiv \neg\beta_j)$ is L-consistent for each non empty subset Δ' of Δ, and L=EC;
– $((\bigwedge_{\alpha_i \in \Delta'} \alpha_i) \equiv \neg\beta_j)$ is L-consistent for each subset Δ' of Δ, and L=ECN;
– Δ is empty or $((\bigwedge_{\alpha_i \in \Delta} \alpha_i) \wedge \neg\beta_j)$ is L-consistent, and L=EMC;
– $((\bigwedge_{\alpha_i \in \Delta} \alpha_i) \wedge \neg\beta_j)$ is L-consistent, and L=EMCN.

Assume that L=EC or L=ECN. The straightforward implementation of the corresponding condition may lead to an exponential number of checks in the cardinality $|\Delta|$ of Δ. More carefully, for each conjunct $\neg\Box\beta_j$ in μ, we can perform at most $|\Delta| + 1$ checks if

1. for each formula α_i in Δ, we first check whether $(\neg\alpha_i \wedge \beta_j)$ is consistent in L. Let Δ' be the set of formulas for which the above test fails. Then,
2. in case L=ECN or $\Delta' \neq \emptyset$, we perform the last test, checking whether $((\bigwedge_{\alpha_i \in \Delta'} \alpha_i) \wedge \neg\beta_j)$ is consistent in L.

Furthermore, the result of the consistency checks performed in the first step can be cached in a matrix M analogous to the one used in the previous subsection.

4 Implementation and comparative analysis

*SAT is built on top of SATO ver. 3.2 [4]. We have chosen SATO as the basis for our system since it is fast and has many options, including various splitting heuristics and backjumping. We have inherited some of these options, and they are available for experimentation. Also, SATO has been written using some Software Engineering conventions which have made and will make much easier to tune it for our goals. Besides the options inherited from SATO, our system allows for other possibilities that we have developed while implementing the system. It is out of the goals of this paper to describe *SAT structure. See [13] and the manual distributed with *SAT for a more detailed presentation of the system. To understand the experimental results, it suffices to say that the core of *SAT is a C implementation of the procedures LSAT and LCONSIST in Figures 1, 2, 3. Also, we run *SAT with the following options enabled:

Early-pruning. Before each splitting step in LSAT, the L-consistency of the assignment generated so far is checked by a call to LCONSIST.

Caching for K. In the case of the logic K, *SAT uses an additional data structure which allows to associate to any formula φ the result of LSAT(φ). Before invoking LSAT on a formula ψ, LCONSIST checks whether the K-consistency of ψ has already been determined.

The availability of decision procedures for the logics we consider varies significantly. For EMCN, that we recall is equivalent to K, there are many implemented decision procedures available, see, e.g., [14, 15]. For E, EM and EMC, Gasquet and Herzig [16] provide a reduction to normal modal logics: by implementing this reduction we indirectly obtain decision procedures for these logics. Fitting [17] calls U the logic EM, and defines a tableau system for it. More recently, Governatori and Luppi [18] define a tableau-like proof system for classical, monotonic and regular modal logics. We are not aware of any implementation of this tableau system. For EN, EC, EMN and ECN we are not aware of any other implemented decision procedure, nor of any reduction into a formalism for which a decision procedure is available.

We restrict our analysis to E. In fact, both our decision procedures for E and EM, and Gasquet and Herzig's reductions for E and EM, are similar. We expect that the experimental analysis for EM would lead to results similar to the ones we have for E. For EMC, Gasquet and Herzig's reduction is to a normal modal logic for which we do not have a system available.[3]

Gasquet and Herzig [16] provide a translation which maps any formula φ into a formula φ_{GH} in K_2, i.e., the smallest normal modal logic with two modal

---

[3] The reduction maps the consistency problem for a formula φ in EMC, into the consistency problem for a formula φ' in the smallest normal modal logic with two modal operators $\Box_1$, $\Box_2$ and augmented with the schema $\psi \supset \Box_1 \psi$.

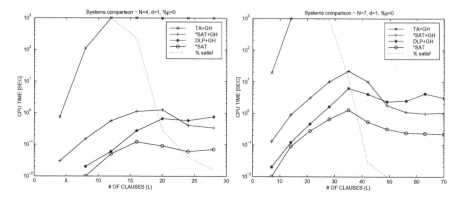

Fig. 4. Logic E. *SAT, *SAT+GH, DLP+GH, and TA+GH median CPU time. $N = 4, 7$. $p = 0\%$. 100 samples/point. Background: satisfiability percentage.

operators $\Box_1$ and $\Box_2$. The translation is such that φ is satisfiable in E iff φ_{GH} is satisfiable in K_2. This translation is defined in the following way:

- $\varphi_{GH} = \varphi$, if φ is a propositional variable,
- $\varphi_{GH} = \neg\Box_1\neg(\Box_2\psi_{GH} \wedge \Box_1\neg\psi_{GH})$, if $\varphi = \Box\psi$,

and homomorphic for the cases of the propositional connectives.

Consider a formula φ. We compare *SAT performances on φ with respect to *SAT, DLP [19] and TA [20] performances on φ_{GH}. We remember that DLP is one of the fastest of the currently available systems for K. TA, given a modal formula φ, first determines a corresponding first order formula φ^* and then it performs conventional first-order theorem proving. In our tests, as in [20], TA uses FLOTTER to convert φ^* in a set of clauses $Cl(\varphi^*)$, and then the theorem prover SPASS to solve $Cl(\varphi^*)$. For a brief description of FLOTTER and SPASS, see [21]. To make evident when a system is run using Gasquet and Herzig's translation, we append the string "+GH" to the name of the system. Therefore, in the following, we will have the systems *SAT, *SAT+GH, DLP+GH, and TA+GH.

In E, the 3CNF$_K$ test methodology is not suited. Indeed, it is no longer the case that for any modal formula φ there exists a 3CNF$_K$ formula which is E-satisfiable iff φ is E-satisfiable. Furthermore, checking the consistency of an assignment μ in E amounts to determine the consistency of $(\alpha \equiv \neg\beta)$ for each pair of conjuncts $\Box\alpha$ and $\neg\Box\beta$ in μ: most of these tests, in case α and β are 3CNF$_K$ clauses, can be trivially satisfied.

We therefore consider sets of 3CNF$_E$ formulas. A 3CNF$_E$ formula is a conjunction of 3CNF$_E$ clauses, each with three disjuncts. Each disjunct in a 3CNF$_E$ clause is either a propositional literal or a formula having the form $\Box C$ or $\neg\Box C$, where C is a 3CNF$_E$ formula. For example,

$$\Box((\Box(l_1 \vee l_2 \vee l_3) \vee l_4 \vee l_5) \wedge (l_6 \vee l_7 \vee l_8))$$

where each l_i ($1 \leq i \leq 8$) is a propositional literal, is a 3CNF_E formula. For any formula φ, there exist a 3CNF_E formula which is E-consistent iff φ is E-consistent.

Sets of 3CNF_E formulas can be randomly generated according to the following parameters:

(i) the modal depth d;
(ii) the number L of clauses at depth $d = 0$;
(iii) the number N of propositional variables;
(iv) the probability p with which a disjunct occurring in a clause at depth $< d$ is purely propositional.
(v) the number C of clauses at depth $d > 0$

Parameters (i) through (iv) are the same used used to generate 3CNF_K formulas. A 3CNF_K is thus a 3CNF_E formula in which $C = 1$.

A problem set is characterized by N and p: d and C are fixed to 1 and L respectively; L is given increasing values in such a way to empirically cover the "100% satisfiable – 100% unsatisfiable" transition. We also check that in each sample there are no multiple occurrences of a formula in a clause, at the same ensuring that the propositional vs. the modal structure of the formula only depends on p. Notice that while increasing L also C is increased. As a consequence, for each pair of formulas $\Box\alpha_i$ and $\neg\Box\beta_j$ in an assignment satisfying a 3CNF_E formula, the recursive E-consistency check for $(\alpha_i \equiv \neg\beta_j)$ has itself a phase transition from 100% satisfiable to 100% unsatisfiable when increasing L. Overall, for low [resp. high] values of L we expect that each satisfying assignment should be trivially determined to be E-consistent [resp. not E-consistent].

For each L in a problem set, 100 3CNF_E formulas are randomly generated, and the resulting formulas are given in input to the procedure under test. A timeout stops the execution of the system on a formula after 1000 seconds of CPU time. We consider the following problems sets:

- PEN4p0, PEN5p0, PEN6p0, PEN7p0 in which $p = 0\%$ while $L = 4, 5, 6, 7$ respectively, and
- PEN4p50, PEN5p50, PEN6p50, PEN7p50 in which $p = 50\%$ while $L = 4, 5, 6, 7$ respectively.

Given the huge amount of time that FLOTTER takes to prepare the formula for SPASS, we run TA+GH only on the problems sets PEN4p0 and PEN4p50. For PEN7p0 and PEN7p50, we run TA+GH only on the initial points. We only take into account the time the systems take for the main processing of the formula. In particular, for each system, we do not take into account the time needed to perform the Gasquet and Herzig's conversion; and for TA+GH we take into account only the time taken by SPASS. For the lack of space, only the median plots of the systems on PEN4p0 and PEN7p0 are shown in Figure 4. The behavior of *SAT, *SAT+GH and DLP+GH on PEN5p0 and PEN6p0 is indeed very similar to what is shown in Figure 4.

Consider Figure 4. As can be observed, *SAT is the fastest: the gap with the other systems is of more than one order of magnitude for certain values of

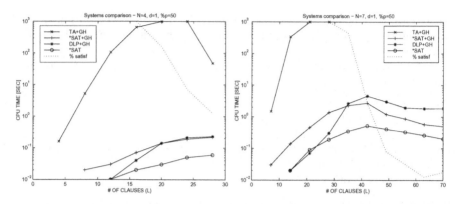

Fig. 5. Logic E. *SAT, *SAT+GH, DLP+GH, and TA+GH median CPU time. $N = 4, 7$. $p = 50\%$. 100 samples/point. Background: satisfiability percentage.

L. However, both *SAT+GH and DLP+GH perform quite well, better than one could have imagined given that the consistency problem for E and K_2 belongs to two different complexity classes. However, a closer look to Gasquet and Herzig's reduction reveals that, considering a 3CNF$_E$ formula φ, and an assignment $\mu = \bigwedge_{i=1}^{m} \Box\alpha_i \wedge \bigwedge_{j=1}^{n} \neg\Box\beta_j \wedge \gamma$ (as usual we assume that γ is a propositional formula) in the language of φ,

1. μ satisfies φ iff μ_{GH} satisfies φ_{GH}.
2. for checking the E-consistency of μ, *SAT performs at most $2mn$ consistency checks involving the formulas $\alpha_1, \ldots, \alpha_m, \beta_1, \ldots, \beta_m$.
3. for checking the K_2-consistency of μ_{GH}, *SAT+GH and DLP+GH perform at most $2mn$ consistency checks involving $\alpha_{1GH}, \ldots, \alpha_{mGH}, \beta_{1GH}, \ldots, \beta_{mGH}$.

The first two points are obvious. To understand the last, it suffices to notice that μ_{GH} is propositionally equivalent to

$$\bigwedge_{i=1}^{m} \neg\Box_1\neg(\Box_2\alpha_{iGH} \wedge \Box_1\neg\alpha_{iGH}) \wedge \bigwedge_{j=1}^{n} \Box_1(\neg\Box_2\beta_{jGH} \vee \neg\Box_1\neg\beta_{jGH}) \wedge \gamma.$$

Given that both *SAT+GH and DLP+GH use caching, these procedures will perform at most a quadratic number of checks in the number of subformulas of φ_{GH}. This is not the case for TA+GH, since SPASS does not have any caching mechanism. This explains the good behavior of *SAT+GH and DLP+GH, and the bad behavior of TA+GH.

For $N = 4, 7$ and $p = 50\%$, *SAT, *SAT+GH, DLP+GH and TA+GH median times are plotted in Figure 5. As before, for the lack of space, we did not show the results for PEN5p50 and PEN6p50. As it can be observed, the situation is very similar to the case in which $p = 0\%$. The only difference is that now *SAT+GH performs better than DLP+GH for a lower value of L. This is reasonable, since for each L, the number of consistency checks performed by *SAT+GH because of early pruning, diminishes when p increases.

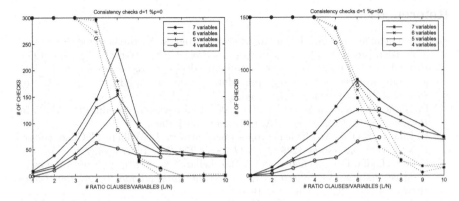

Fig. 6. Logic E. *sat median number of calls to LSAT. $N = 4, 5, 6, 7$. $p = 0\%$ (left) and $p = 50\%$ (right). 100 samples/point. Background: satisfiability percentages.

Finally, notice the easy-hard-easy pattern of *sat. To better appreciate it, Figure 6 shows the number of calls to LSAT done by LCONSIST on PEN4p0-PEN7p0 (left), PEN4p50-PEN7p50 (right) against the ratio $\frac{L}{N}$ between L and N. As can be observed, *sat performs a number of LSAT calls whose maximum roughly correspond to the 50% of satisfiable formulas. This transition happens when $\frac{L}{N}$ is close to 5 for $p = 0\%$ and to 6 for $p = 50\%$. This behavior reflects the above stated intuition according to which for low [resp. high] values of L all the formulas should be easily determined to be E-consistent [resp. not E-consistent]. Notice also that:

- the easy-hard-easy pattern in the plots of Figure 6 becomes more evident when increasing the number of variables and the phenomenon is even clearer when $p = 0\%$; and
- the shape of the transition seems to be independent from the number of variables.

5   Conclusions

We have presented a set of SAT-based decision procedures for eight classical modal logics. We implemented the decision procedures in our system *sat which is the only system that is able to deal with EN, EC, ECN and EMN. We have defined a testing methodology which generalizes the 3CNF$_K$ methodology by Giunchiglia and Sebastiani [2], and which is suitable for testing systems for non-normal modal logics. The experimental evaluation shows that *sat+GH performs better than or as well as other state of the art systems on the sets of randomly generated 3CNF$_E$ formulas that we consider. In all such tests, *sat performs better than systems exploiting Gasquet and Herzig's reduction to multimodal normal logics.

References

1. E. Giunchiglia, F. Giunchiglia, R. Sebastiani, and A. Tacchella. More evaluation of decision procedures for modal logics. In *Proc. KR'98*, Trento, Italy, June 1998.
2. F. Giunchiglia and R. Sebastiani. Building decision procedures for modal logics from propositional decision procedures - the case study of modal K. In *Proc. CADE-96*, LNAI. Springer Verlag.
3. F. Giunchiglia and R. Sebastiani. A SAT-based decision procedure for ALC. In *Proc. of KR'96*, Cambridge, MA, USA, November 1996.
4. H. Zhang. SATO: An efficient propositional prover. In William McCune, editor, *Proc. CADE-14*, volume 1249 of *LNAI*, pages 272–275, 1997. Springer.
5. E. Giunchiglia, F. Giunchiglia, and A. Tacchella. *SAT, KSATC, DLP and TA: a comparative analysis. In *Collected Papers from the International Description Logics Workshop (DL'99)*. CEUR, July 1999.
6. B. F. Chellas. *Modal Logic – an Introduction.* Cambridge University Press, 1980.
7. Richard Montague. Pragmatics. In R. Klibansky, editor, *Contemporary Philosophy: A Survey. I*, pages 102–122. La Nuova Italia Editrice, Florence, 1968.
8. Krister Segerberg. *An Essay in Classical Modal Logic.* Philosophical Studies, Uppsala, 1 edition, 1971.
9. R. Fagin, J.Y. Halpern, Y. Moses, and M. Y. Vardi. *Reasoning about knowledge.* MIT Press, 1995.
10. R. Sebastiani and F. Giunchiglia. From Tableau-based to SAT-based procedures - preliminary report. Technical Report 9711-14, IRST, Trento, Italy, 1997.
11. M. Davis and H. Putnam. A computing procedure for quantification theory. *Journal of the ACM*, 7:201–215, 1960.
12. Moshe Y. Vardi. On the complexity of epistemic reasoning. In *Proceedings, Fourth Annual Symposium on Logic in Computer Science*, pages 243–252. IEEE Computer Society Press.
13. Armando Tacchella. *SAT system description. In *Collected Papers from the International Description Logics Workshop (DL'99)*. CEUR, July 1999.
14. E. Franconi, G. De Giacomo, R. M. MacGregor, W. Nutt, C. A. Welty, and F. Sebastiani, editors. *Collected Papers from the International Description Logics Workshop (DL'98)*. CEUR, May 1998.
15. H. de Swart, editor. *Automated Reasoning with Analytic Tableaux and Related Methods: International Conference Tableaux'98*, number 1397 in LNAI. Springer.
16. O. Gasquet and A. Herzig. From classical to normal modal logics. In Heinrich Wansing, editor, *Proof Theory of Modal Logics*, volume 2 of *Applied Logic Series*, pages 293–311. Kluwer Academic Publishers, 1996.
17. M. Fitting. *Proof Methods for Modal and Intuitionistic Logics.* D. Reidel Publishing, 1983.
18. G. Governatori and A. Luppi. Labelled tableaux for non-normal modal logics. In *Proc. AI*IA '99*, Bologna, Italy, September 14–17, 1999.
19. P. F. Patel-Schneider. DLP system description. In E. Franconi, G. De Giacomo, R. M. MacGregor, W. Nutt, C. A. Welty, and F. Sebastiani, editors, *Collected Papers from the International Description Logics Workshop (DL'98)*, pages 87–89. CEUR, May 1998.
20. U. Hustadt and R.A. Schmidt. On evaluating decision procedures for modal logic. In *Proc. IJCAI-15*, 1997.
21. C. Weidenbach, B. Gaede, and G. Rock. SPASS & FLOTTER version 0.42. In M.A. McRobbie and J.K. Slaney, editors, *Proc. CADE-13*, volume 1104 of *LNAI*, pages 141–145, New Brunswick, New Jersey, USA, July/August 1996. Springer.

Local Search Techniques for Disjunctive Logic Programs

Nicola Leone[1], Simona Perri[2], and Pasquale Rullo[2]

[1] Institut für Informationssysteme,
Technische Universität Wien
Favoritenstrasse 9, A-1040 Vienna, Austria
leone@dbai.tuwien.ac.at
[2] Dipartimento di Matematica
Università della Calabria
I-87036 Rende (CS), Italia
{sperri,rullo}@si.deis.unical.it

Abstract. In this paper we propose a heuristic approach to solve the following (hard) problem: "given a disjunctive logic program P and a set C of constraints, determine a minimal model of P satisfying all constraints in C (if any)". The approach is based on the idea of using a heuristic technique for solving the SAT problem to efficiently compute a model M of P satisfying all constraints in C. The reduction of M to a minimal model of P is then performed by using an (exact) algorithm for SAT applied to a formula derived from both P and M. This way, the computational cost needed to find a solution is drastically reduced (to the detriment of completeness). In particular, the proposed algorithm runs in polynomial time on the important class of head cycle free programs.

1 Introduction

Disjunctive logic programming (DLP) is a very expressive formalism for modeling commonsense reasoning. For instance, it allows to represent in a very simple and natural way non-monotonic reasoning, incomplete knowledge, diagnostic problems, planning and, more in general, problems with high computational complexity. In [4], it is shown that DLP supports the representation of problems up to Σ_2^P-complete (by 'brave reasoning'). In order to increase the modeling capability of DLP, logic programs are often coupled with a set of constraints (empty-head rules). A disjunctive logic program with constraints (DLPC) is thus a pair $\pi = \langle P, C \rangle$ where P is a set of disjunctive rules and C a set of constraints. The semantics of π is the set of minimal models of P satisfying C. Thus, constraints play the role of discarding the minimal models of P violating the imposed conditions. For instance, let us consider the well-known problem of 3-colorability, which consists in the assignment of three colors to the nodes of a graph in such a way that adjacent nodes have different colors. This problem is known to be NP-complete. Let us suppose that the nodes and the arcs are represented by a set F of facts with predicates *node* (unary) and *arc* (binary),

E. Lamma and P. Mello (Eds.): AI*IA 99, LNAI 1792, pp. 107–118, 2000.
© Springer-Verlag Berlin Heidelberg 2000

respectively. Then, the following DLPC program allows us to determine the admissible ways of coloring the given graph.

$r_1 :$ $color(X, red) \vee color(X, yellow) \vee color(X, green) \leftarrow node(X)$

$c_1 :$ $\leftarrow arc(X, Y), color(X, C), color(Y, C)$

Rule r_1 above states that every node is colored red or yellow or green; while the constraint c_1 forbids the assignment of the same color to two adjacent nodes. The minimal models of $F \cup \{r_1\}$ are all possible ways of coloring the graph (note that minimality guarantees that every node is assigned with only one color). If a minimal model of $F \cup \{r_1\}$ satisfies the constraint c_1, then it represents an admissible 3-coloring for the graph. Thus, there is a one-to-one correspondence between the solutions of the 3-coloring problem and the minimal models of $F \cup \{r_1\}$ satisfying c_1. The graph is 3-colorable if and only if there exists one of such minimal models.

Exact methods for computing the minimal models of DLP programs can be found in [7]. The difficulty of solving the problem is determined by two sources of computational complexity: indeed, both computing a model and testing its minimality are hard problems (NP-hard the former, co-NP-complete the latter). As a consequence, for the time being, there is only one system, namely the dlv system [5], fully supporting DLP.

In this paper, we consider the following problem (that we call *MMC*):

given a DLP program with constraints $\langle P, C \rangle$, determine a minimal model of P satisfying C (if any)

and propose heuristic techniques for an efficient solution. To this end, we rely on the use of well-known techniques for the satisfiability problem (SAT), such as GSAT [9]. In particular, we compute in polynomial time a model M for a DLPC $\langle P, C \rangle$ and, then, using an exact algorithm for SAT applied to a formula derived from P and M, possible "assumptions" are discarded from M thus obtaining a minimal model for P. Such an approach, which is shown to be correct (but not complete), drastically reduces the computational effort, thus allowing the construction of AI systems based on disjunctive logic programming. It is worth emphasizing that the proposed approach is polynomial for a large and meaningful class of DLP programs, called *head cycle free*[1] [1, 7]. This class, for instance, includes the above program for 3-colorability.

This paper is organized as follows. In Section 2 we give preliminaries on disjunctive logic programming. In Section 3 we describe how the minimality checking of a model can be reduced to the unsatisfiability problem. Then, in Section 4 we describe our approach to the efficient computation of a minimal model of a disjunctive logic program. We draw our conclusions in Section 5.

---

[1] Clearly, also on this class the method is not complete

2   Disjunctive Logic Programming

2.1   Sintax

A variable or constant is a *term*[2]. An *atom* is $a(t_1, ..., t_n)$, where a is a *predicate* of arity n and $t_1, ..., t_n$ are terms. A *(positive disjunctive) rule* r is a clause of the form

$$a_1 \vee \cdots \vee a_n \leftarrow b_1, \cdots, b_m \qquad n \geq 1, \ m \geq 0$$

where $a_1, \cdots, a_n, b_1, \cdots, b_m$ are atoms. The disjunction $a_1 \vee \cdots \vee a_n$ is the *head* of r, while the conjunction $b_1, ..., b_m$ is the *body* of r. We denote by $H(r)$ the set $\{a_1, ..., a_n\}$ of the head atoms, and by $B(r)$ the set $\{b_1, ..., b_m\}$ of the body atoms. A *disjunctive logic program* (often simply "DLP program") is a finite set of rules with not empty head (note that we do not allow negation in a DLP program).

An *(integrity) constraint* is a rule with empty head:

$$\leftarrow b_1, \cdots, b_m \qquad m \geq 1$$

A *disjunctive logic program with constraints* is a pair $\langle P, C \rangle$, where P is a disjunctive logic program and C is a finite set of constraints. In the following, we will often refer to a disjunctive logic program with constraints simply by "DLPC program".

A term, an atom, a rule, a constraint or a program is *ground* if no variables appear in it. A ground program is also called a *propositional* program.

2.2   Semantics

Let $\pi = \langle P, C \rangle$ be a DLPC program. The *Herbrand universe* U_π of π is the set of constants appearing in π (i.e., either in P or in C). The *Herbrand base* B_π of π is the set of all possible ground atoms that can be constructed from the predicates appearing in π and the terms occurring in U_π. Obviously, both U_π and B_π are finite.

Given a rule r appearing in π, a *ground instance* of r is a rule obtained from r by replacing every variable X in r by $\sigma(X)$, where σ is a mapping from the variables occurring in r to the terms occurring in U_π. Define $ground(P)$ (resp. $ground(C)$) as the set of all the ground instances of the rules belonging to P (resp. C).

An *interpretation* for P is a set of ground atoms, that is, a subset I of B_π. A ground atom A is *true* (resp. *false*) w.r.t. I if $A \in I$ (resp. $A \notin I$).

Let r be a ground rule of $ground(P)$. The head of r is *true* w.r.t. I if $H(r) \cap I \neq \emptyset$. The body of r is *true* w.r.t. I if every atom in the body is true w.r.t I, i.e. $B(r) \subseteq I$, and is *false* otherwise. The rule r is *satisfied* (or *true*) w.r.t. I if its head is true w.r.t. I or its body is false w.r.t. I. Hence, a constraint is satisfied if its body is false w.r.t. I. An interpretation M for P is a *model* for P if every rule

---

[2] Function symbols are not considered in this paper

$r \in ground(P)$ is satisfied w.r.t. M. A model M for P is *minimal* if no model N for P exists such that N is a proper subset of M. The set of all minimal models for P, denoted by $\mathrm{MM}(P)$, in [8] is defined as the semantics of DLP programs. Each model can be regarded as a possible view of the reality represented by P.

Example 1. For the program $P_1 = \{a \vee b \leftarrow\}$ the interpretations $\{a\}$ and $\{b\}$ are its minimal models (i.e. $\mathrm{MM}(P) = \{\ \{a\},\ \{b\}\ \})$.

For the program $P_2 = \{a \vee b \leftarrow;\ b \leftarrow a;\ a \leftarrow b\}$, $\{a,b\}$ is the only minimal model. □

The semantics of $\pi = \langle P, C \rangle$ is the following set of models of P:

$$\{M \in \mathrm{MM}(P) : M \text{ satisfies all the constraints in } ground(C)\}$$

Example 2. Consider the DLPC program $\pi_1 = \langle P_1, \{\leftarrow a\} \rangle$, where $P_1 = \{a \vee b \leftarrow\}$. The semantics for π_1 is given by the model $\{b\}$ of P_1, as the other model $\{a\}$ of P_1 doesn't satisfy the constraint $\leftarrow a$. □

2.3   Unfounded Sets

Next we provide a characterization of minimal models in terms of an extension to DLP programs of the classical notion of unfounded sets [7].

Definition 1. *Let I be a model for a DLP program P. A set $X \subseteq B_\pi$ is an unfounded set for P w.r.t. I if for each $a \in X$, for each rule $r \in ground(P)$ such that $a \in H(r)$, at least one of the following conditions holds:*

1. *$B(r) \not\subseteq I$, that is the body of r is false w.r.t. I.*
2. *$B(r) \cap X \neq \emptyset$ that is some body atom belongs to X.*
3. *$(H(r) - X) \cap I \neq \emptyset$, that is an atom of $H(r)$, which does not belong to X, is true w.r.t. I.* □

Conditions 1 and 2 above coincide with those given for non-disjunctive logic programs. In turn, condition 3 expresses that a disjunctive rule cannot derive more than one head atom. Intuitively, an unfounded set is a set of atoms that cannot be derived from the rules of the program and, thus, can be considered false.

Theorem 1. *[7] Let M be a model for a DLP program P. M is minimal iff no nonempty set of atoms contained in M is an unfounded set for P w.r.t. M.* □

Next we define two operators that we use for the computation of the minimal models of a DLP program.

Definition 2. *Let P be a DLP program, I and X sets of ground atoms. We define the operators, $\Phi_{P,I}$ and $\mathcal{T}_{P,X}$ as follows:*

- $\Phi_{P,I}(X) = \{a \mid \forall\ r \in ground(P)\ s.t.\ a \in H(r),\ (H(r) - \{a\}) \cap I \neq \emptyset\ or\ B(r) \cap X \neq \emptyset\}.$

- $\mathcal{T}_{P,X}(I) = \{a \mid \exists \, r \in ground(P) \; s.t. \; a \in H(r), \; H(r) - \{a\} \subseteq X \; and \; B(r) \subseteq I\}$. $\qquad\qquad\qquad\qquad\qquad\qquad\qquad\qquad\qquad\qquad\qquad\qquad\qquad\qquad\square$

Intuitively, I (resp. X) represents a set of atoms whose truth (resp. falsity) has already been proven. $\Phi_{P,I}(X)$ derives further atoms which, according to the definition of unfoundedness, can be considered false; while $\mathcal{T}_{P,X}(I)$ (first defined in [7]) derives further atoms which are necessarily true if the atoms in I are true and the atoms in X are false. Note that $\mathcal{T}_{P,X}(I)$ is a skeptical operator as an atom a is derived from a rule r provided that each other atom in the head of r is false. The following proposition is a consequence of results shown in [7]. In particular, it follows from the propositions 5.6 and 5.12 in [7].

Proposition 1. *Given a DLP program P, let $\{W_n\}_{n \in \mathcal{N}}$ and $\{X_n\}_{n \in \mathcal{N}}$ be the sequence $W_0 = X_0 = \emptyset$, $W_n = \mathcal{T}_{P,X_{n-1}}(W_{n-1})$, $X_n = \Phi_{P,W_{n-1}}(X_{n-1})$. Then:*

1. *$\{W_n\}_{n \in \mathcal{N}}$ converges finitely to a limit $\mathcal{W}_P^\infty$.*
2. *$\{X_n\}_{n \in \mathcal{N}}$ converges finitely to a limit $\mathcal{X}_P^\infty$.*
3. *$\mathcal{W}_P^\infty$ is contained in every minimal model of P.*
4. *The atoms in $\mathcal{X}_P^\infty$ are false in every minimal model of P.*
5. *In the propositional case $\mathcal{W}_P^\infty$ and $\mathcal{X}_P^\infty$ are computable in polynomial time.*

$\qquad\qquad\qquad\qquad\qquad\qquad\qquad\qquad\qquad\qquad\qquad\qquad\qquad\qquad\qquad\qquad\square$

3   Minimality Checking

3.1   The General case: Reduction to UNSAT

Verifying the minimality of a model M of a DLP program P is a hard task (co-NP-complete for propositional programs). In this section, we show a transformation, proposed in [6], reducing our problem to UNSAT, the complement of satisfiability (SAT), a well-known problem in AI for which many efficient algorithms have been proposed [9].

We recall that a CNF formula on a set A of atomic propositions is a conjunction of the form $\varphi = c_1 \wedge ... \wedge c_n$, where $c_1, ..., c_n$ are clauses on A. The formula φ is *satisfiable* if there exists a truth assignment for the propositions in A such that φ is true. Thus, UNSAT is the following decision problem: Given a CNF formula φ, is it true that φ is unsatisfiable?

In [6], where the reader is referred for further details, it has been shown that verifying the minimality of a model M of a DLP program P is equivalent to verifying the unsatisfiability of the formula $\Gamma_M(P)$ defined by the transformation of figure 1.

Theorem 2. *[6] Let P be a DLP program, let M be a model for P and $\Gamma_M(P)$ the CNF formula obtained by applying the transformation shown in figure 1. X is a model for $\Gamma_M(P)$ iff X is an unfounded set for P w.r.t. M.* $\qquad\square$

Corollary 1. *[6] Given a model M for a DLP program P, let $\Gamma_M(P)$ be the formula computed by the algorithm in figure 1 with inputs P and M. Then M is a minimal model for P iff $\Gamma_M(P)$ is unsatisfiable.* $\qquad\qquad\square$

Input: A ground DLP program P and a model M for P.
Output: A CNF formula $\Gamma_M(P)$.
var: P': DLP program; S: Set of clauses;

begin
1. Delete from P each rule whose body is false w.r.t. M;
2. Remove all false atoms (w.r.t. M) from the heads of the resulting rules;
3. $S := \emptyset$;
4. Let P' be the program resulting from steps 1-2;
5. **for** each rule $a_1 \vee \cdots \vee a_n \leftarrow b_1, \cdots, b_m$ in P' **do**
6. $S := S \cup \{\, b_1 \vee \cdots \vee b_m \leftarrow a_1 \wedge \cdots \wedge a_n \,\}$
7. **end for**;
8. $\Gamma_M(P) := \bigwedge_{c \in S} c \wedge (\bigvee_{x \in M} x)$;
9. **output** $\Gamma_M(P)$;
end;

Fig. 1. Computation of $\Gamma_M(P)$

3.2 A Tractable Case: HCF Programs

Deciding whether a model M of a DLP program P is minimal is co-NP-complete
for general propositional programs. However, this problem is tractable if P
is *head cycle free (HCF)* [1]. Intuitively, head cycle freeness forbids recursion
through disjunction. Formally, we associate to P a directed graph $DG_P = (N, A)$, called the *dependency graph* of P, where each atom in P is a node in N
and there is an arc in A from node a to node b iff there exists a rule r in P such
that $b \in H(r)$ and $a \in B(r)$. A program P is HCF if there is no rule r in P such
that two atoms $a, b \in H(r)$ belonging to the same cycle of DG_P.

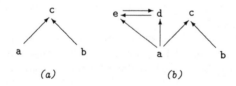

Fig. 2. Graphs (a) DG_{P_1}, (b) DG_{P_2}

Example 3. Consider the program P_1 consisting of the following rules:

$$a \vee b \leftarrow \qquad\qquad c \leftarrow a \qquad\qquad c \leftarrow b$$

and the program P_2, obtained by adding to P_1 the rules

$$d \vee e \leftarrow a \qquad\qquad d \leftarrow e$$

The dependency graphs given in Figure 2 reveals that program P_1 is HCF and that program P_2 is not HCF, as rule $d \vee e \leftarrow a$ contains in its head two predicates belong to the same cycle of DG_{P_2}.

Proposition 2. *Let M be a model for a DLP propositional program HCF P.*

1. *[7] Verifying the minimality of M is feasible in polynomial time.*
2. *[1] A minimal model M' of P contained in M is computable in polynomial time.*   □

4   A heuristic algorithm for DLP programs with constraints

In this section, we show how previous results can be combined with heuristics for SAT for the computation of a minimal model of a DLPC program, i.e., to solve the *MMC* problem. To this end, we first discuss the computational complexity of *MMC*.

For propositional programs, *MMC* is $\Delta_2^P[O(\log n)]$-hard [2, 3]; it is therefore both NP-hard and co-NP-hard. The precise complexity of *MMC* has been determined in in [3]. The problem remains NP-hard even if the input program is head cycle free (but it is not co-NP-hard in this case). To give an intuition of the two main sources of complexity in *MMC*, we next provide a simple reduction from a NP-hard problem and from a co-NP-hard problem to *MMC*.

To check co-NP-hardness, we reduce 'minimal model checking' (a well-known co-NP-hard problem [4]) to *MMC*. Given a model M for a DLP program P, let us construct the DLPC program $\pi = \langle P, C \rangle$ where $C = \{\leftarrow a : a$ is false in M$\}$. M is a minimal model of P iff it is the (unique) solution of the instance π of *MMC*.

Clearly, *MMC* is NP-hard as well. Indeed, as shown in the Introduction, 3-colorability can be reduced to *MMC*. Moreover, since the DLP program used in the reduction is HCF, it turns out that *MMC* remains NP-hard even if the input program is head cycle free.

It is unlikely that a co-NP problem can be solved in polynomial time by using heuristics. Therefore, we employ a heuristic method which cuts down the NP source of complexity of *MMC*, resulting in an (incomplete) polynomial time procedure for solving *MMC* on the class of HCF programs (where the co-NP complexity component is not present). In the general case, our method runs in polynomial space and single exponential time.

Let $\pi = \langle P, C \rangle$ be a DLPC program. Let us first consider the set $\mathcal{W}_P^\infty$ which, as already seen (see proposition 1), is contained in every minimal model of P. Thus, if there exists a constraint $c \in ground(C)$ which is violated in $\mathcal{W}_P^\infty$, then no model exists for π (as no minimal model of P can satisfy all constraints).

Otherwise (i.e., if every constraint is satisfied in $\mathcal{W}_P^\infty$), let P' be the program obtained from $ground(P)$ as follows:

a) for each atom $a \in \mathcal{W}_P^\infty$, discard from $ground(P)$ every rule r such that $a \in H(r)$.
b) discard from $ground(P)$ every rule r such that $B(r) \cap \mathcal{X}_P^\infty \neq \emptyset$.
c) for each remaining rule in $ground(P)$, rule out every atom $a \in B(r)$ such that $a \in \mathcal{W}_P^\infty \cup \mathcal{X}_P^\infty$.

Informally, the program P' consists of only those rules that can give further contribution to the construction of a minimal model for P. Now, since $\mathcal{W}_P^\infty$ is contained in every minimal model of P, it turns out that for every minimal model M of P there exists a minimal model M' of P' such that $M = M' \cup \mathcal{W}_P^\infty$. On the contrary, if M' is a minimal model of P' then $M' \cup \mathcal{W}_P^\infty$ is a minimal model of P. Therefore, from now on we can concentrate on the minimal models of P' (looking for those satisfying the constraints in C).

To this end, let us consider the CNF formula ψ resulting from the conjunction of the rules in P' and the constraints in C. More precisely,

$$\psi = \bigwedge_{r \in P'} clause(r) \bigwedge_{c \in ground(C)} clause(c),$$

where, for a given rule or constraint $x = a_1 \vee \cdots \vee a_n \leftarrow b_1, \cdots, b_m$ $(n, m \geq 0)$, $clause(x)$ is the clause $a_1 \vee \cdots \vee a_n \vee \neg b_1 \vee \cdots \vee \neg b_m$.

Since ψ contains also the constraints in C, its models are precisely those of P' satisfying all constraints in C. Thus, if I is a model for ψ then $I \cup \mathcal{W}_P^\infty$ is a model for π (i.e., a model for P satisfying C).

Then, we apply to the CNF ψ an algorithm for the satisfiability problem that we denote by $SAT(\psi)$. Now, if ψ is satisfiable then $SAT(\psi)$ returns a model M for ψ (recall that M is a model for P' satisfying the constraints in C). Unfortunately M is not in general minimal. However, as we shall see later on this section, we can iteratively extract suitable subsets of M eventually converging to a minimal model of P (satisfying the constraints in C).

In particular, if P' is a HCF program, then the computation of a minimal model starting from the model M can be carried out in a simple and efficient way (see proposition 2). Otherwise (i.e., P' is not HCF) we apply the satisfiability algorithm to the CNF formula $\Gamma_M(P')$ obtained by the rewriting algorithm of figure 1. Now, if $\Gamma_M(P')$ is unsatisfiable, from corollary 1, it turns out that M is a minimal model for P', so that $M \cup \mathcal{W}_P^\infty$ is a minimal model for P satisfying C.

On the contrary, if $SAT(\Gamma_M(P'))$ generates a truth assignment X (i.e., $\Gamma_M(P')$ is satisfiable), by therorem 2, X is an unfounded set of P' w.r.t. M. Further, thanks to the following theorem, we have that $(M - X)$ is a model for P'.

Theorem 3. *Let P be a DLP program, M a model for P and X an unfounded set of P w.r.t. M. Then $(M - X)$ is a model for P.*

CMMC Algorithm

Input: A $DLPC$ program $\pi = \langle P, C \rangle$
Output: A minimal model of P satisfying all constraints in C.
var: P': DLP Program; φ, ψ: Clause; M, M', Min: Interpretation;
begin
1. $M := \mathcal{W}_P^\infty$
2.   **if** $(\exists(\leftarrow a_1, \cdots a_n) \in ground(C)$ such that $\{a_1, \cdots a_n\} \subseteq \mathcal{W}_P^\infty)$ **then**
3.   **output** "No minimal model of P satisfies C"
4. $P' := \text{Simp}(P, M)$
5. $\psi := \text{CNF}(P', C)$
6. $\text{GSAT}(\psi, M', \text{is-sat})$
7.   **if** (**not** is-sat) **then**
8.   **output** "No model has been found"
9.   **elseif** (P' is HCF program) **then**
10. $\text{Comp-HCF-Minimal}(P', M', Min)$;
11.   **else**
12.   minimal:=false
13.   **while**(not minimal) **do**
14. $\varphi := \Gamma_{M'}(P')$
15. $\text{Sat}(\varphi, X, \text{is-sat})$
16.   **if** (**not** is-sat) **then**
17.   minimal:=true; $Min := M'$;
18.   **else** $M' := M' - X$
19.   **end-while**;
20.   **end-if**;
21.   **return** $Min \cup \mathcal{W}_P^\infty$;
end.

Fig. 3. Computation of a minimal model for a DLPC program

Proof. We show that every rule $r \in ground(P)$ is true w.r.t. $M - X$. To this end, it suffices to consider only those rules whose head has some atom in X. Let $r \in ground(P)$ such that $H(r) \cap X \neq \emptyset$. From the definition of unfounded set we have that, for each $a \in X$ and for each $r \in ground(P)$ such that $a \in H(r)$, one of the following conditions holds: either (1) the body $B(r)$ is false w.r.t. M and, hence, is false w.r.t. $M - X$; thus, r is true w.r.t. $M - X$; or (2) $B(r) \cap X \neq \emptyset$ which implies $B(r) \not\subseteq (M - X)$ and, thus, r is true w.r.t. $M - X$; or (3) $(H(r) - X) \cap I \neq \emptyset$, i.e., there is an atom b such that $b \in M - X$, that is the head of r is true w.r.t. $M - X$. Thus, $M - X$ is a model for P. $\qquad\square$

Now, let us consider the sequence of models $\{M_i\}_{i \in N}$ defined as follows:

$$M_0 = M; \qquad M_j = (M_{j-1} - X_{j-1})$$

where, if $\Gamma_{M_j}(P')$ is satisfiable, then X_j is a model for $\Gamma_{M_j}(P')$ (that is, an unfounded set of P' w.r.t. M_j), otherwise X_j is the empty set.

Proposition 3. $\exists j \in N$ t.c. $M_j = M_{j-1}$. M_j is a minimal model for P.

Proof. It is easy to recognize that $\{M_i\}_{i \in N}$ is a monotonically decreasing sequence. Hence, there exists a natural j such that $M_j = M_{j-1}$. If $M_j = M_{j-1}$ then $X_{j-1} = \emptyset$, i.e., $\Gamma_{M_{j-1}}(P')$ is unsatisfiable (by definition). Then, from corollary 1, it follows that M_{j-1} (and, hence, M_j) is a minimal model for P. $\square$
Therefore, once the limit of the sequence $\{M_n\}$ has been reached, we have found a desired minimal model.

In figure 3 is represented the algorithm *CMMC* that, based on the above results, evaluates a minimal model satisfying the integrity constraints. The algorithm uses the following functions:

- *Simp*(P, M) : given a DLP program P and an interpretation M, it returns a program P' obtained by applying to P the transformation rules a), b) e c) above described;
- *CNF*(P', C) : given a DLPC π, it returns the equivalent CNF formula;
- *GSAT*$(\psi, M', is\text{-}sat)$: is an implementation of a (polynomial) heuristic algorithm for the satisfiability problem such as *GSAT* or *WSAT* [9]. Given a CNF ψ, it returns the boolean value *is-sat* which is true if a model for ψ has been found, false otherwise. In case of success, the parameter M' is a model of ψ.
- *Comp-HCF-Minimal*(P', M', Min) given a model M' for a HCF disjunctive logic program P', it returns in Min a minimal model of P' contained in M'. The function runs in polynomial time (see prop. 2).
- *Sat*$(\varphi, X, is\text{-}sat)$: is an implementation of an exact algorithm for the satisfiability problem such as, for instance, *SATO* [10]. Given a CNF φ, the variable *is-sat* returned by the procedure is set to true iff φ is satisfiable. In such a case, the parameter M' is a model of φ.

We point out that the algorithm *CMMC* is correct. That is, if a model M is computed by *CMMC*, then M is a minimal model for P satisfying all constraints in C.

Concerning completeness, we note that the program P could have no minimal model satisfying the constraints. In such a case, the clause ψ is unsatisfiable and thus the algorithm *GSAT* doesn't generate any model. On the other hand, *GSAT* is incomplete, that is, it could fail even if ψ is satisfiable. It turns out that, in case of failure of the *CMMC* algorithm, we never know the reason.

Concerning the complexity of *CMMC*, the following holds. (Obviously, we assume that the functions employed in *CMMC* behave as decribed above and, in particular, that *GSAT* runs in polynomial time.)

Proposition 4. *Given a propositional DLP program P and a set C of constraints*

a) *the algorithm CMMC terminates in polynomial time if P is HCF;*
b) *in the general case, CMMC runs in polynomial space and single exponential time.*

Proof. Instructions 1–8 are evidently polynomial time executable (recall that the external heuristic function GSAT is assumed to be polynomial). If the program is HCF, and the algorithm did not terminate at instruction 8, then the algorithm terminates after the execution of Comp-HCF-Minimal which is also polynomial by virtue of proposition 2. Therefore, *CMMC* always terminates in polynomial time if the program P is HCF.

In the general (not HCF) case, the execution of the **while** loop of lines 13–19 is needed. This loop is executed at most $|M'|$ times, where $|M'|$ is the cardinality of the model M' (which is linear in the input), because a non-empty set X is subtracted from M' at each loop iteration. The only expensive instruction in the loop is the call to the external Sat procedure, which is well known to run in polynomial space and single exponential time. Thus, even in the worst case, the algorithm runs in polynomial space and single exponential time.   □

Thus, thanks to the application of a heuristic approach for the computation of an initial model satisfying the constraints, *CMMC* removes the NP source of complexity and becomes polynomial for HCF programs (where the co-NP component is absent).

5   Conclusion

We have studied the possibility to apply heuristic methods to the computation of minimal models disjunctive logic programs with integrity constraints. A heuristic method computing minimal models of disjunctive logic programs in polynomial time appears hard to be found in the general case, because the problem has a co-NP complexity source. Thus, we have designed a heuristic method which runs in polynomial time on the meaningful class of HCF programs; while running in single exponential time on general programs.

Future work is concerned with the implementation of the proposed approach in the context of the *dlv* system [5] and the experimentation on real applications.

References

1. Ben-Eliyahu, R. and Palopoli, L. (1994), Reasoning with Minimal Models: Efficient Algorithms and Applications, *in* "Proc. Fourth International Conference on Principles of Knowledge Representation and Reasoning (KR-94)," pp. 39–50.
2. Cadoli, M. (1992), On the complexity of model finding for nonmonotonic propositional logics. In A. Marchetti Spaccamela, P. Mentrasti, and M. Venturini Zilli, editors, *Proceedings of the Fourth Italian Conference on Theoretical Computer Science*, pages 125–139. World Scientific Publishing Co.
3. Chen, Z., and Toda, S., (1995), The complexity of selecting maximal solutions. *Information and Computation*, 119:231–239.
4. Eiter,T., Gottlob, G., and Mannila, H. (1997), Disjunctive datalog, *ACM Trans. on Database Systems*, 22(3):315-363, September 1997.
5. Eiter,T., Leone, N., Mateis, C., Pfeifer, G., Scarcello, F. (1998), The KR System dlv: Progress Report, Comparisons and Benchmarks. Proc. KR'98, pp.406-417.

6. Koch,C., Leone, N., (1999) "Stable Model Checking Made Easy", *Proceedings of the 16th International Joint Conference on Artificial Intelligence – IJCAI '99*, Stockolm, August 1999.
7. Leone, N. , Rullo, P., Scarcello, F. (1997), Disjunctive Stable Models: Unfounded Sets, Fixpoint Semantics and Computation, *Information and Computation*, 135(2):69-112.
8. Minker, J. (1982), On Indefinite Data Bases and the Closed World Assumption, *in* "Proc. of the 6th Conference on Automated Deduction (CADE-82)," pp. 292–308.
9. Selman,B., Kautz,A., Cohen,B. (1993), Local Search Strategies for Satisfiability Testing, *in* "Second DIMACS Challenge on Cliques, Coloring, and Satisfiability".
10. Zhang,H. (1997), SATO: An efficient Propositional Prover. *Proc. CADE-97.*

Labelled Tableaux for Non-Normal Modal Logics

Guido Governatori[1] Alessandro Luppi[2]

[1] School of CIT, Griffith University, Nathan, QLD 4111, Australia
[2] Department of Philosophy, University of Bologna, Via Zamboni 38, 40122, Italy

Abstract. In this paper we show how to extend KEM, a tableau-like proof system for normal modal logic, in order to deal with classes of non-normal modal logics, such as monotonic and regular, in a uniform and modular way.

1 Introduction

Non-normal modal logics have a long tradition, however, despite their heritage they have been the subject of a very few recent attempts of mechanization [6,8,9]. One of the main reasons for this underdeveloppement is that modern automated proof techniques are mainly semantic based, and non-normal modal logics have more complex semantic structures than normal modal logics. Nevertheless Hilbert systems for non-normal modal logics are very close to those for normal modal logics: they lack the axiom $\Box\top$ or the equivalent rule of necessitation $(A/\Box A)$.

The second objection to non-normal modal logics we would like to answer to is that concerning their possible applications. The necessitation rule is a very strong inference rule and it comports significant consequences; for example under the epistemic interpretation of the modal operators, it implies omniscience: the agent must be an ideal agent, i.e., it must be a perfect reasoner and it must have unlimited computational ability. This seems to be a very unrealistic assumption so some scholars (see, among others, [4,13,11,12,14]) suggested to use non-normal modal logics to model epistemic reasoning. On the other hand one could argue this does not obtain when more exact disciplines such as mathematics are involved. However, this is not the case: it is well known that provability in Peano arithmetic can be represented with the normal modal logic GL, but some classes of arithmetic formulas (i.e., Σ_1-sentences) are represented by a non-normal modal logic [2].

It is not the aim of this work to investigate applications of non-normal modal logics. Instead we want to present a tableau-like proof system (called KEM) for classes of non-normal modal logics, namely: regular and monotonic. The main feature of KEM is its label formalism studied to simulate the semantics of modal logics. The differences between the various classes of modal logics are embedded in the definition of the basic unification; however, the various extensions (in each class) arising from modal axioms are dealt with in a uniform way wrt the various classes.

In Section 1 we shall resume briefly the basic of non-normal modal logic, then, in the following sections we shall describe KEM in details. More precisely

E. Lamma and P. Mello (Eds.): AI*IA 99, LNAI 1792, pp. 119–130, 2000.
© Springer-Verlag Berlin Heidelberg 2000

in Section 4 we introduce the label formalism, then, in Section 5, we describe the unification mechanism for dealing with the various classes of non-normal modal logic, and in Section 6 we present KEM inference rules. Finally, in Section 7, we outline the soundness and completeness proofs.

2   Non-Normal Modal Logics

We shall consider only modal logics extending classical propositional logic, and where the modal operators $\Box$ and $\Diamond$ are the dual of each other (i.e., $\Box \leftrightarrow \neg\Diamond\neg$).

The rules we use to extend classical propositional logic are:

$$\frac{\vdash (A_1 \wedge \cdots \wedge A_n) \to A}{\vdash (\Box A_1 \wedge \cdots \wedge \Box A_n) \to \Box A} \; n \geq 0 \tag{RK}$$

and, in particular, we shall consider

$$\frac{\vdash A}{\vdash \Box A} \; (\text{RK}, n = 0) \tag{Nec}$$

$$\frac{\vdash A \to B}{\vdash \Box A \to \Box B} \; (\text{RK}, n = 1) \tag{RM}$$

$$\frac{\vdash (A \wedge B) \to C}{\vdash (\Box A \wedge \Box B) \to \Box C} \; (\text{RK}, n = 2) \tag{RR}$$

We can now classify modal logics according to their deductive power.

Definition 1. A modal logic Σ is:

1. *monotonic* iff it is closed under RM;
2. *regular* iff it is closed under RR;
3. *normal* iff it is closed under RK.

We can now formulate the relationships between the various classes of modal logics

Theorem 2.

1. *Every regular logic is monotonic;*
2. *Every normal logic is regular, and therefore monotonic.*

Proof. For the proof see [3, 235].

According to [3] the smallest regular logic is called R, the smallest monotonic logic M, and the smallest normal logic K.

The semantics of non-normal modal logic is given in terms of neighborhood semantics. A model is a structure

$$\mathcal{M} = \langle W, N, v \rangle$$

where W is a set of possible worlds, N is a function from W to $\mathscr{P}(\mathscr{P}(W))$ and v is an evaluation function: $v : WFF \times W \mapsto \{T, F\}$, where WFF is the set of well-formed formulas.

Before providing the evaluation clauses for the formulas we need to define the notion of truth set.

Definition 3. Let $\mathscr{M}$ be a model and A be a formula. The truth set of A wrt to $\mathscr{M}$, $\|A\|^{\mathscr{M}}$ is thus defined:

$$\|A\|^{\mathscr{M}} = \{w \in W : v(A, w) = T\} \ .$$

The evaluation clauses for atomic and boolean formulas are as usual while those for modal operators are given below.

Definition 4. Let w be a world in $\mathscr{M} = \langle W, N, v \rangle$:

1. $w \vDash \Box A \iff \|A\|^{\mathscr{M}} \in N_w$;
2. $w \vDash \Diamond A \iff W - \|A\|^{\mathscr{M}} \notin N_w$.

It is natural to add some conditions on the function N in neighborhood models. The conditions relevant for the present work are given in the following definition.

Definition 5. Let $\mathscr{M}$ be a model. For every world $w \in W$ and every proposition A, and B.

(m) If $\|A\| \cap \|B\| \subseteq N_w$, then $\|A\| \in N_w$ and $\|B\| \in N_w$;
(c) If $\|A\| \in N_w$ and $\|B\| \in N_w$, then $\|A\| \cap \|B\| \in N_w$;
(n) $W \in N_w$.

According as the function N in a neighborhood model satisfies condition (m), (c), or (n), we shall say that the model is *supplemented*, is *closed under intersections*, or *contains the unit*. When a model is both supplemented and closed under intersections then we shall call it a *quasi-filter*; when a quasi-filter contains the unit it is a *filter*.

We are now able to state the correspondence theorem for non-normal modal logics.

Theorem 6.

1. M *is characterized by the class of supplemented models;*
2. R *is characterized by the class of quasi-filters;*
3. K *is characterized by the class of filters.*

Proof. For the proof see [3, 257]

From now on we shall use $\vDash_{\Sigma} A$ to denote that A is valid in the class of model characterizing Σ.

3   KEM

KEM (see [1,10]) is a labelled analytic proof system based on a combination
of tableau and natural deduction inference rules which allows for a suitably restricted ("analytic") application of the cut rule; the label scheme arises from an
alphabet of constant and variable "world" symbols. A "world" label is either a
world-symbol or a "structured" sequence of world-symbols called "world-path".
Constant and variable world-symbols denote worlds and set of neighbors respectively (in a neighborhood model), while a world-path conveys information about
access between the worlds in it. We attach labels to signed formulas (i.e., formulas prefixed with either a "T" or a "F") to yield *labelled signed formulas*
(*LS-formulas*). An *LS*-formula TA, i (FA, i) means that A is true (false) at the
(last) world (on the path) i. In the course of proofs labels are manipulated in
a way closely related to the modal semantics and "matched" using (specialized,
logic-dependent) unification algorithms.

4   Label Formalism

The set $\Im$ of labels arises from two (non empty) sets $\Phi_C = \{w_1, w_2, \dots\}$ (the set
of *constant world symbols*), and $\Phi_V = \{W_1, W_2, \dots\}$ (the set of *variable world
symbols*) through the following

Definition 7.

$$\Im = \bigcup_{1 \leq i} \Im_i \text{ where } \Im_i \text{ is :}$$
$$\Im_1 = \Phi_C \cup \Phi_V;$$
$$\Im_2 = \Im_1 \times \Phi_C;$$
$$\Im_{n+1} = \Im_1 \times \Im_n, \ n > 1.$$

That is, a world-label is either (i) an element of the set Φ_C, or (ii) an element
of the set Φ_V, or (iii) a path term (k', k) where (iiia) $k' \in \Phi_C \cup \Phi_V$ and (iiib)
$k \in \Phi_C$ or $k = (i', i)$ where (i', i) is a label. From now on we shall use $i, j, k, \dots$
to denote arbitrary labels.

For any label $i = (k', k)$ we shall call k' the *head* of i, k the *body* of i,
and denote them by $h(i)$ and $b(i)$ respectively. Notice that these notions are
recursive (they correspond to projection functions): if $b(i)$ denotes the body of
i, then $b(b(i))$ will denote the body of $b(i)$, $b(b(b(i)))$ will denote the body of
$b(b(i))$; and so on. We call each of $b(i)$, $b(b(i))$, etc., a *segment* of i. Let $s(i)$
denote any segment of i (obviously, by definition every segment $s(i)$ of a label i
is a label); then $h(s(i))$ will denote the head of $s(i)$.

For any label i, we define the length of i, $\ell(i)$, as the number of world-symbols
in i, i.e., $\ell(i) = n \Leftrightarrow i \in \Im_n$. $s^n(i)$ will denote the segment of i of length n, i.e.,
$s^n(i) = s(i)$ such that $\ell(s(i)) = n$. We shall use $h^n(i)$ as an abbreviation for
$h(s^n(i))$.

For any label $i, \ell(i) > n$, we define the *countersegment-n* of i, as follows:

$$c^n(i) = h(i) \times (\cdots \times (h^k(i) \times (\cdots \times (h^{n+1}(i), w_0)))) \quad (n < k < l(i))$$

where w_0 is a dummy label. In other words the countersegment-n of a label i is the label obtained from i by replacing $s^n(i)$ with a dummy world symbol.

Let us exemplify the notions introduced above: let us consider the label $i = (w_5, (W_4, (w_3, (w_2, w_1))))$. Obviously, the length of i, $\ell(i)$, is 5: there are five world symbols in i. The head of i, $h(i)$, is the label w_5, while its body, $b(i)$, is $(W_4, (w_3, (w_2, w_1)))$. The segment of length 2 of i, $s^2(i)$, is (w_2, w_1) and the corresponding countersegment, $c^2(i)$, is the label $(w_5, (W_4, (w_3, w_0)))$, where w_0 stands for $s^2(i)$. However, it is worth noting that when we deal with countersegments w_0 is conceived as world symbol.

5   Unifications

The key feature of KEM is that in the course of proof labels are manipulated in a way closely related to the semantics of modal operators and "matched" using a specialized unification algorithm. That two labels i and k are unifiable means, intuitively, that the set of worlds they "denote" have a non-null intersection. The basic element of the unification is the substitution function which maps each variable in labels to a label, and each constant to itself.

The label unification is the core of KEM. The unifications for the various logics, as usual, are defined from a substitution and imposing conditions on the substitution produces the basic unification for the classes of logics we are dealing with.

Let ρ^C be a substitution function defined on labels. We first build a basic unification for the classes of logics, then we define the unifications corresponding to the various modal axioms relying on basic unifications, finally we compose the axiom unifications into the unifications for the corresponding logics.

First of all a label substitution ρ^C is built upon a "world" substitution θ^C as follows:

$$\rho^C(i) = \begin{cases} i & \text{if } i \in \Im_1 \text{ ;} \\ (\theta^C(k), \rho^C(k')) & \text{if } i = (k, k') \text{ .} \end{cases}$$

For two labels i and j, and a substitution ρ, if ρ is a unifier of i and j then we shall say that i, j are σ^C-*unifiable*. We shall use $(i, j)\sigma^C$ to denote both that i and j are σ^C-unifiable and the result of their unification. In particular

$$\forall i, j, k \in \Im, (i, j)\sigma^C = k \text{ iff } \exists \rho^C (\rho^C(i) = \rho^C(j) \text{ and } \rho^C(i) = k) \text{ .}$$

On this basis we may define several specialised, logic-dependent notions of σ-unification characterizing the various modal logics. The first step in order to define the unifications characterizing the various modal logic is to define unifications (axiom unifications) corresponding to the modal axioms. Then in the same way a modal logic is obtained by combining several axioms we define combined unifications, that, when applied recursively, produce logic unifications.

Let A be a modal axiom, then the general form of a σ^{CA} unification corresponding to A is:

$$(i,j)\sigma^{CA} \iff (f_A(i), g_A(j))\sigma_C \text{ and } C^A$$

where f_A and g_A are given logic-dependent functions from labels to labels and C^A is a set of constraints (see [10,1,7] for examples of axiom and logic unifications).

A combined unification $\sigma^{CA_1 \cdots A_n}$ is generally defined as the combination of the axiom unifications for the axioms $A_1, \ldots, A_n$ characterizing the logic Σ.

$$(i,j)\sigma^{CA_1 \cdots A_n} \iff \begin{cases} (i,j)\sigma^{CA_1} & C^{A_1} \; ; \\ \vdots & \vdots \\ (i,j)\sigma^{CA_n} & C^{A_n} \; . \end{cases}$$

Applying recursively the above $\sigma^{CA_1 \cdots A_n}$ unification we obtain the logic unification σ_Σ.

$$(i,j)\sigma_\Sigma = \begin{cases} (i,j)\sigma^{CA_1 \cdots A_n} \; , \\ (c^n(i), c^m(j))\sigma^{CA_1 \cdots A_n} \end{cases}$$

where $w_0 = (s^n(i), s^m(j))\sigma_\Sigma$.

We shall denote the constants occurring in labels obtained as the result of an unification with $*$, and we shall denote the set of such constants by Φ_C^*.

It is worth noting that the variables can be mapped on more than a label in the course of a proof; imposing restrictions on the number of labels a variable can be mapped to in the course of a proof makes us able to characterize the classes of modal logics at hand. More precisely the world substitutions for the classes of logics under analysis are:

Monotonic Logics

$$\theta^M : \Phi_V \mapsto \Im_{\text{branch}} \qquad\qquad \text{injective}$$
$$\mathbf{1}_{\Phi_C^*}$$

The condition for monotonic logics states that a variable can be mapped to a unique label in a branch of a KEM-proof, while constants are mapped to themselves only if they are the result of a unification. It is worth noting that it is possible to map a variable to different labels if they occur in distinct branches.

Regular Logics

$$\theta^R : \Phi_V \mapsto \Im$$
$$\mathbf{1}_{\Phi_C^*}$$

For regular logics the restriction on variables is released, while that on constants still obtains.

Normal Logics

$$\theta^K : \Phi_V \mapsto \Im$$

$$\mathbf{1}_{\Phi_C}$$

The substitution for normal logics is obtained from that for regular by dropping the restriction on constants: each constant is mapped to itself.

To explain the mechanics of the unifications we consider the regular logic R4 —R plus the axiom 4 ($\Box A \rightarrow \Box\Box A$). The axiom unification for 4 in R is

$$(i,j)\sigma^{4R} = \begin{cases} c^{\ell(i)}(j) & \ell(j) > \ell(i), h(i) \in \Phi_V \text{ and} \\ & w_0 = (i, s^{\ell(i)}(j))\sigma^R ; \\ c^{\ell(j)}(i) & \ell(i) > \ell(j), h(j) \in \Phi_V \text{ and} \\ & w_0 = (s^{\ell(j)}(i), j)\sigma^R . \end{cases}$$

Accordingly, $i = (w_5, (w_4, (w_3, (W_1, w_1))))$ and $j = (W_2, (w_2, w_1))$ $\sigma^4 R$-unify on $(w_5, (w_4, (w_3, (w_2, w_1))))$ since $c^3(i) = (w_5, (w_4, w_0))$, and $w_0 = (s^3(i), j)\sigma^R$: it is immediate to see that $s^3(i) = (w_3, (W_1, w_1))$ and j σ^R-unify.

From the above unification we obtain the combined unification for R4, namely:

$$(i,j)\sigma^{R4} = \begin{cases} (i,j)\sigma^R & \ell(i) = \ell(j) ; \\ (i,j)\sigma^{4R} & \ell(i) \neq \ell(j) . \end{cases}$$

The logic unification for R4 is given by the recursive iteration of the combined unification σ^{R4}.

$$(i,j)\sigma_{R4} = \begin{cases} (i,j)\sigma^{R4} , \\ (c^n(i), c^m(j))\sigma^{R4} \end{cases}$$

where $w_0 = (s^n(i), s^m(j))\sigma_{R4}$. Then the labels $(w_5, (w_4, (w_3, (W_1, w_1))))$ and $(W_2, (w_2, w_1))$ σ_{R4}-unify since they σ^{4R}-unify; the labels $(w_3, (W_1, w_1))$ and $(W_2, (w_2, w_1))$ σ_{R4}-unify since they σ^R-unify. We consider now the labels $i = (W_2, (w_3, (w_2, w_1)))$ and $j = (w_5, (w_4, (W_1, w_1)))$. It is immediate to see that they do not σ^{4R}- nor σ^R-unify. However, $c^3(i) = (W_2, w_0)$ and $c^2(j) = (w_5, (w_4, w_0))$ σ^{R4}-unify, and so do $s^3(i) = (w_3, (w_2, w_1))$ and $s^2(i) = (W_1, w_1)$. Therefore i and j σ_{R4}-unify.

6   Inference Rules

In displaying the rules of KEM we shall use Smullyan-Fitting α, β, ν, π unifying notation [6]. If X is an LS-formula, X^C denotes the *conjugate* of X, i.e., the result of changing the sign of X to its opposite; two LS-formulas X, i and X^C, k such that $(i,k)\sigma_\Sigma$ will be called σ_Σ-*complementary*.

$$\frac{\alpha, i}{\alpha_n, i}[n = 1, 2] \tag{α}$$

The α rules are just the familiar linear branch-expansion rules of the tableau method.

$$\frac{\beta, i}{\beta^C_n, j}{\beta_{3-n}(i,j)\sigma_\Sigma}[(i,j)\sigma_\Sigma, \; n=1,2] \tag{β}$$

The β are nothing else than natural inference patterns such as Modus Ponens, Modus Tollens and Disjunctive syllogism generalized to the modal case. In order to apply such rules it is required that the labels of the premises unify and the label of the conclusion is the result of their unification.

$$\frac{\nu, i}{\nu_0, (W_n, i)}[W_n \text{ new}] \tag{ν}$$

$$\frac{\pi, i}{\pi_0, (w_n, i)}[w_n \text{ new}] \tag{π}$$

ν and π rules allow us to expand labels according to the intended semantics, where, with "new" we means that the label does not occur previously in the tree. It is worth noting that the proviso "W_n new" is not necessary for normal logics, but this is not the case for non-normal ones; this is due to the fact that the meaning of W_n wrt to normal modal logic is the set of worlds accessible from i, while for non-normal modal logic it denotes a set of neighbors of i, and a world may have several sets of neighbors.

$$\frac{}{X, i \qquad X^C, i}[i \text{ restricted}] \tag{PB}$$

PB (the "Principle of Bivalence") represents the (LS-version of the) semantic counterpart of the cut rule of the sequent calculus (intuitive meaning: a formula A is either true or false in any given world).

$$\frac{X, i}{X^C, j}{\times}[(i,j)\sigma_\Sigma] \tag{PNC}$$

PNC (the "Principle of Non-Contradiction") corresponds to the familiar branch-closure rule of the tableau method, saying that from a contradiction of the form (occurrence of a pair of σ_Σ-complementary LS-formulas) X, i and X^C, j on a branch we may infer the closure of the branch. The $(i,j)\sigma_\Sigma$ in the "conclusion" of PNC means that the contradiction holds "in the same world".

As usual with refutation methods, a proof of a formula A of Σ consists of attempting to construct a counter-model for A by assuming that A is false in some arbitrary model for Σ. Every successful proof discovers a contradiction in the putative counter-model. In what follows by a KEM-*tree* we shall mean a tree generated by the inference rules of KEM. A branch τ of a KEM-tree will be said to be σ_Σ-*closed* if it ends with an application of PNC. A KEM-tree $\mathcal{T}$ will be said to be σ_Σ-closed if all its branches are σ_Σ-closed. Finally, by a Σ-proof of a formula A we shall mean σ_Σ-closed KEM-tree starting with FA, i, where i is a constant world-symbol. We shall use $\vdash_{\text{KEM}(\Sigma)} A$ to denote that there is a Σ-proof of A.

To illustrate the proof procedure we consider the formula $C = \Box A \wedge \Box B \to \Box(A \wedge B)$. C is a theorem of every regular logic but not of monotonic logics.

$$
\begin{array}{lll}
1. & F\Box A \wedge \Box B \to \Box(A \wedge B) & w_1 \\
2. & T\Box A \wedge \Box B & w_1 \\
3. & F\Box(A \wedge B) & w_1 \\
4. & T\Box A & w_1 \\
5. & T\Box B & w_1 \\
6. & FA \wedge B & (w_2, w_1) \\
7. & TA & (W_1, w_1) \\
8. & TB & (W_2, w_1) \\
9. & FB & (w_2^*, w_1)
\end{array}
$$

The steps from 1 to 8 are straightforward. 9 has been derived from an application of a β rule on 6 and 7. If we are in a monotonic logic then the tree is completed, every non atomic formula has been analysed and it is not possible to apply PNC on 8 and 9, since their labels do not unify: the variable W_2 cannot be mapped to w_2, because W_1 is already mapped to w_1, and θ^M must be injective. Otherwise, in a regular logic, θ^R is not required to be injective, thus W_2 can be mapped to w_2. In this way the formulas in 8 and 9 become complementary, therefore PNC is applicable, the tree is closed, and thus we have a KEM-proof of C.

7 Soundness and Completeness

In order to prove soundness and completeness of KEM with respect to the classes of logics and models of Theorem 6, we have to show that the rules RM, RR, and RK are derived rules in KEM. This can be easily achieved by drawing a KEM-proof for them. Here we just provide the proof for RM in M; the proofs for the remaining rules and logics are similar.

$$
\begin{array}{lll}
1. & F\Box A \to \Box B & w_1 \\
2. & T\Box A & w_1 \\
3. & F\Box B & w_1 \\
4. & TA & (W_1, w_1) \\
5. & FB & (w_2, w_1)
\end{array}
$$

$$
\begin{array}{llll}
6. & TA \to B \ (w_2, w_1) & 7. & FA \to B \ (w_2, w_1) \\
8. & TB \qquad (w_2^*, w_1) & 10. & B \qquad\qquad (w_2^*, w_1) \\
9. & \times \qquad (w_2^*, w_1) & 11. & \times
\end{array}
$$

To show that there is a KEM-proof we have to provide a closed KEM-tree for $F\Box A \to \Box B$ given that a KEM-tree ($\mathcal{B}$) for $FA \to B$ closes. The steps 1–5 are immediate; at this point we apply PB wrt to $A \to B$, and label (w_2, w_1). In the left branch we can apply a β-rule on 4 and 6, thus obtaining 8 and closing the branch. In the right branch we can repeat the proof for $FA \rightarrow B$ with label (w_2^*, w_1), and so also this branch is closed.

D'Agostino and Mondadori [5] have proved that Modus Ponens (if $\vdash A$, and $\vdash A \rightarrow B$, them $\vdash B$) is a derived rule of KE, the propositional modulo of KEM. Moreover they proved that KE is sound and complete with respect to classical propositional logic.

From the above considerations and Theorem 6 we can conclude

Theorem 8. $\vDash_\Sigma A \Rightarrow \vdash_{KEM(\Sigma)} A$.

To prove the second part of the correspondence theorem for KEM, we have to show that KEM rules and unifications are sound with respect to the appropriate model. To this end we define some functions mapping LS-formulas on elements of a model, according to the structure of the labels.

Let g be a function from $\Im$ to $\mathscr{P}(W)$ such that:

$$g(i) = \begin{cases} h(i) = \{h(i)\} & h(i) \in \Phi_C \\ h(i) = \{w_i \in W \ : \exists \mathcal{X}(\mathcal{X} \in N_{g^*(b(i))} \wedge w_i \in \mathcal{X})\} & h(i) \in \Phi_V \end{cases}$$

where g^* is a selection function over $g(i)$; if $h(i) \in \Phi_C$ and $\ell(i) > 1$:

$$g(i) = \{h(i)\} \subseteq \{w_i \in W \ : \exists \mathcal{X}(\mathcal{X} \in N_{g^*(b(i))} \wedge w_i \in \mathcal{X})\}$$

Let r be a function from $\Im$ to N such that:

$$r(i) = \begin{cases} \emptyset & \ell(i) = 1 \\ g(i^n) \in N_{g^*(i^{n-1})}, \ (n > 1) & \ell(i) > 1 \end{cases}$$

Finally let f be a function from the set of LS-formulas to v such that:

$$f(SA, i) =_{def} v(A, w_j) = S$$

for every $w_j \in g(i)$.

Let $\mathcal{F}$ be a set of LS-formulas and $\mathcal{L}$ be the set of labels occurring in $\mathcal{F}$; the function g_Σ, $\Sigma = M, R$, from $\mathcal{L}$ to $\mathscr{P}\mathscr{P}(W)$ produces an Σ-model starting from the LS-formulas in $\mathcal{F}$.

$g_\Sigma : \mathcal{L} \mapsto N$ such that $\forall i, j, k \in \mathcal{L}$

  $\Sigma = M$: if $g(i) \subseteq g(k)$ and $g(i) \in N_{g^*(j)}$ then $g(k) \in N_{g^*(j)}$;

  $\Sigma = R$: if $g(i) \in N_{g^*(j)}$ and $g(k) \in N_{g^*(j)}$ then $g(i) \cap g(k) \in N_{g^*(j)}$;

Moreover it satisfies the following condition: let i, and j be label; if $h(i) \in \Phi_V$, $h(j) \in \Phi_C$, and there exists a world substitution θ^C such that $\theta^C(h(i)) = h(j)$, then $g(j) \subseteq g(i)$.

A KEM-tree with n branches is a collection of $\mathcal{F}_1, \ldots, \mathcal{F}_n$ where $\bigcap \mathcal{F}_n \neq \emptyset$ since it contains at least the origin of the tree.

Lemma 9. For any $i, k \in \Im$ if $(i, k)\sigma_L$ then $g(i) \cap g(k) \neq \emptyset$.

Proof. The proof is similar to that given by [1,10] for normal modal logics.

This lemma shows that if two labels unify, then the result of their σ_Σ-unification corresponds to an element of the appropriate model. In this way, we are able to build the neighborhood model for the labels involved in a KEM-proof, and so we can check every rule of KEM in a standard semantic setting:

Theorem 10. $\vdash_{KEM(\Sigma)} A \Rightarrow \vDash_\Sigma A.$

From theorems 8 and 10 we obtain:

Theorem 11. $\vdash_{KEM(\Sigma)} A \iff \vDash_\Sigma A.$

8   Conclusion

In this paper we have provided a uniform and modular automated proof system for non-normal modal logics. The system enjoys two orthogonal kinds of modularity: the first one with respect to the substitutions determining the classes of modal logic and the second one with respect to the unifications corresponding to the various modal axioms.

It is possible to claim that the system here presented is more efficient than the system proposed in [6]. Such a method takes a direct approach and uses prefixes to keep trace of the relation among possible worlds. However, it suffers from the drawback of duplicating formulas. It is easy to see that when the duplicate formulas behave disjunctively, the duplication implies an exponential increase of the complexity. On the other hand the complexity of KEM unification algorithm is linear (at least for the basic cases), so we can build examples such that the length of KEM proof is linear while Fitting's prefix tableaux has exponential proofs.

Acknowledgments

We would like to thank Giovanna Corsi for her helpful discussions. This research was partially supported by the Australian Research Council under Large Grant No. A49803544.

References

1. Alberto Artosi, Paola Benassi, Guido Governatori, and Antonino Rotolo. Shake-spearian modal logic. In M. Kracht, M. de Rijke, H. Wansing, and M. Za-kharyaschev, editors, *Advances in Modal Logic*, pages 1–21. CSLI Publications, Stanford, 1998.
2. George Boolos. *The Logic of Provability*. Cambridge University Press, Cambridge, 1993.
3. Brian Chellas. *Modal Logic: An Introduction*. Cambridge University Press, Cambridge, 1980.

4. Max J. Cresswell. The interpretation of some Lewis systems of modal logic. *Australasian Journal of Philosophy*, 45:198–206, 1967.
5. Marcello D'Agostino and Marco Mondadori. The taming of the cut. *Journal of Logic and Computation*, 4:285–319, 1994.
6. Melvin Fitting. *Proof Methods for Modal and Intuitionistic Logics*. Reidel, Dordrecht, 1983.
7. Dov M. Gabbay and Guido Governatori. Dealing with label dependent deontic modalities. In Paul McNamara and Henry Prakken, editors, *Norms, Logics and Information Systems. New Studies in Deontic Logic*, pages 311–330. IOS Press, Amsterdam, 1998.
8. Olivier Gasquet and Andreas Herzig. From classical to normal modal logic. In H. Wansing, editor, *Proof Theory of Modal Logic*, pages 293–311. Kluwer, Dordrecht, 1996.
9. Enrico Giunchiglia, Fausto Giunchiglia, and Armando Tacchella. SAT-based decision procedures for classical modal logics. *Journal of Automated Reasoning*, forthcoming.
10. Guido Governatori. *Un modello formale per il ragionamento giuridico*. PhD thesis, CIRFID, University of Bologna, Bologna, 1997.
    http://www.cit.gu.edu.au/~guido/papers/PhD.pdf
11. Liwu Li. Possible world semantics and autoepistemic logic. *Artificial Intelligence*, 71:281–320, 1994.
12. Luc Lismont and Philip Mongin. A non-minimal but very weak aximotization of common belief. *Artificial Intelligence*, 70:363–374, 1994.
13. Nicholas Resher and Arnold Vander Nat. On alternatives in epistemic logic. *Journal of Philosophical Logic*, 2:119–135, 1973.
14. Moshe Vardi. On epistemic logic and logical omniscience. In J.Y. Halpern, editor, *Theoretical Aspects of Reasoning About Knowledge,*, pages 293–305, San Matteo, CA, 1986. Morgan & Kaufmann.

Pairing Transitive Closure and Reduction to Efficiently Reason about Partially Ordered Events

Massimo Franceschet   Angelo Montanari

Dipartimento di Matematica e Informatica, Università di Udine
Via delle Scienze, 206 – 33100 Udine, Italy
{*francesc*|*montana*} *@dimi.uniud.it*

Abstract

In this paper, we show how well-known graph-theoretic techniques can be successfully exploited to efficiently reason about partially ordered events in Kowalski and Sergot's Event Calculus and in its skeptical and credulous modal variants. We replace the traditional generate-and-test strategy of (Modal) Event Calculus by a generate-only strategy that operates on the transitive closure and reduction of the underlying directed acyclic graph of events. We prove the soundness and completeness of the proposed strategy, and thoroughly analyze its computational complexity.

1   Introduction

The problem of efficiently computing which facts must be or may possibly be true over certain time periods, when only partial information about event ordering is available, is fundamental in a variety of applications, including planning and plan validation [2, 4, 8]. In this paper, we show how well-known graph-theoretic techniques can be successfully exploited to efficiently reason about partially ordered events in Kowalski and Sergot's Event Calculus (*EC* for short) [7] and in its skeptical and credulous modal variants [1]. Given a set of events, *EC* is able to infer the set of maximal validity intervals (*MVIs*) over which the properties initiated and/or terminated by them hold uninterruptedly. Events can be temporally qualified in several ways. We consider the relevant case where either the occurrence time of an event is totally unspecified or its relative temporal position with respect to (some of) the other events is given. Partial ordering information about events can be naturally represented by means of a directed acyclic graph $G = \langle E, o \rangle$, where the set of nodes E is the set of events and, for every $e_i, e_j \in E$, there exists $(e_i, e_j) \in o$ if and only if it is known that e_i occurs before e_j.

EC updates are of additive nature only and they just consist in the acquisition of new events and/or of further ordering information about the given events [6]. Hence, update processing in *EC* reduces to the addition of such data, provided that they are consistent with the current binary acyclic relation o. The set of *MVIs* for any given property p has been traditionally computed at query time

E. Lamma and P. Mello (Eds.): AI*IA 99, LNAI 1792, pp. 131–142, 2000.
© Springer-Verlag Berlin Heidelberg 2000

according to a simple (and expensive) *generate-and-test* strategy: *EC* first blindly picks up every candidate pair of events (e_i, e_t), where e_i and e_t respectively initiate and terminate p; then, it checks whether or not e_i precedes e_t; finally, it looks for possible events e that occur between e_i and e_t and interrupt the validity of p. Checking whether e_i precedes e_t or not reduces to establish if the edge (e_i, e_t) belongs to the transitive closure o^+ of o as well as checking if there exists an interrupting event e requires to verify if both (e_i, e) and (e, e_t) belong to o^+. In [3], Chittaro et al. outline an alternative (and efficient) *generate-only* strategy for *MVIs* computation when all recorded events are concerned with the same unique property p (*single-property* case). According to such a strategy, the graph $G = \langle E, o \rangle$ is replaced by its *transitive reduction* $G^- = \langle E, o^- \rangle$, which must be maintained whenever a new consistent and non-redundant pair of events (e_i, e_j) is entered (the addition of a new event e to E does not affect o^-). Since any event $e \in E$ either initiates or terminates p, the set of *MVIs* for p can be obtained by searching G^- for edges (e_i, e_j) such that e_i initiates p and e_j terminates it. Being G^- the transitive reduction of G ensures us that there are no interrupting events for p that occur between e_i and e_j. It is not difficult to prove that such a strategy properly works also when all recorded events are concerned with a set of pairwise incompatible properties. In this paper, we show how it can be generalized to the (general) *multiple-property* case[1]. The resulting strategy is organized in three steps: first, it determines (and maintains) the transitive closure $G^+ = \langle E, o^+ \rangle$ of G; then, for every property p, it extracts from G^+ the subgraph induced by the set of events that initiate or terminate p, or a property incompatible with p; finally, it derives the set of *MVIs* for any property p by applying the strategy for the single-property case to the transitive reduction of the subgraph for p.

As pointed out in [1], when only partial information about the occurred events and their exact order is available, the sets of *MVIs* derived by *EC* bear little relevance, since the acquisition of additional knowledge about the set of events and/or their occurrence times might both dismiss current *MVIs* and validate new *MVIs*. In [1], Cervesato and Montanari propose a modal variant of *EC*, called *Modal Event Calculus* (*MEC*), that allows one to identify the set of *MVIs* that cannot be invalidated no matter how the ordering information is updated, as far as it remains consistent (*necessary MVIs*), and the set of event pairs that will possibly become *MVIs*, depending on which ordering data are acquired (*possible MVIs*). They extend the generate-and-test strategy for *MVIs* computation in *EC* to *MEC*, without any rise in computational complexity. In the last part of this paper, we show that the proposed generate-only strategy for *MVIs* computation in *EC* can be easily adapted to *MEC*.

The paper is organized as follows. In Section 2, we introduce some background knowledge. In Section 3, we propose a sound and complete generate-only strategy

---

[1] The generalization to the multiple-property case sketched in [3] is not guaranteed to properly work whenever there exist two or more non-transitive paths of different length between an ordered pair of events that respectively initiate and terminate a given property.

for *MVIs* computation in *EC* and show how to adapt it to cope with *MEC*. The increase in efficiency of the proposed strategy with respect to the traditional generate-and-test one is demonstrated by the complexity analysis of Section 4.

2   Preliminaries

In this section, we first introduce some basic notions about ordering relations, transitive closure, and transitive reduction; then, we briefly recall syntax and semantics of the basic Event Calculus [7] and of the Modal Event Calculus [1].

2.1   On ordering relations, transitive closure and reduction

Let us first remind some basic notions about ordering relations and ordered sets upon which we will rely in the following.

Definition 1. (DAGs, generated DAGs, induced DAGs)

Let E be a set and o a binary relation on E. o is called a (strict) *partial order* if it is irreflexive and transitive (and, thus, asymmetric), while it is called a *reflexive partial order* if it is reflexive, antisymmetric, and transitive. The pair (E, o) is called a *directed acyclic graph* (*DAG*) if o is a binary acyclic relation; a *strictly ordered set* if o is a partial order; a *non-strictly ordered set* if o is a reflexive partial order. Moreover, given a DAG $G = \langle E, o \rangle$ and a node $e \in E$, the subgraph $G(e)$ of G consisting of all and only the nodes which are accessible from e and of the edges that connect them is called the graph *generated by e*. Finally, given a DAG $G = \langle E, o \rangle$ and a set $T \subseteq E$, the subgraph of G *induced by T* consists of the nodes in T and the subset of edges in o that connect them.

In this paper, we will make a massive use of the notions of transitive closure and reduction of a *DAG*.

Definition 2. (Transitive closure and reduction of DAGs)

Let $G = \langle E, o \rangle$ be a DAG. The *transitive reduction* of G is the (unique) graph $G^- = \langle E, o^- \rangle$, with the smallest number of edges, such that, for any pair $e_i, e_j \in E$ there is a directed path from e_i to e_j in G if and only if there is a directed path from e_i to e_j in G^-. The *transitive closure* of G is the (unique) graph $G^+ = \langle E, o^+ \rangle$ such that, for any pair of nodes $e_i, e_j \in E$ there is a directed path from e_i to e_j in G if and only if there is an edge $(e_i, e_j) \in o^+$ in G^+.

Notice that, given a DAG $G = \langle E, o \rangle$ and its transitive closure G^+, for every $T \subseteq E$, the subgraph of G^+ induced by T is a transitive closure (we will exploit this property of transitive closure in Section 3).

In the following, we will use the notations $o \uparrow (e_i, e_j)$ and $o \downarrow (e_i, e_j)$ as shorthands for $(o \cup \{(e_i, e_j)\})^+$ and $(o \cup \{(e_i, e_j)\})^-$, respectively. Furthermore, we will denote the sets of all binary acyclic relations and of all partial orders on E as O_E and W_E, respectively. It is easy to show that, for any set E, $W_E \subseteq O_E$. We will use the letters o and w, possibly subscripted, to denote binary acyclic relations and partial orders, respectively. Clearly, if (E, o) is a DAG, then (E, o^+) is a strictly ordered set. Two binary acyclic relations $o_i, o_j \in O_E$ are *equally informative* if $o_i^+ = o_j^+$. This induces an equivalence relation $\sim$ on O_E. It is easy to prove that, for any set E, $O_E / \sim$ and W_E are isomorphic.

2.2   Basic and Modal Event Calculus

A compact model-theoretic formalization of Kowalski and Sergot's *Event Calculus* has been provided by Cervesato and Montanari in [1]. It distinguishes between the time-independent and time-dependent components of *EC*. The time-independent component is captured by means of the notion of *EC-structure*.

Definition 3. (EC-structure)

A *structure* for the *Event Calculus* (abbreviated *EC-structure*) is a quintuple $\mathcal{H} = (E, P, [\cdot\rangle, \langle\cdot],]\cdot,\cdot[)$ such that:

- $E = \{e_1, \ldots, e_n\}$ and $P = \{p_1, \ldots, p_m\}$ are finite sets of *events* and *properties*, respectively;
- $[\cdot\rangle : P \to 2^E$ and $\langle\cdot] : P \to 2^E$ are respectively the *initiating* and *terminating map* of $\mathcal{H}$. For every property $p \in P$, $[p\rangle$ and $\langle p]$ represent the set of events that initiate and terminate p, respectively;
- $]\cdot,\cdot[\subseteq P \times P$ is an irreflexive and symmetric relation, called the *exclusivity relation*, that models incompatibility among properties.

The time-dependent component is formalized by specifying a binary acyclic relation o, called *knowledge state*, on the set of events E.

Given a structure $\mathcal{H} = (E, P, [\cdot\rangle, \langle\cdot],]\cdot,\cdot[)$ and a knowledge state o, *EC* permits inferring the *maximal validity intervals* (*MVIs*) over which a property p holds uninterruptedly. An *MVI* for p is represented as $p(e_i, e_t)$, where e_i and e_t are the events that initiate and terminate the interval over which p maximally holds, respectively. The *query language* $\mathcal{L}(EC)$ of *EC* is the set of formulas of the form $p(e_1, e_2)$, for every $p \in P$ and $e_1, e_2 \in E$. The task performed by *EC* reduces to deciding which of the elements of $\mathcal{L}(EC)$ are *MVIs* and which are not, with respect to o^+. The elements of $\mathcal{L}(EC)$ are interpreted relative to the set W_E of partial orders on E ($W_{\mathcal{H}}$ hereafter).

Definition 4. (Intended model of EC)

Let $\mathcal{H} = (E, P, [\cdot\rangle, \langle\cdot],]\cdot,\cdot[)$ be a EC-structure and $w \in W_{\mathcal{H}}$ be the transitive closure of a knowledge state o. The *intended EC-model* of $\mathcal{H}$ is the propositional valuation $v_{\mathcal{H}} : W_{\mathcal{H}} \to 2^{\mathcal{L}(EC)}$, where $v_{\mathcal{H}}$ is defined in such a way that $p(e_1, e_2) \in v_{\mathcal{H}}(w)$ if and only if

i. $(e_1, e_2) \in w$; **ii.** $e_1 \in [p\rangle$; **iii.** $e_2 \in \langle p]$;
iv. $br(p, e_1, e_2, w)$ does not hold, where $br(p, e_1, e_2, w)$ abbreviates

$$\exists e \in E \, \exists q \in P \, ((e_1, e) \in w \wedge (e, e_2) \in w \wedge (e \in [q\rangle \vee e \in \langle q]) \wedge (]p, q[\vee p = q))$$

In the case of partially ordered events, the set of *MVIs* derived by *EC* is not stable with respect to the acquisition of new ordering information. Indeed, if we extend the current partial order with new pairs of events, current *MVIs* might become invalid and new *MVIs* can emerge. The *Modal Event Calculus (MEC)* [1] allows one to identify the set of *MVIs* that cannot be invalidated no matter how the ordering information is updated, as far as it remains consistent, and the set of event pairs that will possibly become *MVIs* depending on which ordering data are acquired. These two sets are called *necessary MVIs* and *possible MVIs*, respectively, using $\Box$-*MVIs* and $\Diamond$-*MVIs* as abbreviations. The query language $\mathcal{L}(\mathrm{MEC})$ of *MEC* consists of formulas of the forms $p(e_1, e_2)$, $\Box p(e_1, e_2)$, and $\Diamond p(e_1, e_2)$, for every property p and events e_1 and e_2 defined in $\mathcal{H}$. The intended model of *MEC* is obtained by shifting the focus from the current knowledge state to all knowledge states that are accessible from it. Since $\subseteq$ is a reflexive partial order, $(W_{\mathcal{H}}, \subseteq)$ can be naturally viewed as a finite, reflexive, transitive, and antisymmetric modal frame. This frame, together with the straightforward modal extension of the valuation $v_{\mathcal{H}}$ to the transitive closure of an arbitrary knowledge state, provides a modal model for *MEC*.

Definition 5. (Intended model of MEC)

Let $\mathcal{H}$ be an EC-structure and $v_{\mathcal{H}}$ be the propositional valuation defined as in Definition 4. The *MEC-frame* $\mathcal{F}_{\mathcal{H}}$ of $\mathcal{H}$ is the frame $(W_{\mathcal{H}}, \subseteq)$. The *intended MEC-model* of $\mathcal{H}$ is the modal model $\mathcal{I}_{\mathcal{H}} = (W_{\mathcal{H}}, \subseteq, v_{\mathcal{H}})$. Given $w \in W_{\mathcal{H}}$ and $\varphi \in \mathcal{L}(\mathrm{MEC})$, the truth of φ at w with respect to $\mathcal{I}_{\mathcal{H}}$, denoted by $\mathcal{I}_{\mathcal{H}}; w \models \varphi$, is defined as follows:

$$\mathcal{I}_{\mathcal{H}}; w \models p(e_1, e_2) \quad \text{iff} \quad p(e_1, e_2) \in v_{\mathcal{H}}(w);$$
$$\mathcal{I}_{\mathcal{H}}; w \models \Box p(e_1, e_2) \quad \text{iff} \quad \forall w' . (w' \in W_{\mathcal{H}} \wedge w \subseteq w') \to \mathcal{I}_{\mathcal{H}}; w' \models p(e_1, e_2);$$
$$\mathcal{I}_{\mathcal{H}}; w \models \Diamond p(e_1, e_2) \quad \text{iff} \quad \exists w' . w' \in W_{\mathcal{H}} \wedge w \subseteq w' \wedge \mathcal{I}_{\mathcal{H}}; w' \models p(e_1, e_2).$$

The sets of *MVIs* that are necessarily and possibly true in w correspond respectively to the $\Box$- and $\Diamond$-moded atomic formulas which are valid in w. We denote by $MVI(w)$, $\Box MVI(w)$, and $\Diamond MVI(w)$ the sets of *MVIs*, necessary *MVIs*, and possible *MVIs* with respect to w, respectively. It is immediate to see that $p(e_1, e_2) \in \Box MVI(w)$ if and only if e_1 initiates p, e_2 terminates p, $(e_1, e_2) \in w$, and no event can interrupt the validity of p over (e_1, e_2). An event e can possibly interrupt the validity of p over (e_1, e_2) if it either initiates or terminates p, or a property which is incompatible with p, and it can consistently be located between e_1 and e_2 in w. Let $S(w)$ be the set of atomic formulas $p(e_1, e_2)$ such that all other events in E that either initiate or terminate p, or a property incompatible with p, are ordered with respect to e_1 and e_2 in w. Formally,

$$S(w) = \{p(e_1, e_2). \; \forall e \in E \; ((\exists q \in P \; ((e \in [q\rangle \vee e \in \langle q]) \wedge (q = p \vee]p, q[))) \\ \to (((e, e_1) \in w \vee (e_1, e) \in w) \wedge ((e, e_2) \in w \vee (e_2, e) \in w)))\}$$

It is easy to prove that $p(e_1, e_2) \in \Box MVI(w)$ if and only if $p(e_1, e_2) \in MVI(w)$ and $p(e_1, e_2) \in S(w)$. Similarly, $p(e_1, e_2) \in \Diamond MVI(w)$ if and only if e_1 initiates p, e_2 terminates p, (e_1, e_2) is consistent with w, that is, $(e_2, e_1) \notin w$, and there are no already known interrupting events for p that occur between e_1 and e_2.

Let $C(w)$ be the set of atomic formulas $p(e_1, e_2)$ such that e_1 initiates p, e_2 terminates p, and e_1 and e_2 are unordered in w. Formally,

$$C(w) = \{p(e_1, e_2).\ e_1 \in [p\rangle \wedge e_2 \in \langle p] \wedge (e_1, e_2) \notin w \wedge (e_2, e_1) \notin w\}$$

It is not difficult to show that $p(e_1, e_2) \in \Diamond MVI(w)$ if and only if $p(e_1, e_2) \in MVI(w)$ or $p(e_1, e_2) \in C(w)$.

Proposition 6. *Let $\mathcal{H} = (E, P, [\cdot\rangle, \langle\cdot],]\cdot, \cdot[)$ be an EC-structure and $w \in W_{\mathcal{H}}$ be the transitive closure of a knowledge state o. It holds that:*

$$\Box MVI(w) = MVI(w) \cap S(w) \text{ and } \Diamond MVI(w) = MVI(w) \cup C(w)$$

3   A generate-only strategy for EC

In this section, we first propose a sound (resp. complete) generate-only strategy for *MVIs* computation in *EC* that exploits the notion of transitive reduction (resp. closure) of the ordering graph; then, we show how to pair transitive reduction and closure to devise a sound and complete algorithm; finally, we generalize such an algorithm to compute necessary and possible *MVIs* in *MEC*.

3.1   Two partial generate-only strategies

We start by describing a sound (but incomplete) and a complete (but unsound) generate-only strategy for *MVIs* computation in *EC*. The first strategy stores and maintains the transitive reduction of a knowledge state. Let $\mathcal{H} = (E, P, [\cdot\rangle, \langle\cdot],]\cdot, \cdot[)$ be an *EC*-structure, o^- be the transitive reduction of a knowledge state o, and (e_1, e_2) be an ordered pair of events. The addition of (e_1, e_2) to o^- is dealt with as follows (update processing). First, (e_1, e_2) is checked for consistency and redundancy with respect to o^-. If (e_1, e_2) is neither inconsistent $((e_2, e_1) \notin o^+)$ nor redundant $((e_1, e_2) \notin o^+)$, then o^- is replaced by $o^- \downarrow (e_1, e_2)$. The set $o^- \downarrow (e_1, e_2)$, which can be proved to be the transitive reduction of $o \cup \{(e_1, e_2)\}$, is obtained as follows: first, the ordered pair (e_1, e_2) is added to o^-; then, the set of nodes from which e_1 is accessible ($\mathrm{Pred}(e_1)$) and the set of nodes which are accessible from e_2 ($\mathrm{Succ}(e_2)$) are computed; finally, any pair $(e', e'') \in o^-$ such that $e' \in \mathrm{Prec}(e_1)$ and $e'' \in \mathrm{Succ}(e_2)$ is deleted from $o^- \cup \{(e_1, e_2)\}$.

if $(e_1, e_2) \notin o^+$ **and** $(e_2, e_1) \notin o^+$ **then**
    $o^- \leftarrow o^- \cup \{(e_1, e_2)\}$
    put in $Prec(e_1)$ the nodes from which e_1 is accessible
    put in $Succ(e_2)$ the nodes accessible from e_2
    for each $e' \in Prec(e_1)$ **do**
        for each $e'' \in Succ(e_2)$ **do**
            if $(e', e'') \in o^-$ **then** $o^- \leftarrow o^- \setminus \{(e', e'')\}$

Given two events e_i and e_j, testing whether $(e_i, e_j) \in o^+$ or not can be performed by visiting depth-first the subgraph of (E, o^-) generated by e_i, searching for the node e_j. The set $\text{Succ}(e_2)$ can be computed by executing a depth-first visit of the subgraph of $(E, o^- \cup \{(e_1, e_2)\})$ generated by e_2 and retrieving all the visited nodes. In order to compute the set $\text{Prec}(e_1)$, we first replace each $(e', e'') \in o^- \cup \{(e_1, e_2)\}$ by (e'', e'); then, we execute a depth-first visit of the subgraph (of the resulting graph) generated by e_1 and retrieve all the visited nodes.

At query time, for every property p, the algorithm selects as $MVIs$ for p the p-edges of the transitive reduction o^-, i.e. the edges $(e_1, e_2) \in o^-$ such that e_1 initiates p and e_2 terminates p.

$MVI \leftarrow \emptyset$
for each $p \in P$ **do**
　　　　for each $(e_1, e_2) \in o^-$ **do**
　　　　　　　　if $e_1 \in [p\rangle$ **and** $e_2 \in \langle p]$ **then** $MVI \leftarrow MVI \cup \{p(e_1, e_2)\}$
return MVI

Such a strategy is *sound*: (e_1, e_2) is selected as an MVI for p if e_1 initiates p, e_2 terminates p, e_1 precedes e_2, and there are no events between e_1 and e_2 (the truth of this last condition immediately follows from the fact that (e_1, e_2) is an edge of the transitive reduction o^-); hence, by definition, $p(e_1, e_2)$ is an MVI. As shown in [3], this strategy is also complete in the single-property case. Unfortunately, it is *incomplete* in the general multiple-property case. Consider the following simple scenario, where p and q are two compatible properties:

Since e does not interrupt the validity of p, $p(e_1, e_2)$ is an MVI for p; however, since there is not an edge from e_1 to e_2, the proposed algorithm does not return $p(e_1, e_2)$.

Let us now describe a *complete* (but not sound) generate-only algorithm for $MVIs$ computation. The idea is to store and maintain the transitive closure of the knowledge state, instead of its transitive reduction. Let $\mathcal{H} = (E, P, [\cdot\rangle, \langle\cdot],]\cdot, \cdot[)$ be an EC-structure, $w \in W_{\mathcal{H}}$ be the transitive closure of a knowledge state o, and (e_1, e_2) be an ordered pair of events. The addition of (e_1, e_2) to w is dealt with as follows (update processing). Whenever both $(e_1, e_2) \notin w$ and $(e_2, e_1) \notin w$, the update procedure derives $w \uparrow (e_1, e_2)$ by executing the following steps: first, the edge (e_1, e_2) is added to w; then, for every pair of events $e', e'' \in E$ such that $(e', e_1) \in w$, $(e_2, e'') \in w$, and $(e', e'') \notin w$, the edge (e', e'') is added to $w \cup (e_1, e_2)$. It is worth noting that, since w is transitive, the set of predecessors (resp. successors) of e_1 (resp. e_2) coincides with the set of nodes from which e_1 is accessible (resp. accessible from e_2).

if $(e_1, e_2) \notin w$ **and** $(e_2, e_1) \notin w$ **then**
　　$w \leftarrow w \cup \{(e_1, e_2)\}$

put in $I\_Pred(e_1)$ the predecessors of e_1
put in $I\_Succ(e_2)$ the successors of e_2
for each $e' \in I\_Pred(e_1)$ **do**
      for each $e'' \in I\_Succ(e_2)$ **do**
          if $(e', e'') \notin w$ **then** $w \leftarrow w \cup \{(e', e'')\}$

At query time, for every property p, the algorithm retrieves as *MVIs* for p the p-edges of w.

The proposed strategy is *complete*: if $p(e_1, e_2)$ is an *MVI*, then, by definition, e_1 initiates p, e_2 terminates p, and e_1 precedes e_2; hence, the interval (e_1, e_2) is selected as an *MVI* for the property p. Unfortunately, it is immediate to show that such a strategy is *not sound*. Consider the following scenario, where p and q are incompatible properties:

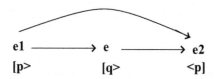

$p(e_1, e_2)$ is not an *MVI* for p, since e interrupts the validity of p over (e_1, e_2). However, since there is an edge from e_1 to e_2, $p(e_1, e_2)$ is retrieved as an *MVI* for p.

3.2   A sound and complete generate-only strategy

In this section, we pair the notions of transitive closure and reduction to obtain a sound and complete algorithm for *MVIs* computation in *EC*. Let $\mathcal{H}$ be an *EC*-structure, w be the transitive closure of a knowledge state o, and (e_1, e_2) be an ordered pair of events. The addition of (e_1, e_2) to w is dealt with as follows (update processing):

1. if $(e_1, e_2) \notin w$ and $(e_2, e_1) \notin w$, then w is replaced by $w \uparrow (e_1, e_2)$;
2. for every property $p \in P$, the subgraph w_p induced by the set of events affecting p, that is, the events that initiate or terminate either p or a property incompatible with p, is extracted from $w \uparrow (e_1, e_2)$;
3. for every property $p \in P$, the transitive reduction w_p^- of the graph w_p is computed by using one of the standard algorithms, e.g. [5, 9].

The set of *MVIs* for p includes all and only the p-edges of w_p^-. Hence, for every property p, query processing reduces to the retrieval of the p-edges of w_p^-.

$MVI \leftarrow \emptyset$
for each $p \in P$ **do**
      for each $(e_1, e_2) \in w_p^-$ **do**
          if $e_1 \in [p\rangle$ **and** $e_2 \in \langle p]$ **then** $MVI \leftarrow MVI \cup \{p(e_1, e_2)\}$
return MVI

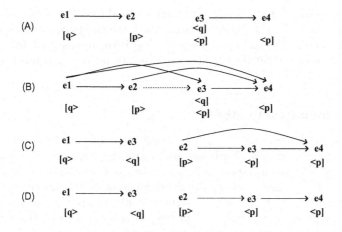

Fig. 3.1. *MVI*s computation using the proposed generate-only strategy

An example of *MVI*s computation using the proposed generate-only strategy is given in Figure 3.1. Let the initial situation be that depicted in Figure 3.1 - A, where p and q are two compatible properties. Once the edge (e_2, e_3) is entered, the transitive closure of the resulting graph is computed (cf. Figure 3.1 - B). Then, the subgraphs induced by the events that respectively affect q and p are extracted from the original graph (the two resulting subgraphs are described in Figure 3.1 - C). Finally, the transitive reductions w_q^- and w_p^- are computed (cf. Figure 3.1 - D). At query time, $q(e_1, e_3)$ and $p(e_2, e_3)$ are returned as *MVI*s for q and p, respectively.

Theorem 7. *The proposed generate-only strategy for* MVI*s computation is sound and complete with respect to the given semantics of* EC.

Proof. Let $\mathcal{H} = (E, P, [\cdot\rangle, \langle\cdot],]\cdot, \cdot[)$ be an *EC*-structure and w be the transitive closure of a knowledge state o. To prove that the proposed strategy is sound, we must show that if (e_1, e_2) is a p-edge of w_p^-, then $p(e_1, e_2)$ is an *MVI* for p with respect to w and $\mathcal{H}$. The proof is by contradiction. If $p(e_1, e_2)$ is not an *MVI*, then one of the following propositions must hold: e_1 does not initiate p, e_2 does not terminate p, $(e_1, e_2) \notin w$, or there exists an interrupting event e for p that occurs between e_1 and e_2. If e_1 does not initiate p or e_2 does not terminate p, then (e_1, e_2) is not a p-edge. If $(e_1, e_2) \notin w$, then $(e_1, e_2) \notin w_p^-$, since $w_p^- \subseteq w$, and thus (e_1, e_2) is not a p-edge of w_p^-. Finally, if there exists an interrupting event e for p such that both $(e_1, e) \in w$ and $(e, e_2) \in w$, then there exist a path $e_1 \rightsquigarrow e$ and a path $e \rightsquigarrow e_2$ in w_p^-. Hence, the edge (e_1, e_2) is a transitive one, and thus it does not belong to w_p^-. This allows us to conclude that (e_1, e_2) is not a p-edge of w_p^-.

To prove that the proposed strategy is complete, we must show that if $p(e_1, e_2)$ is an *MVI* for p with respect to w and $\mathcal{H}$, then (e_1, e_2) is a p-edge of w_p^-. By hypothesis, e_1 initiates p, e_2 terminates p, and $(e_1, e_2) \in w$. It follows that (e_1, e_2) is a p-edge of w_p. Moreover, since there are no interrupting events for p that occur between e_1 and e_2, the edge (e_1, e_2) is the unique path from e_1 to e_2 in w_p. This implies that the edge (e_1, e_2) is not transitive, and thus it is a p-edge of w_p^-.   □

3.3   The generalization to MEC

Given an EC-structure $\mathcal{H} = (E, P, [\cdot\rangle, \langle\cdot],]\cdot,\cdot[)$ and the transitive closure w of a knowledge state o, two efficient algorithms, that respectively compute the necessary and possible *MVIs* with respect to $\mathcal{H}$ and w, can be obtained by exploiting Proposition 6 taking advantage of the algorithm for basic *MVIs* computation.

We assume P to be lexicographically sorted. As in *EC*, given a pair (e_1, e_2) of events, update processing consists in replacing w with $w \uparrow (e_1, e_2)$. Moreover, for every property p, the set w_p^- is computed and maintained lexicographically sorted (this can be done without any significant increase in complexity). Finally, the sets $C(w)$ and $S(w)$ are obtained as follows. $C(w)$ is computed by selecting all property-labeled pairs of events $p(e', e'')$ such that e' initiates p, e'' terminates p, and neither (e', e'') nor (e'', e') belong to w. The computation of $S(w)$ is more involved. Let $U(w)$ be the subset of $E \times P$ including all and only the pairs (e, p) for which there exists $e' \neq e$ such that e' initiates or terminates either p or a property incompatible with p, and neither (e, e') nor (e', e) belong to w. It is easy to prove that if $(e, p) \in U(w)$, then e can neither initiate nor terminate a □-*MVI* for p. The set $S(w)$ consists of those atomic formulas $p(e_1, e_2)$ such that e_1 initiates p, e_2 terminates p, and neither (e_1, p) nor (e_2, p) belong to $U(w)$. Query processing in *MEC* reduces to the computation of the sets $MVI(w)$, □MVI(w), or ◇MVI(w). The basic steps of $MVI(w)$ computation have been described in Section 3.2. Since both P and w_p^-, for every property p, are sorted, $MVI(w)$ can be sorted without any additional cost. The set □MVI(w) is obtained by intersecting the ordered sets $MVI(w)$ and $S(w)$ by using a simple variant of the algorithm for merging sorted vectors. In a similar way, the set ◇MVI(w) can be obtained as the union of $MVI(w)$ and $C(w)$.

4   Complexity analysis

In this section, we analyze the worst-case computational complexity of the proposed algorithms for update and query processing in *EC* and *MEC*. Given an *EC*-structure $\mathcal{H} = (E, P, [\cdot\rangle, \langle\cdot],]\cdot,\cdot[)$ and a knowledge state o, we determine the complexity of computing the set of *MVIs* with respect to o and $\mathcal{H}$, that is, of determining the set of formulas $p(e_1, e_2)$ such that $w \models p(e_1, e_2)$, by means of the proposed generate-only strategy. We assume that the set of events E can grow arbitrarily, while the set P of relevant properties characterizes the considered application domain and thus it is fixed once and for all. As a consequence, we choose the number n of events in E as the size of $\mathcal{H}$, and consider the number of properties as a constant. We measure the complexity in terms of the size n

of $\mathcal{H}$ and the size m of the knowledge state o, or the size m^- (resp. m^+) of its transitive reduction o^- (resp. closure o^+)[2]. As already pointed out, we assume P to be lexicographically sorted. Furthermore, we assume that the knowledge state o as well as the sets $[p\rangle$ and $\langle p]$, for every property $p \in P$, are (maintained) sorted. Under such assumptions, given an event e and a property p, the tests $e \in [p\rangle$ and $e \in \langle p]$ cost $\mathcal{O}(\log n)$, while given two distinct events e_1 and e_2, the test $(e_1, e_2) \in o$ costs $\mathcal{O}(\log m)$. The test $(e_1, e_2) \in o^+$ can be performed in $\mathcal{O}(m + n)$ by executing a depth-first visit of the subgraph of (E, o) generated by e_1. The overall complexity of the generate-only strategy for $MVIs$ computation in EC is stated by the following theorem.

Theorem 8. *Let $\mathcal{H} = (E, P, [\cdot\rangle, \langle\cdot],]\cdot,\cdot[)$ be an EC-structure, w be the transitive closure of a knowledge state o, and (e_1, e_2) be an ordered pair of events. The complexity of update processing is $\mathcal{O}(n \cdot m^- + n^2 \cdot \log n)$, while the complexity of query processing is $\mathcal{O}(m^- \cdot \log n)$, where m^- is the cardinality of $(w \uparrow (e_1, e_2))^-$.*

Proof. Update processing is performed in three steps. At the first step, EC verifies that neither (e_1, e_2) nor (e_2, e_1) belong to w. If this is the case, it determines the set $\hat{w} = w \uparrow (e_1, e_2)$. Let m^+ be the cardinality of $\hat{w}$. The tests $(e_1, e_2) \notin w$ and $(e_2, e_1) \notin w$ cost $\mathcal{O}(\log m^+)$. The set $\hat{w}$ is computed as follows: first, the edge (e_1, e_2) is added to w; then, for every pair of events $e', e'' \in E$ such that $(e', e_1) \in w$, $(e_2, e'') \in w$, and $(e', e'') \notin w$, the edge (e', e'') is added to $w \cup (e_1, e_2)$. The sets of predecessors and successors of a given node can be computed in $\mathcal{O}(n)$ and have both cardinality $\mathcal{O}(n)$, and the addition of (e', e'') to $w \cup (e_1, e_2)$ (checking whether or not $(e', e'') \in w$) costs $\mathcal{O}(\log m^+)$; hence, the complexity of computing $\hat{w}$ is $\mathcal{O}(n^2 \cdot \log m^+)$. The second step consists in the extraction of $\hat{w}_p$ from $\hat{w}$, for every property p. For every property p, $\hat{w}_p$ contains the edges (e', e'') of $\hat{w}$ such that both e' and e'' affect either p or a property incompatible with p. Since each test costs $\mathcal{O}(\log n)$, this step has complexity $\mathcal{O}(m^+ \cdot \log n)$. The last step is the computation of the transitive reduction $\hat{w}_p^-$, for every property p. Since $\hat{w}_p$ is acyclic, $\hat{w}_p^-$ can be computed in $\mathcal{O}(n \cdot m^-)$. The resulting cost of update processing is thus $\mathcal{O}(n \cdot m^- + m^+ \cdot \log n + n^2 \cdot \log m^+) = \mathcal{O}(n \cdot m^- + n^2 \cdot \log m^+) = \mathcal{O}(n \cdot m^- + n^2 \cdot \log n)$. Query processing consists in picking up, for every property p, the p-edges of $\hat{w}_p^-$. Since the cardinality of $\hat{w}_p^-$ is $\mathcal{O}(m^-)$ and verifying whether or not an edge is a p-edge costs $\mathcal{O}(\log n)$, the complexity of query processing is $\mathcal{O}(m^- \cdot \log n)$. □

The complexities of update and query processing in MEC are given by the following theorem.

Theorem 9. *Let $\mathcal{H} = (E, P, [\cdot\rangle, \langle\cdot],]\cdot,\cdot[)$ be an EC-structure, w be the transitive closure of a knowledge state o, and (e_1, e_2) be an ordered pair of events. As for the computation of necessary and possible MVIs, the complexity of update processing is $\mathcal{O}(n \cdot m^- + n^2 \cdot \log n)$, while the complexity of query processing is $\mathcal{O}(n^2 + m^- \cdot \log n)$, where m^- is the cardinality of $(w \uparrow (e_1, e_2))^-$.* □

---

[2] It is well-known that m, m^-, and m^+ are $\mathcal{O}(n^2)$.

5 Conclusions

In this paper, we have shown how the graph-theoretic notions of transitive closure and reduction of a directed acyclic graph can be successfully exploited to efficiently reason about partially ordered events in EC and MEC. Even though we developed our solution in the context of (Modal) Event Calculus, we expect it to be applicable to any formalism for reasoning about partially ordered events.

The (worst-case) complexities of update and query processing of the standard generate-and-test strategy for EC are $\mathcal{O}(n^2)$ and $\mathcal{O}(n^5)$, respectively. The alternative generate-only strategy we outlined moves computational complexity from query to update processing and features an absolute improvement of performance: the (worst-case) complexities of update and query processing in EC become $\mathcal{O}(n^3)$ and $\mathcal{O}(n^2 \log n)$, respectively. In particular, whenever the size of the transitive reduction is $\mathcal{O}(n)$ (we expect this case to be the most frequent) update and query processing can be performed in $\mathcal{O}(n^2 \cdot \log n)$ and $\mathcal{O}(n \cdot \log n)$, respectively (the factor $\log n$ can actually be eliminated by using suitable hashing techniques).

References

1. I. Cervesato and A. Montanari. A general modal framework for the event calculus and its skeptical and credulous variants. *Journal of Logic Programming*, 38(2):111–164, 1999.
2. D. Chapman. Planning for conjunctive goals. *Artificial Intelligence*, 32:333–377, 1987.
3. L. Chittaro, A. Montanari, and I. Cervesato. Speeding up temporal reasoning by exploiting the notion of kernel of an ordering relation. In *Proc. of the 2nd International Workshop on Temporal Representation and Reasoning — TIME'95*, pages 73–80, Melbourne Beach, FL, 26 April 1995.
4. T. Dean and M. Boddy. Reasoning about partially ordered events. *Artificial Intelligence*, 36:375–399, 1988.
5. A. Goralcikova and V. Koubek. A reduct and closure algorithm for graphs. In *Proc. of the 8th Symposium on Mathematical Foundations of Computer Science. LNCS 74*, pages 301–307, Olomouc, CZ, 1979. Springer.
6. R. Kowalski. Database updates in the event calculus. *Journal of Logic Programming*, 12:121–146, 1992.
7. R. Kowalski and M. Sergot. A logic-based calculus of events. *New Generation Computing*, 4:67–95, 1986.
8. B. Nebel and C. Bäckström. On the computational complexity of temporal projection, planning, and plan validation. *Artificial Intelligence*, 66:125–160, 1994.
9. K. Simon. An improved algorithm for transitive closure on acyclic digraphs. *Theoretical Computer Science*, 58(1-3):325–346, 1988.

TimeNetManager – A Software Tool for Generating Random Temporal Networks

Amedeo Cesta, Angelo Oddi and Angelo Susi

IP-CNR, National Research Council of Italy
{*cesta, oddi, susi*}*@pst.ip.rm.cnr.it*

Abstract. This paper describes a system, named *TimeNetManager* or *TNM*, that generates and manipulates random constraint networks corresponding to the so called Simple Temporal Problem (STP). The software tool satisfies both the requirements to build some common benchmarks useful to compare different research results, and to create a tool for supporting intensive test of new algorithms for temporal constraints management. The paper gives an overview of the functionalities of the software system and describes in detail the random generator able to fast generate sets of temporal networks controlled by a set of macro-parameters that characterize the topology and the temporal flexibility of the networks.

1 Introduction

The problem of a correct experimental evaluation is crucial in several areas of AI research, in particular when a computationally intensive test of specific algorithms is needed. This paper describes a system, named *TimeNetManager*, or *TNM*, that generates and manipulates random constraint networks corresponding to the so called Simple Temporal Problem (STP) defined in [8]. An STP is a constraint network where nodes represent temporal variables and edges represent temporal duration constraints. All constraints are binary (they concern pairs of variables) and the specification of disjunctive constraints between a pair of variables is not allowed.

Our attention to the problem generates from previous work on the synthesis of specialized dynamic algorithms for managing STPs [2, 3]. In that work the need arose for reliable benchmarks, like a library of problems having different characteristics, and some preliminary solutions were given. Such solutions found difficult acceptance for their supposed lack of generality, their limited reproducibility and usability by people different from the authors. In this paper we address the problem of creating a software infrastructure to specifically cope with those limitations. In particular we address the problem of defining a set of random networks according to a number of well designed parameters and their management by a "facilitating" software environment.

When in need of benchmarks two approaches can be followed. A first possibility consists of collecting problems made public by other people (typically on

E. Lamma and P. Mello (Eds.): AI*IA 99, LNAI 1792, pp. 143–154, 2000.

a Web page). This approach, quite common nowadays, is very useful to gather significant examples of real world problems (see for example the "Planning and Scheduling Benchmarks" page [1]). A second possibility is to create random benchmarks. Such a rather different goal, pursued also in this paper, is required in the experimental analysis of algorithms for a well defined research problem, where the need exists of identifying particular structural cases in which one algorithm can be better then another, etc. (see [11, 12] for discussions of several aspects related to the empirical evaluations of algorithms). The generation of random problems is seldom seen in AI as a separate research problem but it is usually described in subparagraphs of papers mostly aimed at presenting technical results about algorithms that solve those random problems. This paper addresses the generation of random STPs as a separate research problem. Such an approach is often followed by the operation research community (see for example [18] for job-shop scheduling or [13] for project scheduling) and is less frequent in AI.

A further question the reader may have is the following "why to address such an effort for the quantitative scheduling problem STP which seems very specific?". The study of the efficiency of STP manipulation is relevant because the management of this temporal problem is the basis of all the approaches to complex scheduling problems [6, 7, 16, 4] not only the ones based on constraint satisfaction. STPs are also concern of attention for the creation of future generation multimedia presentation systems and workflow management tools. It is worth observing that most of the experimental analysis for temporal constraint networks have concerned qualitative constraints (see for example [19, 15]) while no specific work exists for the STPs. It is worth mentioning that some work exists that deals with "general CSP" random generation (see for example [9, 10]).

This paper is organized as follows: Sections 2 shortly introduces the Simple Temporal Problem and the reasoning it requires; Section 3 presents the technical details of the random network generator proposed in this paper; Section 4 describes the general software architecture TNM, its capabilities to offer an experimental workbench and gives some example of randomly generated STPs. Some concluding remarks end the paper.

2   A Basic Definition of STP

The temporal constraint problem named *Simple Temporal Problem (STP)* is defined in [8] and involves a set of integer temporal variables $\{X_1, \ldots, X_n\}$, having convex domains $[lb_i, ub_i]$ and a set of constraints $a \leq X_j - X_i \leq b$, where $b \geq a \geq 0$. A special variable X_0 is added to represent the *Reference-Point* (the beginning of the considered temporal horizon) and its domain is fixed to $[0, 0]$. A solution of the STP is a tuple $(x_1 \ldots x_n)$ such that $x_i \in [lb_i, ub_i]$ and every constraint $a \leq X_j - X_i \leq b$ is satisfied. An STP is *inconsistent* if no solution exists.

---

[1] http://www.neosoft.com/~benchmrx/

A STP can be also represented by a *time-map*. A time-map is defined as a direct graph $TM = \langle V, E, L \rangle$, where V is the set of time points i which represents the variables X_i; E is the set of edges, such that $\langle i, j \rangle \in E$ if the constraint $a \leq X_j - X_i \leq b$ exists; L is a labeling function defined on the set E, such that $L(\langle i, j \rangle) = [a, b]$ for each constraint $a \leq X_j - X_i \leq b$.

2.1 Reasoning Capabilities for an STP

STP networks are used as subcomponents in software systems in several application areas. Such subcomponents can be seen as separate representation and reasoning modules that offer specialized services. An STP stores information about temporal events (time-points) and temporal constraints between events. The possibility may exist of also retracting previous information. In general we can list the main *Tell* and *Ask* primitives of the reasoning service. Among the *Tell* functions of an STP module are the following:

- *Create_time_point* that adds a new time point to the net and links it to the reference-point t_0;
- *Delete_time_point(i)* that deletes the time point specified in the signature of the function;
- *Add_constraint(i, j, [a, b])* that adds the constraint of label $[a, b]$ between time-points i and j;
- *Remove_constraint(i, j, [a, b])* that removes the constraint of label $[a, b]$ between i and j.

Given a certain configuration of a time-map the basic operation is realized by a *propagation function* that computes the domains $[lb_i, ub_i]$ for every time variable i according to the current constraints. The propagation is usually automatically called after any activation of the Tell functions to leave the information on the network in a consistent state (Figure 1 shows an example of time-map where the domains $[lb_i, ub_i]$ have been computed. The boxes labelled "Ref" and "Hor" represent the beginning and end of the temporal horizon).

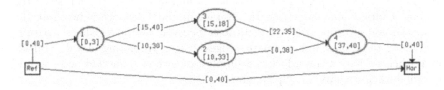

Fig. 1. A propagated time-map

Several *Ask* primitives may be used to extract particular information from a time-map. Two of the more frequent are:

- *time_point_bounds(i)* that returns the bounds associated to a time point i;
- *temporal_distance(i, j)* that returns the interval describing the minimum and maximum distance between the specified time points.

Further primitives can be added for specific tasks according to application requirements. As a service module called into play quite frequently a time-map manager should be rather efficient but addressing this aspect is out of the scope of this paper (for examples of managing algorithms see [8, 2, 3]). We are here interested in two aspects: creating random time-maps as we describe in the next section, and realizing a software environment for easily managing time-maps for different aims as described in Section 4.

3   Generating Random Temporal Networks

In this section we describe the basic ideas followed to generate random temporal networks based on the STP model. The procedure builds temporal networks by using a set of parameters to control the structure of the temporal graphs.

The generation algorithm controls four main graph's characteristics: (1) the number of nodes n, (2) the edges density (also called *connection degree*) D, (3) the *network topology* and (4) the *temporal flexibility*. We believe that by changing these characteristics it is possible to generate a significantly representative subset of all possible STP networks. The proposed procedure is able to generate either a large benchmark set with several levels of difficulty to test the average performance of a reasoning algorithm or to create a particular instance to test such an algorithm in "extreme situations".

The meaning of the first two parameters is straightforward: they determine the number of nodes and edges of the graph. The temporal flexibility is defined as a measure of how the time points can be moved with respect to each other without generating temporal inconsistency. The greater the temporal flexibility, the greater will be the set of the possible solutions of the associated Simple Temporal Problem. As far as the network topology is concerned, we introduce a measure which in practice is the opposite of the definition of *graph diameter* given in [1]. Given a graph G, we consider its undirected version and define the *average minimal diameter* d_m as the average minimal distance between all the couple of nodes in the graph. The distance between two nodes along a path is considered to be the number of path's edges. It is worth noting that d_m is maximal when we have a tree which is a simple sequence of connected nodes and is minimal when we have a complete graph.

The Grid. In order to control both the network topology and the temporal flexibility, we use a reference structure called *grid*. This is a matrix of points with discrete dimensions $T \times P$, (see Figure 2), where the horizontal dimension represents the *time* and the vertical one represents a quantity called *degree of parallelism* which intuitively represents the maximum number of contemporaneous events (time points) in the same time period.

The basic idea is to randomly map the set V of time points on the set of grid points, in this way we fix the average position of all the time points along the time (hence the number of grid points is always greater or equal of the number of graph's nodes n). The random mapping is controlled by two parameters: the *grid ratio* α and the *grid density* β. The first one is the ratio between the dimensions of the grid $\alpha = P/T$ and is one of the basic parameters to control the *average minimal diameter* d_m of the random graph. The second parameters gives the ratio between the number of grid points and the number of nodes $|V|$. In this case the greater β the greater will be the probability of a large scattering of the time points over the time line.

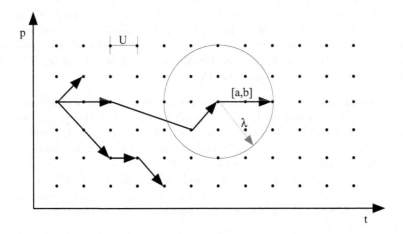

Fig. 2. The grid

The other aspect to control is the temporal flexibility (and also the consistency of the network). As we know, each edge (i, j) represents a temporal constraint between the time points i and j that describes the minimum and the maximum temporal distance between them. The generator randomly produces a set of intervals $[a, b]$ that represents a set of consistent temporal constraints. To this aim we use the metric defined on the grid to generate consistent constraints. That is, we select an interval which contains the distance between i and j computed on the horizontal dimension of the grid. In addition, in order to control the amplitude of the interval (which is directly related to the temporal flexibility) we introduce two real and nonnegative slack parameters S_{min} and S_{max}. The actual generation algorithm can produce only sets of consistent constraints; we are now modifying it for producing also inconsistent time networks.

3.1   The Generation Procedure

The algorithm is shown in Figure 3. It takes as input the parameters n, α, β, D, S_{min}, S_{max} and U and produces a temporal network $TN = \langle V, E, L \rangle$. The algorithm can be divided in three main blocks (or phases): *initialization* (Steps 1-3), *tree generation* (Steps 4-11) and *graph completion* (Steps 12-22).

Initialization. During the *initialization* phase the random mapping is realized between the set of nodes V and the set of points in the grid (Step 1). At Step 2 the neighborhood sets N_i of each time points i are initialized with a set of time points N_i^o. The definition of these sets is related to the grid. In fact, for each node $i \in V$ mapped on the grid, we find a "circular area", with i in the center and having a radius λ, called the *locality*. Here the idea is that it is possible to put only edges (i, j) with $j \in N_i$; λ is defined as the minimum value, such that, the set of nodes contained in the neighborhoods N_i is enough to build a graph of density D. Hence, with regard to the value α and a fixed (and low) value of the edge density D, the smaller the value α, the greater will be the average minimal diameter d_m of the generated graph. Finally at Step 3, a variable F_T (fathers set) is initialized which is used during the *tree generation* phase.

Tree Generation. In order to guarantee the connectivity of the final time map TN, a tree is created and used as basic graph for the completion phase. Steps 4 to 11 implement a quite simple idea. A set F_T (initialized to the origin time point 0), contains the set of nodes currently included in the tree. A father node i and a child node are randomly selected respectively from sets F_T and $N_i \setminus F_T$; hence an edge (i, j) is posted between the nodes i and j with a label $[a, b]$. After that, the node i is included in the set F_T (i becomes a father) and the neighborhoods N_i and N_j are updated. The previous steps continue until a random tree connects the set of nodes V.

It is worth observing the difference between the selection of a child or a father node. The first one is randomly selected with respect to a uniform probability distribution ($Rnd\_Selection()$). The second one is selected by using a dynamic probability distribution ($Tree\_Rnd\_Selection()$) which assigns to each node a variable probability in a way that the more often a point has been involved in a selection as a father the smaller is the probability for it to be selected.

The function $Add\_Constraint(i, j)$ is used to add a labeled edge to the graph. We use two values of time slacks, S_{min} and S_{max}, to generate a random label $[a, b]$ that contains the distance d_{ij} along the grid time line. The distance d_{ij} is computed as $d_{ij} = U|t_j - t_i|$. The edge is always posted according to increasing temporal order. U is an input parameter that gives the number of temporal units per each grid interval and t_j and t_i are the projection of the grid points on the time axis. Hence, the label $[a, b]$ (that contains the distance d_{ij}) are computed as $a = max\{0, \lceil d_{ij}(1 - S_{min}r) \rceil\}$ and $b = \lfloor d_{ij}(1 + S_{max}r) \rfloor$, where r is random number in the interval $[0, 1]$. In the special case of two points selected on the same column of the grid ($d_{ij} = 0$), a specific random function adds either the label $[0, \infty]$ (simple precedence constraint) or the label $[0, 0]$ with equal probability.

INPUT: $n, \alpha, \beta, D, S_{min}, S_{max}, U$
OUTPUT: $TN = \langle V, E, L \rangle$

1. $Rnd\_Mapping(V)$
2. $N_i \leftarrow N_i^o$ (for $i = 1 \ldots n$)
3. $F_T \leftarrow \{0\}$

4.   **for** $k = 1$ **to** $(n - 1)$ **do begin**
5. $i \leftarrow Tree\_Rnd\_Selection(F_T)$
6. $j \leftarrow Rnd\_Selection(N_i \setminus F_T)$
7. $F_T \leftarrow F_T \cup \{j\}$
8. $Add\_Constraint(i, j)$
9. $N_i \leftarrow N_i \setminus \{j\}$
10. $N_j \leftarrow N_j \setminus \{i\}$
11.   **end**

12.   **while** $(Current\_Density(TN) < D)$ **do begin**
13.   **if** $(\exists N_i \neq \emptyset)$
14.   **then begin**
15. $i \leftarrow Rnd\_Selection(\{k \,|\, N_k \neq \emptyset\})$
16. $j \leftarrow Rnd\_Selection(N_i)$
17. $Add\_Constraint(i, j)$
18. $N_i \leftarrow N_i \setminus \{j\}$
19. $N_j \leftarrow N_j \setminus \{i\}$
20.   **end**
21.   **else** $N_i \leftarrow Ns\_Updating(N_i)$ (for $i = 1 \ldots n$)
22.   **end**

Fig. 3. Generation Algorithm

Graph Completion. In the last phase other edges are added to the graph until the density D is reached. The algorithm proceeds similarly to the tree generation phase with two notable differences. First, we use only uniform probability distribution to make random selections. Second, we have to consider the possibility that all the neighborhood sets became empty and at the same time the value of edges density D is not reached. This is possible, because at Step 2 we generate the sets N_i^o with respect to an estimation of the locality λ. At Step 13 we check if at least a neighborhood is not empty, if not we update the locality to a larger value such that at least one neighborhood N_i becomes not empty (Step 21); otherwise we insert edges as previously explained.

4   The TNM Software Architecture

To exploit the capabilities of the time-map generator we have inserted it in a software tool that allows a flexible interaction between a user, an STP reasoning system and the random generator. The software environment TNM has been designed as a building block for two main goals:

 – experimental comparative testing of algorithms;
 – intensive debugging of time-map reasoning systems.

It turns out that the system we have built is very useful to be used also as a
didactic tool to describe a quantitative constraint manager based on STP.

The architecture of TNM is shown in Figure 4. We can see the three basic
modules: (1) the TN Generator (TN-G) that is responsible for creating random
networks according to the previous description; (2) a TN Representation and
Reasoning Module (TN-RR) that gives the basic service of constraint management; (3) a TN Interaction Module that allows a user to interact and use all
the features of the two basic modules. In the figure dashed lines remark that
two components can be substituted by or integrated with others. In particular
the software architecture is designed to allow the use of different TN-RR modules. We have built the TNM system for the aim of testing the efficiency of the
time-map manager of the scheduling architecture O-OSCAR [5] but the careful
object-oriented design allows the easy integration of a different representation
module and/or of new management algorithms. A further aspect considered as
"TNM independent" is the visualization of the time-map. As well known graph
drawing is a research topic *per se*, so we are using for this task a public domain
system VCG [17] [2] that guarantees quite an amount of useful features. The whole
TNM is implemented in C++, the graphical user interface has been developed
using the Amulet toolkit [14] [3].

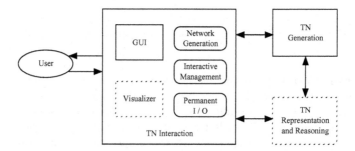

Fig. 4. Overview of the software architecture

4.1   The TNM Interaction Services

As depicted in Figure 4 the TNM Interaction Module (TN-IM) is composed by
a graphical user interface (GUI) that allows to call the visualizer and to interact
with three specific groups of functionalities:

---

[2] http://www.cs.uni-sb.de/RW/users/sander/html/gsvcg1.html

[3] http://www.cs.cmu.edu/afs/cs/project/amulet/www/amulet-home.html

- *Network Generation* is the modality that allows to interact with TN-G to produce sets of random networks giving in input a set of appropriate parameters as previously described;
- *Interaction Manager* allows the user to directly manipulate a time-map executing single Tell or Ask functions towards the TN-RR. In this way it is possible to either modify a pre-existent random network, or specify a network step by step from scratch. This functionality is particularly useful while debugging new reasoning modules because it allows the user to execute particular operations on the network after inspecting the visualization of the network for example.
- *Permanent I/O* allows to load and save in several file formats the networks and their characteristics. The possibility is included to produce files readable from a graph visualizer. This modality is deeply used to reproduce experiments because allows to save whole networks, the random seeds, etc.

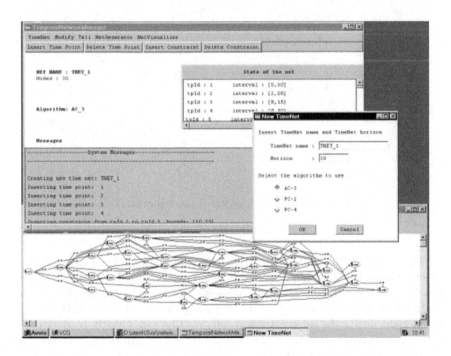

Fig. 5. Typical screen of TNM in operation

Figure 5 shows a dump screen of TNM at work. It is possible to recognize: the general menu bar that allow the selection of basic functionalities and/or interaction modalities; a specialized menu-bar of the Interaction Manager that allows to perform the basic Tell functions specified above on a give time-map (visualized in the background). It is to be noted the constant possibility of naming and saving a current network, of choosing particular propagation algorithms to be used, of inspecting single aspects of the active network, etc.

4.2   Using the Random Network Generation

We now show examples of the ability of TN-G at creating time-maps of different shapes. In Figure 6 we have omitted from the drawing the information of distances because we aim at showing the possibility of producing different topologies.

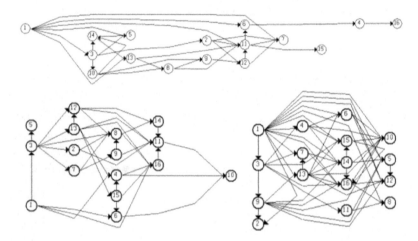

Fig. 6. Examples of generated random networks

The graph in the first row of the figure is an example of network "almost serial and loosely connected" and has been produced with the parameters $\langle \alpha = 0.33, \beta = 3.5, D = 0.18 \rangle$. In the left of the second row a graph is shown "parallel and loosely connected" with the parameters $\langle \alpha = 1, \beta = 3.5, D = 0.18 \rangle$. In the right side of the second row a graph "parallel and strongly connected" is shown (generation parameters: $\langle \alpha = 1, \beta = 4, D = 0.4 \rangle$). All the networks in the examples have 16 time-points.

It is not possible here to show the effectiveness of the work performed by the generation algorithm in deciding random durations, we just report the fact that first experimentation we are performing is quite satisfactory.

It is worth noting that TN-G opens the possibility to create a number of random network with similar parameters and all different on a random basis, and also the possibility of creating benchmarks with and equilibrate presence of networks of different shape.

By using a TN-IM dialogue window it is possible to ask for the creation of a set of random problems within certain generation parameters, set a name to each of them and store them on separate directories. It is alternatively possible to create a random temporal network for immediate use in the TN-RR and the subsequent store of it.

5 Conclusions

This paper has addressed the problem of producing random STP networks for experimental analysis of STP reasoning functionalities. This is motivated from one side by the need to build some common benchmarks to compare different results as in other research fields like scheduling; from the other by the need to produce tools for doing tests during the development of new algorithms for temporal constraints managing. We have developed a software tool called *Temporal Networks Manager* (TNM) that can satisfies both this requirements. The system has a temporal network generator that allows the user to fast generate sets of random temporal networks controlling this process through a set of macroscopic parameters that characterize the topology and the temporal flexibility of the networks. This way is possible to produce collections of networks for testing the algorithms used in the temporal representation managing. The system also allows the user to manually modify these networks or to produce from scratch other networks with particular properties, useful to tests the algorithms in critical situations. It is possible to interact with the system trough graphical user interface that allows to load, save, generate and edit the networks. The system has a modular design and this made easy to expand or modify single parts of it. In particular it is possible to redefine the temporal representation module allowing the user to put its own representation of temporal domains in the system only respecting the predefined interface between modules.

Acknowledgments

Thanks to the AI*IA reviewers for their detailed comments. This research has been developed in the framework of the project "A toolkit for the synthesis of interactive planners for complex space systems" supported by ASI (Italian Space Agency).

References

1. B. Bollobás. *Random Graphs*. Academic Press, 1985.
2. R. Cervoni, A. Cesta, and A. Oddi. Managing Dynamic Temporal Constraint Networks. In *Artificial Intelligence Planning Systems: Proceedings of the Second International Conference (AIPS-94)*, 1994.
3. A. Cesta and A. Oddi. Gaining Efficiency and Flexibility in the Simple Temporal Problem. In *Proceedings of the Third International Workshop on Temporal Representation and Reasoning (TIME-96)*, 1996.

4. A. Cesta, A. Oddi, and S.F. Smith. An Iterative Sampling Procedure for Resource Constrained Project Scheduling with Time Windows. In *Proceedings of the 16th Int. Joint Conference on Artificial Intelligence (IJCAI-99)*, 1999.

5. A. Cesta, A. Oddi, and A. Susi. O-OSCAR: A Flexible Object-Oriented Architecture for Schedule Management in Space Applications. In *Proceedings of the Fifth International Symposium on Artificial Intelligence, Robotics and Automation in Space (i-SAIRAS-99)*, 1999.

6. C. Cheng and S.F. Smith. Generating Feasible Schedules under Complex Metric Constraints. In *Proceedings 12th National Conference on AI (AAAI-94)*, 1994.

7. B. De Reyck, E. Demeulemeester, and W. Herroelen. Algorithms for Scheduling Projects with Generalized Precedence Relations. In J. Weglarz, editor, *Handbook on Recent Advances in Project Scheduling*. Kluwer, 1998.

8. R. Dechter, I. Meiri, and J. Pearl. Temporal Constraint Networks. *Artificial Intelligence*, 49:61–95, 1991.

9. I.P. Gent, A.S. Grant, E. MacIntyre, P. Prosser, P. Shaw, B. Smith, and T. Walsh. How Not To Do It. Technical Report 97.27, University of Leeds, School of Computer Studies, 1997.

10. I.P. Gent, E. MacIntyre, P. Prosser, B. Smith, and T. Walsh. Random Constraint Satisfaction: Flaws and Structure. Technical Report 98.23, University of Leeds, School of Computer Studies, 1998.

11. J.N. Hooker. Needed: An Empirical Science of Algorithms. *Operations Research*, 42:201–212, 1994.

12. J.N. Hooker. Testing Heuristics: We Have It All Wrong. *Journal of Heuristics*, 1:33–42, 1996.

13. R. Kolish, A. Sprecher, and A. Drexl. A Characterization and Generation of a General Class of Resource-Constrained Project Scheduling Problems. *Management Science*, 41:1693–1703, 1995.

14. B. A. Myers, R. G. McDaniel, R. C. Miller, A. Ferrency, A. Faulring, B. D. Kyle, A. Mickish, A. Klimovitski, and P. Doane. The Amulet Environment: New Models for Effective User Interface Software Development. *IEEE Transactions on Software Engineering*, 23:347–365, 1997.

15. B. Nebel. Solving Hard Qualitative Temporal Reasoning Problems: Evaluating the Efficiency of Using the ORD-Horn Class. *Constraints*, 1(3):175–190, 1997.

16. W.P.M. Nuijten and C. Le Pape. Constraint-Based Job Shop Scheduling with ILOG-SCHEDULER. *Journal of Heuristics*, 3:271–286, 1998.

17. G. Sander. Graph Layout through the VCG Tool. In R. Tamassia and I. G. Tollis, editors, *Graph Drawing, DIMACS International Workshop GD'94, Proceedings*, pages 194–205. Lecture Notes in Computer Science 894, Springer Verlag, 1995.

18. E. Taillard. Benchmarks for Basic Scheduling Problems. *European Journal of Operational Research*, 64:278–285, 1993.

19. P. van Beek and D. W. Manchak. The Design and Experimental Analysis of Algorithms for Temporal Reasoning. *Journal of Artificial Intelligence Research*, 4:1–18, 1996.

A fuzzy extension of Allen's Interval Algebra

S. Badaloni[1], M. Giacomin[2]

(1) Dept. of Electronics and Computer Science
Via Gradenigo 6A - 35100 Padova - Italy
(2) DEA - University of Brescia
via Branze 38, 25123 Brescia, Italy
email: badaloni@ladseb.pd.cnr.it, giacomin@ing.unibs.it

Abstract. The aim of this work is to integrate the ideas of flexibility and uncertainty into Allen's interval-based temporal logic [1], defining a new formalism which extends classical Interval Algebra (IA). Some results obtained in the framework of Fuzzy Constraint Satisfaction Problem (FCSP) approach [3] are used in the specific domain of temporal reasoning. A new fuzzy interval algebra IA^{fuz} is defined. Classical concepts of consistency and minimality are generalized to deal with IA^{fuz}. Path-consistency and branch & bound algorithms are shown. A tractable sub-algebra of IA^{fuz} is defined.

1 Introduction

Allen's Interval Algebra relies on the framework of Constraint Satisfaction Problem (CSP), from which it inherits two fundamental limitations, as pointed out in [3, 9]:

1. Constraints (including temporal constraints) in real world problems are seldom hard and CSPs are often idealizations that do not account for preference among feasible solutions.
2. As pointed out in [9], there is a weak representation of uncertainty. A constraint between two intervals is a set of atomic relations which can hold between them. It is impossible to express more refined knowledge regarding the priority of the constraints that have to be satisfied or about the uncertainty affecting them. In real situations the presence of some constraints may be uncertain, depending for example on the environmental conditions, but we could have some idea of their degree of "plausibility"; this kind of knowledge cannot be expressed in Interval Algebra.

The aim of this work is to integrate the ideas of flexibility and uncertainty into Allen's interval-based temporal logic, defining a new formalism which extends classical Interval Algebra (IA). Possibility theory offers a rich and powerful setting for the representation and treatment of the time information pervaded with imprecision and uncertainty. Compared to the probabilistic representations which are intrinsically quantitative, the possibilistic approach is likely to be more robust to imprecision of parameters because, being an ordinal model [2], it offers

E. Lamma and P. Mello (Eds.): AI*IA 99, LNAI 1792, pp. 155–165, 2000.
© Springer-Verlag Berlin Heidelberg 2000

a more qualitative representation of knowledge.

The imprecision and vagueness which are inherent in almost all problem domains can be represented in the framework of Fuzzy Constraint Satisfaction Problem (FCSP) [3] in which constraints are satisfied to a degree, rather than satisfied or not satisfied, and the acceptability of a potential solution becomes a gradual notion. FCSP has been applied in job-shop scheduling problems to deal with quantitative temporal information [4], but in the present work we focus our attention exclusively on representing the qualitative aspect of temporal knowledge in a qualitative temporal reasoner, as a first step to developing a possibilistic planning system.

Two notions of flexible constraints are introduced in the temporal framework:

- soft constraint which enables us to express preferences among solutions;
- prioritized constraint which indicates how essential it is that a constraint be satisfied; thus, less important constraints can be automatically discarded on the basis of their priority weights.

2   The Fuzzy Interval Algebra

The relations of Allen's Interval Algebra are qualitative, expressed as disjunctions of the thirteen atomic relations of Figure 1. The corresponding Interval Algebra can be viewed as a special case of CSP, since an interval can be interpreted as an element of $\mathcal{R}^2$ and a relation between a pair of intervals as a subset of $\mathcal{R}^2 \times \mathcal{R}^2$. In order to relax the definition of such constraints, we make this subset fuzzy, assigning a preference degree α_i to every atomic relation rel_i. According to the definition of "soft constraint" given in [3] as that constraint which directly expresses preferences among solutions, α_i indicates the degree of preference of the corresponding assignment among the others.

So, we deal with relations between intervals I_1 and I_2 in the form

$$I_1(rel_1[\alpha_1], rel_2[\alpha_2]\ldots)I_2 \tag{1}$$

where α_i is the preference degree of rel_i ($i = 1, \ldots, 13$), belonging to the interval $[0, 1]$. If α_i belongs to $\{0, 1\}$ we re-obtain the classical framework.

rel		eq	b	a	d	di	o	oi	m	mi	s	si	f	fi
rel^{-1}		eq	a	b	di	d	oi	o	mi	m	si	s	fi	f

Fig. 1. Allen's atomic relations and their inverse

An atomic relation with a degree α is a fuzzy subset of $\mathcal{R}^2 \times \mathcal{R}^2$ defined as follows: those pairs of intervals which satisfy "classically" the same atomic relation have membership degree α; all the others have membership degree 0.

The semantics of (1) is the relation obtained by the union (or sum) of fuzzy subsets corresponding to every $rel_i[\alpha_i]$. For example, the fuzzy relation

$$I_1(b[0.3], m[0.7])I_2$$

is represented in Figure 2.

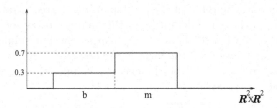

Fig. 2. Example of $\mathrm{IA}^{\mathrm{fuz}}$ relation.

Thus interval algebra has been extended to a new fuzzy algebra. We call it $\mathrm{IA}^{\mathrm{fuz}}$ and define it as follows:

$\mathrm{IA}^{\mathrm{fuz}}$ is defined on the set

$$I = \{b[\alpha_1], a[\alpha_2], m[\alpha_3], mi[\alpha_4], d[\alpha_5], di[\alpha_6], o[\alpha_7],$$
$$oi[\alpha_8], s[\alpha_9], si[\alpha_{10}], f[\alpha_{11}], fi[\alpha_{12}], eq[\alpha_{13}]\}$$
$$\text{where } \alpha_i \in [0,1], \alpha_i \in \mathcal{R}, i = 1, \ldots, 13$$

This set is closed under the following operations [8]:
1. Inverse
2. Conjunctive Combination
3. Composition

In the following, if $\alpha_i = 0$ then rel_i will be omitted, while $rel_i[1]$ will be equivalent to rel_i.

The operations between relations have been obtained from the classical ones by generalization. In particular, given the relation $R = (rel_1[\alpha_1], \ldots, rel_{13}[\alpha_{13}])$, we define the unary operator of *inversion* R^{-1} as

$$R^{-1} = (rel_1{}^{-1}[\alpha_1], \ldots, rel_{13}{}^{-1}[\alpha_{13}]) \tag{2}$$

where $rel_i{}^{-1}$ is defined as in Figure 1, e.g., the constraint $I_1(b[0.3], m[0.5])I_2$ is equivalent to $I_2(a[0.3], mi[0.5])I_1$.

Given any two relations R' and R'', where $R' = (rel_1[\alpha'_1], \ldots, rel_{13}[\alpha'_{13}])$ and $R'' = (rel_1[\alpha''_1], \ldots, rel_{13}[\alpha''_{13}])$, we define the *conjunctive combination* $R = R' \otimes R''$ as

$$R = (rel_1[\alpha_1], \ldots, rel_{13}[\alpha_{13}]) \quad \alpha_i = \min\{\alpha'_i, \alpha''_i\} \, i \in \{1, \ldots, 13\} \tag{3}$$

It assigns to every atomic relation the corresponding degree of satisfaction of both R' and R'', according to the usual definition of the intersection of fuzzy sets.

Given any two relations R' and R'', we define the *disjunctive combination* (or sum) $R = R' \oplus R''$ as

$$R = (rel_1[\alpha_1], \ldots, rel_{13}[\alpha_{13}]) \ \alpha_i = \max\{\alpha'_i, \alpha''_i\} \ i \in \{1, \ldots, 13\} \qquad (4)$$

It assigns to every atomic relation the corresponding degree of satisfaction of R' or R'', according to the usual definition of the union of fuzzy sets.

We start the extension of classical *composition* by first supposing that R_{ik} and R_{kj} are atomic relations of the form $R_{ik} = (rel_1[\alpha_1])$, $R_{kj} = (rel_2[\alpha_2])$. Let $rel_1 \circ rel_2 = (rel'_1, rel'_2, \ldots, rel'_l)$ be the classical composition, as defined by the transitivity table. Composition is defined as [8]

$$R_{ik} \circ R_{kj} = rel_1[\alpha_1] \circ rel_2[\alpha_2] \quad = \quad (rel'_1[\alpha], rel'_2[\alpha], \ldots, rel'_l[\alpha])$$
$$\text{where } \alpha = \min\{\alpha_1, \alpha_2\} \qquad (5)$$

For example, if $R_{ik} = o[0.5]$ and $R_{kj} = b[0.9]$ then $R_{ik} \circ R_{kj} = b[0.5]$. In the case of non-atomic relations, we can use distributivity of composition on the sum. For example, consider the constraints $I_i R_{ij} I_j$ and $I_j R_{jk} I_k$, where $R_{ij} = (o[0.5], m[0.7])$ and $R_{jk} = b[0.9]$. As shown in Figure 3, I_i is before I_k, otherwise R_{ij} or R_{jk} would be completely violated. Moreover, the greatest degree to which both R_{ij} and R_{jk} can be satisfied if I_i is before I_k is 0.7. In fact, $R_{ij} \circ R_{jk} = (b[0.5] \oplus b[0.7]) = b[0.7]$.

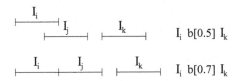

Fig. 3. Example of composition

3   Prioritized Constraints and Uncertainty

In the FCSP framework [3] it is possible to express prioritized constraints. Let's apply this notion to our temporal framework. A priority degree is attached to each temporal constraint, indicating the degree of necessity of its satisfaction.

The temporal constraint

$$C' : I_1(rel_1[\alpha'_1], \ldots, rel_{13}[\alpha'_{13}])I_2 \text{ with priority } \alpha$$

is represented by the relation

$$I_1(rel_1[\alpha_1], \ldots, rel_{13}[\alpha_{13}])I_2 \ \alpha_i = \max(\alpha'_i, 1 - \alpha)$$

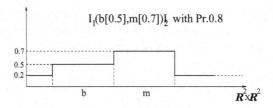

$I_1(b[0.5],m[0.7])$, with Pr.0.8

Fig. 4. Example of prioritized constraint.

An example of prioritized constraint is shown in Figure 4.

By means of prioritized constraints uncertainty can be integrated into our formalism. Suppose that an uncertain IA^{fuz} problem is defined by a set of possible soft constraints

$$C = \{C_1, \ldots, C_m\}$$

where C_i is of the kind $I_{1i}(rel_1[\alpha_{i_1}], rel_2[\alpha_{i_2}], \ldots, rel_{13}[\alpha_{i_{13}}])I_{2i}$

We are not sure about what constraints of C define the real problem, but we have a possibility distribution expressing the "plausibility" that each constraint belongs to it:

$$\Pi_r : C \to [0,1]$$

It can be proved [3] that a solution which maximizes the necessity of satisfying the real problem is a solution of an equivalent problem defined by the constraints of C, with a priority degree attached to every constraint C_i equal to the corresponding plausibility degree $\Pi_r(C_i)$. In our formalism, the equivalent IA^{fuz} problem is defined by the constraints

$$C_i' : I_{1i}(rel_1[\alpha_{i_1}'], rel_2[\alpha_{i_2}'] \ldots, rel_{13}[\alpha_{i_{13}}'])I_{2i}$$
$$\alpha_{i_j}' = \max\{\alpha_{i_j}, 1 - \Pi_r(C_i)\} \ j = 1, \ldots, 13$$

4   Path consistency and minimality

The classical concepts of consistency and minimality of an interval-based network have been extended in order to deal with IA^{fuz} networks [8], where nodes represent intervals, and arcs are labelled with IA^{fuz} relations.

In classical IA networks an assignment is locally consistent if it satisfies all the constraints involved in the relative subnetwork and if it is consistent (i.e. there exists an interval for each node involved which satisfies the chosen atomic relations). In our framework local consistency is graded, expressed by a degree of satisfaction of the soft constraints involved in the sub-network. We define the *degree of local consistency* of an assignment as follows:

1. If the assignment is inconsistent then this degree is equal to 0;
2. otherwise, it is equal to the preference degree of the least satisfied constraint.

For example, the assignment $(I_1 m I_2, I_2 m I_3, I_1 b I_3)$ for the subnetwork of Figure 5 has a degree of local consistency 0.5, while the assignment $(I_1 m I_2, I_2 m I_3, I_1 m I_3)$ has a degree 0, as it is classically inconsistent.

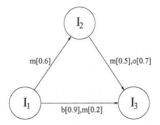

Fig. 5. Example of IA^{fuz} network.

Following the ideas of Dubois et al. [3], we define the *degree of global consistency* of an assignment as the highest degree of local consistency through which it can be extended to a complete labelling of the whole network. A complete assignment of the network is a *solution* if its degree of global consistency, in this case equal to the degree of local consistency, is not null. Solutions with the maximum degree of global consistency are said to be optimal, and this degree is called the *problem consistency*.

An IA^{fuz} network is called *k-consistent* if and only if, for every set of $k-1$ nodes, every assignment with a degree of local consistency α is extensible to any other k-th variable maintaining the same degree α.

A network is path consistent if it is 3-consistent. For example, the network of Figure 5 is not path-consistent: if we consider the relation $I_1 m I_3$ no solution exists. Furthermore, the assignment $I_1 b I_3$ can be extended to a global assignment with degree at most 0.6. Notice that the composition of R_{12} and R_{23} is exactly $b[0.6]$.

A network is *minimal* if and only if, for every relation R_{ij} between a pair of intervals (I_i, I_j), $\forall rel_k[\alpha] \in R_{ij}$ there is a "classical" consistent instantiation of the whole network, such that $R_{ij} = rel_k$, with a degree of satisfaction equal to α.

5   Algorithms

We develop a path-consistency algorithm, starting from the basic one proposed by van Beek and Manchak [12], where transitivity rules are applied to determine more explicit constraints, and a list L is used to maintain the edges that are modified and can further constrain other relations of the network. If an edge is not labelled it is considered equal to I (all the 13 atomic relations) and it cannot constrain other relations of the network. So, a first refinement adopted by van Beek and Manchack is to propagate only the constraints whose relations are defined. In the case of IA^{fuz} networks we cannot adopt the same technique, as the not-labelled edges cannot be neglected, but there is a mechanism which upper-bounds problem consistency (as defined in section 4). Let us consider the network (i, j, k) [Figure 6] where α_{ij}^* is the maximum of the preference degrees of edge (i, j) and R_{jk} is undefined. So $R_{ij} \circ R_{jk} = I[\alpha_{ij}^*]$, and the operation $R_{ik} \leftarrow R_{ik} \otimes (R_{ij} \circ R_{jk})$ modifies the preference degrees of R_{ik}, which are truncated to α_{ij}^*. This has an intuitive explanation: path consistency requires that every assignment of R_{ik} could be extended to the 3-subnetwork maintaining its preference degree, but no solution of the subnetwork can have a degreee of satisfaction greater than α_{ij}^*; thus, the preference degrees of (i, k) can be limited to α_{ij}^* achieving path consistency and maintaining the equivalence of the subnetwork.

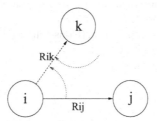

Fig. 6. Transitivity rule with a not-labelled edge.

This suggests that the following upper bound to the problem consistency can be computed:

$$\text{Cons-Sup} = \min_{(i,j)} \{ \alpha^*_{ij} \} \tag{6}$$

During constraint propagation, the value of Cons-Sup is updated and, of course, it can only decrease. Every time Cons-Sup decreases all the preference degrees of every edge can be upper-bounded by its value. In this way a first improvement of the algorithm is obtained. But it is not necessary to scan every edge when Cons-Sup decreases. Only the preference degrees of those edges involved in the current step of the algorithm can be cut to Cons-Sup, if a final truncation of all the degrees of the network is performed in the last step.

We also note that if an edge has all its preference degrees greater than or equal to Cons-Sup it does not modify by propagation any other edge. Taking into account the distributivity property

$$(R_{ij} \otimes I[\alpha]) \circ (R_{jk} \otimes I[\alpha]) = (R_{ij} \circ R_{jk}) \otimes I[\alpha]$$

we obtain the following algorithm, in which every edge is cut to Cons-Sup only in the final step:

PATH-CONSISTENCY
1. $L \leftarrow \{(i,j) \mid 1 \le i < j \le n, \min_{ij}{}^* < \text{Cons-Sup}\ \}$
2. **while** (L is not empty)
3. **do** extract an edge (i,j) from L
4   **if** $\min_{ij}{}^* < \text{Cons-Sup}$
5.   **then for** $k \leftarrow 1 \ldots n,\ k \ne i, k \ne j,\ (j,k) \mid \min_{jk}{}^* < \text{Cons-Sup}$
6.   **do** $t \leftarrow R_{ik} \otimes (R_{ij} \circ R_{jk})$
7.   **if** (t is different from R_{ik} in a degree $< \text{Cons-Sup}$)
8.   **then** $R_{ik} \leftarrow t,\ R_{ki} \leftarrow t^{-1}$
9. $\text{Cons-Sup} \leftarrow \min(\text{Cons-Sup}, \alpha_{ik}{}^*)$
10. $L \leftarrow L \cup \{(i,k)\}$
11.   **for** $k \leftarrow 1 \ldots n, k \ne i \ \text{e} \ k \ne j,\ (k,i) \mid \min_{ki}{}^* < \text{Cons-Sup}$
12.   **do** $t \leftarrow R_{kj} \otimes (R_{ki} \circ R_{ij})$
13.   **if** (t is different from R_{kj} in a degree $< \text{Cons-Sup}$)
14.   **then** $R_{kj} \leftarrow t,\ R_{jk} \leftarrow t^{-1}$
15. $\text{Cons-Sup} \leftarrow \min(\text{Cons-Sup}, \alpha_{kj}{}^*)$
16. $L \leftarrow L \cup \{(k,j)\}$
17. $\forall(i,j),\ R_{ij} \leftarrow R_{ij} \otimes I[\text{Cons-Sup}]$

where n is the number of nodes, $\min_{ij}{}^*$ is the minimum of the preference degrees of the edge (i,j) and $\alpha^*{}_{ij}$ is the maximum.

The classical problem of finding a solution of an IA network corresponds to find an optimal solution of an IA^{fuz} network; so classical backtracking algorithm with incremental path-consistency is generalized to a branch and bound algorithm. Let β_{ij} be a generic atomic relation of the edge (i,j) and $\alpha_{\inf}$ the degree of satisfaction of the current best solution. The basic steps are:

1. Application of the path consistency algorithm; $\alpha_{\inf} = 0$, $\alpha_{\sup} = \text{Cons-Sup}$.
2. If Cons-Sup > 0 (otherwise the problem has no solutions), consider every edge in a fixed order.
3. For every edge (i,j) choose β_{ij} such that $\text{pref}(\beta_{ij}) > \alpha_{\inf}$, set R_{ij} equal to $\beta_{ij}[\text{pref}(\beta_{ij})]$ and apply incremental path consistency.
4. If Cons-Sup $\le \alpha_{\inf}$ then choose another β_{ij} (returning to point 3) or if necessary backtrack to the precedent edge.
5. When the atomic assignment is complete, Cons-Sup gives its degree of satisfaction. If Cons-Sup is strictly greater than $\alpha_{\inf}$, record it as the current best solution, and let $\alpha_{\inf}$ be Cons-Sup. If $\alpha_{\inf}$ has reached $\alpha_{\sup}$ the searching process can be halted.

Notice that in point 3 if there is only one β_{ij} such that $\text{pref}(\beta_{ij}) > \alpha_{\inf}$ then incremental path consistency can be skipped, because it would modify only degrees not greater than $\alpha_{\inf}$.

6   A tractable sub-algebra of IA^{fuz}

It is well known that Allen's Interval Algebra is non-tractable. In particular, the problem of finding a consistent scenario and the problem of computing the minimal network are NP-complete. This issue has been addressed by many authors [7, 11]. One of the possible approaches is to limit the expressive power of the temporal language, restricting it to a subset whose problems are solvable in polynomial time. More specifically, the Path-Consistency algorithm is complete when applied to SA_c networks [13]; a corresponding result can be obtained in our framework too, i.e. a corresponding tractable sub-algebra of IA^{fuz} can be found, which we call SA_c^{fuz} .

We can define a fuzzy point temporal algebra in the same way as IA^{fuz}. We call it PA^{fuz} ; it is defined on the set

$$I = \{< [\alpha_1], = [\alpha_2], > [\alpha_3]\}$$
$$\text{where } \alpha_i \in [0,1], \, \alpha_i \in \mathcal{R}, \, i = 1, 2, 3$$

closed under the operations of Inversion, Conjunctive Combination and Composition.

Some IA^{fuz} relations between intervals can be translated to PA^{fuz} relations between their endpoints, as shown in Figure 7. We call the subset of IA^{fuz} composed by these relations SA^{fuz} .

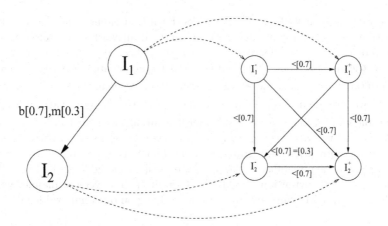

Fig. 7. Translation of a SA^{fuz} relation to a PA^{fuz} relation.

A tractable sub-algebra of PA^{fuz} can be defined in a similar way as PA_c . We call it PA_c^{fuz} and we define it on the set

$$I = \{< [\alpha_1], = [\alpha_2], > [\alpha_3]\}$$
$$\text{where } \alpha_i \in [0,1], \, \alpha_i \in \mathcal{R}, \, i = 1, 2, 3$$
$$\alpha_2 \geq \min\{\alpha_1, \alpha_3\}$$

It can be shown [8] that PA_c^{fuz} is an algebra (i.e. closed under inverse, conjunction and composition), and the proof by van Beek and Cohen about the completeness of Path-Consistency algorithm for PA_c networks [13] can be extended to PA_c^{fuz} networks.

Now let us define SA_c^{fuz} as the subset of IA^{fuz} made up of the relations which can be translated to PA_c^{fuz} relations. SA_c^{fuz} is an algebra and Path-Consistency algorithm achieves minimality when applied to SA_c^{fuz} networks too [8].

7   Conclusions and future work

In this work we have provided an extension of Allen's Interval Algebra in order to take into account the notions of flexibility and uncertainty. We use Possibility Theory because it is a well-suited framework to model qualitative information, and it can be used even if probabilities based on statistical measures are not available. This choice distinguishes our work from all probabilistic approaches, such as [6].

Other works in the literature deal with possibilistic temporal constraints (e.g. [4, 5, 9]). In comparison with them, our approach is focused on the qualitative aspect of temporal knowledge representation, as it does not require any numerical specification. Our approach seems particulary promising for planning applications.

In order to deal with IA^{fuz} networks, Path-Consistency and Backtracking algorithms have been generalized to our fuzzy framework; we observe that if we let all the preference degrees belong to $\{0, 1\}$ these algorithms would be the same as the classical ones, their complexity being augmented at most by a factor equal to the number of the levels of preference used to define the IA^{fuz} network. Finally, we have defined a tractable sub-algebra of IA^{fuz}, and we are addressing the problem of finding the maximal tractable sub-algebras of IA^{fuz}.

As for future work, we are studying how the temporal system could be used in planning applications, integrated in an autonomous robot architecture. Some approaches for a possibilistic planner have been proposed (e.g. [2, 10]), all of them based on an extension of STRIPS. Our aim is to develop a planner which can handle explicitly time and uncertainty, relying on our temporal logic.

8   Acknowledgments

This work has been developed at LADSEB-CNR of Padova. It has been partially funded by the Italian Ministry of University, Science and Technology.

References

1. J.F.Allen *Maintaining Knowledge about temporal intervals* Communication of the ACM, 26(1), pp. 832-843, 1983

2. C.Da Costa Pereira, F.Garcia, J.Lang, R.Martin-Clouaire *Planning with Graded Nondeterministic Actions: A Possibilistic Approach* International Journal of Intelligent Systems, Vol. 12, pp. 935-962, 1997

3. D.Dubois, H.Fargier, H.Prade *Possibility Theory in Constraint Satisfaction Problems: Handling Priority, Preference and Uncertainty* Applied Intelligence 6, pp. 287-309, 1996

4. D.Dubois, H.Fargier, H.Prade *Fuzzy constraints in job-shop scheduling* Journal of intelligent Manufacturing, Vol. 6, pp. 215-235, 1995

5. D.Dubois, H.Prade *Processing Fuzzy Temporal Knowledge* IEEE Trans. on Systems, Man and Cybernetics, Vol. 19, no. 4, pp. 729-743, 1989

6. H.Fargier, J.Lang *Uncertainty in constraint satisfaction problems: a probabilistic approach* Proceedings of ECSQARU 1993, Granada, pp. 97-104, 1993

7. A. Gerevini, L.Schubert *On computing the minimal labels in time point algebra networks* Computational Intelligence, 11 (3), pp. 443-448, 1995

8. M.Giacomin *Estensione Fuzzy di Reti di Vincoli Temporali* Tesi di Laurea dell' Università di Padova, 1998

9. L.Godo, L.Vila *Possibilistic Temporal Reasoning based on Fuzzy Temporal Constraints* Research Report 95/09, IIIA-CSIC, 1995

10. E.Guere, R.Alami A Possibilistic Planner that deals with non-determinism and contingency Proceedings of IJCAI 1999, pp.996-1001, 1999

11. B.Nebel, H.J.Burckert *Reasoning about temporal relations: a maximal tractable subclass of Allen's interval algebra* Journal of the Association for Computing Machinery, 42 (1), pp. 43-66, 1995

12. P.van Beek, D.W. Manchak *The Design and Experimental Analysis of Algorithms for Temporal Reasoning* Journal of Artificial Intelligence Research 4, pp. 1-18, 1996

13. P. van Beek, R. Cohen *Exact and approximate reasoning about temporal relations* Computational Intelligence, 6, pp. 132-144, 1990

Non Binary CSPs and Heuristics for Modeling and Diagnosing Dynamic Systems[*]

Andrea Panati

Dipartimento di Informatica — Università di Torino
Corso Svizzera 185 – 10149 Torino, Italy
E-mail: panati@di.unito.it

Abstract In this paper we concentrate on practical aspects of qualitative modeling and reasoning about physical systems, reporting our experience within the VMBD project[1] in applying Constraint Programming techniques to the task of diagnosing a real-life automotive subsystem.

We propose a layered modeling approach: qualitative deviations equations as a high level model description language, and Constraint Satisfaction Problems (CSPs) with non binary constraints as underlying implementation formalism.

An implementation of qualitative equations systems based on non binary constraints is presented, discussing the applicability of various heuristics. In particular, a greedy heuristic algorithm for cycle cutset decomposition and variable ordering is proposed for efficient reasoning on CSPs derived from qualitative equations.

A prototype implementation of a constraint-based diagnostic engine has been developed using $CLP(FD)$ and C++, and some preliminary results on the proposed modeling approach and heuristics are reported.

Keywords: qualitative modeling, diagnosis, constraint programming heuristics, non-binary constraints.

1   Introduction

In Model-Based Diagnosis there is an increasing interest in the diagnosis of dynamic controlled systems [7, 8] given that most of the technical systems that demand for some form of automated diagnosis share these properties.

In this paper we address the diagnosis task focusing on modeling issues that arise when dealing with continuous dynamic systems, proposing a layered modeling approach: qualitative deviations equations as high level model description language, and Constraint Satisfaction Problems (CSPs) with non binary constraints as underlying formalism for model implementation, supporting Constraint Programming techniques and heuristics for efficient reasoning.

---

[*] Partially supported by the European Commission, DG XII (project BE 95/2128).

[1] VMBD (Vehicle Model-Based Diagnosis) is a Brite-Euram project concerning the application of model-based diagnostic techniques in automotive domains.

E. Lamma and P. Mello (Eds.): AI*IA 99, LNAI 1792, pp. 166–177, 2000.

$\oplus$	-	0	+
-	-	-	-, 0, +
0	-	0	+
+	-, 0, +	+	+

Table1. Qualitative addition.

$\otimes$	-	0	+
-	+	0	-
0	0	0	0
+	-	0	+

Table2. Qualitative multiplication.

The paper is organized as follows. Section 2 introduces the relevant concepts of Qualitative Reasoning. Section 3 discusses why and how CSPs can be an effective framework for qualitative reasoning. Section 4 concerns some CSP-based heuristics and their applicability. In particular, subsection 4.2 presents a cutset reduction heuristic for solving CSPs derived from qualitative equations. In section 5 a layered modeling approach for translating qualitative equations models into CSPs (with associated heuristics) is proposed. In section 6 we apply the modeling methodology and heuristics discussed above to a real-world application studied within the VMBD project, the Common Rail. Some preliminary results and suggestions for future work are provided in section 7.

2   Sign Equations and Qualitative Deviations Modeling

Qualitative Reasoning (QR) about continuous systems requires domain *discretization* over a finite set of values. Many systems described in the QR literature are based on a set of 3 qualitative values $S = \{-, 0, +\}$, which correspond to real number signs. On this set it is possible to define arithmetic operations such as qualitative addition ($\oplus$) and multiplication ($\otimes$), see tables 1 and 2.

2.1   Qualitative Deviation Models

Applying model-based diagnosis to dynamic controlled systems is one of the main focuses of research in the field. In [7], an approach based on qualitative deviations has been introduced. The system is modeled in terms of differential equations that include appropriate *parameters* for components, whose values correspond to different (correct or faulty) *behavior modes* of the component. From these equations, corresponding equations on qualitative deviations are derived as follows:

1. For each variable x, its deviation $\Delta x(t)$ is defined as $\Delta x(t) = x(t) - x_{ref}(t)$, where $x_{ref}(t)$ is a reference behavior;
2. From any equation $A = B$, the deviation equation $\Delta A = \Delta B$ is derived;
3. The corresponding qualitative equation $[\Delta A] = [\Delta B]$ is derived; it equates the signs of the two deviations ([.] is the sign operator).

For an example of model translation, see section 6.2.

This form of qualitative modeling has been chosen for dynamic systems in which some observable variables are varying according to a number of inputs, therefore a *normal range* of values cannot be given. This means that reasoning in terms of absolute values would be very difficult. A main problem in applying this approach is however the choice of the reference behavior. We regard the reference behavior as the evolution of the system when all components are not faulty. As discussed in [8], this choice has strong influences on fault detection.

3 Practical Modeling: From Qualitative Equations to CSPs

In order to implement a qualitative equation system in a language which supports efficient inference methods, there are several choices, see e.g. [1] for a comparison of Integer Linear Programming and Constraint Programming over Finite Domains $(cp(FD))$. In this work, non binary CSPs and $cp(FD)$ have been chosen for several reasons:

- CSPs provide a well-known declarative semantics and expressive power;
- $cp(FD)$ gains expressive power from non binary constraints (also called symbolic constraints) and treats integral constraints in a very efficient way, thus providing efficient support for qualitative abstractions over fixed sets of values (of which sign equations are an instance);
- Constraint Programming provides a well-studied framework for heuristic integration in problem solving, which is particularly necessary when tackling intractable problems (as diagnosis) on real-life instances.

3.1 Qualitative Equations Systems as CSPs

In the following we restrict our attention to qualitative equations systems in which each qualitative equation can be written in the form:

$$s = (f_{11} \otimes \ldots \otimes f_{1k_1}) \oplus \ldots \oplus (f_{p1} \otimes \ldots \otimes f_{pk_p}) \tag{1}$$

where s and f_{ij} are qualitative variables over the sign domain S, and $\oplus$ and $\otimes$ are the qualitative operations discussed above[2]. Qualitative subtraction ($\ominus$) can be trivially defined in terms of qualitative addition, so it can be considered a form of syntactic sugar.

Ternary Constraints Model. Qualitative operators can be seen as ternary relations over S. Observe that even the basic operation of qualitative addition ($\oplus$) is not linear, and the relation is satisfied by 13 combinations of values, out of the 27 possible ones. Then we can expect, in general, that solving CSPs with such kind of constraints would not be "easy". Recent contributions to the field of phase transition [3] show that hardest CSPs are often characterized by constraints being satisfied by about 50% of the possible value assignments. Similar considerations apply for the qualitative multiplication relation.

Operation	Symbol	Constraint	Semantics
Addition	$\oplus$	qadd(X, Y, Z)	$X \oplus Y = Z$
Subtraction	$\ominus$	qdiff(X, Y, Z)	$X \ominus Y = Z$
Multiplication	$\otimes$	qmul(X, Y, Z)	$X \otimes Y = Z$

Table3. Qualitative operations as ternary constraints.

However, this simple approach yields a straightforward implementation of (1) as a CSP with ternary constraints (table 3).

The translation from qualitative equation (1) to a set of ternary constraints on variables over domain S is done as follows:

1. For each term of the form $x \otimes y$, a new variable z and a new constraint $z = x \otimes y$ (i.e. $qmul(x, y, z)$) are added to the model, and z is substituted in the original equation for $x \otimes y$;
2. The above step is repeated until no $\otimes$ operator appear in the equation; the equation now has the form:

$$s = a_1 \oplus \ldots \oplus a_q \qquad (2)$$

3. For each term of the form $x \oplus y$, a new variable z and a new constraint $z = x \oplus y$ (i.e. $qadd(x, y, z)$) are added to the model, and z is substituted for $x \oplus y$;
4. The above step is repeated until no $\oplus$ operator appear in the equation.

As we will discuss in section 5, this translation can be conveniently done automatically.

Higher arity constraints of the form $qsum(Addends, Sum)$ can be used instead of the $qadd$ ternary constraint in order to implement (2):

$$qsum([a_1, \ldots, a_q], s) \qquad (3)$$

Notice that (3) is equivalent to the disjunction of the following 3 constraints:

$$s = \text{'}0\text{'} \wedge atleast(q, [a_1, \ldots, a_q], \text{'}0\text{'})$$
$$s = \text{'}0\text{'} \wedge atleast(1, [a_1, \ldots, a_q], \text{'}+\text{'}) \wedge atleast(1, [a_1, \ldots, a_q], \text{'}-\text{'})$$
$$s \neq \text{'}0\text{'} \wedge atleast(1, [a_1, \ldots, a_q], s)$$

where the constraint $atleast$ has the standard meaning, i.e.:
$atleast(n, [a_1, \ldots, a_q], val)$ is satisfied iff at least n variables a_i have value val.

---

[2] Most considerations are easily extensible to other fixed set of values, given appropriate redefinition of the qualitative operators.

4   Model Solving: Heuristics

The considered qualitative constraints ($qadd$, $qmul$, $qsum$) appear to be "hard" and do not give rise to good propagation inference. This is well-known in qualitative reasoning, since the qualitative abstraction over real numbers introduces a loss of information. For instance, given the constraint $qadd(x, y, z)$ and values for x and y, it is not guaranteed that we can infer a value for z, or even restrict its domain: if $(x = +) \land (y = -) \land z \in \{-, 0, +\}$, we cannot restrict the domain of z after propagating over the $qadd$ constraint.

Considering that real-life models will contain hundreds of such constraints, if we want to solve similar CSPs in an efficient way, we should exploit some structural property of the problem at hand. In the following, we will propose a few heuristics that proved to be effective on the class of CSPs considered here, relying on the structure of the constraint graph.

4.1   Cycle-Cutset Heuristic

In this section we propose the application of a Constraint Programming technique called *cycle cutset* decomposition [5] for solving qualitative equations systems modeled as CSPs, then we motivate this choice, and we show its effectiveness on (a fragment of) a real example.

The basic idea of the *cycle cutset* decomposition technique is the following: any given constraint graph can be made a tree after deleting certain vertices such that all the cycles from the graph are removed. This set of vertices is called the *cycle cutset*. If a small cycle cutset can be (easily) found, than a good heuristic is to first instantiate all the variables in the cycle cutset and then solve the resulting tree-structured CSPs. In fact, it is known from the literature [6] that tree-structured constraint graphs can be efficiently solved without backtracking simply at the cost of achieving arc consistency.[3]

The problem of computing a minimal cycle cutset is however NP-hard. So we can usually conveniently rely on an approximate solution, i.e. on a cycle cutset which is not minimal but can be easily computed. The effectiveness of this heuristic on CSPs derived from qualitative equations systems comes from the following observations:

- In most practical cases, the number of variables appearing in more than one qualitative equation is a small fraction (less than $1/3$) of the total number of variables;
- Each equation of the form (1) (if it does not contain more than one reference to the same variable) gives rise to a tree-structured constraint graph.

Given this last observation and a system of qualitative equations of the form specified in (1), a naive approach for finding a non-minimal cycle cutset is to compute the set C of variables that appear in more than one equation (and thus

---

[3] If the size of a cycle cutset of an n-variables CSP is m, then the original CSP can be solved in $O(d^m + (n - m)d^2)$ steps, where d is the size of the largest domain.

are potentially responsible for introducing cycles in the constraint network). This can be done in linear time and space in the number of variables.

4.2   Greedy Cutset Reduction Heuristic

Variables in C (section 4.1) are good candidates for early labeling. But C may consist of several variables when dealing with complex systems, so we want to:
 – reduce the cardinality of C, but at a low computational cost;
 – label the remaining variables in a "convenient" order.
To address these issues we propose the following cutset-reduction heuristic:

1. Construct the bipartite graph $(E \cup C, A)$. where E is the set of qualitative equations, C is the set of variables which occur in more than one equation (initial cutset, as discussed above), and A is the set of edges representing the relation of "occurrence" of a variable into an equation (fig. 2);
2. Sort nodes in C by decreasing degree (i.e. number of incident arcs), resolving ties with some efficient heuristic such as a fixed ordering[4];
3. Let $C' = \emptyset$ be the reduced cutset we are going to compute, and $X = E$ the set of equations we should check;
4. Until $|C| < 2$ or $|E| < 2$ do:
 – if a node $e \in X$ with $deg(e) < 2$ exists then call $check\_node(e, (E \cup C, A))$;
 – else choose the first node $v \in C$ using the order computed in step 2; let $C' = C' \cup \{v\}$, $X = \{e \in E | (v, e) \in A\}$ (i.e. X is the set of nodes connected to v); delete node v and all the arcs incident on v from the graph;
5. Return C' as reduced cutset.

```
procedure check_node (node e, graph (E ∪ C, A))
      d_e = deg(e)
      if d_e < 2 then
            remove node e from E
            if d_e = 1 then
                  remove arc (e, v) from A
                  check_node (v, (E ∪ C, A))
            endif
      endif
endproc
```

The problem of finding a cycle cutset in the constraint graph reduces to finding a cycle cutset in the bipartite graph $(E \cup C, A)$. Then the algorithm is essentially a greedy heuristic for cycle cutset determination in a bipartite

---

[4] In other words, define a total order $first$ on the set C such that $\forall v_i, v_j \in C :$
$v_i \ first \ v_j \leftrightarrow (deg(v_i) \geq deg(v_j) \vee (deg(v_i) = deg(v_j) \wedge i < j))$, where $deg(v)$ denotes the degree of node v.

graph. Notice that we use the a priori knowledge that all original qualitative equations (and all corresponding sets of constraints in the CSP model) are tree-structured, thus we reason on clusters of constraints (one for each qualitative equation) and not on single constraints; this drastically reduces the complexity of the algorithm. This heuristic reduces the size of the initial cutset, and provides a variable ordering for labeling variables in C' (the order *first*).

The worst case time complexity of the algorithm (which occurs when the bipartite graph is complete) is $O(|C||E|)$, since we consider each node $v \in C$ and then check its adjacent nodes; this requires $O(|E|)$ steps[5]. This is a substantial improvement over cutset decomposition algorithms which operate directly on the constraint graph.

4.3   Heuristics for the qsum Constraint

Sometimes, it is possible to identify "preferred" labelings for variables involved in high arity constraints. In our modeling formalism, variables represent qualitative deviations from their reference values, then some heuristic (i.e. minimal deviation) could be exploited in practical applications.

For instance, in a diagnostic framework, we could require that at most one single fault is present in the system at any given time (or first look for a single fault). This assumption, often useful in order to cope with complexity in diagnostic problem solving, leads to the following heuristic: when checking a constraint of the form (3) to determine if it is consistent with a given fault mode (i.e. a given set of value assignments) first try to satisfy the *qsum* constraint with minimal deviation assignments for variables $a_1, \ldots, a_q$, i.e. value assignments that minimize the objective function $h = \sum_{i=1}^{q} |a_i|$. [6]

The main problem of this kind of heuristics is that they depend on model-specific information, and then they are usually difficult to derive and reuse. For these reasons, we preferred the more general CSP-based heuristics discussed in section 4.2 for our implementations.

5   The Layered Modeling Approach

In our modeling approach, two different modeling languages (abstraction layers) with different objectives are used:

1. The **qualitative equations language**, a very high level formalism, directly related to the mathematical (qualitative) model of the system;
2. The **constraint language**, an implementation framework, which is more adequate for supporting the inferential mechanisms and heuristics.

---

[5] Moreover, $O(|C| \log |C|)$ steps are required for sorting nodes in C; in all practical cases, $\log |C| << |E|$, so this initial cost is negligible.

[6] Of course h can be generalized to embed probabilistic, statistical or structural information through the introduction of appropriate weights w_i.

We claim that this layered modeling approach has great advantages, both for the user and for the developer of the inference engine:

- The user works with a convenient high level language, ignoring the underlaying kind of constraints and heuristics (generated by the translator);
- The translation from qualitative equations to CSPs (described in section 3.1) can be done automatically by an LR parser;
- The translator acts as an additional abstraction, allowing the implementation formalism (kind of constraints, constraint propagators, search algorithms, heuristics) to change without requiring any revision of the higher level model; this allows better model reusability from the user perspective and easier (i.e. cheaper) software evolution from the software developer point of view;
- The translation, as discussed above, is not only a syntactical transformation, it also involves the computation of ad-hoc heuristics which will be exploited by the inference engine (constraint propagator).

6   The Example System

In this section we present a fragment of a case study (a continuous dynamic controlled system studied within the VMBD project) and we apply the modeling methodology and CSP-based heuristics described so far.

6.1   The Common Rail system

The Common Rail is a fuel injection system for diesel engines designed in order to be able to control the injection pressure, as well as injection amount and timing; this allows better engine performance and lower noise and emissions. To this end, pressurized fuel is stored in the rail and its pressure is controlled by an Electronic Control Unit (ECU) through a pressure regulator.

If the rail pressure, measured by the pressure sensor, deviates from the target value, the command to the pressure regulator is varied in order to reduce the difference between the measured pressure and the target value. For a detailed description of the system, including possible recovery actions and diagnostic tests, please refer to [2].

6.2   Common Rail qualitative deviations modeling

Qualitative deviations modeling has been chosen for this system especially because the fuel pressure in the rail is rapidly varying, according to the position of the accelerator pedal and a number of other inputs, therefore a *normal range* of values cannot be given.

The model used for our experiments is shown in the block diagram in figure 1. Some simplifications have been done with respect to a model that would be derived from models of individual components. In particular, the low pressure part of the system has been abstracted to a single component; similarly for the rail and the high pressure pipes. Variable names on the arcs correspond to pairs of interface variables of components, which are imposed to be equal by the connection. Observable variables are in italic.

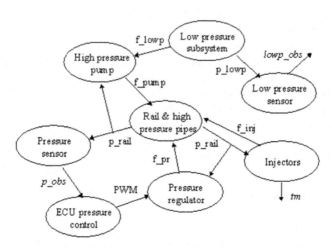

$-f_{lowp}$: flow from low pressure system; $-p_{obs}$: pressure sensor in the rail;
$-p_{lowp}$: pressure in low pressure system; $-pwm$: command to pressure regulator;
$-lowp_{obs}$: sensor for low pressure system; $-f_{pr}$: flow through pressure regulator;
$-f_{pump}$: outflow of high pressure pump; $-f_{inj}$: flow through the injectors;
$-p_{rail}$: pressure in the rail; $-tm$: torque measurement.

Figure1. Block diagram of the Common Rail and meaning of interface variables.

The qualitative deviations model for the general behavior of the example system is the following:[7]

$$\text{High pressure pump} \quad \Delta f_{pump} = c_p \otimes \Delta f_{lowp} \oplus \Delta c_p \ominus \Delta p_{rail} \quad (4)$$

$$\text{High pressure pipes and rail} \quad \Delta \partial p_{rail} = \Delta f_{pump} \ominus \Delta f_{pr} \ominus \Delta f_{inj} \ominus \Delta f_{leak} \quad (5)$$

$$\text{Pressure regulator} \quad \Delta f_{pr} = open_{pr} \otimes \Delta p_{rail} \oplus \Delta open_{pr} \quad (6)$$

$$\Delta open_{pr} = c_{reg} \ominus \Delta pwm \otimes k_{reg} \quad (7)$$

$$\text{Pressure sensor} \quad \Delta p_{obs} = \Delta k_s \oplus \Delta p_{rail} \oplus \Delta c_s \quad (8)$$

$$\text{Injectors} \quad \Delta f_{inj} = i \otimes \Delta p_{rail} \oplus \Delta i \oplus \Delta f_{inj\_rec} \quad (9)$$

$$\text{Low pressure system} \quad \Delta f_{lowp} = \Delta p_{lowp} \quad (10)$$

$$\text{Electronic Control Unit} \quad \Delta \partial pwm = c_{ecu} - \Delta p_{obs} \quad (11)$$

In addition to the model of general behavior, we considered 13 fault modes for the Common Rail components; each one is modeled as a set of pairs $\langle v, value \rangle$,

---

[7] We omit the sign operator [.] on all qualitative variables for brevity.

where v is a variable (parameter), and *value* is a particular qualitative value for v which characterizes the specific fault. In the CSP-based framework presented here, fault modes are additional constraints used by the consistency-based diagnostic algorithm. Refer to [2] for a detailed description of the considered faults.

As an example of qualitative deviations modeling, consider equation (5), which models the general behavior of the pipes and rail component. As an example of fault mode, consider the constraints on the Δf_{leak} parameter, which represents the flow through possible leaks: the "ok" mode for the rail component imposes $\Delta f_{leak} = 0$ (i.e., there are no leaks), while the fault mode "leaking" imposes $\Delta f_{leak} = +$.

6.3   Common Rail CSP model

The qualitative model of the Common Rail based on ternary constraints is derived from the qualitative deviations model. For example, from equation (5) the following constraints are derived:

$$a_{21} = \Delta f_{pump} \ominus \Delta f_{pr}, a_{22} = a_{21} \ominus \Delta f_{inj}, \Delta \partial p_{rail} = a_{22} \ominus \Delta f_{leak}$$

Notice the new variables a_{ij} introduced by the translation process in order to connect constraints derived from the same equation.

6.4   CSP-based Heuristics

In the example considered here, only 7 of the 24 variables of the model appear in more than one equation. However, the minimal cycle cutset contains only the variable Δp_{rail}. Labeling this variable (i.e. removing this node and its incident arcs from the constraint graph) yields a set of tree-structured networks (2 in this example).

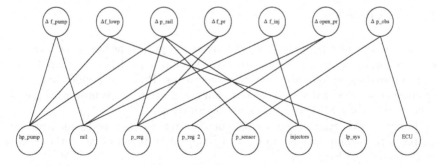

Figure2. Relation between variables and equations as a bipartite graph.

Thus, the greedy heuristic algorithm works on a bipartite graph with only 7 variable nodes (figure 2) and computes a cutset which is of minimal cardinality in this case. Performances in solving the example CSP for diagnostic purposes (i.e. checking consistency with the 13 considered fault modes) have been measured using a $CLP(FD)$ implementation. The results with and without applying the cutset heuristic are 512 and 2954 variable instantiations during the labeling phase, respectively (i.e. 83% reduction of search when the heuristic decomposition approach is used), with a similar ratio for execution times; then the cost of the algorithm is negligible with respect to the overall CPU time.

7   Preliminary Results and Future Work

The models and algorithms described here have been implemented using a $CLP(FD)$ language (ECL^iPS^e) and C++. Some experiments with simplified models of real-life systems show that the greedy approach for cycle cutset reduction gives good results (the cardinality of the computed cutset is usually a small fraction of the total number of variables of the CSP). One of these case studies has been discussed in section 6. Of course more detailed investigation is needed to evaluate practical applicability of the approach to large complex systems featuring hundreds of equations.

The ternary constraints approach is easy to implement in constraint languages. Moreover, it has the advantage of being easy to integrate with dependency recording mechanisms, in particular with Assumptions Based Truth Maintenance Systems (ATMSs), an implementation approach we experimented with our C++ prototype. However, the overhead of maintaining information about performed inferences (i.e. domain reductions) is too high compared with the time saved in the propagation phase (for a comparison between ATMS and CSP techniques, see [4]). The integration of reasoning and retrieving mechanisms for problem solving is however an important area for future investigation.

8   Conclusions

From the modeling point of view, the layered approach proves to be essential, even on simple case studies, in order to develop a model with limited effort and automatically compute associated heuristics. Practical applications (such as consistency-based diagnosis of our example system) have proven to greatly benefit from the CSP-based heuristics described here.

From the Constraint Programming perspective, we proposed some heuristics for problem decomposition/solving which appear to be effective on the class of CSPs considered here.

Moreover, we notice that most research in the field of CSP heuristics has been done on binary CSPs. On one hand, binary CSPs are easy to randomly generate and provide a general and uniform ground for algorithm evaluation. On the other hand, however, we believe that binary CSPs are not representative enough of "real" CSPs (those implementing real-world models), at least under the modeling and the heuristic evaluation point of view.

References

1. A. Bockmayr and T. Kasper. Branch-and-infer: A unifying framework for integer and finite domain constraint programming. *INFORMS J. Computing*, 10(3):287 – 300, 1998.
2. F. Cascio, L. Console, M. Guagliumi, M. Osella, A. Panati, S. Sottano, and D. Theseider Dupré. Generating on-board diagnostics of dynamic automotive systems based on qualitative models. *AI Communications*, 12:33–43, June 1999.
3. A. Davenport and E. Tsang. An empirical investigation into the exceptionally hard problems. *Proc. Workshop on Constraint-based Reasoning*, pages 46–53, 1995.
4. J. de Kleer. A comparison of ATMS and CSP techniques. *Int. Joint Conference on Artificial Intelligence*, 1989.
5. R. Dechter. Enhancement schemes for constraint processing: Backjumping, learning, and cutset decomposition. *Artificial Intelligence*, 41:273–312, 1990.
6. V. Kumar. Algorithms for constraint satisfaction problems: A survey. *AI Magazine*, 13(1):32–44, 1992.
7. A. Malik and P. Struss. Diagnosis of dynamic systems does not necessarily require simulation. *Proc. 7th Int. Workshop on Principles of Diagnosis*, 1996.
8. D. Theseider Dupré and A. Panati. State-based vs simulation-based diagnosis of dynamic systems. In *Proc. 9th International Workshop on Principles of Diagnosis*, pages 40–46, Cape Cod (USA), May 1998.

Relational Learning: Hard Problems and Phase Transitions

M. Botta[(1)], A. Giordana[(2)], L. Saitta[(2)], and M. Sebag[(3)]

[(1)] Dipartimento di Informatica -Università di Torino
Corso Svizzera 185 - 10149 Torino, Italy
botta@di.unito.it

[(2)] Dipartimento di Scienze e Tecnologie Avanzate
Università del Piemonte Orientale "Amedeo Avogadro"
Corso Borsalino 54 - 15100 Alessandria, Italy
{attilio, saitta}@al.unipmn.it

[(3)] Laboratoire de Méchanique des Solides - Ecole Polytechnique
91128 Palaiseau, France
sebag@cmapx.polytechnique.fr

Abstract. This paper focuses on a major step of machine learning, namely checking whether an example matches a candidate hypothesis. In relational learning, matching can be viewed as a Constraint Satisfaction Problem (CSP). The complexity of the task is analyzed in the Phase Transition framework, investigating the impact on the effectiveness of two relational learners: FOIL and G-NET.

The critical factors of complexity, and their critical values, are experimentally investigated on artificial problems. This leads to distinguish several kinds of learning domains, depending on whether the target concept lies in the "mushy" region or not. Interestingly, experiments done with FOIL and G-NET show that both learners tend to induce hypotheses generating matching problems located inside the phase transition region, even if the constructed target concept lies far outside. Moreover, target concepts constructed too close to the phase transition are hard and both learners fail. The paper offers an explanation for this fact, and proposes a classification of learning domains and their hardness.

1 Introduction

In several classes of computationally difficult problems, such as K-Satisfiability, Constraint Satisfaction problems (CSP), graph K-coloring, and the decision version of the Traveling Salesman problem, a phenomenon termed *phase transition* occurs (see [12] for a comprehensive presentation). A *phase transition* consists in an abrupt change in the probability of a problem being solvable, and it is coupled with a peak in the computational complexity [3,4,5,6,11,13,16,17,18,19].

The CSP class exhibits a typical phase transition with respect to the number of constraints [9,13]. Proving a conjunctive formula true or false in a given universe (referred to as *matching problem*, in the following) is a CSP, and has been proven to have exponential complexity in the worst case. On the other hand Giordana et al. [9] have shown that this task is characterized by typical phase transitions with respect to

E. Lamma and P. Mello (Eds.): AI*IA 99, LNAI 1792, pp. 178–189, 2000.

the number of predicates in a formula and the number of constants in the universe in which the proof occurs.

This paper investigates the influence on relational learning of phase transition in the matching problem. For any relational learner, the induction process can be modeled as a cycle, where inductive hypotheses (logical formulas) are continuously generated and verified on a set of instances of the target relation, checking for consistency. In the verification step, every pair <inductive hypothesis, learning example> defines a matching problem. When a matching problem lies in the mushy region the complexity may be prohibitive, and the learner might not be able to terminate within the limits imposed by the available resources.

This point has been experimentally investigated using a suite of artificial problems. As described later on, every learning problem has been constructed by choosing a specific target formula and then by generating a set of positive and negative instances for it, which defined matching problems in different positions with respect to the phase transition. Two learners (FOIL and G-NET) have been challenged to discover the original formula, or at least a semantically equivalent one.

The two results we obtained are both quite surprising: first, both learners tend to select hypotheses defining matching problems inside the mushy region. This occurs independently of the location of the original target concept. Second, when the target concept defines matching problems located too close to the mushy region, the learners get confused and produce definitions consisting of many small disjuncts, very little predictive on a test set. These findings are analyzed and some explanations are provided.

The paper is organized as follows: Section 2 summarizes the findings described by Giordana et al. [9] showing that the matching problem presents a phase transition with respect to the number of predicates and the constants in the universe, used as order parameters. Section 3 describes the context and the goal of the experimentation, whose results are reported in Section 4. Section 5 presents a discussion of the results, whereas some concluding remarks are contained in Section 6.

2 Phase Transition in the Matching Problem

We first propose some order parameters to analyze the relational matching problem. These are used to design artificial random matching problems.

2.1 Order parameters

An instance of the matching problem is a pair $<\varphi,U>$, being φ a conjunctive formula in First Order Logic (FOL), and U a universe. The instance is solvable if there exists at least one model of φ in U. The problem can be reformulated as a *Constraint Satisfaction Problem* (CSP): the goal of a CSP is to assign a value a_i to each variable x_i $(1\leq i\leq n)$, such that every constraint $R_j(x_1, x_2, ..., x_n)$ $(1\leq j\leq m)$ in a set **R** is satisfied. A constraint R_j is described as the set of all tuples $v_1, ..., v_n$ such that $R_j(v_1, v_2, ..., v_n)$ holds.

A formula φ to match can clearly be reformulated as a set of constraints (corresponding to the literals in φ), and the universe U contains all tuples satisfying the constraints (closed world assumption). In the following, we restrict ourselves to only consider binary relations. The corresponding CSP is then termed *binary* [18].

Phase transitions in binary CSP have been both experimentally and theoretically investigated [13,17,18]. Two parameters account for the constrainedness degree of CSP: the *constraint density* p_1, defined, for binary constraints, as the fraction of constrained variable pairs among all possible pairs, and the *constraint tightness* p_2, defined as the average number of value pairs ruled out by any one of the constraints [13]. Unlike the literature of the main stream, we will use other two parameters, which are related to p_1 and p_2, but are more useful in order to analyze the matching problem in relational learning.

For the sake of simplicity, we assume that all variables have the same domain of size L, and that the extensions of all relations have the same size N (number of atoms built on any given predicate symbol). The constrainedness degree of a matching problem is then studied with respect to two order parameters: the number m of constraints and the number L of constants in the universe (the size of any variable domain); a third parameter, namely the number N of atoms built on any predicate symbol, is kept constant in the present investigation.

2.2 Artificial Problem Generation

The experimental analysis reported in the following is based on artificial matching problems <φ,U> generated as follows. Let x_1, x_2, ..., x_n denote a set of variables, and α_1, α_2, ..., α_r denote the predicate symbols. Formula φ is generated in two steps. In order to guarantee the connectivity of φ, we first construct a connected formula φ_s as:

$$\varphi_s(x_1, x_2, ..., x_n) = \alpha_{\sigma(1)}(x_1, x_2) \wedge ... \wedge \alpha_{\sigma(n-1)}(x_{n-1}, x_n), \tag{1}$$

where $\alpha_{\sigma(i)}$ is uniformly selected in the predicate symbols. Formula φ is constructed from φ_s by adding random literals $\alpha_\kappa(x_i, x_j)$ until a total number of m literals is reached (assuming of course that $m \geq n-1$), such that all literals in φ are distinct. Formula φ, constructed in this way, contains exactly n variables and m literals, and the same pair of variables may appear in literals built on different predicate symbols.

Universe U is constructed by selecting, for each predicate α_t, exactly N pairs of values (a_k, a_h), where a_j ranges over the set of all L possible values. The selection is uniform without replacement (all N pairs being distinct). In summary, the matching problems we consider are defined by a 4-tuple (n, m, L, N).

3   Observing Phase Transitions

The probability for a matching problem to be satisfiable is experimentally investigated. The phase transition region, where the probability of satisfiability abruptly drops from 1 to 0, is delineated. We then discuss the difficulty of a learning domain, depending on its position with respect to the phase transition.

3.1 Evidence of Phase Transitions

An extensive experimentation [8] considered the following settings: the cardinality of

the relations N is set to 100; the number of variables n ranges in {4, 6, 10, 12, 14};
moreover, each pair (L, m) with L in [10, 50] and m in [5, 50], has been considered.
For each problem, we compute if φ is satisfiable (i.e., it admits at least one model in
U). We associate to each 4-tuple (n,m,L,N) the fraction P_{sol}(n,m,L,N) of matching
problems that are solvable, out of 100 problems generated along these parameters.

Figure 1 plots P_{sol}(10,m,L,100) as a function of m and L, with n and N respectively
fixed to 10 and 100. When m and L are both low, all problems are solved (P_{sol} is 1).
Then, P_{sol} dramatically drops to almost zero along a very regular hyperbolic curve.
The dashed region in the (L, m) plane shows all problems for which P_{sol} belongs to the
interval [.15, .85]: this region is quite narrow, witnessing how steep the transition is
from solvable to non-solvable problems. This is the phase transition, or *mushy*,
region.

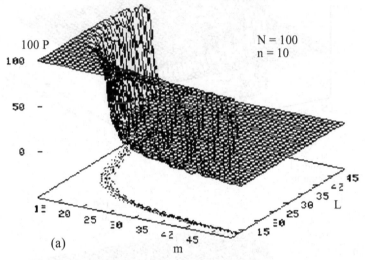

Fig. 1. 3-Dimensional plot of the probability of solution P_{sol} for n = 10, when N = 100. In the
(L, m) plane some contour level curves, corresponding to P_{sol} values in the interval [0.15, 0.85]
have been drawn.

We also analyze the complexity of solving a problem (φ,U), measured as the
number of explored nodes using a depth-first search. The region of highest
complexity corresponds to the mushy region (Figure 2(a)), but it is more irregular and
much broader, like a mountain chain. And the variance is high (Figure 2(b)): not all
problems in the mushy region are equally difficult to solve.

3.2 Concept Learning in the (L, m) Plane

In the following we adopt the learning framework defined by Giordana et al., [7],
where an example *e* of a relational concept corresponds to a universe U_e. With respect
to a target relation φ, the positive and negative examples of the concept thus
correspond to different universes: a learner solves many matching problems <φ, U_e>,
for *e* ranging over the positive and negative examples. Assuming that all variable
domains still have same size L, all examples belong to a line parallel to axis L in the

(L,m) plane. This remark allows us to distinguish several cases.

(a) The easiest case is when positive examples, satisfying φ, fall to the left of the phase transition region, whereas negative examples fall to the right. Here, static estimates based on the value of m and L, would suffice to separate positive from negative examples (the transition phase itself being the separating surface, as in Figure 1).

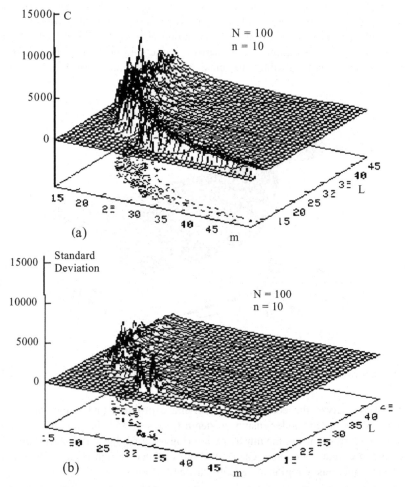

(a)

(b)

Fig. 2. (a) Plot of the complexity C (for n = 10), measured as the number of expanded nodes by a depth-first searcher, averaged over 100 problem instances in each point. (b) Plot of the standard deviation of the complexity.

(b) A second case is when positive and negative examples fall within the phase transition region: the matching complexity is high in any case. This implies that positive examples would contain very few models of the target concept, and that negative examples almost match the target concept (near-misses).

(c) A third case is when all positive and negative instances fall to the right of the phase transition. This entails that positive examples are very far from being random: by construction, random universes would hardly have any chance to match φ. But indeed, examples illustrating an interesting target concept should contain regularities: one should expect these regularities to be naturally or artificially emerging from the random noise.

(d) The last case, complementary to the previous one, is when all positive and negative instances fall to the left of the phase transition. This symmetrically implies that negative examples are very far from being random. However, though it is always possible to construct formulas and artificial examples satisfying these formulas whatever their size (see next section), it might be impossible to construct a negative instance to the left of the phase transition when the value of L is too small.

4   Hardness of the Learning Problems

The conjectures made in the previous section are confronted to the actual performance of FOIL using artificial problems.

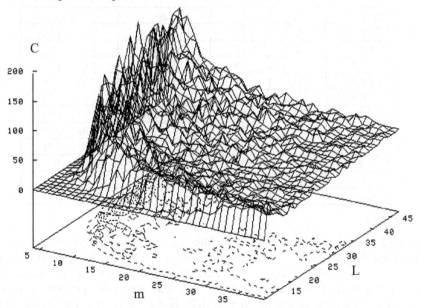

Fig. 3. Complexity peak at the phase transition for a formula of four variables.

4.1 Experimental Setting

The analysis considers problems falling under the categories (c) and (d) shown above. In order to keep the problems to a reasonable complexity, we restricted ourselves to consider concepts with four variables (n=4). In this comparatively simple case, the phase transition still occurs (see Figure 3), but the complexity peak is small enough to guarantee that the matching problem can always be solved in a reasonable time.

Artificial learning problems are constructed as follows, with relation size N=100 in all cases. In case (b), a formula φ lying in the phase transition region, and 500 examples (universes) are randomly generated as detailed in Section 2.2. The class of each example is positive if it contains at least one model of φ, negative otherwise. Examples are divided into a 200-training and a 300-test set. By construction, since φ lies in the phase transition region, positive and negative examples of φ are quasi balanced (Table 1).

In case (c), a formula φ lying to the right of the phase transition has been randomly generated by suitably choosing L and m, together with 500 examples (universes). But none of these examples will satisfy φ. We then select one half of these examples (100 in the training set and 150 in the test set), and transform each one of them into a positive example by adding to it a model of φ.

Five problems in the region (b) and six problems in the region (c) are generated, as summarized in Table 1.

Table 1. Artificial problems used for the experimental analysis. The symbol (*) denotes the problems located at the phase transition where the probability of solution is about 1/2.

Problem	M	L	LS	TS
LP_1*	9	19	118^+, 72^-	168^+, 132^-
LP_2*	8	22	95^+, 105^-	147^+, 153^-
LP_3*	7	25	116^+, 84^-	189^+, 111^-
LP_4*	6	30	135^+, 65^-	215^+, 85^-
LP_5*	6	35	71^+, 129^-	101^+, 199^-
LP_6	12	25	100^+, 100^-	150^+, 150^-
LP_7	12	30	100^+, 100^-	150^+, 150^-
LP_8	18	20	100^+, 100^-	150^+, 150^-
LP_9	18	23	100^+, 100^-	150^+, 150^-
LP_{10}	18	30	100^+, 100^-	150^+, 150^-
LP_{11}	18	50	100^+, 100^-	150^+, 150^-

4.2 Results

The hardness of the artificial learning problems generated as above is estimated from the results obtained by two relational learners that use different strategies: FOIL [14], and G-Net [1,2]. Both learners explore candidate hypotheses ψ lying on a line $L = L_U$, being L_U the number of constants in the example universes. FOIL performs a general to specific search, and moves from left to right on the line $L = L_U$. The number m of literals in the candidate hypothesis increases along the search. The hypothesis to be considered and specialized is selected on the basis of its information gain.

G-Net is based on an evolutionary search: it considers a population of hypotheses lying also on the line $L = L_U$, and moves back and forth as evolution determines whether these hypotheses should be specialized or generalized. Furthermore, the selection of the hypotheses to be considered and refined is guided by the MDL principle.

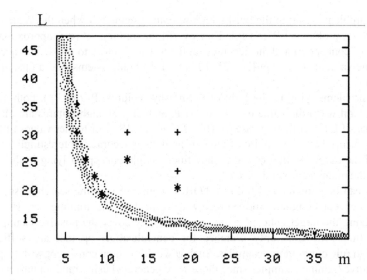

Figure 4 – Contour plots of the probability of solution. The symbol "+" denotes problems where FOIL succeeded, whereas symbol "*" denotes problems where FOIL failed.

Being FOIL faster than G-Net, the experiments have been primarily done using FOIL. G-Net has been run for comparison only on the learning problems that seemed most significant to us. In all cases, the two systems have been surprisingly in agreement, reporting minimal differences in the classification rate. The results are summarized in Table 2, and in Figure 4 a graphical representation of the generated learning problems is reported, together with an indication of success/failure.

Table 2. Summary of the experimental results obtained by FOIL for the set of learning problems described in Table 1.

Problem	# of Clauses	Complexity	Class. Rate (LS) [%]	Class. Rate (TS) [%]	CPU Time [sec]	Avg. # of Models
LP_1*	10	<7-13> 8.9	88	50	398.2	1.7
LP_2*	11	<6-11> 8.6	92	53	624.7	2.0
LP_3*	15	<7-11> 8.9	98.5	52	513.9	4.9
LP_4*	1	6	100	100	43.3	2.1
LP_5*	1	6	99.9	100	132.6	1.25
LP_6	12	<1-12> 6	81	58	825.4	10.7
LP_7	1	6	100	96	73.4	34.6
LP_8	6	<1-11> 5	98.5	75.3	723.8	1.4
LP_9	1	9	100	99.6	620.1	1.0
LP_{10}	1	6	100	99.6	36.9	4.2
LP_{11}	1	6	100	99.6	72.2	9.1

For problems lying in the mushy region, both systems fail when the value of L is low (L ≤ 25, problems LP_1 to LP_3). They overfit the training set (φ is approximated as a dozen of concept ψ) and the accuracy on the test set is close to the default accuracy. When the value of L is high (L > 25, LP_4 and LP_5) both systems find a quasi-perfect solution.

For problems lying to the right of the mushy region (LP_6 to LP_{11}), both systems similarly fail when the value of L is low (LP_6 and LP_8), though failures are observed for values of L lower than in case (b) (L = 22 for m = 18). For higher values of L both systems succeed from the point of view of predictive accuracy. Interestingly, they do not find the exact solution φ; rather they find a single concept ψ lying in the mushy region (the number of literals is 6 or 7).

This can be explained as follows. FOIL is bound to stop the search as soon as it finds a concept complete and correct with respect to the training set. But all ψ generalizing the target concept φ are complete: they cover the positive examples by construction. One thus only searches for generalizations ψ that are sufficiently specific to rule out random examples. Such ψ would then be consistent with respect to the negative training examples since those were generated using random universes.

Considering generalizations of φ on the right side of the mushy region, these will rule out most negative instances: and given the relatively small datasets we used, they will likely be consistent with respect to the training and test sets.

FOIL will end up exploring the generalizations of φ lying in the mushy region; provided there exists a sufficient number of such generalizations, it will succeed in finding a complete and correct solution ψ. Though G-Net might explore more specific concepts than FOIL, it is also biased toward generality (using MDL principle instead of information gain): it will thus end up discovering more or less the same complete and correct generalization of φ as FOIL.

5   Discussion

As shown in the previous section, both FOIL and G-Net find hard, and actually fail to solve, learning problems including few constants (low values of L). Why is it so?

Let us first consider the case where the target concept φ lies in the mushy region (case (b)). In this case, negative examples fail to match φ by only a few traits, i.e. they are "near-misses" of φ. In the left side of the mushy region, all concepts ψ, including the generalizations of φ, match on average any example. Let $M(m, L)$ denote the average number of models of a m-literals formula in universes including L constants. From [8,13], the number $M(m, L)$ increases as L decreases (the extension N of any predicate and the number m of literals being constant).

Further, the variance of $M(m, L)$ is high: this can be inferred from the high variance of the matching complexity (Figure 2(b)). Indeed, the complexity depends on the probability of finding a model, and hence, on the total number of models of the current formula in the current universe: the complexity thus exponentially decreases with the number of models in the universe.

Figure 2(b) shows that the variance reaches its maximum on the edge of the mushy region. FOIL starts the search in the left side of the mushy region, where any example matches on average any formula. The information gain criterion then fails to guide the search; further, FOIL tends to be misled by the fluctuations of the number of models of the candidate hypotheses. When L decreases, the left side of the mushy region is larger, and the complexity landscape is more rugged: both facts explain the increasing difficulties met by FOIL search strategy.

Practically, experiments give an order of idea of M(m, L): for problem LP_1 (m=4, L=35), M is 66; for problem LP_2 (m=4, L=19), M is 667. But, when increasing the number of literals, M rapidly decreases. In 10 other experiments done with (m=6, L=19), M is 62 on average.

When FOIL explores too general concepts, it fails to find consistent hypotheses; it then specializes the candidate hypotheses, until it ends up exploring the concepts with the right level of generality, in the mushy region. But then, the high number of models hinders the search. The system then specializes again the candidate hypotheses, until the number of models falls down to tractable values.

But these hypotheses are then too specific compared to the target concept: many of them must then be retained in order to cover all positive examples. Ultimately, these concepts show a low predictive accuracy on the test set. Incidentally, such a behavior closely accounts for the small disjunct phenomenon [10].

G-Net meets the same difficulties, which is more surprising given the fact that it goes back and forth, specializing and generalizing the candidate hypotheses. However, it soon dismisses all hypotheses lying on the right side of the mushy region, since these hardly cover any positive example. G-Net is then bound to explore the same regions, and meet the same difficulties as FOIL.

Let us now consider the case where the target concept φ lies on the right side of the mushy region (case (c)). These problems were expected to be very hard, since the target concept is hardly satisfiable. But surprisingly, both FOIL and G-Net succeed on such learning domains, provided again that L is low enough.

The explanation proposed for this fact is the following. The distribution of the positive examples was altered from the random generation, to ensure that they include at least one model of φ. If we consider the generalizations of φ, their number of models is thus artificially increased, compared to the random (negative) examples: the information gain criterion hence favors the selection of these generalizations. (Experimentally, 4-literals generalizations of φ in LP_9 admit 244 models on average for positive examples, and 225 models on average for negative examples). On one hand, the search is biased toward exploring generalizations of φ, and it stops when it meets a generalization of φ in the mushy region.

On the other hand, the number of k-literals generalizations of φ varies with $\binom{m}{k}$, (being m the number of literals in φ): the more specific the target concept, the more likely its generalizations are explored. The complexity analysis of G-net offers evidence supporting this fact. The system explores 28,000 hypotheses in LP_7 (m=12) against 15,000 in LP_{10} (m=18).

6 Conclusions

This paper focuses on the average case analysis of the matching problem, considered as a constraint satisfaction problem. Problems in the mushy region are expected to be hard for two reasons. On one hand positive and negative instances are very similar and so intrinsically difficult to discriminate. On the other hand, verifying hypotheses in the mushy region may be very complex.

Unexpectedly, experiments on artificial problems suggest that learning an almost unsatisfiable target concept is not always a hard learning problem: many generalizations of the target concept appear to be consistent with respect to the training set provided that they are sufficiently specific. Generality-biased learners would then end up with a complete and correct solution belonging to the mushy region. Some care must however be exercised in interpreting these results, as we actually considered random negative examples.

Further research will examine what happens when negative examples are no longer random, e.g. when the learning problem is to separate examples of two different target concepts. Other complexity parameters should then be defined to account for the degree of difference of these concepts.

Another perspective of research is concerned with learning a target concept in the mushy region. In this case, there is no other possibility than learning exactly the target concept: any generalization (resp. specialization) would unlikely to be consistent (resp. complete). One possibility is to take advantage of the fact that negative examples fail to match the target concept by only a few traits, i.e. they are near-misses.

Ultimately, the major obstacle to relational learning remains the complexity of dealing with hypotheses in the mushy region: as was shown, exploring this region is unavoidable in truly relational learning domains. When target concepts include a low number of variables (4 or 5), the search complexity remains affordable. Otherwise, the learning search fully faces with the exponential complexity of matching.

This difficulty could be alleviated by relaxing the matching task, e.g. by replacing the exhaustive exploration of the universe with a stochastic exploration: as discussed in [8,15], stochastic matching gives correct and probabilistically complete answers within bounded resources (any-time matching). A perspective for further research is to study how the phase transition would be affected by using a stochastic resolution process.

References

1. Anglano C., Giordana A., Lo Bello G., and Saitta L. (1997). "A Network Genetic Algorithm for Concept Learning". In *Proc. 7th Int. Conf. on Genetic Algorithms* (East Lansing, MI), pp. 434-441.
2. Anglano C., Giordana A., Lo Bello G., and Saitta L. (1998). "An Experimental Evaluation of Coevolutive Concept Learning". In *Proc. 15th Int. Conf. on Machine Learning* (Madison, WI), pp. 19-27.
3. Cheeseman P., Kanefsky B., and Taylor W.M. (1991). "Where the *Really* Hard Problems Are". In *Proc. 12th Int. Joint Conf on Artificial Intelligence* (Sidney, Australia), pp. 331-

337.

4. Crawford J.M., and Auton L.D. (1996). "Experimental Results on the Crossover Point in Random 3-SAT". *Artificial Intelligence, 81,* 31-58.

5. Freeman J.W. (1996). "Hard Random 3-SAT Problems and the Davis-Putnam Procedure". *Artificial Intelligence, 81,* 183-198.

6. Gent I.P., and Walsh T. (1996). "The TSP Phase Transition". *Artificial Intelligence, 88,* 349-358.

7. Giordana A., Neri F., Saitta L., and Botta M. (1998). "Integrating Multiple Learning Strategies in First Order Logics". *Machine Learning, 27,* 209-240.

8. Giordana A., and Saitta L. (1998). "Phase Transition in Learning with FOL Languages", TR 97-25, Dipartimento di Informatica, Università di Torino.

9. Giordana A., Saitta L., and Botta M. (1999). "An Experimental Study of Phase Transitions in Matching", in *Proc. 16th Int. Joint Conf. on Artificial Intelligence,* (Stockholm, Sweden), pp. 1198-1203.

10. Holte R.C., Acker L.E., and Porter B.W. (1989). "Concept learning and the problem of small disjuncts". In *Proc. 11th Int. Joint Conf. On Artificial Intelligence* (Detroit, MI), pp. 813-818.

11. Hogg T. (1996). "Refining the Phase Transition in Combinatorial Search". *Artificial Intelligence, 81,* 127-154.

12. Hogg T., Huberman B.A., and Williams C.P. (Eds.) (1996). *Artificial Intelligence, Special Issue on Frontiers in Problem Solving: Phase Transitions and Complexity, 81 (1-2).*

13. Prosser P. (1996). "An Empirical Study of Phase Transitions in Binary Constraint Satisfaction Problems". *Artificial Intelligence, 81,* 81-110.

14. Quinlan R.J. (1990). "Learning Logical Definitions from Relations", *Machine Learning, 5,* 239-266.

15. Sebag M., and Rouveirol C. (1997). "Tractable Induction and Classification in FOL". In *Proc. 15th Int. Joint Conf. on Artificial Intelligence* (Nagoya, Japan), pp. 888-892.

16. Selman B., and Kirkpatrick S. (1996). "Critical Behavior in the Computational Cost of Satisfiability Testing". *Artificial Intelligence, 81,* 273-296.

17. Smith B.M., and Dyer M.E. (1996). "Locating the Phase Transition in Binary Constraint Satisfaction Problems". *Artificial Intelligence, 81,* 155-181.

18. Williams C.P., Hogg T. (1994). "Exploiting the Deep Structure of Constraint Problems". *Artificial Intelligence, 70,* 73-117.

19. Zhang W., and Korf R.E. (1996). "A Study of Complexity Transition on the Asymmetric Travelling Salesman Problem". *Artificial Intelligence, 81,* 223-239.

A Machine Learning Approach to Web Mining

Floriana Esposito
Donato Malerba

Luigi Di Pace
Pietro Leo

Dipartimento di Informatica
Università degli Studi di Bari
via Orabona, 4
70126 Bari
{esposito | malerba}@di.uniba.it

Java Technology Center
IBM SEMEA Sud
via Tridente, 42/14
70125 Bari
{luigi_dipace | pietro_leo}@it.ibm.com

Abstract. In this paper a Web mining tool for content-based classification of Web pages is presented. The tool, named WebClass, can be used for resource discovery purposes. Information considered by the system is both the textual contents of Web pages and the layout structure defined by HTML tags. The representation language adopted for Web pages is the bag-of-words, where words are selected from training documents by means of a novel scoring measure. Three different classification models are empirically compared on a classification task: Decision trees, centroids, and k-nearest-neighbor. Experimental results are reported and conclusions are drawn on the relevance of the HTML layout structure for classification purposes, on the significance of words selected by the scoring measure, as well as on the performance of the different classifiers.

1   Introduction

It has been estimated that the size of the public Web as of January 1997 was about 80 million HTML pages, with a predicted annual doubling rate [17]. Search engines are not even able to index all pages [4], and often return imprecise and incomplete references. Thus the problem of finding all and only Web pages of interests for a single user or a group of users is attracting many researchers. Because of the huge volume of pages to be analyzed, it can be easily drawn an analogy with the problem of finding interesting patterns in a database (*data mining*). The main difference is that data reported in Web pages are semi-structured (in the case of text) or not structured at all (in the case of images, sounds and executable). The term *Web mining* is usually referred to the application of specific algorithms for extracting patterns from *resources* (documents and services) distributed in the Web. It is possible to identify three different activities in Web mining [7]:
1. *Resource discovery*, that is locating documents and services on the Web.
2. *Information extraction*, that is extracting information from newly discovered resources.
3. *Generalization*, that is learning about the Web itself.
    First of all, Web users need locate information of interest. Current resource discovery tools are based on Web robots, or *spiders*, that scan millions of Web pages and build a term-based index of the retrieved documents. Often indices built by such

E. Lamma and P. Mello (Eds.): AI*IA 99, LNAI 1792, pp. 190–201, 2000.

robots include partial or irrelevant information. More powerful resource discovery systems should apply automatic text categorization techniques in order to customize the classification of Web pages indexed by search engines. These techniques are also helpful in information extraction. In this case, textual content of pages is parsed and specific pieces of information are extracted in order to fill pre-defined *templates* [19]. Once we have automated the discovery and extraction of information from Web sites, the next step is learning about the Web itself. Some problems faced in this generalization step are: 1) definition of a similarity between Web pages; 2) clustering of Web documents; 3) characterization of how pages change over time [5].

In this work we are interested in applying text categorization techniques to customizable Web resource discovery systems. Differently from other works [3] we intend to exploit machine learning methods in order to derive the classification rules that can be used for document categorization. The main challenge set by typical text categorization problems to machine learning methods resides in the very large number of categories. In text categorization the problem is even more complicated since categories may overlap. Fortunately, a Web user may be interested to a limited number of categories, for instance those identified by the folders of her/his browser bookmarks. In this context, it is possible to apply several machine learning techniques in order to learn users' interests (*user profile*).

In this paper some learning issues met in the design of *WebClass*, a Web mining tool for the automated classification Web documents, are presented. In particular, a novel scoring measure for the selection of relevant words in the preprocessing phase is introduced in Section 3, while the different approaches adopted for the automated categorization are described in Section 4. Empirical results on different training sets are reported and discussed in Section 5.

2   The learning issues

Many issues are related to the goal of building a Web page classifier. Firstly, it is necessary to determine which kind of information in a Web page is relevant. In this work, it is assumed that the relevance of a page for the group of users depends exclusively on both the *textual content* and the HTML *layout structure* of the Web page. Hence, the following factors are not considered in this study:

- External factors, such as the novelty or the reliability of the information in the document.
- Multimedia components of a page, such as pictures, videos, animations and audios, which take 80% of a typical Web site [17].
- Contextual information reported in a link to an HTML document [3].
- Possible dependencies among classes of Web documents.

Thus, the learning problem can be formulated as follows:

Given

- a set of classes of documents $C_1, C_2, ..., C_r$,
- a finite Web space W structured as a directed graph over Web documents,
- a set of Web documents $D \subseteq W$ described in a language L_D,

Find

a model or hypothesis H which maps Web documents to a class and maximizes predictive accuracy on, possibly unseen, documents in the Web space W.

The second issue concerns the representation language L_D adopted for Web documents. Typically, documents are represented as feature-vectors, where features correspond to specific words (*1-grams*) or groups of words (*n-grams*, *n*>1). This representation, also known as *bag-of-words*, is that adopted in this work, although two variants have been tested: *Plain* frequency vector representation and *emphasized* representation. The latter takes into account the information related to all the HTML tags enclosing occurrences of words.

The third issue is feature selection. Thousands of features can be generated even from a small set of pages. Generally, only a subset of features is relevant, and their selection has been proven beneficial for the computational complexity and the accuracy of the page classifiers [9]. Several approaches have been proposed in the literature: Most of them simply score words according to some measure and select the best firsts. An experimental comparison, based on a two-class problem, between scoring measures based on the *Odds ratio* and scoring measures based on *information gain* has led to conclusions in favor of former ones [13]. Joachims [8] extends the well-known TF-IDF measure, originally proposed for information retrieval purposes [16], to text categorization with more than two categories for the definition of a probabilistic classifier of documents. In all investigated methods, however, words extracted from documents of different classes are pooled. Thus it may happen that words extracted from documents of the majority class are favored with respect to words extracted for poorly represented classes. In the next section, a feature selection process that extracts orthogonal sets of features for each document class is described and a novel scoring measure appropriate for feature selection in multi-class text categorization problems is presented.

The last issue concerns the construction of classifiers. Once again, several solutions have been proposed in the literature: Bayesian classifiers [15], decision trees [2], some adaptations of Rocchio's algorithm to text categorization [8], and *k*-nearest neighbor [12]. An empirical comparison of these techniques has been performed by Pazzani and Billsus on the problem of learning the user profile. In our case the three classifiers are based on three different views of classes: *k*-nearest neighbor (extensional view), decision trees (classical intensional view), and centroids (exemplar intensional view). Conclusions drawn from experiments are at variance with those reported in the work by Pazzani and Billsus (see Section 4).

3   The preprocessing phase

WebClass preprocesses the training documents in order to extract the relevant words to be used in the bag-of-words representation (see Fig. 1). All training documents are initially tokenized, and tokens (words) shorter than three characters are removed. The set of tokens is filtered in order to remove HTML tags, punctuation marks, numbers and stopwords, such as articles, prepositions and conjunctions (stopwords are taken from glimpse.cs.arizona.edu). In this preprocessing phase, the structural information of HTML is not taken into account (e.g., no difference is made between words in the title and words in the body of the page) and a simple stemming algorithm is applied to remove suffixes *-s*, *-es* and *-ies*.

The selection of features is based on a variant of TF-IDF. More precisely, given the j-th training document of the i-th class, for each token t the frequency $TF(i,j,t)$ of the token in the document is computed. Then, for each class i and token t, the following statistics are computed:

- $MaxTF(i,t)$, the maximum value of $TF(i,j,t)$ on all training documents of class i;
- $PF(i,t)$, the *page frequency*, that is the percentage of documents of class i in which the token t occurs.

The union of sets of tokens extracted from Web pages in one class defines an "empirical" *class dictionary* used by documents on the topic specified by the class. By sorting the dictionary with respect to $maxTF(i,t)$, words occurring frequently only in one long HTML page might be favored. This problem is known as *spamming*: Web page authors usually "hide" a number of occurrences of "key" words in the HTML code in order to force search engines to rank that page in the first positions of the returned lists of Web references. In order to reduce the effect of spamming, each class dictionary is ordered according to the product $maxTF(i,t)*PF(i,t)^2$, shortly denoted as $MaxTF\text{-}PF^2$ (Max Term Frequency - Square Page Frequency) measure.[1]

In this way, common words used in documents of a given class will appear in the first entries of the corresponding class dictionary. Some of these words are actually specific of that class, while others are simply common English words (e.g., "information", "unique", "suggestion", "time" and "people") and should be considered as *quasi-stopwords*. In order to move quasi-stopwords down in the sorted dictionary, the $MaxTF\text{-}PF^2$ of each term is multiplied by a factor $1/CF(t)$, where $CF(t)$ (*category frequency*) is the number of class dictionaries in which the word t occurs. In this way, the sorted dictionary will have the most representative words of each class in the first entries, so that it will be enough to choose the first N words per dictionary in order to define the set of attributes. For instance, the first seven entries for the classes *Astronomy*, *Jazz*, *Auto* and *Motorcycle* considered in one experiment are reported in Table 1. Note that the sets of features defined in this way are "orthogonal", in the sense that documents of the i-th class will typically contain many occurrences of terms in the i-th set and few or no occurrences of terms in the j-th sets, with $j \neq i$. As empirically proven later, this property is very useful for

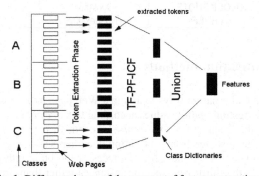

Fig. 1. Different phases of the process of feature extraction.

---

[1] Using the plain $PF(i,t)$ factor was also tried, but was found to decrease performance slightly. For the small sets of training documents we considered in our experiments, the term $PF(i,t)$ might not be small enough to reduce the effect of very frequent words in single documents.

document classification purposes.

Once the class dictionaries are determined, a unique set of features is selected to represent documents of all classes. Currently, the user defines the number of features.

Table 1. First entries in the class dictionaries found in one experiment

Astronomy	Sky	solar	Astronomy	eclipse	earth	Sun	telescope
Jazz	Jazz	music	Composer	band	recording	Artist	art
Auto	Car	vehicle	Auto	drive	fuel	Automobile	brake
Motorcycle	Motorcycle	bike	Harley	yamaha	honda	Ride	riding

Once the set of features has been determined, training documents can be represented as feature vectors. WebClass can adopt two different representations: Plain and emphasized. In the latter representation, the frequency of a word is multiplied by an *emphasis factor*, which is computed in two different ways:
1. *Additive* emphasis: The emphasis factor of a word is computed by summing weights associated to the HTML layout structures where the word occurs;
2. *Multiplicative* emphasis: The product of weights is considered.

In Table 2, weights for selected tags are reported. It is worthwhile to observe that tags concerning *physical* styles, such as <B> (bold) and <I> (italics), have standard weight (1.0), since they are generally used to improve rendering and not to emphasize the text. The effect of the emphasis on the results is described in Section 5.

Table 2. Special HTML tags and relative weight used in the emphasized representation.

HTML tag	Meaning	Weight
<TITLE>	Title	10
<H1>	Heading level 1	9
<H2>	Heading level 2	8
<H3>	Heading level 3	7
<H4>	Heading level 4	6
<ST>	Strong emphasis	5
<EM>	Emphasis	4
<BLOCKQUOTE>	Quotation	3
<A HREF>	Hypertext link	2

4   The classification methods

WebClass has three alternative ways to assign a Web page to a class:
1. By sequentially testing feature values according to a *decision tree*.
2. By computing the distance from the *centroids* of the different classes.
3. By computing the distance from all training documents (*k-nearest-neighbor*).

In the first two ways, a training phase is necessary to build either the decision tree or the centroids. In the third way, specific instances rather than pre-built abstractions are used during the prediction task.

WebClass generates a univariate decision tree, by means of the system OC1 [14], for each class C_i, by considering training documents of class C_i as positive examples and all remaining documents as negative examples.[2] Therefore, the result of the classification process can be: 1) no classification (the document is not stored); 2) single classification (the document is stored as instance of the corresponding class); 3) multiple classification (the document is stored as instance of more than one class). The choice of this system has been initially motivated by numerical nature of the adopted document representation. Nevertheless, from first experiments it has been evident that the generation of oblique trees degraded the performance of the system, thus the decision to run the system in the standard ID3-like operation mode was taken.

The computation of centroids is based on a simple formula. Let v_1, v_2,..., v_{ni} be the feature vectors corresponding to the n_i training pages of class C_i. Let $v_j(k)$, denote the k-th component of v_j, $k=1, 2, ..., N$. Then the *centroid* is an N-dimensional feature vector whose components are computed by averaging on the corresponding components of the training documents. In order to classify a document, the centroid most similar to the document description has to be found. The similarity measure considered is the *cosine correlation* [11], which computes the angle spanned by two vectors (the document and the centroid). The mathematical formulations of both the centroid and the similarity measure are the following:

$$P(k) = \frac{\sum_{j=1}^{n_i} v_j(k)}{n_i} \qquad sim(P,V) = \frac{\sum_{k=1}^{N} P(k)V(k)}{\sqrt{\sum_{k=1}^{N} P(k)^2 \sum_{k=1}^{N} V(k)^2}}$$

The cosine correlation returns a particularly meaningful value when vectors are highly dimensional and features define orthogonal directions. In our application, both conditions are satisfied, although orthogonality refers to the group of features extracted from each class dictionary rather than to the individual features.

The cosine correlation is also used in the third classification approach implemented by WebClass, the *k*-nearest-neighbor. In principle, we should expect low performances for this approach, because of the sensitivity of instance-based algorithms to irrelevant features [1]. However, as we will observe in the next section, this problem has not occurred in our experiments.

5   Design of the experiments and results

A set of experiments has been designed in order to test the performances of the Web mining tool with alternative document representations, different classifiers and different training sets. Four classes of Web pages have been considered: *Astronomy, Jazz, Auto* e *Motorcycle*. The first two categories are semantically distant, although it is not easy to find the set of words that describe them effectively. On the contrary, *Auto* and *Motorcycle* both concerns vehicles, and it might be difficult to find proper words that can easily discriminate them. Additionally, it is possible to have term

---

[2] It is noteworthy that the construction of the classifiers can be reformulated as a set of two-class problems, although the feature selection process is based on a multi-class approach. In fact, by using the same set of features for all classes, it is possible to adopt a centroid-based classification and to compare it with more sophisticated techniques, such as decision trees.

sharing among classes. The main advantage for choosing these topics is that they correspond to Yahoo! categories. Thus, a subset of the pre-classified Web pages proposed in the Yahoo! ontology has been considered for training purposes. One hundred and ninety-two pages[3] have been selected according to the following criteria: 1) random selection of proposed links;[4] 2) pages are written in English;[5] 3) equal distribution of pages among the four classes.

Five experiments with different training set sizes have been designed in order to study the learning curve of the three classification techniques (see Table 3). For each experiment, a three-fold cross-validation has been performed, thus realizing fifteen trials in all. For each trial, 66% of the selected documents has been used for training while the remaining pages are used to compute the statistics precision and recall. All classes are equally represented in each training set. A set of twenty-five features per class has been selected for each trial, therefore, each Web page is represented by a vector of one hundred numerical features (about 1% of distinct non-stopping words extracted in the fifth experiment).

Table 3. Distribution of pages for the five experiments.

Experiment	1	2	3	4	5
Total number of Web pages	24	48	60	96	192
Number of pages per class	6	12	15	24	48
Number of training pages	16	32	40	64	128
Number of test pages	8	16	20	32	64

Some interesting conclusions can be drawn by analyzing the fifteen different sets of selected features. Firstly, the most frequently selected features are semantically close to the topics of the classes, independently of the number of training instances (see Table 4). Secondly, the percentage of features that have a semantic relevance for the four topics increases with the number of training documents (see Table 5). This phenomenon is explained by the increasing effect of the inverse category frequency factor, $1/CF$.

Table 4. The four most frequently selected features on the fifteen trials.

Astronony	Auto	Jazz	Motorcycle
Earth	Car	Blue	bike
Planet	Fuel	Jazz	Motorcycle
Solar	Cylinder	Music	yamaha
Moon	Vehicle	Recording	ride

In the classification phase, three classifiers have been applied for each trial: Decision trees, centroids, and 7-nearest neighbor. Statistics collected for each trial are *precision* and *recall*, which are traditionally used in information retrieval and text

---

[3] See http://www.di.uniba.it/~malerba/software/webclass/webclass.htm for both a public version of the system WebClass and the set of 192 Web pages used in this experiment.

[4] The textual content of a page has not been seen before selecting the link.

[5] This preference is due to the fact that stopwords we considered refers to the English language.

Table 5. Some selected features extracted in the fifteen trials: Semantically relevant (on the left) and spurious (on the right).

Semantically relevant features:

Feature	1.1	1.2	1.3	2.1	2.2	2.3	3.1	3.2	3.3	4.1	4.2	4.3	5.1	5.2	5.3
Astronomy															
sky				X	X	X	X		X	X	X	X	X	X	X
star					X		X	X	X		X	X			X
mass						X	X	X	X		X	X			
atmosphere										X	X	X			X
Auto															
automotive										X	X	X	X	X	
wheel										X	X	X	X	X	
oil										X	X	X			X
transmission												X	X	X	
Jazz															
rhythm	X				X		X	X	X	X	X	X	X	X	X
black										X	X	X			X
festival													X		X
instrument												X			X
Motorcycle															
scooter				X	X	X	X	X	X		X	X	X		
riding					X	X				X	X	X	X	X	X
road									X	X	X	X	X	X	X
harley	X													X	X

Spurious features:

Feature	1.1	1.2	1.3	2.1	2.2	2.3	3.1	3.2	3.3	4.1	4.2	4.3	5.1	5.2	5.3
Astronomy															
ray	X	X		X			X								
distance				X	X	X		X							
contain	X	X		X											
tidal				X			X			X					
Auto															
technology	X			X	X	X		X	X						
conversion				X	X					X					
compressed							X	X							
energy	X	X													
Jazz															
davis				X			X								
disc	X	X													
soundtrack				X	X										
talent	X			X											
Motorcycle															
sidecar	X			X	X										
perception	X			X											
statnekov	X	X													
fault				X											

categorization [10]. Experimental results obtained with plain representation are shown in Fig. 2. It is worthwhile to note that, after an initial unstable behavior, both precision and recall stabilizes above 90% as the training set size increases. These encouraging results for relatively small training sets, for all classifiers and all classes, are an indication of the effectiveness of the feature selection phase. In particular, for the classes *Auto* and *Motorcycle*, WebClass shows high performances although the class dictionaries presented many common entries.

As further test, an independent set of web pages concerning the four topics above was built by means of the metasearcher ProFusion, which bases its results on well-known Internet search engines, such as Altavista and Excite. Queries for the four classes are reported below:

Astronomy	astronomy	astronomy & planet	astronomy & planet & telescope
Auto	car	car & vehicle	car & vehicle & automotive
Jazz	jazz	jazz & music	jazz & music & band
Motorcycles	motorcycle	motorcycle & bike	motorcycle & bike & rider

The first twenty-five links retrieved by the metasearcher were selected, thus collecting seventy-five pages per class. From the three hundred links, those pointing to pages in the training set or returning "not found" pages were removed. The remaining 283 pages were used for testing. The best classifiers obtained in the previous experiment have been used to classify the new test pages. In all cases, plain document representations have been used. Results reported in Table 6, confirm the system performances observed with cross-validation.

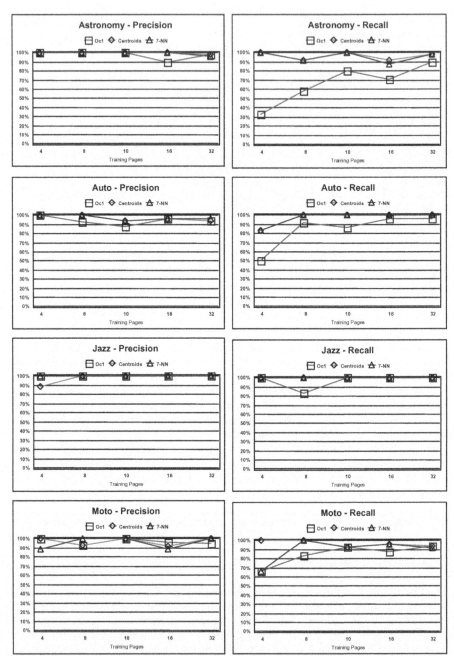

Fig. 2. Precision (left) and recall (right) of different classifiers (plain representation).

Table 6. *Precision* and *Recall* for the set of 283 test pages.

	Centroid		OC1		NN	
	Precision	**Recall**	**Precision**	**Recall**	**Precision**	**Recall**
Astronomy	98,5%	97,1%	100,0%	100,0%	97,1%	97,1%
Auto	97,3%	100,0%	94,6%	95,9%	100,0%	98,6%
Jazz	100,0%	97,0%	100,0%	92,5%	97,1%	100,0%
Moto	98,6%	100,0%	96,0%	100,0%	100,0%	98,6%

In order to investigate the effect of the information of the HTML layout structure on the performance of the classifier, a parallel set of experiments have been performed with the two emphasized representations (additive and multiplicative). From results on one hundred and twenty-eight training documents (fifth experiment), no clear indication that some classification technique generally benefits from the HTML structural information was found (see Table 7). In fact, in several cases the introduction of an emphasis factor can even worsen the predictive accuracy. As an illustrative examples, consider the title "MCS&L December - Yamaha Drag Star and Royal Star" of a page of the class Moto. By emphasizing the term "star" the system might erroneously associate the document to the class Astronomy.

Table 7. *Precision* and *recall* for different representations.

%	*Classifier*	*Emphasis*	*Astronomy*	*Auto*	*Jazz*	*Moto*
P		*No*	97.9	94,1	100	100
R	*Centroid*	*Additive*	100	94.0	100	97.9
E		*Multiplicat.*	98.0	93.4	100	88.5
C		*No*	95.9	96.1	100	100
I	*7-NN*	*Additive*	95.9	94.0	100	97.9
S		*Multiplicat.*	95.9	88.4	100	97.9
I		*No*	97.9	94,0	100	94.7
O	*Oc1*	*Additive*	97.7	93.9	100	96.3
N		*Multiplicat.*	95.5	85.1	100	96.3
R		*No*	97.9	100	100	93.7
	Centroid	*Additive*	97.9	97.9	100	95.8
E		*Multiplicat.*	95.8	93.7	100	91.7
C		*No*	97.9	100	100	91.6
A	*7-NN*	*Additive*	97.9	97.9	100	91.6
L		*Multiplicat.*	97.9	95.8	97.9	87.5
L		*No*	89.6	95.8	100	93.7
	Oc1	*Additive*	87.5	91.7	100	93.7
		Multiplicat.	87.5	89.6	100	93.7

6   Discussion of results and conclusions

Web mining is revealing a source of new interesting and challenging problems for machine learning. One of the main issues is the automatic selection of features to describe the document. This is part of the preprocessing step, whose result strongly affects the subsequent learning phases. A novel scoring measure for the selection of relevant features from training pages has been reported in the paper. This measure combines three different factors: term frequency (TF) and page frequency (PF), which favor the selection of frequent words in all documents of a given class, and inverse category frequency(ICF), which penalizes words common to different classes. The aim is that of selecting orthogonal sets of terms, one for each class. This means that Web pages of a class C_i will have many occurrences of terms selected for that class, and very few occurrences of terms selected for the other classes. Since the feature space is the same for all classes, it is possible to adopt distance based-approaches (e.g., centroids and k-nearest neighbor) to classify new documents. The cosine correlation is a similarity measure especially suitable for feature spaces spanned by orthogonal sets of features. For instance, by computing the inverse of the Euclidean distance as similarity metric, the orthogonal vectors $(1,1,0,0)$ and $(0,0,1,1)$ are considered similar to some extent, while the cosine correlation equals zero.

Experiments performed under well-controlled conditions have given encouraging results on the effectiveness of the feature selection process. Indeed, the study of selected features for training sets of different size has shown that features semantically close to (distant from) the topic of a class are selected (discarded) as the number of training cases increases.

That also explains the better performance of all document classifiers as the training set increases. Indeed, an empirical comparison of three classification methods, namely decision trees, centroids and k-nearest-neighbor, perform almost equally well on four distinct domains. In particular, the encouraging results obtained with the naive method based on centroids are a clear indication that extracted features allow training documents to cluster in distinct regions of the feature space.

It is noteworthy that WebClass performs well with a reduced number of features (1% of distinct non-stopwords extracted from documents). This result agrees with Yang and Pedersen's observation that a rather small feature subset should be used for text categorization, since it gives either better or good results as the whole set of features [18]. Nevertheless, the feature selection process adopted by Yang and Pedersen has an important difference with that reported in this paper: Terms extracted from documents of different classes are pooled. Thus, in the case of unbalanced class distribution, it may happen that terms extracted from documents of the majority class are favored more than terms extracted from documents of poorly represented classes. This problem does not occur in WebClass, since the number of features extracted for each class is the same.

In this paper a feasibility study has been reported, and the work can be extended in several directions. First, no semantic information has been considered in this work. For instance, the terms *jazz* and *music* are strongly correlated, but WebClass ignores it. Therefore, the similarity measure will be extended in order to take into account some ontological relations, such as hyponyms, hyperonyms, and synonyms. Second, the addition of new training documents or classes requires the computation of a new set of features from scratch. Thus, "incremental" feature extraction techniques and easily modifiable classifiers will be studied in order to extend the set of applications of the WebClass system. Third, further experiments on different data sets and with different parameters is planned for the next future in order to understand whether the relative importance of the HTML structure is confirmed on different domains. Fourth, an empirical comparison with competitive approaches to text classification has being performing. Finally, WebClass is being integrated into a shared workspace in order to support the search activity of geographically distributed groups of people with common interests in browsing the Web [6].

Acknowledgments

The authors would like to thank Giulio De Luise and Giorgio Vespucci for their contribution to the development of WebClass.

References

1. Aha, D.W. , Kibler, D., Albert, M.K.: Instance-based learning algorithms. Machine Learning Journal 6 (1991) 37-66
2. Apté, C. , Damerau, F., Weiss, S.M.: Automated learning of decision rules for text categorization. ACM Trans. on Information Systems 12 3 (1995) 233-251
3. Attardi, G. , Di Marco, S. , Salvi, D. , Sebastiani, F.:. Categorisation by context. On-line Proc. of the 1st Int. Workshop on Innovative Internet Information Systems   (1998). http://www.idt.ntnu.no/~monica/iii-98/proceedings_on_line.html
4. Bharat, K., Broder, A.: A technique for measuring the relative size and overlap of public Web search engines. Proc. of the 7th Int. WWW Conf., Brisbane Australia (1998) 379-388. http://decweb.ethz.ch/WWW7/1937/com1937.htm
5. Broder,   A.,   Glassman,   S.,   Manasse,   M.:   Clustering   the   Web. http://www.research.digital.com/SRC/articles/199707/cluster.html
6. Esposito, F. , Malerba, D., Di Pace, L., Leo P.: A learning Intermediary for Automated Classification of Web Pages. Proc. of the ICML-99 Workshop on Machine Learning in Text Data Analysis, Bled, Slovenia   (1999) 37-46
7. Etzioni O. : The World-Wide Web: Quagmire or gold mine? Communications of the ACM 39 1 (1996) 65-68
8. Joachims, T. : A probabilistic analysis of the Rocchio algorithm with TFIDF for text categorization, Proc. of the 14th Int. Conf. on Machine Learning (1997) 143-151
9. Koller, D., Sahami, M.: Toward optimal feature selection. Proc. of the 13th Int. Conf. on Machine Learning (1996) 284-292
10. Lewis, D.D.: Evaluating and optimizing autonomous text classification systems. Proc. of the 19th Annual Int. ACM SIGIR Conf. on Research and Development in Information Retrieval (1995) 246-254
11. Lewis, D.D, Schapire, R.E, Callan, J.P., Papka, R.: Training algorithms for linear text classifiers. In H.-P. Frei, D. Harman, P. Schauble, & R. Wilkinson, (ed.), Proceedings of the 19th Annual Int. ACM SIGIR Conf. on Research and Development in Information Retrieval (1996) 298-306
12. Masand, B., Linoff, G., Waltz, D.: Classifying new stories using memory based reasoning. Proceedings SIGIR'92 (1992) 59-65
13. Mladenic, D.: Feature subset selection in text-learning. In C. Nédellec, & C. Rouveirol (Eds.), Machine Learning: ECML-98, Lecture Notes in Artificial Intelligence, 1398, 95-100, Springer Berlin (1998)
14. Murthy, S.K., Kasif, S., Salzberg S.: A system for induction of oblique decision trees. Journal of Artificial Intelligence Research, 2 (1994) 1-32
15. Pazzani, M., Billsus   D.: Learning and revising user profiles: The identification of interesting web sites. Machine Learning Journal 23 (1997) 313-331
16. Salton, G., Buckley, C.: Term weighting approaches in automatic text retrieval. Information Processing and Management 24(5) (1988) 513-523
17. Smith. Z.: The truth about the Web: Crawling towards the eternity. Web Techniques Magazine (1997) http://www.webtechniques.com/features/1997/05/burner/burner.shtml
18. Yang, Y., Pedersen, J.O.: A comparative study on feature selection in text categorization. Proceedings of the 14th Int. Conf. on Machine Learning, (1997) 412-420.
19. Wilks, Y.: Information Extraction as a core language technology. Information Extraction SCIE-97 Springer Verlag (1997).

Experiences with a Logic-based Knowledge Discovery Support Environment

Fosca Giannotti[1], Giuseppe Manco[1], Dino Pedreschi[2], Franco Turini[2]

CNUCE – CNR
Via S. Maria 36, 56126 Pisa, Italy
{G.Manco,F.Giannotti}@cnuce.cnr.it

Dipartimento di Informatica
Università di Pisa
Corso Italia 40, 56125 Pisa, Italy
{pedre,turini}@di.unipi.it

Abstract. We introduce a Logic-Based Knowledge Discovery Support Environment, capable of integrating knowledge extraction and knowledge manipulation. Its flexibility and expressiveness in supporting the process of knowledge discovery in databases is illustrated by presenting two case studies, market-basket analysis and audit planning strategy in fraud detection. We show that the query language deals effectively and uniformly with data preparation, model extraction and model evaluation and analysis, thus providing a powerful formalism where methodologies for classes of challenging applications can be conveniently designed.

1 Introduction

Context. Most knowledge-intensive data analysis applications require the combination of two kinds of activities: knowledge acquisition, and reasoning on the acquired knowledge according to the expert rules that characterize the business. Data mining techniques are an answer to the first issue, in that they extract from raw data knowledge that is implicit and, more importantly, that is at a higher abstraction level. However, the ability of combining the results of knowledge extraction with expert rules is a key factor of success when building decision support systems.

Many applications of the above mentioned kind, in domains such as those selected in this paper for illustration purposes: *market basket analysis* and *fraud detection*, are challenging applications, for a variety of reasons.

1. *Multiple abstraction levels and separation of concerns*. Manipulation and reasoning over knowledge and data at different abstraction levels is required, in a way that closely follows the database design methodology:
   - a *conceptual* level, where the key issue is semantic integration of domain knowledge, expert (business) rules and extracted knowledge, as well as a uniform knowledge representation layer supporting the semantic integration of different analysis paradigms;
   - a *logical* level, where the key issue is the mapping to relational databases, and the design of required analyses in terms of a query language suitably integrated with mining capabilities;
   - a *physical* level, where the key issue is interoperability among various system components: DBMS's, data mining tools, desktop tools, as well as

E. Lamma and P. Mello (Eds.): AI*IA 99, LNAI 1792, pp. 202–213, 2000.

optimization of queries, mining operations and their combination, including choice of loose vs. tight coupling between the query language and the specialized mining tools.

2. *Management of the KDD process, and its tailoring to specific domains.* The specification and monitoring of a complex process, the so-called *KDD process*, is required. Little support is provided in this sense by the currently available technology. The management of the overall process, from data selection and preprocessing to data mining to knowledge evaluation, is limited in currently available data mining platforms to version control of data mining experiments. What is needed is a high-level design and development environment for vertical data analysis applications, where data mining tools and models are combined, geared, presented and evaluated in a way which is pertinent to the specific domain.

3. *Integration of extracted knowledge and domain knowledge.* The role of *domain*, or *background, knowledge* is relevant at each step of the KDD process: which attributes discriminate best, how can we characterize a correct/useful profile, what are the interesting exception conditions, etc., are all examples of domain dependent notions. Notably, in the evaluation phase we need to associate with each inferred knowledge structure some *quality function* that evaluates its information content in the specific domain. The notion of quality strictly pertains to the business decision process. However, while it is possible to define quantitative measures for certainty (e.g., estimated prediction accuracy on new data) or utility (e.g., gain, speed-up, etc.), notions such as novelty and understandability are much more subjective to the task, and hence difficult to define. More generally, a logically uniform representation of data, domain knowledge and extracted knowledge is required, in order to express easily high-level business rules.

Position. The position that we maintain in this paper is that a coherent formalism, capable of dealing uniformly with induced knowledge and background, or domain, knowledge, would represent a breakthrough in the design and development of decision support systems, in diverse application domains. The advantages of such an integrated formalism are, in principle:

- a high degree of expressiveness in specifying expert rules, or business rules;

- the ability to formalize the overall KDD process, thus tailoring a methodology to a specific class of applications;

- the separation of concerns between the specification level and the mapping to the underlying databases and data mining tools.

As a small step towards this ambitious goal, this paper tries to demonstrate how a suitable integration of deductive reasoning, such as that supported by logic database languages, and inductive reasoning, provides a powerful formalism, where methodologies for classes of data analysis applications are conveniently specified. Two case studies are briefly discussed, from two relevant application domains, to the purpose of illustrating the benefits of a uniform representation of induced knowledge and domain knowledge:

- *market basket analysis*, which requires the development of business rules of value for the market analyst, and
- *fraud detection*, which requires the construction and the evaluation of models of fraudulent behavior.

In fact, the objective of the rest of this paper is to demonstrate how a logic-based database language can support the various steps of the KDD process.

In the following we adopt the LDL++ [10,11] deductive database system, a rule-based language with a Prolog-like syntax, and a semantics that extends that of relational database query languages with recursion. Other advanced mechanisms, such as non-determinism and non-monotonicity, make LDL++ a highly expressive query language, and a viable system for knowledge-based applications [6]. Data mining extensions, discussed in this paper, are extensively studied in [2,4,5,10].

2 A market basket analysis application

Association rules are often too low-level to be directly used as a support of marketing decisions. Market analysts expect answers to more general questions, such as "Is supermarket assortment adequate for the company's target class of customers?" "Is a promotional campaign effective in establishing a desired purchasing habit in the target class of customers?" These are business rules, and association rules are necessary, albeit insufficient, basic mechanisms for their construction. Business rules require also the ability of combining association rule mining with deduction, or *reasoning*: reasoning on the temporal dimension, reasoning at different levels of granularity of products, reasoning on the spatial dimension, reasoning on association rules themselves. It is clear that a language where knowledge extraction and knowledge manipulation are integrated can provide flexibility and expressiveness in supporting the process of knowledge discovery in databases [9]. By focusing on association rules, we show that the query language deals effectively and uniformly with data preparation, rule extraction, analysis and construction of business rules.

A general way of dealing with data mining in a deductive framework is to directly define queries, which implement such mining needs. Aggregates are basic tools to start with. For example, the following program defines two-dimensional associations between the items of a market basket (the basket(Transaction,Item) relation), by using the predefined count aggregate.

```
pair(I₁,I₂, count<T>) ← basket(T, I₁),basket(T,I₂).

rules(I₁,I₂) ← pair(I₁,I₂,C),C ≥ 20.
```

The first rule generates and counts all the possible pairs of items in the same transaction, and the second one selects the pairs with sufficient support (i.e., at least 20). As a result, predicate rules specifies associations, i.e. rules that state that certain combinations of values occur with other combinations of values with a certain frequency.

Using combinations of rules and aggregates it is easy to define concepts of rule interestingness, that are different from the usual statistical parameters. Thus, other interesting measures, such as financial measures, may be defined. For example, if we are interested in discovering the associations between the cities and the products where the sales are less than 30% w.r.t. the average, we can define the following query:

average(avg<Sales>) ← sales(City,Product,Date,Sales).

avg_cp(City,Product,avg<Sales>) ← sales(City,Product,Date,Sales).

answer(City,Product) ← average(A), avg_cp(City,Product,P),P ≤ 0.7 × A.

The first rule computes the average on the whole sales. The second rule computes the averages related to the tuples <City,Product>, and the third rule selects the relevant rules.

However, the idea of using the query language to directly implement mining algorithms is not a novelty and it raises obvious concerns about efficiency. In our proposal, we use aggregates as the means to introduce mining primitives into the query language, and to implement such aggregates by exploiting another characteristics of the LDL++ system, namely, its open architecture, which supports easy connectivity with a variety of external systems and components. In our language, association rules are computed by an aggregate, as illustrated in the following rule:

rules(patterns<(m_s,m_c,Y_1,...,Y_n)>) ← q(X_1,...,X_m).

In this rule, the variables Y_1,...,Y_n are a subset of the variables X_1,...,X_m of q. The aggregate patterns computes the set of quadruples (L,R,S,C) where:

- L and R are respectively the left and right side of an association rule L ⇒ R,
- L=<l_1,...,l_i> and R=<r_1,...,r_k> where the tuple <l_1,...,l_i,r_1,...,r_k> is a rearranged subset of the values of Y_1,...,Y_n in a tuple resulting from the evaluation of q.
- S,C are respectively the (normalized) support and confidence of the rule L ⇒ R, such that S ≥ m_s and C ≥ m_c.

As an example, the following program computes the two-dimensional association rules with a minimum 40% support:

rules(patterns<0.4,0, I1,I2>) ← basket(T, I1), basket(T, I2).

Here, by querying rules(L,R,S,C), we obtain tuples such as rules(milk,bread,0.66,1).

The main advantage of the approach is that an external ad hoc induction algorithm computes the patterns (by applying ad hoc optimizations [1]), while the deductive engine has the only task of exchanging the data with the inductive engine on demand.

More significant examples of the power of the integration between induction and deduction are shown in solving the following problems.

- *"Which rules survive/decay up or down the product hierarchy?"* We can directly represent domain knowledge, such as taxonomies, and define abstractions at different levels of the products. To extract the rules which are preserved in an abstraction step, we can compute rules separately at each abstraction level, and select those which occur both at a level I and at level I+1:

rules_at_level(I, pattern<S,C,Itemset>) ← abstraction(I, Tid, Itemset).

preserved_rules(Left,Right) ← rules_at_level(I, Left, Right, _, _), rules_at_level(I+1, Left₂, Right₂, _, _), is_a(Left,Left₂),i s_a(Right,Right₂).

Where the abstraction predicate defines the generalization of a transaction according to a hierarchy level.

- *"What happens after promoting some product?"* We can give an answer by representing the promotion domain knowledge, and finding those rules which have been established by the promotion (i.e. rules which did not hold before the promotion, which were raised during the promotion and persisted after the promotion):

interval(before, -∞, 3/7/1998).
interval(promotion, 3/8/1998, 3/30/1998).
interval(after, 3/31/1998, +∞).

itemset_partition(Label, Tid, <Item>) ← transaction(Tid, Date, ..., Item),interval(Label, Start, End), Start ≤ Date, Date ≤ End.

rules_partition(Label, pattern<S,C, Itemset>)← itemset_partition(Label, _, Itemset).

preserved_rules(Left, Right) ←rules_partition(promotion,Left,Right,_,_), ¬rules_partition(before, Left,Right,_,_), rules_partition(after,Left,Right,_,_).

- *"How do rules change along time?"* One way to answer is given by computing rules valid in the whole dataset and then checking their support and confidence in predefined intervals. We then obtain a description of the evolution of rules in time, which can be used for instance to check whether a rule holds uniformly along time or has some peak in an interval, or shows some kind of periodicity.

check_support(Set, Label, count<Tid>) ← itemsets_partition(Label, Tid, Itemset), subset(Set, Itemset).

rules_evolution(Left, Right, Label, Supp) ← rules(Left, Right, _, _), union(Left, Right, All), check_support(All, Label, Supp).

3 Planning audit strategies in fraud detection

The second case study is about fiscal fraud detection. It was developed within a project aimed at investigating the adequacy and sustainability of KDD in the detection of tax evasion, and is fully described in [2].

Audit planning is a difficult task, which has to take into account constraints on the available resources, both human and financial. Therefore, planning has to face two conflicting issues:

- maximizing audit benefits, i.e., define subjects to be selected for audit in such a way that the recovery of evaded tax is maximized, and

- minimizing audit costs, i.e., define subjects to be selected for audit in such a way that the resources needed to carry out the audits are minimized.

The capability of designing systems for supporting this form of decisions poses technically precise challenges [3,7]: is there a KDD methodology for audit planning which may be tuned according to these options? What and how data mining tools may be adopted? How extracted knowledge may be combined with domain knowledge to obtain useful audit models? Our experience in the case study indicates that classification-based KDD [8] is an extremely promising direction for fiscal fraud detection. However, our approach is aimed at abstracting from the particular case study, and identifying the lines of a methodology for a whole class of applications – those centered on planning audit strategies. In this section, we briefly sketch the methodology for constructing profiles of fraudulent behavior based on classification, and aimed at supporting audit planning.

The dataset used in the case study consists of information from tax declarations, integrated with data from other sources, such as social benefits paid by taxpayers to employees and official budget documents. Each tuple in the dataset corresponds to a (large or medium-sized) company that filed a tax declaration in a certain period of time: we shall use the word *subject* to refer to such companies. The initial dataset consists of 80643 tuples, with 175 numeric attributes (or features), where only a few of which are categorical. From this dataset, 4103 tuples correspond to *audited* subjects: the outcome of the audit is recorded in a separate dataset with 4103 tuples and 7 attributes, one of which represents the *amount of evaded tax ascertained by the audit*: such feature is named *recovery*. The recovery attribute has value zero if no fraud is detected.

Audits are very expensive in both human and financial resources, and therefore it is important to focus audits on subjects that presumably return a high recovery. The challenging goal is therefore to build a classifier, which selects those interesting subjects. To this purpose, *a cost model* is developed, as follows. We define two derived attributes, *audit_cost* and *actual_recovery*, representing respectively an estimation of the cost of an audit in proportion to the size and the complexity of the subject to be audited, and the recovery of an audit after the audit cost. The target variable of our analysis is hence defined from *actual_recovery*, for each tuple i:

$$car(i) = \begin{cases} negative \text{ } \textbf{if} \text{ } actual\_recovery(i) \leq 0 \\ positive \text{ } \textbf{if} \text{ } actual\_recovery(i) > 0. \end{cases}$$

The decision trees are trained to distinguish between positive *car* (fruitful audits) and negative *car* (unfruitful audits). Once the training phase is over, the test-set is fed to the classifier, to check whether it is effective in selecting the new tuples. In our case, not only the misclassification rate of the classifier on the test-set is relevant, but also the actual recovery obtained from the audits of the subjects from the test-set that are classified as positive. This value can be matched against the real case, where all (366) tuples of the test-set are audited. This case, which we call *Real*, is characterized by the following:

- actual_recovery(*Real*) = $\sum_{i \in \text{test-set}}$ actual_recovery(i) = 159.6 ME

- audit_costs(*Real*) = $\sum_{i \in \text{test-set}}$ audit_costs(i) = 24.9 ME

where recovery and costs are expressed in million euro's. As the whole dataset consists of audited subjects, by comparing the previous values of the *Real* case with those of the subjects classified as positive by the various classifiers, it is possible to evaluate the potential improvement of using data mining techniques to the purpose of planning the audits.

Therefore, the classifiers resulting from our experiments are evaluated according to the following metrics, which represent domain-independent (1 and 2) and domain-dependent (3 through 6) indicators of the quality of a classifier *X*:

1. *confusion_matrix*(*X*), which summarizes the prediction of classifier *X* over the test-set tuples.

2. *misclassification_rate*(*X*), which is the percentage of misclassified tuples.

3. *actual_recovery*(*X*), which is the total amount of actual recovery for all tuples classified positive by *X*.

4. *audit_costs*(*X*), which is the total amount of audit costs for all tuples classified as positive by *X*.

5. *profitability*(*X*), which is the average actual recovery per audit, i.e., the ratio between the total actual recovery and the number of audits suggested by *X*.

6. *relevance*(*X*), which relates profitability (a domain-dependent measure) and misclassification rate (a domain-independent measure).

In particular, the confusion matrix is a table of the form:

Negative	Positive	← classified as
# TN	# FP	*car* = negative
# FN	# TP	*car* = positive

where the sets **TN** (*True Negative*), **TP** (*True Positive*), **FN** (*False Negative*), **FP** (*False Positive*), are defined as follows, using the notation $pred_X(i)$ to denote the *car* (either positive or negative) of a tuple *i* predicted by classifier *X*:

- **TN** = $\{i \mid pred_X(i) = car(i) = \text{negative}\}$

- **FP** = $\{i \mid pred_X(i) = \text{positive} \wedge car(i) = \text{negative}\}$, non fraudulent subjects which will be audited, according to *X*, with a negative actual recovery (an audit at a loss);

- **FN** = $\{i \mid pred_X(i) = \text{negative} \wedge car(i) = \text{positive}\}$, fraudulent subjects which will not be audited, according to *X*, although the audit would have a positive actual recovery (a loss for missing a fruitful audit);

- **TP** = $\{i \mid pred_X(i) = car(i) = \text{positive}\}$

We can consider two distinct approaches to classifier construction: on one hand, we can aim at keeping *FP* as small as possible, in order to minimize wasteful costs. On the other hand, we can aim at keeping *FN* as small as possible, in order to maximize evasion recovery. The two policies are clearly conflicting: as *FP* shrinks, *TP* shrinks accordingly, while *FN* (and *TN*) inevitably grows; the situation is dual when *FN* shrinks. In practice, it is needed to find an acceptable trade-off between the two conflicting policies, by balancing the level of actual recovery with the resources needed to achieve it. The classifier construction method can be adequately tuned to reach the desired trade-off.

We present here only one classifier, referred to as *A*, and assess its quality and adequacy to the objectives. *A* simply uses the original training-set, and therefore we obtain a classifier construction biased towards the majority class of training-set, i.e., the negative car. As a consequence, we enforce the "minimize *FP*" policy. To reduce errors, we employ 10-trees adaptive boosting. The confusion matrix of the obtained classifier is the following:

Negative	Positive	← classified as
237	11	*car* = negative
70	48	*car* = positive

The classifier *A* prescribes 59 audits (11 of which wasteful), and exhibits the following quality indicators:

- *misclassification_rate*(*A*) = 22%   (81 errors)
- *actual_recovery*(*A*) = 141.7 ME
- *audit_costs*(*A*) = 4 ME
- *profitability*(*A*) = 2.401 ME
- *relevance*(*A*) = 1.09

Profitability of model *A* is remarkable: 141 ME are recovered with only 59 audits, which implies an average of 4,649 ME per audit. If compared with the case *Real*, model *A* allow to recover 88% of the actual recovery of *Real* with 16% of audits. The following chart compares recovery and number of audits in the two cases.

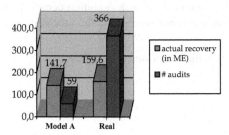

The entire methodology, including data preparation, training-set and test-set construction, model construction, prediction, quality evaluation, and complex combination of classifiers, can be formalized using the logic-based language. Even in this case, the features of the logic language that provide a uniform environment are the use of aggregates to import the results of algorithmic analyses into the logical framework, and the rule-oriented nature of the language that provide the most natural support to reason on the results of the mining phase.

The original datasets are organized in two tables: the table subject(ID:integer, F1:integer, ... , F20:integer) containing the tuples with all their features, say F1, ..., F20, and the table audit(ID:integer, Recovery:integer), containing the historical records of auditing outcomes. Subjects in the two tables are connected through the primary key ID. Addition of the cost model can be achieved through the following rule:.

```
audited_subject(ID, F1, ..., F20, Audit_Cost, Actual_Recovery, CAR) ←audit(ID, Recovery), subject(ID, F1, ..., F20),
                          audit_cost(F1, ..., F20,Audit_Cost),
                          Actual_Recovery = Recovery – Audit_Cost,
                          if (Actual_Recovery>0
                          then CAR = pos else CAR = neg).
```

The effect of this rule is to create the view audited_subject, as the join of the relations audit and subject on the ID key, extended with derived attributes. Other phases of data preparation, such as data cleaning and attribute selection, are not described here, although easily expressible in LDL++.

We exploit the open architecture of LDL++ to interface to the external classification algorithm (C5.0), which is invoked by the tree_induction predicate, with the following parameters: pruning factor level (PF), misclassification costs (MC) and boosting (BO). The following rule manages the process by first constructing a training-set of a specified size, and then calls the external induction program on the training-set.

```
tree_rules(Tree_name, P, PF, MC, BO, Rules_list) ← training_set(P, Cases_list),
                          tree_induction(Cases_list, PF, MC, BO, Rules_list).
```

The tree is returned to the tree_rules relation in the form of a list of rules, where each rule is in turn a list. In our case study, each subject has 20 features, so each rule is a list of 21 elements, one element for each feature and the final element for the predicted class. More precisely, $Rule_i = [C_1, C_2, ... , C_{20}, Predicted\_CAR]$, where:

- for $j=1,...,20$, C_j is either a condition on feature F_j, if such condition occurs in the precondition of rule $Rule_i$, or nil if feature F_j is not involved in the precondition of rule $Rule_i$;

- Predicted_CAR is the class (pos or neg) in the conclusion of rule $Rule_i$.

For instance, the rule:

```
if  feature2 > 12000 and feature5 <= 4300
    then class pos
```

is represented by the following list:

```
[nil, (>,12000), nil, nil, (<=, 4300), nil, ..., nil, pos].
```

Once a tree has been built, we want its rules to classify test cases. The predicate prediction establishes the class predicted by a given tree (Tree_name) for the test tuple identified by ID.

```
prediction(Tree_name, ID, CAR, Predicted_class) ← tree_rules(Tree_name, _ ,_ , _ , Rules_list),
                                 test_subject(ID, F1, ..., F20,Actual_cost, Actual_Recovery, CAR),
                                      classify(Rules_list ,[F1, ..., F20], Predicted_class).
```

The relation classify, whose definition is omitted, looks for the first rule in the tree, if any, whose precondition is satisfied by the feature values of a test-set tuple.

The quality indicators of a classifier may be conveniently defined by using the aggregates provided by LDL++. An incomplete list is the following:

- # *misclassification errors*: count the tuples where predicted class and actual class differ

```
tree_errors(Tree_name, count<ID>) ←  prediction(Tree_name, ID, CAR, Predicted_class),CAR ≠ Predicted_class.
```

- # *audits*: count the tuples classified as positive

```
tree_audits(Tree_name, count<ID>) ←prediction(Tree_name, ID, CAR, pos).
```

- *actual recovery*: sum actual recovery of all tuples classified as positive

```
tree_actual_recovery(Tree_name,sum<Actual_Recovery>) ←prediction(Tree_name, ID, CAR, pos),
                                 test_subject(ID, F1, ..., F20, Actual_cost, Actual_Recovery, CAR).
```

- # *TP*: count positive tuples classified as positive

```
tree_TP(Tree_name, count<ID>) ←prediction(Tree_name, ID, pos, pos).
```

Finally, model combination can be conveniently formalized. For instance, the following rules specify tree conjunction: a tuple is classified as positive by T1 ∧ T2 iff both T1 and T2 predict the tuple as positive.

```
tree_conjunction(T1, T2, ID, CAR, pos) ←prediction(T1, ID, CAR, pos, _),prediction(T2, ID, CAR, pos, _).
```

```
tree_conjunction (T1, T2, ID, CAR, neg) ←test_subject(ID, F1, ..., F20, C, E, CAR),
                                 ~ tree_conjunction(T1, T2, ID, CAR, pos).
```

4 Final remarks

In following the initial intuition that a logic-based language can be the right framework for integrating data mining techniques and reasoning, we adopted an application-driven approach. The most useful properties that we experimented are flexibility, capability to adapt to analysis needs, and modularity, i.e., possibility to clearly separate the various components, and provide a simple interface for their interaction.

Our future plans are now the systematization of our findings into a syntactically and semantically coherent linguistic framework. The issues that will be further investigated are:

- The formal specification of methodologies adequate to the classes of applications we have studied. Different classes of similar applications in fact may require different methods to specify and control the overall KDD process.

- The complete design of the logic formalism able to combine induction and deduction. The underlying language should be able to represent different tools pertaining to different applications and phases of the KDD process.

- An in-depth tackling of the implementation problem. A trade-off between loose and tight coupling of mining algorithms with the query language must be defined. A tight coupling allows directly integrating domain knowledge in the mining process, but often at the cost of worsening performance.

5 References

1. R. Agrawal, R. Srikant. *Fast Algorithms for Mining Association Rules.* In Procs. of 20th Int'l Conference on Very Large Databases, 1994.

2. F. Bonchi, F. Giannotti, G. Mainetto, D. Pedreschi. *A Classification-Based Methodology for Planning Audit Strategies in Fraud Detection.* In Proc. 5th ACM-SIGKDD Int. Conf. on Knowledge Discovery & Data Mining, KDD'99, pages 175-184. ACM Press, August 1999.

3. P.K. Chan, S.J. Stolfo. *Learning with Non-uniform Class and Cost Distributions: Effects and a Multi-Classifier Approach.* Machine Learning Journal, 1999, 1-27.

4. Giannotti, F., M. Nanni, G. Manco, D. Pedreschi, F. Turini. *Integration of Deduction and Induction for Mining Supermarket Sales Data.* In Proc. PADD'99, Practical Application of Data Discovery, Int. Workshop, p. 79-94. The Practical Applications Company, London, 1999.

5. Bonchi, F., Giannotti, F., G. Mainetto, D. Pedreschi. *Using Data Mining Techniques in Fiscal Fraud Detection.* In Proc. DaWak'99, Int. Conf. on Data Warehousing and Knowledge Discovery, Firenze 1999.

6. F. Giannotti, G. Manco, M. Nanni, D. Pedreschi. *Query Answering in Nondeterministic, Nonmonotonic, Logic Databases.* In Procs. of the Workshop on Flexible Query Answering, number 1395 in LNAI, 1998.

7. Fawcett, T and Provost, F. "Adaptive Fraud Detection", *Data Mining and Knowledge Discovery, Vol. 1, No. 1*, pp. 291-316, 1997.

8. Quinlan, J. R., *C4.5: Programs for Machine Learning*, Morgan Kaufman, 1993.

9. J. Han. Towards On-Line Analytical Mining in Large Databases. In *Sigmod Records*, 27(1):97--107, 1998.

10. W. Shen, K. Ong, B. Mitbander, and C. Zaniolo. Metaqueries for Data Mining. *In Advances in Knowledge Discovery and Data Mining*, pages 375--398. AAAI Press/The MIT Press, 1996.

11. C. Zaniolo, N. Arni, K. Ong. *Negation and Aggregates in Recursive Rules: The LDL++ Approach*. In Procs. DOOD93, LNCS vol.760, 1993.

12. C.Zaniolo, H.Wang. *Logic-Based User-Defined Aggregates for the Next Generation of Database Systems*. In The Logic Programming Paradigm: Current Trends and Future Directions. Springer Verlag, 1998.

Conceptual Change in Learning Naive Physics:
The Computational Model as a Theory Revision Process

F. Esposito, G. Semeraro, N. Fanizzi, S. Ferilli

Dipartimento di Informatica, Università di Bari
Via E. Orabona 4, 70126 Bari, Italy
{esposito, semeraro, fanizzi, ferilli}@di.uniba.it

Abstract. This work concerns a research project aiming at studying whether a machine learning system could reproduce the changes in the concept of force observed in children. The theoretical framework proposed considers learning as a process of formation and revision of a logical theory. INTHELEX, an incremental learning system, was used to emulate the transitions occurring in the human learning process. The experiment proved very interesting both for improving the computational model and for supporting a conceptual change by means of a model shift.

1   Introduction

This paper reports the results of a research initiative aiming at studying whether a machine learning system which learns from positive and negative examples by inductive inferential mechanisms could reproduce the changes in the concept of force observed in children. The study was developed in collaboration with a Cognitive Psychology team within the LHM (Learning in Humans and Machines) European Project, founded by the European Science Foundation.

According to the theoretical framework proposed by Vosniadou [1994], children's concepts concerning the physical world are embedded within larger theoretical structures that promote but also constrain their development. This framework has been proved successful in describing the development of the concept of force in young children. Research conducted with Greek elementary and high school children identified a number of important changes in the development of the concept of force, which were explained as changes in mental models, beliefs or presuppositions.

The theoretical framework proposed by the Machine Learning team considers learning as a process of formation and revision of a logical theory, where a logical theory is viewed as a set of conditions that are necessary and sufficient to explain a number of observations in a given environment. Revisions of a logical theory are caused by a shift in the language (*representation shift*) and a change in the number and meaning of the concepts involved (*conceptual change*): in the proposed framework these changes are obtained through induction mechanisms by generalization and specialization processes.

The incremental learning system INTHELEX (INcremental THEory Learner from EXamples) [Esposito et al., 1998] is used in order to test if a computational learning model based on revision processes triggered by inductive mechanisms is sufficient for modeling *conceptual change* in learning naive physics.

E. Lamma and P. Mello (Eds.): AI*IA 99, LNAI 1792, pp. 214–225, 2000.

On these grounds, a set of training examples for the artificial systems was extracted by the psychology team from a set of empirically derived hypotheses, concerning the kind of observations that may be critically related to the development of the concept of force in children.

INTHELEX has been used to emulate the transitions occurring in the human learning process when, starting from an empty theory and providing just an observation at a time, it is possible to model and to monitor the refinement process of a theory. The system tries to develop two models of force proposed by the psychologists, trying to maintain consistency of the logical theory through its operators.

The goal was investigating the validity of a particular Machine Learning system that may be categorized as an ILP (Inductive Logic Programming) system: whether it is able to simulate the very complex phenomena related to the process of acquiring concepts of naive physics by creating these conceptualizations and refining them on the ground of new evidences.

In next Section, the fundamental issues concerning the modeling of the conceptual change are discussed from different perspectives. Section 3 describes the incremental learning system INTHELEX, which has been used in the experiment, presented in Section 4, that aimed at testing the validity of the computational model in acquiring the concept of force. Finally we draw our conclusion in Section 5.

2   Modeling Conceptual Change as Theory Revision

The problem of modeling conceptual change that takes place in learning naive physics is faced using a theoretical framework proposed by [Vosniadou, 1994], which hypothesizes that children's explanations of physical phenomena could be justified considering that they make consistent use of generic mental representations (mental models) of the physical world, constrained by strong underlying beliefs an presuppositions.

Trying to interpret the development of the concept of force in younger children, different "initial mental models" were identified [Vosniadou et al., 1998].

This paper focuses on two mental representations of force, model 1 (*internal force*), which is very frequent in kindergarten children, and model 4 (*acquired force*), which is the dominant model for 6th grade children. These results show that many children start with a representation of force as something like a property of objects that are "big and heavy". Children explained that big/heavy objects have force because it is difficult for someone to lift or move those objects. It seems that these children believe that there is a force within those objects that can provide resistance. The potential of objects to provide resistance is considered as a function of their weight and not of other factors like their position or motion. The above evidence is an indication that young children do not differentiate force from weight.

By grade 6 many children seemed to have revised their initial models of force and to believe that force is a property of moving objects only. According to children's explanations this force is imparted to the objects by the agent who set them in motion (e.g. the man who threw or pushed the object), and continues to exist only while the object is moving. The interpretation of force as "internal force" in the big/heavy inanimate objects was not found among those of the older students who used the model of "acquired force".

The adoption of the model of acquired force requires a differentiation between force and weight. It also requires a distinction between animate and inanimate objects with respect to force.

In the acquired force model, force still continues to be perceived as a property of objects. In addition, this explanation seems to be constrained by the epistemological presupposition that the movement of inanimate objects is a phenomenon that needs to be explained and that the explanation ought to be a causal one.

From the machine learning point of view, if we assume that the only source of knowledge available is represented by a set of examples and no prior knowledge can be exploited, the process of formulating a new theory is bound to be progressive. Starting from contingent observations, it is not possible to define concepts that are regarded as correct. The validity of the theory itself extends to the available knowledge. Conversely, new observations can point out the inadequacies in the current formulation of the concepts. In such a case, a process of theory revision should be activated.

Two problems arise while trying to do this. First of all, we must decide which representation formalism and representation language should be used in the description of the examples and of the generated theories. Then we must decide, in the framework of representation change, which operators should be modeled in order to perform a process of automated knowledge revision in an effective way.

In the following section a machine learning system, which is able to revise and refine a theory in an incremental way will be presented. It maintains the inferred set of concept definitions consistent with all the examples as they become available so that the hypotheses generated step by step are continuously updated in the light of new evidence. This behavior seems in strict analogy with the human one.

3   The Learning System INTHELEX

INTHELEX (INcremental THEory Learner from EXamples) is a fully incremental, multi-conceptual closed loop learning system for the induction of hierarchical theories from examples. In detail, *full incrementality* avoids the need of a previously generated version of the theory to be available, so that learning can start from an empty theory and from the first example; *multi-conceptual* means that it can learn simultaneously various concepts, possibly related to each other; a *closed loop system* is a system in which the learned theory is checked to be valid on any new example available, and in case of failure a revision process is activated on it, in order to restore the completeness and consistency properties.

Incremental learning is necessary when either incomplete information is available at the time of initial theory generation, or the nature of the concepts evolves dynamically. The latter situation is the most difficult to handle since time evolution needs to be considered. In any case, it is useful to consider learning as a *closed loop* process, where feedback on performance is used to activate the theory revision phase.

INTHELEX learns theories, expressed as sets of Datalog^{OI} clauses [Semeraro et al., 1995], from positive and negative examples described in the same language. It adopts a full memory storage strategy - i.e., it retains all the available examples, thus the learned theories are guaranteed to be valid on the whole set of known examples.

The system integrates refinement operators based on the notion of Object Identity. Their effectiveness and efficiency (*ideality*, according to the definition given in [van der Laag & Nienhuys-Cheng, 1994]) was proven in [Esposito et al., 1996a]. Indeed, the process of theory revision explores a search space whose properties are different from those induced by the θ-subsumption ordering that causes the non-existence of ideal refinement operators as proven in [van der Laag & Nienhuys-Cheng, 1994]. Revisions performed by these operators are always minimal, since for the language bias all clauses in the theory contain only variables as arguments. Moreover these operators change the *answer set* of the theory (by answer set, we mean the set of examples that are satisfied by the theory). Therefore, INTHELEX is a system for theory revision rather than for *theory restructuring* [Wrobel, 1996].

In order to deal with the new examples INTHELEX makes use of an (optional) initial theory, of a graph reporting the dependence relationships among the concepts to be learned, and of a historical memory of all the past (positive and negative) examples that led to the current theory. A thorough description of the process of logical theory revision can be found in [Semeraro et al., 1995].

Since the system learns hierarchical theories, the dependence graph consists of a directed acyclic graph of concepts, in which it is assumed that offspring can concur to the definition of parent nodes. For example, the following tree represents the concept hierarchy for the induction of the concept *bicycle*:

bicycle		
Chassis	*wheel*	*handle-bar*
	tire	*rim*	

An instance of a positive example for INTHELEX is:

bicycle(b) :-   has_wheel(b,r1), has_wheel(b,r2), has_saddle(b,s),
          has_handlebar(b,h).

which means "*b* is a bicycle *since* it has two wheels, *r1* and *r2*, a saddle *s* and a handle-bar *h*"; a negative example could be:

not(bicycle(m)) :- has_wheel(m, w1), has_wheel(m, w2), has_engine(m, e).

to be read as "*m* is not a bicycle, *since* it has two wheels *w1* and *w2* and an engine, *e*".

Furthermore, the following could be a clause in an INTHELEX theory:

bicycle(X) :- has_wheel(X,Y), has_wheel(X,Z), not(has_engine(X,W)).

to be interpreted as "Something that has two wheels and has not an engine is a bicycle".

Examples cannot contain variables or negated literals in the body, while clauses of a hypothesis can contain negated literals in the body, to be interpreted according to the *negation-as-failure* rule [Clark, 1978].

Whenever a new example is considered, it is first checked to see if other concepts in the dependence graph are recognizable in its description, in which case (opportunely instantiated) literals concerning those concepts are added to its description. For instance, given:

computer(c) :- has_monitor(c,m), has_printer(c, p), has_CPU(c,u), part_of(c,k),
          has_keys(k, 102), italian(k).

as a new example, and the rule in the theory

keyboard(X) :- has_keys(X, Y), italian(X).

the literal *keyboard(k)* can be added to the body of the example.

If the example is negative and is not covered or positive and covered, no revision of the theory is needed. When a positive example is not covered, a generalization of the theory is needed. First of all, the system chooses a clause of the wrong concept to be generalized (*blame assignment*), then it tries to compute the least general generalization under object identity (lgg_{oi}) [Esposito et al., 1996a] of this clause and the example. If one of the clauses in the lgg_{OI} is consistent with all the past negative examples, then it replaces the chosen clause in the theory, or else a new clause is chosen to compute the lgg_{OI}. If no clause in an incomplete hypothesis of a theory can be generalized so that the resulting theory is complete and consistent, the system checks if the example itself, with the constants properly turned into variables, is consistent with the past negative examples and such a clause is added to the theory, or else the example itself is added as an exception to the theory.

On the other hand, if a negative example is covered, a specialization of the theory must be performed. Among the program clauses occurring in the SLD-derivation of the example, INTHELEX tries to specialize one whose concept is at the lowest possible level in the dependence graph, by adding to it one (or more) positive literal(s), which can discriminate all the past positive examples from the current negative one. We decided to specialize lower level concepts since they may appear in the definition of many higher level concepts; the underlying heuristic is that the latter will hopefully benefit from the better definition of the former. In case of failure, the operator tries to add the negation of a literal, which discriminates the negative example from all the past positive ones, to the first clause of the SLD-derivation.

If still none of the clauses obtained makes the theory complete and consistent, then the negative example is added to the theory as an exception. New incoming observations are always checked with respect to the exceptions before the rules of the related concept.

It is worth noting that, in analogy with human behavior, INTHELEX never rejects examples, but always refines the theory.

This purely inductive system has been further developed by providing it with an additional operator, namely an abductive proof procedure which could help in managing situations in which not only the set of all observations is partially known, but each observation could be incomplete too. In particular, we adopted the algorithm by Kakas and Mancarella [1990], modified as in [Esposito et al., 1996b].

Currently abduction is exploited to complete the (possibly) partial information of the examples. The observations are completed in such a way that they could be either covered (if positive) or ruled out (if negative) by the already generated theory, avoiding in such a way, whenever possible, the use of the operators and the modification of the theory. This solution limits the influence of abduction when it is not necessary, and, as a consequence, bounds the amount of information that was not directly observed in the theory. The set of abduced literals that are generated to be added to the description of an observation is minimal, so that the integrity constraints of the theory that are not involved in that observation are not taken into account.

When a new example is available, the abductive proof procedure is started. If it succeeds, the resulting set of assumptions that were necessary to correctly classify the observation is added to the example description before storing it. Otherwise the usual refinement procedure (generalization or specialization) is performed.

The negative literals that might be abductively assumed [Kakas & Mancarella, 1990] are not added to the description. Instead, they are handled by means of the Closed World Assumption [Lloyd, 1987].

It should be noted that this system is only able to perform changes at the representation language level: representation changes on the formalism level are still the exclusive domain of the human system design by means of changes in the concept hierarchy. Thus, sometimes inferred concepts might seem trivial or ingenuous if compared with the human ones.

4   The Experiment

The experiment concentrated on the process of simulating the type of transitions occurring in the children's learning process: Accretion, tuning or restructuration [Rumelhart & Norman, 1977]. The main underlying assumption is that, starting from an empty theory and providing a learning system with just one example at a time, it is possible to single out which learning operators are more appropriate for refining children's incorrect belief.

In order to state the problem and to plan the experiments, we designed a set of predicates which could be able to describe all the necessary, sufficient characteristics (for our experiment) of the observations and scenes presented to the children by the cognitive psychologists during their experimentation, that allowed the formulation of mental models of *force*.

Since our learning system does not perform predicate invention, we have to state, for each example of *force* submitted, whether it is *inner* or *acquired*. To do this, we must try to interpret children definitions of the concept of *force*, distinguishing among situations where the force is *inner* or *acquired* depending on the scene presented to children. The goal of the computational model is, for each of these two classes of *force*, to discover which features characterize/discriminate all the instances, and to compare this with the interpretations of the corresponding verbal definitions given by the children for that particular kind of force.

The supervised learning paradigm constrained us to give examples of *inner* and *acquired force*, explicitly denoted. We know that inner force is something inferred (it is our interpretation of the meaning children give to the word force), but here the goal is simply to validate the system refinement operators in order to see if they could change the initial representations correctly. These concepts should be interpreted according to the intuitive notions deriving from the observation of the corresponding phenomena (even though they could be, and often are, completely erroneous from the point of view of Physics).

It is worth noting that, considering the mental models of force developed by students ranging in age from five to fifteen years, the acquisition of the model concerning the concept *acquired force* requires rather complex inferences based on observations like "if an object is inanimate then there can be no self-initiated motion", "if there is motion, then force must have been exerted", "if motion continues, then force exerted (or part of it) must have become acquired force", "if motion stops, then acquired force has dissipated". Consequently, some examples regarding the concept *acquired force* need to be described as a temporal sequence of scenes, thus requiring a modification of the representation language to be able to express such a sequence.

The best solution to this problem appeared to be the addition to each predicate, representing some property that could change over the time, of an argument stating the moment in which that property is true. Moreover, we introduced the two predicates *before(X,Y)* and *after(X,Y)* to express the fact that "moment X precedes or follows, respectively, moment Y in the temporal flow". The use of temporal relationships also allows more generality, since in this way some actions learned in the moment they were in progress can be recognized in some past or future moments of other examples. In addition, it is necessary to decide *a priori* the number of time intervals occurring in the observation, and to chain them only through the predicates *before* and *after*, starting from the present. Under these assumptions, the rules

after(X,Y) :- after(X,Z), after(Z,Y).

before(X,Y) :- before(X,Z), before(Z,Y).
should be assumed, in order to temporally connect moments that do not immediately follow each other as well.

The complete list of predicates in the representation language used for the experiment, along with the corresponding interpretations, is given in Table 1.

The experiment simulated the situation in which the initial theory was empty and the observations contributed to its creation and refinement. For each example used to train the system, we will give first a description in natural language, then the internal representation of INTHELEX (in Prolog style). The graphical representation of such examples is given in Figure 1.

The first part of the experiment concerns the concept *inner_force*, to be interpreted as the capability of someone/something to resist an attempt to move it. The first example (Figure 1a) is: "A big, heavy man, who does not move when pushed by a child, has inner force" (*n* being the moment in which the scene takes place).

has_inner_force(m,n) :- man(m), dimension_high(m), weight_high(m), quiet(m,n),
*   child(c), dimension_low(c), weight_low(c), quiet(c,n),*
*   pushes(c,m,n).*

Note that, in the logical clause, the fact that the man is not moving has been transformed into the positive information that he is quiet. This because the example clauses must contain only positive literals in the body.

The computer generalizes this example to any man:

has_inner_force(X,Y)	X has inner force at moment Y
has_acquired_force(X,Y)	X has acquired force at moment Y
must_acquire_motion(X,Y)	X must acquire motion at moment Y
acquiring_motion(X,Y)	X is acquiring motion at moment Y
animate(X)	X is animate
inanimate(X)	X is inanimate
man(X)	X is a man
child(X)	X is a child
stone(X)	X is a stone
chair(X)	X is a chair
table(X)	X is a table
box(X)	X is a box
dimension_low(X)	X is small
dimension_medium(X)	X has medium dimension
dimension_high(X)	X is big
weight_low(X)	X is light
weight_medium(X)	X has medium weight
weight_high(X)	X is heavy
quiet(X,Y)	X is quiet at moment Y
moving(X,Y)	X is moving at moment Y
pushes(X,Y,Z)	X pushes Y at moment Z
exerts_force(X,Y,Z)	X is exerting force on Y at moment Z
before (X,Y)	Moment X immediately precedes moment Y
after(X,Y)	Moment X immediately follows moment Y

Table 1.   List of predicates used in the experiment along with the corresponding natural language interpretation.

has_inner_force(X,T) :- man(X), dimension_high(X), weight_high(X), quiet(X,T),
child(Y), dimension_low(Y), weight_low(Y), quiet(Y,T),
pushes(Y,X,T).

Children say that "Big/heavy objects have force".

In order to refine this concept, the example: "A big, heavy stone, which does not move when pushed by a big, heavy man, has inner force" (Figure 1b) is given

has_inner_force(s,n) :- stone(s), dimension_high(s), weight_high(s), quiet(s,n),
man(m), dimension_high(m), weight_high(m), quiet(m,n),
pushes(m,s,n).

INTHELEX generalizes the first inference, and produces a rule whose natural language translation is "Any big and heavy object, which does not move when pushed by something, has inner force"

has_inner_force(X,T) :- dimension_high(X), weight_high(X), quiet(X,T),
quiet(Y,T), pushes(Y,X,T).

For the children, "Big/heavy objects have force".

The results produced by INTHELEX suggest that there is possibly confusion of the concept *inner_force* with the concept of *weight*.

The experiment regarding the concept *acquired_force* is more complex. The system is provided with the information that stones, chairs and tables are inanimate, by handling these requirements as constraints.

First, INTHELEX must learn that inanimate objects do not move by themselves by

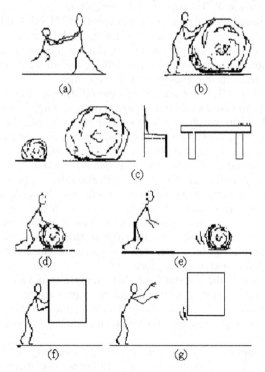

Figure 1. Graphical representation of the examples given to the children in the experiment.

exploiting the examples depicted in Figure 1c.

Here, the first problem arises. INTHELEX learns from positive and negative examples: this choice allows the system to produce complete and consistent theories that could be revised incrementally in the light of new evidences. The system cannot learn the negation of a concept; so, these examples should be handled either as negative ones for the concept motion or as positive ones for some new concept (say *must_acquire_motion*).

The first solution would not improve the inferred theory, and the learning system would just store the examples (since the current theory itself does not cover them). Conversely, if we provide INTHELEX with the following positive instances of the concept *must_acquire_motion* (so that it will also use them as negative instances of the concept acquired_force):

must_acquire_motion(s,n) :- stone(s), quiet(s,n), dimension_medium(s),
                            weight_medium(s).
must_acquire_motion(s,n) :- stone(s), dimension_high(s), weight_high(s), quiet(s,n).
must_acquire_motion(c,n) :- chair(c), quiet(c,n), dimension_medium(c),
                            weight_medium(c).
must_acquire_motion(t,n) :- table(t), quiet(t,n), dimension_medium(t),
                            weight_medium(t).

it learns that "quiet inanimate objects must acquire motion" (since they cannot move by themselves):

must_acquire_motion(X,T) :- inanimate(X), quiet(X,T).

It is worth noting that, in the given examples, INTHELEX ignored the type and dimensions of the inanimate object, which are irrelevant details for the concept. If we now consider a counterexample for this concept, representing a man who cannot move a big stone (which would be covered by the above definition), the system specializes the previous inference in the following one:

must_acquire_motion(X,T) :- inanimate(X), quiet(X,T), not(weight_high(X)).

that is, "quiet, inanimate and not heavy objects must acquire motion".

The second situation concerns a stone, which is moving because of the force exerted on it by a man (Figure 1d). It is important to point out that this is not yet an instance of the concept *acquired_force*, so the above-mentioned problem arises again. This time, we introduce the concept of *acquiring_motion* for the same reason as above. Thus, we provide INTHELEX with the example: "A stone of medium weight and dimension, that moves when a man exerts a force on it, is acquiring motion"

acquiring_motion(s,n) :- stone(s), weight_medium(s), dimension_medium(s),
                        moving(s,n), man(m), weight_medium(m),
                        dimension_medium(m), moving(m,n), exerts_force(m,s,n).

Such an example can be considered a negative instance for both the concepts *must_acquire_force* and *acquired_force*.

INTHELEX turns the constants of this example into variables, and adds the information that the stone is inanimate and the man is animate.

Now, the observation in Figure 1f is given as a further example of acquiring force: "A box of light weight and big dimension, that moves when a man throws it, is acquiring motion"

acquiring_motion(b,n) :- box(b), weight_low(b), dimension_high(b), moving(b,n),
                        man(m), weight_medium(m), dimension_medium(m),
                        moving(m,n), exerts_force(m,b,n).

It causes the system to generalize producing the rule:

acquiring_motion(X,T) :- inanimate(X), moving(X,T), man(Y), animate(Y),
weight_medium(Y), dimension_medium(Y),
moving(Y,T), exerts_force(Y,X,T).

which means that "an inanimate object which moves when a man exerts a force on it is acquiring motion".

Children say that "If inanimate objects move, then a force is being exerted on them".

The next example (Figure 1e) claims that: "If the stone continues moving even after the man stops pushing it, then it has acquired force"

has_acquired_force(s,n) :- stone(s), weight_medium(s), dimension_medium(s),
man(m), moving(s,n), weight_medium(m),
dimension_medium(m), moving (s,b), moving(m,b),
quiet(s,a), exerts_force(m,s,b), before(b,n), after(a,n).

This is exploited by INTHELEX as a counterexample for the concepts *must_acquire_motion* and *acquiring_motion*.

INTHELEX produces the following rule:

has_acquired_force(X,T) :- inanimate(X), stone(X), animate(Y), man(Y),
weight_medium(X), weight_medium(Y),
dimension_medium(X), dimension_medium(Y),
moving(X,T), moving(X,B), moving(Y,B), quiet(X,A),
exerts_force(Y,X,B), before(B,T), after(A,T),
acquiring_motion(X,B), must_acquire_motion(X,A).

i.e., briefly, "A stone has acquired force if it acquired motion in the past, is now moving and in the future will stop".

The last example (Figure 1g) shows a big box that is moving in the air after having been thrown by a man and that stops after a while.

has_acquired_force(b,n) :- box(b), weight_low(b), dimension_high(b), man(m),
moving(b,n), weight_medium(m), dimension_medium(m),
moving (m,p), moving(b,p), quiet(b,a),
exerts_force(m,b,p), before(p,n), after(a,n).

INTHELEX can refine the previous rule yielding as a result the following clause:

has_acquired_force(X,T) :- inanimate(X), animate(Y), man(Y), weight_medium(Y),
dimension_medium(Y), moving(X,T), moving(X,B),
moving(Y,B), quiet(X,A), exerts_force(Y,X,B),
before(B,T), after(A,T), acquiring_motion(X,B),
must_acquire_motion(X,A).

Note that this definition is very specific, due to the fact that only one example for each concept was examined.

Children say that "If animate objects continue to move, then some force must be exerted on them (acquired force). When this force dissipates, the object stops".

5 Conclusion

The aim of this study was to see whether learning systems which learn from positive and negative examples by inductive inferential mechanisms could reproduce the changes in the concept of force observed in children. It has been suggested that children develop their concept of *force* on the basis of their interpretation of the observations and information from their cultural background. Given some empirically derived hypotheses about the development of the concept of force, it was possible to extract the kinds of observations and/or information that are needed for the development to take place. These observations were used to validate the inferential power of a learning system able to produce from examples concepts related to the two models of "internal" and "acquired" force which were found in the developmental studies.

The experiment concentrated on the process of theory revision; INTHELEX was used to emulate the transitions occurring in the human learning process when, starting from an empty theory and providing just an observation at a time, it is possible to model and to monitor the refinement process of a theory. Some initial interesting results have been obtained although a direct comparison with the children acquisition mechanisms is not possible.

From the Machine Learning point of view, considering that the models proposed by the cognitive psychologists are very useful, the experiment proved very interesting both for improving the computational model and for supporting a conceptual change based on language shift instead of a model shift or a paradigm change [Wrobel, 1994]. Indeed, in our experiment the computational model changed the learned concept definitions only through generalization/specialization. The learning system succeeded, at a first very simple level, in inferring the naive physics concept definitions, despite of the few (and trivial, if compared to the complex human ones) inference mechanisms it integrates. It seems enough accurate in performing the conceptualization process, for two basic reasons: a) changes of the initial theory caused by a new observation go through a process of refinement and it is not necessary to re-start the whole learning process from the beginning when a new instance is presented; b) it can take into account temporal relations albeit in a very simplistic way.

On this ground, we may expect that even another objective could be reached: supervising in a more controlled way conceptual changes that happen when learning concepts from examples. However, it could be interesting to use the incremental system in a larger experiment with the aim of discovering how the order of the observations and the kind of the negative examples and exceptions supplied by the trainer could influence the formation of a correct theory. Unfortunately, running new experiments of this kind is feasible only if the results of previous, similar experiments carried out with the children by the cognitive psychologists are available to make the comparison possible.

References

[Clark, 1978] K.L. Clark, Negation as failure. *Logic and Data Bases*, Gallaire, H. and Minker, J., (Eds.), Plenum Press, 293-322, 1978.

[Esposito et al., 1996a] F. Esposito, A. Laterza, D. Malerba, and G. Semeraro. Locally Finite, Proper and Complete Operators for Refining Datalog Programs. *Foundations of Intelligent Systems, Lecture Notes in Artificial Intelligence 1079*, Z.W. Ras and M. Michalewicz (Eds.), Springer, 468-478, 1996.

[Esposito et al., 1996b] F. Esposito, E. Lamma, D. Malerba, P. Mello, M. Milano, F. Riguzzi, G. Semeraro. Learning Abductive Logic Programs. *ECAI 96 Workshop on Abductive and Inductive Reasoning, Workshop Notes*, 1996.

[Esposito et al., 1998] F. Esposito, G. Semeraro, N. Fanizzi, and S. Ferilli. Multistrategy Theory Revision with INTHELEX. *Proceedings of the 4th International Workshop on Multistrategy Learning*, MSL-98, F. Esposito, R.S. Michalski and L. Saitta (Eds.), 65-74, 1998.

[Kakas & Mancarella, 1990] A.C. Kakas, and P. Mancarella. On the Relation of Truth Maintenance and Abduction. *Proceedings of the 1st Pacific Rim International Conference on Artificial Intelligence, PRICAI 90*, Nagoya, Japan, 1990.

[Lloyd, 1987] J.W. Lloyd. *Foundations of Logic Programming*, Springer-Verlag, 2nd edition.

[Rumelhart & Norman, 1977] D.E. Rumelhart, and D.A. Norman. Accretion, Tuning and Restructuring: Three modes of Learning. *Semantic Factors in Cognition*, J.W. Cotton and R.L. Klatzky, Erlbaum, Hillsdale, NJ, 1977.

[Semeraro et al., 1995] G. Semeraro, F. Esposito, N. Fanizzi, and D. Malerba. Revision of Logical Theories. *Topics in Artificial Intelligence, Lecture Notes in Artificial Intelligence 992*, M. Gori and G. Soda (Eds.), Springer, 365-376, 1995.

[van der Laag & Nienhuys-Cheng, 1994] P.R.J. van der Laag, and S.-H. Nienhuys-Cheng. Existence and Nonexistence of Complete Refinement Operators. *Machine Learning: ECML-94 - Proceedings of the European Conference on Machine Learning, Lecture Notes in Artificial Intelligence 784*, F. Bergadano and L. De Raedt (Eds.), 307-322, Springer-Verlag, 1994.

[Vosniadou, 1994] S. Vosniadou. Capturing and modeling the process of conceptual change. *Learning and Instruction*, 4, 1994.

[Vosniadou et al., 1998] S. Vosniadou, C. Ioannides, A. Dimitracopoulou, D. Kayser, M. Champesme, F. Esposito, G. Semeraro, D. Malerba, S. Ferilli. Modelling Conceptual Changes in Mechanics: An Interdisciplinary Perspective. *Proceedings of the 2nd European Conference on Cognitive Modelling (ECCM-98)*, E. Ritter and R. M. Young (Eds.), Nottingham UK, 1998.

[Wrobel, 1994] S. Wrobel. Concept Formation and Knowledge Revision, Kluwer Academic Publishers, 1994.

[Wrobel, 1996] S. Wrobel. First Order Theory Refinement. Advances in Inductive Logic Programming, L. De Raedt (Ed.), 14-33, IOS Press, Amsterdam, 1996.

Using the Hermite Regression Formula
to Design a Neural Architecture with Automatic
Learning of the "Hidden" Activation Functions

S.Gaglio[1], G.Pilato[2], F.Sorbello[1] and G.Vassallo[3]

[1] Dip. di Ingegneria Automatica e Informatica, Univ. of Palermo, Italy
and CERE-CNR, Palermo, Italy
{gaglio,sorbello}@unipa.it

[2] Dip. di Ingegneria Elettrica, Univ. of Palermo, Palermo, Italy
pilato@csai.unipa.it

[3] CRES – Centro per la Ricerca Elettronica in Sicilia, Monreale (PA) – Italy
vassallo@cres.it

Abstract. The value of the output function gradient of a neural network, calculated in the training points, plays an essential role for its generalization capability.

In this paper a feed forward neural architecture (αNet) that can learn the activation function of its hidden units during the training phase is presented. The automatic learning is obtained through the joint use of the Hermite regression formula and the CGD optimization algorithm with the Powell restart conditions. This technique leads to a smooth output function of αNet in the nearby of the training points, achieving an improvement of the generalization capability and the flexibility of the neural architecture.

Experimental results, obtained comparing αNet with traditional architectures with sigmoidal or sinusoidal activation functions, show that the former is very flexible and has good approximation and classification capabilities.

1. Introduction

It is well known that artificial neural networks are powerful tools in the pattern recognition field. Feed-forward architectures can approximate boundary surfaces, hence they are universal classifiers[14]; in particular Multilayer perceptrons (MLPs), thanks to the compromise realized between recognition rate, recognition speed and memory resources, are used for both approximation and classification tasks.

It has been shown that a feed-forward neural architecture with one hidden layer can approximate various kind of functions defined on compact sets in $\mathbf{R}^n$[5].

However, the generalization capability of a MLP is strongly dependent on the training set characteristic. In fact, the training set should be consisting of a large number of elements which should be also equally distributed[15]

In the field of the handwritten character recognition, to increase the generalization

E. Lamma and P. Mello (Eds.): AI*IA 99, LNAI 1792, pp. 226–237, 2000.
© Springer-Verlag Berlin Heidelberg 2000

capability of a neural network, the training set can be artificially enhanced adding slightly rotated characters to the original training patterns[1]. This technique leads to a low gradient of the output function learned by the neural architecture, according to the results achieved by Le Cun in[4]. Similarly, other methods used to increase the generalization capability of feed forward neural networks are reported in [6].

Besides, the value of the output gradient, calculated in the training points, of the function learned by the network after the training phase is strongly related to the generalization skill of feed-forward neural architectures [2][3].

In [7][8] Hwang et al., to better the statistical performances of the PPL[9], used a orthogonal polynomial regression method obtaining a smooth function approximation.

The choice of the activation function of the hidden units is also crucial to obtain a good generalization quality[1]. Three-layered feed-forward networks usually adopt sigmoidal activation function in their hidden units. However, it is known that, despite the computational properties and the very simple derivative form of this kind of functions, they are not suitable for a lot of regression applications[7][8].

In this paper it is introduced a feed-forward neural architecture, called αNet, with two fundamental characteristics: it is enhanced the generalization capability of the architecture obtaining, after that the learning phase is over, a low gradient of the output function in the nearby of the points used for the training; besides it is enhanced the flexibility of the network, adopting hidden units that can change the shape of their activation function during the training phase.

The two above mentioned features can be reached making a joint use of the Hermite regression formula and the Conjugate Gradient Descent algorithm with Powell's restart conditions[10]: each activation function belonging to the hidden layer is expressed as the weighted sum of the first R Hermite orthonormal functions; the coefficients of the sum are continuously changed during the training phase together with the weights of the connections between the units of the network using the CGRD algorithm. Hence each activation function of the hidden layer changes its shape until the minimum of the error over the training set is reached.

The choice of the Hermite regression algorithm is due to the fact that the use of this algorithm leads to a smooth interpolation and that it is possible to calculate easily and accurately the values of the approximated function and its first derivative[7][8].

The remainder of this paper is organized as follows: section 2 deals with theoretical background; in section 3 it is introduced in detail the αNet neural architecture and its way of learning; section 4 deals with experimental results obtained with αNet and two traditional neural architectures that use hidden units with sigmoidal or sinusoidal activation functions; in section 5 conclusions are then given.

2. Theoretical Background

Since the proposed solution makes a joint use of the Hermite regression formula and the Conjugate Gradient Descent technique with the Powell's restart conditions, here they are briefly summed up.

2.1 The Hermite Regression Formula

Let H_R the r-th Hermite orthogonal polynomial and $\Phi(x)$ a gaussian function with zero mean and unitary variance, then the r-th Hermite orthonormal function can be defined as[7][8]:

$$h_r(x) \equiv (r!)^{-\frac{1}{2}} \cdot \pi^{\frac{1}{4}} \cdot 2^{-\frac{r-1}{2}} \cdot H_r(x) \cdot \Phi(x) \qquad -\infty < x < \infty \qquad (1)$$

and the desiderated approximating smooth function is given by:

$$f^*(x) = \sum_{r=1}^{R} c_r^* h_r(x) \qquad (2)$$

and the value of its first derivative can easily be calculated:

$$\frac{d}{dx} f^*(x) = \sum_{r=1}^{R} c_r^* h_r'(x) = \sum_{r=1}^{R} c_r^* \left[(2r)^{\frac{1}{2}} h_{r-1}(x) - x h_r(x) \right] \qquad (3)$$

2.2 The CGRD Algorithm

The algorithm is based on the conjugate gradient descent (CGD) optimization technique which is faster than the steepest descent method and does not require any choice of critical parameters like learning rate or momentum[1][10].

The search of the minimum of the error surface is based on the determination of a set of directions, so that the minimization gain on a particular direction does not interfere with the minimization obtained before.

The chosen algorithm employs the optimization technique of the conjugate gradient descent algorithm; such a technique substitutes the steeepest descent method with one of minimization along a set of non-interfering directions. These directions are usually called conjugate directions.

An optimal result might be to have a set of linearly independent conjugate directions, which can be searched with a recursive formula, first developed by Powell[10].

3. The Proposed Solution

The regularity of the output functions plays an essential role for the generalization capability of a neural network[1]; furthermore, it has been shown in a previous work[3] that the approximation capability is strictly related to the classification capability by the value (in the training points) of the gradient of the output function learned by the network after the training phase. Hence, a good interpolator is also a good classifier.

Let **O** be the input-output mapping learned by a feed-forward neural network and **p** be the generic pattern used for the network training; to obtain a good classification ability it is necessary to minimize the quantity $\nabla \mathbf{O}|_p$, i.e. it is necessary to keep the gradient of the output function in the nearby of the training points as low as possible. The αNet feed-forward network has been hence designed to achieve a twofold advantage:

1. to obtain a three-layered feed-forward network without shortcuts that requires as few as possible connections between its units to reduce the computational cost of the network during the production phase;

2. to obtain a low value of the gradient, in the nearby of the training points, of the output function of any unit belonging to the output layer thus trying to obtain a better generalization capability [1];

3.1 The Computational and the Gradient Costs

Let us consider a typical three-layered feed-forward network without shortcuts (see fig.3.1);

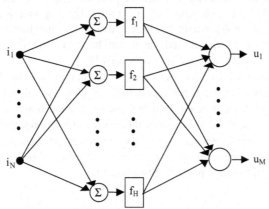

Fig. 3.1. A typical three-layered feed-forward network with no shortcuts

if H is the number of hidden units, N is the number of the input units, M is the number of output units of the network, to measure the number of connections between the network units it has been introduced[2][3] the *Computational Cost of the Production Phase* $\mathbf{C_C}$:

$$C_C \equiv H \cdot (N + M)$$

If u_k is the k-th output of the network, $\mathbf{x}_r$ is the r-th training pattern and P is the number of input-output patterns of the training set, to measure the average gradient, in the nearby of the training points, of the output function of any unit belonging to the output layer it has been introduced[2][3] the *Gradient Cost* **C_G**:

$$C_G \equiv \frac{1}{P} \sum_{r=1}^{P} \left(\sum_{k=1}^{M} \left| \nabla u_k \right|_{\mathbf{x}_r}^2 \right)$$

3.2 αNet Architecture

Having introduced the quantities C_C and C_G, it is necessary to keep them as low as possible; to reach this goal it has been introduced the αNet architecture whose *k-th* hidden unit has the activation function $f^*_k(x)$ given by (2):

$$f_k^*(x) = \sum_{r=1}^{R} c_{rk}^* h_{rk}(x)$$

where $h_{rk}(x)$ are the first R orthonormal functions of Hermite calculated in the point x and the coefficients c^*_{rk} are the expansion coefficients of the Hermite approximation algorithm; this approximation function has been chosen in order to obtain a smooth representation of the output function of any unit belonging to the output layer; moreover the Hermite polynomials have the advantages that they can be easily calculated in a recursive manner and, as it can be seen from (3), that the first derivative can also be calculated in a very easy way[7][8]
The activation function of the units belonging to the output layer of αNet is linear while the architecture of the units belonging to the hidden layer of αNet is different from that one of a traditional neural unit that uses activation functions arranged in advance. In fact, in figure 3.2 it is shown the typical unit belonging to the hidden layer of αNet: the dashed square represents the activation function block. It is worthwhile to point out that each block h_r, representing the orthonormal function of Hermite, is calculated from the preceding two (eq. 1).

3.3 αNet Learning

The number H of the hidden units and the number R of the Hermite orthonormal functions are experimentally chosen by hand.
The R weights c_{rk}^* of the k-th unit belonging to the hidden layer of αNet are set before starting the training phase so that $f^*_k(x)$ results the approximation of a bell-shaped function. In fact, it has been seen experimentally that this configuration of expansion coefficients leads to better generalization results.
During the training phase the coefficients c_{rk}^* are changed together with the weights of the connections between the units of αNet using the CGRD algorithm with the Powell's restart conditions[10]. Therefore each activation function of each hidden

unit of αNet is continuously changed until the minimum of the error over the training set is reached.

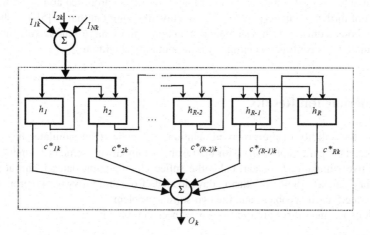

Fig. 3.2. It is represented the typical k-th hidden unit of αNet: note that the first R orthonormal Hermite functions h_r are calculated and each of them is then multiplied for the respective weight c_{rk}^*. The weights c_{rk}^* are changed during the training phase according to the CGRD optimization algorithm.

The decision of choosing the Conjugate Gradient Descent optimization algorithm with the restart conditions of Powell has matured because of very good results obtained in training MLPs with this technique with respect to other optimization algorithms[1]; the main features of this algorithm are:

- high learning speed
- optimal performances for high-grade polynomial functions;
- reasonable amount of memory needed: memory requirements increase linearly with the number of variables needed.

The computational complexity of the learning algorithm, supposing a quadratic approximation, is linearly increasing with the number $H \cdot (N+M+R)$ of αNet weights[10]. However, it is worthwhile to point out that the R weights c_{rk}^* of the k-th unit belonging to the hidden layer of αNet should not be considered as "true weights" of the network. When the training phase is over, every coefficient c_{rk}^* has been fixed and each hidden unit activation function does not change anymore. After the training phase, each hidden unit activation function could be coded in a $(x, f_k^*(x))$ lookup table, hence the coefficients c_{rk}^* do not appear in the expression of the Computational Cost of the Production Phase C_C.

αNet can be used for managing classification tasks: the approach is to have one output unit for each desired class. During the training phase the output unit, corresponding to the class the input pattern belongs to, assumes the value +1, while the other output units assume the value −1. During the production phase an unknown input pattern will be then classified according to the associated output unit that gives the highest output value.

A formal analysis of the approximation capabilities of the proposed architecture will be object of further studies. However, it is worthwhile point out that in [5] it is shown that the boundedness of the sigmoidal functions plays an essential role in the approximation, as contrast to continuity or monotonity condition.

4. Experimental Results

To prove the validity of the proposed solution, a C-code αNet simulator has been developed. This paragraph deals with the results obtained with some benchmarks for comparative simulations, in particular the splice classification dataset, the add-10 regression dataset (both of them downloaded from http://www.cs.utoronto.ca/~delve/), the 5-parity problem and the two-spirals problem.

For each experiment three architectures have been compared:

- a traditional feed-forward network with sigmoids as activation functions of the hidden units that uses the CGRD algorithm with the restart conditions of Powell to reach minimum of the error over the training set;

- a traditional feed-forward network with sinusoidal activation functions of the hidden units that uses the same CGRD optimization algorithm;

- the αNet architecture that uses the Hermite regression formula to dynamically change the activation functions belonging to the hidden layer; the starting configuration of such functions is a gaussian function with zero mean and unitary variance; the network uses the same CGRD algorithm of the previous three architectures.

It has been used the same simulator for all networks to ensure that, having fixed the architecture and the optimization algorithm, the difference in results is due only to the adoption of the Hermite regression formula.

If P is the number of patterns that form the training set, $t_j^{(i)}$ is the j-th element of the i-th output vector of the training set; $o_j^{(i)}$ is the j-th output of the network corresponding to the i-th pair of input-output patterns of the training set, the error obtained over the training set is defined as[2][3]:

$$Q_E \equiv \frac{1}{P} \sum_{i=1}^{P} \sum_{j=1}^{M} \left(t_j^{(i)} - o_j^{(i)} \right)^2$$

The value of Q_E should be close to zero for all networks, then the factors C_C and C_G are calculated to compare the computational cost during the production phase and the generalization capability of the architectures to exam.

4.1 DNA Splice Junction Type Determination

Splice junctions are points on a DNA sequence at which "superfluous" DNA is removed during the process of protein creation in higher organisms.

The problem posed here is to recognize, given a sequence of DNA, the boundaries between the parts of the DNA sequence kept after splicing (exons) and the parts of DNA that are spliced out (introns); this task can be subdivided in two subproblems: recognizing exon/intron boundaries (EI sites) and recognizing intron/exon boundaries (IE sites).

The task of the network is to recognize, given a DNA sequence coded in 240 boolean elements, if there is a EI boundary, a IE boundary or neither of them, hence there are 3 output units.

To prove the validity of the αNet architecture, 4 training sets have been used, each of them consisting of 400 patterns of 240 binary elements; the following results have been obtained:

NETWORK ARCHITECTURE	Q_E	C_G	C_C
Traditional network 240-5-3 using sigmoids	0	172.03	1215
Traditional network 240-4-3 using sinusoids	0	178.69	972
αNet 240-4-3 using the first 14 Hermite polynomials	0	170.76	972

Note that a lower value of C_G is obtained using the αNet architecture with automatic learning of the hidden units activation function than using the traditional feed-forward network with fixed sigmoidal or sinusoidal activation functions of the units belonging to the hidden layer. A lower value of C_C is also obtained using the αNet architecture.

It has been also conducted the verification method of the test set with 4 test sets, each of them consisting of 1575 test patterns; the following table shows the misclassification error obtained:

NETWORK ARCHITECTURE	% Misclassified patterns
Traditional network 240-5-3 using sigmoids	9.2 %
Traditional network 240-4-3 using sinusoids	10.9 %
αNet 240-4-3 using the first 14 Hermite polynomials	10.3 %

The networks behavior, with respect to the test set, is more or less the same; as a matter of fact, because of the high dimensionality of the problem under exam, the test set method could be non-indicative of the network generalization capability.

4.2 The Add-10 Regression Problem

The problem is to predict the output of a function of 10 variables; this function has been suggested by J. Friedman in[11] to provide an example where some input are irrelevant for predictions and where the function has a predominantly additive structure:

$$f(x_1, x_2, \ldots, x_{10}) = 10 \cdot sin(\pi \cdot x_1 \cdot x_2) + 20 \cdot (x_3 - 0.5)^2 + 10 \cdot x_4 + 5 \cdot x_5 + n$$

where n is zero mean unit variance Gaussian noise given by $x_6, \ldots, x_{10}$ variables. The inputs $x_1, x_2, \ldots, x_{10}$ are sampled independently from a uniform [0,1] distribution; the used dataset has been downloaded from the Delve archive.

To prove the validity of the αNet architecture, 8 training sets have been used, each of them consisting of 50 patterns; the following results have been obtained:

NETWORK ARCHITECTURE	Q_E	C_G	C_C
Traditional network 10-5-1 using sigmoids	0	9.57	55
Traditional network 10-4-1 using sinusoids	0	11.3	44
αNet 10-5-1 using the first 6 Hermite polynomials	0	8.25	55

Note that a lower value of C_G is obtained using the αNet architecture with automatic learning of the hidden units activation function than using the traditional feed-forward network with fixed sigmoids or sinusoids as activation function of the units belonging to the hidden layer.

To have an evidence of the better generalization capability obtained with αNet it has been also conducted the verification method of the test set; in doing this it has been introduced the quantity E_T, defined as:

$$E_T \equiv \frac{1}{P} \sum_{i=1}^{P} \sum_{j=1}^{M} \left(t_j^{(i)} - o_j^{(i)} \right)^2$$

where P is the number of patterns that form the test set; $t_j^{(i)}$ is the j-th element of the i-th output vector of the test set; $o_j^{(i)}$ is the j-th output of the network corresponding to the i-th pair of input-output patterns of the test set.

The average value of E_T has then been calculated over 8 test sets; the results are shown in the following table:

NETWORK ARCHITECTURE	E_T
Traditional network 10-5-1 using sigmoids	1.16
Traditional network 10-4-1 using sinusoids	1.13
αNet 10-5-1 using the first 6 Hermite polynomials	0.79

It is worthwhile observing that there is an average improvement greater than 30% in approximating the desired output of the function using the αNet architecture.

4.3 The 5-Parity Problem

The 5-parity problem consists in determining the minimum number of hidden nodes to let the hidden network learn the 2^5 possible configurations of the training set. Hence the network structure is the following: five inputs, H hidden units and one output that can assume the values "0" or "1" if the number of "1" in the five inputs is even or odd respectively.

In general, for the N-bit parity function, no less than (1+N/2) hidden-unit sigmoid functions are required[12]. The following results have been obtained:

NETWORK ARCHITECTURE	Q_E	C_G	C_C
Traditional network 5-6-1 using sigmoids	0	297.97	36
Traditional network 5-1-1 using sinusoids	0	13.5	6
αNet 5-1-1 using the first 9 Hermite polynomials	0	12.42	6

Note that lower values of C_G are obtained using the αNet architecture with automatic learning of the hidden units activation function than using the traditional feed-forward network with fixed sigmoids or sinusoids as activation function of the units belonging to the hidden layer.

4.4 The Two Spirals Problem

The benchmark of the two-spirals consists in classifying the points in the x-y plane belonging to one of two interlocked spirals. This problem is not linearly separable and is extremely hard to resolve for a traditional MLP[13].

Here the problem is treated as interpolation to point out the correlation between the approximation and the classification capabilities of a neural network: an architecture with two inputs (the x,y pairs), h hidden units and one output unit is therefore needed; the output can assume the values +1 if the input pair belongs to the "diamond" spiral and -1 if the input pair belongs to the "x" spiral. It has been chosen to use this method to point out the correlation between interpolation and classification ability of a neural network.

The following results have been obtained:

NETWORK ARCHITECTURE	Q_E	C_G	C_C
Traditional network 2-60-1 using sigmoids	0.02	327.9	180
Traditional network 2-30-1 using sinusoids	0.02	178.69	90
αNet 2-13-1 using the first 14 Hermite polynomials	0,02	23,75	39

It is worthwhile to point out the lower value obtained of C_G using αNet than using a traditional network with sigmoids; this result leads to the supposition that the αNet should have a better skill in classifying the two spirals than the traditional architecture.

This assumption is confirmed looking at fig 4.1(B-D) where three samples of results obtained with all three architectures are shown. αNet, besides, is able to learn the input-output relationship with just 13 hidden units instead of the 60 or 30 hidden units required by the traditional network that uses fixed sigmoids or sinusoids as hidden units activation function respectively; therefore the value of C_C obtained using αNet is lower than the C_C obtained with the traditional architecture.

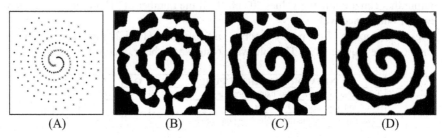

| (A) | (B) | (C) | (D) |

Fig 4.1. In A is represented the training set for the two-spirals problem; in B it is shown the result obtained with a traditional feed-forward network 2-*60*-1 with sigmoidal activation functions; in C it is shown the result obtained with a traditional feed-forward network 2-*30*-1 with sinusoidal activation functions; in D it is represented the result obtained with the αNet 2-*13*-1 network using the first 14 Hermite polynomials.

5. Conclusions

In this work it has been introduced αNet: a feed-forward neural network in which the activation function of the hidden units, starting from a gaussian-shaped function, is dynamically changed during the training phase by the joint use of the Hermite function regression formula and the Conjugate Gradient Descent optimization algorithm with the restart conditions of Powell. The use of these techniques leads to a very flexible neural architecture with very good generalization capability.

Experimental results show that αNet has a better skill of classification and interpolation often requiring less hidden units than a traditional feed-forward network that uses, in the hidden units, fixed sigmoidal or sinusoidal activation functions.

References

1. Gioiello G.A.M., Tarantino A., Sorbello F., Vassallo G.: Simple Techniques for an Efficient Recognition of Handwritten Characters Using a MLP. The Journal of Intelligent Systems. Vol 6 No 3/4 (1997) 199-221
2. Pilato G., Sorbello F., Vassallo G.: An Innovative Way to Measure the Quality of a Neural Network without the Use of the Test Set. Proc. of

IEEE Int. Workshop on Intelligent Signal Processing, Budapest (Hungary) 4-7 Sept. 1999 pp. 278-282

3. Pilato G., Sorbello F., Vassallo G.: Using the Hermite Regression Algorithm to Improve the Generalization Capability of a Neural Network. XI Italian Workshop on Neural Nets WIRN'99, Vietri sul Mare (Italy) 20-22 May 1999 (in press)

4. Simard P., Le Cun Y. Denker J. Victorri B.: An Efficient Algorithm for Learning Invariances in Adaptative Classifiers. Proc of 11th IAPR International Conference on Pattern Recognition, (1994) 651-655

5. Chen T., Chen H., Liu R.: Approximation Capability in $C(R^n)$ by Multilayer Feed-forward Networks and Related Problems. IEEE Trans. Neural Networks, vol 6 No 1, (1995) 25-30

6. Russell R., Robert J., Marks I., Seho O.: Similarities of Error Regularization, Sigmoid Gain Scaling, Target Smoothing, and Training with Jitter. IEEE Trans. on Neural Networks Vol.6 No. 3, (1995) 529-538

7. Hwang J. N., Lay S. R., Meachler M., Martin D., Schimert J.: Regression Modeling in Back-Propagation and Projection Pursuit Learning. IEEE Trans. Neural Networks, Vol 5 No 3, (1994) 342-353

8. Hwang J. N., You S. S., Lay S. R., Jou I. C.: What's Wrong with a Cascaded Correlation Learning Network: A Projection Pursuit Learning Perspective. ftp://ftp.cis.ohio.state.edu/pub/neuroprose/

9. Friedman J. H., Stuetzle W.: Projection Pursuit Regression. Journal of the American Statistical Association. Vol.76 No.376 (1981) 817-823

10. Powell M. J. D.: Restart Procedures for the Conjugate Gradient Method. Mathematical Programming Vol 12 (1977) 241-254

11. Friedman J.: Multivariate Adaptive Regression Splines. Technical Report No. 102, Laboratory for Computational Statistics, Department of Statistics, Stanford University, Nov. 1988

12. Minor J. M.: Parity With Two Layer Feed-Forward Nets. Neural Networks Vol.6 No.5 (1993) 705-707

13. Fahlman S.E., Lebiere C.: The Cascade-Correlation Learning Architecture Advances in Neural Information Processing Systems - D.S. Touretzky ed, San Mateo Calif: Morgan Kaufmann. Vol.2 (1990) 524-532

14. Hornik K., Multilayer Feed-forward Networks Are Universal Approximators, Neural Networks, Vol. 2, (1989) 359-366

15. Zhang M., Suen C.Y., Bui T.D., An Optimal Pairing Scheme in Associative Memory Classifier and its Application in Character Recognition, Proc. Of 11th IAPR Int. Conf. On Pattern Recognition (1994) 50-53

XIG: Generating from Interchange Format using Mixed Representations

Emanuele Pianta and Lucia M. Tovena

ITC-IRST
{pianta,tovena}@itc.it

Abstract. We present the C-STAR Italian Generator (XIG), a system for generating Italian text from the interlingua content representation (Interchange Format) adopted within the C-STAR II speech to speech translation project. The constraints of the application scenario led us to follow a Mixed Representions approach to text generation and to adopt for the sentence planner an architecture based on cascades of default rules.

1 Introduction

We present a system for generating Italian sentences from the interlingua content representation (Interchange Format) adopted inside the C-STAR II[1] project. The target of this consortium is to build a speech to speech translation system able to treat spontaneous speech. The application domain is tourist information.[2]

The Interchange Format (IF) is based on a predefined set of Dialogue Acts (DAs) with attributes[3]. We developed a generator that takes IF representations in input and feeds in a speech synthesizer [Balestri et al. 1993] with full/part of sentences. The particular scenario we are working with imposes a number of constraints which add to those common to a generation task. First, the input representation is partially underspecified and its full interpretation relies on implicit domain knowledge. Second, the output must be in spoken language, which is characterized by frequent use of idiomatic forms, fragmentary phrases, etc. Third, the application scenario imposes a strong requirement for time efficiency and robustness. As an answer to these constraints we developed a generator based on Mixed Representations, a solution that allowed us to achieve high efficiency. The system is implemented in Prolog and a demonstrator is available via Internet: `http://ecate.itc.it:1025/projects/cstar/cstar.html`.

---

[1] Consortium for Speech Translation Advanced Research `http://www.c-star.org`

[2] As far as academic requirements are concerned, Tovena takes official responsibility for sections 1, 2.1, 2.2, 3, 6, Pianta takes official responsibility for 2.3, 4, 5, 7, 8.

[3] IF is the result of joint effort by the members of C-STAR II who adopt the interlingua approach to machine translation. See [Tovena 1998].

E. Lamma and P. Mello (Eds.): AI*IA 99, LNAI 1792, pp. 238–248, 2000.

2   C-STAR II requirements for text generation

The XIG generator has to satisfy a number of requirements specific to the C-STAR II project. In the following, we discuss the requirements posed to the XIG system by the given input (Interchange Format), the expected output (spoken language), and the application scenario (speech to speech translation).

2.1   Generating from IF representations

An *IF representation* constitutes the minimal generation unit. It encodes a dialogue fragment and does not necessarily correspond to a full sentence. Each representation is structured into three levels indicating different aspects of the utterance. It can be formally expressed as follows.

$$speaker: \underbrace{speech\ act}_{level\ 1}\ \underbrace{[concept*]}_{level\ 2}\ \underbrace{[attribute*]}_{level\ 3}$$

The first level is the *speech act*, which encodes the communicative intention of the speaker. This is the only necessary and sufficient part of the representation, together with the information on the speaker, i.e. the agent (**a**) or the client (**c**).

The second level is made of *concepts* encoding the informational focus of the utterance. Concepts and speech acts can be combined to build Dialogue Acts (DAs), according to a predefined regular grammar. For instance, in the DA (1) the speech act `request-information` is concatenated with the two concepts `availability` and `hotel`.

(1)   `request-information+availability+hotel`

The third level is made by *attributes*, which convey specific content of the utterance. Attributes are optional and their use is licensed by specific concepts. For instance, the set of possible attributes for (1) is the union of the legal attributes for `hotel`, e.g. `[hotel-name, hotel-type, location]`, and for `availability`, e.g. `[time, location, price]`. Attributes are independent from each other and are given as an unordered sequence.

A first remark to be made is that the interpretation of an IF representation is partially domain dependent. Some information peculiar to hotel reservation transactions is not overtly coded. For instance, in (2) a correct mapping of the IF representation into English requires the use of the modal of possibility as in (2'). Any other modal, for instance *must*, would be inappropriate.

(2)   `a:give-information+payment (method=mastercard)`

(2')   *Può pagare con Mastercard* (You can pay with Mastercard)

Analogously, (3) refers to an action which is going to be performed, cf. (3'), not to a past one. In sum, tense and modality are left unspecified.

(3)   `c:give-information+temporal+arrival`
    `(location=pittsburgh, time=sunday)`

(3')   *Arrivo a Pittsburgh domenica* (I will arrive in Pittsburgh on Sunday)

Furthermore, in many cases the subject of the action is not specified and this piece of information has to be worked out from the DA and domain knowledge. Consider, for instance, the DA `give-information+payment`. In the hotel reservation domain the subject of the action of paying is always the client. Instead, when interpreting the DA `give-information+send`, we can always assume that the subject of the sending is the agent.

Finally, IF does not supply a formal semantics for its DAs. However, as argued in [Tovena and Pianta 1999], DAs have an internal structure that allows them to be assigned a meaning in a intuitive way. As a matter of fact, so far this vagueness has not undermined the enterprise of using IF as interlingua for speech to speech translation. To a certain extent, vagueness can work as 'flexibility', which is needed for an enterprise that puts together several teams working with different methodologies and different languages. The Interchange Format was developed in the field as an answer to the concrete needs of the different research communities involved in the project (speech recognition and synthesis, understanding, generation and translation).

Any system generating sentences from IF representations needs to cope with the semantic underspecification and semantic vagueness characterising the input representation. On the one hand the system needs to make explicit the kind of domain dependent knowledge that has been discussed above, on the other hand it requires a number of heuristic rather than formal methods to assign a correct interpretation to the representations. In both cases there is a risk of producing a huge number of *ad hoc* rules. To avoid this risk we developed a sentence planner based on cascades of default rules, as illustrated in sect. 5 and 6.

2.2   Generating for speech

Constraints on the generation system come from the expected output. Spoken language is characterized by the frequent occurrence of linguistic phenomena such as idiomatic forms, ellipsis, telegraphic style. The following are some expressions that our generator is expected to output: *due singole fanno 280 mila* (two singles are 280 thousand) to say *il prezzo di due stanze singole è 280 mila lire* (the price for two single rooms is 280 thousand liras); *partenza martedì* (departure Tuesday); *scadenza 2001* (expiration date 2001).

Note that sentence generators based on deep techniques are very good at generating sentences featuring complex syntactic phenomena such as unbounded dependences or quantifier scoping, but may have difficulties in generating incomplete phrases or idiomatic expressions. On the contrary, such phenomena can be handled quite easily by cascades of default rules combined with Mixed Representation, see sect. 3 and 4.

2.3   Generating for speech to speech translation

The application setting imposes a few more constraints on the whole system.

- efficiency is crucial; in a dialogue setting, a speech to speech translation system should produce a correct translation almost instantaneously. For this reason we are expected to compress as much as possible the time taken by the generation component.
- robustness primes over linguistic sophistication; the generator should always produce some output conveying as much information as possible; an awkwardly phrased—but understandable—utterance is better than none.

Robustness is an issue from two points of view: coverage and ill-formed input. Coverage problems arise mostly during IF interpretation. As mentioned above, the meaning of a DA must be derived from its building blocks, i.e. speech act and concepts, using heuristics rather than formal compositional rules. Moreover, the global interpretation of a DA depends on the speaker (client or agent), as different speakers imply different sets of default domain assumptions, and may depend on the presence or absence of certain attributes. The two IF representations in (4) and (5) share the same DA but have different speakers and attributes. Notice how much they differ in their interpretation, given as English paraphrase in (4') and (5').

(4) a:give-information+temporal+trip
     (duration=(quantity=2, time-unit=day))

(4') *Il viaggio dura due giorni* (The trip will take two days)

(5) c:give-information+temporal+trip
     (time=(early, january), destination=pittsburgh)

(5') *Andrò a Pittsburgh ai primi di gennaio* (I'll travel to Pittsburgh in early January)

As for ill-formed input, consider that the analysis chain of the translation system can produce ill-formed IF representations. Whatever the flaw in the input, the generator is expected to produce an output, and more specifically the best output compatible with the information contained in the ill-formed IF representation. Let us look at the real example in (6). This IF representation is supposed to encode a source utterance by which the client accepts one first class ticket offered by the agent. However the chosen speech act is wrong, because **affirm** should be used only for formulaic expressions of agreement such as *yes, ok* etc. As a result, the attributes encoding the information on the type of ticket are not licensed by the DA.

(6) c:affirm (admission-type=(ticket,quantity=1), class=first)

Even if (6) is ill-formed, it includes interpretable chunks of meaning, which convey most of the source utterance. Therefore, a robust generator should be able to produce something like (6').

(6') *sì un biglietto di prima classe* (yes a first class ticket)

Mixed Representations are our solution for the efficiency requirement, as they allow the generation process to skip any intermediate representation and computation whenever this is desirable. Cascades of default rules are our solution for robustness, as they allow the system to generate a sub-optimal solution whenever the optimal one is not available, either because of the incomplete coverage of the generator or the ill-formedness of the input.

3   The Mixed Representation approach

A clear distinction is generally made between deep generation and template based approaches [Reiter 1995]. Template based approaches are usually rated as efficient but not flexible, while deep generation is considered flexible but inefficient and resource demanding. Also, deep generation systems are usually difficult to update and require specialized support, while template based systems can be maintained by non linguists. However, the distinction between these two approaches tends to become less clear-cut. In the last few years, templates have been used within NLG architectures in order to overcome some of the drawbacks of NLG, first of all time inefficiency and resource development cost. [Reiter and Mellish 1993] introduce pointers to KB individuals among fixed strings and insert canned text as the value of a frame representing the meaning of a sentence. [Cancedda et al. 1997] insert templates as leaf nodes of a textual plan produced by classical NLG techniques. Hybrid techniques are also used by [Busemann 1996] and [Busemann and Horacek 1998]. All these attempts to integrate templates within NLG architectures can be characterized as using Mixed Representations, which are absent from both pure NLG and static templates.

Our approach to text generation aims at mixing representation levels in a systematic and principled way. From a practical perspective, this amounts to using precompiled generation knowledge whenever possible, while retaining the possibility of using a full-fledged NLG approach when strictly necessary [Pianta and Tovena 1999]. For instance, in the hotel reservation domain, it is very common to find sentences with the following structure *I'd like to book* <object> *in a hotel*. A Mixed Representation approach allows us to restrict the use of flexible generation techniques only to the <object> of the sentence.

Before presenting a practical implementation of the proposed approach, let us see how it compares with the received view about the separation of representation levels. Standard NLG architectures map an input message to an output text passing through a number of intermediate representations such as a text plan and a list of sentence representations. Each representation level is the input and/or output of a separate component coping with specific linguistic phenomena, e.g. communicative intentions, text structure, referring expressions, morphology, etc. In the accepted view, representation levels should be kept carefully separated, on the grounds that separation enhances modularity and reflects different levels of linguistic analysis. In the Mixed Representation approach both these motivations are challenged. On the one hand, we argue that representation levels can be mixed while preserving the modularity of the linguistic components. On the other hand, we argue that, while the strict separation of representation levels is crucial when taking a competence point of view on language, mixing representations is acceptable in a more performance oriented perspective. In practical terms, we consider it plausible that human speakers produce discourse by mixing dynamic planning with precompiled knowledge about the structure and relevance of texts, and produce sentences by mixing flexible sentence planning and realization with all kind of (semi)idiomatic expressions, (semi)fixed descriptions of individuals, precompiled sentence patterns, phrases stored in the short-term memory, etc.

4   The Hyper Template Planning Language

In this section we present an implementation of the Mixed Representation approach, namely the Hyper Template Planning Language (HTPL), see [Cancedda et al. 1997] and [Pianta and Tovena 1999] for a more detailed description of the formalism and its interpretation mechanisms. Here we focus on the linguistic objects that can be represented and mixed in an HTPL expression. They are:

message representation: a formula in some content representation formalism. In C-STAR this is an IF representation or a part of it. When specifying a message representation, one should also specify the formalism and the type of message object which is being described. For instance, `msg('IF', attributes, [location=Location])` can be used in HTPL to represent an IF attribute. This expression is handled by a specialized component during the HTPL interpretation process.

phrase representation: an abstract representation of a phrase which can feed some context free tactical generator. In C-STAR we specify phrases in terms of grammatical functions such as subject, verb, object, adjuncts, determiner etc., in the spirit of LFG. These specifications feed a very simple Definite Clause Grammar that can handle constituency and agreement phenomena.

morphological bundles: sets of morphological features that are mapped onto potential words[4]. For example, the bundle `morpho([cat=noun, pred=room, num=plur])` is mapped onto the potential word `w(noun, rooms)`. When used in HTPL expressions, the values of morphological features can be variables: `morpho([cat=noun, pred=room, num=Num])`. Morphological variables make it easier to treat agreement phenomena, which are awkward to handle with static templates.

potential word: a word form which can undergo phonological adjustment. It is described by a term specifying the lexical category of the word and its form: `w(noun, albergo)`. Sequences of potential words are mapped onto sequences of strings: for example in Italian `[w(preposition, di), w(article, il), w(noun, albergo)]` becomes `["dell'albergo"]`.

string: a sequence of characters inserted in the text without modification, for example: `"hotel reservation"`.

The representation levels have been listed following an ordering that we defined as decreasing by convention. This ordering is relevant for the HTPL interpreter, but it is also meaningful from a linguistic point of view. For example a

---

[4] See the following paragraph for a definition.

potential word is a more abstract object than a string, whereas a phrase representation belongs to a constituency level that is more complex than a morphological bundle.

Mixing representation levels can be done in two ways: by concatenation or by embedding. Mixing by *concatenation* means building a list of objects pertaining to different levels. For instance one can think of a list with the following structure [<string>, <potential word>, <sentence representation>, <string>]. Mixing by *embedding* means that an object of a certain level is included inside the structure of a different level. For instance in the phrase representation (7), the values of all grammatical functions are HTPL expressions: `subject` is assigned a list of potential words, the value of `verb` is a string, while the value of `adjuncts` is a message representation.

```
(7)  phrase(sentence,
         [subject=htpl([w(article, il),
                        w(noun, viaggio)]), /* the trip*/
          verb=htpl(["dura"])              /* lasts */
          adjuncts=htpl([msg('IF', attributes, Duration)])])
```

Let us assume that the representation level of a mixed HTPL expression is equal to the highest level of the objects it contains. The interpretation of an HTPL expression boils down to a progressive reduction of its representation level. Thus, first all message representations are reduced to objects of lower levels, by calling a specialized planning component, then phrase representations are reduced by calling a syntactic component, etc., until only strings are left.

5   Architecture

The XIG architecture includes four components; the sentence planner, the syntactic component, the morphological synthesizer and the phonetic adjustment component. The last three components are standard and are reused from a previous system [Cancedda et al. 1997]. In the rest of this section we will concentrate on the sentence planner, as this component has been specifically designed for the XIG system.

The aim of the sentence planner is to map an IF representation onto the functional representation of a sentence. Mapping rules are grouped in five decreasingly specific layers: sentence specific rules, sentence default rules, phrase specific rules, phrase default rules, lexical rules. Each layer incrementally instantiates the functional representation, while progressively consuming the IF representation. Specific rules apply to classes of IF representations or even to a single IF representation, whereas default rules apply to any IF representation. Examples of specific rules are presented in the following section. Here is an example of a sentence default rule: map the first concept after the speech act onto the verb and the remaining concepts onto the object.

In HTPL terms, the sentence planner is the component that is called by the HTPL interpreter to reduce message representations. As mentioned above, message representations must contain a flag specifying the type of message objects that is being described. In our case the legal types are: **if** (full IF representation), **concepts** (list of concepts, informational focus), **atts** (list of attributes), **lex** (atomic IF expression, a speech act, a concept or the atomic value of an attribute).

Note that mapping rules can set the value of any grammatical function as an HTPL expression. This means that any unnecessary intermediate level can be shortcut; thanks to this, formulaic expressions typical of the reservation domain can be easily generated.

6   Discussion

Let us see in more detail an example of generation, focussing on the contribution of the different rule types. We start from the full IF representation in (8).

(8)   a:give-information+price+room
       (hotel-name=ramada, price=(quantity=115,per-unit=night),
       bed-type=(double, quantity=2))

This can be paraphrased roughly as "The agent intends to give some information about the price of a room; the room is at the Ramada Hotel, the price is 115 per night, the room contains two double beds". A specific **if**-rule maps the full IF representation in (8) into sentence level grammatical functions.

(9)   map_if_to_sentence(

```
          /* lefthand */
          [speech_act=give-information,
          concepts=[price|OtherConcepts],
          attributes=[price=Price]],

          /* righthand */
          [subject=htpl(msg('IF', concepts, [price|OtherConcepts]))
          verb=htpl(["#", "e'"]),
          object=htpl([msg('IF', attributes, [price=Price])])]).
```

The rule states that if the speech act is **give-information** and the list of concepts has **price** as first item, then the list of concepts must be realized as subject and the **price** attribute as object of the output sentence; the verb is to be realized as the string *è* (is). The hash sign tells the synthesizer to produce a short pause. Notice that grammatical functions are instantiated with two message representations and a string.

All HTPL expressions are then passed to the HTPL interpreter, that will try to reduce them. Let us consider the subject in the right hand side of (9), a message representation of type **concepts**. A specific **concepts**-rule applies to the sequence of concepts **price+room**.

(10)   `map_concepts_to_noun_phrase(`

```
        /* lefthand */
        [concepts=[price, room] ],

        /* righthand */
        phrase(noun_phrase,
           [det=htpl([w(article, il)]),
           noun=htpl(["prezzo"]),
           modifier=[preposition=htpl([w(preposition, di)]),
                   noun=htpl([msg('IF', concepts, [room])]),
                   position=after]])).
```

The rule in (10) states that the list **price+room** should be realized as the noun phrase *il prezzo di una stanza* (the price of a room). The determiner is realized as a potential word because the whole noun phrase could be preceded by a preposition, in which case a phonological adjustment should apply. The head noun of the **modifier** is instantiated by a message representation so that the rules that attach attributes to concepts can apply recursively. In fact, in our example two attributes of the input IF representation, namely **hotel-name** and **bed-type**, should be realized as modifiers of the **room** concept, e.g. *a room with two double beds at the Ramada Hotel.*

Finally, let us see how the atomic attribute value **double** is mapped by a **lex**-rule.

(11)   `has_translation(double,`

```
           htpl([template(noun(letto, Agr)),
               template(adjective(doppio, Agr))]),
           context=attribute(bed-type)).
```

(12)   `has_translation(double,`

```
           htpl([template(noun(doppia, agr(f, _, _)))]),
           context=attribute(room-type)).
```

double is a legal value of both the **bed-type** and **room-type** attributes, and in the two cases Italian requires different expressions. Hence, two context sensitive rules are devised. Note in (11) and (12) the template calls **noun** and **adjective** which expand into morphological bundles. The **Agr** variable realises the agreement between noun and adjective. The resulting text is (13).

(13)   Il prezzo di una stanza con 2 letti doppi al Ramada Hotel è 115 a notte
       (the price of a room with 2 double beds at the Ramada Hotel is 115 per
       night)

7 Results

The current version of the system has been tested against the official data base of the C-STAR consortium. This is a collection of about a hundred spontaneous dialogues, annotated by hand with IF representations. It contains 4150 IF representations using about 550 distinct DAs.

The generation succeeds on all the IF representations. The quality of the output has been assessed by a panel of judges, who rated 90% of the sentences as acceptable, cf. [Pianesi et al. 1999] for details.

Generating the whole database of sentences on a Ultra SPARC 1 takes 70 seconds. Memory allocation is about 2 MB.

The table below shows how the number of rules grew as the system was extended from one (hotel reservation) to two (hotel reservation and travel info) subdomains. As you can see, while the number of lexical rules has doubled, the other rules exhibit a much slower growing rate.

Type of rule	nb. for 1 subdom.	nb. for 2 subdom.
sentence	252	318
noun phrase	25	40
adjuncts/modifiers	136	168
verb	18	25
lexicon	462	820

8 Conclusions and future work

We presented a system that generates Italian sentences annotated for speech synthesis from IF representations. The system adopts a Mixed Representation approach, allowing a generation system to choose, according to the needs, between the full flexibility of NLG and the efficiency of using precompiled intermediate representations. The approach is implemented through the Hypertext Template Planning Language. The sentence planner component is called by the HTPL interpreter to map IF content representations into linguistic objects of less abstract level. Specific mapping rules are tried first; they produce accurately worded phrases, but have limited application. More general rules are tried later; they may produce less elegant phrased but guarantee a robust behaviour to the system. The XIG generator is time and space efficient, and is easy to maintain and scale up thanks to his structural simplicity.

Currently the generator treats only one IF representation at the time. We plan to enable XIG to treat a whole dialogue turn (possibly made of more sentences). Also, the system could benefit from a record of the dialogue history to improve the generation of referring expressions. Note that in a machine translation system one could expect that all the information necessary to generate felicitous referring expressions (for example the novel/familiar status of referred entities) should be available in the interlingua representation of the source phrase. However, this is an ideal situation that is hardly met by real machine translation systems. As already mentioned, the current version of the Interchange Format has a number of limitation on the kind of information that can be represented. Currently, XIG copes with the problem of missing information through domain dependent heuristics. For example the novel/familiar status of referents can be guessed from the current speech act, concept and speaker. Keeping a record of the dialogue history would allow the generation system to reconstruct pieces of information that got lost in the IF coding in a more general and principled way.

References

[Balestri et al. 1993] Balestri M., Lazzaretto S., Salza PL. and Sandri S. The CSELT system for Italian text-to-speech synthesis. In *Eurospeech*, pages 2091–2094, Berlin, 1993.

[Busemann 1996] Busemann S. Best-first surface realization. In *INLGW-8*, pages 101–110, Sussex, 1996.

[Busemann and Horacek 1998] Busemann S. and Horacek H. A flexible shallow approach to text generation. In *INLGW-9*, Niagara Falls, 1998.

[Cancedda et al. 1997] Cancedda N., Kamstrup G. and Pianta E. Sax: Generating hypertext from SADT models. In *Proceedings of NLDB'97*, Vancouver, 1997.

[Pianesi et al. 1999] Pianesi F., Pianta E. and Tovena LM. Comparing methodologies for evaluating the generator in a speech-to-speech translation system. In *Proceedings of EWNLG'99*, pages 145–154, Toulouse, 1999.

[Pianta and Tovena 1999] Pianta E. and Tovena LM. Mixing representation levels: The hybrid approach to automatic text generation. In *Proceedings of AISB'99*, pages 8–13, Edinburgh, 1999.

[Reiter 1995] Reiter E. Nlg vs. templates. In *EWNLG*, Leiden, 1995.

[Reiter and Mellish 1993] Reiter E. and Mellish Ch. Optimizing the costs and benefits of natural language generation. In *Proceedings of IJCAI*, pages 1164–1169, 1993.

[Tovena 1998] Tovena LM. A user's point of view on the interlingua IF. Technical Report 9809-01, ITC-IRST, Trento, 1998.

[Tovena and Pianta 1999] Tovena LM. and Pianta E. Generating felicitous sentences from underspecified semantic representations. In *Proceedings of IWCS-3*, pages 410–412, Tilburg, The Netherlands, 1999.

Natural Language Access to Public Administration Data: the TAMIC-P System

Clara Bagnasco[1], Amedeo Cappelli[2], Bernardo Magnini[3] and Diego Zamatteo[4]

[1] Quinary S.p.A., Milano, Italy
[2] CNR-ILC, Istituto di Linguistica Computazionale, Pisa, Italy
[3] ITC-Irst, Istituto per la Ricerca Scientifica e Tecnologica, Trento, Italy
[4] INPS, Sede Regionale per il Trentino Alto Adige, Trento, Italy
e-mail: {bag@quinary.it, amedeo@ilc.pi.cnr.it, magnini@irst.itc.it, DirTec.Trentino@inps.it}

Abstract. The main goal of the TAMIC-P[1] project is to demonstrate the opportunities offered by the use of Natural Language Processing technologies in the human-machine interaction, in particular related to data access in complex environments.

The Natural Language interface has been proposed as a modality of access complementary to other techniques, such as graphical interfaces. It shows its power when used in scenarios characterised by a relevant number of distributed information sources, in which current interfaces do not offer appropriate solutions to the complexity of data handling, and often generate difficulties in navigation. These problems turn out to become even more critical in the presence of not skilled users, having low technical knowledge.

Using Natural Language, as normally used between persons for communicating, reduces the skill requirements and enhances the system usability. The evaluation tests performed on the TAMIC-P system confirm this point, showing that upon just a short training, a non-skilled operator is able to operate with effectiveness.

1. Introduction

The use of natural language to access databases is suitable to avoid the necessity of learning an artificial database management language, with its syntax and semantics, thus enabling a user to formulate queries in a simple and natural way. As a consequent benefit, anaphoric and elliptical expressions can be used with a relevant simplification and economy in the man machine communication process. In the second half of the eighties, several NL based interfaces have been realized (NLDB), including many experimental (TEAM [Grosz 1987], IRUS [Bates 1986], JANUS [Resnik 1989], SHOPTALK [Cohen 1992]) and commercial prototypes (INTELLECT [Harris 1984], PARLANCE [BBN 1989], English Wizard). Even if many of the above mentioned products have demonstrated their effective use for specific limited domains, nowadays natural language interfaces to databases are not so widely used as one could expect. There is more than one reason for that fact. Androutsopoulos (1995) highlights some specific problems that, from a computational point of view, are hard to be solved, among others: the opacity both of

---

[1] TAMIC-P (Transparent Access to Multiple Information for the Citizen – Pensions) is a European Union funded project (LE-4253).

E. Lamma and P. Mello (Eds.): AI*IA 99, LNAI 1792, pp. 249–260, 2000.
© Springer-Verlag Berlin Heidelberg 2000

the linguistic capabilities and of the domain knowledge a system exhibits, reference, context-sensitive interpretation of expressions etc.

Apart from technical problems, although natural language is a powerful modality to achieve certain tasks, it is highly ineffective for others. For instance, the selection of visible objects on a screen is more efficient through pointing than by means of a linguistic description. Selecting and acting on virtual objects contained in a graphical interface is an ecologically valid transposition of what humans do in the real world when they isolate relevant targets by attention, to perform purposive behaviors. So, graphical interfaces have been often preferred to natural language interfaces.

However, in the last years, many relevant results have been achieved in the field, from which new technologies have emerged (CLE [Alshawi 1992], CLARE [Alshawi et al. 1992]). Recently, a new approach has been experimented which tries to combine and integrate different communication modalities in man-machine interfaces. In this multimodal view, each modality performs specific tasks in order to achieve specific results and, in collaboration with the others, many of its specific limits are overcome [Maybury 1997, Cohen and Sullivan 1989, Stock 1993].

As an example, direct manipulation of objects is a valid means to overcome certain difficulties in language understanding and can mitigate the opacity problem by enabling a user to directly learn (i.e. see) what are the objects and their possible appropriate manipulations in a system. However, in a graphical interface, effective manipulation is allowed only when a limited number of actions are to be performed in a given time and when objects to be manipulated are unambiguously displayed on the screen. Indeed, natural language allows referring to non present objects through complex descriptions, taking advantage of both lexical variations and free compositions of sentences.

The aim of TAMIC-P is to realize a NL based interface system able to support Public Administration desk operators during an information session with a citizen. For this purpose, many of the above mentioned problems have been approached and, in particular, an extensive study of the communicative modalities in the chosen domain has been carried out.

The project follows a feasibility study [Bagnasco et al. 1996], which pointed out three main requirements in the relationship between Public Administration and citizen: (i) the transparency of the information access, both for the operator and for the citizen; (ii) the ease of use of the interface, particularly for non expert operators; (iii) the need to integrate data from different archives, in order to promote the realization of multi-function desks. For the project prototype, the *social insurance* domain has been chosen, which involve about 19 M Italian people. Information is currently distributed over different systems and environments, and is accessible by means of several data access procedures. For each procedure, the operator needs to know the proper format of the transactions to be activated, the sequence and the content of the input/output panels, and the meaning of the codes describing the citizen data. Besides this technical knowledge, the operator is required to deeply understand the domain, including norms and bureaucratic procedures.

As a result, a multimodal interface has been designed and implemented which has, as its core engine, a natural language front end, but which combines other modalities suitable to solve specific interaction problems. The interaction uses a scenario based on the metaphor of a card file. By presenting the structure of a card, the language of a user is naturally reduced to the use of complex noun phrases describing the content of the fields of a card, in this way reducing the linguistic opacity problem. Furthermore, the structure and the content of a card inherently limit the types of concepts to be searched and the types of inferential processes to be applied to such concepts. By this presentation of the data, the user can easily realize what are the conceptual and inferential limits of the system. He is also facilitated in this operation, since he has, at his disposal, the possibility to directly manipulate visible objects and to verbalize actions to be triggered on them.

2. Prototype Functionalities

The prototype is a work environment for the Public Administration desk operator, in which three main functionalities, all accessible by natural language, are implemented:

- access to users archives containing personal information about citizens;
- access to a technical dictionary, providing general information on domain concepts and their relationships;
- access to a textual database containing information on laws and norms in the social insurance area.

TAMIC-P is based on the idea of consulting *information cards*. In order to access a card through natural language it is sufficient to enter a short description of the card content in the character input field of the graphical interface. For example, as an answer to an input sentence like *"voluntary contributions between 1980 and 1990"* a list of contributions of the given kind and for the chosen time period is obtained.

In the following, some of the main features of the TAMIC-P system are presented.

Linguistic Flexibility. Descriptions in natural language are flexible both with respect to the syntactic structure, (e.g., either *"contributions after 1980 voluntary"* or *"voluntary contributions after 1980"*) and the used terms (e.g., either *"voluntary payments from 1980"* or *"voluntary contributions"*). The language may be telegraphic and synthetic, as in *"Cig contributions 1970-1975"*(where "Cig" stands for lay-off fund), but even redundant or partially inappropriate queries are accepted (e.g.: *"contributions for the lay-off fund administration from year 1970 to year 1975"*).

Synthetic and Analytical Views. Due to the complexity of the available information, two views are enabled: a *synthetic view*, with the minimum needed information, used to review data lists (for example a list of contribution periods), and an *analytical view*, with all the available information on a subject, used to inspect details, for example concerning a single contribution period.

Information Integration. The citizen personal data are always displayed with links both to their technical explanations and to the related norms. Thanks to this mechanism, after an input request like *"contributions for University degree redemption"* three kinds of information may be obtained on the specific subject of the contributions for University degree redemption.

Hypertextual Navigation. Each card is a hypertext, where the presented information are active objects, which can be inspected for further details. By means of the hypertextual navigation modality it is possible to move from one subject to another, even without a detailed knowledge on the underlying domain. At any moment, the operator can move from the hypertextual navigation to the natural language modality, in a complete transparent way.

Contextualization. Natural language queries are interpreted by the system in the context of the preceding queries. This allows follow-up sequences, which turn out to be quite natural and effective during the consultation of complex data. For example the sequence:

> *contributions*
> *deemed*
> *for Lay-off pay fund*

gradually restricts the output data by using the power of the contextualization mechanism.

> *contributions as employee from 1980*	"Employee" stands for "obligatory employed worker": the use of terminology is flexible.
> *salaries*	Interpretation is contextual with respect to the preceding request: only the salaries related to the above contributions are shown.
> *uncovered periods*	These data are calculated, since they are not present in the archives.
> *deemed*	Interpretation is contextual: deemed contributions are meant.
> *Cig only*	Technical expressions: "Cig" is an acronym for "Cassa integrazione guadagni"(Lay-off pay fund).

Fig. 1. Example of dialogue (commented) in natural language with TAMIC-P.

Correction of Typing Errors. The most common typing errors (e.g. inversions of adjacent keys on the keyboard or omissions of a character in a word) are automatically corrected. In these cases, the correct word replaces the wrong one. Only in the case of very complex errors, the system asks the user to choose among possible corrections.

Analysis of Abbreviations. Because of the frequent use of abbreviations, in particular by specialized operators, a highly effective abbreviations recognizer has been realized. For example, a query like:

> *contr. serv. mil.*

is correctly interpreted by the system as "*contributions for the military service*", automatically eliminating other less plausible interpretations, such as "*contract related to military service*", or "*control of military service*".

Personalized Presentations. The TAMIC-P system allows different presentations of the same data. For example, the list of contributions of a citizen may be ordered by time periods, starting from the oldest contribution to the most recent one. The same list may also be ordered by type, resulting in homogeneous groups of contributions. In order to obtain a particular presentation, it is sufficient to perform a query in natural language by specifying the desired order, as in:

> *contributions by type*

Fig. 1 shows a short operator-system dialogue with some of the main TAMIC-P system features.

3. Architecture

The TAMIC-P application is highly heterogeneous both with respect to the kind of knowledge it is based on (i.e. lexicon, domain knowledge and data) and with respect to the data stores to which it makes access (hierarchical, relational, file systems). In order to scale the application complexity and to facilitate its maintenance, a considerable effort has been spent on the definition of a modular architecture and on the representation of declarative knowledge, including the relationships (mappings) among representation structures belonging to different knowledge levels. The four main components of TAMIC-P are (see Fig. 2):

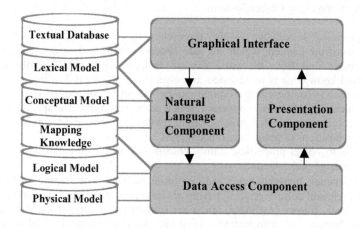

Fig. 2. Main components and knowledge bases.

- the graphical interface, which defines all the allowed interactions between the user and the application;
- the linguistic component, which carries on the basic steps of natural language interpretation: tokenization and morphological analysis, parsing, construction of a semantic representation, contextualization;
- the data access component, which groups all the modules which manage the communication with the data stores;

- the presentation component, which aggregates retrieved data and displays them in the most convenient output format.

Section 3.1 presents the TAMIC-P information sources, while section 4 describes the main software modules which drive the interaction with the system.

3.1 Knowledge Bases

TAMIC-P is based on different information sources: *linguistic knowledge*, namely the lexicon and the grammar, *conceptual knowledge*, the domain model, *textual knowledge*, the texts of the norms, *logical knowledge*, the data model, and *physical knowledge*, the data location and format.

The *lexical* knowledge is composed of the terms used by an INPS desk operator when speaking about the domain (the insurance area), and is represented and organized in the *Lexical Knowledge Base*, a WordNet-like conceptual dictionary [Miller et *al.* 1990; TAMIC-P 1999-3]. The dictionary contains about 2000 technical terms pertaining to the insurance domain and a quite large set of commonly used words which increase the system robustness. Terms are organized into a hierarchy of sets of synonyms. Each set of synonyms (i.e. a synset) is characterized by a group of properties, among which: an identifier, a list of synonyms, a list of pointers to direct hypernyms and hyponyms, an explanatory gloss, a logical form (used to build the semantic representation of the NL query, see below), and a set of pointers to text documents containing related norms. The Lexical Knowledge Base is implemented in CLOS (Common Lisp Object System).

The *conceptual* knowledge is the representation of objects, relationships and constraints of the domain, which are independent both from the organization of the data archives and from the particular words used when speaking about them. Conceptual knowledge is represented in a *Conceptual Model* (CM), implemented in CLOS, which is composed of a limited number (about 50) of frames, organized into an ISA hierarchy. A frame contains relevant information about a specific class of domain objects (e.g. contributive situation, payments, insured person, etc.). Filler values can be atoms or pointers to other frames.

In addition to object properties, frames contain information used in the process of natural language understanding:

- A distinction between *basic* and *non-basic* frames: basic frames represent the most relevant domain entities, having also complex structures (e.g. *contribution*). Non-basic frames (e.g. *date*, *town*) are introduced to support the definition of basic frames. This information is used both for deriving the Logical Form from the parsing tree and for some contextualization operations. All frames subsumed by a Basic Frame are in turn considered Basic Frames.
- When more than one slot in a frame has the same filler restriction, one of them has to be marked as *focalized*. For example the *contribution* frame has at least two slots constrained to be a *date* (i.e. *start-date* and *end-date*). It is a domain dependent choice that *start-date* is the focalized one, allowing the correct interpretation of a request like "*contributions of 1992*" where the relation is left unspecified. This information plays a crucial role during the contextualization phase, in particular when two turns have to be connected each other with an implicit relation.

- Certain slots are annotated for presentation purposes. A *presentation* slot will be always displayed to the user by default. For example if the user asks for the *"amount of contributions from 1993"* a list of contributions is displayed, each of them described with the "presentation" slots (e.g. the *type*, the *start-date*, the *end-date*) together with the explicitly required information (i.e. the *amount*).
- A *default presentation order* is defined over the slots of a frame, to be used to determine the default view of a frame for direct manipulation.

Knowledge about the *logical* organization of the data is represented by an entity-relationship model [Chen 1976], the *Logical Model*, and is implemented into a relational database and into a set of CLOS frames, which play the role of a data catalog. The logical model is the unified model of all the interesting data which can be downloaded from the user (i.e. INPS) archives: a number of integration and homogenization procedures convert these data into the Logical Model structure [TAMIC-P 1999-1].

The *physical* knowledge about the native format and location of the data in the user archives is modeled and recorded into a *Physical Model*, implemented as a relational database.

Texts containing the relevant norms have been annotated using HTML as a markup language, and have been recorded into a *textual* database.

Finally, the *mapping knowledge* describes the data structure transformations which must be performed to share information among modules at different levels. One of the most crucial is the mapping between the logical and the conceptual model, where quite complex transformations are described, such as the transformation of a flat record into a hierarchy, the possibility to aggregate data, the transformation of a relationship represented with external keywords into a relationship among frames, and the transformation of values performed by decoding functions.
Given the complexity of this mapping, a declarative mapping language has been developed: Fig. 3 shows a fragment of a mapping statement describing the relationships between the logical model item "contribution_file" and the conceptual model frame "contributive_situation". In general, the meaning of a mapping statement is the following: the instances of a CM frame are the result of the application of a set of transformation clauses (':with' clauses in Fig. 3) to the collection of instances of a LM item(s).

Other mappings require less complex specifications. For instance, the mappings between the conceptual model and the lexical model are represented by a logical form whose predicates and constants relate the terms contained in the synset to the items (frames and slots) of the conceptual model. An example of the resulting Logical Form is reported in Fig. 4. The mappings between the physical and the logical model are maintained in a support database. Finally, the relationships between the text documents in the textual database and the lexical model are established by indexing the documents with respect to the lexical knowledge base: each document can be related to one or more synsets in the dictionary.

```
(defmapping cm::contributive_situation
 (lm::contribution_file
 :with
     cm::type = lm::contribution_code
     Direct mapping between the slot cm::type and the property lm::contribution_code.

 cm::has_holder = lm::person
     Although this appears to be the same as the one above, here lm::person is an
     entity. This case implies that: (i) cm:: holder contains a pointer to a CM frame;
     (ii) a mapping statement exists between such CM frame and lm::person; (iii) the
     LM defines foreign keys relating lm::contribution_file and lm::person.

 cm::total_contribution =
 AGGR(sum lm::contribution_amount
 lm::contribution_period)
     Aggregation: cm::total_contribution is the sum of lm::contribution_amount from
     all lm::contribution_period pertaining to a given  lm:: contribution_file.
 ............ . )
```

Fig. 3. Example of a mapping statement. Conceptual Model items are prefixed by "cm::", while Logical Model items are prefixed by "lm::".

4. Components and Modules

The interaction among the four main components of the system is driven by a Control Manager, which coordinates the execution of complex tasks. Each component can be thus considered as an agent which activates itself in response to a message sent by the Control Manager. In turn, each module communicates the computation results to the Control Manager which, on the basis of the received output, can fire a subsequent interpretation phase or transfer the control to an Error Handling module. The main components of the system are briefly described in the following.

4.1 Graphical Interface and Presentation Component

The system interface includes two components: the Presentation Component, implemented in Lisp, and the Graphical Interface, implemented in Tcl/Tk. Communication between the two components relies on a socket-based message exchange protocol: the Lisp module is the server while the Tcl/Tk module is the client. The Graphical Interface handles the graphic widgets and visualizes the output of the Presentation Component which defines the proper presentation of the output data [TAMIC-P 1999-4].

4.2 Natural Language Interpretation

Natural Language Interpretation is based on the integration of linguistic knowledge, represented in the lexical knowledge base, with domain knowledge, represented in the conceptual model. The interpretation process is split into different phases, each one implemented by a dedicated module [TAMIC-P 1999-2]. Communication among the modules is supported by a common data structure, implemented as a language independent Quasi Logical Form (QLF), which is also the output of the linguistic interpretation. A QLF is a conjunction of predicates, which refer to slots (if binary) or to frames (if unary) in the Conceptual Model. Constants are atomic values of the Conceptual Model. QLF predicates are partitioned into three groups, according to the functional role of a predicate in the user query:

- The *argument* group represents the main object referred by the user in a turn. It is always a predicate denoting a "basic concept" in the Conceptual Model, and it determines the kind of objects the system will display as output to the user. As an example, the QLF shown in Fig. 4 represents the query *"amount of the deemed contributions from 1990 to 1995"*, interpreted in the context of the interaction with a particular citizen. When the argument is not present in the query it is determined through a search in the previous turns.

- The *restriction* group collects those predicates which express constraints on the argument, resulting in a subset of the entities denoted by the argument. These predicates can be either explicitly expressed in the user query, as the starting-date predicate in Fig. 4, or automatically supplied by the system during the contextualization procedures, as it is the case of the predicate *holder*.

- The *specification* group indicates the particular information requested by the user about the argument; for example the amount of money of a particular contribution. This group collects also those predicates not explicitly mentioned in the user query, but which refer to properties of the argument object the user wishes to see by default (for example the number of weeks in Fig. 4).

Argument:	(contribution ?x)
Restriction:	((starting-date ?x ?y)(year ?y) (>= ?y 1990) (end-date ?x ?y)(year ?y) (<= ?y 1995)) (type ?x «deemed») *(holder ?x ?q) (person ?q)* *(surname ?q «Rossi»)* *(name ?q «Mario»)*
Specification:	((amount ?x ?z) (amount ?z) *(starting-date ?x ?p1)(date ?p1)* *(end-date ?x ?p2) (date ?p2)* *(type ?x ?p3) (string ?p3)* *(weeks ?x ?p4) (number ?p4))*

Fig. 4. QLF representing the query «*amount of the deemed contributions from 1990 to 1995*». Predicates in Italics represent context information, automatically added by the system.

The following are the main phases of the linguistic interpretation.

Segmentation and Morphological Analysis. This module is responsible for the tokenization and for the morphological analysis of the input string. The output is a list of all possible morphological interpretations for the words included in the input string, which constitute the input of the parser. Linguistic phenomena handled at this level are: multiwords (*"voluntary contribution"*), abbreviations, dates, acronyms, cardinals (*"last 10 contributions"*), proper nouns, typing errors.

Parsing. Given an input words sequence, the parser builds a semantic representation of the query, i.e. a QLF, by unifying the logical forms attached to the lexical entries in the conceptual dictionary. Phenomena handled at this level are: preposition and article omissions, syntactic agreement and the treatment of structural ambiguities (in particular pp-attachment).

The parser is a chart parser based on a typed feature logic and is coupled with a proper unification algorithm. The grammar is written adopting an HPSG-like style, and each rule is regarded as Typed Feature Structure. In the current prototype, the grammar coverage is limited to very simple nominal sentences formed by a series of nouns together with their modifiers.

Semantic Interpretation. This phase includes a normalization procedure of the QLF and a consistency check against the Conceptual Model and the contextualization procedure.

Normalization is the process by means of which a QLF produced by the parser is put into correspondence with actual objects (i.e. frames, slots and fillers) in the Conceptual Model. Normalization is based on the substitution of patterns matching information stored in the Conceptual Model. For instance the expression "*amount*" has to be matched (i.e. normalized) with the slot actually named "amount_ivs", which is the proper technical name.

Consistency is the process of checking a given QLF against the Conceptual Model. The consistency algorithm takes as input a QLF and recursively checks that all its unary predicates refer to a frame, all its binary predicates insisting on a frame refer to a slot of that frame, and all the constants refer to an allowed slot filler. The output of the consistency check is a true/false value. A consistent QLF can always be interpreted in the Conceptual Model and, given the mapping to the Logical Data Model, it always has an interpretation, possibly empty, in the Local Data Base.

Contextualization is handled by a dialogue manager based on a decision tree structure. Rules are called with two QLFs: the QLF of the last turn and the QLF associated to one of the previous queries. The rule is fired if a test is satisfied and its action (i.e. the result it produces) is a new QLF, which merges the two input QLFs. For example, the second dialogue turn in Fig. 1, "*salaries*" produces a QLF where only the specification field is filled. After the contextualization procedure a new QLF is built where both the argument (i.e. "*contributions*") and the restriction (i.e. "*as employee*" and "*from 1980*") have been supplied from the previous dialogue turn. Of course, if the QLF of the last turn is complete, the merge process leaves it unchanged.

4.3 Data Access

The data access component retrieves needed data from the INPS archives and records them in a temporary local database which implements the logical data model, where integration and homogenization are performed. Data access includes several modules, written in LISP and C, which:

1. transform the QLF, that is the input of the data access component, into an SQL query to the local database;
2. compile and execute a set of middleware messages which gather data from the physical archives;
3. integrate the gathered data into the local database and execute the SQL query;
4. transform the result tuples into a set of conceptual model instances.

Mappings between the conceptual model and the logical model are used to compile the SQL query and to transform the tuples into instances (point 1 and 4), while mappings between the logical model and the physical model are used to compile the middleware messages and to perform integration and homogenization operations in the local database (point 2 and 3).

5. Evaluations and Conclusions

The prototype has been designed taking into account the "user centered" methodology [Norman and Draper 1986] which required a deep and accurate experimentation of the user requirements. In order to establish the degree of usability, three defined dimensions have been taken into account: ease of learning, user satisfaction and ease of remembering the use of the system after a certain period of time [Nielsen 1993]. At the very beginning of our work, a simulation of the system with the *Wizard of Oz* technique has been tested. Thirty INPS operators, divided into two groups, according to their working area and competence, were involved in the experiment. The aim of this test was to compare the ability of an operator in the use both of the current non NL based system of INPS and of TAMIC-P proposed solution. TAMIC-P hypothesis showed immediately its validity: after a training of only twenty minutes, the user could reach the same degree of interactive efficacy reached with current INPS systems, for a simple task; for a more complex or unknown task, the performances of INPS systems substantially decreased, while those of TAMIC-P remained stable.

The evaluation of TAMIC-P in real working situations demonstrated its flexibility and adaptability. Because of its multimodality and its chosen scenario, it can be adapted to aims and competencies of different types of users. As an example, an expert operator uses TAMIC-P as a communicative means with a non expert citizen, while a less expert operator tries to exploit the whole set of TAMIC-P functionalities in order to obtain information for his own use, including what he needs to better understand the application domain and the system behavior. In this task, an effective help is given by a flexible error manager, which can properly handle different types or errors, either linguistic or conceptual. The file card scenario, and the combination of the two chosen modalities, also helps in making the interaction more robust, since the user can always recover the focus of his dialogue with the machine.

In conclusion, the key factor of the success of TAMIC-P is its interface, which integrates NL and direct manipulation of visual objects. In particular, the introduction of state of art NL technologies allowed to obtain relevant advantages in making interaction more easy and natural, in facilitating navigation through complex environments (data bases, conceptual data modeling, text retrieval), in aggregating heterogeneous data in a flexible way, and, finally, in increasing the transparency of the man-machine communication. In this way, many benefits can be obtained, in particular: reduction of the technical knowledge required for its use and reduction of the time required for learning. Transparency also increases the degree of participation of the citizen into the social affairs and, at the same time, it makes the interaction between the public administration and the citizen more effective and clear.

References

Alshawi H. 1992 ed. *The Core Language Engine*. Cambridge Mass: MIT Press.

Alshawi H., Carter D., Crouch R., Pulman S., Rayner M. and Smith A. 1992. CLARE - A Contextual Reasoning and Cooperative Response Framework for the Core Language Engine. Final Report, SRI International.

Androutsopoulos I., Ritchie G.D. and Thanisch P. 1995. Natural Language Interfaces to Databases - an Introduction. *Natural Language Engineering* 1(1).

Bagnasco C., Bresciani P., Magnini B. and Strapparava C. 1996. Natural Language Interpretation for Public Administration Database Querying in the TAMIC Demonstrator. In R.P. van de Riet, J.F.M Burg, A.J. van der Vos (eds.), *Applications of Natural Language to Information Systems*, IOS Press, Amsterdam, Netherlands.

Bates M., Moser M. G. and Stallard D. 1986. The IRUS transportable natural language database interface. In L. Kerschberg (ed.) *Expert Database Systems*, Benjamin/Cummings.

BBN System and Technologies. 1989. BBN Parlance Interface Software – System Overview.

Chen P. P. 1976. The entity-relationship model - Toward a Unified View of Data. *ACM TODS* 1:1.

Cohen, P. R. 1992. The Role of Natural Language in a Multimodal Interface. In Proceedings of *UIST'92*, pp. 143-149. ACM Press, New York

Cohen, P. R. and Sullivan, J. W. 1989. Synergistic Use of Direct Manipulation and Natural Language. *CHI-89* Conference Proceedings, New York: ACM Press, 227-233.

Grosz, B.J., Appelt D.E., Martin P.A., Pereira, F.C.N. 1987. TEAM: An Experiment in the Design of Transportable Natural-Language Interfaces. *Artificial Intelligence*, 32:173-243.

Harris L.R. 1984. Experience with INTELLECT: Artificial Intelligence Technology Transfer. *The AI Magazine*, 5(2):43-50.

Maybury, M. T. 1997 ed. *Intelligent Multimedia Information Retrieval*, MIT Press.

Miller, G. A., Beckwith R., Fellbaum C., Gross D. 1990. Introduction to WordNet: an on-line lexical database. *International Journal of Lexicography* 3 (4), pp. 235 - 244.

Nielsen, J. 1993. *Usability Engineering*. San Diego: Academic Press.

Norman, D. A. and Draper, S. W. 1986. *User Centered System Design: New Perspectives on Human-Computer Interaction*. Hillsdale, New Jersey: Lawrence Erlbaum Associates.

Resnik P. 1989. Access to Multiple Underlying Systems in JANUS. BBN report 7142, Bolt Beranek and Newman Inc., Cambridge, Mass.

Shneiderman, B. 1992. *Designing the User Interface-strategies for Effective Human-Computer Interaction*. Reading, MA: Addison-Wesley, 1992.

Stock, O. and the Alfresco project team. 1993. Alfresco: enjoying the combination of Natural Language processing and hypermedia for information exploration. In M. Maybury (ed.) *Intelligent Multimedia Interface*, AAAI Press/ MIT Press, Menlo Park, CA.

Stock O., Strapparava C. and Zancanaro M. 1995. Explorations in a Natural Language Multimodal Information Access Environment. Proceedings of the workshop *Intelligent Multimedia Information Retrieval*, IJCAI 95, Montreal.

TAMIC-P 1997. Deliverable 2.0.2: User Requirements.

TAMIC-P 1999-1. Deliverable 3.0.4: DB Conceptual Model and Data Access Layer.

TAMIC-P 1999-2. Deliverable 4.0.5: Italian NL Access.

TAMIC-P 1999-3. Deliverable 6.0.4: Technical Dictionary.

TAMIC-P 1999-4. Deliverable 7.0.5: User Interface.

TAMIC-P 1999-5. Deliverable 9.0.4: Demonstrator Validation.

On the application of personalization techniques to news servers on the WWW

Liliana Ardissono, Luca Console, Ilaria Torre

Dip. Informatica, Università di Torino
Corso Svizzera 185 - 10149 Torino (Italy)
{liliana,lconsole,ila.torre}@di.unito.it

Abstract. This paper describes how the generation of hypertexts for accessing on-line news servers can be tailored to different users. News servers contain huge amounts of information, concerning different topics. The aim of our system is to present the most appropriate set of news (and advertisements) to each user, choosing the "right" level of detail for each news item. This is obtained by using knowledge representation, user modeling and flexible hypermedia techniques.

1 Introduction

For several years the aims of providing customized services and reaching customer satisfaction have been the focus of communication and marketing strategies. Now the World Wide Web seems to offer very big possibilities to satisfy these needs. Thus, several efforts are being made to exploit this potential at its best. In this paper we focus on a specific service: accessing large amounts of information (news). The number of Web sites delivering news is rapidly growing (e.g., newspapers, broadcasting companies, portals in general). As these sites contain huge amounts of data, the search for relevant information is a difficult task; therefore, the possibility of presenting news in a personalized way is at the same time a need and an interesting opportunity. Moreover, as the income of these sites comes mainly from advertisements, showing the "right" advertisements to each user is also of paramount importance.

The personalization of the interaction with the user is based on the generation of *user models* containing data about her/his needs, interests and preferences: user modeling techniques (see [29,20,10]) have been widely exploited to design adaptive interfaces [5] in several areas, such as intelligent tutoring systems [7,9,12,16], electronic catalogues [24,8,21,23], information filtering and recommender systems [19,3,25,18,22,4,15]. Many systems in the first two areas use well-structured databases and sophisticated Natural Language techniques to provide the user with customized presentations. On the other hand, most of the information filtering systems, which operate on large data sources, use various types of techniques to select a set of information items to be displayed (e.g., [6, 13,17]), but are usually unable to present the selected items in a personalized way.

E. Lamma and P. Mello (Eds.): AI*IA 99, LNAI 1792, pp. 261–272, 2000.
© Springer-Verlag Berlin Heidelberg 2000

In this paper we describe our approach to the generation of adaptive hypermedia for accessing on-line electronic news servers: the system we designed presents the "right" set of news to each user, with the appropriate detail level for each piece of news; moreover, it also tailors the advertisements added to the pages to the user's interests [1]. In order to achieve these goals, we exploit user modeling techniques to identify the user's interests and capabilities and we make use of a news database where news are represented in a structured way and organized in a taxonomy of sections corresponding to their topics.

The user models are handled by exploiting *stereotypical information* and *user modeling acquisition techniques*. If the users give their permission, their models are stored in a users database at the end of the interaction, for future reference. Stereotypical knowledge describes the interests and capabilities of classes of readers/customers and is exploited to initialize the models of the readers who access the news server for the first time. The classification is based on a small set of data that each new user provides in an initial registration form. This step is not needed for a user that is already registered: her/his model is retrieved from the users database. The user modeling acquisition techniques are then applied to update the user models while the readers browse the news server (hypertext): in this way, on the one hand, we can refine the model of the user to reflect her/his actual individual interests and capabilities; on the other hand, we can track the possible changes in users' interests.

The news server we designed is formed by four main modules:

1. Databases of news and advertisements (Sect. 2).

2. A user modeling component; in particular, Sect. 3 describes how user models are initialized using stereotypical knowledge, while Sect. 6 discusses how the user's behavior is tracked and her/his model is updated/revised dynamically.

3. A knowledge base relating the features in the user model to what has to be presented: which sections (i.e., topics), which news, which detail level for each section or news item, which advertisements (Sect. 4).

4. A module for the dynamic generation of the Web pages of the news server (Sect. 5).

2   Databases for news and advertisements

Three aspects are relevant in the structure of our news database.

First of all, news are organized in a taxonomy of sections, which includes titles such as politics (with subsections such as internal and foreign politics), sport, economics, technology, culture, and so forth.

Second, we introduced the concept of "news" as the main structured entity in our database. News have a set of associated attributes that define their components: title and subtitle; author(s); abstract; text (article); a set of graphics summarizing the content of the text; photos, video or audio clips; commentaries, interviews, agency reports; raw data and/or detailed (technical) charts/graphics, etc. Some of the attributes are optional or can be multi-valued (e.g., more than one photo may be associated with a news item); moreover, the same object (e.g., a video clip) may be associated with more than one news item. Thus, each news item corresponds to a chunk of information to be conveyed to a reader.

Finally, the database is an historical one, so we can store information concerning several days. In particular, the same news item can be present in the database on different days, possibly with different components.

A second database contains the advertisements that can be inserted into the pages. Each advertisement has two attributes: (i) a topic, in relation to the sections of the news server (in order to insert into each page advertisements that are in accordance with the content of the page); and (ii) a target, i.e., the segment(s) of population to which it is directed.

Our approach is different with respect to most approaches to information filtering. In fact, many of such approaches do not assume any structure and use techniques like *TF/IDF* (term frequency, inverse document frequency) to index and classify the documents [27]. The personalized selection is then based on a match between these indices and keywords representing users' interests. Not imposing any structure has some advantages in terms of flexibility: in fact, the techniques can be used on any repository of documents, including collections of text files. However, this approach does not support a personalized presentation of the documents: although semantic labels can be exploited to annotate linked documents (e.g., to express recommendation degrees), the documents cannot be presented in different ways: i.e., either a document is selected, or it is not. Other approaches exploit *annotations* in the documents (like HTML tags) to improve indexing; yet others *generate summaries* of the documents [11], but need to apply sophisticated natural language techniques; thus, they are mainly applicable in restricted domains. Instead, the *structure* we impose allows us to apply sophisticated personalization strategies for presenting news at different detail levels (as we shall see in the next sections), without requiring the introduction of specific domain-dependent knowledge for the dynamic generation of the components of the news, tailored to the user's interests. At the same time, our approach does not prevent the adoption of other information retrieval and filtering techniques.

3   Creating the initial user model

We distinguish two phases in the management of the user models: the generation of an initial model for a new user and the refinement of an existing user model. In fact, the problems that arise in the two phases are different: we regard the creation of an initial user model as a classification problem, aimed at generating initial predictions about the user; instead, the refinement of the model consists in revising these predictions, based on the observation of the user's behavior. In this section, we describe the first task, while the description of the techniques for updating the user models is deferred to section 6.

The user models are initialized by classifying users in stereotypical descriptions [26], representing the features of classes of readers/customers. The data used in the classification are those asked to the user in a registration form: age and gender; education level and field; type and field of job; whether her/his access to the news server is for work or not; how frequently (s)he connects to the Web, her/his hobbies or priorities (how much (s)he likes traveling, doing sport, following sport, shopping, etc.).

The information about the user that is needed to customize the news server includes quite heterogeneous features. In fact, the selection of the (sub)sections and news to be presented depends on the user's interests and capabilities; the detail level is related also to her/his expertise and receptivity; finally the selection of the advertisements must be related to her/his priorities (life-style). Thus, the stereotypes must provide a first (coarse) prediction on all these aspects. Having a single classification that takes into account all these aspects would require a combinatorial number of stereotypes. Thus, we decided to decompose the problem into different dimensions for dealing independently with each one of the aspects above. In particular, we defined four families of stereotypes: a user is classified independently in each family and the predictions are merged. The families use partially overlapping classificatory data and make predictions on different user features (a similar idea has been experimented in [2]):

- **Interests**. Starting from classificatory data such as the age, gender, type and field of job, purpose of the access to the server, hobbies, these stereotypes make a first prediction on the user's interest level in each (sub)section.

- **Cognitive characteristics**. This group of stereotypes makes a prediction on the user's receptivity, a parameter used to determine the amount and detail of the information that can be presented to her/him. These stereotypes use classificatory data such as the user's age, education level, job and familiarity in reading Web pages (derived from her/his frequency of access to the Web).

- **Domain expertise**. Starting from data such as the degree and area of education and field of job, these stereotypes make predictions on the user's expertise on the topics of each (sub)section of the news server.

- **Life styles**. These stereotypes classify the users according to their psychographic features, which include socio-demographic data and priorities [14]. They do not make specific predictions: the relevant prediction is the class to which a user belongs. The classes in this family correspond to the targets that can be associated with the advertisements in the database.

Figure 1 shows the "Professional financial reader" stereotype, belonging to the "Interests" family. Two groups of slots can be recognized: profile and prediction slots.

Profile. The profile of the users belonging to the stereotype is described by means of a set of slots, each one corresponding to a user feature. For each feature F_i we consider a set of linguistic values $\{v_{i1}, \ldots, v_{ik}\}$; we associate with each v_{ij} a numeric value $x_{ij} \in [0, 1]$, representing the compatibility of $F_i = v_{ij}$ with the stereotype. More precisely, x_{ij} can be regarded as the frequency (probability) of $F_i = v_{ij}$ for the individuals belonging to the stereotypical class. For example, the slot "age" in figure 1 specifies that 10% of the professional financial readers are between 20 and 25 years old, while 20% are between 26 and 35.

Classification of the user. The degree of match between a user and each stereotype is computed by matching the user's data with the profile of the stereotype.

PROFESSIONAL FINANCIAL READER:
profile:
age: <20: 0; 20-25: 0.1; 26-35: 0.2; 36-45: 0.3; 46-65: 0.3; >65: 0.1
gender: M: 0.8; F: 0.2
job: manager: 0.57; self-trader: 0.3; self-employed: 0.05; ...; student: 0.01
job field: financial, banking, insurance: 0.8; politics, law, civil services: 0.14; ...
reason of connection: work: 0.9; personal: 0.1
hobbies: theatre: a lot: 0.1; some: 0.3; a little: 0.4; not at all: 0.2;
hobbies: following sports: a lot: 0.4; some: 0.3; a little: 0.2; not at all: 0.1;
...
predictions on interests:
economy: high: 1; medium: 0; low: 0; null: 0
politics: high: 0.7; medium: 0.3; low: 0; null: 0
sport: high: 0.2; medium: 0.4; low: 0.3; null: 0.1
culture: high: 0; medium: 0.2, low: 0.5; null: 0.3
technology: high: 0; medium: 0.3; low: 0.6; null: 0.1
...

Fig. 1. An example of a stereotype.

If we know, for the user under examination, that $F_i = v_{ij}$, then x_{ij} can be interpreted as the compatibility of the user with that specific feature of the stereotype. Since we are interested in matching all the features simultaneously, we compute the degree of match of the user with a stereotype as the product (i.e., the conjunction) of the contributions of all the individual slots (in the computation we also take into account an a-priori probability distribution of the stereotypes, estimated in the population of readers). This is in accordance with the theoretical framework in [28] and corresponds to assuming that the features are independent. Indeed, this is reasonable since our goal is to rank the stereotypes in the same family and these stereotypes contain exactly the same set of profile slots. Thus, the ranking can be obtained after normalizing the degrees of match obtained with the computation above. In this way we have, for each stereotype of each family, a number $p(stereotype)$ which is a normalized match between the user and the stereotype itself.

Predictions. These slots make predictions on features used by the system to personalize information to the user.[1] Again we consider a set of linguistic values for each feature and we associate with each linguistic value v'_{ij} of each feature F'_i a numeric value $x'_{ij} \in [0, 1]$. This number represents the strength of the prediction and is the conditional probability that $F'_i = v'_{ij}$, given that the user belongs to the stereotype $(p(F'_i = v'_{ij}|stereotype))$. For example, the predictions of the "Professional financial reader" stereotype concern the interest level in the various sections of the news server, as, e.g., in its first slot:

---

[1] No predictions are associated with the stereotypes of the "Life styles" family. In fact, the granularity needed for selecting advertisements is coarser than that needed for selecting news and their detail levels.

1) title, subtitle, authors

2a) abstract, summarizing graphics   2b) full text, summarizing graphics

3a) pictures, video/audio   3b) pictures, video/audio
    titles relative to other days   titles relative to other days

4b) comments, interviews, agency reports

5b) technical graphics, raw data

Fig. 2. Detail levels in the presentation of news

$$p(interest\ in\ economy = high \mid Professional\ Financial\ Reader) = 1.$$

The prediction for a specific user is obtained by combining this value and the degree of match between the user and the stereotype ($p(stereotype)$), computed using the profile slots):

$$p(F_i' = v_{ij}') = p(F_i' = v_{ij}' | stereotype) * p(stereotype)$$

Merging the stereotypical predictions. Since the user may partially match more than one stereotype, the corresponding predictions have to be merged. We assume that the contributions by different stereotypes are independent and we use an additive formula to combine them; i.e., if $p(F_i' = v_{ij}') = X$ (using a stereotype A) and $p(F_i' = v_{ij}') = Y$ (using a stereotype B), then the combined prediction is $p(F_i' = v_{ij}') = X + (1 - X) * Y$. The final predictions are computed by normalizing the values obtained for the different linguistic values of each feature F_i'.

4   Selecting relevant information for each user

In this section we discuss how the model of a user is related to what has to be presented: (i) which sections/subsections and news should be selected and at which detail level, and (ii) which advertisements should be displayed.

The selection of the detail level requires a brief discussion. In our approach, different detail levels for presenting news can be obtained as different aggregations of the attributes of news, considering that some attributes provide more detailed and technical information than others. In principle, several alternatives could be considered; in our experiments we defined a fixed set of presentation formats (each one corresponding to a different aggregation of attributes) and a partial ordering between them, as shown in figure 2. Each node of the tree corresponds to one way of presenting a news item to the user. The root corresponds to the minimum detail. Moving to a descendant corresponds to increasing the detail level by adding further attributes. For example, the node 2a corresponds to presenting: title, subtitle, authors, abstract and summarizing graphics (if any). Notice that 2a and 2b (and 3a and 3b) correspond to alternative choices.

The selection of the detail level for the presentation of news relies on a knowledge base formed by different sets of rules and on a heuristic scoring approach.

Taking into account interest and expertise. A first set of rules is used to evaluate, for each (sub)section and for each possible presentation format (detail level), the probability that the user wants to read the news of the (sub)section at that level. In order to make this computation we use a matrix that specifies the probability of each detail level for a generic section S, given all possible pairs $< X, Y >$ of linguistic values of the interest and expertise in the subject of S:

$p(level = i \ for \ section \ S \mid interest \ in \ S = X, \ expertise \ in \ S = Y)$

For example, an entry could be:

$p(level = 4 \ for \ S \mid interest \ in \ S = medium, \ expertise \ in \ S = medium) = 0.7$

specifying that the conditional probability of level 4 (defined in figure 2), given that the user has a medium interest and expertise, is 0.7. Notice that the rules include a level 0, that corresponds to disregarding the (sub)section.

The rules are applied for each (sub)section s. Since the user model contains the probability distribution for the interest and expertise in s, the rules enable the computation of a probability for each detail level for each section. For example, if the user model predicts for section s that $p(interest \ in \ s = high) = 0.8$ and $p(expertise \ in \ s = high) = 0.9$, then $p(level = 4 \ for \ section \ s)$ would be $0.9 * 0.8 * 0.7 = 0.504$.

Taking into account the receptivity. In a second step we use information about the user's receptivity and the scores computed by the rules above to decide which (sub)sections should be presented and their detail level. This is done in two sub-steps:

a) Selecting the (sub)sections to be presented. This decision is made by considering the scores computed by the first set of rules. All the (sub)sections for which the level 0 has the highest score or for which the cumulative scores of levels 0 and 1 is over a threshold (0.7) are excluded. Those for which the level 5 has the highest score or such that the cumulative scores of levels 4 and 5 is over a threshold (0.7) are included in the set of (sub)sections to be presented. The remaining (sub)sections are ranked according to the distribution of the scores.

b) Selecting the detail level on the basis of receptivity. For each (sub)section S selected in step *a)*, the system considers the detail level L with the highest score and evaluates whether it is compatible with the user's receptivity. If it is, then this is the detail level for S. If L is too detailed, then the system searches for a lower level representing a good compromise between the scores computed by the first group of rules and the user's receptivity. If L is low with respect to the receptivity, then there are two cases. If the cumulative scores of the levels higher than L is over a threshold (0.5), this means that the user's expertise and interest are compatible with detail levels higher than L; thus, the system increases the detail, again looking for a compromise between the scores and the user's receptivity. Otherwise, L remains the level of presentation.

If the selected level is 2 or 3, a decision between 2a and 2b (3a and 3b) has to be made. The choice between the abstract and the full article is based on the user's interest and expertise on the topic of the section under examination, and on her/his receptivity: the full article is presented only when, for all these features, the probabilities of the values low and null are close to zero. Moreover, in case there are alternatives (e.g., between a picture or a video clip), the choice is based on the user's past preferences.

Selecting the advertisements. The selection of the advertisements to be included in each page depends on: (i) the topic of the page, that is the (sub)section to which it belongs, and (ii) the classification of the user according to the "Life Styles", which specifies a degree of compatibility between the user and each stereotype in that family. The selection is performed as follows: first we consider the stereotypes whose compatibility is over a threshold; then we select advertisements that are compatible with the topic of the page and whose target includes these stereotypes, with frequency proportional to the compatibility values.

5   Dynamic generation of the hypertextual presentation

The pieces of information selected using the techniques described in the previous section are the input to a module that generates the Web pages to be sent to the user's browser. We chose a simple hypertextual structure which is very easy to navigate and allows the user to modify the system's choices, both as regards the sections and news selected by the system and as regards their detail level. This is important for two reasons: on the one hand, we believe that the personalization techniques should never impose their choices to the user, who must have the possibility of accessing the whole set of data available in the server; on the other hand, changing the system's settings is the basis for refining user models dynamically (see next section).

The first page of the hypertext contains a list of the sections considered of interest to the user. Each section name is a link to the page corresponding to the section. A "delete" button is associated with each section and can be used to suppress it. Moreover, a menu allows the user to explore sections that were not selected by the system. The pages corresponding to sections organized into subsections have a similar structure.

Figure 3 shows a page corresponding to a subsection containing news. Three areas can be recognized: on the left, a list of the titles of the news in the section ("delete" buttons can be used to suppress each item, while a menu — the hotword "visualizza altre notizie" — allows the user to explore the news items not selected by the system); when a title is selected, the corresponding news item is presented in the central part of the frame; advertisements are located in the right part. In the example, the news item is presented with limited detail (level 2a); however, the hidden attributes are included as links which can be selected to display the corresponding pieces of information. On the other hand, "delete" buttons can be used to suppress the displayed pieces of information (attributes).

6   Dynamic updating of the user model

In this section we discuss how the user model is revised after tracking the user's actions during the navigation. Such a refinement/update is needed because the user model initialized by the stereotypes may be imprecise and generic, due to the limited amount of data asked in the initial registration form.

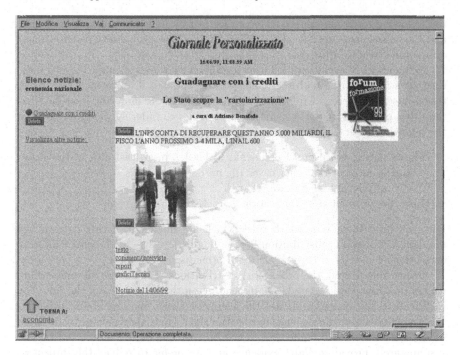

Fig. 3. An example of a page presenting the news in section "economy".

The user model can be revised after monitoring the user's behavior. To this purpose, several events are recorded by the server:

- The number of connections per week and month, and the amount of time devoted by the user to each (sub)section;
- The (sub)sections (and news) that the system has selected and the user has suppressed;
- The (sub)sections or news that were not selected by the system and that the user asks to display;
- The details about a news item presented by the system and suppressed by the user;
- The user's requests for more detail (on a specific news item) than that selected by the system;
- The selection of specific advertisements.

The actions taken by the user are collected and periodically analyzed by the system (after the user moves to a new section, and at the end of each session). Thus, the user model is modified after having analyzed the user's behavior across time, and not after each single action.

In order to update the user models, we pursue again the idea of considering separate dimensions (the user's interests, domain expertise, receptivity and life style) and we use four sets (families) of user modeling acquisition rules, having

270 L. Ardissono, L. Console, and I. Torre

the following form: the antecedents are formed by logical conditions on events and the consequents specify new predictions (i.e. new probability distributions) over some features of the user.

Different set of events are relevant to different families of rules. For instance, the user's interest in a (sub)section has to be updated if, in most of the cases, the user selects pieces of information at a level that is more (or less) detailed than that predicted by the system. Thus, the rules considering the interests have the following general pattern:

> **if** in section X the user selected links at level L in at least 60% of the cases
>   **and** in most of the other cases the user selected links
>   at a level higher/lower than L'
> **then** the user's interest for section X is M;

For each level there is a set of rules which are instances of this pattern. M provides a probability distribution for the linguistic values of the user's interest on section X, i.e.: $M = (p(null), p(low), p(medium), p(high))$.

Once a rule is fired, the probability distributions of the user's features occurring in its consequent are updated, depending on the predictions of the rule. For each feature, the system evaluates the average between the probability values in the user model and those suggested by the rule. Thus, the changes to the user model are smooth. We made this choice because the events monitored by the system rarely provide definite evidence and we prefer to reduce the impact of new information with respect to the past history, avoiding abrupt changes in the user model. This is a conservative choice; other alternatives will be explored.

Revising the user model may change the (sub)sections and news to be presented, or the detail level to be used for some news. Since making changes during a consultation may create confusion to the user, the changes are effective immediately only on the generation of the pages ((sub)sections and/or news) that s/he has not yet seen during the session. The other changes are effective only the next time the user will connect to the server.

7   Conclusions

In the paper we described the architecture of an adaptive WWW news server, focusing on the user modeling and personalization techniques exploited to customize the presentation of the news to each user. The user models are initialized using stereotypes and are then updated dynamically. The peculiarity of our approach is that we partitioned the knowledge about users in several dimensions, to describe and handle in parallel different user features. Besides allowing us to cope with the complexity of the problem, this approach has a further advantage: some groups of stereotypes can be used across different applications. Indeed, for example, the stereotypes related to the life style of readers/customers are the same used in adaptive electronic commerce [2].

The system tailors the presentation of news to the peculiarities of the user by exploiting a structured database of news where items are classified in a hierarchy of topics and are characterized by a set of attributes. These attributes can be shown or hidden, depending on the contents of the user model. This is a significant difference with respect to other approaches to personalized information filtering, which do not assume information is structured but then have difficulties in the selection of contents, especially as regards the detail level. Filling in the database of news is additional work. However, this task is not very different from what has to be done in the software systems that are being used in the editorial offices of some newspapers. These systems require that the author of a paper submits her/his work to a specific section and, in case there are photos or extra items, s(he) must specify the paper to which these items are related (this is used to define the layout of the pages).

It is worth noting, in conclusion, that there is a difference between the goals of personalization in our approach and those pursued in systems for the personalization of electronic catalogues [21] or archives, such as virtual museums [11, 23] or information kiosks). In fact, we aim at defining the "right" detail level for presenting news on a given topic by aggregating different attributes of the news, while they generate personalized linguistic descriptions for presenting in different ways the items in the database.

A first prototype of the system has been implemented and we recently started a first qualitative evaluation of its performance. In these initial tests (whose main aim is that of evaluating and refining the knowledge bases) we obtained interesting results as regards the ability of the system to tailor the presentation to (very) different typologies of users. More extensive and systematic testing will be performed in the next months.

References

1. L. Ardissono, L. Console, and I. Torre. Exploiting user models for personalizing news presentations. In *Proc. 2nd Workshop on adaptive systems and user modeling on the World Wide Web*, pages 13–20, Banff, Canada, 1999.

2. L. Ardissono, A. Goy, R. Meo, G. Petrone, L. Console, L. Lesmo, C. Simone, and P. Torasso. A configurable system for the construction of adaptive virtual stores. *World Wide Web*, 2(3):143–159, 1999.

3. F. Asnicar and C. Tasso. ifWeb: a prototype of user model-based intelligent agent for document filtering and navigation in the World Wide Web. In *Proc. workshop "Adaptive Systems and User Modeling on the World Wide Web"*, pages 3–12, 1997.

4. Autonomy. Technology white paper. http://www.autonomy.com.

5. D. Benyon. Adaptive systems: a solution to usability problems. *User Modeling and User-Adapted Interaction*, 3:65–87, 1993.

6. D. Billsus and M. Pazzani. A personal news agent that talks, learns and explains. In *Proc. 3rd Int. Conf. on Autonomous Agents (Agents '99)*, pages 268–275, 1999.

7. P. Brusilovsky, E. Schwartz, and G. Weber. ELM-ART: An intelligent tutoring system on World Wide Web. In *Proc. 3rd Int. Conf. on Intelligent Tutoring Systems (ITS-96)*, Montreal, 1996.

8. R.D. Burke, K.J. Hammond, and B.C. Young. The FindMe approach to assisted browsing. *IEEE Expert*, pages 32–39, 1997.

9. L. Calvi and P. De Bra. Proficiency-adapted information browsing and filtering in hypermedia educational systems. *User Modeling and User-Adapted Interaction*, 7:257–277, 1997.

10. D.N. Chin. Acquiring user models. *Artificial Intelligence Review*, 7:185–197, 1993.

11. R. Dale, S.J. Green, M. Milosavljevic, and C. Paris. Dynamic document delivery: Generating natural language texts on demand. In *Proc. 9th Int. Conf. and Workshop on Database and Expert Systems Applications (DEXA '98)*, Vienna, 1998.

12. B.N. De Carolis. Introducing reactivity in adaptive hypertext generation. In *Proc. 13th Conf. ECAI*, Brighton, UK, 1998.

13. J. Domingue and P. Scott. KMi Planet: a web based news server. In *Asia Pacific Computer Human Interaction Conference (APCHI'98)*, Kanagwa, Japan, 1998.

14. Eurisko. Sinottica.

15. D.R. Greening. LikeMinds: Building consumer trust with accurate product recommendations. http://likeminds.com/technology/white_papers/websell/.

16. N. Henze and W. Nejdl. Adaptivity in the KBS hyperbook system. In *Proc. 2nd Workshop on adaptive systems and user modeling on the World Wide Web*, Banff, Canada, 1999.

17. T. Joachims, D. Freitag, and T. Mitchell. WebWatcher: a tour guide for the World Wide Web. In *Proc. 15th IJCAI*, pages 770–775, Nagoya, Japan, 1997.

18. T. Joerding. Intelligent multimedia presentations in the web: Fun without annoyance. In *Proc. of the 7th World Wide Web Conference (WWW7)*, Brisbane, Australia, 1998.

19. J. Kay. Vive la difference! individualised interaction with users. In *Proc. 14th IJCAI*, pages 978–984, Montreal, 1995.

20. M.F. McTear. User modelling for adaptive computer systems: a survey of recent developments. *Artificial Intelligence Review*, 7:157–184, 1993.

21. M. Milosavljevic and J. Oberlander. Dynamic hypertext catalogues: Helping users to help themselves. In *Proc. 9th ACM Conf. on Hypertext and Hypermedia*, 1998.

22. A. Nill, J. Fink, and A. Kobsa. Adaptable and adaptive information for all users, including disabled and elderly people. *New review of Hypermedia and Multimedia*, 1999.

23. D. Petrelli, A.De Angeli, and G. Convertino. A user centered approach to user modelling. In *Proc. 7th Int. Conf. on User Modeling*, pages 255–264, Banff, Canada, 1999.

24. H. Popp and D. Lödel. Fuzzy techniques and user modeling in sales assistants. *User Modeling and User-Adapted Interaction*, 6:349–370, 1996.

25. P. Resnick and H.R. Varian, editors. *Special Issue on Recommender Systems*, volume 40. Communications of the ACM, 1997.

26. E. Rich. Stereotypes and user modeling. In A. Kobsa and W. Wahlster, editors, *User Models in Dialog Systems*, pages 35–51. Springer Verlag, Berlin, 1989.

27. G. Salton and M.J. McGill. *An Introduction to Modern Information Retrieval*. McGraw-Hill, 1983.

28. P. Torasso and L. Console. Approximate reasoning and prototypical knowledge. *International Journal of Approximate Reasoning*, 3(2):157–178, 1989.

29. W. Wahlster and A. Kobsa. *User Models in Dialog Systems*. Springer Verlag, 1989.

Levels of Delegation and Levels of Adoption as the basis for Adjustable Autonomy

Rino Falcone, Cristiano Castelfranchi

IP-CNR, Group of "Artificial Intelligence, Cognitive Modeling and Interaction"
Viale Marx, 15 - 00137 ROMA - Italy
E-mail: {falcone,castel}@ip.rm.cnr.it

Abstract. "Adjustable autonomy means dynamically adjusting the level of autonomy of an agent depending on the situation" [1]. Our claim is that in studying how to adjust the level of autonomy and how to arrive to a dynamic level of control, it could be useful an explicit theory of delegation able to specify different kinds and levels of autonomy.
In this paper, we present our model of delegation and help. On such a basis, it is possible to analyze the adjustable autonomy of an agent both by considering the level of delegation allowed to the contractor by the client, and the possibility for the contractor itself to adjust its own autonomy by restricting or by expanding the received delegation. We consider also possible conflicts due to the initiative of the delegated agent (contractor) or to an inappropriate delegation by the client: conflicts due to the contractor's willingness to help the client better and more deeply (collaborative conflicts).

1 Introduction

"Adjustable autonomy means dynamically adjusting the *level of autonomy* of an agent depending on the situation. For real-world teaming between humans and autonomous agents, the desired or optimal *level of control* may vary over time. Hence, effective autonomous agents will support adjustable autonomy." [1] But which level of autonomy are we speaking about? And what kind of autonomy?

In this paper we will analyze a specific view of autonomy strictly based on the notions of delegation and adoption. In fact, in several situations the MA plan, the co-operation between user and agent (or between the delegating agent (*client*) and the delegated one (*contractor*)) requires a strict collaboration, and a flow of the control between the partners, either in order to maintain the client's trust [2] or in order to avoid breakdowns, failures and unsatisfactory solutions.

Moreover, mixed initiative is necessary since, in fact, it is necessary (but also dangerous) the initiative of the delegated agent. A real collaborator, not a simple tool [3], should be able to intelligently take care of the client's interests. This implies the capability and the initiative either to be less autonomous than the client/user expected (in case of lack of competence, of conditions, or of knowledge), or to go beyond the user/client requests and expectations. In other words, 'the adjustable autonomy concept includes the ability.... for agents to adjust their own autonomy' [1] either by restricting or by expanding the received delegation.

This problem is particularly relevant also because delegation to agents is not only based on 'weak dependence' [4] i.e. on the possibility but not on the necessity to delegate. A client does not delegate only tasks that it could manage/perform by itself and it prefers to allocate

E. Lamma and P. Mello (Eds.): AI*IA 99, LNAI 1792, pp. 273–284, 2000.

to other agents. Software and autonomous agents will not be useful only for relieving human agents from boring and repetitive tasks; they will be mainly useful for situations where delegation and autonomy are necessary ('strong dependence', [5,6]) because the user/client will not have the local, decentralised and updated knowledge, or the expertise, or the just-in-time reactivity, or some physical skill that requires some local control-loop. Thus autonomy and initiative are not simply optional features for Agents, they are obligatory directions of study. However, control cannot be completely lost and delegation cannot be complete, not only for reasons of confidence and trust, but for reasons of distribution of goals, of knowledge, of competence, and for an effective collaboration: humans needs autonomous artificial collaborators, but artificial agents needs human collaboration and supervision.

Our claim is that in studying how to adjust the level of autonomy and how to arrive to a dynamic level of control, it is useful an *explicit theory of delegation* (and of trust) able to specify different dimentions and levels, and able to link to these the notion and the levels of autonomy. Thus, we propose in this paper our plan-based analysis of levels of delegation, of levels of help, of the notion of autonomy, and of possible conflicts due to collaborative initiative.

In this paper we will consider this framework only marginally in a dynamic perspective. A dynamic perspective of the levels of delegation should specify:

- how the delegation or help levels can vary over time and in a reactive way (depending on the intermediate results of co-operation);
- how the levels of delegation, of trust, and of autonomy can be different for different aspects and dimensions of the same task.

Why is delegation so important and central in a theory of autonomy?

If we consider an agent delegated to take care of a given *task,* it has to choose among different possible recipes (plans), or to adapt abstract or previous plans to suit new situations; it has to find additional (local and updated) information; it has to solve a problem (not just to execute a function, an action, or implement a recipe); sometimes it has to exploit its "expertise". In all these cases this agent takes care of the interests or goals of the delegating agent "remotely" i.e. far from it and without its monitoring and intervention (control), and autonomously. This requires what we will call an "open delegation": basically the delegation "to bring it about that ...". The agent is supposed to use its knowledge, its intelligence, its ability, and to exert some degree of discretion (in this paper we do not consider as part of the agent's autonomy that the agent itself could have its *own goals* to pursue, and the consequent possible conflicts).

Moreover, given that the knowledge of the delegating agent/user (client) concerning the domain and the helping agents is limited (possibly both incomplete and incorrect) the "delegated task" (the request or the elicited behaviour) might not to be so useful for the client itself. Either the expected behaviour is useful but cannot be executed, or it is useless or self-defeating, or dangerous for the client's other goals, or else there is a better way of satisfying the client's needs; and perhaps the helping agent is able to provide greater help with its knowledge and ability, going beyond the "literally" delegated task. We will call this kind of help: "over-help" or "critical-help". To be really helpful this kind of agent must take the initiative of opposing (not for personal reasons/goals) the other's expectations or prescriptions, either proposing or directly executing a different action/plan. To do this it must be able to recognise and reason about the goals, plans and interests of the client, and to have/generate different solutions.

However, of course, there is a trade-off between pros and cons both in open delegation and in over(critical)-help: the more intelligent and autonomous the agent (able to solve problems, to choose between alternatives, to think rationally and to plan) the less quickly and passively "obedient" it is. The probability that the solution or behaviour provided does not correspond to what we expect and delegate exactly increases.

In addition, possible conflicts arise between a "client" delegating certain tasks to an agent, and the "contractor" or in general the agent adopting and/or satisfying those tasks; conflicts which are either due to the intelligence and the initiative of the delegated agent or to an inappropriate delegation by the client: we are interested here only in conflicts due to the agent's willingness to collaborate and to help the other better and more deeply: a sort of "collaborative conflict".

2 Delegation and Adoption: Analyzing the Cooperation Theory

Delegation and adoption are two basic ingredients of any collaboration and organization [7]. In fact, the huge majority of DAI and MA, CSCW and negotiation systems [8], communication protocols, cooperative software agents [9], are based on the idea that *cooperation works through the allocation of some task (or sub-task) by a given agent (individual or complex) to another agent*, via some "request" (offer, proposal, announcement, etc.) meeting some "commitment" (bid, help, contract, adoption, etc.).

In [10] we in fact described a theory of cooperation among agents by identifying the elementary mechanisms on which any collaboration must be founded.

Our research is based on three fundamental claims:

i) only on the basis of a principled theory of cooperation will it be possible both to really understand the human cooperation and to design cooperation among artificial agents, among humans and artificial agents, among humans through artificial agents;

ii) this theory must be founded on the main actions of *delegation* and *adoption*;

iii) the analysis of the delegation/adoption theory must be based on the *plan model* of the action.

We will propose a definition of delegation and adoption, the identification of their various levels, the characterization of their basic principles and representations. The aim of this analysis is to provide some instruments for characterizing high levels of agent's cooperativeness and autonomy.

2.1 Delegation/Adoption Theory

The notion of delegation is already explicitly present in the theory of MAS, of collaboration [7], and team-work. However, we have based our analysis on much more basic notions.

Informally, *in delegation an agent A needs or likes an action of another agent B and includes it in its own plan. In other words, A is trying to achieve some of its goals through B's* *actions; thus A has the goal that B performs a given action.*A is constructing an MA plan and B has a "part" (Fig.1), a share in this plan: B's task (either a state-goal or an action-goal).

On the other hand: *in adoption an agent B has a goal since and for so long as it is the goal of another agent A, that is, B usually has the goal of performing an action since this action is included in the plan of A* (Fig.2). So, also in this case B plays a part in A's plan (sometimes A has no plan at all but just a need, a goal).

In our model, *delegation and adoption are characterized in terms of the particular set of mental states (cognitive ingredients) of the agents involved in the interaction.*

In fact, a delegation (or an adoption) is a set of agent's (agents') beliefs, goals, intentions, commitments, etc.: externally there may be no interaction between the agents, the delegation (adoption) being only in the mind of one of the agents (unilateral delegation/adoption) [10]. At this basic level delegation (adoption) can be established also between a cognitive and a non cognitive agent.

We assume that *to delegate an action necessarily implies delegating some result of that action.* Conversely, *to delegate a goal state always implies the delegation of at least one action (possibly unknown to A) that produces such a goal state as result.* Thus, we consider the action/goal pair $\tau=(\alpha,g)$ as the real object of delegation, and we will call it 'task'. Then by means of τ, we will refer to the action (α), to its resulting world state (g), or to both.

Delegation is generally a social action [5, 6], and also a meta-action, since its object is an action. We introduce an operator of delegation with four parameters:

Delegates(A B τ), where A,B are agents, $\tau=(\alpha,g)$.

This means that A delegates the task τ to B. In analogy with delegation we introduce the corresponding operator for adoption: Adopts(B A τ). This means that B adopts the task τ for A.

A (Client)   B (Contractor)   A (Client)   B (Contractor)

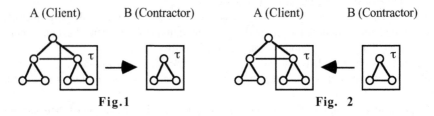

Fig.1   Fig. 2

Dimentions of Delegation

We could consider several dimentions of delegation. In this paper we focus our attention on three main dimentions:

- *Interaction-based types of delegation* (the various levels at which the behaviour of the delegated agent is influenced by the delegating agent in the delegation relationship);
- *Specification-based types of delegation* (the various levels at which the delegated task is specified in the delegation relationship);
- *Delegation of the control* (the various possibilities at which the control of the delegated task is realized).

It is interesting to note that each of these dimentions implies in fact a specific aspect of the autonomy in delegation.

Weak Delegation

We call *weak delegation* the delegation based on exploitation, on the passive achievement by A of the task. In it there is no agreement, no request or even influence: A is just exploiting in its plan a fully autonomous action of B. In fact, A has only to recognize the possibility that B will realize τ by itself and that this realization will be useful for A, which "passively" awaits the realization of τ.
More precisely,

  a) The achievement of τ (the execution of α and its result g) is a *goal* of A.

  b) A believes that there exists another agent B that has the *power of* achieving τ.

  c) A believes that B will achieve τ in time.

  c-bis) A believes that B *intends* to achieve τ in time (in the case that B is a cognitive agent).

  d) A *prefers*[1] to achieve τ through B.

  e) The achievement of τ through B is the goal of A.

  f) A has the goal (*relativized* to (e)) of not achieving τ by itself.

We consider (a, b, c, and d) what the agent A views as a "*Potential for relying on*" the agent B, its *trust*; and (e and f) what A views as the "*Decision to rely on*" B. We consider "Potential for relying on" and "Decision to rely on" as two constructs temporally and logically related to each other.

Delegation-Adoption (Contract)

We will call *strict delegation* , delegation based on explicit agreement, on the active achievement by A of the task through an agreement with B. It is based on B's adopting A's task in response to A's request/order. We will call *strict adoption* , the adoption based on explicit agreement, on the active achievement by B of the task delegated/requested by A.
In *Strict Delegation*, the delegated agent knows that the delegating agent is relying on it and accepts the task; in *Strict Adoption*, the helped agent knows about the adoption and accepts it (very often both these acceptations are preceded by a process of negotiation between the agents). In other words, *Strict Delegation requires Strict Adoption, and viceversa*: they are two facets of a unitary social relation that we call "delegation-adoption" or "contract".
There is a delegation-adoption relationship between A and B for τ, when:
1) there is a "*Potential for request of contract*" from A to B:
  - From A's point of view:

  a) The achievement of τ (the execution of α and its result g) is a *goal* of A.

  b) A believes that there exists another agent B that has the *power of* achieving τ.

  c) A *prefers* to achieve τ through B.

  - From B's point of view:

  d) B believes that B has the *power of* achieving τ.
2) After the "*Agreement*": a series of mutual beliefs (MB) are true:

  (MB A B (a) The achievement of τ (the execution of α and its result g) is a *goal* of A.

  b) A believes that there exists another agent B that has the *power of* achieving τ.

  c) A *prefers* to achieve τ through B.

---

[1] This means that, either relative to the achievement of τ or relative to a broader goal g' that includes the achievement of τ, A believes to be dependent on B.

d) B believes that B has the *power of* achieving τ.

e) A believes that B will achieve τ in time.

f) The achievement of τ through B is the goal of A.

g) A has the goal (*relativized* to (e)) of not achieving τ by itself.

h) B is *socially committed* to A to achieve τ for A.

i) B believes that the achievement of τ is a *goal* of A.

l) B *intends* to achieve τ for A.   )

Delegation based on the specification of the task

An important dimension of the delegation/adoption problem concerns how the task is specified in the delegation action; how this specification influences the contractor's autonomy, how different interpretations of the specification of the task (or different levels of granularity in the interpretation of the task specification) for client and contractor could produce misunderstanding and conflicts.

The object of delegation (τ) can be minimally specified (*open delegation*), completely specified (*close delegation*) or specified at any intermediate level.
Let us consider two extreme main cases:

- *Pure Executive (Close) Delegation:* from the client's (contractor's) point of view: when the delegating (delegated) agent believes it is delegating (adopting) a completely specified task (Fig. 4): what A expects from B is just the execution of an (or more) elementary action(s) (what B believes A delegated to it is simply the execution of an (or more) elementary action(s)).

A (Client)   B (Contractor)   A (Client)   B (Contractor)

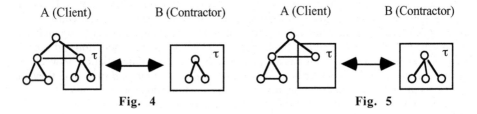

Fig. 4   Fig. 5

- *Open Delegation:* there are in fact two kinds of Open Delegation. One is relative to the delegated (sub)plan, the other is relative to the opportunity to act or not.
As for the first kind let us say that the client (contractor) believes it is delegating (adopting) an incompletely specified task (Fig. 5): either A (B) is delegating (adopting) a complex or abstract action, or it is delegating (adopting) just a result (state of the world). The agent B can (or must) realize the delegated (adopted) task by exerting its autonomy.
As for the second kind, it is the case of commands like the following one: "If it is the case, then does τ". This is a special case of *conditional delegation* like "If q then does τ". With q fully specified, we have a form of delegation of control, even if it is not Open since everything is fully specified[2].

---

[2] In fact, notice that also in this case B has some discretion about performing or not its task, since it is delegated to autonomously test the condition for its action. Consider also that performing the test might be a complex action, requiring an autonomous plan and discretion about it. In this case also this is Open delegation.

In the *Open-conditional* form "If it is the case, then does τ", B is completely free to accertain and decide when and how it is the case to do τ. The condition is not specified at all and is up to the agent to specify it (Fig. 6). The importance of *open delegation* in collaboration theory should be examined.

On the one hand, we would like to stress that *open delegation* is not only due to client's preference (utility) or limited know-how or limited skills. Of course, when A is delegating τ to B, it is dependent *on* B as for τ [6]: it needs B's action for some of its goals (either some domain goals or goals like saving time, effort, resources, etc.). However, *open delegation* is fundamental because it is also due to A's ignorance about the world and its dynamics. In fact, frequently enough *it is not possible or convenient to fully specify* τ because some local and updated knowledge is needed in order for that part of the plan to be successfully executed.

Open delegation is one of the bases of the *flexibility* of distributed and MA plans. To be radical, delegating actions to an autonomous agent always requires some level of "openness": the agent at least cannot *avoid monitoring and adapting* its own actions, during their execution.

Moreover, the distributed character of the MA plans derives from *open delegation*.

As we saw, A can delegate to B either an entire plan or some part of it (*partial delegation*). The combination of *partial delegation* (where the contractor can ignore the other parts of the plan) and *open delegation* (where the client can ignore the sub-plan chosen and developed by the contractor) creates the possibility that A and B collaborate in a plan that they do not share and that *nobody* knows fully: that is to say a truly *distributed plan* [3, 5]. However, for each part of the plan there will be at least one agent that knows it.

The object of the delegation can be a practical or *domain action* as well as a *meta-action* (searching, planning, choosing, problem solving, and so on). When A is open delegating to B some domain action, it is necessarily also delegating to B some meta-action: at least searching for a plan, applying it, and sometimes deciding between alternative solutions. We call B's *discretion* concerning τ the fact that some decision about τ is delegated to B.

A (Client)   B (Contractor)

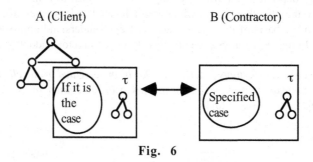

Fig. 6

Delegation of the Control

The control (or check up) is an action aimed at ascertaining whether another action has been successfully executed (or if a given state of the world has been realized or maintained).

Controlling an action means verifying that its relevant results hold (including the execution of the action itself). Plans typically contain control actions of some of their actions. When the client is delegating a given object-action, what about its control actions?

Considering, for the sake of simplicity, that the control action is executed by a single agent, when Delegates(A B τ) there are at least four possibilities:

i) A delegates the control to B: the client does not (directly) verify the success of the delegated action to the contractor; ii) A delegates the control to a third agent; iii) A gives up the control: nobody is delegated to control the success of α; iv) A maintains the control for itself.

Each of these possibilities could be explicit or implicit in the delegation of the object-action, in the roles of the agents (if they are part of a social structure), in the preceding interactions between the client and contractor, etc.

Delegation of Initiative

The notion of initiative is often ambiguous and too broad. Agents should be characterised at least by two forms of initiative:

- *Motu proprio*: Agents do not execute the required action/plan under the direct and immediate command of their client or user; they take care of and also "decide" the appropriate moment for the execution of the task (which can be ignored by the client or user). Their behaviour is not fired or elicited by the user or the request, but by the agent's autonomous relation with its environment. It takes the initiative of executing the task where and when appropriate, also depending on its internal state (this can be considered also as another aspect of "discretion").

- *Spontaneous interaction or pro-active help*: Agents can act "for us" (or for the client) also without any request or beyond the request. The agent might spontaneously help the other or over-help it (doing more or better than requested) or spontaneously starting an interaction for example by offering some help. They may anticipate the user/client request and even desires.

Levels of Adoption

In order for the adoption be an effective help (*deep cooperation*), the contractor should consider/foresee the client's plan (in which the delegated task is inserted), its goals and interests and, on the basis of the circumstances, deeply-understand/improve/preserve the requested help. In this way it is possible to classify the contractor's adoption at the various levels:

Literal help: *the contractor adopts exactly what has been delegated by the client* (see Fig. 7).

Overhelp: *the contractor goes beyond what has been delegated by the client without changing the client's plan* (see Fig. 8).

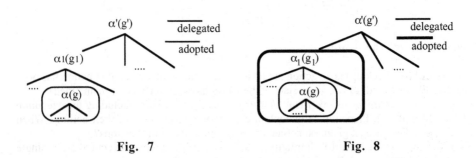

Fig. 7   **Fig. 8**

<u>Critical help</u>: *the contractor achieves the relevant results of the requested plan/action, but modifies the plan/action* (see Fig. 9).

<u>Critical overhelp</u>: *the contractor implements an overhelp and in addition modifies/changes the plan/action* (see Fig. 10).

<u>Hyper-critical help</u>: *the contractor adopts goals or interests of the client that the client itself did not take into account: by doing so, the contractor neither performs the delegated action/plan nor totally achieves the results that were delegated* (see Fig. 11).

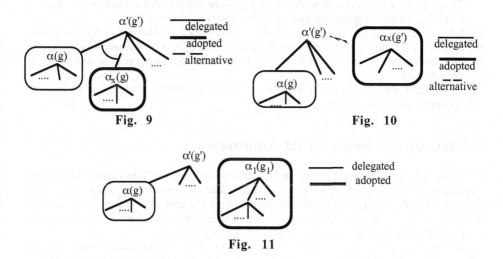

Fig. 9   Fig. 10

Fig. 11

3 Conflicts Due to the Level of Adoption of the Contractor

Given our characterisation of delegation and adoption, we can derive a series of conflicts arising between the two agents when there is a mismatch between the intended delegation and the intended adoption. These mismatches are neither due to simple misunderstandings of A's request/expectation nor to B's offer, nor to a wrong or incomplete plan/intention recognition of B. We are mainly interested in *collaborative conflicts* which come from B's intention to help A beyond its request or delegation and to exploit its own knowledge and intelligence (reasoning, problem solving, planning, and decision-making skills) for A [11].
- *Conflicts due to the contractor's over-help, critical help, critical over-help, hyper-critical help*
In any case of over, critical and hypercritical adoption there is apparently a conflict, since A has the goal that B does α, while B is doing or intends to do something different for A. Normally these conflicts can be quickly solved, for two reasons. First, B's intention is to help A, it's a collaborative intention; second, normally B is "entitled"[3] by A (either explicitly or implicitly) to provide this deeper help, and A is expecting this initiative and autonomy. Thus, normally there is no real conflict since A is *ready to accept* B's collaborative initiative. However, sometimes these cases trigger serious conflicts which have to be negotiated. This is specially true in organizations and among different roles.

---

[3] We will say that B is *entitled* by A to τ through the delegation Delegates(A B τ), when there is common (to A and B) knowledge that A is committed not to oppose, not to be astonished, etc., if B pursues τ.

Leaving aside possible cases of misunderstanding between client and contractor about A's request/expectation or B's offer (or to a wrong plan/intention by B), we can distinguish the reasons for conflict (i.e., A is against B's initiative) into two main classes:

i) *Trouble for A's goals:* B can jeopardize the A's goal achievement; this is possible for:

   i1) *Lack of coordination:* A plan is composed of many actions (assigned to several agents, when there is a partial delegation), so a unilateral initiative on the part of one agent to change that plan without reconsidering the general plan might be fatal (because of interference) or lead to a waste of resources, time, etc. (because of redundancy).

   i2) *Disagreement about action results:* A knows or believes that the action executed by B does not bring about the results expected or believed by B itself.

ii) *Role and Status:* in this case the conflict is relative to the entitlement of B by A to take the initiative of changing the delegated task. For reasons of power, job, subordination, role B while doing such a sub/over/critical help is going beyond what it is permitted to do (according to A).

This important aspect concerning conflicts extends beyond the plan-based analysis of delegation we are illustrating here.

4 Bilateral and Bidirectional Adjustment

Given the delegation/adoption theory, and the related kinds and levels of interaction between client and contractor (kinds and levels that determine the contractor autonomy), it is clear that not only the delegating agent can try to adjust the autonomy of the contractor in realizing τ, but also the delegated agent can try to change its own autonomy with respect to the delegation itself. In this sense we speak of *bilateral adjustment*.

On the one hand, the *client's adjustment* is, in general, linked with the reasons that had produced the delegation and that in our view reside in the trust model. More specifically, the adjustment depends either from the change the client's beliefs about contractor's competence and/or disposition, or from the change the client's beliefs about its own dependence and/or preferences (included its attitude toward the risk).

On the other hand, the *contractor's adjustment* is, in general, always motivated by a delegation conflict (that sometimes could be a collaborative conflict [12]). The contractor, either from the start of interaction or during the interaction itself, wants to change the level of delegation because disagrees about the levels of trust.

Adjustment of delegation is not only in the direction of restricting, and constraining autonomy. Both client and contractor (trustor and trustee) could try to modify the initial (previous) level of delegation and autonomy by enlarging it. Trustor can in fact revise its opinions or predictions about the trustee's abilities, or the difficulty of the task, or the obstacles and opportunities, or trustee's willingness and loyalty. On such a basis it can place more trust in trustee or in the circumstances, leave to the trustee more discretion and independence in adapting and executing the task or in solving some problem. On the other side, the trustee/contractor can believe that it is more able than expected by trustor, or that the circumstances are more favourable, or the task more simple; or it can perceive that some local, situated and adaptive sub-plan and decision is needed (the task should not have been completely and rigidly pre-specified); or the delegated plan is partially wrong for trustor's goals or is pratically impossible while it knows a better or possible plan [10].

The same bilateral initiative holds obviously for restricting autonomy by specifying delegation or increasing monitoring, control, and intervention.

5 Levels of Autonomy

On the basis of the previous analysis of the delegation dimentions, it is possible to specify a n-dimentional space (three -dimentional, in the specific case) in which the autonomy of an agent could be described. In the same way it could be possible to specify a n-dimentional space for the adoption dimentions.

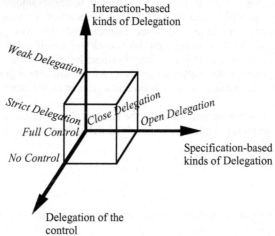

Fig. 12

Types and levels of delegation characterize the autonomy of the delegated agent.
There are at least two meanings of "autonomy": one is equal to *self-sufficiency*, not being dependent on others for our own goals [6]; on this side the less dependent B is on A regarding the resources necessary for the task, the more autonomous B is of A regarding that task. The other meaning is related to action and goals and to their levels. One could distinguish between *performance or executive autonomy* (the agent is not allowed to decide anything but the execution of the entire delegated plan [5]: in our terms, given an agent A and a plan α, α is completely specified in the delegation itself); *planning autonomy* (the agent is allowed to plan by itself, to choose its own plan to obtain the goal delegated, for example α is not completely specified in the delegation itself); *goal autonomy* (the agent is allowed to have/find goals). Here we ignore the autonomous goals of the delegated agent, so we can characterise different degrees of autonomy in delegation as follows. The autonomy of the contractor vis-à-vis the client increases along various dimensions: i) the more *open the delegation* (the less specified the task is), or ii) the more *control actions* given up or delegated to B by A, or iii) the more delegated decisions (*discretion*), the more autonomous B is of A regarding that task.

6 Concluding Remarks

As we said, we presented here only our basic framework as a possible background for the theory of the Adjustable Autonomy to be developed and for the future work about its dynamics.
Let us in particular stress how in this future development a merging between the theory of trust and the theory of delegation and help levels will be necessary.

To delegate a task or a role, in fact, a given *degree of trust* is necessary, based on some evaluation and agent modelling. However, trust is not only the global final result of the evaluation, that determines if one delegates or not that task to that agent. It should be articulated along several dimensions. Our claim is that it is precisely an articulated trust which determines the level and kind of delegation. For example, -as we said- open delegation presupposes that the client has a model of the agent 'intellectual' competence and that specifically trusts its ability to find or build a plan, to chose among different possible plans, to intend a given plan and to persist in its execution, to assess or provide the necessary resources and conditions, and to successfully control its own performance. If the client does not delegate all these things, and takes back to himself either the control, or the planning, or the discretion, etc. it is precisely because he trusts some capabilities of the agents but not the others. He has *different degree of trust relative to different aspects* of the complex task, and he delegates more or less on one aspect or on the other depending on this *differential reliance*.

To model this process -that we believe to be the basis of Adjustable Autonomy- we claim that it is necessary to merge the theory of levels of delegation [10] with the theory of the degrees of trust [2].

7 References

[1] Call for Papers, 1999 *AAAI Spring Symposium on Agents With Adjustable Autonomy*, March 22-24, 1999, Stanford University.

[2] Castelfranchi C., Falcone R., Principles of trust for MAS: cognitive anatomy, social importance, and quantification, *Proceedings of the International Conference of Multi-Agent Systems (ICMAS'98)*, pp. 72-79, Paris, July, 1998.

[3] B. Grosz, Collaborative Systems. *AI Magazine* (summer 1996) 67-85.

[4] Jennings. N.R. 1993. Commitments and conventions: The foundation of coordination in multi-agent systems. *The Knowledge Engineering Review*, 3, 223-50.

[5] R. Conte & C. Castelfranchi, Cognitive and Social Action (UCL Press, London, 1995).

[6] Sichman, J, R. Conte, C. Castelfranchi, Y. Demazeau. A social reasoning mechanism based on dependence networks. In *Proceedings of the 11th ECAI*, 1994.

[7] A. Haddadi, Communication and Cooperation in Agent Systems (the Springer Press, 1996).

[8] Rosenschein, J.S. and Zlotkin, G. Rules of encounters Designing conventions for automated negotiation among computers. Cambridge, MA: MIT Press. 1994.

[9] Werner, E., Cooperating agents: A unified theory of communication and social structure. In L.Gasser and M.N.Huhns, editors, *Distributed Artificial Intelligence*: Volume II. Morgan Kaufmann Publishers, 1990.

[10] Castelfranchi, C., Falcone, R. (1998), Towards a Theory of Delegation for Agent-based Systems, *Robotics and Autonomous Systems*, Special issue on Multi-Agent Rationality, Elsevier Editor. Vol. 24, pp. 141-157.

[11] J. Chu-Carroll, S. Carberry, Conflict detection and resolution in collaborative planning, IJCAI-95 *Workshop on Agent Theories, Architectures, and Languages*, Montreal, Canada (1995).

[12] Castelfranchi, C., Falcone, R., (1997), Delegation Conflicts, in M. Boman & W. Van de Velde (eds.), Proceedings of the 8th European Workshop on Modelling Autonomous Agents in A Multi-Agent World (MAAMAW'97), Multi-Agent Rationality, Lecture Notes in Artificial Intelligence, 1237 (Springer-Verlag) 234-254.

Notes on formalizing coordination[*]

Alessandro Agostini

Università di Siena
LOMIT - Dipartimento di Matematica
via del Capitano, 15
53100 SIENA
Italy
agostini@unisi.it

Abstract. This paper concerns with 2-agents coordination games—we call them *paradigms of coordination*. To coordinate, agents' behaviour must eventually stabilize to a set of basic formulas that express a suitable part of agents' "nature". Four paradigms are advanced and discussed. Several new perspectives are provided to coordinating agents. Coordination via belief revision and cooperation by team work are two.

1   Introduction

A real problem in extending single agent systems to cooperative settings is determining methods of *coordination*. However, agents may be based on different languages, they may have different behaviours, they may use different representations of information and reasoning strategies, and they may have different interaction capabilities. We will refer to all this as to *the coordination problem*. Investigations into the coordination problem can be divided into three general classes: those based on convention, those based on communication, and those based on learning. Some example in the first class was given in AI by Shoham and Tennenholtz [25, 24], where some social laws or 'conventions' [11] are imposed by the system designer (see also [20]) so that optimal joint action is assured. In the second class, agents' coordination is based on communication (see for instance [28]). This second class might be thought as a special case of the normative class, where the communication language is assumed to be the convention. So, what makes this class different is rather the emphasis it gives to the communicative agents' skills with regard to agents' coordination problems. In this class, it does make sense to speak about *failure messages* that prevent the agents from coordinating (see for instance [30] for some further remarks and references on the infulence of the *speech act theory* in communication). In the third class, coordination might be learned through repeated interaction (see for instance [2, 22,

---

[*] I thank Franco Montagna and Dick de Jongh for fundamental feedback on the first draft of this article and for research guidance. I am indebted to Daniel Osherson for early fruitful discussions on coordination and to Fausto Giunchiglia for invaluable suggestions. This work has been done at ILLC, Amsterdam. I kindly thank ILLC for the excellent research environment.

E. Lamma and P. Mello (Eds.): AI*IA 99, LNAI 1792, pp. 285–296, 2000.
© Springer-Verlag Berlin Heidelberg 2000

29] and the bibliography cited). It is evident that the coordination problem is central in several contemporary disciplines like Sociology, Artificial Intelligence, Game Theory, Computer Science. We shall not here attempt to synthesize this vast literature save to remark that a general understanding of the conditions under which coordination can be achieved, and exactly how it relates to agents' learning ability and their background knowledge and beliefs, are problems that have not yet been thoroughly explored.

Our ultimate goal is to provide a framework and a methodology which will allow us to investigate the coordination problem from a *learning-by-discovery* [29] perspective. To achieve this goal, we need a suitable formalism. We focus on the model-theoretic tradition of *Formal Learning Theory*—say [23, 7, 19, 18, 12], that descends from the pioneering studies on inductive inference developed by [27, 21, 8, 1]. The work in the recursive-theoretic tradition concerns algorithms for inferring recursive functions from finite samples of their graphs, and has been adapted successively to characterize abstract languages in the limit. The model-theoretic tradition is more recent; its main aim is to provide a formal framework for learning first order theories and models. The recursive-functional approach to learning has been extended to characterize recursive functions by means of coordination in the limit. A natural question is whether a similar framework can be developed to investigate the coordination problem. What follows is an attempt to present such a conception, and to describe what place coordination has within it. There are many definitions, some remarks, no theorems, and a great deal left to be investigated.

Our discussion begin in Section 2 with an intuitive idea of the coordination problem we are thinking on. In Section 3 we then proceed by presenting the logical framework. Four paradigms of coordination are advanced. We conclude in Section 4 with a discussion of several issues that promise to make the boorderline between formal learning theory and agent theory an exciting area of research for the foreseeable future.

2   Coordination as a 2-agents game

We start with a concrete example intended to help the reader interpret some of the abstract concepts described later. Thus, we can image two "worlds-based agents", say **A**lfonso and **B**arbara, whose "background world" is represented by two nonempty classes of structures **A** and **B** of a given signature, and whose aim is to coordinate, *e.g.* to solve a common problem. For doing this, **A**lfonso and **B**arbara try to communicate with each other in order to respectively end up with a description of two structures $\mathcal{A} \in \mathbf{A}$ and $\mathcal{B} \in \mathbf{B}$ such that $\mathcal{A}$ is sufficiently close to **B** and $\mathcal{B}$ is sufficiently close to **A**. We expect that the more **A**lfonso is like **B**arbara, the better chance **A**lfonso and **B**arbara have of reaching coordination. To dramatize, let us suppose that each agent does not know the "background world" of the other agent, and that agents were never before in a similar situation, so they cannot rely on past experience to solve their coordination problem—no common knowledge arises between agents despite of their

common language. This "drama" is indeed a basic ingredient of what we called
the coordination problem. We also image that the agents are "rational" (*e.g.* in
their "communication ability") and both know that joint cooperation is better
than joint defection, but each has no idea what sort of agents the opponent is.
Alfonso and Barbara's decisions have a strategic component. Since strategic interactions are best modeled by game theory, we image the agents' coordination
problem as a form of 2-players game, which we qualify as a *coordination game*.

To start the game, Alfonso is conceived as choosing one member from **A** to
be his "actual world"; Alfonso's choice is initially unknown to Barbara. Alfonso
then provides a "clue" (the Alfonso's *behaviour*) about his world. Barbara does
her choice as well (we image the game is *synchronous*, *i.e.* both agents are not
taking turns but rather are choosing simultaneously), and provides Alfonso with
a clue about her actual world. We can assume that Alfonso and Barbara are
allowed to change their actual world at each step of the game, provided that they
remain coherent with the behaviour they have shown since then. Clearly, it is
safe to begin with a behaviour coherent on many worlds in the class. In this way,
if say Alfonso realizes that the structure he has in mind, *i.e.* his actual world,
is not close enough to Barbara's world, he can change it, and vice versa. Agents
may provide "bad clues", in principle. Thus, we can consider a paradigm of
coordination-by-failure according to which an agent can give to the other agent
a 'failure message'. In such a case, the agents are allowed to start the game
again from the beginning. Of course, to reach coordination this should occur
only finitely often. Alfonso's clues constitute the data upon which Barbara will
base her hypotheses on Alfonso's background world, that eventually become
themselves a clue for Alfonso about Barbara's world. And so forth. Each time
Alfonso provides a new clue, Barbara may produce a new hypothesis, and a
new clue for Alfonso as well. Alfonso and Barbara *win the game*—and we say
that they solve their coordination problem, if the successive clues about their
own background worlds eventually stabilize to a consistent set of hypotheses
satisfiable in one of the other agent's worlds. Both lose otherwise. As a necessary
condition for winning, each agent's behaviour must be consistent with agent's
own background world.

3   Logical framework

Five concepts figure in the foregoing game-theoretic picture of coordination:
worlds, agents, clues, descriptions, success. We formalize them as follows.

Notation. We fix a (countable, decidable) first-order language $\mathcal{L}_{form}$ with vocab-
ulary $\mathcal{L}$ and countable set of variables *Var*. Unless stated otherwise, $\mathcal{L}$ and *Var*
will remain fixed. We use $\mathcal{L}_{sen}$ and $\mathcal{L}_{basic}$ to denote, respectively, the set of sentences (or *closed formulas*, that is no free variables occur) and the set of literals
(or *basic formulas*) of $\mathcal{L}_{form}$. We are particularly interested in the collection of
all the *finite* sequences over $\mathcal{L}_{basic}$. We denote such collection by *SEQ*. Some
further notation is as follows. The set $\{0, 1, 2, ...\}$ of natural numbers is denoted
by N. If X is a set, $pow(X)$ is the set of all subsets of X and X^{ω} is the set of

infinite sequences over X. A sequence in X^ω is called an ω-*sequence* (over X). Let τ be an ω-sequence. We write $\tau(i)$, $i \in N$, for the finite sequence $\langle \tau_0 \ldots \tau_i \rangle$, and $\tau|_i$ for the proper initial segment of length i in τ. We write $length(\eta)$ for the length of a finite sequence and η_i for the ith element of η, $0 \leq i < length(\eta)$. We write $range(\eta)$ for the set of elements of any sequence. We denote the finite sequence of length zero by $\emptyset$.

Otherwise, our semantic notions are standard.[1] In particular, $\mathcal{L}$-structure $\mathcal{S}$ is a model of $\Gamma \subseteq \mathcal{L}_{form}$, and Γ is said to be *satisfiable in* $\mathcal{S}$, if there is an assignment $h : Var \longrightarrow |\mathcal{S}|$ with $\mathcal{S} \models \Gamma[h]$. Γ is *satisfiable* if it is satisfiable in some structure. The class of models of Γ is denoted: $MOD(\Gamma)$.

3.1   Worlds

We begin to give substance to our view of coordination by representing the possible realities, or "worlds", where the coordination problem may arise. By *world* we shall here mean any countable structure that interprets $\mathcal{L}$. Worlds may be conceived as the "possible truths" for the agents. We are interested in aggregations of such worlds, namely, countable collections of worlds. These collections may be intuitively thought as the set of realities of a given agent. To see how, we must first say what we mean by an "agent".

3.2   Agents

What has to be termed *agent* and what does not is a long debate in Artificial Intelligence (see for instance [5]; also [30] for a survey). Here we do not try a full explanation of our conception of "agent" from this more general perspective. In the sequel, rather, agents are conceived as systems that examine (partial) evidence coming from other agents' behaviours or empirical data and emit hypotheses and clues. Agents are possibly bounded-resource systems and can fail on some input. We shall address some question about bounded-resource agents later in this paper, with the proviso that a deeper discussion of "real", say computable, agents is to come.

To formalize the mixture of data and failures we need, let us extend $\mathcal{L}$ with the symbol $\bot$ for 'message failure'. We will thus be interested in the collection of all the *finite* sequences whose elements are basic formulas and $\bot$. We denote such collection: *FSEQ*. Any member σ of *FSEQ* is to be interpreted as a finite evidence available to agents at time $t = length(\sigma)$. Thus, σ may be thought as an "evidential status" or a "situation" that recapitulate the information available to agents about an underlying world at a certain moment of observation. Note that *FSEQ* is countable, because of $\mathcal{L}_{basic}$ does. We now record the official definition of "agent".

Definition 1. *A (basic)* agent *is any mapping from FSEQ to* $\mathcal{L}_{basic} \cup \{\bot\}$.

---

[1] See for instance [14] for a standard reference.

We say that $\mathcal{L}$ is the *agent's language*. A basic agent might be partial or total, recursive or nonrecursive. Thus, agents examine data recorded in a finite representation and emit hypotheses or "clues" about the world to be represented by the data, or also they "suspend the judgement" by saying $\bot$. For $\sigma \in FSEQ$ being the input of agent Ψ, Ψ's output $\Psi(\sigma)$ represents Ψ's behaviour with respect to the sequence σ of facts observed. In particular, $\Psi(\sigma) = \bot$ may be interpreted as Ψ's "suspension of coordination" if σ collects the clues from some agent's output, and as "suspension of the judgement" if σ collects data elsewhere, say from Nature.

Agents as functions are not enough. Indeed, agents of Definition 1 do not capture the basic ingredients of agency (see for instance, [30] and the references cited there). Moreover, according to the intuitive picture drawn in Section 2, when faced with any coordination problem an agent is conceived as trying to coordinate to the other agent advancing successive clues about his or her own "background world". If an agent realizes that his "actual world" (*i.e.* the world he "has in mind") is not close enough to some world of the other agent, he can change his actual world or break off the coordination process by playing $\bot$. To state all this precisely, basic agents must be restricted to "worlds-based agents". We rely on the following definition.

Definition 2. *Let Ψ_0 be a basic agent and $\mathbf{A}$ be a nonempty class of worlds. We say that $\Psi = \langle \Psi_0, \mathbf{A} \rangle$ is a* worlds-based agent.

For all $\sigma \in SEQ$, we then write $\Psi(\sigma)$ for $\Psi_0(\sigma)$. Moreover, to shorten the terminology we allow ourselves to say "$\langle \Psi_0, \mathbf{A} \rangle$ is an agent" in place of "$\langle \Psi_0, \mathbf{A} \rangle$ is a worlds-based agent". The class of all such worlds-based agents is denoted: Δ. As basic agents, worlds-based agents may be computable or noncomputable. Of the two components of Ψ, Ψ_0 is said to be the *communication ability of Ψ* and $\mathbf{A}$ is said to be the *background world of Ψ*. We also say that Ψ is *based on* $\mathbf{A}$. To fix intuitions one might think of a background world as representing the agent's belief space. In this case, background worlds generalize the scientist's "mono-world" habitat of the first-order paradigm of inquiry [13]. Thus, the scientist'question: "What is true in my world?" (cf. [13], p. 63) might be generalized here as: "What is true in my and *your* world?". This "*your*" is indeed a fundamental motivation that underlines our work on coordination in a whole, and the further developments in this paper.

3.3   Environments, enumerations, descriptions

We consider the information made available to agents. This information is of two different kinds, and comes from *environments* and *descriptions* as defined below. We assume to have a *full assignment* to all worlds we will consider in the sequel.[2] Our formulation of environments is a restatement of [19] (Definition 3.1A).

---

[2] The notion of *full assignment* we use is standard. For structure $\mathcal{S}$, a *full assignment to $\mathcal{S}$* is any mapping of *Var* onto the domain of $\mathcal{S}$. See for instance [3] for a reference.

Definition 3. *Let ω-sequence e over $\mathcal{L}_{basic}$, $\mathcal{L}$-structure $\mathcal{S}$, full assignment h to $\mathcal{S}$ and nonempty class of worlds $\mathbf{K}$ be given.*

(a) e is a (basic) environment.

(b) e is for $\mathcal{S}$ via h just in case $\mathrm{range}(e) = \{\beta \in \mathcal{L}_{basic} \mid \mathcal{S} \models \beta[h]\}$.

(c) e is for $\mathbf{K}$ just in case e is an environment for some $\mathcal{S} \in \mathbf{K}$.

Thus, an environment is a sequence of increasing, consistent or inconsistent sets of basic formulas. In particular, an environment for $\mathcal{S}$ (via full assignment h) lists the basic diagram of $\mathcal{S}$ using h to supply temporary names for the members of $|\mathcal{S}|$.[3] Finite initial segments of environments thus recapitulate the information available to a single agent about the underlying structure of evidence at a certain time of observation.

Enumerations. When an agent is involved in a coordination game, environments take the form of the (finite, consistent) behaviour of the opponent. We now consider this second kind of information. In contrast to environments, information *by enumeration* is "active" as it comes from interacting agents. Of course, this is possible only for systems with more than one agent. Hence, we suppose there are at least two agents around.[4] Agents should be made able to manage information from different information sources as environments and enumerations. Otherwise, only one-way interaction is possible, that is the interaction between the agent and his "passive" environment. Notice that the information we are looking for does not depend on worlds, but only on the communication abilities of the agents. Thus, next terminology involves basic agents only, leaving worlds-based agents out for further developments.

Definition 4. *Let agents Ψ and Φ be given.*

(a) The enumeration from Ψ and Φ *is the pair $[\overline{\psi}, \overline{\phi}]$ of ω-sequences defined by induction as follows: $\overline{\psi}_0 = \Psi(\emptyset)$ and $\overline{\phi}_0 = \Phi(\emptyset)$. Let $\overline{\psi}(n) = \langle \overline{\psi}_0 \cdots \overline{\psi}_n \rangle$ and $\overline{\phi}(n) = \langle \overline{\phi}_0 \cdots \overline{\phi}_n \rangle$. Then, we define $\overline{\psi}_{n+1} = \Psi(\overline{\phi}(n))$ and $\overline{\phi}_{n+1} = \Phi(\overline{\psi}(n))$.*

(b) Let $k \in N$ be given. The enumeration from Ψ and Φ starting at k *is the pair $[\overline{\psi}^{(k)}, \overline{\phi}^{(k)}]$, where $\overline{\psi}^{(k)}$ and $\overline{\phi}^{(k)}$ are obtained from $\overline{\psi}$ and $\overline{\phi}$ by deleting the first $k + 1$ elements.*

The following terminology will also be useful. Let agent Ψ be given. We say that ω-sequence $\overline{\psi}$ is an *enumeration from Ψ* just in case $[\overline{\psi}, \overline{\phi}]$ is the enumeration from Ψ and Φ for some agent Φ. We say that $\overline{\psi}$ is an *enumeration* just in case $\overline{\psi}$ is an enumeration from Ψ. We say that $[\overline{\psi}, \overline{\phi}]$ is the *enumeration from worlds-based agents* $\langle \Psi_0, \mathbf{A} \rangle$ and $\langle \Phi_0, \mathbf{B} \rangle$ just in case $[\overline{\psi}, \overline{\phi}]$ is the enumeration from Ψ_0 and Φ_0. To return briefly to the game-theoretic meaning of coordination, let us note that an enumeration $[\overline{\psi}, \overline{\phi}]$ is *the play* in a coordination game between agents Ψ and Φ. It follows directly from the definition of enumeration that coordination games are *infinite games*. Nevertheless, it is important to observe that *finite* coordination games are possible, and even useful when modeling coordination phenomena within real systems.

---

[3] We use "basic diagram" as "diagram" in the sense of A. Robinson; see *e.g.* [3].

[4] To simplify matters, we consider here systems of *exactly* two agents.

Descriptions. There are several ways in which agents $\langle \Psi_0, \mathbf{A} \rangle$ and $\langle \Phi_0, \mathbf{B} \rangle$ may stabilize to a consistent behaviour. To coordinate, agents' successive conjectures must eventually stabilize to a set of formulas that gives them a sufficiently accurate information about one of other agent's worlds. Two concepts must thus be defined: "stabilization" and "sufficient accuracy." Stabilization comes first.

Definition 5. *Let $k \in N$, agent Ψ and nonempty class of worlds $\mathbf{K}$ be given.*

(a) Ψ ultimately describes $\mathbf{K}$ just in case enumeration $\overline{\psi}$ is an environment for some $\mathcal{S} \in \mathbf{K}$.

(b) Ψ ultimately describes $\mathbf{K}$ starting at k just in case enumeration $\overline{\psi}^{(k)}$ is an environment for some $\mathcal{S} \in \mathbf{K}$.

In these cases, $\overline{\psi}$ and $\overline{\psi}^{(k)}$ are said to be full descriptions *for $\mathbf{K}$.*

If $\overline{\psi}$ or $\overline{\psi}^{(k)}$ is an environment for some world, Ψ eventually reaches the necessary information to coordinate. Full descriptions are a kind of information made explicit by some agent, and represent the formal, "active" counterpart of the information provided to agents by "passive" environments. However, this information is not sufficient to coordinate, as we see in next section.

3.4 Success criteria.

By Definition 5 we give a meaning to "stabilization for an agent in a coordination game": An agent *stabilize* if he or she eventually ends up with an enumeration that is an environment for some world, viz., a full description. How "accurate" such a description have to be to coordinate is the meaning of next definition.

Definition 6. *Let $n, k \in N$, agents $\langle \Psi_0, \mathbf{A} \rangle$, $\langle \Phi_0, \mathbf{B} \rangle$ and enumeration $[\overline{\psi}, \overline{\phi}]$ from $\langle \Psi_0, \mathbf{A} \rangle$ and $\langle \Phi_0, \mathbf{B} \rangle$ be given.*

(a) $\langle \Psi_0, \mathbf{A} \rangle$ cognitively matches with $\langle \Phi_0, \mathbf{B} \rangle$ at n just in case $\overline{\psi}(n)$ is satisfiable in some $\mathcal{B} \in \mathbf{B}$ and $\overline{\phi}(n)$ is satisfiable in some $\mathcal{A} \in \mathbf{A}$.

(b) $\langle \Psi_0, \mathbf{A} \rangle$ cognitively matches with $\langle \Phi_0, \mathbf{B} \rangle$ at n starting at $k \leq n$ just in case $\overline{\psi}^{(k)}(n)$ is satisfiable in some $\mathcal{B} \in \mathbf{B}$ and $\overline{\phi}^{(k)}(n)$ is satisfiable in some $\mathcal{A} \in \mathbf{A}$.

Observe that $\mathcal{A}$ and $\mathcal{B}$ may depend on n. Moreover, "cognitively matches with" is a reflexive and symmetric binary relation (on Δ). Definition 6 takes two agents to be cognitively matched at some time of the play if there exist two worlds, one for each agent's background world, which satisfy the enumeration provided so far in the play by the other agent. Our conception of coordination simply extends the idea to agents that hold consistency, *i.e.*, agents that ultimately describe some world. What background worlds can provide worlds-based agents to coordinate? To answer that we must first say what we mean by the question. We will distinguish four senses in which two agents could be said to coordinate. In what follows, f, s, l and mf may be read as "full," "slow," "local," and "message-failure," respectively.

Definition 7. *Let agents* $\langle \Psi_0, \mathbf{A} \rangle$, $\langle \Phi_0, \mathbf{B} \rangle$ *and enumeration* $[\overline{\psi}, \overline{\phi}]$ *from* $\langle \Psi_0, \mathbf{A} \rangle$ *and* $\langle \Phi_0, \mathbf{B} \rangle$ *be given.*

(a) Let $\mathbf{K}$ *be a nonempty class of worlds.* $\langle \Psi_0, \mathbf{A} \rangle$ *and* $\langle \Phi_0, \mathbf{B} \rangle$ *lf-coordinate just in case both* $\langle \Psi_0, \mathbf{A} \rangle$ *and* $\langle \Phi_0, \mathbf{B} \rangle$ *ultimately describe some* $\mathbf{K}$ *and for every* $n \in N$, $\overline{\psi}(n)$ *is satisfiable in some* $\mathcal{A} \in \mathbf{A}$, $\overline{\phi}(n)$ *is satisfiable in some* $\mathcal{B} \in \mathbf{B}$ *and* $\langle \Psi_0, \mathbf{A} \rangle$ *cognitively matches with* $\langle \Phi_0, \mathbf{B} \rangle$ *at* n.

(b) $\langle \Psi_0, \mathbf{A} \rangle$ *and* $\langle \Phi_0, \mathbf{B} \rangle$ *f-coordinate just in case* $\langle \Psi_0, \mathbf{A} \rangle$ *ultimately describes* $\mathbf{A}$, $\langle \Phi_0, \mathbf{B} \rangle$ *ultimately describes* $\mathbf{B}$ *and for every* $n \in N$, $\langle \Psi_0, \mathbf{A} \rangle$ *cognitively matches with* $\langle \Phi_0, \mathbf{B} \rangle$ *at* n.

(c) $\langle \Psi_0, \mathbf{A} \rangle$ *and* $\langle \Phi_0, \mathbf{B} \rangle$ *sf-coordinate just in case for some* $k \in N$, $\langle \Psi_0, \mathbf{A} \rangle$ *ultimately describes* $\mathbf{A}$ *starting at* k, $\langle \Phi_0, \mathbf{B} \rangle$ *ultimately describes* $\mathbf{B}$ *starting at* k *and for all* $n \geq k$, $\langle \Psi_0, \mathbf{A} \rangle$ *cognitively matches with* $\langle \Phi_0, \mathbf{B} \rangle$ *at* n *starting at* k.

(d) Suppose that for almost all $i \in N$, $\overline{\psi}_i \neq \bot$ *and* $\overline{\phi}_i \neq \bot$. *Let* k *be maximal such that either* $\overline{\psi}_k = \bot$ *or* $\overline{\phi}_k = \bot$. $\langle \Psi_0, \mathbf{A} \rangle$ *and* $\langle \Phi_0, \mathbf{B} \rangle$ *mf-coordinate just in case* $\langle \Psi_0, \mathbf{A} \rangle$ *ultimately describes* $\mathbf{A}$ *starting at* k, $\langle \Phi_0, \mathbf{B} \rangle$ *ultimately describes* $\mathbf{B}$ *starting at* k *and for all* $n \geq k$, $\langle \Psi_0, \mathbf{A} \rangle$ *cognitively matches with* $\langle \Phi_0, \mathbf{B} \rangle$ *at* n.

4   Discussion

"Local full" coordination is the most liberal paradigm, and provides us a model for the more popular problem of coordination between agents. By local coordination agents are allowed to fully describe an arbitrary but common world. In this case, one would say that agents take an *agreement on* that world. The information on the background world that each agent gives to the other agent is thus assured by adding the request for each agent's output to be finitely consistent with some world in his or her own background world. A question is what classes $\mathbf{A}$, $\mathbf{B}$ and $\mathbf{K}$ allow agents to *lf*-coordinate. Of course, a similar local paradigm may be defined as a generalization of *sf*-coordination. "Full" coordination is a stringent version of local coordination, where each agent must provide a full description of a world in *his* or *her* own background world in place of an arbitrary world taken from the class of all worlds. "Slow full" coordination is a paradigm of coordination *by failure*. Agents are free to stabilize to a suitable description of their worlds after a finite number of failures (disagreements). For this reason, we qualified this paradigm of "slow" coordination. *sf*-coordination arises if agents fail to communicate their clues in the play. According to this paradigm, agents can restart finitely many often, but after the last failure message they must eventually coordinate. The last paradigm, *mf*-coordination, is a particular version of coordination by failure; agents are permitted to explicitly state their coordinating problems by outputing a special atom of their language: $\bot$. Again, for agents Ψ and Φ, $\overline{\psi}_i$ and $\overline{\phi}_i$ must differ from $\bot$ for infinitely many $i \in N$, *i.e.* there are only finitely many failure messages. An interesting question on "slow" coordination is how *sf*-coordination compares with *mf*-coordination, and precisely how the use of explicit failure relates with success in any coordination play. It seems likely that something is gained in the efficiency of coordination.

Other definitions of coordination are possible, of course, and an interesting question concerns for what pairs of background worlds what communication abilities provide agents (based on the first and the second element of the pairs, and having that communication abilities) to coordinate. We will not attempt to answer the question save to remark that if the background world of both agents is a singleton, f-coordination models a situation rather close to that of Ehrenfeucht games for elementary equivalence in model theory (see for instance [4] for backgound on Ehrenfeucht games). It seems likely that f-coordination is equivalent to the interactive construction of partial isomorphisms between the worlds of the agents involved, but we have no proofs to give.

There are many potentially interesting generalizations of the logical framework just described:

1. Environments of the kind introduced here are *basic environments*, in the sense the their expressive power goes along with basic formulas. However, it is sometimes useful to have more expressive environments. An agent's observation may require more information than is captured in basic formulas. Thus, it could be both necessary and useful to extend environments over quantified formulas. Of course, this enrichment rises new problems when extending the resulting framework towards computational settings, our next point.

2. One can develop the conceptual framework into computational issues. A restriction to computer simulable agents as well to *finite* coordination games is required to study the coordination problem within real multi-agent systems. Computable agents can be obtained by considering agents based on recursive classes of finite worlds to recursive, or possibly P-TIME communication abilities. Agents might be bounded in their computation time, *i.e.* as a function of the length of the input. The speed of coordination may be taken into account. Thus, given worlds-based agent Ψ and $n \in N$, one can define the collection of worlds-based agents Φ such that Ψ changes his actual world (coordinating with Φ according to each paradigm) no more than n times (cf. [9] for some reference on "mind changes" in inductive inference).

3. So far, no mention has been given to how coordination can be used to problem solving. By extending the agents' outputs with a second component ranging over arbitrary sets of formulas, coordination is suitable to investigate *Team*-solvability. Coordination moves to *cooperation*. Then the question is: What classes of worlds are solvable (according to some paradigm of inquiry; we refer the reader to [13, 12, 16]) by a *team* of agents? A team of $m \geq 3$ agents can be defined as a set of pair of agents that coordinate according to some paradigm of coordination. A similar approach to team solvabiliy—called *Team*-identification, has been developed within *Formal Learning Theory* (see [9], Chapter 9). However, a definition of *Team*-identifiability is given for total recursive functions (Smith, [26]) and recursive enumerable formal languages (Osherson *et. al.*, [17]). As far as we know, no *Team*-identifiability is given for first-order structures. More important, definitions by Smith and Osherson *et. al.* "fail to formalize one aspect of scientific pratice that is central to the informal idea of team work." ([9], Chapter 9, pp.198-199). "The hypotheses of the individual scientists [agents] in

team scientific discovery influence each other in a way that is not captured by Smith and Osherson *et. al.* definitions." The paradigms of coordination are a suitable starting point to capture the hint of the informal idea of teamwork we look at, and provide the "formation rule" for teams of collaborative agents.

4. The problem of belief change—how an agent should revise her beliefs upon learning new information—can be taken into account. One can investigate belief changes by limiting a slightly modified version of the paradigms of coordination to agents based on background worlds that are expressible by a finite set of basic formulas. For such finite sets, one can put *revision* into the communicative ability Ψ_0 of agent $\langle \Psi_0, \mathbf{A} \rangle$ by assuming $\Psi_0 = \lambda \sigma.K \dot{\#} \sigma$, where $\dot{\#} : pow(\mathcal{L}_{basic}) \times SEQ \longrightarrow pow(\mathcal{L}_{basic})$ is a suitable revision function and $\mathbf{A} = MOD(K)$. One can take $\dot{\#}$ to be "rational" according to some principle of rationality (see for instance [6, 10, 13, 12] and the reference listed there). Agents of this new sort have "rational" communication abilities in this strict sense. It is then possible to investigate the coordination game of $\langle \lambda \sigma.A \dot{\#}_a \sigma, \mathbf{A} \rangle$ and $\langle \lambda \sigma.B \dot{\#}_b \sigma, \mathbf{B} \rangle$ into three winning strategies: (a) strategies that hold constant the background *belief sets* A and B, and then determine what kind of revision functions allow agents to coordinate; (b) strategies that hold constant the revision functions and determine what kind of belief sets allow agents to coordinate; (c) strategies that hold constant both belief sets and revision functions, and determine what kind of coordination paradigm allow agents to coordinate.

In the context of related work, there is a previous framework for analyzing the problem of coordination in the limit. That account, due to Franco Montagna and Daniel Osherson [15], is in the spirit of the recursion-functional tradition of inductive inference in something like the way that the framework given here is in the spirit of model-theoretic's. In Montagna and Osherson's work, the agent's communication skills are investigated by defining several kinds of players that interactively "learn to coordinate". Montagna and Osherson take the coordination problem of two agents or *players* that want to coordinate by repeatedly showing each other one of two possible behaviours. The problem of coordination the players are faced with follows from the shifting constraints on their behaviours. Each player tries to predict the other's behaviour, and their predictions are based on no more than the history of earlier events. One player "learns" the other's behaviour if her or his own behaviour matches the other's forever after. There is no an unique winner in the coordination game. To keep matters simple, Montagna and Osherson consider two players facing the same two options on each trial, and they denote the options by 0 and 1. A player is therefore be identified with a function from the set of all finite binary sequences into $\{0, 1\}$, where any such sequence is conceived as the history of moves of an opposing player. There are several obvious differences in the frameworks, some of which being a direct consequence of the language in use (recursive-theoretic vs. first-order), and one that is not obvious but which is the most important: *sf*-coordination extends the learning to coordinate Montagna and Osherson's paradigm, in the sense that coordination arises between Montagna and Osherson's players if and only if *sf*-coordination arises between a special kind of agents defined on them.

References

1. L. Blum and M. Blum. Toward a mathematical theory of inductive inference. *Information and Control*, 28(2):125–155, 1975.
2. P. Brazdil, M. Gams, S. Sian, L. Torgo, and W. van de Velde. Learning in distributed systems and multi-agent environments. In Y. Kodratoff, editor, *Machine Learning - European Working Session on Learning*, pages 412–423. Springer-Verlag LNAI 482, 1991.
3. C.C. Chang and J.M. Keisler. *Model Theory - 3rd edition*. North Holland, 1990.
4. H-D Ebbinghaus and J. Flum. *Finite Model Theory*. Springer, 1995.
5. S. Franklin and A. Graesser. Is it an agent, or just a program?: A taxonomy for autonomous agents. In J. P. Müller, M. J. Wooldridge, and N. R. Jennings, editors, *Intelligent Agents III - Agent Theories, Architectures, and Languages*, pages 21–35. Springer-Verlag LNAI 1193, 1997.
6. P. Gärdenfors. *Knowledge in Flux: Modeling the Dynamics of Epistemic States*. MIT Press, Cambridge, MA, 1988.
7. C. Glymour. Inductive inference in the limit. *Erkenntnis*, 22:23–31, 1985.
8. E. M. Gold. Language identification in the limit. *Information and Control*, 10:447–474, 1967.
9. S. Jain, D. Osherson, J. Royer, and A. Sharma. *Systems That Learn - An Introduction to Learning Theory, 2nd edition*. The MIT Series in Learning, Development, and Conceptual Change, v. 22. MIT Press, Cambridge, MA, 1999.
10. K. T. Kelly. *The Logic of Reliable Inquiry*. Oxford University Press, New York, NY, 1996.
11. D. K. Lewis. *Conventions. A Philosophical Study*. Harvard University Press, Cambridge, MA, 1969.
12. E. Martin and D. Osherson. Scientific discovery based on belief revision. *Journal of Symbolic Logic*, 62(4):1352–1370, 1997.
13. E. Martin and D. Osherson. *Elements of Scientific Inquiry*. MIT Press, Cambridge, MA, 1998.
14. E. Mendelson. *Introduction to Mathematical Logic - 3rd edition*. The Wadsworth & Brooks/Cole mathematics series. Wadsworth, Monterey, CA, 1987.
15. F. Montagna and D. Osherson. Learning to coordinate: A recursion theoretic perspective. *Synthese*, in press.
16. D. Osherson, D. de Jongh, E. Martin, and S. Weinstein. Formal Learning Theory. In J. van Benthem and A. ter Meulen, editors, *Handbook of Logic and Language*, pages 737–775. Elsevier Science Publishers B.V., 1997.
17. D. Osherson, M. Stob, and S. Weinstein. *Systems That Learn*. The MIT Series in Learning, Development, and Conceptual Change, v. 4. MIT Press, Cambridge, MA, 1986.
18. D. Osherson, M. Stob, and S. Weinstein. A universal inductive inference machine. *Journal of Symbolic Logic*, 56(2):661–672, 1991.
19. D. Osherson and S. Weinstein. Identification in the limit of first order structures. *Journal of Philosophical Logic*, 15:55–81, 1986.
20. E. Plaza, J. L. Arcos, and F. Martín. Cooperative case-based reasoning. In G. Weiß, editor, *Distributed Artificial Intelligence meets Machine Learning*, pages 180–201. Springer-Verlag LNAI 1221, 1997.
21. H. Putnam. Trial and error predicates and a solution to a problem of Mostowski. *Journal of Symbolic Logic*, 30(1):49–57, 1965.

22. S. Sen, M. Sekaran, and J. Hale. Learning to coordinate without sharing information. In *Proceedings of the Twelfth National Conference on Artificial Intelligence*, pages 426–431, Seattle, 1994.

23. E. Shapiro. Inductive inference of theories from facts. In J-L. Lassez and G. Plotkin, editors, *Computational Logic: Essays in honor of Alan Robinson*. MIT Press, 1991.

24. Y. Shoham and M. Tennenholtz. Emergent conventions in multi-agents systems: Initial experimental results and observations. In *Proceedings of the Third International Conference on Principles of Knowledge Representation and Reasoning*, pages 225–231, Cambridge, 1992.

25. Y. Shoham and M. Tennenholtz. On the synthesis of useful social laws for artificial agent societiesp. In *Proceedings of the Tenth National Conference on Artificial Intelligence*, pages 276–281, San Jose, 1992.

26. C. Smith. The power of pluralism for automatic program synthesis. *Journal of the ACM*, 29:1144–1165, 1982.

27. R. J. Solomonoff. A formal theory of inductive inference. *Information and Control*, 7:7–22, 1964.

28. G. Weiß. Learning to coordinate actions in multi-agent systems. In *Proceedings of the Thirteenth International Joint Conference on Artificial Intelligence*, pages 311–316, Chambery, France, 1993.

29. G. Weiß. Adaptation and learning in multi-agents systems: Some remarks and a bibliography. In G. Weiß and S. Sen, editors, *Adaptation and Learning in Multi-Agent Systems*, pages 1–21. Springer-Verlag LNAI 1042, 1995.

30. M. J. Wooldridge and N. R. Jennings. Agent theories, architectures, and languages: A survey. In M. J. Wooldridge and N. R. Jennings, editors, *Intelligent Agents*, pages 1–39. Springer-Verlag LNAI 890, 1995.

Autonomous Spacecraft Resource Management: A Multi-Agent Approach

N.Monekosso[1] and P. Remagnino[2]

[1]Surrey Space Centre, University of Surrey, GU2 5XH, UK
[2]Digital Imaging Research Centre, Kingston University, Surrey KT1 2EE, UK
N.Monekosso@ee.surrey.ac.uk

Abstract. The paper presents a multi-agent system that learns to manage the re-sources of an unmanned spacecraft. Each agent controls a subsystem and learns to optimise its resources. The agents can co-ordinate their actions to satisfy user requests. Co-ordination is achieved by exchanging sched-uling information between agents. Resource management is implemented using two reinforcement learning techniques: the Montecarlo and the Q-learning. The paper demonstrates how the approach can be used to model the imaging system of a spacecraft. The environment is represented by agents which control the spacecraft sub-systems involved in the imaging activity. The agent in charge of the resource management senses the information regarding the resource requested, the resource conflicts and the resource availability. Scheduling of resources is learnt when all subsystems are fully functional and when resources are reduced by random failures.

1 Introduction

The paper presents a novel multi-agent spacecraft architecture (MASA) for use in the resource management of an unmanned spacecraft. All agents are modelled alike [9], but each independent agent has a specialisation which allows it to control a different spacecraft subsystem. The agents have a single common top level goal and must co-operate to plan and execute it. For the purpose of planning and scheduling activities, each agent works as a client or the server of the resource. An agent working as a server manages the resource in order to meet the clients' requirements. Because spacecraft resources are limited, the resource manager agent cannot always meet all requests. It supplies its resource optimally, making sure that the resource is distributed to enhance the achievement of the mission goals. Resource management is used for onboard spacecraft activities such as payload operations (e.g. science observations) and other routine engineering operations. Certain activities, such as the imaging of a target, have a tightly constrained time window of opportunity. Moreover most resources are time varying and reusable. At present the scheduling of spacecraft is manually operated from ground and activities are ranked by priority. A priority depends on the mission phase and other factors that determine the criticality of the related activity. If a conflict within a schedule cannot be solved through a move

E. Lamma and P. Mello (Eds.): AI*IA 99, LNAI 1792, pp. 297–308, 2000.

of a task to a new start time, then the last resort is to postpone the activity with the least priority to the next scheduling horizon. The objective of the general resource-constrained scheduling is to minimise the length of the schedule. In the context of the paper the global objective is to maximise the number of satisfied spacecraft operation goals. The paper proposes an implementation of reinforcement learning techniques as part of the multi-agent architecture to optimally manage resources within the spacecraft. The imaging system is used to demonstrate a possible application. Section 2 describes current literature on resource management. Section 3 introduces the proposed approach. Section 4 and 5 propose an application and Section 6 related results. Section 7 concludes the paper.

2   Background

The MASA approach proposes resource allocation cast as a distributed scheduling problem with a single resource manager per resource type. This differs from the resource allocation problem where all agents manage one or more resources of the same type, for instance job scheduling on a network of computers [2], or the Airline Ground services scheduling problem [4]. In the case of the network of computers, a market-based control technique is employed where bids are made for a resource as in [2]. Only the agent that manages a resource has the knowledge of all constraints imposed on the resource. Individual agents cannot generate a complete schedule involving resources that belong to other agents. This means that some sort of communication between agents is required to exchange information during the scheduling process. Co-operation and co-ordination between scheduling agents are needed to arrive at a feasible schedule. For each agent, the problem is a resource-constrained scheduling problem. The constraints are the task start and completion times, the resource requirements, the task ordering and the relative priorities be-tween the tasks. Unlike in the job shop problem the scheduling of science observations allows for less slack. There may be only one opportunity to make a science observation. This makes the domain more restrictive. Constrained resource scheduling problems are commonly solved with operational research (OR) and artificial intelligence (AI) techniques. In this paper we discuss only the latter. The most used AI techniques employ either rule-based or knowledge-based systems. Of interest here is the knowledge-based approach, where the scheduling problem is viewed as a constraint satisfaction problem. The problem is represented in terms of a set of variables, a set of domains for the variables and a set of constraints on two or more variables. A schedule is an assignment to all the variables, which satisfy all the constraints. In general the job shop problem is formulated by finding a consistent set of start times for each involved operation [1]. The constructive and the iterative repair methods are two standard scheduling approaches. ISIS [6], the first constraint-based scheduling system, uses the constructive method from an order perspective. The schedule is incrementally extended until it is complete. OPIS [10] uses the constructive method from an order and a resource perspective. The Micro-Boss [8] uses the constructive method to schedule one activity at a time as opposed to an order as in OPIS. The repair method came about in an attempt to overcome the poor performance on real problems and the need for incremental rescheduling that minimises changes to the original schedule. Zweben [7] and others [5][7] use the iterative repair method, which starts with an unfeasible initial solution and proceeds by eliminating constraint violations in the schedule. More recently, Reinforcement learning (RL) has been applied to the scheduling problem. Zhang [12] applies RL to the task of scheduling payload processing for the NASA space shuttle program. As with the iterative repair approach, a critical path schedule, possibly unfeasible, is constructed. This is used as the starting state for the reinforcement learning solution. Operators are applied to move from one state to the next.

3   The Proposed Approach

The scheduling of resources is a complex problem because the state space is very large. Designing a model, which can take into account all possible configurations, is an unfeasible task. Machine learning lends itself well as a tool to learn the scheduling of tasks in different conditions. The MASA scheduler presented in this paper applies a reinforcement learning approach to the distributed scheduling problem. Reinforcement learning is a means of learning to act (in this case how to schedule) by trial and error. Scheduling with RL consists of two phases: an off-line or training phase and an online phase. During the training phase, the RL scheduler, presented with training problem instances, learns to a policy. This policy is used during the online phase to construct a schedule. The paper proposes a variation of the RL scheduling methodology proposed by Zhang [12] by applying it to a distributed problem. The approach adopted in the MASA architecture uses reinforcement learning to solve the resource-constrained allocation problem. However, whereas the objective of the general resource-constrained scheduling is to minimise the length of the schedule, in the MASA domain, the objective is to minimise the number of re-assigned requests. Requests that cannot be satisfied in the current scheduling horizon are as-signed to the next horizon. The scheduling comprises two phases. The first phase during which each agent constructs asynchronously an initial schedule, the critical path schedule. The second phase, where the agents must exchange information with co-operating agents. These will allow the complete conflict-free schedule to be constructed. In the second phase, iterative repair and co-operative repair take place simultaneously within the scheduler. An autonomous user driven imaging mission is used to demonstrate the proposed MASA approach. The goal is to allow users, distributed across the globe, to request the imaging of targets on Earth. The spacecraft autonomously schedules the imaging activities and downloads the image data to the user. A system was developed to simulate the spacecraft receiving the imaging goals. The simulator serves two purposes. Firstly, it provides a tool to generate any number of problem examples used to learn the scheduling under different conditions. Secondly, it simulates realistic requests for a spacecraft with an autonomous user driven imaging system. The simulator is an indispensable tool since no spacecraft exist with an autonomous on-board imaging system. The simulator comprises the data generator and the scheduling agents. The data generator models the spacecraft in the orbit receiving requests to image targets on the Earth. The requests for imaging arrive randomly throughout the track repeat period[1]. The track repeat period is taken as the scheduling horizon. The requests for imaging during horizon h_{i+1} are submitted throughout horizon h_i. Prior to the start of the horizon, the resource manager schedules the requests for the horizon. The second part of the simulator is the resource-managing agent. It implements the algorithm that constructs the schedules and the reinforcement learning algorithm that removes constraint violations from the initial schedules to produce a conflict free schedule. Although the basic scheduling problem in the chosen domain is deterministic, the problem becomes non-deterministic when failures are considered. Failures occur in the spacecraft altering resource availability. The reinforcement learning agent learns to schedule in failure situation as well as in nominal conditions. In the context of this paper the simulator generates failure data as well as the imaging goals. The failure data consist of variations in resource capacity, some intermittent others permanent. A fault in any of the spacecraft systems is modelled as a resource unavailability. For example a fault in an imaging instrument resulting in an inability to take an image is modelled by a reduction in the number of imaging instruments. A fault in the power system causing a reduction or unavailability of electrical power is modelled by a reduction in the power capacity. Similarly a fault affecting the data storage is modelled as a reduction in storage capacity. The resource manager learns a new policy to schedule despite of the failures.

4   Spacecraft Imaging Application

The problem and solution are demonstrated in the simulation of an autonomous user driven imaging system of a satellite in Earth orbit. The requests for images are asynchronously transmitted by the users to the spacecraft. Any point on the Earth surface is defined by the time at which the spacecraft passes over that point. The track repeat period[2] is defined as the time between two successive pass over the same point on the Earth. The request for an image capture will normally be received during the track period preceding the expected image acquisition time. The time interval between a request arriving and the actual imaging time is variable. Once the image is acquired, the file is downloaded at the user co-ordinates. Certain assumptions were made about the spacecraft. First of all the cameras are body mounted and fixed. This means that the spacecraft pointing determines the camera pointing. The second assumption is that the acquired images are transferred from the imager local storage to mass storage immediately following the image acquisition to release the local storage for the next image. The mass storage device is emptied between each planning horizon.

---

[1] The time between the spacecraft passing over the same point on the Earth.
[2] Also called the *scheduling horizon*.

A single imaging activity is a goal or in job scheduling terminology a job for which a request is placed. A number of actions must be performed to achieve this goal. The spacecraft sub-systems involved in the imaging activity are the power system, the attitude (pointing) control system, the imaging system and the mass storage device. The power system provides the power to the imager, the attitude control system and the mass storage device during the imaging activities. Prior to initiating an image acquisition, the spacecraft must be stable and pointing in the required direction. Following the image acquisition, the data are transferred to the mass storage device to await downloading to Earth. The timelines for the resource are shown in Figure 1. The power timeline shows the

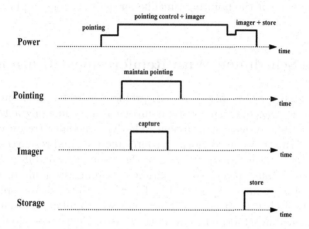

Fig. 1. Resources Timelines

amount of power requested. The available capacity for the power resource varies throughout the orbital period. Multiple requests for power resource to cater for more overlapping imaging goals will not require additional resource. The same applies to the pointing resource. Multiple activities can be supported if each activity requires the same configuration. The storage like the power resource is a capacitated resource, with a fixed amount of storage space available. The available storage capacity diminishes with each image stored but the capacity is restored once the image data is downloaded. Each request for storage reduces the total resource capacity by a certain amount. More than one request might be submitted requiring the image acquisition of the same target. This will generate a conflict that is referred to as an overlap conflict. Only one of the requests needs to be fulfilled to satisfy all users.

Another case occurs when adjacent or partially overlapping targets are to be imaged. When this occurs one or more goals are re-assigned for imaging at the next track period. Because the spacecraft passes over the target at a fixed time, all the requests for resources are constrained by the pass time and are defined in relation to this time. The duration of the power and the pointing requests is constrained by the duration of the image capture task. The image capture time has duration governed by the imager maximum capture rate. The capture rate is not only a function of the camera imaging rate limitations but also of the data transfer rate from the imaging system local storage to the mass storage device. The start time of the request for storage coincides with the end of the image capture request and the end time is the time at which the data is transmitted to ground. Overlapping or conflicting imaging goals do not require additional power or pointing resource. Except in the case of failure, it is assumed that there will always be sufficient power and pointing resources irrespective of the number overlapping imaging goals. Therefore there is no conflict on either the power timeline or the pointing timeline for multiple imaging jobs in nominal conditions.

5   Image Scheduling With Reinforcement Learning

Image scheduling can be cast as an RL problem. The RL environment is represented by the spacecraft sub-systems involved in an imaging activity as well as the spacecraft physical environment. The RL scheduler (resource manager) senses the information regarding the resource requests and resource conflicts together with the information pertaining to the resource availability. When faults occur, the agent must receive information regarding the fault in the form of a reduction of a resource capacity. The RL task is intrinsically episodic. Each episode starts with the initial schedule containing conflicts and ends with the conflict free schedule. Information from the environment takes the form of information about resource conflicts and resource availability. Each state is a possible ordering of tasks (or schedule) with or without resource conflicts. Hence the state space encompasses all possible schedules. In the search for a conflict free schedule, the scheduling agent searches through the state space. The size of the state space (i.e. the number of states) depends on the number of tasks and all possible assignments of task start time. Depending on the number of tasks involved and the slack for each task, the state space can be very large. When applying RL to large state space problems, the size of the state space must somehow be reduced to a manageable size otherwise the problem becomes computationally intractable. For a large state space, the processing and storage requirements are unfeasible. In an attempt to reduce the state space, the resource conflicts are classified and the number of states is a function of the number and the types of conflicts. An alternative is to use function approximation for the value function. Neural networks have been trained [3][12] to learn the value function. There are two types of conflicts. The overlap conflict where two or more requests overlap in time and only one needs to be serviced to satisfy both requests. The partial-overlap conflict where more requests partially overlap in time and one of the requests must be moved or postponed to resolve the constraint violation. All possible combinations of conflicts, including the no conflict, yield eight states. An additional co-ordinate state is entered when the resource-managing agents

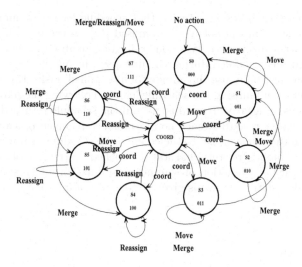

Fig. 2. The State Machine Automaton

must exchange scheduling information. Figure 2 shows the state machine for the scheduling problem. The circles represent the states. Each orientated arc is labelled with the actions that are legal from the starting to the arriving state. The actions are categorised into two classes. The first class deals with resolving conflicts in the schedule (or repairing the schedule). The second class includes actions, which deal with agent co-ordination. To resolve a conflict the RL scheduler can either move or re-assign or merge tasks. If a task has slack, it can be moved to a new start time. If no slack is available, the task is re-assigned to the next scheduling horizon. If the conflict comprises two or more requests for the same targets, the resource manager agent will merge the duplicate requests. The resource-managing agents must co-ordinate action to enable the exchange of information. As with the iterative repair method [7] an operator is applied to the tasks involved in the constraint violation. In our scheduling problem, these actions are the operators. Table 1 illustrates the implemented operators. In ap-

Table 1. The Operators

Operator	Action	Criterion
Move	Move task to new start time	resource excess priority
Re-assign	Delay task to next imaging horizon	Unresolvable constraint violation
Merge	Tasks are merged	Entirely overlapping tasks
Co-ordinate	Agents co-ordinate	Joint request for more resources

plying reinforcement learning to a resource-constrained scheduling problem, the reward scheme must be designed such that schedule length is minimised, and the number of steps in the policy is minimised [12]. In the particular problem, because an image capture activity is constrained by an absolute time of capture[3] if a task cannot be scheduled during the first pass, it may be rescheduled. The reward scheme must minimise the number of 'postponed' tasks, this in effect has the same effect as minimising the schedule length. Following the move, re-assign or merge actions, a negative reward is given if the schedule returned is not conflict free. A negative reward at each non-terminal step encourages a search for a shorter path to the solution, i.e. to the conflict free schedule. A reward of zero is given when the conflict free terminal state is reached. In the case of a co-ordinate action, the reward is a function of whether co-ordination information was used or not. A small negative reward is given if exchange of information did not take place.

6   Results

In the first experiment, learning performance is measured for the Montecarlo (MC) and the Q-Learning (QL) techniques [11]. In the second experiment, it is shown how the system deals with failures. When a system fails, there is a reduction in the resource capacity provided by the system. Thus failure is manifested by a reduction in resources. It is seen that the performance degrades as failures reduce the resources of a subsystem. The final experiment shows agent co-ordination. Failure again is used to demonstrate that coordination is taking place.

6.1   Learning Performance

In the process of searching for a conflict-free schedule, the RL scheduler resolves one constraint violation at each step, i.e. it performs a schedule repair at each step. The repairs also include the co-ordination steps. The number of repairs to arrive at a conflict free schedule is a measure of performance. In the first phase (or training phase), policies are learnt with a different number of problem instances. In the second phase (or online phase), the policies learnt are used to solve one problem and the number of repairs is recorded. For the online phase, the number of repairs performed to arrive at the final schedule is a good measure of the performance of the scheduler. The plots in Figure 3 and Figure 4 show the number of repairs. Figure 3 and Figure 4 show the trend lines for the number of repairs using policies obtained using the MC and QL schedulers respectively. In the figures, each graph corresponds to a different degree of training. The scheduling agent was trained for 2, 10, 50 and 100 epochs. One epoch corresponds to a problem instance i.e. starting from the initial schedule and terminating with the conflict free schedule. The number of repairs is recorded at the end of each epoch. In the case of the MC learning (Figure 3), the difference in the average

---

[3] The time at which the spacecraft passes overhead the imaging target.

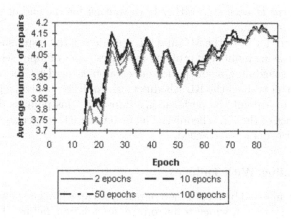

Fig. 3. Average Number of Repairs per Conflict vs. Epoch for Directed Montecarlo

number of repairs is small. The trend lines for the epochs 2, 10 and 50 are very close, the difference is quite small. The MC technique learns on an episode basis and therefore the performance is slower to improve. However it is seen clearly that after 100 epoch training the corresponding trend line for the repairs is lower meaning that less repairs are required to arrive at the final schedule. After a 100 epochs there is no improvement in the learning. In the case of QL learning (Figure 4), the trend lines for the number of repairs are further apart as shown in Figure 4. The difference in number of repairs after training for 2 epochs and for 10 epoch is much greater here. But at 50 and above training epochs the trend lines merge. The QL is quicker to improve its performance

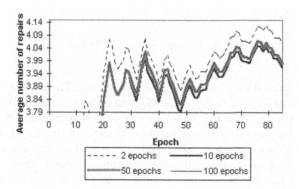

Fig. 4. Average number of repairs per conflicts vs. Epoch for directed Q-Learning

because it learns at each step rather than waiting for the end of the episode as does the MC technique.

As expected, for both the MC and QL techniques, the result show that training on an increasing number of problem instances (a set of input scheduling data) improves the scheduling agent performance as measured by the number of repairs. The better trained the RL schedulers, the quicker it solves a given problem instance. Up to a point the performance improves, this point is determined by the convergence of the RL scheduler. The faster the RL converges, the faster the maximum performance is reached.

6.2   Scheduling With Failures

A failure is manifested by a reduction in resource capacity. The power system was chosen as the system in which to introduce degradation/failure. The scheduling agent is trained off-line with a failure in a single agent and a policy is obtained. During the on-line phase, this policy is used to construct a schedule. The RL

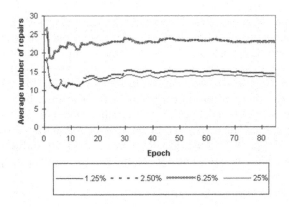

Fig. 5. Average Number Of Repairs

scheduler was trained with increasing power reduction. The percentage reduction in power was 1.25%, 2.5%, 6.25%, and 25% respectively. These figures could also represent the gradual reduction in solar array power during the mission lifetime. The number of repairs is used as a measure of the performance of the scheduler when scheduling with failures. Recall the number of repairs is the number of steps to achieving the final conflict free schedule. Figure 5 shows the running average for the number of repair for the scheduling agent with the failure. Each graph cor-responds to a resource capacity reduction of 1.25%, 2.5%, 6.25% and 25%. The number of repairs increases with decreasing resource capacity, this is explained by the increasing number of constraint violations caused by the reduction in resource. This is expected, as there are more constraints violations. The number of repairs reaches a maximum when there is insufficient resource capacity for scheduling the activities in which case all the goals are re-assigned to the next scheduling horizon. This is shown by the curves for 6.26% and 25% merging.

6.3   Co-ordination

In this section, we demonstrate that co-ordination takes place between two or more scheduling agents. Two agents A, and B are scheduling and a failure (a reduction in the capacity of the agent's resource) is introduced in one agent (agent A). The effect on the scheduling in agent B is observed. In Figure 6the number of repairs versus the epoch is shown for agent B. Note that agent B has no failure. Each graph represents a larger reduction of the resource managed by agent A. The graphs in Figure 6 show that there is increasing activity (more

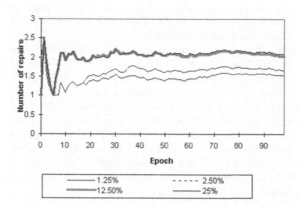

Fig. 6. Co-ordination With Failures

repairs) in agent B due to the failures in agent A. With each additional failure, agent A has additional constraint violations to resolve which in turn create additional co-ordination activity with agent B. The number of repairs levels off when there is insufficient resource to schedule any activity and all the goals are re-assigned. Despite the failures, the RL scheduler is still able to schedule albeit with an increased number of repairs.

7   Conclusions

The paper has introduced a multi-agent model for an unmanned spacecraft. An application was described, an autonomous user driven imaging system. Users based on the ground submit request for the imaging capture of targets on the Earth. In the multi-agent spacecraft each agent manages a resource. The agent must optimise the distribution of their resources. Users submit goals to the space-craft. The spacecraft carry out the goal submitted by the users on the ground or by spacecraft agents. When a goal involves the use of more than one resource, agents co-ordinate to satisfy the goal. The results show that the RL schedulers improve their performance with increased training. It was also has been demonstrated that resources can be managed in presence of subsystem failures. A sensitivity analysis proves that the more serious is the failure the slower is the agent to cope with the problem and with the co-ordination with other agents.

References

1. C.C.Cheng and S.F.Smith. "Applying constraint satisfaction techniques to job shop scheduling". "CMU-RI-TR-95-03", CMU, January 1995.
2. A. Chavez, A.Moukas, and P.Maes. "Challenger: A multi-agent system for distributed resource allocation". In 1st Conference on Autonomous Agents, pages 323–331. ACM Press, February 5-8 1997.
3. R.H. Crites and A.G. Barto. "Improving elevator performance using reinforcement learning". In D.S. Touretzky, M.C. Mozer, and M.E. Hasselmo, editors, Advances in Neural Information Processing Systems, pages 1017–1023. MIT Press, 1996.
4. D.E.Neiman and V.R.Lesser. "A Co-operative repair method for a distributed scheduling system". In $3^{r}d$ International Conference on Artificial Planning Systems, pages 166–173. AAAI Press, 1996.
5. A.S. Fukunaga, G. Rabideau, and S. Chien. "SPEN: An Application Framework for Automated Planning and Scheduling of Spacecraft Control and Operations". In i-SAIRAS, pages 181–187, Tokyo, Japan, 1997.
6. M.Fox. "ISIS, a retrospective". In M.Zweben and M.Fox, editors, Intelligent scheduling, pages 3–28. Morgan Kaufmann Press, 1994.
7. M.Zweben, B.Daun, E.Davis, and M.Daele. "Scheduling and re-scheduling with iterative repair". In M.Zweben and M.Fox, editors, Intelligent scheduling, pages 241–256. Morgan Kaufmann Press, 1994.
8. N.Sadeh. "Micro-opportunistic scheduling". In M.Zweben and M.Fox, editors, Intelligent scheduling, pages 99–136. Morgan Kaufmann Press, 1994.
9. Y. Shoham. "Agent-Oriented Programming". Artificial Intelligence, 60:51–92, 1993.
10. S.F. Smith. "Reactive scheduling system". In D.E. Brown and W.T.Scherer, editors, Intelligent scheduling systems. Kluwer Press, 1995.
11. Richard S. Sutton and Andrew G. Barto. "Reinforcement Learning An Introduction". MIT Press, 1998.
12. W. Zhang and T.G. Dieterich. "Solving combinatorial optimisation tasks by reinforcement learning: A general methodology applied to resource constrained scheduling". Artificial Intelligence Research, 1, 1998.

Multi-Agent Scene Interpretation

P. Remagnino, J. Orwell, G.A. Jones

Digital Imaging Research Centre,
Kingston University, Surrey KT1 2EE, United Kingdom
P.Remagnino@kingston.ac.uk

Abstract. A multi-agent architecture is presented for implementing scene understanding algorithms in the visual surveillance domain. To achieve a high level description of events observed by multiple cameras, many inter-related, event-driven processes must be executed. We use the *agent* paradigm to provide a framework in which these processes can be managed. Each camera has an associated *camera agent*, which detects and tracks moving events (or *regions of interest*). Each camera is calibrated so that image co-ordinates can be transformed into *ground plane* locations. Each camera agent instantiates and updates *object agents* for each stable image event it detects. Object agents are responsible for continually updating a 3D trajectory, a view-independent chromatic appearance model, a description of the event's behaviour, and from these a classification of the object type itself. Camera agents synchronously supply each of its associated object agents with current chromatic and 3D positional observations of the tracked events. Each object agent classifies itself from a range of predefined activities each evaluated using a trained hidden Markov model. The combination of the agent framework, and visual surveillance application provides an excellent environment for development and evaluation of scene understanding algorithms.

1 Introduction

In the proposed car park monitoring system, the physical environment is monitored by multiple cameras with overlapping viewpoints. Events such as a vehicle or person passing through the environment may be simultaneously visible in more than one camera. Moreover the object may move in and out of the view volumes of several cameras in a sequential manner as the object progresses through the car park. An agent-based architecture for performing visual surveillance in a multi-camera environment is described. The loosely-coupled nature of the agent approach and the ability to neatly partition responsibilities is ideal for solving such complex issues as *target handover* between cameras, *data fusion* and description of inter-object situations.

Much of the previous work on *motion detection* and *tracking*[4, 8, 10, 14, 11] has been based on pixel differencing techniques which assume that objects move against a static scene (and hence static camera). Other approaches for tracking motion include segmentation and temporal matching of image features such as *greylevel correlation*[5, 7], *corner points*[12], *greylevel and colour regions*[1, 9] and

E. Lamma and P. Mello (Eds.): AI*IA 99, LNAI 1792, pp. 309–320, 2000.

moving regions[4]. While these different methods have enjoyed some degree of success, most require significant computational resources for realtime implementation. For a stationary platform, moving objects can be detected, tracked and extracted by pixel differencing at speeds approaching frame-rate. Not only is this an efficient means of recording the evolving scene, it literally provides an object oriented format for the image data, allowing a simple interface to object-specific processes.

The analysis of behaviour is an increasingly popular area of investigation particularly in the context of visual surveillance. Buxton and Shaogong[6] introduced Bayesian networks, based on the work of Pearl[13], to detect the foci of attention of a dynamic scene and to provide interpretations of traffic situations. Bogaert *et al*[3] have worked on the surveillance of subways and metropolitan stations to monitor vandalism. Bobick[2] proposed a novel approach for the description of human activities, while Remagnino[15, 17] combine human and vehicle model-based trackers to create a language description of a carpark scene.

Agent technology, originally formalised in the seminal paper of Shoham[18], is nowadays used in many disciplines. Intelligent user interfaces, electronic commerce and communication systems in general have put most of the agent theory into practice. Agent technology has currently become an artificial intelligence paradigm in its own right, and computer vision[6, 2] has adopted it to implement intelligence more formally. The advantages of the agent methodology are clear. A team of agents provides a flexible distributed platform where parallel processing can take place in an optimised manner. Computer-based visual surveillance represents an ideal application for the agent technology. The hierarchy of information, from detected motion, through object descriptions, to classification of behaviour, is passed between independent agents, which co-operate to infer the most plausible scene understanding. The agent paradigm provides an appropriate framework to orchestrate all the processing necessary to optimise the interpretation of dynamic visual data.

Overview of Agent Architecture

Each camera is managed by its own *camera agent* responsible for detecting and tracking all moving objects as they traverse its view volume. All cameras are calibrated to a common ground plane coordinate system. For each event, the bottom most image location is used by the camera agent to generate the 3D position of the event in the view volume. The smallest enclosing colour subimage around the event is used to store all relevant pixels. The tracking algorithm is described in considerable detail in Section 3. For each event detected, the camera agent instantiates an *object agent*. Three-dimensional positional and colour observation data of the event are continually streamed to each existing object agent. Each object agent uses this data to continuously update internal colour and trajectory models of the event (see Section 4).

Each object agent is responsible for continually updating a complex description of itself. The data streamed by each camera is combined with knowledge of the activity of the ground plane to generate the following knowledge about the event:

Appearance Model A view-independent chromatic appearance model.

Trajectory Each position observation supplied by the camera is used to update an acceleration, velocity and positional trajectory model.

Behaviour Analysis The object agent attempts to classify its dynamics against a number of pre-stored set of activities *e.g.* people walking in the car park, people getting out of a vehicle, or vehicles entering the car park and parking.

Event Classification Label the event from a set of carpark domain-specific classifications *i.e.* person, car and cyclist.

Activities are identified by each object agent using a hidden Markov model (HMM) formulation as described fully in section 5. Each activity HHM model makes use of *activity map* storing the prior probabilities of activity at the location for different times of the day. Moreover, the regions of interest in the scene are semantically labelled off-line (*e.g.* parking areas, entrances, exits and vehicle, bicycle and pedestrian *through routes*), and stored along with the activity maps in the *activity agent*. When instantiated, each object downloads from the activity agent the temporally relevant activity maps which are used to classify an objects behaviour. Once an object is deactivated its trajectory history is passed to the activity agent to update the activity maps.

Figuratively speaking, a community of camera agents will continuously detect events and populate the shared ground plane with object agents. The resultant population of object agents both model their motion within the semantically labelled ground plane, and their interactions with other objects as well as attempting to classify themselves. A number of important problems can be elegantly handled by requiring that all object agents periodically communicate with each other. The handover of events between cameras, or the fusion of data from multiple overlapping cameras, is facilitated by allowing neighbouring object agents to compare trajectory and colour data. When pair of object agents determine that they refer to the same event, they are merged to create a single object agent which inherits both sets of camera data links. The internal colour and trajectory models are updated from both sources of information.

In the context of visual surveillance applications, many interesting activities are signalled by the close proximity of objects, for instance associating cars and owners or identifying potential car theft. When such situations arise, the agents of the proximal objects communicate to provide a basic interpretation of the interaction.

2   Agent Anatomy

In our approach all entities involved in the process of visual interpretation are *controlled* by agents. In the proposed work an agent is multi-layered.

The idea behind the proposed approach is to make use of an object-oriented architecture. The agent anatomy works at three different levels of abstraction.

At the lowest level there is the software which implements the basic algorithms used to process visual data, to analyse the features and the trajectory of an object. At the intermediate level the agent makes use of the object-orientated paradigm to provide a means of communication with other agents. Finally at the highest level there lies the software used to analyse the behaviour of an object and in future its own identity. The proposed approach resembles the old Artificial Intelligence paradigm used for scene interpretation where a clear distinction existed between low vision processes and high level interpretation processes. However what is proposed here is somewhat very different. The idea is to make use of a unified framework all based on Bayesian calculus. Since shape and chromatic features, trajectory and behaviour information follow stochastic models the inference from low level to high level, what is commonly called the scene interpretation, is all performed in a unified framework which is mathematically sound and able to capture the uncertain nature of the underlying processes. Moreover, the probabilistic approach can handle incomplete information caused by lack of communication. The orientated nature of the approach makes the framework distributed and the very nature of the high level processes involved in the interpretation of the scene makes the framework artificially intelligent. In the next sections the agents will be analysed in greater detail.

3   The Camera Agent

In the proposed architecture, an agent is assigned to each camera and has the responsibility of tracking events in its field of view. To perform this function reliably a number of tasks need to be performed:

- Maintain the planar homography between image plane and ground plane.
- Learn and continuously update a model of the appearance of the scene.
- Detect and track moving events within the scene.
- Invoke an *object agent* for each stable tracked event in the view volume.
- Integrate within the tracker 3D position and colour feedback supplied by each object agent.

The role of a tracker is to associate moving objects between frames and with a high degree of temporal and spatial coherence. In summary, the presented tracker works as follows. First, the pixels in each new frame are classified as *moving* or *not-moving* by comparing pixel greylevels with an adaptive reference image. Next, moving regions are recovered and annotated by appropriate region statistics. Finally, an inter-frame matching procedure is used to establish the temporal continuity of the moving regions. This procedure is made robust to the spatial and temporal fragmentation exhibited by any segmentation technique based on pixel differencing. All cameras are calibrated via a plane-to-plane homography to a common ground plane coordinate system. For each event, the bottom most image location is used by the camera agent to generate the 3D position of the event in the view volume. At 5Hz, these camera agents recover dense tracks ideal for trajectory estimation on the ground plane. The excellent temporal stability established by the 5Hz tracker is best demonstrated using the frequency of track lengths. The mean track length of real events has been manually determined to be 35 frames. There were 50 people and 75 car events within the carpark itself.

4   Scene Interpretation using Object Agents

Once instantiated, the object agent is obliged to pursue the goal of describing its activity and classifying itself from a limited domain of carpark classes *i.e.* vehicle, person, cyclist, *etc.* This knowledge is derived from the trajectory T and appearance model A of the event - see figure 1(a). A data link between the camera agent and object agent is established and maintained while the 3D event is being successfully tracked. Down this connection, the image tracker synchronously streams both pixel data and the computed location of the event on the ground plane. Figure 1(b) shows the observations of two people walking within the field of views of two cameras (the red and blue polygons). The 2D image positions have been converted into ground plane coordinates and overlaid along with their associated covariance ellipses. Note that each person is represented by two almost coincident tracks. The pixel and positional data streams are absorbed by

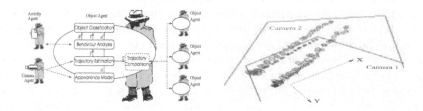

Fig. 1. (a) Object Agent Anatomy (b) Fusing Events from Two Cameras

the *Appearance Model* and *Trajectory Estimation* processes respectively to continually update a colour and spatial appearance model A and an estimate of the trajectory T. An object agent updates its estimate of a simple second-order trajectory model using a Kalman filter formulation. The motion model is composed of an acceleration, velocity and positional terms. This trajectory information is employed in four ways. First, the *Trajectory Comparison* process recovers trajectory data from all neighbouring object agents to determine whether one of the neighbouring agents represents the same ground plane event seen from a different camera - see figure 1(b). If so, the two agents are merged to create a single object linked to two cameras. Second the *Behaviour Analysis* process uses the trajectory to classify the activity using pre-trained HMMs. Third, the Object Classification process combines the trajectory information with appearance A and behavioural data B to classify the object. Finally the object trajectories are used by the activity agent to update the activity maps associated with each activity.

5   Probabilistic Framework for Behavioural Analysis

A probabilistic framework is applied to perform an analysis of the object dynamics. This framework combines the agent paradigm proposed by Shoham[18], and the Markov modelling studied by Rabiner[16]. In addition to maintaining an estimate of its trajectory, each *object agent* attempts to interpret the activity of its event. A number of predefined activities are allowed for the particular problem context [1]. The proposed approach makes use of the Markov learning technique. A training set of tracks for people and vehicles is pre-classified to build Markov models for the required activities occurring in the analysed environment. On invocation, each agent loads a copy of the model for each possible activity. Each updated trajectory estimate is then used continually by each agent to calculate the likelihood of all the available models and infer the most likely activity of the object.

5.1   Markov models for scene understanding

The Markov model is an ideal probabilistic technique for learning and matching activity patterns. A Markov model is a stochastic state automaton, where each state is associated a prior probability and all transitions between states have associatedtemporal conditional probabilities. In our formulation, the states are the various regions of interest in the scene, classified by an operator in an offline procedure from a series of semantic labellings *e.g. parking areas, vehicle entrance* and *exit, pedestrian path, etc.* A hidden Markov model represents each possible activity of people or vehicles moving on the ground plane. Each ground plane region R_i represents a separate state q_i of a hidden Markov model which may or may not be accessible to another adjacent region R_j, depending on the ground plane topological constraints *i.e.* imagine a fence normally barring access between two regions. The duration of an activity within a region can also be captured by the model, and used in a second stage to determine unpredictable events or even employed as a source of object classification. Slow objects are most likely people walking along, while faster objects are likely to be vehicles. The ground plane is tessellated by an array of rectangular bins. The enclosing region is used to assign each bin to a particular state. These bins are used to construct a spatial probability density function for each region (and hence state) and for each activity by allowing pre-classified trajectories to vote for each bin they visit.

   In a learning phase, the dynamics of objects moving in the scene are used to train each hidden Markov model by building the following

---

[1] In our car park application, the set of activities include: People activities: walking through the car park, reaching or getting out of a vehicle and Vehicle dynamics: passing near, through or parking in the car park

prior probability π_i for each state q_i *i.e.* the probability that a particular region R_i is the starting point for a track,

transitional probabilities a_{ij} between two regions R_i and R_j *i.e.* the probability that an object moves from one region to another given all possible transitions from that region,

spatial probability density function for each region $b_j(\mathbf{o}_t)$ *i.e.* the probability that a track visits a particular bin of a region given that the object is in that region,

duration density function $p_i(d)$ for each state of the model, *i.e.* the probability that the object spends duration d inside a region R_i.

Priors are readily learnt by counting the frequency that a region is the first state of a track. Similarly transitional probabilities are learnt by counting the number of times a transition between regions occurs normalised to all occurred transitions. The pdfs for each region are then calculated by using the bins as accumulators and normalising each region to a unitary volume. This is done by accumulating evidence during the training phase for the bins and regions visited by an object. These learned probability functions effectively act as a long term memory for predefined activities and can be continuously updated with the information of a new track once the object has left the scene. Each region R_i of the tessellated ground plane is represented by a pdf $b_i(\mathbf{o})$ where $\mathbf{o}$ is the position vector (x, y) of an observed event on the ground plane. The duration density function is learnt by assuming a parametric state model such as a Gaussian where $p_i(d) = \mathcal{N}(d, \mu_i, \sigma_i)$. The duration d is assumed to follow a Gaussian trend where μ_i represents the mean time spent by the object in a state, and σ_i its variance. Once the hidden Markov models have been learned they can be used to describe the dynamic evolution of the scene. Models are learnt to provide the most plausible explanation for the observed dynamics. In the case of a car park, the parking dynamics of vehicles and the various movements of pedestrians represent two classes of models. Typical activities include people approaching or coming out of vehicles and vehicles manoeuvring in the car park.

Model selection can be performed using a *Maximum A Posterior* probability (MAP) scheme which finds the activity model λ from the set of possible activities Λ which yields the highest likelihood $P(\mathbf{O}|\lambda)$ for the sequence of N observations $\mathbf{O} = (\mathbf{o}_1, \ldots \mathbf{o}_N)$ *i.e.*

$$\hat{\lambda} = \underset{\lambda \in \Lambda}{\operatorname{argmax}} \, P(\lambda|\mathbf{O}) \tag{1}$$

For equally likely activities, the MAP scheme is equivalent to maximising the class conditional probabilities $P(\mathbf{O}|\lambda)$ which from the theorem of total probability can be written as

$$P(\mathbf{O}|\lambda) = \sum_{\forall \mathbf{q}} P(\mathbf{O}|\mathbf{q}, \lambda) P(\mathbf{q}|\lambda) \tag{2}$$

where $\mathbf{q} = \{q_1, \ldots, q_T\}$ is one possible traversal of a sequence of T states by the N observations, and $\forall \mathbf{q}$ represents all possible n-tuple sequences of T states. The conditional probability $P(\mathbf{q}|\lambda)$ represents the joint probability of a particular traversal of states given a particular model λ, and may be written in terms of the prior and transitional probabilities as

$$P(\mathbf{q}|\lambda) = \pi_{q_1} a_{q_1 q_2} \times \ldots \times a_{q_{T-1} q_T} \qquad (3)$$

while $P(\mathbf{O}|\mathbf{q}, \lambda)$ represents the joint probability of a particular set of observations given a particular model λ and sequence of states which may be written as

$$P(\mathbf{O}|\mathbf{q}, \lambda) = b_{q_1}(\mathbf{o}_1) p_{q_1}(d_1) \times \cdots \times b_{q_T}(\mathbf{o}_N) p_{q_T}(d_T) \qquad (4)$$

where $p_{q_i}(d_i)$ represents the probability that state q_i lasts for a duration interval d_i.

$$P(\mathbf{O}|\lambda) = \sum_{\forall \mathbf{q}} \pi_{q_1} p_{q_1}(d_1) b_{q_1}(\mathbf{o}_1) a_{q_1 q_2} \times \cdots \times a_{q_{T-1} q_T} p_{q_T}(d_T) b_{q_T}(\mathbf{o}_N) \qquad (5)$$

At each moment in time all models are tested and the most likely used to explain the current scene dynamics. Each agent makes use of the data provided by the camera as observations to test all available Markov models.

Efficient Model Selection The HMM framework employs the computationally efficient *forward* iterative procedure[16] to calculate the likelihood of a given model λ given a set of observations $\mathbf{O}$. This three step procedure makes use of the *forward* variable $\alpha_t(i)$ defined as the likelihood that the partial set of observations $\mathbf{O}_t = \{\mathbf{o}_1, \ldots, \mathbf{o}_t\}$ finishing in state q_i are described by the model λ *i.e.*

$$\alpha_t(i) = P(\mathbf{o}_1, \ldots, \mathbf{o}_t, q_i | \lambda) \qquad (6)$$

Initialisation The forward probabilities for each state q_i are computed from the prior probability of starting in this state and the probability that the first observation belongs to this state.

$$\alpha_1(i) = \pi_i p_i(1) b_i(\mathbf{o}_1), \qquad i \in [1, N] \qquad (7)$$

Induction The likelihood $\alpha_t(i)$ at time t is evaluated from possible transitions from all previous states and all possible durations in the new state

$$\alpha_t(i) = \sum_{j=1}^{N} \left\{ a_{ji} \sum_{d=1}^{D} \left\{ \alpha_{t-d}(j) a_{ji} p_i(d) \prod_{s=t-d+1}^{t} b_j(\mathbf{o}_s) \right\} \right\}, \qquad i \in [1, N] \qquad (8)$$

where D is the maximum duration within any state.

Evaluation At each moment in time t a sequence of observations $(\mathbf{o}_1, \ldots, \mathbf{o}_t)$ provide sufficient information to calculate the probability that one of the learned models is likely to represent the current scene evolution. The highest probability provides a means of selecting the most likely activity

$$P(\mathbf{O}_t|\lambda) = \sum_{i=1}^{N} P(\mathbf{o}_1, \ldots, \mathbf{o}_t, q_i | \lambda) = \sum_{i=1}^{N} \alpha_t(i) \qquad (9)$$

5.2   Car park surveillance with Markov models

Experiments have been carried out to prove the robustness of the Markov modelisation in the specific application of car park visual surveillance. The ground plane has been manually segmented into regions of interests corresponding to different areas of the car park and the neighbouring areas and tessellated into a 25 × 25 array of voting bins. Parking lots, entrance, neighbouring road and the car park drive-through were chosen as areas of interest. Figure 2(a) illustrates the segmentation of the car park scenario used in the experiments. Each region represents a separate state within a number of activities. Superimposed, are the states used in hidden Markov model for the scene and the possible inter-state transitions. The topology of the hidden Markov model was designed to capture exclusively all activities usually taking place in a car park. Topological links, such as the one between regions separated by a wall were removed. The design is aimed at activity classification and also identification of unusual or bizarre sets of actions, such as the one of a person entering the car park from a non-authorised entrance.

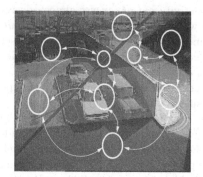 

Fig. 2. (a)Hidden Markov model (b) Spatial PDF for *Drive Through* Activity

A set of activities were chosen for pedestrians and vehicles normally moving into the defined areas. The footnote [2] illustrates the defined activities. In order to test the method data provided by the tracker was pre-classified. The classification entailed going through all vehicle and person tracks, and assign a label to each one of them from a set of predefined activities. A percentage of the data was used to learn the Markov models, while the remaining data was used to test the models. Figure 2(b) shows the spatial probability density function for vehicle *drive-through* activity. Darker regions show larger degrees of activity. This PDF built from two overlapping images shows large degrees of activity in the entrance and interior road regions.

---

[2] Person activity: walking by, getting into car, getting out of car, walking through; Vehicle dynamics: driving by, parking, pulling out, driving through

A large set of object tracks was used to train the hidden Markov models corresponding to the predefined 8 activities. Object tracks were pre-classified into person and vehicle activity and then used to learn the different Markov models. A smaller set of 100 object tracks was used to measure the performance of the system. Table 1 shows the scatter matrix for the person object type and Table 1 shows the scatter matrix for the vehicle object type. Each row of the scatter matrices represents the probability of correct classification for the ensemble of analysed tracks. The *to-car* and the *walk-by* activities were correctly

Activity	to-car	out o'car	w-thro'	walk-by	Activity	park	unpark	d-thro'	drive-by
to-car	1.00	0.00	0.00	0.00	park	1.00	0.00	0.00	0.00
out o'car	0.00	0.95	0.05	0.00	unpark	0.09	0.73	0.09	0.09
w-thro'	0.10	0.40	0.50	0.00	d-thro'	0.00	0.05	0.95	0.00
walk-by	0.00	0.00	0.00	0.99	drive-by	0.00	0.03	0.00	0.97

Table 1. Scatter matrix for person and vehicle activities

identified for all tested object tracks. The activity *out-of-car* was almost always identified, while the activity *walk-through* was partially confused with the *out-of-car* activity. The confusion is not symmetrical due to the fact that the set actions involved in getting out of a car are more selective and therefore easier to identify. The activities *park* and *drive-by* was correctly classified. The activity *drive-through* was almost always correctly classified. For the vehicle object type the *unpark* activity was only partially classified.

The results show that object activity can indeed be classified using the Markov modelisation. Although the method is not too computationally demanding, it still does not run in real time. The current set of activities is minimal, however it captures the most common car park events and can indeed be used to perform scene understanding with a fairly high degree of confidence. It is the authors' intention to improve the Markov modelisation to include more complex activities and to classify longer film footage in real time.

6   A note on multi-agent programming

The paper presented a multi-agent framework to infer scene interpretation from visual information provided by a multi-camera system. The advantages of a multi-agent framework are clear and they were mentioned in the introduction. There the discussion was mainly concerned with the design of distributed and intelligent visual surveillance systems. Here a note is intended on the actual implementation detail of such architecture. The presented work described in detail a number of algorithms which have been implemented over the last year at our site. At present the very first implementation of the architecture exists as a two camera system linked to a single cpu. The very nature of the proposed architecture is distributed and as such it introduces a number of standard communication problems. On one hand a fully distributed communication system represents a feasible solution. This entails that each newly created object agent broadcasts its existence or the termination of it to all the others opening all channels. On the other end one could imagine a communication architecture where all agents do not communicate directly but they rather do so through a centralised agent which could be identified with the ground plane agent. Finally one could imagine an intermediate architecture where each semantic region is assigned an agent whose job is to keep the local communication under control. The three proposed alternatives represent by no means an exhaustive set of choices. We do believe that the spectrum is much wider and we intend to investigate hybrid choices as well where for instance objects agents are free to communicate between them only when needed, not to create bottlenecks in the communication *floor*. Thus far only the centralised choice has been implemented, however this was simply dictated by our need to have a very first prototype. The design proposed here is extremely flexible. It is our intention to investigate the alternative architectures and to compare them quantitatively.

7   Conclusion

A framework for visual surveillance has been presented, consisting of society of camera and object agents. A *camera agent* processes the raw bitstream of observed video data into foreground and background elements. Individual foreground data are segmented into regions, and tracked through the image plane. Calibrating each camera relative to a common ground plane enables each camera agent to convert these into 3D observations of an event. For each event detected, the camera agent instantiates an *object agent*. Three-dimensional positional and colour observation data of the event are continually streamed to each existing object agent. Each object agent uses this data to continuously update internal colour, trajectory and activity models of the event. Each object agent can interrogate each other's properties, which may be used to update their own, and thus the distributed representation of the scene interpretation. As an example, a formal technique for object fusion was presented, by which two object agents, spawned by different cameras, may ascertain if they are actually the same object.

An inportant element of any scene understanding system is the recovery of descriptions of the activities within the scene. An approach based on Hidden Markov models has been implemented which employs a pre-defined set of domain-specific behaviours. On invocation, An object agent loads the current activity models, transitional probabilities and spatial probability density functions on invocation, and continually updates its belief about the activity of the event. A simple demonstration was shown, in which vehicle and pedestrian movements were classified into one of four categories.

References

1. A. Bakowski and G.A. Jones. "Visual Surveillance Tracking using Colour region Adjacency Graphs". In *Proceedings of IEE Image Processing and Applications*,

Manchester, July 1999.

2. A.F. Bobick. "Computers Seeing Action". In *Proceedings of the British Machine Vision Conference*, volume 1, pages 13–22, Edinburgh, September 1996.

3. M. Bogaert, N. Chleq, P. Cornez, C. Regazzoni, A. Teschioni, and M. Thonnat. "The PASSWORD Project". In *Proceedings of International Conference on Image Processing*, pages 675–678, 1996.

4. F. Bremond and M. Thonnat. "Tracking multiple non-rigid objects in a cluttered scene". In *Scandinavian Conference on Image Analysis*, pages 643–650, Lappeeranta, Finland, June 1997.

5. S. Brock-Gunn and T. Ellis. "Using colour templates for target identification and tracking". In *British Machine Vision Conference*, Leeds, September 1992.

6. H. Buxton and S. Gong. "Visual Surveillance in a Dynamic and Uncertain World". *Artificial Intelligence*, 78(1-2):431–459, 1995.

7. A. Carbonaro and P. Zingaretti. "Object tracking in a varying environment". In *IEE International Conference on Image Processing and Its Applications*, Dublin, July 1997.

8. M. Hotter, R. Mester, and M. Meyer. "Detection of moving objects using robust displacement estimation including statistical error analysis". In *International Conference Pattern Recognition*, Vienna, August 1996.

9. H.S.Parry, A.D.Marshall, and K.C.Markham. "Region template correlation for FLIR target tracking". In *British Machine Vision Conference*, Edinburgh, September 1996.

10. G.A. Jones. "Motion Detection in Security Applications using Tracking and Hierarchy". In *International Society of Optical Engineering*, San Diego, September 1994.

11. J.Segen and S.Pingali. "A camera-based system for tracking people in real-time". In *IEEE International Conference on Pattern Recognition*, Vienna, August 1996.

12. L.S.Shapiro, H.Wang, and J.M.Brady. "A matching and tracking strategy for independently moving objects". In *British Machine Vision Conference*, Leeds, September 1992.

13. Judea Pearl. *"Probabilistic Reasoning Intelligent Systems: Networks of Plausible Inference"*. Morgan Kaufmann, 1988.

14. P.L.Rosin and T.Ellis. "Image difference threshold strategies and shadow detection". In *British Machine Vision Conference*, 1995.

15. P.Remagnino, T.Tan, and K.Baker. "Agent Orientated Annotation in Model Based Visual Surveillance". In *Proceedings of IEEE International Conference on Computer Vision*, pages 857–862, Bombay, India, January 1998.

16. L.R. Rabiner and B.H. Juang. *"Fundamentals of Speech Recognition"*. Prentice-Hall, 1993.

17. P. Remagnino, S. Maybank, R. Fraile, K. Baker, and R. Morris. *Advanced Video-based Surveillance Systems*, chapter 'Automatic Visual Surveillance of Vehicles and People', pages 97–107. Kluwer Academic Publishers Press, Hingham, MA., USA, 1998. Edited by C.S. Regazzoni, G. Fabri and G. Vernazza.

18. Y. Shoham. "Agent-Oriented Programming". *Artificial Intelligence*, 60:51–92, 1993.

An Algorithm for Recruitment of Agents in Agency Design

Francesco Amigoni, Mauro Villa

Artificial Intelligence and Robotics Project
Dipartimento di Elettronica e Informazione; Politecnico di Milano
Piazza Leonardo da Vinci 32; I-20133 Milano (MI); Italy
amigoni@elet.polimi.it; villa@airlab.elet.polimi.it

Abstract. Multiagent systems, also denoted as *agencies*, are a matter of growing importance in distributed artificial intelligence. Whereas several applications have been addressed by means of agencies, little effort has been devoted to identify and define general methodologies for developing agencies. The purpose of this paper is to propose and analyze an algorithm that, given a formalized initial exigency, recruits, from an inventory of agents, the components that form the better agency for addressing the exigency. This algorithm for composing an agency can be naturally applied in very flexible environments, such as Web applications, in which both the reconfiguration of systems and the reuse of agents for different applications play a fundamental role.

1 Introduction

Multiagent systems are a subject of growing importance in distributed artificial intelligence. We denote, following the wording introduced by Minsky [14], a multiagent system as *agency* in order to stress the uniqueness of the machine that results from the integration of complex entities called *agents*. Whereas several applications have been addressed by agencies, little effort has been devoted to identify and define general methodologies for developing agencies.

The purpose of this paper is to propose, describe, and analyze an algorithm that, given a formalized initial exigency, recruits the components, namely the agents, that form the better agency for addressing the exigency. More precisely, the designer expresses an *ideal op semiagency* that represents a description of the operative functions that are required to address an initial exigency. This request is matched by the algorithm to the availability, namely to the real op semiagents that can be recruited from an *inventory* to implement the ideal op semiagents and that constitute the better, according to some metric, *real op semiagency*. The proposed algorithm is intended to be a contribution toward the definition of a general methodology for developing agencies.

The paper is structured as follows. In Section 2, we introduce the concept of agency. In Section 3, we present the main steps of the agency design process. In Section 4, we define the metric for quantifying the distance between ideal op semiagency and real op semiagency. In Section 5, we describe the recruitment

E. Lamma and P. Mello (Eds.): AI*IA 99, LNAI 1792, pp. 321–332, 2000.

algorithm for finding the optimal, according to the defined metric, real op semi-agency that covers the ideal op semiagency. Some experimental evaluations of the algorithm are illustrated in Section 6, where applications of the algorithm are also proposed. Finally, Section 7 concludes the paper.

2   Agencies in Distributed Artificial Intelligence

Minsky [14] firstly introduced the concept of *agency* in order to provide a description of the complex nature and performances of the human mind. According to Minsky, the human intellectual activities are of such complexity that a single model is not adequate to fully describe each one of them. Therefore, Minsky proposed to adopt several competing and cooperating models, called paradigms, each one embedded in an *agent*, for expressing the knowledge about the mind. The set of interrelated agents constitutes the "society of mind", which is also called agency.

The idea of agency has further evolved, from Minsky's conception, within the field of distributed artificial intelligence [6, 7]. In this area, an agency is considered as a particular *multiagent system* in which each agent is a computer or a robot with inferential ability that it exploits for performing some functions [4]. The adoption of the wording 'agency' instead of 'multiagent system' emphasizes our conception of a multiagent system as a unique machine, even if composed of several entities, namely agents, that can be very complex in their nature.

A lot of agencies have been presented in literature for addressing several different applications including industrial applications, commercial applications, medical applications and entertainment applications [11, 12]. On the other hand, little effort has been dedicated to the definition of general methodologies for designing and building agencies, namely to the methodologies that, independently of any particular application field, provide guidelines for the development of agencies [16]. However, the availability of such methodologies is invoked by several authors. For example, Jennings et al. stress that "what is required is a systematic means of analyzing the problem, of working out how it can best structured as multiagent system, and then determining how the individual agents can be structured" [11]. Also in [9], the necessity of a general methodology for multiagent systems is emphasized: "as the field matures, the broader acceptance of agent-oriented systems will become increasingly tied to the availability of well-founded techniques and methodologies for systems development" (likewise, see [10] for a similar point of view).

The proposal presented in this paper aims to constitute a first step in addressing the above requests for a general development methodology for multiagent systems. In section 7, we compare our approach with some of the few others presented in literature.

3   Agency Design Process

During the design of an agency, a fundamental critical problem, called *Babel Tower Aporia*, arises and stimulates interesting, important, and modern research directions, as also recognized in [12]. The Babel Tower Aporia is encountered in the development of an agency when we consider that, on one hand, it is useful to have agents that are specialized, namely that are able to perform specialized functions. In fact, in this way, many problems can be addressed by the agency that can exploit the heterogeneous functions provided by the composing agents. On the other hand, it is necessary to have a uniform cooperation framework in which agents can perform the homogeneous information exchanging that is the base of cooperation. Thus, in order to build an agency, we are facing the problem of uniformly integrating the specialized agents, namely we have to tackle the Babel Tower Aporia.

Our previous work has addressed [2,3] the solution of the Babel Tower Aporia by proposing an architectural structure of each agent belonging to an agency as arranged in a couple of semiagents (Fig. 1(a)). The first semiagent is called *op semiagent* and it is devoted to operate, the second semiagent is called *co semiagent* and it is devoted to cooperate. Therefore, the op semiagent represents the specialized and particular part of an agent, whereas the co semiagent represents the uniform and general part of an agent. Hence, the architecture of each agent of an agency involves the coexistence of the op semiagent, which is different in each agent of the agency, and of the co semiagent, which is uniform in all agents of the agency.

Formally, we define a semiagent, either op semiagent or co semiagent, as follows (see [1,5] for a more comprehensive and detailed illustration of the formal subjects presented in this section).

Definition 1 (semiagent) *A semiagent a is a couple $a = (N, T)$ where*

- *N is an identifier and represents the* name *of the semiagent;*
- *T is a set $\{f_1, f_2, \ldots, f_k\}$ of functions[1] and represents the* type *of the semiagent.*

We explicitly note that the above definition of semiagent is quite general and encompasses, for example, robotic semiagents and software semiagents. In the following, we do not specify the physical nature of semiagents. Hence, our methodology is not bound to a particular way of implementing agents.

The bipartite architecture of each agent envisages the possibility of constructing an agency by starting from existing heterogeneous agents, which are considered as mere op semiagents, and which are successively integrated with homogeneous co semiagents in order to form an agency. More precisely, it is interesting, at this point, to present the process (Fig. 1(b)) of design that brings, following some phases, to the construction of an agency (see [1,2] for a more circumstantial description of such methodology).

---

[1] A function is a primitive action that can be performed by a semiagent. For example, for a robotic op semiagent, functions can be navigation, vision, and so on.

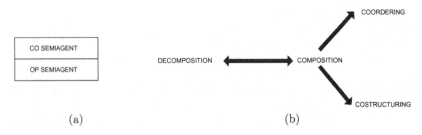

Fig. 1. The architectural structure of an agent as a couple of semiagents (a) and the agency design process (b).

The first phase of the agency design process is the *decomposition* of the problem (or of the class of problems) that represents the initial exigency that stimulates the development of an agency. The problem is decomposed into a set of subproblems that are simpler than the original problem, although they are not trivial. In fact, each subproblem requires, for its solution, some operative functions that identify an *ideal op semiagent*, which performs the requested functions and that is, therefore, related to the subproblem. Thus, at the end of the decomposition, it is identified an *ideal op semiagency* composed of ideal op semiagents. The ideal op semiagency is a representation of the requirements for addressing the given problem. The requirements are expressed in terms of operative functions (i.e., the types of ideal op semiagents, see Definition 1).

The second phase in designing an agency is the *composition* of the real op semiagency. Starting from an ideal op semiagency, the designer covers the ideal op semiagents with some of the available *real op semiagents* in order to form a *real op semiagency*. We can consider the available real op semiagents as organized in an *inventory* according to the functions they perform (namely to their types, see Definition 1). Hence, the composition can be seen as the *recruitment*, from the inventory, of a set of real op semiagents that functionally cover the ideal op semiagents. The real op semiagency is the results of the matching between the request, represented by the ideal op semiagency, and the availability, represented by the inventory. The real op semiagency is the operative part of an agency, namely it is composed of agents that may be heterogeneous in their cooperation abilities since they may have been developed by different designers and companies. These agents (considered as real op semiagents) have been recruited for their operative functions, but they lack common cooperation framework.

Decomposition and composition are not performed in a static order but the designer performs them dynamically jumping from one to another and vice versa, until a real op semiagency that covers the ideal op semiagency is found. This fact can be expressed by saying that the decomposition depends on the availability. More precisely, a designer can decompose an initial problem in several ways, namely several ideal op semiagencies can be identified. The one that is adopted is determined also by the real op semiagents that are available in the inventory.

For the purposes of this paper, we define an op semiagency, either ideal op semiagency or real op semiagency, as follows (see [1,5] for a more complete definition that considers topology as well).

Definition 2 (op semiagency) *An op semiagency A is a set $\{a_1, a_2, \ldots, a_n\}$, where each a_i, for $i = 1, 2, \ldots, n$, is an op semiagent.*

The set of functions performed by the op semiagents of an op semiagency is called functionality and it is defined as follows.

Definition 3 (functionality) *The* functionality $\mathcal{F}(A)$ *of an op semiagency A is defined as*
$$\mathcal{F}(A) = \{f | \exists a = (N, T) \in A \wedge f \in T\}.$$

On the basis of the previous definitions, we formally describe the composition as the recruitment of a set of real op semiagents from the inventory in order to form a real op semiagency A_R such that $\mathcal{F}(A_R) \supseteq \mathcal{F}(A_I)$, where A_I is the ideal op semiagency to cover.

Since, as already noticed, the real op semiagents of the inventory could be designed and built by different designers and companies, it is required a common agreement (or ontology) to ensure that a function f of an op semiagent a has the same meaning for the different subjects involved in agency design. More precisely, for our methodology to work, f has to represent the same function for every designer of real op semiagents and for the designer of the whole agency.

We stress that the real op semiagency is composed of incomplete agents since each agent has only the op semiagent and there is no common and uniform framework of cooperation. Thus, the real op semiagency is not able to solve any specific problem (belonging to the more general class of problems denoted as initial exigency) until in each agent the co semiagent is inserted. For this reason, in the following of the paper, we call *fixed agency* the real op semiagency.

We can identify two opposite ways for inserting the co semiagent in each real op semiagent of a fixed agency (Fig. 1(b)). The first one is called *costructuring* and brings to a *static agency*. The second one is called *coordering* and brings to a *dynamic agency* (for further details, see [1–3]). In this paper we do not further discuss costructuring and coordering, but we concentrate on composition, namely on the matching between request and availability.

4   Distances between Op Semiagencies

The goal of the composition, namely of the recruitment of real op semiagents from the inventory, is to obtain a fixed agency that corresponds as many as possible, in particular in the distribution of functions among op semiagents, to the ideal op semiagency.

More formally, a fixed agency that implements an ideal op semiagency can be obtained by selecting an *association* for every ideal op semiagent. An association is a couple $(a_I, \{a_{R1}, a_{R2}, \ldots, a_{Rh}\})$ with the meaning that a_{Ri} contributes to (it is part of the set of real op semiagents that) implement a_I. If $a_I = (N, T)$, $a_{R1} = (N_1, T_1)$, $a_{R2} = (N_2, T_2), \ldots, a_{Rh} = (N_h, T_h)$, then an association is such that $T_1 \cup T_2 \cup \ldots \cup T_h \supseteq T$. This means that the real op semiagents cover the functions required by the ideal op semiagent. A set of associations is *exact* when, for each association, $h = 1$, $T_1 = T$, and each real op semiagent is associated to one and only one ideal op semiagent. We note that, in general, a real op semiagent can be associated to more ideal op semiagents. If, in the inventory, there is not a set of real op semiagents that is exactly associated to the ideal op semiagents, then the designer selects a set of associations that realize, in the better way, the ideal op semiagency. We have identified the following four ways for implementing, by means of non-exact associations, ideal op semiagents in a non-optimal manner. Each one of these ways is related to an index of the (below defined) metric that quantifies the distance of fixed agency from ideal op semiagency.

Sharing. To h ideal op semiagents of type T, namely $a_{I1} = (N_1, T)$, $a_{I2} = (N_2, T), \ldots, a_{Ih} = (N_h, T)$, is associated a unique real op semiagent $a_R = (N, T)$. We call *sharing* the associations $(a_{I1}, \{a_R\}), (a_{I2}, \{a_R\}), \ldots, (a_{Ih}, \{a_R\})$.

For example, consider a fleet of four robotic ideal op semiagents, each one performing the function of cleaning the floor of a room (f_1 in Fig. 2(a)). If, in the inventory, there are only three robotic real op semiagents of type $\{f_1\}$, then we can recruit all the available robotic real op semiagents for implementing the ideal op semiagency by means of sharing associations. A function of a real op semiagent a_R that belongs to the type of at least two of the ideal op semiagents associated to a_R is called *shared*.

Sharing is related to the index $I_{sh} = |T|$ (in Fig. 2(a), $I_{sh} = |\{f_1\}| = 1$). The index I_{sh} measures the number of shared functions, namely it measures how many functions a recruited real op semiagent performs to implement ideal op semiagents of the same type. Sharing associations account for the situations in which a real op semiagent of the real (implemented) system has to carry on the work of many ideal op semiagents of the same type of the ideal (required) system.

Merging. To h ideal op semiagents $a_{I1} = (N_1, T_1)$, $a_{I2} = (N_2, T_2), \ldots, a_{Ih} = (N_h, T_h)$ is associated a real op semiagent $a_R = (N, T)$, such that $T = T_1 \cup T_2 \cup \ldots \cup T_h$. We call *merging* the associations $(a_{I1}, \{a_R\}), (a_{I2}, \{a_R\}), \ldots, (a_{Ih}, \{a_R\})$.

For example, consider two ideal op semiagents that perform, respectively, the function of searching Web sites for a given item (f_1 in Fig. 2(b)) and the function of buying a given item (f_3 in Fig. 2(b)). If, in the inventory, there are not real op semiagents of such types, then we can recruit a single real op semiagent that covers the required functions $\{f_1, f_3\}$.

Merging is related to the index $I_m = h - 1$ (in Fig. 2(b), $I_m = 2 - 1 = 1$). The index I_m measures the number of ideal op semiagents that lack an exclusively corresponding real op semiagent. Merging associations account for the situations in which a real op semiagent of the real system has to carry on the work of many ideal op semiagents of different types of the ideal system.

Expansion. To an ideal op semiagent $a_I = (N, T)$ are associated h real op semiagents $a_{R1} = (N_1, T_1), a_{R2} = (N_2, T_2), \ldots, a_{Rh} = (N_h, T_h)$, such that $T = T_1 \cup T_2 \cup \ldots \cup T_h$. We call *expansion* the association $(a_I, \{a_{R1}, a_{R2}, \ldots, a_{Rh}\})$.

For example, consider a robotic ideal op semiagent performing the functions of navigation, vision, and manipulation (respectively, f_1, f_2, f_3 in Fig. 2(c)). If, in the inventory, there is no robotic real op semiagent of such type, then we can recruit two robotic real op semiagents, one performing navigation and vision functions (f_1, f_2) and one performing manipulation function (f_3), for implementing the robotic ideal op semiagent.

Expansion is related to the index $I_e = h - 1$ (in Fig. 2(c), $I_e = 2 - 1 = 1$). The index I_e measures the number of real op semiagents that contribute to implement an ideal op semiagent (minus one gives account for the fact that at least a real op semiagent is always required). Expansion association accounts for the situations in which many real op semiagents of different types of the real system have to carry on the work of an ideal op semiagent of the ideal system.

Substitution. To an ideal op semiagent $a_I = (N_I, T_I)$ is associated a real op semiagent $a_R = (N_R, T_R)$, such that $T_R \supseteq T_I$. We call *substitution* the association $(a_I, \{a_R\})$.

For example, let us require a robotic ideal op semiagent that performs the function of navigation (f_2 in Fig. 2(d)). If, in the inventory, there is no robotic real op semiagent of such type, then we can implement the robotic ideal op semiagent by means of a robotic real op semiagent that performs the functions of navigation and manipulation (f_2, f_5 in Fig. 2(d)). A function of a real op semiagent a_R that does not belong to any of the ideal op semiagents associated to a_R is called *useless*.

Substitution is related to the index $I_{su} = |T_R - T_I|$ (in Fig. 2(d), $I_{su} = |\{f_2, f_5\} - \{f_2\}| = |\{f_5\}| = 1$). The index I_{su} measures the number of useless functions, namely it measures how many functions a recruited real op semiagent does not use to implement the corresponding ideal op semiagents. Substitution association accounts for the situations in which a real op semiagent is only partially utilized for implementing an ideal op semiagent.

We note that the listed non-exact associations are neither all primitive nor independent. In fact, for example, sharing can be viewed as a peculiar case of merging. Notwithstanding, we consider all these types of associations because they provide an expressive characterization of the non-optimality in implementing an ideal op semiagency, as we have induced from several examples. Moreover, we note that, in order to implement an ideal op semiagent, more non-exact associations can be employed. For example, a substitution and an expansion can be necessary for finding a set of real op semiagents that implement an ideal op semiagent. Therefore, sharing, merging, expansion, and substitution can be composed together for implementing an ideal op semiagency with the availability of the inventory.

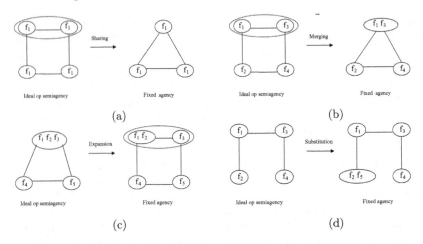

Fig. 2. The sharing associations (a), the merging associations (b), the expansion association (c), and the substitution association (d). Each node of the graphs, namely each op semiagent, is labeled by the corresponding type.

The indexes are integrated in a weighted sum in order to obtain a *metric* that, given an ideal op semiagency and a fixed agency, defines the *distance* between them as:

$$d = w_{sh}I_{sh} + w_m I_m + w_e I_e + w_{su}I_{su}.$$

The weights w permit to consider a type of non-exact association as preferable than another on the basis of the addressed problem. For example, if the functions of ideal op semiagents are such that it is not desirable to split them for the nature of the particular application addressed, then we can give high value (e.g., 100) to w_e and low values (e.g., 1) to other weights. In this way, we penalize fixed agencies that are built by means of expansions and, thus, the best fixed agency (with the minimum distance to the optimum) is likely to be composed without expansion.

Some associations can not be applied in particular problems (for example, it is not possible to split, by expansion, vision and navigation functions of a robotic ideal op semiagent composing an ideal op semiagency for exploring environments). This leads to consider, in some applications, a set of the following constraints on associations.

- *Coexistence constraint* is a couple $(a_I = (N_I, T_I), \{f_1, f_2\})$, where $f_1, f_2 \in T_I$ are the functions that can not be divided among real op semiagents that implement a_I.
- *Incompatibility constraint* is a triple $(a_I = (N_I, T_I), f_1, f_2)$, where $f_1 \in T_I$ and $f_2 \notin T_I$ are the functions that can not be merged in real op semiagents that implement a_I.
- *Non-sharing constraint* is a couple $(a_I = (N_I, T_I), f)$, where $f \in T_I$ is the function that can not be shared by real op semiagents that implement a_I.

We note that, whereas the selection of weights in the metric brings to consider some types of associations better than others, the definition of a constraint forbids the application of some types of associations in implementing an ideal op semiagency.

5   An Algorithm for Recruitment

In this section, we propose a simple algorithm to cope with the problem of matching ideal op semiagency and inventory. The depicted algorithm is based on the metric defined in the previous section.

Given an ideal op semiagency, we can divide the automatic recruitment in two steps: (1) finding all the possible associations for every ideal op semiagent, (2) selecting, for each ideal op semiagent, an association among the possible ones.

To address step (1), we have devised an algorithm derived from those used to solve set covering problems within the synthesis of digital circuits [13]. This algorithm, called *(1) algorithm*, considers the associations of an ideal op semiagent with a set of *essential* real op semiagents, namely with real op semiagents that contribute in an exclusive manner to cover some of the required functions. The (1) algorithm has a complexity that is not polynomial: with m ideal op semiagents and n real op semiagents, we have 2^n combinations to evaluate in order to check if they can be associated to an ideal op semiagent: so the complexity is $O(m2^n)$. However, for each ideal op semiagent we consider only a subset of the real op semiagents of the inventory (excluding, for example, the non-essential ones), so the temporal complexity of (1) algorithm is a sum of m exponential functions, each one with an exponent lesser or equal than n. During the determination of every possible association for an ideal op semiagent, the algorithm avoids to consider the associations that violate coexistence and incompatibility constraints. The third constraint, namely non-sharing constraint, can not be detected at this stage because its violation depends on the entire set of associations selected to realize the fixed agency.

To address step (2), we have devised an heuristic algorithm, called *(2) algorithm*, based on a greedy policy to reach a solution of the recruitment in a polynomial time, even if this solution could be sub-optimal. The (2) algorithm is sketched in the following.

```
FOR every ideal op semiagent a
    IF exists an association between a and real op semiagent a'
            that is not yet associated and with the same type
        THEN associate a to a'
END FOR
FOR every ideal op semiagent a not associated in the
        previous cycle
    select the association for a that produces the minimum
            increment of the distance from ideal op semiagency
```

```
                    considering the fixed agency built so far
END FOR
```

The complexity of (2) algorithm is polynomial ($O(2m)$ with m ideal op semi-agents). It performs two cycles on the ideal op semiagents: firstly, it implements the part of ideal op semiagency that has exact associations with real op semiagents and, secondly, it implements the part that has not exact associations with real op semiagents. In this second cycle, (2) algorithm chooses the associations that are metrically nearer the ideal op semiagency, with respect to the part of fixed agency already built. During the two cycles the (2) algorithm does not share any function that is subject to a non-sharing constraint.

6   Experimental Results and Applications

We have implemented our algorithm in CLIPS [8] and we have compared it to an exhaustive recruitment algorithm that evaluates all the possible fixed agencies suitable to implement an ideal op semiagency and that, thus, always finds the optimal fixed agency. The examples for comparison have been random generated with up to 10 ideal op semiagents and up to 15 real op semiagents in the inventory. Some results are summarized in the following table (we have considered $w_{sh} = 50$, $w_m = 30$, $w_e = 10$, and $w_{su} = 1$).

EXPERIMENT #	EXHAUSTIVE ALGORITHM		OUR ALGORITHM	
	distance	time (s)	distance	time (s)
1	130	10	130	3
2	141	3	141	3
3	50	2	50	1
4	30	4	33	2
5	5	445	15	4
6	202	1	202	1
7	22	55	22	3
8	42	55	42	3
9	44	1710	56	5

Since (2) algorithm is composed of two cycles in which every ideal op semiagent is considered only once, the particular order in which ideal op semiagents are considered influences the result of the algorithm. We have determined that our algorithm reaches the optimal solution when the choice of an association that contributes to a local minimum does not influence the optimality of the choice of other associations. This is always the case except when the selected associations involve useless functions. However, in the tests we have made there is always a particular order of ideal op semiagents with which the optimal solution is detected. Usually, an empirical rule is the following one: if an order of ideal op semiagents leads to a suboptimal solution, then the opposite order leads to the optimal solution.

Finally, we note that our algorithm recruits a, sometimes suboptimal, fixed agency in a very short time. Hence, the natural application areas for the algorithm are highly dynamic, flexible, and variable environments, in which the on-the-fly reconfiguration of a multiagent system addressing a problem and the reuse of the components of a system are required. For example, a Web application that supports the user to buy some items on the Internet by means of "shopping agents" can reconfigure itself, changing the agents on the basis of the exigency expressed by the user (e.g., to buy a book or a music CD). In this case, the application can benefit from the dynamic (i.e., on-line) recruitment of specialized shopping agents on the basis of the user request.

7   Conclusions

In this paper, we have presented an algorithm for composing an agency, namely a multiagent system of distributed artificial intelligence, on the basis of an exigency that the designer expresses in form of an ideal op semiagency. Among the several fixed agencies that can be composed starting from the availability of real op semiagents of the inventory, the algorithm tries to select the one that is nearest to the ideal op semiagency according to the defined metric.

The work illustrated in this paper is one of the few methodological approaches for developing multiagent systems that have been presented in literature. Among them, we deem as significantly related to our work the ones reported in [15, 17]. In particular, in [15], it is promoted the reusability of some design results that had been demonstrated successful. Our contribution goes beyond this conception and emphasizes the reusability of agents and the on-the-fly reconfiguration of a complex multiagent system. The uncoupling of the *roles* of the system from the *interactions* among roles is pointed out as a fundamental feature of the design methodology proposed in [17]. This uncoupling is similar to our division between operation and cooperation, although the proposal of [17] does not emphasize the reuse of agents. This is, from our perspective, an important issue since our final aim is to build a multiagent system starting from existing agents.

To reach this ultimate goal, further research work has to include an enhancement of the two steps of the algorithm in order to reach more frequently the optimal solution without significantly increasing the time complexity. More generally, future research activities will address the automation of the design and construction processes of agencies in order to bring the user of the agency to be also its designer. In fact, in this perspective, the user, by expressing an exigency, stimulates the automated development of an agency that addresses the exigency.

Acknowledgements. The authors are particularly glad to express sincere gratitude to Prof. Marco Somalvico for his guidance in carrying out this work.

References

1. F. Amigoni. *Dynamic Agency: A Methodology and Architecture for Multiagent Systems.* PhD thesis, Politecnico di Milano, Milano, Italy, January 2000.

2. F. Amigoni and M. Somalvico. Dynamic agencies and multi-robot systems. In T. Lueth, R. Dillmann, P. Dario, and H. Wörn, editors, *Proceedings of the Fourth International Symposium on Distributed Autonomous Robotic Systems*, pages 215–224, Karlsruhe, Germany, May 25-27 1998. Springer-Verlag.

3. F. Amigoni and M. Somalvico. Dynamic agencies: Concepts and applications. In *Proceedings of the Sixth Symposium of Italian Association for Artificial Intelligence (AI*IA)*, pages 196–200, Padua, Italy, September 23-25 1998.

4. F. Amigoni, M. Somalvico, and D. Zanisi. A theoretical framework for the conception of agency. *International Journal of Intelligent Systems*, 14(5):449–474, May 1999.

5. F. Amigoni and M. Villa. An algebraic description of agency design. In *Proceedings of the Eleventh European Summer School in Logic, Language and Information (ESSLLI99) Workshop on Foundations and Applications of Collective Agent Based Systems (CABS)*, Utrecht, The Netherlands, August 16-20 1999.

6. A. H. Bond and L. Gasser. *Readings in Distributed Artificial Intelligence*. Morgan Kaufmann, San Mateo, CA, USA, 1988.

7. B. Chaib-Draa, B. Moulin, R. Mandiau, and P. Millot. Trends in distributed artificial intelligence. *Artificial Intelligence Review*, 6:35–66, 1992.

8. CLIPS. http://www.ghg.net/clips/clips.html.

9. M. d'Inverno and M. Luck. Development and application of a formal agent framework. In *Proceedings of the First IEEE International Conference on Formal Engineering Methods*, Hiroshima, Japan, 1997.

10. C. A. Iglesias, M. Garijo, and J. C. González. A survey of agent-oriented methodologies. In *Proceedings of the Workshop on Agent Theories, Architectures and Languages*, Paris, France, July 1998.

11. N. R. Jennings, K. Sycara, and M. Wooldridge. A roadmap of agent research and development. *International Journal of Autonomous Agents and Multi-Agent Systems*, 1(1):7–38, 1998.

12. N. R. Jennings and M. Wooldridge. *Agent Technology: Foundations, Applications and Markets*, chapter Applications of Intelligent Agents, pages 3–28. Springer-Verlag, 1998.

13. G. De Micheli. *Synthesis and Optimization of Digital Circuits*. McGraw-Hill, 1994.

14. M. L. Minsky. *The Society of Mind*. Simon & Schuster, New York, USA, 1985.

15. Y. Tahara, A. Ohsuga, and S. Honiden. Agent system development method based on agent patterns. In *Proceedings of the 1999 International Conference on Software Engineering (ICSE99)*, pages 356–367, Los Angeles, USA, May 16-22 1999. ACM.

16. M. Wooldridge and N. R. Jennings. Pitfalls of agent-oriented development. In *Proceedings of the Second International Conference on Autonomous Agents (Agents-98)*, Minneapolis, USA, 1998.

17. M. Wooldridge, N. R. Jennings, and D. Kinny. A methodology for agent-oriented analysis and design. In *Proceedings of the Third Interantional Conference on Autonomous Agents (Agents-99)*, Seattle, USA, 1999.

Towards a Conceptual Representation of Actions

Antonio Chella[1], Marcello Frixione[2], and Salvatore Gaglio[1]

[1] Dip. di Ingegneria Automatica e Informatica, Univ. of Palermo, Italy
and CERE-CNR, Palermo, Italy
{chella,gaglio}@unipa.it
[2] Dip. di Scienze della Comunicazione, Univ. of Salerno, Italy
frix@dist.unige.it

Abstract. An autonomous robot involved in missions should be able to generate, update and process its own actions. It is not plausible that the meaning of the actions used by the robot is given form the outside of the system itself. Rather, this meaning should be anchored to the world through the perceptual abilities of the robot. We present an approach to conceptual action representation based on a "conceptual" level that acts as an intermediate level between symbols and data coming form sensors. Symbolic representations are interpreted by mapping them on the conceptual level through a mapping mechanism based on artificial neural networks.

1 Introduction

An autonomous robot engaged in complex missions as surveillance in unstructured environments [4], space missions [14], must perform long sequences of actions. The robot needs high-level planning capabilities in order to generate the correct action sequences according to the current task and the environmental context. High-level planning requires the ability of build and process rich inner representations of the environment and of the agents acting in it, included the robot itself and its own actions.

The AI community developed several approaches to the description of actions and the generation of robot plans (Penberthy and Weld [16], Blum and Furst [3], Weld, Anderson and Smith [18]). Although the proposed planners allow for rich and expressive descriptions of actions and tasks, they manage only in a very limited way the problem of linking perception with action. Generally, a typical symbolic planner delegates to some sort of execution module the burden of taking into account the "situatedness" of the robot in the environment (see, e.g., PLANEX [8]).

On the other side, researchers involved in mobile robot architectures developed working robots rich of sensors that effectively "situate" the robot in the environment (see Kortenkamp, Bonasso and Murphy [11] for a review). Although the operations of these robots are impressive, the role of the high-level action planning is generally limited to a search in suitable action graphs.

Our aim is to develop a representation of actions based on a principled integration of the approaches of mobile robot architectures and of symbolic planners.

E. Lamma and P. Mello (Eds.): AI*IA 99, LNAI 1792, pp. 333–344, 2000.

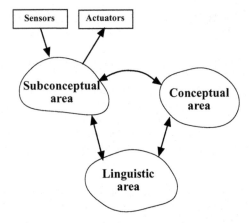

Fig. 1. The three computational areas of the system and the relationships among them.

We assume that this integration requires the introduction of a missing link between these two kinds of approaches. The role of such a link is played by the notion of *conceptual space* (Gärdenfors [10]). Briefly, a conceptual space (CS) is a representation where information is characterized in terms of a metric space defined by a number of *cognitive* dimensions, that are independent from any specific representation language. The CS acts as an intermediate action representation level between "subconceptual" (i.e., reactive) actions, and symbolic actions.

In this perspective, our system is organized in three computational areas (Fig. 1). They must not be interpreted as a hierarchy of levels of higher abstraction; rather, they are concurrent computational components working together on different commitments (Chella, Frixione and Gaglio [5, 6]).

The *subconceptual* area is concerned with the low level processing of perceptual data coming from the robot sensors. The term *subconceptual* suggests that information is not yet organized in terms of conceptual structures and categories. Our subconceptual area includes reactive behavior modules, as a *self-localization* module and a *wandering and obstacle detection* module and some *3D reconstruction* modules. In the *linguistic area*, representation and processing of actions are based on a logic oriented formalism.

The mapping between the conceptual and the linguistic areas plays the role of interpreting linguistic representations on structures in CS, and it is implemented by suitable recurrent neural networks (Frasconi, Gori and Soda [9]).

The proposed system has been implemented on a *Real World Interface* RWI-B12 autonomous robot equipped with an Ethernet radio link and a vision head composed of a pan-tilt in which a CCD video camera is mounted. The robot environment is a laboratory area populated by big white boxes, vases, persons and other obstacles.

2   Conceptual spaces

The theory of conceptual spaces provides a principled way for relating the low level, unstructured, representation of data coming out from the robot sensors with a high level, linguistic formalism. A *conceptual space CS* is a *metric space* whose dimensions are strictly related to the quantities processed in the subconceptual area. By analogy with the term *pixel*, we call *knoxel* a point in *CS*. A knoxel is the epistemological primitive element at the considered level of analysis.

The basic blocks of our representations of robot actions in *CS* are the *superquadrics* [17]. Superquadrics are 3D geometric shapes derived from the quadrics parametric equation with the trigonometric functions raised to two real exponents. The parametric form of a superquadric is:

$$f(\eta, \omega) = \begin{bmatrix} a_x \cos^{\varepsilon_1} \eta \cos^{\varepsilon_2} \omega \\ a_y \cos^{\varepsilon_1} \eta \sin^{\varepsilon_2} \omega \\ a_z \sin^{\varepsilon_1} \eta \end{bmatrix} \tag{1}$$

where $-\pi/2 \leq \eta \leq \pi/2$ and $-\pi \leq \omega < \pi$. The quantities a_x, a_y, a_z are the lengths of the superquadric axes, and the exponents $\varepsilon_1, \varepsilon_2$, are the *form factors*: ε_1 acts in terms of the longitude, and ε_2 in terms of the latitude of the object's surface. A value less than 1 let the superquadric take on a squared form, while a value near 1 let the superquadric take on a rounded form. Eq. (1) describes a superquadric in canonical form; to describe a superquadric in general position in the 3D space, three center coordinates p_x, p_y, p_z and three orientation parameters φ, ϑ, ψ should also be considered. So, a generic superquadric **m** is represented as a vector in $\mathbb{R}^{11}$ space: $\mathbf{m} = \begin{bmatrix} a_x a_y a_z \varepsilon_1 \varepsilon_2 p_x p_y p_z \varphi \vartheta \psi \end{bmatrix}^T$.

An example of 3D reconstruction of robot scenes in terms of superquadrics is shown in Fig. 2 in which our robot is in front of a box.

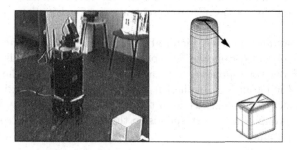

Fig. 2. An example of 3D reconstruction by means of superquadrics.

To take into account the dynamic aspects of robot actions, e.g., when the robot moves towards the box, we need a conceptual space *CS* in which each point represents a whole *simple motion* of a superquadric. In this sense, the space is *intrinsically dynamic* since the generic motion of an object is represented in its wholeness, rather than as a sequence of single, static frames.

The decision of which kind of motion can be considered *simple* is not straightforward, and it is strictly related to the problem of motion segmentation. Marr and Vaina [13] adopt the term *motion segment* to indicate simple movements. According to their *State-Motion-State* schema, a *simple motion* consists of the motion interval between two subsequent (eventually instantaneous) rest states. We generalize this schema by considering a *simple motion* as a motion interval between two subsequent generic discontinuities in the motion parameters.

Let us call $\mathbf{m}(t)$ a function associated to a generic superquadric, that gives the vector of the geometric parameters of the superquadric during a *simple motion*: $\mathbf{m}(t) = \left[a_x(t) a_y(t) a_z(t) \varepsilon_1(t) \varepsilon_2(t) p_x(t) p_y(t) p_z(t) \varphi(t) \vartheta(t) \psi(t) \right]^T$. It should be noted that, in this way, also changes in shape and size of the superquadrics can be taken into account.

If we represent a moving superquadrics in $\mathbb{R}^{11}$ space described above, we obtain a set of points corresponding to subsequent instants of time (the sample values of the function $\mathbf{m}(t)$). This solution is not satisfactory because it does not capture the motion in its wholeness. A possible alternative is suggested by the well known *Discrete Fourier Transform* (*DFT*) [15]. Given a generic parameter of a superquadric, e.g. a_x, consider the function $a_x(t)$, that, for each instant t, returns the corresponding value of a_x. $a_x(t)$ can be seen as a superimposition of a discrete number of trigonometric functions. This allows the representation of the function $a_x(t)$ in a discrete functional space, whose basis functions are trigonometric functions.

By a suitable composition of the time functions of all superquadric parameters, the overall function $\mathbf{m}(t)$ may be represented in its turn in a discrete functional space. This resulting functional space can be adopted as our dynamic conceptual space for the representation of simple motions.

The CS can be taught as an "explosion" of the $\mathbb{R}^{11}$ space in which each main axis is split in a number of new axes, each one corresponding to a harmonic component. A point in the CS represent a superquadric along with its own *simple motion*.

Fig. 3 shows an evocative, pictorial representation of the conceptual space CS. It can be obtained from the $\mathbb{R}^{11}$ space, by exploding each axis into a set of new axes each one corresponding to a harmonic of the motion of the corresponding superquadric parameter. In the left part of the figure, each axis correspond to a superquadric parameter, while in the right part of the figure, representing the CS, each group of axes corresponds to the harmonics of the corresponding superquadric parameter.

3   Situations and actions in conceptual spaces

3.1   Situations

As said before, a *simple motion* of a superquadric corresponds to a knoxel in CS. Let us now consider a scene made up by several moving objects, along with the

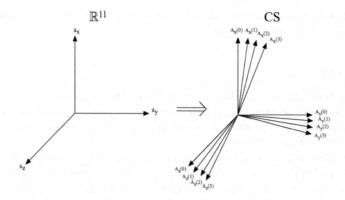

Fig. 3. An evocative, pictorial representation of the conceptual space.

robot itself. Each object may be approximable by one or more superquadrics; e.g., the robot that moves towards the white block as in Fig. 2. We denote this kind of scene a *Situation*; it may be represented in CS by the set of knoxels corresponding to the *simple motions* of its components (see Fig. 4, where $\mathbf{k}_a$ represents the white box and $\mathbf{k}_b$ represents the robot moving towards the box).

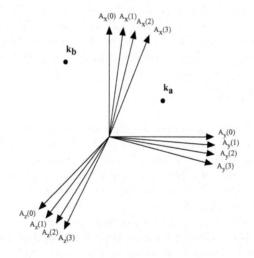

Fig. 4. An evocative picture of the *Situation* of Fig. 2 in CS.

It should be noted that, on the one side, a situation represented in CS may be *perceived* by the robot, i.e., it may correspond to the actual arrangement of the external world as far as it is accessible to the robot itself. On the other side, a situation in CS may be *imagined* by the robot. For example, it may be a *goal* of the robot, or it may correspond to a dangerous state of affairs, that the robot must figure out in order to avoid it.

3.2   Actions

In a *Situation*, the motions in the scene occur simultaneously, i.e. they correspond to a single configuration of knoxels in the conceptual space. To consider a composition of several motions arranged according to a temporal sequence, we introduce the notion of *Action* (Allen [1]).

An *Action* corresponds to a "scattering" from one *Situation* to another *Situation* of knoxels in the conceptual space. We assume that the situations within an action are separated by instantaneous events. In the transition between two subsequent configurations, a "scattering" of at least one knoxel occurs. This corresponds to a discontinuity in time that is associated to an instantaneous event (Marr and Vaina [13]). It should be noted that in this respect, the proposed description of *Action* is strictly anchored to the robot perception, because it is described as a change in the scene perceived by the robot.

The robot may perceive an *Action* passively when it sees some changes in the perceived scene, e.g., a person in the robot environment changing his/her position. More important, the robot may be the *actor* of the action itself, when it moves or when it interacts with the environment, e.g., when it push an object. In all the cases, an action is a scattering from a perceived *Situation* to another.

Fig. 5 shows a simple *Action* performed by the robot. In the figure, the robot goes towards the white box (a), it turns right and it moves (b), then and it turns left in order to to avoid the obstacle (c). This *Action* may be represented in CS (Fig. 6) as a double scattering of the knoxel $\mathbf{k}_b$ representing the robot.

4   Linguistic area

The representation of actions in the linguistic area is based on a high level, logic oriented formalism. In particular, we adopted a hybrid formalism in the KL-ONE tradition (see Donini, Lenzerini, Nardi and Schaerf [7]). In the domain of robot actions, the terminological component contains the description of relevant concepts such as situation, action, time instant, and so on. The assertional component stores the assertions describing specific perceived situations and actions.

Fig. 7 shows a fragment of the terminological knowledge base. In the upper part of the figure is represented some highly general concept. In the lower part, the *Avoid* concept is sketched, as an example of the description of an action in the terminological KB.

Intuitively, a *Situation* is an arrangement of moving objects simultaneously occurring in the CS; in a *Situation* no scattering of knoxels occurs. Every *Situation* is related to *Time_instant* by the roles *start* and *end*, in the sense that a situation has a starting instant and an ending instant. A *Robot* is a moving object occurring in a generic situation. An *Action* involves a temporal evolution (a scattering in CS); it also has a *start* instant and a *end* instant. An *Action*

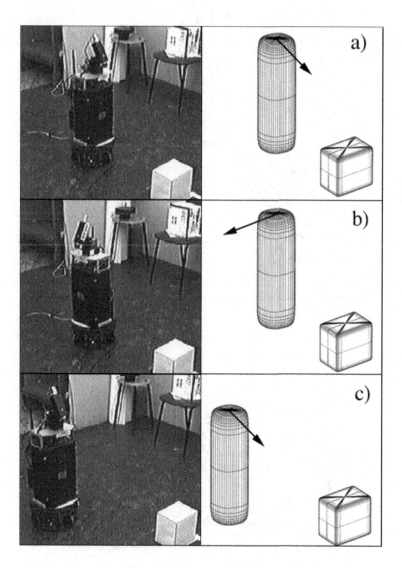

Fig. 5. An example of *Action*.

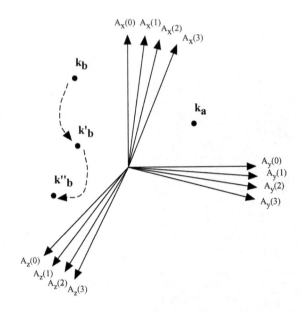

Fig. 6. An evocative picture of the *Action* of Fig. 5 in *CS*.

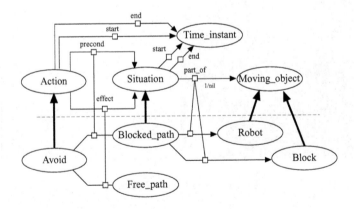

Fig. 7. A fragment of the terminological KB.

has at least two parts that are *Situation* not occurring at the same time: the *precond* (the preconditions) and the *effect* of the action itself.

An example of *Action* is *Avoid*. According to the KB reported in the figure, the precondition of *Avoid* is a *Blocked_path* situation, whose parts are the moving robot and a blocking object. The effect of the *Avoid* action is a *Free_path* situation.

It should be noted that the temporal relations between situations are not explicitly represented in the terminology. The formalism could be easily extended with temporal operators; these extensions have been proposed and deeply studied in the literature (see Artale and Franconi [2]). However, we do not face these aspects. In the following section, we will show how it is possible to deal with many aspects of temporal ordering by means of the mechanism of mapping between the conceptual and the linguistic area.

The *assertional component* contains facts expressed as assertions in a predicative language, in which the concepts of the terminological components correspond to one argument predicates, and the roles (e.g. *precond*, *part_of*) correspond to two argument relations. For example, the following predicates describe that the instance av1 of the *Action* Avoid has as a precondition the instance bl1 of the *Situation* Blocked_path and it has as an effect the *Situation* Free_path:

```
Avoid(av1)
precond(av1,bl1)
effect(av1,fr1)

Blocked_path(bl1)
Free_path(fr1)
```

---

5 Mapping between conceptual and linguistic areas

The mapping between the symbolic representation of actions in the linguistic area and structures in the conceptual space is based on a suitable sequential mechanism of expectations.

The recognition of a certain component of a *Situation* (a knoxel in CS) will elicit the expectation of other related simultaneous components of the same *Situation* in the scene. In this case, the mechanism seeks for the corresponding knoxels in the current CS configuration. For example, when the system recognizes that a knoxel is a moving robot, it generates, among others, the expectation for another knoxel representing, e.g., a box in front of the moving robot. In this way the system recognizes an instance of the *Blocked_path* situation. We call this type of expectation *synchronic* because it refers to a single situation in CS.

The recognition of a certain situation in CS could also elicit the expectation of a scattering in the arrangement of the knoxels in the scene; i.e., the mechanism generates the expectations for another *Situation* in a subsequent CS configuration. We call this expectation *diachronic*, in the sense that it involves subsequent configurations of CS. From the point of view of the description of actions, the role of the *diachronic* expectation is to express the link between a *Situation* perceived as the precondition of an *Action*, and the corresponding *Situation* expected as the effects of the action itself. Therefore, the *diachronic* expectation generates the expected situation resulting as the effect of an action. Continuing the previous example, when the robot recognizes the instance of the *Blocked_path* situation, it generates the expectations for the *Free_path* situation as the *effect* of the *Avoid* action.

We take into account two main sources of expectations. On the one side, expectations could be generated on the basis of the structural information stored in the symbolic knowledge base, as in previous example of the action *Avoid*. We call *linguistic* these expectations. As soon as a *Situation* is recognized and the situation is the *precond* of an *Action*, the symbolic description elicit the expectation of the *effect* situation.

On the other side, expectations could also be generated by purely associative, Hebbian mechanism between situations. Suppose that the robot has learnt that when it sees a person with the arm pointing on the right, it must turn on the right. The system could learn to associate these situations and to perform the related action. We call *associative* these expectations.

In the present model, the mapping between the conceptual space and the linguistic area is implemented by means of recurrent neural networks. In particular, each concept C in the linguistic area is associated with a suitable recurrent neural network which acts as a "predictive filter" on the sequences of knoxels corresponding to C. In particular, we have adopted multi layered neural networks with local feedback in the hidden units (Frasconi, Gori and Soda [9]).

6   Planning in conceptual spaces

The proposed framework for the description of robot actions may be adopted to allow the robot to choose its own sequence of actions. Let us suppose that the robot has recognized the current situation p, e.g., it is in front of a box; let us also suppose that the robot also knows its "goal" situation g, e.g., to be in a certain position with a certain orientation. Then, the system allows for the generation of all the expected situations $\{e_1, e_2, \dots, \}$ both from the *linguistic* and from the *associative* modalities previously described. All these expected situations are the *effects* related with the possible robot actions $\{a_1, a_2, \dots, \}$ which are compatible with the current situation p.

The robot may choose an action a_i among these possible actions $\{a_1, a_2, \dots, \}$ according to some criteria; e.g., the action whose expected effect situation e_i has the minimum euclidean distance in CS with the "goal" situation g. After having chosen the action a_i, e.g., to avoid the blocking box, the robot can effectively act; then it may update its current situation p according to the new perceptions, and it may restart the mechanism of generation of the expectations.

The *linguistic* expectations are at the basis of the process of the generations of deliberative robot plans, in the sense that the generation of the expectations of the effect situations is driven by the linguistic description of the actions in the linguistic KB. This mechanism is similar to the mechanism of action selection in deliberative forward planners. The *associative* expectations are instead at the basis of the process of reactive robot planning, in the sense that a perceived situation reactively associates the expected effect situation.

The described process of action selections allows the robot to be effectively "situated" in the environment, and at the same time, it allows to have its goals, in the sense of Maes [12]. As a matter of fact, in the proposed action selection schema, the symbols of the robot are always firmly grounded in the robot perceptions.

7   Conclusions

We presented a framework for description of *Situations* and *Actions* at an intermediate "conceptual" level between the subconceptual and the linguistic ones. The main advantage of this framework is to suitably ground the symbols of the robot, needed for reasoning about its own actions and for planning the new actions, to the robot perceptions.

Currently, we are extending the proposed framework to define suitable plans in a multirobot environment. In this case, the knoxels in CS are generated through suitable processes of information fusion of the perceptions of the team of robots. Also the *Situations* and *Actions* must be referred to the whole robot team, which may be considered as a single "autonomous entity" with its own perceptions, actions and a suitable common and shared conceptual space.

Acknowledgements

Authors would like to thank Donatella Guarino, Giuseppe Sajeva and Ignazio Infantino. This work has been partially supported by MURST "Progetto Cofinanziato CERTAMEN".

References

1. J.F. Allen. Towards a general theory of action and time. *Artif. Intell.*, 23(2):123–154, 1984.
2. A. Artale and E. Franconi. A temporal description logic for reasoning about actions and plans. *Journal of Artif. Intel. Research*, 9:463–506, 1998.
3. A. Blum and M. Furst. Fast planning through planning graph analysis. *Artif. Intell.*, 90(1-2):281–300, 1997.
4. H. Buxton and S. Gong. Visual surveillance in a dynamic and uncertain world. *Artif. Intell.*, 78:371–405, 1995.

5. A. Chella, M. Frixione, and S. Gaglio. A cognitive architecture for artificial vision. *Artif. Intell.*, 89:73–111, 1997.

6. A. Chella, M. Frixione, and S. Gaglio. An architecture for autonomous agents exploiting conceptual representations. *Robotics and Autonomous Systems*, 25(3-4):231–240, 1998.

7. F.M. Donini, M. Lenzerini, D. Nardi, and A. Schaerf. Reasoning in description logics. In G. Brewka, editor, *Principles of Knowledge Representation*. CSLI Publication, 1996.

8. R.E. Fikes, P.E. Hart, and N.J. Nilsson. Learning and executing generalized robot plans. *Artif. Intell.*, 3(4):251–288, 1972.

9. P. Frasconi, M. Gori, and G. Soda. Local feedback multilayered networks. *Neural Computation*, 4(1):120–130, 1992.

10. P. Gärdenfors. *Conceptual Spaces*. Lund University Cognitive Science, 1998.

11. D. Kortenkamp, R.P. Bonasso, and R. Murphy, editors. *Artificial Intelligence and Mobile Robots - Case Studies of Successful Robot System*. AAAI Press/MIT Press, 1998.

12. P. Maes. Designing autonomous agents. *Robotics and Autonom. Systems*, 6:1–2, 1990.

13. D. Marr and L. Vaina. Representation and recognition of the movements of shapes. *Proc. R. Soc. Lond. B*, 214:501–524, 1982.

14. N. Muscettola, P.P. Nayak, B. Pell, and B.C. Williams. Remote Agents: to boldly go where no AI system has gone before. *Artif. Intell.*, 103(1-2):5–47, 1998.

15. A.V. Oppenheim and R.W. Shafer. *Discrete-Time Signal Processing*. Prentice Hall, Inc., Englewood Cliffs, N.J., 1989.

16. J.S. Penberthy and D.S. Weld. UCPOP: a sound, complete, partial order planner for ADL. In *Proceedings of KR-92*, pages 103–114, 1992.

17. A.P. Pentland. Perceptual organization and the representation of natural form. *Artif. Intell.*, 28:293–331, 1986.

18. D. Weld, C. Anderson, and D. Smith. Extending Graphplan to handle uncertainty and sensing actions. In *Proc. of 16th AAAI*, 1998.

Cellular Automata based Inverse Perspective Transform as a Tool for Indoor Robot Navigation

Giovanni Adorni, Stefano Cagnoni and Monica Mordonini

Department of Computer Engineering, University of Parma, Italy

Abstract. In this paper we describe a system for perspective-effect removal using the cellular automata paradigm.
The system has been developed as a tool to be included in the vision system of an autonomous robot designed to operate in indoor environments. The navigation of such a robot is guided by traffic signs by means of a neural-network based system. By using such a tool as part of the vision system, it is possible to instruct the neural networks with a training set including only frontal views of the signs, thus simplifying training and making it computationally much lighter. Furthermore, using a low-cost massively parallel architecture implementing the cellular automata paradigm, makes the algorithm much more computationally efficient with respect to sequential implementations, thus making it possible for the robot to perform *just-in-time* operations.

1 Introduction

Most objects we see are not located directly in front of us. What we perceive is an object representation that is distorted by perspective effects with respect to the more natural (usually frontal) view from which we tend to represent objects in our mind. Therefore, the recognition of an object requires that the recovery of such a view be implicitly performed. Similarly, in several cases of robotic vision, the task of recognizing complex landmarks, signs, and other reference objects can be made easier by incorporating a module that recovers a canonical view of objects, eliminating perspective distortions. Using machine learning techniques such as neural networks, training the system only on canonical views of the objects to be detected can lead to better results, besides being much more computationally efficient. In this paper we describe a system for perspective-effect removal, which relies on the cellular automata paradigm [1].
The system was developed as a tool to be included in the vision system of an autonomous robot designed to operate in indoor environments, where objects are most likely to be observed from viewpoints characterized by very small incidence angles. A major requirement in developing the vision system for an autonomous robot is to make it possible for the robot to operate *just-in-time*. This means that the robot must be able to make its decisions (e.g., about the path to be followed or about the operation to be performed), based on the output of the

E. Lamma and P. Mello (Eds.): AI*IA 99, LNAI 1792, pp. 345–355, 2000.

vision system, in right time to anticipate the possible occurrence of hazardous conditions for itself or for the other agents (robots or humans) that are operating in the same environment. Therefore, the vision system must operate as close as possible to real-time. Here it is very useful to rely on low-cost special-purpose architectures that implement some massively-parallel computation paradigm, in order to dramatically reduce the computational complexity of vision algorithms with respect to their sequential implementations.

2   Scene Reconstruction

The Inverse Perspective Transform (IPT) is the process by which an acquired image is transformed to reduce the perspective effects and to make it appear as if it were observed from a preset (frontal) point of view. As the transformation of each pixel is space-dependent, this transform is a non-uniform operation on the image (see, for example, [2, 3]). Using a single camera, it is impossible to obtain

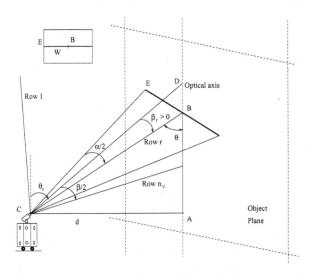

Fig. 1. Computation of the incidence angle.

a full three-dimensional description of a scene, so the inverse transform can be applied only to some known planes: in this case the internal camera system parameters, the angles of pan and tilt, and the distance between the object plane and the camera must be known. Moreover we consider the CCD camera aperture angle to be smaller than $80°$, so that we can suppose the surface of projection is ellipsoidal without the introduction of further distortions in addition to the noise introduced by the digitization process. On the basis of these hypotheses, the vertical and horizontal apertures of the camera can be considered constant over the whole image surface. So, with reference to Figure 1, we can say that the incidence angle (θ_r) for each ray traced between the projection center and each image pixel is given by the algebraic sum of the angles of tilt (θ) and view (β_r) for the central pixel of the same row. That is:

$$\theta_r = (\frac{r-1}{n_v - 1}2\beta - \beta + \theta) \tag{1}$$

where: r is the index of the row, n_v is the vertical resolution of the digitized image, β is the vertical aperture of the camera. Figure 1 shows an example in which $\beta_r > 0$.

The system implementing the IPT is a two-step process (see Figure 2). In the first step rows are rescaled to their actual size by stretching them according to their incidence angle and a *stretched* image is created. In the second step, the algorithm performs the reconstruction of the scene through a reproduction of the *stretched* image rows and produces the output image.

For the scene reconstruction to be of practical use, in the output image a horizontal distance l must represent the same actual length, in cm, as an equal vertical distance, independently of the position in the image where this distance is measured. This corresponds to having the camera axis orthogonal to the image plane. The sizes (in pixels) of the output image are functions of the distance (in cm) represented by its height and of the actual distance, expressed in cm, between two adjacent pixels. In the first step, each row of the original image has to be scaled by a coefficient m.

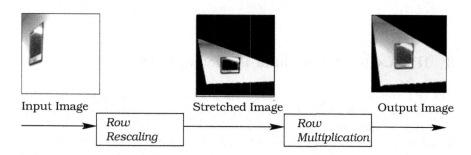

| Input Image | Stretched Image | Output Image |

Row Rescaling → Row Multiplication →

Fig. 2. The two steps of the proposed algorithm.

With reference to Figure 1 we derive m as follows. The length W is a given parameter: the multiplication coefficient m is the actual length divided by W. If the roll angle is zero, the actual length is twice the distance $\overline{EB}$. The angles $\widehat{CBE}$ and $\widehat{CAB}$ are right angles and we can write: $\overline{EB} = \overline{CB}\tan\frac{\alpha}{2}$ and $\overline{CB} = \frac{EB}{\cos\theta_r}$; so $\overline{EB} = \frac{d}{\tan\theta_r}$. Therefore: $\overline{EB} = \frac{d}{\sin\theta_r}\tan\frac{\alpha}{2}$ and $m = \frac{2EB}{W} = \frac{2d\tan\frac{\alpha}{2}}{W\sin\theta_r}$. By replacing θ_r using (1) we obtain:

$$m = \frac{2d\,\text{tg}\,\frac{\alpha}{2}}{W\sin\left(\frac{r-1}{n_v-1}2\beta - \beta + \theta\right)} \tag{2}$$

where: d is the distance between the camera and the plane of projection, r is the index of the row, n_v is the vertical resolution of the digitized image, α and β are the horizontal and vertical aperture angles of the camera, θ is the view angle and W is the width (in cm) of the field of view of the new image.

Once the horizontal zoom is completed, it is necessary to reconstruct the correct proportion also in the vertical dimension. Because the actual distance between two adjacent pixels in height must be the same as between two adjacent pixels in width, the new image becomes $\frac{n_v}{step}$ pixels high, where n_v corresponds to the actual length in cm, of the transformed image height and $step$ is the distance in centimeters between two adjacent pixels. To carry out the vertical reconstruction for each row of the output image we have to choose the row belonging to the *stretched* image that better represents it, and then copy it in the output image. The index a of the *stretched* row that represents the row r of the output image is:

$$a = \frac{\beta_r}{n_v} + \frac{n_v}{2} = \left(\arctan \left(\frac{d}{(n_h - r + 1)step} \right) - \theta \right) \frac{n_v}{\beta} + \frac{n_v}{2} \tag{3}$$

where n_h is the horizontal resolution of digitized image. We obtain the given formula with reference to Figure 1. The angle between the line r and the object plane can be computed using the parameters n_v and $step$:

$$\gamma = \arctan \left(\frac{d}{\frac{d}{\arctan(90-\theta-\frac{\beta}{2})} + (N_v - r + 1)step} \right)$$

Therefore: $\beta_r = \gamma - \theta$.

3   IPT Cellular-Automata Implementation

The IPT can be seen as a reorganization filter for the image pixels, in which pixel displacements are chosen according to the inverse perspective law. In this algorithm we developed the idea of decomposing the motion of each pixel into its horizontal and vertical components and separating the vertical and the horizontal shifts. If we pre-compute the movements that each pixel has to perform to reconstruct the image it is possible to treat the pixel as an independent unit. A cellular automata that performs the perspective effect removal in this way is easy to implement: by the decomposition of pixel motion vectors into horizontal and vertical components the only operations required from the automaton are a horizontal and a vertical shift for each pixel. This also reduces the computation cost of the algorithm because it performs the perspective effect removal by means of two shift operation for each pixel and the shift operation is the most elementary and efficient operation made by a calculator.

Uniform cellular automata (CAs) are discrete dynamical system whose behavior is completely specified in terms of a local relation [1]. A cellular automaton can be thought of as a uniform grid of cells, each of which contains a few bits of data; time advances in discrete steps and there is a single rule (that can be encoded in a small look-up table) through which, at each time step, each cell computes its new state from that of its closest neighbors. Thus, the system laws are local and uniform. In the non-uniform cellular automata paradigm, the property of locality is preserved, but each cell computes a different state-transition function, thus allowing complex and specialized behaviours to be associated with different regions of the grid.

By means of the IPT each image pixel is shifted on the same row to which it belongs. When the values of all pixel shifts are known we can treat each pixel as an independent unit. Therefore, a cellular automata implementation of the IPT can be obtained by associating each image pixel to a cell (of the cellular automaton). The shift value for each pixel can be computed when the camera parameters are known and the set of values can be stored into a *shift matrix* or *shift pattern*. If one wants to change the distance d between the object plane and the camera and/or the incidence angle θ, a different shift matrix has to be computed for each combination of d and θ. It is worth noting that the reconstructed images for two distinct distance values with the same angle of incidence differ only in scale, so only the angle of incidence is needed to obtain a correct scene recovery.

The incidence angle has a range between $0°$ and $180°$ unless application-dependent constraints exist. Within this range, we can select a limited number of incidence angles, store them and their shift matrices in a set of look-up-tables associated to a certain incidence angle range centered around a reference value, and use the matrix corresponding to the selected reference value for each value of incidence. The total number of angles that can be selected depends on the memory available to store the shift matrices, while their values are chosen so that the approximation errors in the pixel shifts are less than a preset value ε for every angle approximation over the whole range of incidence.

To increment the computational efficiency of our algorithm we used the CAM-8 [4], a low-cost architecture for the simulation of uniform cellular automata. Physically, the CAM-8 is a three-dimensional mesh of modules operating in lockstep on pipelined data. In brief, the CAM-8 maps a n-dimensional space $(n >= 1)$ onto a grid of evenly spaced cells. Each cell holds a 16-bit word which represents the cell status. The evolution of the system is computed at discrete time steps; at each new time step the state of each cell is univocally determined by the cell status at the previous step. The status is a 16-bit word, which may be composed by collecting bits from the cell itself and from any other cell in the space.

Because the CAM-8 relies on a uniform-CA model and scene reconstruction is a non-uniform operation on the image, the full transformation has to be carried out in several steps. As all cells have to perform the same computation for each step, only one shift can be applied to all pixels or to a part of them at one time. For each pixel, its total shift size is decomposed into one or more partial shifts. In each time step only the pixels that have to be shifted by the quantity under consideration are selected. At the end of the application of all shifts, all pixels will have been translated by the correct amount. To implement the algorithm on the CAM-8 architecture we consider the values of the *shift matrix* as a sum of powers of 2: if the image resolution is $n \times n$ (with $n = 2^k$) we consider shift values $\frac{n}{8}, \frac{n}{16}, \cdots 2, 1$ and combine them to obtain every shift value up to $\frac{n-1}{4}$. So the shift matrix is divided into ($\log_2 n - 2$) matrices representing the pixels that have to be translated by a certain quantity. Each of them is used during a single step of the CAM-8 in which an identical operation (shift) is applied to each selected pixel, according to the uniform cellular automata paradigm. This provides an algorithm with low computational cost, as its complexity is $\Theta(\log_2 n)$.

4   Testing the System

The proposed technique has been tested and compared with two other approaches to the same problem. The experiments on the CAM-8 demonstrated that the algorithm can perform an image reorganization in 0.02 s for a 512×512 pixel image.

The comparison has been made both in terms of temporal complexity and in terms of quality performance. The first algorithm we have considered is based on

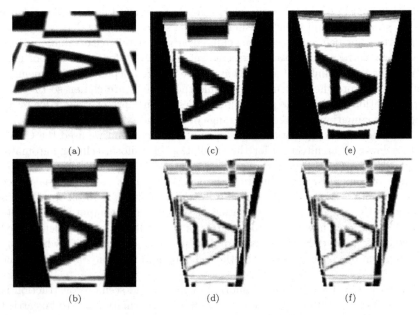

Fig. 3. Comparison between different image recovery techniques: a) original image, b) output of the method based on homogeneous coordinates, c) output of the IPT-based system, d) difference between the images shown in a) and c), e) output of IPM, f) difference between the images shown in a) and e).

the homogeneous coordinate system and acts as the inverse transform process of the projection of a scene onto a plane [5]. It represents the classical approach to the problem and it can be taken as the reference approach. This method returns the exact object plane representation (except for the scale factor) if the camera calibration parameters and the angle of pan and tilt are known. As its serial implementation provides a complexity of $\Theta(n^2)$ and, moreover, it is often impossible to obtain an accurate knowledge of all parameters, some approximated approaches to the problem are described in the literature in order to implement this task on special hardware and obtain real-time perspective effect removal. We have compared our algorithm with the *Inverse Perspective Mapping Transform* (IPM), proposed in [6], which is suitable to be used on a SIMD architecture with a temporal complexity of $\Theta(n)$. This method is used to recover road images acquired from a pair of cameras placed on a moving car. This application is characterized by very small values of the angle formed by a line parallel to the road plane and the optical axis of the camera, that is $h << \overline{DB}$. This condition allows IPM to consider the camera point of view as coincident with its projection D on the road and obtain a good performance on flat road images, but limits the flexibility of the algorithm, which can not therefore be considered as general-purpose.

Figure 3 shows a qualitative comparison of the three algorithm considered, where the original image has a resolution of 256×256 pixels, acquired with an incidence angle of about $45°$ at a height of about 2m. Looking at Figure 3, we can observe that the quality of the result obtained with the cellular approach and with the homogeneous-coordinate method is quite similar. In particular, such algorithms reconstruct correctly the right angles of the square-shape object and preserve lines straight along both the horizontal and the vertical dimensions. On the the other hand, in Figure 3.f the effects of the approximations made in the IPM algorithm are clearly visible. The horizontal lines are reconstructed as arcs of circumferences and the angles of the square-shaped object are only approximately $90°$ in the reconstructed scene. This happens because in this application it is impossible to consider the camera position to be coincident with its projection on the object plane.

In Figure 4 a comparison among the algorithms in term of temporal complexity is shown. We can see that the cellular approach permits a large decrement of the computation cost with respect to both the traditional approach and to IPM on a SIMD architecture. Moreover, using a non-uniform CA, the cellular approach to the removal of the perspective effect could be mapped onto a single lookup table, as the transformation derives from a space-dependent formula that computes the translation by which each pixel must be moved. In this case, the limitations imposed by the CAM-8 are on the width of the neighborhood, which must be at least as wide as the maximum translation to be performed. Without such limitations, the algorithm could have a complexity of $\Theta(1)$ (a single CA step would be sufficient to perform the computation).

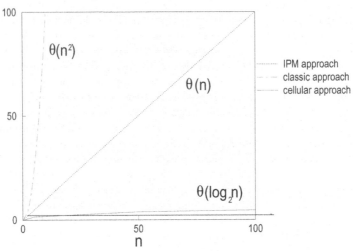

Fig. 4. Temporal complexity of different image reconstruction techniques.

5   IPT as a Tool for Robot Navigation

The previously-described technique can be integrated into the vision system of an autonomous robot designed to operate in indoor environments, to improve its global performance. The robot is able to navigate in partially-structured environments through its perceptive capability to recognize a grammar of (traffic) signs [7]. The sign interpretation is carried out by a neural network system that, in sequence, recognizes the external shape of the sign and the internal symbol. The neural networks have been trained on an appropriate set of marker shapes and internal symbols, obtained through the digitization of real images acquired by the robot CCD camera. The examples in the training set have been chosen so as to include most of the geometrical distortions due to small angles of pan and tilt. The system provides a correct recognition of the whole sign with an accuracy of over 98% when the camera pan and tilt angles are less than 30°, but the systems performance quickly decreases if the the perspective distortion effects are greater. The application of the perspective removal algorithm allows neural network training on frontal views only, thus providing the same confidence level for sign recognition by the same neural network, even where signs are observed by the robot system with angles of pan and tilt up to $60 - 65°$. If the angles are greater than $60 - 65°$, in most images acquired at low resolution the internal symbol becomes connected to the external shape and this does not permit the recognition of the sign.

The perspective-effect removal tool could be used both in navigation tasks and auto-localization tasks. Figure 5 shows a case of navigation guided by lines and signs placed on the floor. In this task all camera parameters are known and remain constant during the navigation. The application of the perspective filter lowers the computational burden of line detection and decreases the possibility of an erroneous match of a sign. In the case of self-localization we put alphanu-

(a)   (b)   (c)

Fig. 5. Example of robot navigation guided by signs.

meric markers on walls, doors, etc. of indoor environments. When given a map of the location of markers, the robot is able to estimate its position from the information extracted through the perceived images. Marker distances and angular displacements make it possible to compute a position-uncertainty region for the mobile robot. In this case the external camera parameters are not constant: the angles of pan and tilt and the distance between the robot and the sign have to be computed by integrating information from other sensors, for example sonars. Even if the computed parameters are affected by errors, the use of neural networks provides a good confidence level for the recognition of partially distorted signs as shown in Table 1.

Experimental results demonstrated that localization is performed with an average position accuracy of within a few centimeters even using visual, common, human-readable markers.

distance error (cm) between object plane and camera	*incidence angle (degree)*	*confidence level (%)*
± 20	± 15-20	98
± 100-150	± 4-5	98

Table 1. Confidence level recognition for different distance errors and incidence angles.

The same approach can be used to detect the free space for robot navigation. By means of a calibrated binocular system we can acquire pairs of frames of the scene in front of the robot during its navigation in an unknown environment. Reconstructing the scenes (left and right) with respect to the floor (used as the reference plane), we obtain pairs of images where all objects on the floor are distorted. We can consider such objects as hypotheses of obstacles and then (if the system is calibrated), by simply computing the difference between the left and right reconstructed frames of each sequence, we can estimate the obstacle-free area: the free space.

Figure 6 shows an example of use of such an approach using a binocular system where two cameras are put on a robot looking in front of itself with the two camera optical axes intersecting with an angle of 170°. Figure 6.a is a left camera frame acquired by a robot during navigation in an indoor environment, while Figure 6.b is the same frame as seen by the right camera.

Figures 6.c and 6.d show the inverse perspective transformations of the two frames with respect to a reference plane, which is the floor of the environment. As a consequence of this transformation every object which is not on the floor is distorted. Figure 6.e shows the difference between the left frame and the right frame with, superimposed in gray, the estimated free space.

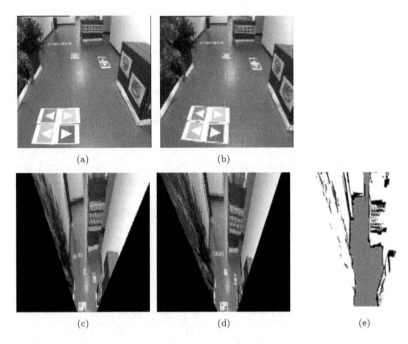

Fig. 6. Example of free space computation: a) a frame of an image sequence acquired by the left camera; b) the same frame acquired by the right camera; c), d) IPT of a) and b) with respect to the floor plane; e) the difference image between c) and d) with the free space superimposed in gray.

6   Conclusions

This paper presented a system for perspective-effect removal based on the cellular automata paradigm. The algorithm was developed as a tool to be included in the vision system of an autonomous robot designed to operate in indoor environments, where objects are most likely to be observed from viewpoints characterized by very small incidence angles. The main goals for which the algorithm was developed are: (i) to allow *just-in-time* robot operation, (ii) to achieve good quality of the reconstructed images, (iii) to make it possible to train the visual system of the robot only on canonical views of the objects that it has to recognize.

The experimental results seem to satisfy the above goals. When compared with the standard approach, the proposed algorithm exhibits a similar quality (in particular it preserves the geometric properties of the objects in the scene) and, in its CAM-8 implementation, it makes it possible to dramatically reduce the temporal complexity (from $\Theta(n^2)$ to $\Theta(\log_2 n)$).

Acknowledgments

This work is partially supported by the Italian "Ministero dell'Università e della Ricerca Scientifica e Tecnologica" under grant MURST 40% "CERTAMEN".

References

1. S. Wolfram, *Theory and Applications of Cellular Automata*, World Scientific Publ. Co, Singapore, 1986.
2. R. Y. Tsai, "A versatile camera calibration technique for high-accuracy 3D machine vision metrology using off-the-shelf TV cameras and lenses", *IEEE Journal of Robotics and Automation*, vol. 3, no. 4, 1987.
3. R. M. Haralick, "Monocular vision using inverse perspective projection geometry: Analytic relations", in *Proc. of CVPR*, 1989.
4. N. Margolus, "CAM-8: a computer architecture based on cellular automata", in *Pattern Formation and Lattice-Gas Automata*. American Mathematical Society, 1994.
5. A. Van Dam J. Foley, S. Feiner, and J. Hughes, *Computer Graphics: Principles and Practice*, Addison-Wesley, Reading, MA, 1995.
6. M. Bertozzi and A. Broggi, "Vision-based Vehicle Guidance", *IEEE Computer*, vol. 30, no. 7, 1997.
7. G. Adorni, M. Gori, and M. Mordonini, "Just-in-Time Sign Recognition in Image Sequences", *Journal of Real-Time Imaging*, , no. 5, pp. 95–107, 1999.

On Plan Adaptation through Planning Graph Analysis

Alfonso Gerevini and Ivan Serina

Dipartimento di Elettronica per l'Automazione
Università di Brescia, via Branze 38, 25123 Brescia, Italy
{gerevini,serina}@ing.unibs.it

Abstract. Fast plan adaptation is important in many AI applications requiring a plan management module. From a theoretical point of view, in the worst case plan adaptation is no more efficient than a complete regeneration of the plan. However, in practice adapting an existing plan can be much more efficient than generating a new one from scratch, especially when the changes to the plan that are required concern only some circumscribed parts of the plan. In this paper we discuss a simple plan-adaptation method based on Blum and Furst's Planning Graphs approach. The method is domain-independent and exploits the planning graph structure for a fast identification of the flaws that are present in the plan, and for fixing them by replanning limited portions of the plan. We present results from some experiments aimed at testing our method with several modifications of planning problems that are hard to solve for current planners based on planning graphs, such as IPP, Graphplan, and Blackbox. These results show that the method in practice is very efficient, especially when the plan can be adapted by changes that are localized in restricted parts of the original plan.

1 Introduction

Plan adaptation is important in many AI applications requiring plan representation and reasoning. A typical plan adaptation task consists of modifying a previously generated plan in order to use it for solving a new problem which is similar to the original one. This process can be either *off-line* (e.g., adapting a plan retrieved from a plan library before its execution), or *on-line* (e.g., adapting a plan during a "mixed-initiative" construction of it [3,4], or during its execution). Fast off-line planning can be important, for example, in case-based reasoning; while fast on-line plan-adaptation is important, for example, when during plan-execution some action fails, or the acquisition of new information affects the world description or the goals of the plan, making the current plan invalid.

From a theoretical point of view, in the worst case plan adaptation is no more efficient than a complete regeneration of the plan [10]. However, we expect that in many practical cases adapting an existing plan should be much more efficient than generating a new one from scratch, especially when the original plan can be adapted by revising restricted portions of the plan.

GPG (Greedy Planning Graph) is a planning system under development that is based on planning graph analysis, and that uses a collection of local and systematic search techniques for solving both plan generation and plan adaptation

E. Lamma and P. Mello (Eds.): AI*IA 99, LNAI 1792, pp. 356–367, 2000.

tasks. In [5] we introduce GPG focusing on plan-generation. In this paper we focus on plan-adaptation tasks, in which the input can be specified in terms of: a planning domain (a set of operators), a valid plan for an old problem P, and a new problem P' that is "similar" to P, in the sense that the initial or goal state of P' contains only few changes with respect to the initial or goal state(s) of P. The output is a valid plan for the new planning problem.

We discuss the systematic plan adaptation module of GPG, presenting results from some experiments aimed at testing the effectiveness of the approach. These tests concern many modifications of some well-known problems, that are hard to solve for IPP [9], Graphplan [1] and Blackbox [7], three state-of-the-art planners based on planning graphs. The results confirm that adapting a plan using our techniques in practice is much more efficient than a complete replanning. This is especially true for modifications requiring changes that are localized in specific parts of the plan, where our method can exploit the planning graph structure to yield fast adjustment of the plan.

In the rest of the paper first we briefly introduce planning graphs; then we present the plan adjustment process of GPG; finally, we give the experimental results.

2   Planning Graphs

This data structure was introduced by Blum and Furst [1], who proposed an approach to planning for STRIPS-like domains based on first constructing a planning graph, and then searching for a particular subgraph of it. A planning graph is a directed acyclic levelled graph with two kinds of nodes and three kinds of edges. The levels alternate between a fact level, containing fact nodes, and an action level containing action nodes. A fact node represents a proposition corresponding to a precondition of one or more operators instantiated at time step t (actions at time step t), or to an effect of one or more actions at time step $t-1$. The fact nodes of level 0 represent the positive facts of the initial state of the planning problem.[1] The last level is a proposition level containing the fact nodes corresponding to the goals of the planning problem.

In the following we indicate with $[u]$ the proposition (action) represented by the fact node (action node) u. The edges in a planning graph connect action nodes and fact nodes. In particular, an action node a of level i is connected by:

- *precondition edges* to the fact nodes of level i representing the preconditions of $[a]$;
- *add-edges* to the fact nodes of level $i+1$ representing the positive effects of $[a]$;
- *delete-edges* to the fact nodes of level $i+1$ representing the negative effects of $[a]$.

Two action nodes of a certain level are *mutually exclusive* if no valid plan can contain both the corresponding actions. Similarly, two fact nodes are mutually exclusive if no valid plan can make both the corresponding propositions true.

---

[1] Planning graphs adopt the closed world assumption.

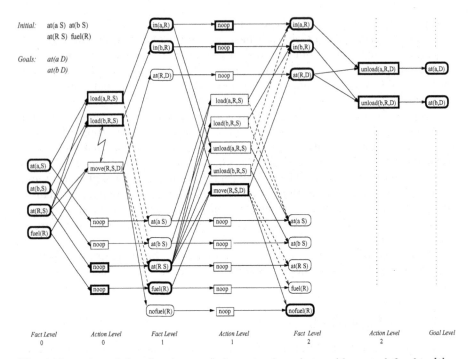

Fig. 1. A portion of the planning graph for a simple rocket problem, as defined in [1], with one rocket R, two objects a and b, a start location S and a destination D. Delete edges (negative effects) are represented by dashed lines, add edges and precondition edges by solid lines. At level 0 we have a mutually exclusive relation imposing that the object b cannot be loaded in R from S while at the same time we move R from S to D. The solution plan is represented by facts and actions with bold boxes.

More precisely, there are two cases in which two actions nodes a and b are marked as mutually exclusive in the graph:

- *Interference*: if either of the actions deletes a precondition or add-effect of the other.
- *Competing Needs*: If there is a precondition node of a and a precondition node of b that are marked as mutually exclusive.

Two proposition nodes p and q in a proposition level are marked as exclusive if all the ways of making proposition $[p]$ true are exclusive with all ways of making $[q]$ true. An action node a of level i can be in a "valid subgraph" of the planning graph (i.e., a subgraph representing a valid plan) only if all its precondition nodes are *supported*, and a is not involved in any mutual exclusion relation with other action nodes of the subgraph. A fact node q of level i is supported in a subgraph $\mathcal{G}'$ of a planning graph $\mathcal{G}$ if either in $\mathcal{G}'$ there is an action node at level $i-1$ representing an action with (positive) effect $[q]$, or $[q]$ is a proposition of the initial state.

Given a problem P in a certain planning domain, the planning graph of P is automatically constructed level by level, starting from level 0 (the initial state) and ending at the first level that contains all the goals of the problem with no mutual exclusive relation among them.

In Figure 1 we give an example of a planning graph for a simple problem in the rocket domain, as formalized in [1]. The action load(b,R,S) is mutually exclusive with move(R,S,D) because they interfere. The fact in(b,R) and at(R,S) are mutually exclusive because all the ways of generating the first (i.e., load(b,R,S)) are exclusive of all the ways of generating the second (i.e., move(R,S,D)).

Given a planning problem P and a planning graph $\mathcal{G}$, a *solution* (plan) for P is a subgraph $\mathcal{G}'$ of $\mathcal{G}$ such that (1) all the precondition nodes of actions in $\mathcal{G}'$ are supported, (2) every goal node is supported, and (3) there are no mutual exclusion relations between action nodes of $\mathcal{G}'$.

3   Systematic Plan Adjustment in GPG

Given a plan $\mathcal{P}$ for a planning problem P and a new problem P', differing from P in some initial or goal fact(s), the systematic plan adjustment process of GPG consists of three main phases:

1. Analysis of the input plan to determine a subset of the actions in $\mathcal{P}$ that are *applicable* to P'.
2. Identification of the set F of *flaws* that are present in $\mathcal{P}$ with respect to P' (a flaw is a pair of mutually exclusive actions or an action with some unachieved precondition(s)).
3. Revision of P to repair the flaws in F and to provide a valid plan $\mathcal{P}'$ for P'.

The first phase is performed by mapping each action of P to an action node of the planning graph $\mathcal{G}$ for the *new* problem (if such a node exists). In this mapping we distinguish three cases: (a) the number of time steps involved in P is the same as the number of levels in $\mathcal{G}$; (b) the number of time steps involved in $\mathcal{P}$ is higher than the number of levels in $\mathcal{G}$; (c) the number of the time steps involved in P is smaller than the number of levels in $\mathcal{G}$.

In case (a) an action at time i in $\mathcal{P}$ is considered applicable if in $\mathcal{G}$ there exists a corresponding action node at level i. In case (b) the applicable actions are determined by first extending $\mathcal{G}$ to have the same number of levels as the time steps of $\mathcal{P}$, and then applying the same definition as in case (a). Finally, in case (c), if $\mathcal{P}$ involves n time steps, the mapping between plan-actions and graph-nodes is done by considering the last n levels of $\mathcal{G}$. E.g., we try to map actions at time n to nodes at the last level of $\mathcal{G}$, actions at time $n-1$ to nodes at the penultimate level of $\mathcal{G}$, and so on. In each of the three cases, if for an action a of $\mathcal{P}$ there is no corresponding action node in $\mathcal{G}$, then we consider a not applicable and we remove it from $\mathcal{P}$.

The second and the third phases of the adaptation process are accomplished by ADJUST-PLAN, an algorithm that we proved to be correct and complete [6]: the adjusted plan is a valid plan for P', and if there exists a plan for P', then an adjusted plan is computed. Figure 3 gives a general description of this algorithm (a more formal description is given in [6]). The first step of ADJUST-PLAN identifies the first level (earliest time step) of $\mathcal{P}$ which contains a flaw. Note that since we are currently considering STRIPS domains, this can be accomplished in

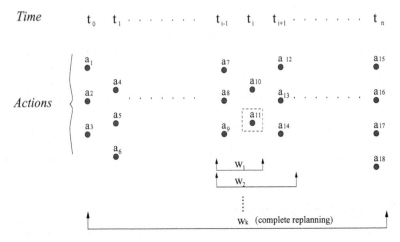

Fig. 2. Example of replanning windows for a plan in which the earliest flaw is at time t_i and consists of an unsatisfied precondition of action a_{11}. The initial replanning window is initially set to w_1 and can be incrementally enlarged up to include all the actions of the plan.

polynomial time by simulating the execution of the plan of $\mathcal{P}$ (similarly, the facts that are necessarily true at any level can be determined in polynomial time).

Then ADJUST-PLAN processes the level i identified at step 1 in the following way. If level i contains a flaw, then it tries to repair it by replanning from level $i-1$ to level i using systematic search. If there exists no plan or a certain search limit is exceeded, then the replanning window is enlarged (e.g., we replan from $i - 1$ to $i + 1$ – see Figure 2).[4] The process is iterated until a (sub)plan is found, the window has been enlarged up to include all the actions of the plan and the (complete) replanning has failed, or the search has reached a predefined CPU-time limit (max-adjust-time).[2]

Note that in our current implementation of ADJUST-PLAN, during replanning (step 4) the actions of $\mathcal{P}$ that are present in the replanning window are ignored (a new planning graph for the replanning problem is constructed). The systematic replanning at step 4 is performed by first constructing the corresponding replanning graph, and then searching it using a complete search method. The current version of GPG uses the same backtracking scheme as IPP [9]; this search method guarantees that if a (sub)plan is found, then this is optimal with respect to the number of time steps that are involved [1, 9].

At step 5 of ADJUST-PLAN the replanning window can be increased going either backward in time (i.e., init-level is decreased), forward in time

---

[2] GPG includes both systematic and local search techniques that can be used in combination. When max-adjust-time is exceeded, GPG activates the local search. However, the local search techniques of GPG are not treated in this paper which focuses on the systematic method.

Algorithm: ADJUST-PLAN

Input: a plan P containing some flaws and a CPU-time limit `max-adjust-time`.

Output: either a correct plan or `fail`.

1. Identify the first level (earliest time step) i in P containing a flaw; if there is no such a level, then return P;
2. If i is the last level of P, then set `init-level` to i − 1 and `goal-level` to i, otherwise set `init-level` to i and `goal-level` to i + 1;
3. While CPU-time ≤ `max-adjust-time`
    4. Systematically replan using as initial facts F(`init-level`) and as goals G(`goal-level`), where F(`init-level`) is the set of facts that are true at level `init-level`, and G(`goal-level`) is the set of preconditions of the actions in P at level `goal-level` (including the no-ops);
    5. If there is no plan from F(`init-level`) to G(`goal-level`), or a search limit is exceeded, then decrease `init-level` or increase `goal-level` (i.e., we enlarge the replanning window), otherwise insert the (sub)plan found into P, removing the existing actions between `init-level` and `goal-level`, and goto 1.
6. Return `fail`.

Fig. 3. Description of the algorithm ADJUST-PLAN used by GPG.

(i.e., `goal-level` is increased), or both.[3] Enlarging a replanning window corresponds to reconsidering a larger portion of the plan under adaptation. Such a portion will be replaced by the subplan solving the replanning problem associated with the enlarged window (when this is found). GPG has a default value for `max-adjust-time` that can be modified by the user. In principle, if `max-adjust-time` is set to sufficiently high values, then ADJUST-PLAN can increase a replanning window up to reach the original initial and goal levels of the planning graph. This would determine a complete systematic search.

The insertion into P of a subplan found at step 4 does not invalidate the rest of the plan. On the contrary, this subplan may be useful for achieving unachieved preconditions at levels following `goal-level`. Once the algorithm has repaired the flaws in a level (i.e., it has replaced a portion of the plan containing this level with a new subplan), it proceeds by considering the next level containing a flaw (if any).

From the previous considerations it can be proved that our plan-adaptation method is complete, in the sense that using a sufficiently high value for `max-adjust-time`, if the new problem is solvable, than the method finds a plan for solving it, otherwise the method detects that the problem is unsolvable [6].

Finally, during replanning within a particular window we impose a search limit that is automatically increased when the replanning window is enlarged.[4]

---

[3] Note that when the replanning window is enlarged by moving the goal state forward, keeping the same initial state, we could use the memoization of unachieved subgoals to prune the search, as indicated in [1, 9].

[4] In the current implementation this limit is defined by limiting the possible number of levels in the *re*planning graph. In our tests this number was initially set to 3, and then automatically increased by 2 each time the replanning window was enlarged of 1 level.

The motivation of this heuristic is that when a replanning problem associated with a certain window is hard to solve, it can be easier to reconsider a larger portion of the plan (instead of dedicating a big effort to the revision of a restricted part of the plan). While this does not affect completeness (in the sense specified above), in practice it can be significantly effective for the efficient computation of an adapted plan.

4   Experimental Results

Figures 4, 5, 6, 7 and 8 give the CPU-times of adapting a plan and of regenerating it "from scratch" (using IPP 3.3) for several problems in the Rocket, Logistics and Gripper domains, which are considered challenging domains for planners based on planning graphs [1, 7, 2].[5]

The tests concerning ADJUST-PLAN were conducted on a Sun Ultra 10 with 64 Mbytes, while the tests concerning IPP were conducted on a PC Pentium II 400 MHz with 64 Mbytes (which is about 1.4 times faster than a SUN Ultra 10). When IPP was not able to find a solution, because it ran out of memory or it consumed a very high amount of CPU-time, the figures plot a default CPU-time of 1000 or 10000 seconds. Each problem modification is named using a number, and is a variant of a known test problem. Each variant contains few changes in the facts of the initial or final state(s) of the original problem, making the input plan for the original problem not valid for solving the revised problem.[6]

Figures 4 and 5 give the adaptation and generation times for Logistics_a and Logistics_b, two problems of the Logistics domain [7]. In this domain there are several cities, and at each city there are several locations (e.g., post offices and airports). Some trucks can be used for carrying packages within the same city, and some airplanes can be used for carrying packages between different cities. Typical goals of a planning problem consist of having some packages delivered to some location, and typical problem modifications consist of having a different initial or final location for some package(s).

Figures 6 and 7 gives results for some modifications of Rocket_a and Rocket_b, two problems in the Rocket domain [7], which has several similarities with the Logistics domain. Finally, Figure 8 gives results for some modifications of Gripper-10 and Gripper-12 as formalized in IPP, two problems in a simple domain where a robot with two arms has to move several balls located in certain rooms to some other rooms.

The modifications of the problems in the domains Logistics and Rocket were obtained by either (a) adding a new object and specifying the corresponding

---

[5] We used the formalization provided in IPP's package, which is available at http://www.informatik.uni-freiburg/~koehler/ipp.html.

[6] Overall we estimated that: about 25% of the problem modifications that we considered required at least 2 changes to the original plan, where a change consists of inserting or removing an action; about 50% required between 3 and 6 changes; about 25% required more than 6 changes. The formalization for all the problems that we tested is available via anonymous FTP from ftp.ing.unibs.it, file /home/gerevini/prob-aiia.tar.

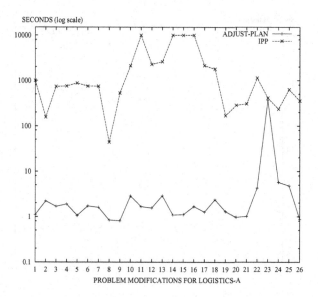

Fig. 4. Graph representation of the CPU-time (log-scale) required by ADJUST-PLAN and by IPP(3.3) for 26 problem modifications of Logistics_a.

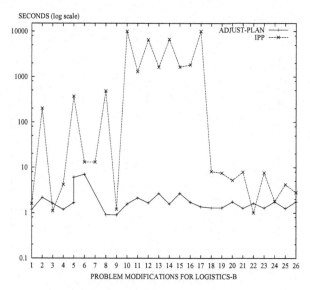

Fig. 5. Graph representation of the CPU-time (log-scale) required by ADJUST-PLAN and by IPP(3.3) for 26 problem modifications of Logistics_b.

location in the initial and final states, (b) changing the initial position of one or two objects of the original problem, or (c) changing the goal position of one or two objects of the original problem. For example, in Logistics_a (Figure 4) problem 1 corresponds to a change of the initial position of "package1" from

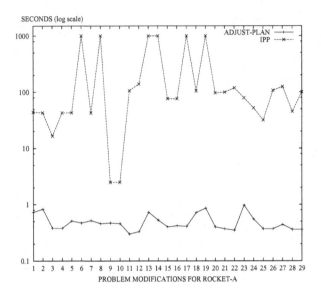

Fig. 6. Graph representation of the CPU-time (log-scale) required by ADJUST-PLAN and by IPP(3.3) for 29 problem modifications of Rocket_a.

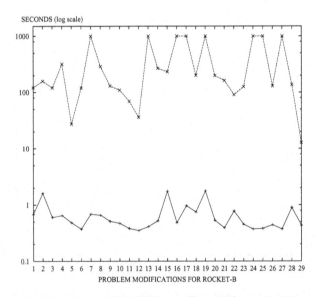

Fig. 7. Graph representation of the CPU-time (log-scale) required by ADJUST-PLAN and by IPP(3.3) for 29 problem modifications of Rocket_b.

the location "pgh-po" to the location "la_airport", which requires many changes to the original plan; problem 19 corresponds to a change of the goal position of "package1" from "bos-po" to "la_po", which requires at least changing four actions in the plan.

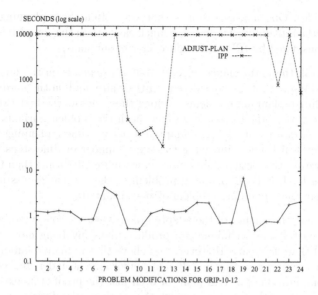

Fig. 8. Graph representation of the CPU-time (log-scale) required by ADJUST-PLAN and by IPP(3.3) for 24 problem modifications of Gripper_10 and Gripper_12.

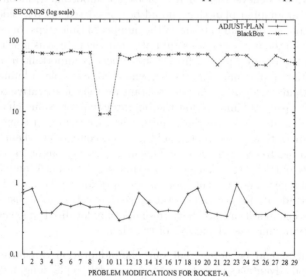

Fig. 9. Graph representation of the CPU-time (log-scale) required by ADJUST-PLAN and by Blackbox (version 3.6) for 29 problem modifications of Rocket_a.

The modifications of the problems in the Gripper domain were obtained by either changing the initial or final location of some (1–4) balls, or adding a new room that becomes the new initial or final location of some (1–4) balls.

The results in the figures show that adapting a plan using our techniques in general is much faster than a complete replanning (up to more than three orders of magnitude). One major reason is that very often the replanning problems defined by the replanning windows are much easier than the complete replanning problem considered by IPP, and require shorter subplans.

In general, the performance of ADJUST-PLAN depends on the number of replanning windows that are considered, on their size, and on the hardness of the corresponding replanning problems. Among these factors the first two seems to be less crucial than the third one. In fact, both the problem variants 10 and 23 of Logistics_a (see Figure 4) were adapted using just one replanning window of length 5, for which plans involving the same number of time steps were computed. However, the variant 23 required much more CPU-time than the variant 10, because for IPP the replanning problem of the variant 23 was much more difficult than the replanning problem of the variant 10.

Concerning the quality of the adapted plans that are computed by ADJUST-PLAN, in general, this technique can produce plans involving more actions (or time steps) than necessary. However, we believe that in many planning applications, such as an agent acting in a dynamic environment under time constraints, the fast computation of a valid plan (or even just the proof of its existence) can be more important than a slow computation of the optimal plan.

Moreover, we believe that there can be an important tradeoff about the "quality" of an adapted plan that should be considered: on one side we would like that the plan is optimal in terms of the number of time steps (or actions) that are involved; on the other side we would like that the plan is as much as possible "similar" to the original plan. This second aspect is important in the context of mixed-initiative planning (e.g., [3,4]), where, for example, a human operator interacts with an artificial intelligent assistant for the collaborative construction of a plan. If during the interaction the operator requests some changes to the initial or goal states (e.g., she/he requires the satisfaction of some additional goal), then the artificial assistant should try to accommodate them minimizing the modifications to the current plan. This minimization can be in contrast with an attempt to optimize the plan, since the time steps optimization might require a substantial revision of the plan. Our plan adaptation method is a first attempt to take this tradeoff into account, in the sense that it tries to adjust the plan by performing some modifications that are temporally localized to specific parts of the plan, leaving unchanged the rest of the plan.

Finally, it should be noted that our plan-adaptation can have significant computational advantages with respect to a complete replanning, independently from the particular replanning algorithm. For example, Figure 9 plots the CPU-time required by Blackbox (version 3.6) for solving the problem modifications considered in Figure 6, together with the CPU-times required by ADJUST-PLAN. This experiment was conducted on a Sun Ultra 10 with 64 Mbytes. We can observe that the advantages of ADJUST-PLAN with respect to Blackbox [7] are similar (though sometimes less dramatic) to the advantages obtained with respect to IPP (see Figure 6). Further experiments for testing Blackbox on the other problem modifications are in progress.

5   Conclusions and further work

Fast plan-adaptation is important in many AI applications requiring a plan management module. We have discussed a simple domain-independent method based on planning graphs that we have experimentally tested on several plan-adaptation tasks. The experimental results show that adapting a plan using our techniques in practice is much more efficient than a complete replanning. This is especially true for plan adaptation problems requiring changes that are localized in restricted parts of the plan.

Further work includes an incremental optimization process that can be used after the computation of a first adapted plan for deriving a succession of improved plans, each of which involves fewer time steps than the previous one. The way we currently compute an improved plan is based on considering alternative replanning windows for all the subplans that have been previously inserted either by ADJUST-PLAN to produce the first adapted plan, or by the previous optimization to obtain a more compact plan. Preliminary results show that in practice this incremental method produce alternative plans that are more compact that the first plan computed by ADJUST PLAN (sometimes they are optimal plans), still requiring much less CPU-time than a complete replanning.

Additional very recent results, partly described in [6], concern further experimental tests to analyze the performance of ADJUST-PLAN, the development of a plan-adaptation method combining ADJUST-PLAN and local search techniques [5], and the study of a more sophisticated mechanism for dealing with the quality of an adapted plan, taking into account both the number of time steps (or actions) in the adapted plan and the number of changes to the original plan.

References

1. A. Blum and M.L. Furst. Fast planning through planning graph analysis. In *Proc. of IJCAI-95*, pages 1636–1642. Morgan Kaufmann, 1995.
2. M. Fox and D. Long. The Detection and Exploitation of Symmetry in Planning Problems. In *Proc.* of IJCAI-99, Stockholm, 1999.
3. G. Ferguson and J. Allen. Arguing about Plans: Plan Representation and Reasoning for Mixed-Initiative Planning. In *Proc. of AIPS-94*, 1994.
4. G. Ferguson and J. Allen. Towards a Mixed-Initiative Planning Assistant. In *Proc. of AIPS-96*, AAAI press, 1996.
5. A. Gerevini, and I. Serina. Fast Planning through Greedy Action Graphs. In *Proc. of AAAI-99*, pages 503–510, AAAI/MIT Press, 1999.
6. A. Gerevini, and I. Serina. 1999. Fast Plan Adaptation through Planning Graphs: Local and Systematic Search Techniques. Technical Report R.T. 2000.01.20. DEA, Univ. di Brescia, Brescia, Italy.
7. H.A. Kautz and B. Selman. Pushing the envelope: Planning, propositional logic, and stochastic search. In *Proc. of AAAI-96*, AAAI Press, 1996.
8. H.A. Kautz and B. Selman. Unifying SAT-based and Graph-based Planning. In *Proc. of IJCAI-99*, Stockholm, 1999.
9. J. Koehler, B. Nebel, Hoffmann J., and Y. Dimopoulos. Extending planning graphs to an ADL subset. In *Proc. of ECP'97*, Springer Verlag, 1997.
10. B. Nebel and J. Koehler. Plan reuse versus plan generation: A complexity-theoretic perspective. *Artificial Intelligence*, 76:427–454, 1995.

Real-Time Motion Planning in Autonomous Vehicles: A Hybrid Approach

Maurizio Piaggio and Antonio Sgorbissa

University of Genova, Department of System Communication and
Computer Science, Via Opera Pia 13, 16145 Genova, ITALY

Abstract. In this paper a multi-agent architecture of an *Autonomous Robot Navigator* for a vehicle that operates in dynamic real-world environments is presented. The vehicle is capable of executing different navigation missions while smoothly avoiding static obstacles in its path as well as moving objects. The navigator architecture is part of a general multi-agent cognitive framework, which is organised into three non-hierarchical components characterised by the type of knowledge they deal with: a *symbolic* component, handling a declarative explicit propositional formalism, a *diagrammatic* component, dealing with analogical, iconic representations, and a *reactive* behaviour based component. The navigator is distributed in all three components combining motion planning on a topological graph with reactive motion planning techniques. It is on these aspects that the paper focuses. Experimental results with our mobile robot will also be provided.

1 Introduction

Recently there has been a growing interest in a specific domain of application of autonomous mobile robots: personal assistive tasks [Simmons et al., 1997][Semerano, 1997]. The reference scenario is that of a service mobile vehicle capable of operating in dynamic real-world civil environments such as hospitals, museums, general stores, executing different navigation missions while smoothly avoiding static obstacles in its path (i.e. tables or chairs) as well as moving objects (i.e. people wandering around, other robots, automatic doors). This paper concentrates on the navigation problems that such a robot is required to face while carrying out its tasks, by proposing a novel hybrid architecture for *Autonomous Robot Navigation*.
The navigator architecture is part of a general multi-agent cognitive framework [Piaggio, 1999], which is organised into three non-hierarchical components (figure 1) characterised by the type of knowledge they deal with: a *symbolic* component (S), handling a declarative explicit propositional formalism, a *diagrammatic* component (D), dealing with

E. Lamma and P. Mello (Eds.): AI*IA 99, LNAI 1792, pp. 368–378, 2000.
© Springer-Verlag Berlin Heidelberg 2000

analogical, iconic representations, and a *reactive* behaviour based component (R).

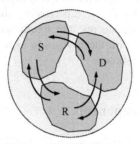

Fig. 1   The general cognitive architecture

The figure suggests that there is no qualitative difference between the three knowledge paradigms and related components. The activity distribution between the components simply depends on the context in which the system is, and thus will vary significantly in time. When a robot has to perform a complex assembling operation most of the activity will be at the symbolic level, in which the explicit assembling plan is represented; when it is following a person the activity will focus on the diagrammatic component that reasons analogically on the different camera snapshots of the environment, in order to track the person movement correctly; when it is avoiding obstacles in its path, reactive behaviours will directly couple sensor data to the robot movement. Analogously, there is not an overall hierarchical organisation in the architecture (i.e. it is not always true that symbolic activities drive diagrammatic activities which in turn drive reactive activities), nor any component is privileged at all times, but the focus of activity, and consequently the partial control of the system, can be taken in different moments by different components. In this sense, different hierarchies in which any of the three components may occupy the top level may be dynamically interchanged depending on internal or external events.

Three levels hierarchical architectures [Ferguson, 1992] [AAAI,1995] [Bonasso et al, 1995] have often been criticised because the overall capabilities of the entire system are bounded to those of the symbolic high levels, which suffer from the known intrinsic limitations when coping with real words (time, uncertainties, monotony and so on) [Brooks,1990]. However, in the proposed architecture all components do not have a predefined hierarchy and operate concurrently with different frequency of intervention: the reactive component will be characterised by a high frequency in order to deal immediately with the real world requirements whereas the diagrammatic and symbolic components will have more relaxed timing constraints. Moreover each component has also a certain degree of autonomy, inspired to the emerging behaviour of complex systems; for example the reactive component will carry out its tasks at its level of knowledge if the other components fail to intervene.

The navigator is distributed in all three components combining motion planning on a topological graph with reactive motion planning techniques. It is on these aspects that the paper focuses. It is organised as follows: the next two sections will describe respectively the symbolic and the diagrammatic/reactive components, the fourth section will deal with the experimental set-up and with the navigation experiments with real robots. Finally conclusions will follow.

2 The Symbolic Component

The symbolic component is responsible of plan selection and adaptation, allowing the robot to execute high-level navigation tasks such as "go into office A". These tasks, depending on the current robot context, may be decomposed into many, possibly concurrent, sub-tasks such as "localise, go to the door, open door, etc..." and eventually into primitive actions to be executed by the diagrammatic and reactive components "go to position (x,y,θ)".

The formalism adopted for the symbolic component is also a hybrid system (in the sense of [Nebel,1990]), combining a terminological and an assertional language. The terminological component is a KL-ONE like network, describing the concepts and the relations concerning the navigation domain. Assertional long term knowledge includes factual generalisations and long term knowledge concerning specific objects of the domain. An assertional knowledge base consists of grounded first order formulas describing the evolution of the actual context. Such assertions describe specific instances of the network concepts.

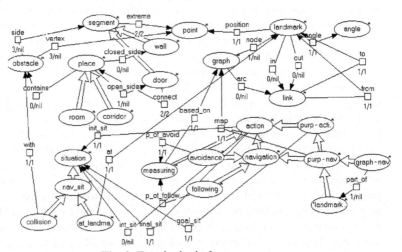

Fig. 2. Terminological component

A portion of a KL-ONE net used for mainly navigational purposes is depicted in figure 2 (double arrows represent *IS-A relations* between concepts; single arrows represent *roles*). The figure depicts simply an example description for an autonomous robot. However, to clarify its content and use within the system, let us briefly discuss it: the concepts describing *actions* are situated on the lower right, *situations* on the lower left, *environment description* on the upper left and finally *path description* on the upper right. It is this last section that mostly concerns the navigation problem.

A path in the environment is characterised by a set of points or *landmarks* linked together forming a graph. A landmark describes the local particular characteristics of region of the environment it relates to: whether it is the centre of a room, a door, a narrow passage or simply a passing point. Each landmark also memorises its absolute *position* in the world, relative to a common frame, and possibly, the *orientation* that the robot must have when passing by that landmark.

It is important to mention that the graph is not a static description. Initially it represents an abstraction of the possible trajectories that the robot might follow: for example, move from landmark A (the centre of the laboratory) to landmark B (the door of the laboratory) and then to landmark C (the end of the corridor). Then, it is continuously updated during the robot's motion by the symbolic information generated by the diagrammatic and reactive components of the architecture such as the really executed robot position (and path) as well the local characteristics of the environment (door, free space, etc.).The role of the symbolic component is to select, using planning on topological graph techniques (currently we are using A*), a suitable sequence of landmarks to be reached by the robot in order to fulfil its mission and to make the sequence available to the diagrammatic and reactive components. While the latter attempts to execute the planned trajectory the symbolic component concurrently monitors what is actually occurring, updates the assertional symbolic information and eventually adapts or simply changes the initial plan.

It is worth emphasising that our system differs greatly from motion planning systems based exclusively on topological graphs. The landmarks do not indicate a precise path but they are simply a rough description of where the robot has to pass. In fact, there could be in theory (and sometimes this is also the case in practice) only two landmarks: the initial robot position and the target position to be reached: for example "move from the current position the entrance of office X". The diagrammatic and reactive components will then have to solve all planning problems autonomously. However, in most cases, in the symbolic component there will be additional prior symbolic information to aid the diagrammatic and reactive components in its tasks as well as more complex symbolic reasoning.

Different methods to provide the initial graph of landmarks have also been investigated. Clearly, one simple method is the direct specification by the system user or programmer. This method allows a complete control on the overall trajectories but it is very time consuming and subject to the operator's sensibility. This problem may be overcome by generating the graph on the basis of analogical image-based data, maps of the environment, either directly available or built using sensor information. For example, in [Piaggio,Zaccaria,1998] the use of roadmaps is combined with abstract potential field techniques to classify regions of space (room centres, narrow passages, etc.) from a bitmap of the environment[1].

3 The Diagrammatic and Reactive Components

The diagrammatic and reactive components are internally organised as a multi-agent architecture as depicted in figure 3. However, while the agents belonging to the reactive component (depicted as ellipses) are responsible of purely reactive behaviours (low-level perception/action, sensor-motor activity), the diagrammatic ones (depicted as rounded rectangles) are responsible for the management of the diagrammatic, iconic representations and have the purpose of trajectory generation and smooth obstacle avoidance. In the figure the shared, image based, analogical representations [Steels,1990] are indicated as grey rectangles.

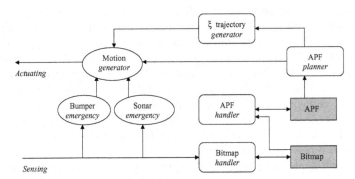

Fig. 3   The navigator architecture

Two representations can be observed: the *bitmap*, an ecocentrical statistical dynamic description of the environment the robot moves in, and the *APF - Abstract Potential Field*, based on the bitmap and on direct sensorial information. These representations are handled and updated to maintain consistency with the real world based on sensor data by two diagrammatic agents: the *APF handler* and the *Bitmap handler* (the details of these agents is beyond the scope of this paper but can be found in [Piaggio,Zaccaria,1997]).

---

[1] an on-line demo is available at "http:// www.robotics.laboratorium.dist.unige.it/ Projects / Roadmap /html"

On the left-hand side of the figure it is possible to notice the reactive agents, which are responsible of simple navigation behaviours. The simplest of these agents is the *motion generator* which receives commands under the form of speed and jog information to be applied to the vehicle and directly controls the actuators. This agent, by itself, is clearly only capable of executing extremely simple trajectories. The *sonar emergency handler* is activated whenever the sonar devices detect an obstacle which is dangerously approaching the robot below a given distance threshold, and feeds the *motion generator* with the appropriate speed and jog values to handle the emergency. The *bumper emergency handler* is activated whenever an obstacle hits the front or the rear bumper of the robot; it feeds the *motion generator* with the appropriate speed and jog values to overcome the anomalous situation. Under normal navigation circumstances, these two agents are never activated: in fact, the agents on the right-hand side of the figure are responsible of calculating a trajectory which the robot has to follow to reach its target while avoiding obstacles in the environment. The ξ *trajectory generator* receives position commands in absolute co-ordinates in the environment. It is capable of executing, relying on a biologically inspired, non linear law of motion (ξ model [Sanguineti,Morasso,1997]), smooth trajectories from the robot current position to the target specified, by periodically modifying the speed/jog values. The agent produces the desired behaviour but only in the absence of obstacles in the robot path. This problem is handled by the *APF planner* which executes a virtual, mental, navigation in the abstract potential field (continuously aligned with the real world by the perceptive agents).

This navigation determines a trajectory and a target position that successfully avoids obstacles but the well-known drawback of this approach is the roughness of the resulting path and therefore the erratic vehicle movement that it would imply. However, in the system, the navigation in the APF is only virtual and it is used only to establish a temporary target position which the ξ *trajectory generator* is instructed to reach.

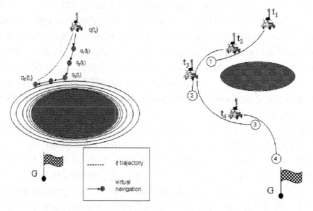

Fig. 4 Virtual navigation in the APF

This mechanism is depicted in figure 4 in which the robot is initially in A and has to reach a target G while avoiding an obstacle in its path. The figure illustrates the equi-potential lines of the APF generated by the obstacle. Instead of using G as a target position, the ξ *trajectory generator* pilots the robot towards a temporary target T found by a virtual navigation in the APF. This still results in effective obstacle avoidance while keeping the executed trajectory smooth and natural. It is important to mention that the temporary targets are never really reached by the robot because the virtual navigation is carried out at each step and thus the virtual target moved until it eventually coincides with the desired goal G.

However the executed trajectory, generated by the ξ *trajectory generator*, clearly differs slightly (at least in smoothness) from the trajectory generated from the virtual navigation in the APF and therefore it may be possible for the robot to collide with some obstacles in the environment. The *APF planner* prevents this from happening: based on the sensorial bitmap and on the APF, in critical conditions it suddenly switches off the virtual navigation and calculates the speed and jog values which are required to directly navigate in the field. Next, it feeds the motion controller with these values, thus correctly avoiding the obstacle. Clearly, these trajectories will no longer be smooth but the probability (and thus the frequency) of this event is very low.

The agents in the architecture communicate using messages conveying the type of information or command to be executed at the appropriate level (planner, trajectory generator, motion generator). However, all agents operate concurrently and the architecture is only partially hierarchical, thus implying a dynamic competition on the allocation of "resources" and, in this specific case, of the vehicle actuators at the motion generator level between the ξ-*trajectory generator*, *APF planner*, *sonar emergency handler* and *bumper emergency handler*. This is solved using an *authority-based* protocol. Each agent is characterised with a specific authority (possibly varying in time) with which it issues command messages. The receiving agent stores the command associated authority and begins its execution (for example speed = 2 cm/s). If the action, as in the given example, continues indefinitely or requires some time to be executed, the agent continues its execution until a contrasting message with a similar or higher authority is received. On the other hand, messages with lower authorities are not considered. For example, in the architecture, the *APF planner* has a higher authority that the ξ-*trajectory generator*, thus, if necessary, overriding any command from the former.

The diagrammatic and reactive components can therefore perform relatively complex navigation tasks that require on-line perception and obstacle avoidance without any external help. However, in most cases, the symbolic component will provide an initial sequence of landmarks to be reached. As with the virtual targets these landmarks are only a suggestion and can be dynamically modified as the context or reasoning horizon evolves. The diagrammatic component, and more specifically the *APF handler*, the *Bitmap Handler* and the *APF Planner*, will also provide symbolic information on the current robot situation: (in free space, in a crowded environment, in a narrow passage, crossing a door, etc.) by classifying, using the local APF, the regions of space in which the robot moves [Piaggio,Zaccaria,1998]. This information is used by the symbolic component to concurrently monitor the mission execution status and expectations.

4 Experimental Results

The system has been implemented and developed on a TRC Labmate. The mobile robot is equipped with an Intel Pentium 133 processor, a positioning system based on active beacons and a belt of 16 proximity sensors. The reactive and diagrammatic components was placed on-board of the robot; they were written in C++ in a programming environment called ETHNOS (Expert Tribe in a Hybrid Network Operating System) [Piaggio,1998]. The robot was then connected throughout a Wavelan® radio link to the off-board remote symbolic component based on the prototype of a terminological system called X-Procne and written mostly in Sicstus Prolog. A simulator has also been developed to test both the functioning of the robot and the implementation of the algorithms used.

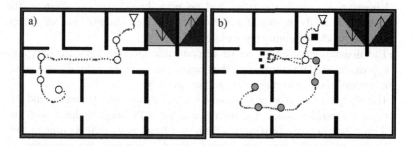

Fig. 5 a) Simulated environment in which the robot performed the superimposed trajectory heading in succession for the different nodes (white circles) in the path. b) The path is obstructed; the symbolic planner re-plans a different sequence of nodes (grey circles) to reach the target.

The remaining part of this section presents two empirical studies. The first study is illustrated in figure 5. The robot was initially placed at the entrance of the large room to the right of the picture (white triangle) and was asked to reach the target position on the bottom left hand side as indicated in figure 5a by the circle at the left end of the robot trajectory. The symbolic component planner on the basis of prior information established a sequence of nodes, white circles in the figure, that the robot had to reach. In figure 5b a different situation is shown, in which the shortest path is obstructed by obstacles. The first square obstacle is avoided in the diagrammatic/reactive components whereas the complete obstruction in corridor can only be handled in the symbolic component: the symbolic planner is forced to re-plan the sequence of nodes (grey circles) to reach the target.

The trajectory demonstrates the ability of the architecture to smoothly avoid obstacles (such as the square-section obstacle met before reaching the first node in figure 5b, the small rectangles in the corridor, etc.) while executing the high-level plan. Moreover, during the execution, the assertional symbolic knowledge is updated. An small portion of the knowledge based generated is presented below as an example in which the navigation history is described: the robot is at landmark 2 at time 1, is about to collide with an obstacle at time 5, is at landmark 3 at time 7, etc.

$$instant(instant\_ass\_0008), \quad instant(instant\_ass\_0007),$$
$$instant(instant\_ass\_0006), instant(instant\_ass\_0005),$$
$$instant(instant\_ass\_0004),......,$$
$$beg\_sit(at\_landmark\_ass\_0002, instant\_ass\_0007).$$
$$beg\_sit(collision\_ass\_0001, instant\_ass\_0005).$$
$$end\_sit(at\_landmark\_ass\_0002, instant\_ass\_0008).$$
$$end\_sit(collision\_ass\_0001, instant\_ass\_0007).$$

Reasoning on this information is carried out concurrently to monitor if the task is being executed correctly. The second study was carried out in our laboratory of which the robot had no prior knowledge, to illustrate the plausibility of the proposed architecture from the computational efficiency and real-world suitability point of view.

The diagrammatic and reactive components operated at a frequency of approximately 50 Hz (meaning that each agent could execute, if required to, its control code on average 50 times per second).

This frequency was exploited only by the ξ-trajectory generator and the motion controller since, the bitmap and the APF were updated with the sensor data from the proximity sensors at a frequency of 20 Hz (due to well known physical sonar limitations), clearly affecting the necessity of intervention by the other agents.

The robot was placed inside the lab in the bottom left side of figure 6 and it was asked to reach the target position marked with a black circle near the door. In this last example the robot operated in a very complex real environment in which navigation, exploration and obstacle avoidance (people wondering about in the lab) had to be carried out dynamically and simultaneously. The difficulties here also arise from the variety of obstacles present among which are tables and chairs which are not easily detected by ultrasonic proximity sensors: this is the main cause of the slight roughness in the robot trajectory which is however sufficiently accurate to allow the robot to complete the task successfully.

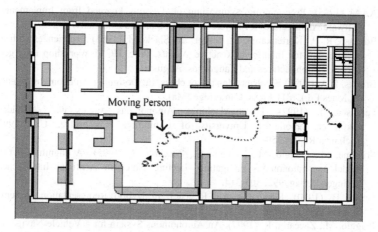

Fig. 6 A real navigation task in our laboratory. The robot trajectory is superimposed over a CAD model of the environment.

5 Conclusions

In this paper a novel architecture for autonomous robots navigating in real complex and dynamic environments was presented. In fact, even though at a first glance it may be classified as yet another three level architecture, there are relevant differences with other approaches that we believe deserve attention. In particular the architecture is non hierarchical with a special emphasis on analogical representations and analogical reasoning [Frixione et al.,1995] which allows to reduce the complexity of the operations that are carried out by the symbolic component as well as to carry out mental simulations. Moreover the symbolic component provides not only a uniform paradigm to describe both short term assertional and long term terminological information but it is also designed to intuitively describe the relations between the different behaviours and situations that may occur. The empirical experimental results show the properties of this architecture and its suitability to the situations mentioned. Moreover the architecture has also been successfully tested and used in museums or shows for public entertainment meeting so far approximately more than 3,000 people.

The degree of autonomy of the different components (and agents within the same component) allows their distribution on different machines as in our experimental set-up with the diagrammatic and reactive components on-board and the symbolic one on a remote station which can also serve as a high-level robot-human interface.

References

AAAI (1995), Proc. Spring Symposium on Lessons Learned from Implemented Software Architectures for Physical Agents, Stanford University.

Bonasso, R. P., Kortenkamp, D., Miller, D., Slack, M. (1995) Experiences with an Architecture for Intelligent Reactive Agents, Proc. IJCAI Workshop on Agent Theories, Architectures and Languages, August.

Brooks, R.A. (1990) Elephants don't play chess, in: Designing Autonomous Agents, (P. Maes Ed.), MIT Press, Cambridge (Ma).

Ferguson, I. (1992), TouringMachines: Autonomous Agents with Attitudes, Computer Laboratory, University of Cambridge, Cambridge, UK, 1992. Technical Report 250.

Frixione, M., Piaggio, M., Vercelli, G., Zaccaria, R. (1995) A cognitive hybrid model for autonomous navigation, Lecture Notes in Artificial Intelligence, Springer-Verlag, 992, 303-314.

Nebel, B. (1990), Reasoning and Revision in Hybrid Representation Systems. Spriger Verlag, Berlin.

Piaggio, M., Zaccaria, R. (1997), An Autonomous System for a Vehicle Navigating in a Partially or Totally Unknown Environment, Proc. Int. Workshop on Mechatronical Computer Systems for Perception and Action MCPA, Pisa, Italy.

Piaggio, M., Zaccaria, R., (1998) Distributing a Robotic System on a Network: the ETHNOS Approach, Advanced Robotics, Vol. 12, N.8, VSP.

Piaggio, M., (1999) HEIR - A Non-Hierarchical Hybrid Architecture for Intelligent Robots, Lecture Notes in Artificial Intelligence, Vol. 1555, Pag. 243-260, Springer-Verlag.

Piaggio, M., Zaccaria, R,. Using Roadmaps to Classify Regions of Space for Autonomous Robot Navigation, Robotics and Autonomous Systems Journal, Vol. 25/3-4, 209-217, Elsevier Science, 1998.

Sanguineti, V, Morasso, P. (1997), Computational maps and target fields for reaching movements,in: Self-organization, Computational Maps, and Motor Control (P. Morasso and V. Sanguineti Eds.), Elsevier Science Publishers, 547-592, Amsterdam, 1997.

Semerano A. (1997) New Promising Applications for Service Robotics: Collective Organization Services, 2nd Workshop IARP (Internation Advanced Robotics Programme), Genoa, Italy.

Simmons, R., Goodwin, R., Zita Haigh, K., Koenig, S., O'Sullivan, J. (1997) A Modular Architecture for Office Delivery Robots, Autonomous Agents, ACM.

Steels, L. (1990), Exploiting analogical representations, in: Designing Autonomous Agents, (P. Maes Ed.), MIT Press, Cambridge (Ma).

Solving Employee Timetabling Problems
by Generalized Local Search

Andrea Schaerf[1] and Amnon Meisels[2]

[1] Dipartimento di Ingegneria Elettrica, Gestionale e Meccanica,
Università di Udine, Via delle Scienze 208, 33100 Udine, Italy
[2] Department of Mathematics and Computer Science
Ben-Gurion University of the Negev, Beer-Sheva, 84-105, Israel

Abstract. Employee timetabling is the operation of assigning employees to tasks in a set of shifts during a fixed period of time, typically a week. We present a general definition of employee timetabling problems (ETPs) that captures many real world problem formulations and includes complex constraints. We investigate the use of several local search techniques for solving ETPs. In particular, we propose a generalization of local search that makes use of a novel search space that includes also partial assignments. We describe the distinguishing features of this generalized local search that allows it to navigate the search space effectively. We show that, on large and difficult instances of real world ETPs, where systematic search fails, local search methods perform well and solve the hardest instances. According to our experimental results on various local search techniques, generalized local search is the best method for solving large ETP instances.

1 Introduction

Employee timetabling problems (ETPs) form a very large family, arising in the diverse commercial world of today. ETPs involve an organization with a set of tasks that need to be fulfilled by a set of employees, each with her/his own qualifications, constraints and preferences. The organization usually enforces some regulations and attempts to achieve global objectives such as lowering the overall cost, or an equitable division of work among employees. Examples of employee timetabling problems include assignment of nurses to shifts in a hospital, assignment of workers to cash registers in a large store, or assignment of phone operators to stations in a service-oriented call-center.

A *task* in the context of ETPs is performed during a predefined time period called a *shift*. Shifts are fixed in time and the term *timetabling employees* refers to a process of *assigning employees* to tasks in shifts. Instead of assigning employees to duties, each in a single weekday, the present model assigns employees to tasks in shifts, where shifts can reside anywhere on the time axis [7]. It is a common view that one major difference between ETPs and generic timetabling problemsis the presence of specific complex constraints due to labour regulations (see e.g., [6, 7]).

We propose a generalization of local search that makes use of a novel search space composed by partial and full assignments. *Generalized local search* aims at reconciling local search with non-systematic constructive search, and it is inspired by various previous approaches to combine them, such as those in [5, 11]. Several aspects of local search have to be reconsidered in this generalized version in order to make it working

E. Lamma and P. Mello (Eds.): AI*IA 99, LNAI 1792, pp. 380–389, 2000.
© Springer-Verlag Berlin Heidelberg 2000

effectively. We describe its novel features and we prove experimentally their impact on the performance of search. We show that, on large and difficult instances of real world ETPs where systematic search fails, local search methods perform well and solve the hardest instances. According to our experimental results, generalized local search is the best method for solving large ETP instances.

The paper is organized as follows. Section 2 introduces the definition of ETPs. Section 3 presents local search and shows how it is applied to ETPs. Section 4 illustrates our generalized local search proposal. Section 5 presents experimental results. Section 6 proposes some variants of our techniques and other ones that we implemented for comparison. Finally, Section 7 discusses related and future work.

2   Employee Timetabling

The Employee Timetabling Problem consists of the (weekly) assignment of employees to tasks in shifts with fixed start and end times. We consider here a search problem formulation. Other variants of the ETP have been proposed in the literature, which also involve an objective function to minimize.

There are m *employees* $E_1, \dots, E_m$, n *shifts* $S_1, \dots, S_n$, and t *tasks* $T_1, \dots, T_t$. We search for an assignment, which can be defined as a 3-dimensional binary matrix $X_{m \times n \times t}$, such that $x_{ijk} = 1$ if employee E_i is assigned to task T_k in shift S_j. The constraints that X is subject to are the following.

Requirements: Each shift S_j is composed of a number of tasks, some of them multiple times. An employee is needed to be assigned for each task belonging to S_j. It is given a non-negative integer matrix $R_{n \times t}$, called *Requirements* matrix, such that R_{jk} denotes the number of occurrences of task T_k in shift S_j, which corresponds to the exact number of employees that must be assigned to task T_k in shift S_j.

Ability: Each employee has qualifications that enable her/him to fulfill certain types of tasks; that is, each employee E_i has a set of tasks $\{T_{i_1}, \dots, T_{i_r}\}$ that E_i can be assigned to. The *qualification* matrix is a binary matrix $Q_{m \times t}$ such that $Q_{ik} = 1$ if employee E_i qualifies for task T_k, $Q_{ik} = 0$ otherwise.

Availability: There are personal preferences of employees, which restrict them to be assigned only to subsets of the shifts. These constraints are represented by a binary matrix of *availabilities* $A_{m \times n}$, where $A_{ik} = 1$ if employee E_i is *available* for shift S_k and $A_{ik} = 0$ otherwise.

Conflicts: Obviously, an employee cannot be assigned to more than one task in the same shift. In addition, employees cannot be assigned to two shift that are in *conflict* with each other. Sources of conflicts could be different: overlap in time, consecutive, or combinations that are forbidden by organizational rules. Conflicts may vary for different employees (because of different contracts) and are described by a 3-dimensional binary *Conflict* matrix $C_{n \times n \times m}$, such that if $c_{ijk} = 1$, then employee E_k cannot be assigned to both shifts S_i and S_j.

Workload: There is an upper and lower limit on the number of tasks that each employee can be assigned to. There are actually a set of limits, because employees can be assigned to a limited total number of tasks per schedule and also to a limited (smaller) number of specific assignments. We therefore define a set of shift sets $G_1, \ldots, G_s$, each one grouping shifts of a specific kind. Then, we define two integer-valued matrices $V_{m \times s}$ and $W_{m \times s}$ such that employee E_i must be assigned to at least V_{ik} and at most W_{ik} shifts of group G_k.

The problem is to find *any* assignment that satisfies all of the above constraints (for the sake of brevity, we omit the mathematical definition). Other definitions include also soft constraints that constitute the objective function (to be minimized). Soft constraints generally regard fair distribution of loads for employees. For example, when a nurse is assigned to two Night_Shifts, it is considered much better to have them spread evenly over the week (e.g., at least two free nights in between).

3 Local Search

We now propose a local search solution to ETP. First, we introduce the general local-search framework, then the search space and neighbourhood structure of ETP. Finally, we define the cost function and several move selection methods for searching the space.

3.1 The Local Search Framework

Given an instance p of a search problem P, we associate a *search space* S to it. Each element $s \in S$ corresponds to a potential solution of p, and is called a *state* of p. An element $s \in S$ that corresponds to a solution that satisfies all constraints of p is called a *feasible state* of p.

Local search relies on a function N which assigns to each $s \in S$ its *neighbourhood* $N(s) \subseteq S$. Each state $s' \in N(s)$ is called a *neighbour* of s. The neighbourhood depends on the structure of P and is generally composed of the states that are obtained by some local change, called *move*, from the current state. We denote by $s \oplus m$ the neighbour obtained from s by applying move m.

A run of a local search algorithm starts from an initial state s_0, obtained with some other technique or generated at random, and enters a loop that *navigates* the search space, stepping from one state s_i to one of its neighbours s_{i+1}.

Local search techniques differ from one another according to the strategies they use to select the move in each state and to stop the search. In all techniques, the search is driven by a *cost function* f that estimates the quality of the state. For search problems, a common cost function counts the number of violated constraints, and the goal of the search is to minimize f to zero (for optimization problems f includes also the objective function of the problem).

Among local search techniques, we focus on *hill climbing* (see Section 6 for a discussion on different techniques). Hill climbing is not a single local search technique, but rather a family of techniques based on the idea of performing only moves that improve or leave unchanged (i.e., *sideways* moves) the value of the cost function f. Hill climbing techniques can thus be described in the following way: At each iteration i, "draw" a move m_i; if $f(s_i \oplus m_i) \leq f(s)$ then let $s_{i+1} = s_i \oplus m_i$ otherwise let $s_{i+1} = s_i$. Different strategies draw their moves differently.

Since hill climbing accepts sideways moves, the search does not stop when it reaches a local minimum. In order not to loop infinitely, we use a stopping criterion based on the number of iterations elapsed from the last strict improvement. Specifically, given a fixed value n the algorithm stops after n iterations that do not improve the value of the cost function, i.e., it stops at iteration j such that $f(s_j) = f(s_{j-1}) = \cdots = f(s_{j-n})$.

To apply hill climbing to ETP we need to define the search space, the neighbourhood structure, the cost function, and the selection rule for their initial solution.

3.2   Search Space

The three-dimensional binary matrix X is not suitable for local search processing. A better form, which corresponds to common manual representations in working places, is a rectangular integer-valued matrix $M_{m \times n}$ with a row for each employee. Each column represents a shift and each cell M_{ij} of the table is assigned a value in the interval $[0..t]$. The value $M_{ij} = 0$ denotes that the employee E_i is not working in shift S_j, and $M_{ij} = k$ (with $k > 0$) denotes that the employee E_i is assigned the task T_k in shift S_j.

This representation automatically rules out the possibility that an employee is assigned to more than one task at the same shift. In addition, we consider only states (and moves) in which the requirements are always satisfied, therefore requirements also do not need to be checked. Conversely, all other constraint types can be violated, and are embedded in the cost function.

3.3   Neighbourhood Structure

We consider here a type of move called **Replace** (others will be considered in Section 4).

Replace: Given a shift S_h, and two employees E_i and E_j, such that $M_{ih} = k$ (with $k \neq 0$) and $M_{jh} = 0$ in S, the state obtained from S after applying the **Replace** move $\langle h, i, j \rangle$ is equal to S with the difference that $M_{ih} = 0$ and $M_{jh} = k$.

That is, an employee E_i doing a task T_k in a shift S_h is replaced by another employee E_j not working at shift S_h. A **Replace** is therefore identified by a triple $\langle h, i, j \rangle$, representing in our search space the swapping of the values M_{ih} and M_{jh} in column h.

Notice that **Replace** moves do not change the number of assignments for shift-task pairs, therefore they preserve the satisfaction of requirement constraints.

3.4   Cost Function and Initial Solution

The cost function is defined to be the total number of constraint violations of the current state. All constraint types (ability, availability, workload, and conflicts) are thus implicitly given the same weight $w = 1$ (see Section 4 for weights for violations).

The initial solution is constructed by a greedy procedure, which will be explained in Section 4. Such construction is compatible with the requirement constraints, so that for each pair (S_h, T_k) it selects R_{hk} distinct employees $E_{i_1}, \ldots, E_{i_{R_{hk}}}$ and assigns $M_{i_j h} = k$, for all $i = 1, \ldots, R_{hk}$.

3.5 Hill Climbing Techniques

The techniques we consider belong to the hill climbing family as explained in Section 3.1. Given a state S, the selection rules that we apply are the following

RHC: Select randomly a legal **Replace** $\langle h, i, j \rangle$

RRSHC: Select a random shift S_h and a random employee E_i, and find E_j so that $f(S \oplus \langle h, i, j \rangle)$ is a minimum (breaking ties randomly) among all employees.

RSSHC: Select a random shift S_h and find E_i, E_j so that $f(S \oplus \langle h, i, j \rangle)$ is minimum (breaking ties randomly) among all pairs of employees.

SHC: Find $m = \langle h, i, j \rangle$ so that $f(S \oplus m)$ is minimum (breaking ties randomly) among all legal **Replace**.

Notice that the techniques differ from each other by the part of the neighbourhood that they explore at each iteration. They are ordered by the "steepness" of the search they perform. Larger parts of the neighbourhood explored imply a steeper search, in the sense that better moves are found at each iteration at the expense of a higher computational cost. The strategy RSSHC corresponds to the min-conflict hill-climbing (MCHC) procedure in [8], in which a move corresponds to changing the value of a variable, the variable is selected randomly and its new value is the one that minimizes the number of conflicts.

4 Generalized Local Search

To describe our generalized local search we first present its search space and its neighbourhood function, then we discuss its cost function, and finally we describe the related move selection strategies.

4.1 Extended Search Space and Neighbourhood

The neighbourhood function includes, beside **Replace**, two new move types:

Insert: Given a shift S_h, an employee E_i, and a task T_k such that $M_{ih} = 0$ in S, the state obtained from the state S after applying the **Insert** move $\langle h, i, k \rangle$ is equal to S with the addition of $M_{ih} = k$.

Delete: Given a shift S_h, an employee E_i, such that $M_{ih} \neq 0$ in S, the state obtained from the state S by applying the **Delete** move $\langle h, i \rangle$ is equal to S with $M_{ih} = 0$.

The full neighbourhood of each state is now constructed by applying all legal **Replace**, **Insert**, and **Delete** moves. The search space includes all possible assignments to the matrix M independently of the fact that the requirements are not satisfied. Most importantly, it contains all *partial states*, i.e., states with fewer assignments than the requirements. This means that the search space includes all the states of the *search tree* visited by a typical backtracking-based algorithm that uses this representation.

4.2   Cost Function Components

In order to explore effectively the extended search space, several modifications have to be introduced into the cost function. First, constraints are split into two classes:

Missings: Minimum requirements and minimum workloads.

Strict Constraints: Maximum requirements, maximum workloads, conflicts, abilities and availabilities.

Intuitively, given a partial state S, strict constraints are those that are present also in any complete state obtained from S, whereas missings are those that might be eliminated by adding assignments.

Furthermore, we introduce a new component in the cost function that takes into account a measure of the possibility for a partial solution to be completed. We call this component, following [11], the *look-ahead factor*, and define it as follows.

Look-Ahead: For all shift-task pairs (S_h, T_k) for which the number of assigned employees in the current (partial) state S is less than the requirements, we sum up the number of employees that have the ability to do T_k, are available in S_h, and are working in at least one shift which is conflicting with S_h for the same employee.

Intuitively, we count the possible employee assignments that are made infeasible only by the presence of other assignments (and not by constraints on that single assignment). The higher the look-ahead factor, the more difficult it is to complete the timetable. For full states(i.e., all requirements satisfied), the look-ahead factor is zero, and it tends to decrease as the state fills up.

The cost function is now composed of three components: missings, strict constraints, and look-ahead. The weights assigned to these three components are crucial for the effectiveness of the search. Our choice is to assign to look-ahead a low weight, which is negligible w.r.t. the others, thus creating a hierarchical cost function. The two weights for missings and strict constraints are adaptively modified using a *shifting penalty* scheme (see [4]) similar to the one proposed in [3].

Specifically, if there are 0 violations of one kind for K consecutive iterations, the corresponding weight is divided by a factor γ randomly chosen between 1.5 and 2. Conversely, if there are more than 0 violations of one kind for H consecutive iterations, the corresponding weight is multiplied by a random factor in the same range (where H and K are parameters of the algorithms). In addition, the weights have strict maximal and minimal limits. The maximal weight for missings is less than the maximum weight for strict constraints, so as to "encourage" the search to move toward partial solutions when, in the initial phase, both types of violations are simultaneously present.

This adaptive scheme allows search to move "up" and "down" in the search space, "exchanging" missing assignments with strict constraint violations. During this vertical oscillation (whose period depends on H and K), which takes into account also the look-ahead factor, all violations eventually tend to disappear.

Similar shifting penalty mechanisms have been proposed in [10] and [13], which rely on relaxing some constraints when a local minimum is reached. Differently from their work, our adaptive relaxation scheme is not a method to deal exclusively with local minima (which are not necessarily perceived), but is a general search guide, which tends to make the overall search more effective.

4.3   Move Selection and Initial Solution

Defining move selection rules for the extended neighbourhood, notice that Insert and Delete moves have three and two degrees of freedom, respectively. In analogy to Replace moves, the same four levels of search steepness can be defined (RSSHC and SHC stay exactly the same for Delete). Therefore, the same four selection strategies are defined, and the corresponding techniques are called GRHC, GRRSHC, GRSSHC, GSHC (where G stands for "generalized").

At each iteration the move type is randomly selected, and subsequently a move of the chosen type is selected based on the steepness currently used. A fifth level of steepness is introduced, called GVSHC (VS for "very steep"), in which the best neighbour of the entire extended neighbourhood is selected. For the other four strategies, the random selection for the move type is not based on an equal distribution, but is biased toward Replace moves, as shown in the experimental results.

The initial solution for both local search and generalized local search is a complete state and it is built by a sequence of only Insert moves, selected by the SHC strategy.

5   Experimental Results

Two different types of instances are used in our experimental study. One type is the timetable of nurses in a department of a hospital. The other type was taken from the schedule of production lines in a factory. In the hospital department problem there are 43 shifts in each week's timetable, 29 employees to be assigned to a total of 102 tasks over 7 days. The production line problem has 21 weekly shifts (three per day, 8 hours each), 50 employees and a total of 280 assignments. The hard constraints of both types of instances included many conflicts arising from regulations on minimal resting periods.

The second type of instances has a larger number of assignment and constraints, which makes them harder. In this section we report the results for 5 instances of the second type, which proved too hard to solve with constructive methods (see Section 6). Similar results where obtained for the nurse cases.

Table 1 presents a general view of the results obtained by the various techniques on the two case studies. We performed 100 runs for each technique for each instance, all starting from the same set of initial solutions. The parameter MaxIters is set to a different appropriate value for each technique, in such a way that the running times for all techniques are approximately the same (300 seconds per run on a SUN Ultra 2 workstation). The shifting penalty mechanism explained in Section 4.2 are used for all local search and generalized local search techniques. The columns Average and Solved give the average number of violations per run, and the percentage of runs that solved the instance (i.e. a 0 violations occurrence), respectively.

The best results in Table 1 are obtained by the technique GRSSHC, and generalized hill climbing outperforms hill climbing for this problem. Notice that the best steepness of search is different for generalized local search and for standard local search. For standard local search, the best results are obtained by the RHC technique. This is intuitively explained by the fact that for generalized local search the cost function includes more

	MaxIters	Average	Solved		MaxIters	Average	Solved
	Standard Local Search				Generalized Local Search		
RHC	20,000,000	0.9	38	GRHC	10,000,000	2.5	0
RRSHC	400,000	1	25	GRRSHC	300,000	1.2	11
RSSHC	150,000	1.4	18	GRSSHC	100,000	0.5	58
SHC	30,000	3.4	0	GSHC	20,000	2.8	0
				GVSHC	5,000	3.5	0

Table 1. General Results

components, and therefore a more accurate move selection is necessary in order to find moves that do not penalize some component for improving the others.

Tables 2, present results that highlights the role played by one single feature of our algorithm. For each set of experiments the parameters associated with one specific feature are varied while all the other parameters are kept at the value of the best overall result. All the results are obtained making a large number of trials of shorter runs with GRSSHC. Specifically, we made 1000 trials for each configuration with MaxIters equal to 1000. What we measure is the average number of violations for the final state.

The top-left part of Table 2 regards the look-ahead mechanism. We consider three possibilities for the computation of the look-ahead factor. Either no look-ahead factor is added to the cost function, or the number of available employees for a pair shift-task in which the requirements are not completely fulfilled are counted two different ways. The non-biased look-ahead counts cost 1 for each employee which cannot do the task, whereas in the biased version, the value is multiplied by the number of missing employees. Intuitively, the biased version emphasizes cases of more than one employee missing per task. The results show a mild advantage for using the biased version.

Look-ahead factor			Average cost	Type Distribution			Average Cost
no look-ahead			9.56	R	I	D	
non-biased look-ahead			6.41	33%	33%	33%	7.43
biased look-ahead			6.25	60%	20%	20%	6.25
				20%	60%	20%	7.75
Weighting regime	H	K	Average cost	20%	20%	60%	8.1
high variations	1	3	6.44	0%	50%	50%	8.9
medium variations	2	10	6.25	80%	10%	10%	6.8
low variations	5	30	6.68	90%	5%	5%	7.2
no variation	∞	∞	8.93	100%	0%	0%	7.4

Table 2. Results for different values for three features of the algorithm

The bottom-left part of the table shows the importance of the shifting penalty mechanism. The results are given for different values of H and K, which determine the variability of the weights, and the last row has fixed weights (both equal to 1). The results show that there is a trade-off associated with the choice of these values.

The importance of biasing the random selection of different move types (R: Replace, I: Insert, D: Delete) is presented in the right-hand side of Table 2. The best results are obtained for a random selection biased toward Replace moves (see second row: 60% of Replace). The last three rows demonstrate that such biasing should be limited. The case (100% Replace) corresponds to standard local search, with no partial states. Selections biased toward Insert or Delete moves perform worse, and, in particular, not using Replace moves at all performs very poorly (fifth row).

6 Discussion

We have implemented some additional search techniques, beside those presented in Sections 3 and 4. First, we implemented an exhaustive forward-checking search using the language ECL^{i}PS^e [1]. This was able to solve a few instances of the nurse problem (102 assignments), but always failed to solve the larger problem.

The ECL^{i}PS^e program was also used as a more informed strategy for finding the initial solution. In particular, a version of it with a time limit was used as the initial (partial) solution for generalized local search. The time limit is implemented in such a way that it makes the maximum number of feasible assignments (similarly to the RFLG algorithm in [12]).

Tabu search [4] can be the basis for generalized local search and we experimented with it for solving our ETP instances. It turned out experimentally that tabu search gave results comparable with RSSHC when using Replace moves. In fact, the difference between our hill climbing procedure and tabu search stems mostly from the prohibition mechanism implemented by the use of the tabu list. For the generalized local search, the combined effect of the shifting penalty mechanism (which changes continuously the quality of moves) and the presence of different move types made the use of the prohibition mechanism not effective in our experiments.

We also experimented with techniques that interleave local search with other constructive (and destructive) phases, similarly to what is proposed in [5]. These techniques, which need further investigation, did not provide good results.

7 Related and Future Work

The presence of many types of complex constraints for ETPs leads naturally to the use of knowledge-based techniques for representations of the constraints and for capturing of domain specific heuristics (cf. [2, 9]). Constraint processing and KB-rules have been combined in the past for solving real world ETPs in [7].

We experimented for comparison with the system in [7]. That system solved the hospital ETPs in a manner that achieves certain additional objectives (e.g. attempting to rotate night shifts among some groups of nurses). It solved the problems with very few backtracks (i.e. 110 assignment attempts for 102 needed) in a few seconds of CPU time. The 280-assignment production line instances of ETPs instead were too difficult to solve by the KB-rules technique. Lacking domain specific knowledge, only 254 feasible assignments out of the needed 280 were found.

An approach similar to ours is provided in [5] for the graph colouring problem. Their method starts from a complete state, which is found with a high-quality heuristics. Thereafter, it alternates local search with a two-phase process which is composed of a destructive phase and a constructive one. The generalized local search takes place when the local search is in a local minimum, and the number of destructive steps that it performs is related to an estimation of the depth of the current local minimum.

In [11] it is proposed an algorithm that interleaves a constructive phase with a local search one. However, the search space only includes partial states of the same level, and no constructive or destructive move is allowed. Our approach generalized this idea, performing constructive and normal moves in a single phase.

In this paper, only the hard constraints of the problems were taken into account. In the future, we plan to apply similar techniques to ETPs with soft constraints, which generally refer to fair load distribution.

References

1. A. Aggoun and *et al. ECL^{i}PS^e User Manual (Version 4.0)*. IC-Parc, London (UK), 1998.
2. J. Collins and E. Sisley. Automated assignment and scheduling of service personnel. *IEEE Expert*, 5:33–38, 1994.
3. M. Gendreau, A. Hertz, and G. Laporte. Tabu search heuristic for the vehicle routing problem. *Management Science*, 40:1276 – 1290, 1994.
4. F. Glover and M. Laguna. *Tabu search*. Kluwer Academic Publishers, 1997.
5. F. Glover, M. Parker, and J. Ryan. Coloring by tabu branch and bound. In D. S. Johnson and M. A. Trick, editors, *Cliques, Coloring, and Satisfiability. Second DIMACS Implementation Challenge*, volume 26 of *DIMACS Series in Discrete Mathematics and Theoretical Computer Science*. American Mathematical Society, 1996.
6. L. Kragelund. Solving a timetabling problem using hybrid genetic algorithms. *Soft. Pract. Exper.*, 27:1121–34, 1997.
7. A. Meisels, E. Gudes, and G. Solotorevsky. Combining rules and constraints for employee timetabling. *Intern. Jou. Intell. Syst.*, 12:419–439, 1997.
8. S. Minton, M. D. Johnston, A. B. Philips, and P. Laird. Minimizing conflicts: a heuristic repair method for constraint satisfaction and scheduling problems. *Artificial Intelligence*, 58:161–205, 1992.
9. E. Morgado and J. Martins. An AI based approach to crew scheduling. In *Proc. of CAIA-93*, pages 71–77, 1993.
10. P. Morris. The breakout method for escaping from local minima. In *Proc. of AAAI-93*, pages 40–45, 1993.
11. A. Schaerf. Combining local search and look-ahead for scheduling and constraint satisfaction problems. In *Proc. of IJCAI-97*, pages 1254–1259, 1997. Morgan-Kaufmann.
12. M. Yoshikawa, K. Kaneko, T. Yamanouchi, and M. Watanabe. A constraint-based high school scheduling system. *IEEE Expert*, 11(1):63–72, 1996.
13. N. Yugami, Y. Ohta, and H. Hara. Improving repair-based constraint satisfaction methods by value propagation. In *Proc. of AAAI-94*, pages 344–349, 1994.

Lecture Notes in Artificial Intelligence (LNAI)

Lecture Notes in Computer Science